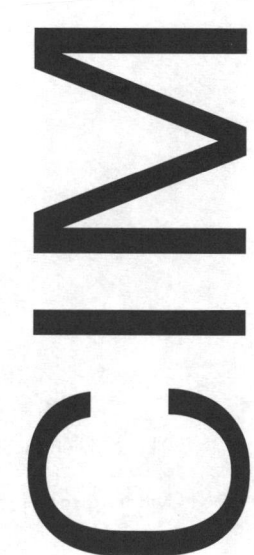

Certificate Paper C2

FINANCIAL ACCOUNTING
FUNDAMENTALS

For assessments in 2005

Practice & Revision Kit

In this January 2005 new edition
- New format for ease of use
- Question formats reflect exam question styles
- Guidance on study planning and techniques
- Three mock assessments for you to attempt under timed conditions

BPP's **i-Pass** product also supports this paper.

First edition January 2005

ISBN 0 7517 1971 4

British Library Cataloguing-in-Publication Data
A catalogue record for this book
is available from the British Library

Published by

BPP Professional Education
Aldine House, Aldine Place
London W12 8AW

www.bpp.com

Printed in Great Britain by
WM Print
45-47 Frederick Street
Walsall
WS2 9NE

All our rights reserved. No part of this publication may be reproduced, stored in a retrieval system or transmitted, in any form or by any means, electronic, mechanical, photocopying, recording or otherwise, without the prior written permission of BPP Professional Education.

We are grateful to the Chartered Institute of Management Accountants for permission to reproduce past examination questions. The answers to past examination questions have been prepared by BPP Professional Education.

©
BPP Professional Education
2005

Contents

Page

Revision

Revising with this Kit iv
Effective revision vi

The assessment

Assessment technique ix
Tackling multiple choice questions xi
Tackling objective test questions xii

Background

Current issues xiv
Useful websites xiv
Syllabus mindmap xv

Question and answer checklist/index xvi

	Questions	Answers

Question practice

Multiple choice questions	3	79
Objective test questions	59	109

Pre-assessment tests

Pre-assessment test 1	125	133
Pre-assessment test 2	128	135

Assessment practice

Mock assessment 1	139	149
Mock assessment 2	157	169
Mock assessment 3	175	187

Review form & free prize draw

Order form

Revising with this Kit

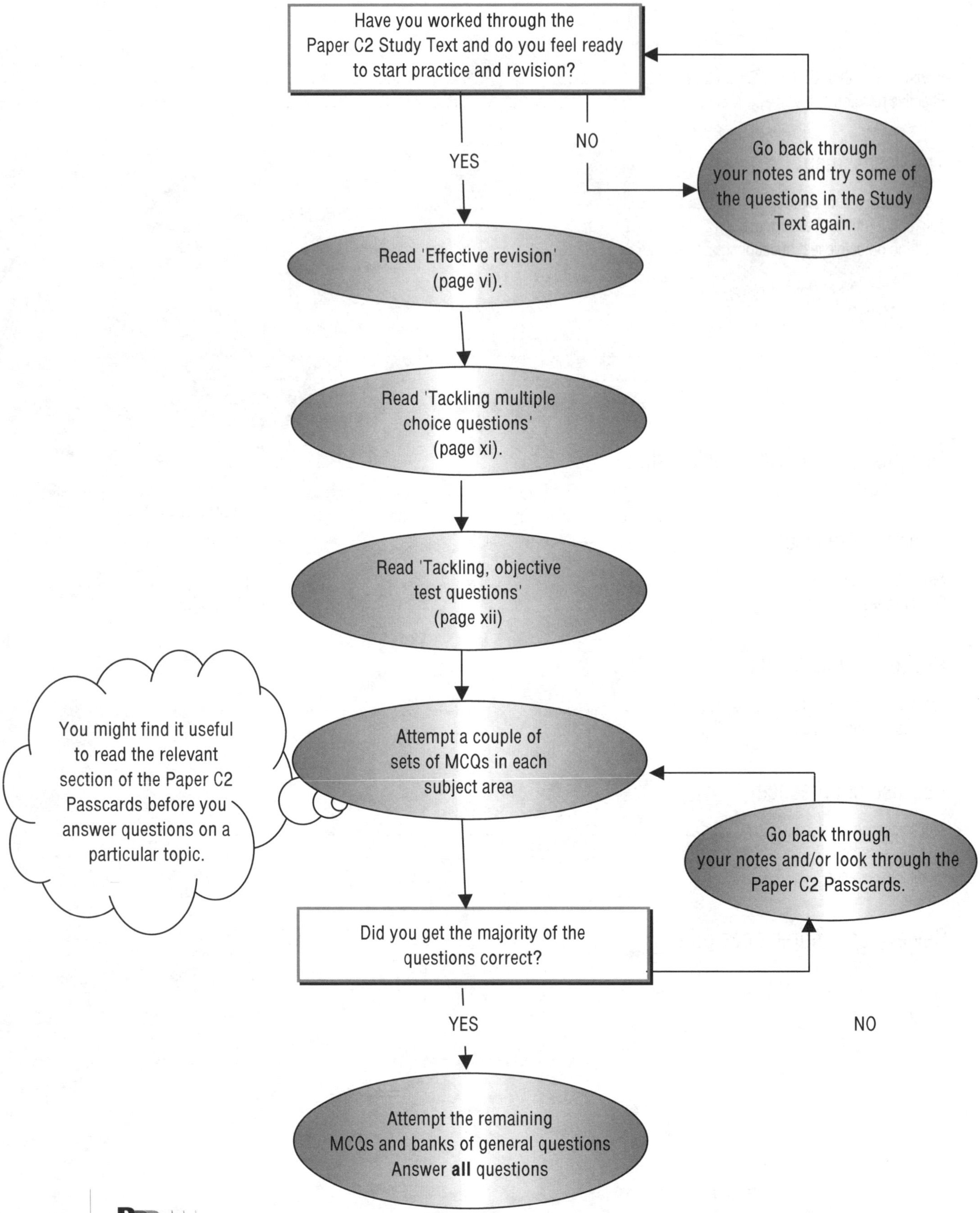

```
                    ┌─────────────────────────────┐
                    │ Have you worked through the │
                    │ Paper C2 Study Text and do  │
                    │ you feel ready to start     │
                    │ practice and revision?      │
                    └─────────────────────────────┘
                       │ YES      NO │
                       ▼             ▼
                                  Go back through your notes and try
                                  some of the questions in the Study
                                  Text again.
```

- Read 'Effective revision' (page vi).
- Read 'Tackling multiple choice questions' (page xi).
- Read 'Tackling, objective test questions' (page xii).
- Attempt a couple of sets of MCQs in each subject area

You might find it useful to read the relevant section of the Paper C2 Passcards before you answer questions on a particular topic.

Did you get the majority of the questions correct?

- **YES** → Attempt the remaining MCQs and banks of general questions. Answer **all** questions
- **NO** → Go back through your notes and/or look through the Paper C2 Passcards.

iv

INTRODUCTION

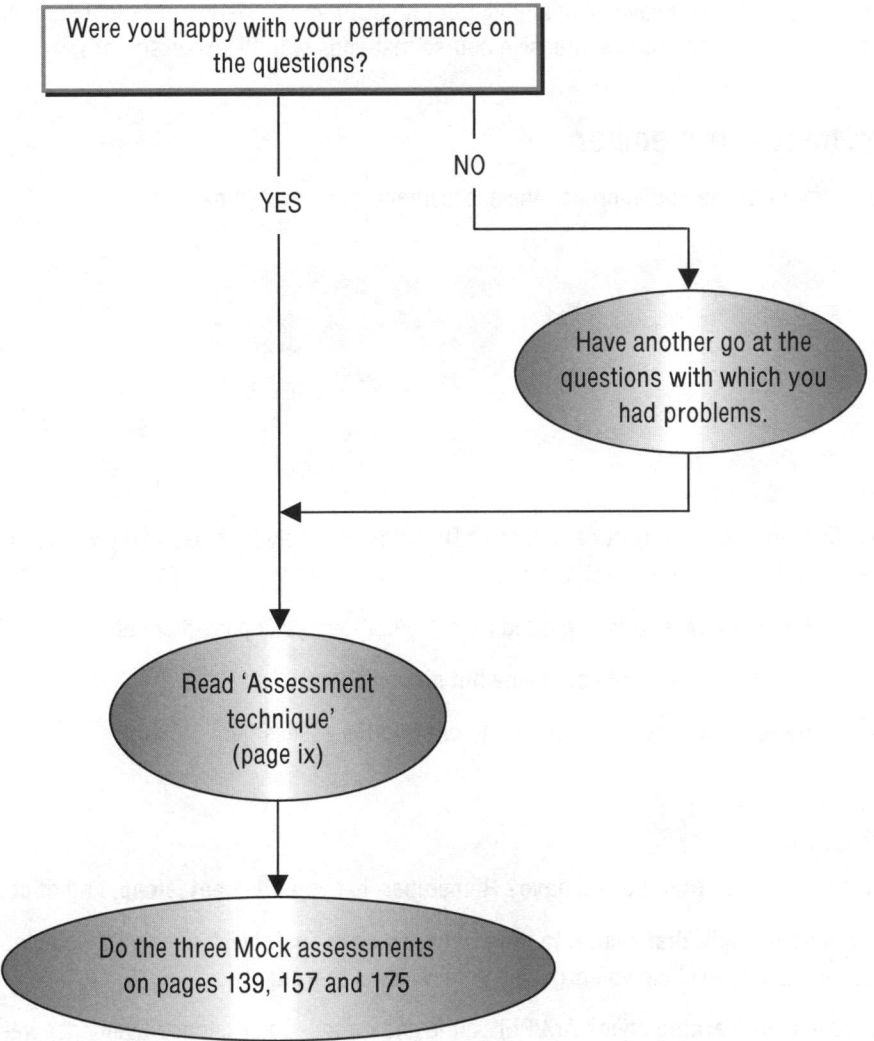

Effective revision

This guidance applies if you have been studying for an exam over a period of time. (Some tuition providers are teaching subjects by means of one intensive course that ends with the assessment.)

What you must remember

Time is very important as you approach the assessment. You must remember:

> **Believe in yourself**
> **Use time sensibly**

Believe in yourself

Are you cultivating the right attitude of mind? There is absolutely no reason why you should not pass this **assessment** if you adopt the correct approach.

- **Be confident** – you've passed exams before, you can pass them again
- **Be calm** – plenty of adrenaline but no panicking
- **Be focused** – commit yourself to passing the assessment

Use time sensibly

1. **How much study time do you have?** Remember that you must **eat**, **sleep**, and of course, **relax**.
2. **How will you split that available time between each subject?** A revision timetable, covering what and how you will revise, will help you organise your revision thoroughly.
3. **What is your learning style?** AM/PM? Little and often/long sessions? Evenings/ weekends?
4. **Do you have quality study time?** Unplug the phone. Let everybody know that you're studying and shouldn't be disturbed.
5. **Are you taking regular breaks?** Most people absorb more if they do not attempt to study for long uninterrupted periods of time. A five minute break every hour (to make coffee, watch the news headlines) can make all the difference.
6. **Are you rewarding yourself for your hard work?** Are you leading a **healthy lifestyle?**

What to revise

Key topics

You need to spend **most time** on, and practise **lots of questions** on, topics that are likely to yield plenty of questions in your assessment.

You may also find certain areas of the syllabus difficult.

> Difficult areas are
> - Areas you find dull or pointless
> - Subjects you highlighted as difficult when you studied them
> - Topics that gave you problems when you answered questions or reviewed the material

DON'T become depressed about these areas; instead do something about them.

- Build up your knowledge by **quick tests** such as the quick quizzes in your BPP Study Text.
- Work carefully through **examples** and **questions** in the Text, and refer back to the Text if you struggle with questions in the Kit.

Breadth of revision

Make sure your revision covers all areas of the syllabus. Your assessment will test your knowledge of the whole syllabus.

How to revise

There are four main ways that you can revise a topic area.

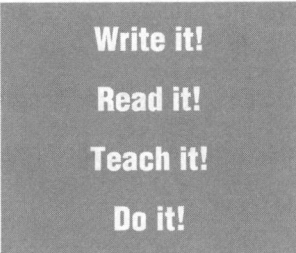

Write it!

Writing important points down will help you recall them, particularly if your notes are presented in a way that makes it easy for you to remember them.

Read it!

You should read your notes or BPP Passcards actively, testing yourself by doing quick quizzes or Kit questions while you are reading.

Teach it!

Assessments require you to show your understanding. Teaching what you are learning to another person helps you practise explaining topics that you might be asked to define in your assessment. Teaching someone who will challenge your understanding, someone for example who will be taking the same assessment as you, can be helpful to both of you.

INTRODUCTION

Do it!

Remember that you are revising in order to be able to answer questions in the assessment. Practising questions will help you practise **technique** and **discipline**, which can be crucial in passing or failing assessments.

1. Start your question practice by doing a couple of sets of multiple choice questions in a subject area. Note down the questions where you went wrong, try to identify why you made mistakes and go back to your Study Text for guidance or practice.

2. The **more questions** you do, the more likely you are to pass the assessment. However if you do run short of time:

    - Make sure that you have done at least some questions from every section of the syllabus
    - Look through the banks of questions and do questions on areas that you have found difficult or on which you have made mistakes

3. When you think you can successfully answer questions on the whole syllabus, attempt the **three mock assessments** at the end of the Kit. You will get the most benefit by sitting them under strict assessment conditions, so that you gain experience of the vital assessment processes.

    - Managing your time
    - Producing answers

BPP's *Learning to Learn Accountancy* gives further valuable advice on how to approach revision. BPP has also produced other vital revision aids.

- **Passcards** – Provide you with clear topic summaries and assessment tips
- **i-Pass CDs** – Offer you tests of knowledge to be completed against the clock
- **Success CDs** – Help you revise on the move

You can purchase these products by completing the order form at the back of this Kit or by visiting www.bpp.com/cima

Assessment technique

Format of the assessment

The assessment will contain 40 questions to be completed in 1½ hours. The assessment will include multiple choice questions and may also include other types of objective test questions, in which case the mark allocation may vary between different questions. The questions will appear in random order.

Passing assessments

Passing assessments is half about having the knowledge, and half about doing yourself full justice in the assessment. You must have the right approach to two things.

> **The day of the assessment**
>
> **Your time in the assessment room**

The day of the assessment

1. Set at least one **alarm** (or get an alarm call) for a morning assessment.
2. Have **something to eat** but beware of eating too much; you may feel sleepy if your system is digesting a large meal.
3. Allow plenty of **time to get to the assessment room**; have your route worked out in advance and listen to news bulletins to check for potential travel problems.
4. **Don't forget** pens and watch. Also make sure you remember **entrance documentation** and **evidence of identity**.
5. Put **new batteries** into your calculator and take a spare set (or a spare calculator).
6. **Avoid discussion** about the assessment with other candidates outside the assessment room.

Your time in the assessment room

1. **Listen carefully to the invigilator's instructions**

    Make sure you understand the formalities you have to complete.

2. **Ensure you follow the instructions on the computer screen**

    In particular ensure that you select the correct assessment (not every student does!), and that you understand how to work through the assessment and submit your answers.

3. **Keep your eye on the time**

    In the assessment you will have to complete 40 questions in 90 minutes. That will mean that you have roughly 2 minutes on average to answer each question. You will be able to answer some questions instantly, but others will require thinking about. If after a minute or so you have no idea how to tackle the question, leave it and come back to it later.

4. **Label your workings clearly with the question number**

    This will help you when you check your answers, or if you come back to a question that you are unsure about.

INTRODUCTION

5 Deal with problem questions

There are two ways of dealing with questions where you are unsure of the answer.

(a) **Don't submit an answer.** The computer will tell you before you move to the next question that you have not submitted an answer, and the question will be marked as not done on the list of questions. The risk with this approach is that you run out of time before you do submit an answer.

(b) **Submit an answer.** You can always come back and change the answer before you finish the assessment or the time runs out. You should though make a note of answers that you are unsure about, to ensure that you do revisit them later in the assessment.

6 Make sure you submit an answer for every question

When there are ten minutes left to go, concentrate on submitting answers for all the questions that you have not answered up to that point. You won't get penalised for wrong answers so take a guess if you're unsure.

7 Check your answers

If you finish the assessment with time to spare, check your answers before you sign out of the assessment. In particular revisit questions that you are unsure about, and check that your answers are in the right format and contain the correct number of words as appropriate.

> BPP's *Learning to Learn Accountancy* gives further valuable advice on how to approach the day of the assessment.

Tackling multiple choice questions

The MCQs in your assessment contain a number of possible answers. You have to **choose the option(s) that best answers the question**. The three incorrect options are called distracters. There is a skill in answering MCQs quickly and correctly. By practising MCQs you can develop this skill, giving you a better chance of passing the assessment.

You may wish to follow the approach outlined below, or you may prefer to adapt it.

Step 1   **Note down how long** you should allocate to each MCQ. For this paper you will be answering 40 questions in 60 minutes, so you will be spending on average 1½ minutes on each question. Remember however that you will not be expected to spend an equal amount of time on each MCQ; some can be answered instantly but others will take time to work out.

Step 2   **Attempt each question**. Read the question thoroughly.

You may find that you recognise a question when you sit the assessment. Be aware that the detail and/or requirement may be different. If the question seems familiar read the requirement and options carefully – do not assume that it is identical.

Step 3   Read the four options and see if one matches your own answer. Be careful with numerical questions, as the distracters are designed to match answers that incorporate **common errors**. Check that your calculation is correct. Have you followed the requirement exactly? Have you included every stage of a calculation?

Step 4   You may find that none of the options matches your answer.

- **Re-read the question** to ensure that you understand it and are answering the requirement
- **Eliminate any obviously wrong answers**
- **Consider which of the remaining answers** is the **most likely** to be correct and select the option

Step 5   If you are still unsure, **continue to the next question**. Likewise if you are nowhere near working out which option is correct after a couple of minutes, leave the question and come back to it later. Make a note of any questions for which you have submitted answers, but you need to return to later. The computer will list any questions for which you have not submitted answers.

Step 6   **Revisit questions** you are uncertain about. When you come back to a question after a break you often find you are able to answer it correctly straight away. If you are still unsure have a guess. You are not penalised for incorrect answers, so **never leave a question unanswered!**

Tackling objective test questions

What is an objective test question?

An objective test (**OT**) question is made up of some form of **stimulus**, usually a question, and a **requirement** to do something.

- **MCQs.** Read through the information on page (xi) about MCQs and how to tackle them.
- **True or false.** You will be asked if a statement is true or false.
- **Data entry.** This type of OT requires you to provide figures such as the correct figure for creditors in a balance sheet, or words to fill in a blank.
- **Hot spots.** This question format might ask you to identify which cell on a spreadsheet contains a particular format or where on a graph marginal revenue equals marginal cost.
- **Multiple response.** These questions provide you with a number of options and you have to identify those that fulfil certain criteria.
- **Matching.** This OT question format could ask you to classify particular costs into one of a range of cost classifications provided, to match descriptions of variances with one of a number of variances listed, and so on.

OT questions in your assessment

CIMA is currently developing different types of OTs for inclusion in computer-based assessments. The timetable for introduction of new types of OTs is uncertain, and it is also not certain how many questions in your assessment will be MCQs, and how many will be other types of OT. Practising all the different types of OTs that this Kit provides will prepare you well for whatever questions come up in your assessment. The OTs other than MCQs in this kit are found in the general question banks. You should assume for OTs where you give more than one answer that one mark is available per answer given. MCQs are worth 2 marks each.

Dealing with OT questions

Again you may wish to follow the approach we suggest, or you may be prepared to adapt it.

Step 1   Work out **how long** you should allocate to each OT. Remember that you will not be expected to spend an equal amount of time on each one; some can be answered instantly but others will take time to work out.

Step 2   **Attempt each question**. Read the question thoroughly, and note in particular what the question says about the **format** of your answer and whether there are any **restrictions** placed on it (for example the number of words you can use).

You may find that you recognise a question when you sit the assessment. Be aware that the detail and/or requirement may be different. If the question seems familiar read the requirement and options carefully – do not assume that it is identical.

Step 3   Read any options you are given and select which ones are appropriate. Check that your calculations are correct. Have you followed the requirement exactly? Have you included every stage of the calculation?

Step 4 You may find that you are unsure of the answer.
- Re-read the question to ensure that you understand it and are answering the requirement
- Eliminate any obviously wrong options if you are given a number of options from which to choose

Step 5 If you are still unsure, **continue to the next question**. Make a note of any questions for which you have submitted answers, but you need to return to later. The computer will list any questions for which you have not submitted answers.

Step 6 Revisit questions you are uncertain about. When you come back to a question after a break you often find you are able to answer it correctly straight away. If you are still unsure have a guess. You are not penalised for incorrect answers, so **never leave a question unanswered!**

Current issues

CIMA recognises a 'revaluation' method of depreciation. What this means is simply that an asset is revalued at the end of the year and any loss of value is treated as depreciation. For instance, if this method were applied to a group of assets:

Opening valuation	100
Cost of additions	20
Proceeds of disposals	(10)
Closing valuation	(80)
Depreciation for the year	30

Useful websites

The websites below provide additional sources of information of relevance to your studies for *Business Law*.

- BPP   www.bpp.com

    For details of other BPP material for your CIMA studies

- CIMA   www.cimaglobal.com

    The official CIMA website

- The Times   www.timesonline.co.uk

- Financial Times   www.ft.com

- The Economist   www.economist.com

- Department of Trade and Industry   www.dti.gov.uk

- UK Government   www.open.gov.uk

INTRODUCTION

Syllabus mindmap

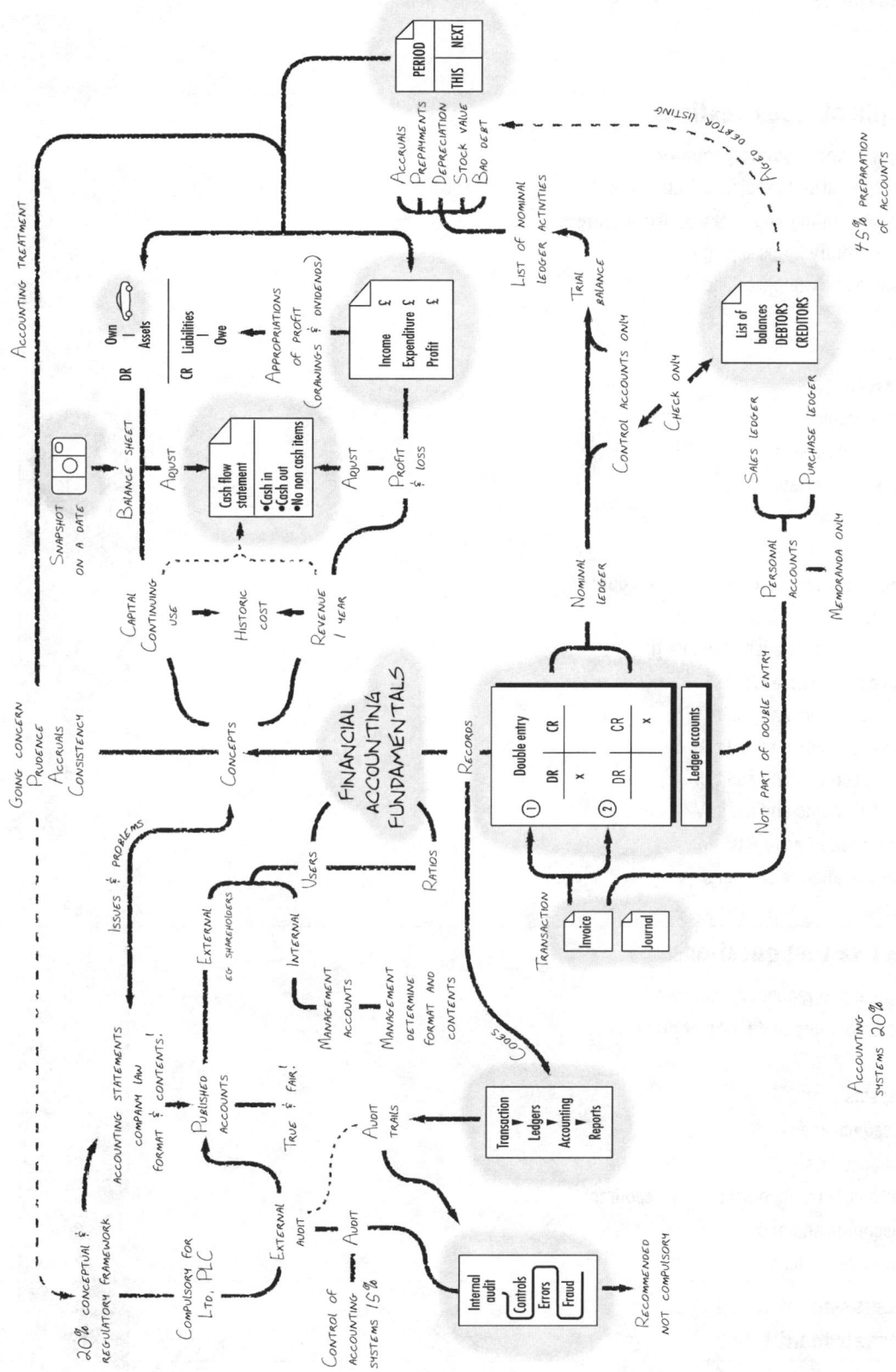

INTRODUCTION

Question and Answer checklist/index

The headings in this checklist/index indicate the main topics of questions, but questions often cover several different topics.

	Page number	
	Question	Answer
Multiple choice questions		
Conceptual and regulatory framework		
1 Conceptual and regulatory framework	3	79
Ledger accounting and books of prime entry		
2 Double entry bookkeeping I	5	80
3 Double entry bookkeeping II	10	82
Stocks		
4 Stocks	14	84
Fixed assets		
5 Fixed assets	18	86
Bank reconciliations		
6 Bank reconciliations	21	88
Control accounts		
7 Control accounts	24	90
Correction of errors and suspense accounts		
8 Errors and suspense accounts I	28	91
9 Errors and suspense accounts II	30	93
Final accounts and audit		
10 Final accounts and audit I	33	94
11 Final accounts and audit II	38	97
12 Final accounts and audit III	42	99
13 Final accounts and audit IV	46	101
Interpretation of accounts		
14 Interpretation of accounts	49	103
15 Ratios	52	104
Objective test questions		
Conceptual and regulatory framework	59	109
Ledger accounting and books of prime entry	59	109
Stocks	62	112
Fixed assets	63	112
Bank reconciliations	64	113
Control accounts	65	114
Correction of errors and suspense accounts	66	115
Final accounts and audit	69	116
Interpretation of accounts	73	119
Pre-assessment test 1	125	133
Pre-assessment test 2	128	135
Mock assessment 1	139	149
Mock assessment 2	157	169
Mock assessment 3	175	187

Multiple choice questions

MULTIPLE CHOICE QUESTIONS

1 Conceptual and regulatory framework

1   The historical cost convention

    A   Fails to take account of changing price levels over time
    B   Records only past transactions
    C   Values all assets at their cost to the business, without any adjustment for depreciation
    D   Has been replaced in accounting records by a system of current cost accounting

2   The *main* aim of accounting is to

    A   Maintain ledger accounts for every asset and liability
    B   Provide financial information to users of such information
    C   Produce a trial balance
    D   Record every financial transaction individually

3   The accounting convention under which items in the accounts are adjusted by reference to the Retail Price Index is known as

    A   Current cost accounting
    B   Historical cost accounting
    C   Alternative accounting rules
    D   Current purchasing power accounting

4   In the time of rising prices, the historical cost convention has the effect of

    A   Understating profits and understating balance sheet asset values
    B   Understating profits and overstating balance sheet asset values
    C   Overstating profits and understating balance sheet asset values
    D   Overstating profits and overstating balance sheet asset values

5   The accounting equation can be rewritten as

    A   Assets plus profit less drawings less liabilities equals closing capital
    B   Assets less liabilities less drawings equals opening capital plus profit
    C   Assets less liabilities less opening capital plus drawings equals profit
    D   Opening capital plus profit less drawings less liabilities equals assets

6   If the owner of a business takes goods from stock for his own personal use, the accounting concept to be considered is the

    A   Prudence concept
    B   Capitalisation concept
    C   Money measurement concept
    D   Separate entity concept

7   Which of the following best explains what is meant by 'capital expenditure'?

Capital expenditure is expenditure

    A   On fixed assets, including repairs and maintenance
    B   On expensive assets
    C   Relating to the issue of share capital
    D   Relating to the acquisition or improvement of fixed assets

MULTIPLE CHOICE QUESTIONS

8   Sales revenue should be recognised when goods and services have been supplied; costs are incurred when goods and services have been received.

   The accounting concept which governs the above is the

   A   Accruals concept
   B   Materiality concept
   C   Realisation concept
   D   Dual aspect concept

9   The capital maintenance concept implies that

   A   The capital of a business should be kept intact by not paying out dividends
   B   A business should invest its profits in the purchase of capital assets
   C   Fixed assets should be properly maintained
   D   Profit is earned only if the value of an organisation's net assets or its operating capability has increased during the accounting period

10 In times of rising prices, the historical cost convention:

   A   Understates asset values and profits
   B   Understates asset values and overstates profits
   C   Overstates asset values and profits
   D   Overstates asset values and understates profits

11 Who issues Financial Reporting Standards?

   A   The auditing practices board
   B   The stock exchange
   C   The accounting standards board
   D   The government

12 Which of the following is *not* an accounting concept?

   A   Prudence
   B   Consistency
   C   Depreciation
   D   Accruals

13 Which of the following statements gives the best definition of the objective of accounting?

   A   To provide useful information to users
   B   To record, categorise and summarise financial transactions
   C   To calculate the taxation due to the government
   D   To calculate the amount of dividend to pay to shareholders

14 According to the ASB 'statement of principles' which of the following is *not* an objective of financial statements?

   A   Providing information regarding the financial position of a business
   B   Providing information regarding the performance of a business
   C   Enabling users to assess the performance of management to aid decision making
   D   Helping to assess the going concern status of a business

15 The ASB statement of principles identified user groups. Which of the following is *not* an information need for the 'Investor' group?

   A   Assessment of repayment ability of an entity
   B   Measuring performance, risk and return
   C   Taking decisions regarding holding investments
   D   Taking buy/sell decisions

16 Which of the following is not a member of the Consultative Committee of Accounting Bodies (CCAB)?

   A   The Chartered Association of Certified Accountants
   B   The Chartered Institute of Management Accountants
   C   The Institutes of Chartered Accountants in England, Wales, Scotland and Ireland
   D   The Association of Accounting Technicians

17 The role of the Financial Reporting Council is to?

   A   Oversee the standard setting and regulatory process
   B   Formulate accounting standards
   C   Review defective accounts
   D   Control the accountancy profession

18 Making bad and doubtful debt provisions and valuing stock on the same basis in each accounting period are examples of which accounting concepts?

	Bad debt provision	*Stock valuation*
A	Accruals	Consistency
B	Accruals	Going concern
C	Prudence	Consistency
D	Prudence	Going concern

19 The prudence concept means that profit is only included in the profit and loss account if it is:

   A   Expected
   B   Material
   C   Realised
   D   Received

20 Which basic accounting concept is being followed when a charge is made for depreciation?

   A   Accruals
   B   Consistency
   C   Going concern
   D   Prudence

2 Double entry bookkeeping I

1   Gross profit for 20X3 can be calculated from

   A   Purchases for 20X3, plus stock at 31 December 20X3, less stock at 1 January 20X3
   B   Purchases for 20X3, less stock at 31 December 20X3, plus stock at 1 January 20X3
   C   Cost of goods sold during 20X3, plus sales during 20X3
   D   Net profit for 20X3, plus expenses for 20X3

MULTIPLE CHOICE QUESTIONS

2 Rent paid on 1 October 20X2 for the year to 30 September 20X3 was £1,200, and rent paid on 1 October 20X3 for the year to 30 September 20X4 was £1,600.

Rent payable, as shown in the profit and loss account for the year ended 31 December 20X3, would be

- A £1,200
- B £1,600
- C £1,300
- D £1,500

3 A decrease in the provision for doubtful debts would result in

- A An increase in liabilities
- B A decrease in working capital
- C A decrease in net profit
- D An increase in net profit

4 If, at the end of the financial year, a company makes a charge against the profits for stationery consumed but not yet invoiced, this adjustment is in accordance with the concept of

- A Materiality
- B Accruals
- C Consistency
- D Objectivity

5 A credit balance of £917 brought down on Y Ltd's account in the books of X Ltd means that

- A X Ltd owes Y Ltd £917
- B Y Ltd owes X Ltd £917
- C X Ltd has paid Y Ltd £917
- D X Ltd is owed £917 by Y Ltd

6 A company received an invoice from ABC Ltd, for 40 units at £10 each, less 25% trade discount, these being items purchased on credit and for resale. It paid this invoice minus a cash discount of 2%. Which of the following journal entries correctly records the effect of the whole transaction in the company's books?

		Debit £	Credit £
A	ABC Ltd	300	
	Purchases		300
	Cash	292	
	Discount allowed	8	
	ABC Ltd		300
B	Purchases	300	
	ABC Ltd		300
	ABC Ltd	300	
	Discount allowed		8
	Cash		292
C	Purchases	300	
	ABC Ltd		300
	ABC Ltd	300	
	Discount received		6
	Cash		294

			Debit £	Credit £
D	ABC Ltd		400	
	Purchases			400
	Cash		294	
	Discount received		106	
	ABC Ltd			400

7   The following is an extract from the trial balance of ABC Ltd at 31 December 20X4.

	Debit £	Credit £
Sales		73,716
Returns	5,863	3,492
Discounts	871	1,267

The figure to be shown in the trading account for net sales is

A   £66,586
B   £66,982
C   £67,853
D   £70,224

8   From the following information, calculate the value of purchases.

	£
Opening creditors	142,600
Cash paid	542,300
Discounts received	13,200
Goods returned	27,500
Closing creditors	137,800

A   £302,600
B   £506,400
C   £523,200
D   £578,200

9   Net profit was calculated as being £10,200. It was later discovered that capital expenditure of £3,000 had been treated as revenue expenditure, and revenue receipts of £1,400 had been treated as capital receipts.

The correct net profit should have been

A   £5,800
B   £8,600
C   £11,800
D   £14,600

10   Stationery paid for during 20X5 amounted to £1,350. At the beginning of 20X5 there was a stock of stationery on hand of £165 and an outstanding invoice for £80. At the end of 20X5, there was a stock of stationery on hand of £140 and an outstanding invoice for £70. The stationery figure to be shown in the profit and loss account for 20X5 is

A   £1,195
B   £1,335
C   £1,365
D   £1,505

MULTIPLE CHOICE QUESTIONS

11 A business received or issues the following invoices and pays or received the invoiced amounts on the following dates:

	Invoice date	Invoice amount	Date paid or received
Purchase	2.6.X1	£200	26.6.X1
	25.6.X1	£300	2.7.X1
Sales	8.6.X1	£400	26.6.X1
	29.6.X1	£600	7.7.X1

There is no stock at the beginning or end of June.

What is the difference between the profit for June calculated on a cash basis, and calculated on an accruals basis?

A   Nil
B   £200
C   £300
D   £500

12 Which of the following would be recorded in the purchase day book?

A   Discounts received
B   Purchase invoices
C   Trade discounts
D   Credit notes received

13 The total of the sales day-book is recorded in the nominal ledger as:

	Debit	Credit
A	Debtors	Debtors Control Account
B	Debtors Control Account	Debtors
C	Sales Account	Debtors Control Account
D	Debtors Control Account	Sales Account

14 Which of the following postings from the cashbook payments side is wrong?

A   The total of the cash paid column to the debit of the cash control account.
B   The total of the discounts column to the credit of the discounts received account.
C   The total of the discounts column to the debit of the creditors control account.
D   The total of the cash paid column to the credit of the cash control account.

15 (i)   A debit entry in the cashbook will increase an overdraft.
    (ii) A debit entry in the cashbook will increase a bank balance.

Are these statements true?

A   Both true
B   Both false
C   (i) true and (ii) false
D   (i) false and (ii) true

16 During the year, £4,000 was paid to the electricity board. At the beginning of the year, £1,000 was owed, and at the end of the year £1,200 was owed?

What is the charge for electricity in the years profit and loss account?

A £3,000
B £4,000
C £4,200
D £5,200

17 On 7 November 20X1, £8,400 rent was paid for the 24 months to 31 September 20X3.

What is the charge for rent in the profit and loss account and the balance sheet entry for the year to 31 December 20X2?

	Profit & Loss	Balance sheet
A	£4,200	Prepayment £3,150
B	£4,200	Prepayment £4,200
C	£5,250	Accrual £3,150
D	£5,250	Accrual £4,200

18 During the year £5,000 rent was received. At the beginning of the year, the tenant owed £1,000, at the end of the year the tenant owed £500.

What is the rent received figure for the year's profit and loss account?

A £4,000
B £4,500
C £5,000
D £5,500

19 During the year, £4,000 was paid for motor expenses. At the end of the year, the charge in the Profit & Loss account was £5,000, with an accrual of £2,500 in the balance sheet.

What was in last year's balance sheet for motor vehicles?

A Accrual £1,500
B Prepayment £1,500
C Accrual £3,500
D Prepayment £3,590

20 These figures relate to debtors:

Balance at 1/1/X1   £2,500
Balance at 31/12/X1   £2,000
Cash from debtors   £10,600
Contra with creditors ledger   £5,000
Increase in doubtful debts provision   £580

What were sales during the year?

A £5,100
B £14,520
C £15,100
D £15,680

21 An employee has a gross monthly salary of £1,000. In September the tax deducted was £200, the employee's national insurance was £60, and the employer's national insurance was £100. What was the charge for salaries in the profit and loss account?

   A   £740
   B   £940
   C   £1,000
   D   £1,100

22 W Ltd is registered for value added tax. The managing director has asked four staff in the accounts department why the output tax for the last quarter does not equal 17.5% of sales (17.5% is the rate of VAT). Which one of the following four replies she received was *not* correct?

   A   The company had some exports that were not liable to VAT
   B   The company made some sales of zero-rated products
   C   The company made some sales of exempt products
   D   The company sold some products to businesses not registered for VAT

23 A business sells goods costing £200 plus VAT at 17.5%. Which of the following entries correctly records this *credit sale*?

   A   Dr   Debtors   £235
        Cr   Sales   £235

   B   Dr   Debtors   £200
        Cr   Sales   £165
        Cr   VAT a/c   £35

   C   Dr   Debtors   £235
        Cr   Sales   £200
        Cr   VAT a/c   £35

   D   Dr   Sales   £200
        Dr   VAT   £35
        Cr   Creditors   £235

3 Double entry bookkeeping II

1 An increase in stock of £250, a decrease in the bank balance of £400 and an increase in creditors of £1,200 result in

   A   A decrease in working capital of £1,350
   B   An increase in working capital of £1,350
   C   A decrease in working capital of £1,050
   D   An increase in working capital of £1,050

2 A credit balance on a ledger account indicates

   A   An asset or an expense
   B   A liability or an expense
   C   An amount owing to the organisation
   D   A liability or a revenue

MULTIPLE CHOICE QUESTIONS

3 Which ONE of the following is not a book of prime entry?

    A   The petty cash book
    B   The sales returns day book
    C   The sales ledger
    D   The cash book

4 A book of prime entry is one in which

    A   The rules of double-entry bookkeeping do not apply
    B   Ledger accounts are maintained
    C   Transactions are entered prior to being recorded in the ledger account
    D   Subsidiary accounts are kept

5 A business has opening stock of £12,000 and closing stock of £18,000. Purchase returns were £5,000. The cost of goods sold was £111,000.

Purchases were

    A   £100,000
    B   £110,000
    C   £116,000
    D   £122,000

6 The double-entry system of bookkeeping normally results in which of the following balances on the ledger accounts?

	Debit balances	Credit balances
A	Assets and revenues	Liabilities, capital and expenses
B	Revenues, capital and liabilities	Assets and expenses
C	Assets and expenses	Liabilities, capital and revenues
D	Assets, expenses and capital	Liabilities and revenues

7 A business commenced with capital in cash of £1,000. Stock costing £800 is purchased on credit, and half is sold for £1,000 plus VAT, the customer paying in cash at once. The VAT rate is 17½%.

The accounting equation after these transactions would show:

    A   Assets £1,775 less Liabilities £175 equals Capital £1,600
    B   Assets £2,175 less Liabilities £975 equals Capital £1,200
    C   Assets £2,575 less Liabilities £800 equals Capital £1,775
    D   Assets £2,575 less Liabilities £975 equals Capital £1,600

8 A sole trader had opening capital of £10,000 and closing capital of £4,500. During the period, the owner introduced capital of £4,000 and withdrew £8,000 for her own use.

Her profit or loss during the period was

    A   £9,500 loss
    B   £1,500 loss
    C   £7,500 profit
    D   £17,500 profit

9 A credit entry of £450 on X's account in the books of Y could have arisen by

    A   X buying goods on credit from Y
    B   Y paying X £450
    C   Y returning goods to X
    D   X returning goods to Y

MULTIPLE CHOICE QUESTIONS

10 At 1 September, the motor expenses account showed 4-months' insurance prepaid of £80 and petrol accrued of £95. During September, the outstanding petrol bill is paid, plus further bills of £245. At 30 September there is a further outstanding petrol bill of £120.

The amount to be shown in the profit and loss account for motor expenses for September is

A   £385
B   £415
C   £445
D   £460

11 A tenant pays us rent of £1,000 a month. At the year-end he had paid 3 months in advance. During the year, £16,000 was received.

What was in our last year's balance sheet in respect of this tenant?

A   £1,000 debit
B   £1,000 credit
C   £7,000 debit
D   £7,000 credit

12 A trial balance contains the following:

	£
Opening stock	1,000
Closing stock	2,000
Purchases	10,000
Purchases returned	200
Carriage inwards	1,500
Prompt payment discounts received	800

What is the cost of sales figure?

A   £8,800
B   £9,500
C   £10,300
D   £12,300

13 A company has been notified that a debtor has been declared bankrupt. The company had previously provided for this doubtful debt. Which of the following is the correct double entry?

	DR	CR
A	Bad and doubtful debts account	The debtor
B	The debtor	Bad and doubtful account
C	Provision for doubtful debts	The debtor
D	The debtor	Provision for doubtful debts

14 A purchase invoice shows 10 items priced at £120 less trade discount 20%. A cash discount of 2½% is allowed if settlement is made within the allowed credit period. How much will be paid if the cash discount applies?

A   £1,170
B   £1,200
C   £936
D   £960

15 Discounts received £800 were treated as discounts allowed when a traders' profit and loss account was prepared. Therefore?

   A   Profits were understated by £800
   B   Profits were overstated by £800
   C   Profits were understated by £1,600
   D   Profits were overstated by £1,600

16 An increase in a provision for bad debts has been treated as a reduction in the financial statements. The amount is £8,000. Which of the following explains the resulting effects?

   A   Net profit is overstated by £16,000, balance sheet debtors overstated by £8,000
   B   Net profit understated by £16,000, balance sheet debtors understated by £16,000
   C   Net profit overstated by £16,000, balance sheet debtors overstated by £16,000
   D   Gross profit overstated by £16,000, balance sheet debtors overstated by £16,000

17 At 1 January 20X1, there was a provision for doubtful debts of £3,000. During the year, £1,000 of debts was written off, and £800 of bad debts was recovered. At 31 December 20X1, it was decided to adjust the bad debts provision to 5% of debtors which are £20,000.

   What is the total bad debt expense for the year?

   A   £200 debit
   B   £1,800 debit
   C   £2,200 debit
   D   £1,800 credit

18 At the beginning of the year, the provision for doubtful debts was £1,000. At the end of the year when debtors were £18,500, a specific provision was made for the whole of Bert's debt of £500 and for 80% of Fred's debt of £1,000. It was decided to make a general provision of 2% of remaining debts.

   What was the closing balance on the provision for the doubtful debts account?

   A   £640
   B   £1,640
   C   £1,644
   D   £2,640

19 Provisions for doubtful debts are an example of which accounting concept?

   A   Accruals
   B   Consistency
   C   Matching
   D   Prudence

20 At the beginning of the year, the provision for doubtful debts was £850. At the year-end, the provision required was £1,000. During the year £500 of debts were written off, which includes £100 previously provided for.

   What is the charge to profit and loss for bad and doubtful debts for the year?

   A   £1,500
   B   £1,000
   C   £650
   D   £550

MULTIPLE CHOICE QUESTIONS

21   What is the correct treatment of discounts allowed and discounts received?

	Discounts allowed	*Discounts Received*
A	Debit creditors control	Credit debtors control
B	Credit creditors control	Credit debtors control
C	Debit debtors control	Credit creditors control
D	Credit debtors control	Debit creditors control

22   Trade debtors and creditors in the final accounts of a VAT registered trader will appear as described by which of the following?

- A   Inclusive of VAT in the balance sheet.
- B   Exclusive of VAT in the balance sheet.
- C   The VAT is deducted and added to the VAT a/c in the balance sheet.
- D   VAT does not appear in the balance sheet because the business simply acts as a collector on behalf of the Government.

23   Net wages paid are?

- A   Debited to P&L as the total employment cost
- B   Debited to wages control a/c
- C   Debited to bank a/c
- D   Credited to wages control a/c

24   A business has the following items extracted from its accounting records. Sales £150,000, opening stock £10,000, closing stock £15,000. The business applies a constant mark up of 25%. Calculate the total purchases for the year.

- A   £115,000
- B   £145,000
- C   £117,500
- D   £125,000

4 Stocks

1   In times of rising prices, the FIFO method of stock valuation, when compared to the average cost method of stock valuation, will usually produce

- A   A higher profit and a lower closing stock value
- B   A higher profit and a higher closing stock value
- C   A lower profit and a lower closing stock value
- D   A lower profit and a higher closing stock value

2   Following the preparation of the profit and loss account, it is discovered that accrued expenses of £1,000 have been ignored and that closing stock has been overvalued by £1,300. This will have resulted in

- A   An overstatement of net profit of £300
- B   An understatement of net profit of £300
- C   An overstatement of net profit of £2,300
- D   An understatement of net profit of £2,300

3   Stock is valued using FIFO. Opening stock was 10 units at £2 each. Purchases were 30 units at £3 each, then issues of 12 units were made, followed by issues of 8 units.

Closing stock is valued at

- A   £50
- B   £58
- C   £60
- D   £70

4   An organisation's stock at 1 July is 15 units @ £3.00 each. The following movements occur:

- 3 July 20X6   5 units sold at £3.30 each
- 8 July 20X6   10 units bought at £3.50 each
- 12 July 20X6   8 units sold at £4.00 each

Closing stock at 31 July, using the FIFO method of stock valuation would be

- A   £31.50
- B   £36.00
- C   £39.00
- D   £41.00

5   Your organisation uses the weighted average cost method of valuing stocks. During August 20X1, the following stock details were recorded:

Opening balance	30 units valued at £2 each
5 August	purchase of 50 units at £2.40 each
10 August	issue of 40 units
18 August	purchase of 60 units at £2.50 each
23 August	issue of 25 units

The value of the balance at 31 August 20X1 was

- A   £172.50
- B   £176.25
- C   £180.00
- D   £187.50

6   During September, your organisation had sales of £148,000, which made a gross profit of £40,000. Purchases amounted to £100,000 and opening stock was £34,000.

The value of closing stock was

- A   £24,000
- B   £26,000
- C   £42,000
- D   £54,000

7   Your firm values stock using the weighted average cost method. At 1 October 20X8, there were 60 units in stock valued at £12 each. On 8 October, 40 units were purchased for £15 each, and a further 50 units were purchased for £18 each on 14 October. On 21 October, 75 units were sold for £1,200.

The value of closing stock at 31 October 20X8 was:

- A   £900
- B   £1,020
- C   £1,110
- D   £1,125

MULTIPLE CHOICE QUESTIONS

8   Stock movements for product X during the last quarter were as follows:

    January   Purchases   10 items at £19.80 each
    February   Sales   10 items at £30 each
    March   Purchases   20 items at £24.50 each
                Sales   5 items at £30 each

    Opening stock at 1 January was 6 items valued at £15 each

    Gross profit for the quarter, using the weighted average cost method, would be

    A   £135.75
    B   £155.00
    C   £174.00
    D   £483.00

9   In times of rising prices, the valuation of stock using the FIFO method, as opposed to average cost, will result in which ONE of the following combinations?

	Cost of sales	Profit	Closing stocks
A	Lower	Higher	Higher
B	Lower	Higher	Lower
C	Higher	Lower	Higher
D	Higher	Higher	Lower

10 Which of the following methods of valuing stocks are allowed under SSAP 9.

    (i)   LIFO
    (ii) Average cost
    (iii) FIFO
    (iv) Replacement cost

    A   (i), (ii), (iii), (iv)
    B   (i), (ii), (iv)
    C   (ii), (iii)
    D   (iii), (iv)

11 Opening stock of raw materials was £58,000, closing stock was £63,000, purchases were £256,000, purchase returns were £17,000. What was cost of sales?

    A   £256,000
    B   £234,000
    C   £239,000
    D   £244,000

12 How should a loss of stock (value £15,000) caused by flooding in the company's warehouse be accounted for? (Assume the stock loss is not insured.)

    A   Dr   Trading a/c   £15,000
             Cr   P&L a/c   £15,000

    B   Dr   P&L a/c   £15,000
             Cr   Trading a/c   £15,000

    C   Dr   Drawings   £15,000
             Cr   Trading a/c   £15,000

    D   Dr   Stock a/c   £15,000
             Cr   Trading a/c   £15,000

13 Net realisable value means? (In relation to the valuation of stock.)

   A   The expected selling price of the stock.

   B   The expected selling price less disposals costs less, in the case of incomplete items, the cost of completion.

   C   The replacement cost of the stock.

   D   The market price.

14 FIFO, LIFO and average cost are stock valuation methods. Which of the following statements is correct?

   A   When prices are rising FIFO will produce the higher profit figure of all these methods.
   B   When prices are rising LIFO will produce the higher profit figure of all these methods.
   C   LIFO is a permissible valuation method under SSAP 9.
   D   Average cost is recomputed following every dispatch or issue of stock.

15 A company has an annual stock take, the factory did not cease production during the stock take and some goods in work in progress (cost £5,500) were later counted again and included in finished goods stock (cost £7,500). As a result profit was?

   A   Overstated by £2,000
   B   Overstated by £7,500
   C   Overstated by £5,500
   D   Overstated by £13,000

16 Which of the following statements are correct?

   (i)   A stock valuation should include carriage in.
   (ii) A stock valuation should exclude carriage out.

   A   Both correct
   B   Both incorrect
   C   (i) correct, (ii) incorrect
   D   (i) incorrect, (ii) correct

17 A company which gives its sales personnel 5% of sales price as commission, has this stock at the year end:

	Quantity	Cost	Per unit Estimated sales price
Beads	2,000	£1.50	£1.53
Buttons	1,500	£1.25	£1.40
Bows	2,000	£1.60	£1.50

   At what value should this stock be recorded in the financial statements?

   A   £7,756
   B   £7,632
   C   £7,875
   D   £8,175

MULTIPLE CHOICE QUESTIONS

5 Fixed assets

1   What is the purpose of charging depreciation in accounts?

    A   To allocate the cost less residual value of a fixed asset over the accounting periods expected to benefit from its use

    B   To ensure that funds are available for the eventual replacement of the asset

    C   To reduce the cost of the asset in the balance sheet to its estimated market value

    D   To comply with the prudence concept

2   Your firm bought a machine for £5,000 on 1 January 20X1, which had an expected useful life of four years and an expected residual value of £1,000; the asset was to be depreciated on the straight-line basis. On 31 December 20X3, the machine was sold for £1,600.

    The amount to be entered in the 20X3 profit and loss account for profit or loss on disposal, is

    A   Profit of £600
    B   Loss of £600
    C   Profit of £350
    D   Loss of £400

3   A fixed asset register showed a net book value of £67,460. A fixed asset costing £15,000 had been sold for £4,000, making a loss on disposal of £1,250. No entries had been made in the fixed asset register for this disposal.

    The balance on the fixed asset register should be

    A   £42,710
    B   £51,210
    C   £53,710
    D   £62,210

4   An organisation's fixed asset register shows a net book value of £135,600. The fixed asset account in the nominal ledger shows a net book value of £125,600. The difference could be due to a disposed asset not having been removed from the fixed asset ledger.

    A   With disposal proceeds of £15,000 and a profit on disposal of £5,000
    B   With disposal proceeds of £15,000 and a net book value of £5,000
    C   With disposal proceeds of £15,000 and a loss on disposal of £5,000
    D   With disposal proceeds of £5,000 and a net book value of £5,000

5   Recording the purchase of computer stationery by debiting the computer equipment account at cost would result in

    A   An overstatement of profit and an overstatement of fixed assets
    B   An understatement of profit and an overstatement of fixed assets
    C   An overstatement of profit and an understatement of fixed assets
    D   An understatement of profit and an understatement of fixed assets

6   Depreciation is best described as

    A   A means of spreading the payment for fixed assets over a period of years
    B   A decline in the market value of the assets
    C   A means of spreading the net cost of fixed assets over their estimated useful life
    D   A means of estimating the amount of money needed to replace the assets

MULTIPLE CHOICE QUESTIONS

7   A business has made a profit of £8,000 but its bank balance has fallen by £5,000. This could be due to

    A   Depreciation of £3,000 and an increase in stocks of £10,000
    B   Depreciation of £6,000 and the repayment of a loan of £7,000
    C   Depreciation of £12,000 and the purchase of new fixed assets for £25,000
    D   The disposal of a fixed asset for £13,000 less than its book value

8   A fixed asset costing £12,500 was sold at a book loss of £4,500. Depreciation had been provided using the reducing balance, at 20% per annum since its purchase.

Which of the following correctly describes the sale proceeds and length of time for which the asset had been owned?

	Sale proceeds	Length of ownership
A	Cannot be calculated	Cannot be calculated
B	Cannot be calculated	2 years
C	£8,000	Cannot be calculated
D	£8,000	2 years

9   On 1 July 20X7, your fixed asset register showed a net book value of £47,500. The ledger accounts showed fixed assets at cost of £60,000 and provision for depreciation of £15,000. It was discovered that the disposal of an asset for £4,000, giving rise to a loss on disposal of £1,500, had not been recorded in the fixed asset register.

After correcting this omission, the fixed asset register would show a balance which was

    A   £3,000 lower than the ledger accounts
    B   £1,500 lower than the ledger accounts
    C   equal to the ledger accounts
    D   £1,000 higher than the ledger accounts

10 A fixed asset was purchased at the beginning of Year 1 for £2,400 and depreciated by 20% per annum by the reducing balance method. At the beginning of Year 4 it was sold for £1,200. The result of this was

    A   A loss on disposal of £240.00
    B   A loss on disposal of £28.80
    C   A profit on disposal of £28.80
    D   A profit on disposal of £240.00

11 The net book value of a company's fixed assets was £200,000 at 1 August 20X8. During the year ended 31 July 20X9, the company sold fixed assets for £25,000 on which it made a loss of £5,000. The depreciation charge for the year was £20,000. What was the net book value of fixed assets at 31 July 20X9?

    A   £150,000
    B   £155,000
    C   £160,000
    D   £180,000

12 Which of the following costs would be classified as capital expenditure for a restaurant business?

    A   A replacement for a broken window
    B   Repainting the restaurant
    C   An illuminated sign advertising the business name
    D   Knives and forks for the restaurant

MULTIPLE CHOICE QUESTIONS

13   On 1 June 20X9 a machine was sold which cost £20,000 on 31 July 20X5. The sale proceeds were £5,500. The depreciation policy for machinery is 20% pa straight line, with a full year being charged in the year of acquisition and none in the year of disposal. The year-end is 31 December.

What is the profit or loss on disposal?

A   Profit £834
B   Loss £834
C   Profit £1,500
D   Loss £1,500

14   On 1 June 20X9 a machine was sold which cost £20,000 on 31 July 20X5. Sale proceeds were £5,500 and the profit on disposal was £1,500. The depreciation policy for machinery is straight line with a full year being charged in the year of acquisition and none in the year of sale.

What is the depreciation rate?

A   20% pa
B   25% pa
C   30% pa
D   35% pa

15   A business buys a machine for £15,000. The depreciation policy for machinery is 15% pa reducing balance. What is the net book value of the machine after two years of use?

A   £10,500
B   £10,837
C   £11,175
D   £12,750

16   A company has recorded its freehold property at its historical cost of £100,000. It now decides to record it at its market value of £280,000, by making which entries?

A	Debit fixed assets	180,000	
	Credit revaluation reserve		180,000
B	Debit revaluation reserve	180,000	
	Credit fixed assets		180,000
C	Debit fixed assets	180,000	
	Credit profit and loss		180,000
D	Debit fixed assets	280,000	
	Credit revaluation reserve		280,000

17   Which of the following would not be included in intangible fixed assets in a company's financial statements?

A   Development costs
B   Goodwill
C   Patents
D   Shares held in a supplier

6 Bank reconciliations

1. Your cash book at 31 December 20X3 shows a bank balance of £565 overdrawn. On comparing this with your bank statement at the same date, you discover the following.

   (a) A cheque for £57 drawn by you on 29 December 20X3 has not yet been presented for payment.

   (b) A cheque for £92 from a customer, which was paid into the bank on 24 December 20X3, has been dishonoured on 31 December 20X3.

   The correct bank balance to be shown in the balance sheet at 31 December 20X3 is

   A   £714 overdrawn
   B   £657 overdrawn
   C   £473 overdrawn
   D   £53 overdrawn

2. The cash book shows a bank balance of £5,675 overdrawn at 31 August 20X5. It is subsequently discovered that a standing order for £125 has been entered twice, and that a dishonoured cheque for £450 has been debited in the cash book instead of credited.

   The correct bank balance should be

   A   £5,100 overdrawn
   B   £6,000 overdrawn
   C   £6,250 overdrawn
   D   £6,450 overdrawn

3. A business had a balance at the bank of £2,500 at the start of the month. During the following month, it paid for materials invoiced at £1,000 less trade discount of 20% and cash discount of 10%. It received a cheque from a debtor in respect of an invoice for £200, subject to cash discount of 5%.

   The balance at the bank at the end of the month was

   A   £1,970
   B   £1,980
   C   £1,990
   D   £2,000

4. The bank statement on 31 October 20X7 showed an overdraft of £800. On reconciling the bank statement, it was discovered that a cheque drawn by your company for £80 had not been presented for payment, and that a cheque for £130 from a customer had been dishonoured on 30 October 20X7.

   The correct bank balance to be shown in the balance sheet at 31 October 20X7 is

   A   £1,010 overdrawn
   B   £880 overdrawn
   C   £750 overdrawn
   D   £720 overdrawn

5. Your firm's cash book at 30 April 20X8 shows a balance at the bank of £2,490. Comparison with the bank statement at the same date reveals the following differences:

	£
Unpresented cheques	840
Bank charges not in cash book	50
Receipts not yet credited by the bank	470
Dishonoured cheque not in cash book	140

   The correct balance on the cash book at 30 April 20X8 is

	A	£1,460
	B	£2,300
	C	£2,580
	D	£3,140

6   Your firm's bank statement at 31 October 20X8 shows a balance of £13,400. You subsequently discover that the bank has dishonoured a customer's cheque for £300 and has charged bank charges of £50, neither of which is recorded in your cash book. There are unpresented cheques totalling £2,400. Amounts paid in, but not yet credited by the bank, amount to £1,000. You further discover that an automatic receipt from a customer of £195 has been recorded as a credit in your cash book.

Your cash book balance, prior to correcting the errors and omissions, was:

    A   £11,455
    B   £11,960
    C   £12,000
    D   £12,155

7   Your firm's cashbook shows a credit bank balance of £1,240 at 30 April 20X9. Upon comparison with the bank statement, you determine that there are unpresented cheques totalling £450, and a receipt of £140 which has not yet been passed through the bank account. The bank statement shows bank charges of £75 which have not been entered in the cash book.

The balance on the bank statement is

    A   £1,005 overdrawn
    B   £930 overdrawn
    C   £1,475
    D   £1,550

8   Which of the following is NOT a valid reason for the cash book and bank statement failing to agree?

    A   Timing difference
    B   Bank charges
    C   Error
    D   Cash receipts posted to creditors

9   The bank statement at 31 December 20X1 shows a balance of £1,000. The cash book shows a balance of £750 in hand. Which of the following is the most likely reason for the difference.

    A   Receipts of £250 recorded in cash book, but not yet recorded by bank
    B   Bank charges of £250 shown on the bank statement, not in the cash book
    C   Standing orders of £250 included on bank statement, not in the cash book
    D   Cheques for £250 recorded in the cash book, but not yet gone through the bank account

10 The cash book balance at 30 November 20X2 shows an overdraft of £500. Cheques for £6,000 have been written and sent out, but do not yet appear on the bank statement. Receipts of £5,000 are in the cash book, but are not yet on the bank statement. What is the balance on the bank statement?

    A   £1,500
    B   £500 in hand
    C   £1,500 in hand
    D   £500 overdrawn

11 A debit entry on a bank statement will have which effect on the level of a bank overdraft and a bank balance?

	Bank overdraft	Bank balance
A	Increase	Increase
B	Decrease	Decrease
C	Increase	Decrease
D	Decrease	Increase

12 When preparing a bank reconciliation it is realised that:

(i)   Cheques with a value of £1,050 have been sent to suppliers and correctly entered in the cash book, but have not yet been presented for payment.

(ii) A cheque for £75 sent to a supplier has been incorrectly recorded in the cash book as £57.

(iii) Before correction, the cash book has a balance of £10,500 credit.

(iv) Bank charges of £175 have not been recorded in the cash book.

The balance of the cashbook after the correction is:

A   £10,307 overdrawn
B   £10,343 overdrawn
C   £10,657 overdrawn
D   £10,693 overdrawn

13 When preparing a bank reconciliation, it is realised that:

(i)   Cheques with a value of £1,050 have been sent to suppliers and correctly entered in the cash book, but have not yet been presented for payment.

(ii) A cheque for £75 sent to a supplier has been incorrectly recorded in the cash book as £57.

(iii) Before correction, the cash book has a balance of £10,500 credit.

(iv) Bank charges of £175 have not been recorded in the cash book.

What is the closing balance shown on the bank statement?

A   £9,257 overdrawn
B   £9,643 overdrawn
C   £11,357 overdrawn
D   £11,743 overdrawn

14 When preparing a bank reconciliation, it is realised that:

(i)   There are unpresented cheques of £8,000
(ii) There are lodgements of £5,000 uncleared
(iii) Bank charges of £67 have not been recorded in the cash book

What adjustment is required to the cash account?

A   Debit £67
B   Credit £67
C   Debit £3,067
D   Credit £3,067

MULTIPLE CHOICE QUESTIONS

15 A company uses the imprest system to control its petty cash, keeping a float of £50.

Since the cash was last replenished it had the following transactions:

1   £12.50 to the milkman
2   £10.00 on taxis
3   £5.70 on stationary
4   £20 advance taken by the director for a taxi fare last week returned unused
5   £18.50 to the cleaner
6   £15 advance to the MD's secretary

How much should now be drawn out of the bank?

A   £50
B   £41.70
C   £46.70
D   £31.70

16 A business has the following cash and bank transactions during January 20X1. Balance 1.1.20X1: cash £500, bank £1,000 overdrawn, receipts of cash £12,600, cash paid £3,200, cash paid to bank £5,500, payments by cheque £8,200. Closing balances: cash £600, bank £6,200 overdrawn. Calculate the total cash and bank drawings.

A   £14,800 (no bank drawings)
B   £860
C   £11,800
D   £6,300

7 Control accounts

1   You are given the following information:

Debtors at 1 January 20X3	£10,000
Debtors at 31 December 20X3	£9,000
Total receipts during 20X3 (including cash sales of £5,000)	£85,000

Sales on credit during 20X3 amount to

A   £81,000
B   £86,000
C   £79,000
D   £84,000

2   A supplier sends you a statement showing a balance outstanding of £14,350. Your own records show a balance outstanding of £14,500.

The reason for this difference could be that

A   The supplier sent an invoice for £150 which you have not yet received
B   The supplier has allowed you £150 cash discount which you had omitted to enter in your ledgers
C   You have paid the supplier £150 which he has not yet accounted for
D   You have returned goods worth £150 which the supplier has not yet accounted for

3   The sales ledger control account at 1 May had balances of £32,750 debit and £1,275 credit. During May, sales of £125,000 were made on credit. Receipts from debtors amounted to £122,500 and cash discounts of £550 were allowed. Refunds of £1,300 were made to customers. The closing balances at 31 May could be

   A   £35,175 debit and £3,000 credit
   B   £35,675 debit and £2,500 credit
   C   £36,725 debit and £2,000 credit
   D   £36,725 debit and £1,000 credit

4   The debit side of a trial balance totals £50 more than the credit side. This could be due to

   A   A purchase of goods for £50 being omitted from the creditor's account
   B   A sale of goods for £50 being omitted from the debtor's account
   C   An invoice of £25 for electricity being credited to the electricity account
   D   A receipt for £50 from a debtor being omitted from the cash book

5   A sales ledger control account had a closing balance of £8,500. It contained a contra to the purchase ledger of £400, but this had been entered on the wrong side of the control account.

   The correct balance on the control account should be

   A   £7,700 debit
   B   £8,100 debit
   C   £8,400 debit
   D   £8,900 debit

6   A trader who is not registered for VAT purposes buys goods on credit. These goods have a list price of £2,000, exclusive of VAT, and the trader is given a trade discount of 20%. The goods carry VAT at 17.5%.

   The correct ledger entries to record this purchase are to debit the purchases account and to credit the supplier's account with

   A   £1,600
   B   £1,880
   C   £2,000
   D   £2,350

7   Your purchase ledger control account has a balance at 1 October 20X8 of £34,500 credit. During October, credit purchases were £78,400, cash purchases were £2,400 and payments made to suppliers, excluding cash purchases, and after deducting cash discounts of £1,200, were £68,900. Purchase returns were £4,700.

   The closing balance was:

   A   £38,100
   B   £40,500
   C   £47,500
   D   £49,900

8   The sales account is

   A   Credited with the total of sales made, including VAT
   B   Credited with the total of sales made, excluding VAT
   C   Debited with the total of sales made, including VAT
   D   Debited with the total of sales made, excluding VAT

MULTIPLE CHOICE QUESTIONS

9   At the end of the month, an organisation needs to accrue for one week's wages. The gross wages amount to £500, tax amounts to £100, employer's national insurance is £50, employees' national insurance is £40, and employees' contributions to pension scheme amount to £30. The ledger entries to record this accrual would be

A	Debit wages expense	£500	Credit national insurance creditor	£90
			Credit income tax creditor	£100
			Credit pension scheme creditor	£30
			Credit wages accrued	£280
B	Debit wages expense	£550	Credit national insurance creditor	£90
			Credit income tax creditor	£100
			Credit pension scheme creditor	£30
			Credit wages accrued	£330
C	Debit wages expense	£280	Credit wages accrued	£500
	Debit national insurance expense	£90		
	Debit income tax expense	£100		
	Debit pension scheme expense	£30		
D	Debit wages expense	£330	Credit wages accrued	£550
	Debit national insurance expense	£90		
	Debit income tax expense	£100		
	Debit pension scheme expense	£30		

10 If sales (including VAT) amounted to £27,612.50, and purchases (excluding VAT) amounted to £18,000, the balance on the VAT account, assuming all items are subject to VAT at 17.5%, would be

    A   £962.50 debit
    B   £962.50 credit
    C   £1,682.10 debit
    D   £1,682.10 credit

11 Which of the following is *not* the purpose of a sales ledger control account?

    A   A sales ledger control account provides a check on the arithmetical accuracy of the personal ledger
    B   A sales ledger control account helps to locate errors in the trial balance
    C   A sales ledger control account ensures that there are no errors in the personal ledger
    D   Control accounts deter fraud

12 The total of the balances in the purchase ledger control account is £1,500 more than the total of the creditor balances extracted from the purchase ledger. Which of the following would explain this difference?

    A   The purchase day book is over added by £1,500.

    B   Discounts received have not been posted in the purchase ledger accounts.

    C   Cash paid to creditors has not been posted in some accounts in the purchase ledger.

    D   A contra entry between the purchase and sales ledgers has been omitted from the purchase ledger but was posted in the control account.

13   When reconciling the list of debtors to the debtors control account, it is discovered that:

(i)   A credit balance of £150 on a customer's account has been treated as a debit balance.
(ii) A debit balance of £120 on a customer's account has been omitted.

What is the required adjustment to the list of balances?

A   Add £30
B   Subtract £30
C   Add £180
D   Subtract £180

14   When reconciling the debtors control account to the list of balances, it was discovered that the sales daybook has been overcast by £50.

What adjustment is necessary to the list of balances?

A   No adjustment
B   Add £50
C   Subtract £50
D   Subtract £100

15   When reconciling the debtors control account to the list of balances, it is discovered that £2,000 of goods returned by customers were not recorded in the nominal ledger.

What is the required adjustment to the debtors control account?

A   Debit £2,000
B   Credit £2,000
C   Debit £4,000
D   Credit £4,000

16   When reconciling control accounts to lists of balances, a casting error in a daybook will require adjustments:

A   To both the control account and the list of balances
B   To neither the control account nor the list of balances
C   To the control account, but not the list of balances
D   To the list of balances, but not the control account

17   On 1 January 20X1, the balance on the debtors control account was £2,050.

During the year:

Sales   £90,000
Sales returns   £4,000
Cash receipts from customers   £72,800
Discounts allowed   £2,570

The cash receipts included £500 from a customer whose debt had been written off last year.

What is the balance on the debtors control account at the year-end?

A   £12,680
B   £13,180
C   £13,680
D   £17,820

18 On 1 January 20X1, the balance on the debtors control account was £2,050, by 31 December it was £5,000. Sales had been £100,000, sales returns £10,000 and cash receipts £85,500.

What was the amount settled by debtor and creditor account contras?

A £1,550
B £3,100
C £3,600
D £11,550

8 Errors and suspense accounts I

1 Splodge plc's accounts contain two errors. A £10,000 bad debt written off has been deducted from sales and a £20,000 credit note received has been added to sales. Before correction, turnover was £1m and cost of sales was £800,000. What is the gross profit margin after correction of these errors?

A 17.8%
B 18.8%
C 21.2%
D 22.2%

2 After calculating your company's profit for 20X3, you discover that:

(a) A fixed asset costing £50,000 has been included in the purchases account;

(b) Stationery costing £10,000 has been included as closing stock of raw materials, instead of stock of stationery.

These two errors have had the effect of

A Understating gross profit by £40,000 and understating net profit by £50,000
B Understating both gross profit and net profit by £40,000
C Understating gross profit by £60,000 and understating net profit by £50,000
D Overstating both gross profit and net profit by £60,000

3 The suspense account shows a debit balance of £100. This could be due to

A Entering £50 received from A Turner on the debit side of A Turner's account
B Entering £50 received from A Turner on the credit side of A Turner's account
C Undercasting the sales day book by £100
D Undercasting the purchases account by £100

4 The capital of a sole trader would change as a result of

A A creditor being paid his account by cheque
B Raw materials being purchased on credit
C Fixed assets being purchased on credit
D Wages being paid in cash

5 You are the accountant of ABC Ltd and have extracted a trial balance at 31 October 20X4. The sum of the debit column of the trial balance exceeds the sum of the credit column by £829. A suspense account has been opened to record the difference. After preliminary investigations failed to locate any errors, you have decided to prepare draft final accounts in accordance with the prudence concept.

The suspense account balance would be treated as

A An expense in the profit and loss account
B Additional income in the profit and loss account
C An asset in the balance sheet
D A liability in the balance sheet

6   Where a transaction is credited to the correct ledger account, but debited incorrectly to the repairs and renewals account instead of to the plant and machinery account, the error is known as an error of

    A   Omission
    B   Commission
    C   Principle
    D   Original entry

7   If a purchase return of £48 has been wrongly posted to the debit of the sales returns account, but has been correctly entered in the supplier's account, the total of the trial balance would show

    A   The credit side to be £48 more than the debit side
    B   The debit side to be £48 more than the credit side
    C   The credit side to be £96 more than the debit side
    D   The debit side to be £96 more than the credit side

8   A suspense account shows a credit balance of £130. This could be due to

    A   Omitting a sale of £130 from the sales ledger
    B   Recording a purchase of £130 twice in the purchases account
    C   Failing to write off a bad debt of £130
    D   Recording an electricity bill paid of £65 by debiting the bank account and crediting the electricity account.

9   An organisation restores its petty cash balance to £500 at the end of each month. During January, the total column in the petty cash book was recorded as being £420, and hence the imprest was restored by this amount. The analysis columns, which had been posted to the nominal ledger, totalled only £400. This error would result in

    A   No imbalance in the trial balance
    B   The trial balance being £20 higher on the debit side
    C   The trial balance being £20 higher on the credit side
    D   The petty cash balance being £20 lower than it should be

10 An invoice from a supplier of office equipment has been debited to the stationery account. This error is known as

    A   An error of commission
    B   An error of original entry
    C   A compensating error
    D   An error of principle

11 Which of these statements are correct?

    (i)   A casting error in a day-book will stop the trial balance balancing.
    (ii)   A transposition error in a daybook will stop the trial balance balancing.

    A   (i) only
    B   (i) and (ii)
    C   (ii) only
    D   Neither (i) or (ii)

MULTIPLE CHOICE QUESTIONS

12 Carriage inwards £5,000 has been recorded in the P&L account as an expense, as a result?

- A Net profit is understated by £15,000
- B Gross profit is overstated by £15,000, net profit is unchanged
- C Gross profit is understated by £15,000
- D Net profit is overstated by £15,000

13 A trial balance has failed to agree. The totals of the debits amounted to £157,800, the credit balances totalled £155,300. The difference was posted to a suspense account. Which of the following would explain this difference?

- A Rates were recorded as
  - Dr   Bank   £2,500
  - Cr   Rates   £2,500
- B An invoice for advertising costs £1,125 debited to advertising a/c and also debited to bank a/c
- C An invoice for the purchase of stock was omitted from the accounts
- D A sundry receipt £1,125 was debited to income and credited to cash

14 When a trial balance was prepared, two ledger accounts were omitted:

Discounts received   £2,050
Discounts allowed   £2,500

To make a trial balance balance, a suspense account was opened.

What was the balance on the suspense account?

- A Debit £450
- B Credit £450
- C Debit £4,550
- D Credit £4,550

15 When a trial balance was prepared, a suspense account was opened. It was discovered that the only error that had been made was to record £2,050 of discounts received on the wrong side of the trial balance.

What is the journal to correct this error?

- A Dr discounts received £2,050   Cr suspense £2,050
- B Dr suspense £2,050   Cr discounts received £2,050
- C Dr discounts received £4,100   Cr suspense £4,100
- D Dr suspense £4,100   Cr discounts received £4,100

16 When a trial balance was prepared, a suspense account was opened. The only error that has been made was that when £400 written off the previous year was recovered, the bookkeeper credited the bad debts expense account and the debtors control account and debited cash.

Which journal is required to correct this error?

- A Dr suspense £400   Cr debtors control £400
- B Dr debtors control £400   Cr suspense £400
- C Dr suspense £800   Cr debtors control £800
- D Dr debtors control £800   Cr suspense £800

9 Errors and suspense accounts II

1   An error of principle would occur if

    A   Plant and machinery purchased was credited to a fixed assets account
    B   Plant and machinery purchased was debited to the purchases account
    C   Plant and machinery purchased was debited to the equipment account
    D   Plant and machinery purchased was debited to the correct account but with the wrong amount

2   An organisation's year end is 30 September. On 1 January 20X6 the organisation took out a loan of £100,000 with annual interest of 12%. The interest is payable in equal instalments on the first day of April, July, October and January in arrears.

How much should be charged to the profit and loss account for the year ended 30 September 20X6, and how much should be accrued on the balance sheet?

	Profit and loss account	Balance sheet
A	£12,000	£3,000
B	£9,000	£3,000
C	£9,000	nil
D	£6,000	£3,000

3   A suspense account was opened when a trial balance failed to agree. The following errors were later discovered.

- A gas bill of £420 had been recorded in the gas account as £240
- A discount of £50 given to a customer had been credited to discounts received
- Interest received of £70 had been entered in the bank account only

The original balance on the suspense account was

    A   Debit £210
    B   Credit £210
    C   Debit £160
    D   Credit £160

4   An error of commission is one where

    A   A transaction has not been recorded

    B   One side of a transaction has been recorded in the wrong class of account, such as fixed assets posted to stock

    C   An error has been made in posting a transaction

    D   The digits in a number are recorded the wrong way round

5   Where a transaction is entered into the correct ledger accounts, but the wrong amount is used, the error is known as an error of

    A   Omission
    B   Original entry
    C   Commission
    D   Principle

MULTIPLE CHOICE QUESTIONS

6   A business's bank balance increased by £750,000 during its last financial year. During the same period it issued shares of £1 million and repaid a debenture of £750,000. It purchased fixed assets for £200,000 and charged depreciation of £100,000. Working capital (other than the bank balance) increased by £575,000.

Its profit for the year was

A   £1,175,000
B   £1,275,000
C   £1,325,000
D   £1,375,000

7   A sole trader's business made a profit of £32,500 during the year ended 31 March 20X8. This figure was after deducting £100 per week wages for himself. In addition, he put his home telephone bill through the business books, amounting to £400 plus VAT at 17.5%. He is registered for VAT and therefore has charged only the net amount to his profit and loss account.

His capital at 1 April 20X7 was £6,500. His capital at 31 March 20X8 was

A   £33,730
B   £33,800
C   £38,930
D   £39,000

8   Which ONE of the following is an error of principle?

A   A gas bill credited to the gas account and debited to the bank account
B   The purchase of a fixed asset credited to the asset account at cost and debited to the creditor's account
C   The purchase of a fixed asset debited to the purchases account and credited to the creditor's account
D   The payment of wages debited and credited to the correct accounts, but using the wrong amount

9   A business can make a profit and yet have a reduction in its bank balance. Which ONE of the following might cause this to happen?

A   The sales of fixed assets at a loss
B   The charging of depreciation in the profit and loss account
C   The lengthening of the period of credit given to customers
D   The lengthening of the period of credit taken from suppliers

10 The purpose of charging depreciation on fixed assets is to

A   Put money aside to replace the assets when required
B   Show the assets in the balance sheet at their current market value
C   Ensure that the profit is not understated
D   Spread the net cost of the assets over their estimated useful life

11 When a trial balance was prepared, the closing stock of £20,400 was omitted. To make the trial balance balance, a suspense account was opened.

What was the balance on the suspense account?

A   Nil
B   Debit £20,400
C   Credit £20,400
D   Debit £40,800

12 When a trial balance was prepared, opening stock of £1,000 was omitted. To make the trial balance balance, a suspense account was opened.

What was the balance on the suspense account?

- A Nil
- B Debit £1,000
- C Credit £1,000
- D Debit £2,000

13 Some stock taken by the owner of a business has not yet been recorded. When this transaction is recorded:

- A Profit will rise and net assets fall
- B Profit will rise and net assets stay the same
- C Profit will fall and net assets rise
- D Profit will fall and net assets stay the same

14 Materials used to improve some machinery have been treated as purchases in the draft accounts. The necessary correction will:

- A Increase both profit and net assets
- B Increase profit and reduce net assets
- C Reduce profit and increase net assets
- D Reduce both profit and net assets

15 A loan repayable in 16 months has been included in current liabilities in the draft balance sheet.

The necessary adjustment will:

- A Increase both current assets and net assets
- B Increase current assets and reduce net assets
- C Reduce current assets and increase net assets
- D Increase net current assets but leave net assets unchanged

16 It is realised that stock which cost £5,000 with a net realisable value of £6,000 was excluded from a stock take. The correction of this omission causes profit to

- A Fall by £1,000
- B Rise by £1,000
- C Fall by £5,000
- D Rise by £5,000

10 Final accounts and audit I

1 Hengist, a sole trader, has calculated that his cost of sales for the year is £144,000. His sales figure for the year includes an amount of £2,016 being the amount paid by Hengist himself into the business bank account for goods withdrawn for private use. The figure of £2,016 was calculated by adding a mark-up of 12% to the cost of the goods. His gross profit percentage on all other goods sold was 20%.

What is the total sales figure for the year?

- A £172,656
- B £177,750
- C £179,766
- D £180,000

MULTIPLE CHOICE QUESTIONS

2   The bookkeeper of Leggit Ltd has disappeared. There is no cash in the till and theft is suspected. It is known that the cash balance at the beginning of the year was £240. Since then, total sales have amounted to £41,250. Credit customers owed £2,100 at the beginning of the year and owe £875 now. Cheques banked from credit customers have totalled £24,290. Expenses paid from the till receipts amount to £1,850 and cash receipts of £9,300 have been lodged in the bank.

How much has the bookkeeper stolen during the period?

A   £7,275
B   £9,125
C   £12,155
D   £16,575

3   A club takes credit for subscriptions when they become due. On 1 January 20X5 arrears of subscriptions amounted to £38 and subscriptions paid in advance were £72. On 31 December 20X5 the amounts were £48 and £80 respectively. Subscription receipts during the year were £790.

In the income and expenditure account for 20X5 the income from subscriptions would be shown as:

A   £748
B   £788
C   £790
D   £792

4   A club takes no credit for subscriptions due until they are received. On 1 January 20X5 arrears of subscriptions amounted to £24 and subscriptions paid in advance were £14. On 31 December 20X5 the amounts were £42 and £58 respectively. Subscription receipts during the year were £1,024.

In the income and expenditure account for 20X5 the income from subscriptions would be shown as:

A   £956
B   £980
C   £998
D   £1,050

5   For many years, life membership of the Tipton Poetry Association cost £100, but with effect from 1 January 20X5 the rate has been increased to £120. The balance on the life membership fund at 31 December 20X4 was £3,780 and membership details at that date were as follows:

	No of members
Joined more than 19 years ago	32
Joined within the last 19 years	64
	96

The Association's accounting policy is to release life subscriptions to income over a period of 20 years beginning with the year of enrolment.

During 20X5, four new members were enrolled and one other member (who had joined in 20X1) died.

What is the balance on the life membership fund at 31 December 20X5?

A   £3,591
B   £3,841
C   £3,916
D   £4,047

6 In the operating profit note of a cashflow statement it is usual to find adjustments for items not involving cash movement. Which one of the following items might appear under such a heading?

A   The profit on disposal of fixed assets
B   The accumulated depreciation on fixed assets
C   The profit and loss account charge for taxation
D   The provision for doubtful debts

7 A company has an authorised share capital of 1,000,000 ordinary shares of £1 each, of which 800,000 have been issued at a premium of 50p each, thereby raising capital of £1,200,000. The directors are considering allocating £120,000 for dividend payments this year.

This amounts to a dividend of

A   12p per share
B   10p per share
C   15p per share
D   12%

8 Your company sells goods on 29 December 20X3, on sale or return; the final date for return or payment in full is 10 January 20X4. The costs of manufacturing the product are all incurred and paid for in 20X3 except for an outstanding bill for carriage outwards which is still unpaid.

The associated revenues and expenses of the transaction should be dealt with in the profit and loss account by

A   Including all revenues and all expenses in 20X3
B   Including all revenues and all expenses in 20X4
C   Including expenses in 20X3 and revenues in 20X4
D   Including the revenue and the carriage outwards in 20X4, and the other expenses in 20X3

9 Which one of the following would you expect to find in the appropriation account of a limited company, for the current year?

A   Preference dividend proposed during the previous year, but paid in the current year
B   Preference dividend proposed during the current year, but paid in the following year
C   Directors' fees
D   Auditors' fees

10 The following information relates to a company at its year end.

	£
Stock at beginning of year	
Raw materials	10,000
Work-in-progress	2,000
Finished goods	34,000
Stock at end of year	
Raw materials	11,000
Work-in-progress	4,000
Finished goods	30,000
Purchases of raw materials	50,000
Direct wages	40,000
Royalties on goods sold	3,000
Production overheads	60,000
Distribution costs	55,000
Administration expenses	70,000
Sales	300,000

The cost of goods manufactured during the year is

- A   £147,000
- B   £151,000
- C   £153,000
- D   £154,000

11 At 31 December 20X1, a business had:

Motor cars	2,000
Stock	500
Debtors	300
Accrued Electricity Expense	50
Rent prepaid	200

At 31 December 20X2, it had:

Motor cars	2,500
Stock	100
Debtors	50
Creditors	600
Accrued Electricity Expense	100
Rent prepaid	250

The owner has drawn £1,000 in cash over the year.

What is the profit or loss?

- A   Loss £250
- B   Profit £250
- C   Loss £750
- D   Profit £750

12 In a balance sheet, capital plus profit less drawings must always equal:

- A   Fixed assets
- B   Current assets
- C   Net current assets
- D   Net assets

13 A sole trader decides to 'net off' the amount he owes to a supplier who is also a customer.

Which of these statements is wrong?

- A   Net assets will not change
- B   Fixed assets will not change
- C   Net current assets will not change
- D   Current assets will not change

14 Which statement is wrong for a balance sheet to balance?

- A   Net assets = Proprietor's fund
- B   Net assets = Capital + profit + drawings
- C   Net assets = Capital + profit − drawings
- D   Fixed assets + net current assets = capital + profit − drawings

15   A business achieves a margin of 25% on sales. Opening stock was £18,000, closing stock was £28,000 and purchases totalled £300,000. Calculate the sales for the period.

       A   £386,666
       B   £362,500
       C   £413,230
       D   £400,000

16   A business has opening stock £15,000, achieves a mark up of 25% on sales, sales totalled £500,000, purchases were £420,000. Calculate closing stock.

       A   £15,000
       B   £20,000
       C   £60,000
       D   £35,000

17   A business sells goods earning a constant 25% mark up. Sales in period amounted to £500,000. Opening stock was £10,000, closing stock is valued at £20,000. Purchases were £450,000. The owner suspects theft, calculate the amount of the stock losses.

       A   £40,000
       B   £65,000
       C   £60,000
       D   £50,000

18   A company achieves a gross profit (margin) of 20% on sales. Opening stock was £5,000, creditors at the start of the period were £4,000. Sales in the period amounted to £50,000. Year end creditors were £6,000 and the business had paid creditors £37,000. All the stock had been stolen at the end of the period, what was it's value?

       A   £nil
       B   £2,000
       C   £6,500
       D   £4,000

19   A debit balance on an income and expenditure account prepared for a club is dealt with by?

       A   Deduction from the club accumulated fund
       B   Addition to the bank balance in the balance sheet
       C   Addition to the club accumulated fund
       D   Inclusion in the balance sheet as a prepayment

20   A club has 200 members, each should pay £20 for subscriptions. At the start of the year 20 members owed subscriptions, at the end of the year 5 members had prepaid subscriptions. 3 members subscriptions were unpaid and written off as uncollectable during the year. Calculate the cash receipts for the year. (Assume the annual subscription remains at £20.)

       A   £3,640
       B   £4,240
       C   £4,560
       D   £4,440

21 Calculate the subscription income for the XYZ Social Club using the following data. Arrears 1.1.20X1 £700, prepaid in advance 1.1.20X1 £1,500, arrears 31.12.20X1 £1,200, paid in advance 31.12.20X1 £3,200, cash received from members £14,200.

   A £13,000
   B £14,200
   C £11,400
   D £17,000

22 Which of the following is the correct accounting treatment of life membership subscriptions paid in advance by members for an indefinite period?

   A Credit to revenue in full in the year of receipt
   B Carry as an asset on the balance sheet
   C Credit to revenue from a life membership fund over a defined period in accordance with club policy
   D Add to the accumulated fund of the club

11 Final accounts and audit II

1 In a not-for-profit organisation, the accumulated fund is

   A Long-term liabilities plus current liabilities plus current assets
   B Fixed assets less current liabilities less long-term liabilities
   C The balance on the general reserves account
   D Fixed assets plus net current assets less long-term liabilities

2 A 'true and fair view' is one which

   A Presents the accounts in such a way as to exclude errors which would affect the actions of those reading them
   B Occurs when the accounts have been audited
   C Shows the accounts of an organisation in an understandable format
   D Shows the assets on the balance sheet at their current market price

3 A business commenced with a bank balance of £3,250; it subsequently purchased goods on credit for £10,000; gross profit mark-up was 120%; half the goods were sold for cash, less cash discount of 5%; all takings were banked.

   The resulting net profit was

   A £700
   B £3,700
   C £5,450
   D £5,700

4 An income and expenditure account is

   A A summary of the cash and bank transactions for a period
   B Another name for a receipts and payments account
   C Similar to a profit and loss account in reflecting revenue earned and expenses incurred during a period
   D A balance sheet as prepared for a non-profit making organisation

5   Revenue reserves are

    A   Accumulated and undistributed profits of a company
    B   Amounts which cannot be distributed as dividends
    C   Amounts set aside out of profits to replace revenue items
    D   Amounts set aside out of profits for a specific purpose

6   A company has £100,000 of ordinary shares at a par value of 10 pence each and 100,000 5% preference shares at a par value of 50 pence each. The directors decide to declare a dividend of 5p per ordinary share.

    The total amount (ignoring tax) to be paid out in dividends amounts to

    A   £5,000
    B   £7,500
    C   £52,500
    D   £55,000

7   The correct ledger entries needed to record the issue of 200,000 £1 shares at a premium of 30p, and paid for by cheque, in full, would be

    A   DEBIT   share capital account   £200,000
        CREDIT   share premium account   £60,000
        CREDIT   bank account   £140,000

    B   DEBIT   bank account   £260,000
        CREDIT   share capital account   £200,000
        CREDIT   share premium account   £60,000

    C   DEBIT   share capital account   £200,000
        CREDIT   share premium account   £60,000
        CREDIT   bank account   £260,000

    D   DEBIT   bank account   £200,000
        DEBIT   share premium account   £60,000
        CREDIT   share capital account   £260,000

8   If work-in-progress decreases during the period, then

    A   Prime cost will decrease
    B   Prime cost will increase
    C   The factory cost of goods completed will decrease
    D   The factory cost of goods completed will increase

9   An organisation's cash book has an opening balance in the bank column of £485 credit. The following transactions then took place.

    (i)   Cash sales £1,450 including VAT of £150
    (ii)   Receipts from customers of debts of £2,400
    (iii) Payments to creditors of debts of £1,800 less 5% cash discount
    (iv)   Dishonoured cheques from customers amounting to £250

    The resulting balance in the bank column of the cash book should be

    A   £1,255 debit
    B   £1,405 debit
    C   £1,905 credit
    D   £2,375 credit

MULTIPLE CHOICE QUESTIONS

10 A club received subscriptions during 20X5 totalling £12,500. Of these, £800 related to 20X4 and £400 related to 20X6. There were subscriptions in arrears at the end of 20X5 of £250. The subscriptions to be included in the income and expenditure account for 20X5 amount to

    A   £11,050
    B   £11,550
    C   £11,850
    D   £12,350

11 During the year, all sales were made at a gross profit margin of 15%. Sales were £25,500, purchases were £22,000 and closing stock was £4,000.

What was opening stock?

    A   £3,675
    B   £4,000
    C   £4,174
    D   £4,325

12 During the year, all sales were made with a 20% mark-up on cost. Sales were £25,500, purchases were £26,000 and closing stock was £10,000.

What was opening stock?

    A   £4,150
    B   £5,250
    C   £10,000
    D   £14,750

13 At 1/1/X1 debtors owed £3,050, at 31/12/X1 they owed £4,000. Cash received from debtors during the year was £22,000 (including £1,000 bad debt recovered). All sales were made at a 20% gross profit margin and no stocks are held.

What were purchases for the year?

    A   £21,950
    B   £18,292
    C   £17,560
    D   £4,390

14 If the mark-up is 30% and the cost of sales is £28,000, and expenses are £14,000, what is the net profit?

    A   Profit £2,000
    B   Loss £2,000
    C   Profit £5,600
    D   Loss £5,600

15 If sales were £25,500, and cost of sales was £21,250, what was the gross profit percentage?

    A   16.67%
    B   20%
    C   83.333%
    D   120%

16 A particular source of finance has the following characteristics: a fixed return, a fixed repayment date, it is secured and the return is classified as an expense.

Is the source of finance

A Ordinary share
B Hire purchase
C Debenture
D Preference share

17 Which of the following items does not appear under the heading 'reserves' on a company balance sheet?

A Share premium account
B Retained profits
C Revaluation surpluses
D Proposed dividends

18 Which of the following statements regarding a company profit and loss account is correct?

A The Companies Act 1985 defines the expenses which are reported under 'cost of sales'.

B 'Depreciation' appears as a separate heading.

C Interest payable is deducted from profit after taxation.

D Bad debts will be included under one of the statutory expense headings (usually administrative expenses).

19 A company has £500,000, 15% debentures which were originally issued at par. The company had paid interest half yearly but the final instalment is outstanding at the year end. Which of the following statements is correct?

A The interest charge in the P&L account will be £75,000
B The interest charge in the P&L account will be £37,500
C The balance sheet will contain a liability for outstanding interest of £75,000
D The interest charge in the P&L account will be £112,500

20 Which of the following would correctly calculate the operating cash flows for a company?

A Operating profit plus stock increase less debtor decrease plus creditor increase
B Operating profit less stock increase less debtor increase plus creditor increase
C Operating profit less stock increase plus debtor decrease less creditor increase
D Operating profit less stock increase less debtor increase less creditor increase

21 A company has the following payments and receipts during its accounting period. Calculate the 'financing' cash flow figure for its cash flow statement. Issue of shares £515,000, debenture repaid £200,000, share premium received £230,000, proceeds of a rights issue £315,000, interest paid £115,000.

A £860,000
B £545,000
C £745,000
D £630,000

22 A company has the following fixed asset transactions. Fixed assets purchased cost £1,200,000, part of the costs of these (£100,000) are unpaid at the year end. Fixed assets value £500,000 are also leased. Fixed assets sold for £50,000. Depreciation for the period is £170,000. Calculate the capital investment cash flow.

  A £880,000 (outflow)
  B £1,050,000 (outflow)
  C £1,100,000 (outflow)
  D £1,150,000 (outflow)

12 Final accounts and audit III

1 A manufacturer has the following figures for the year ended 30 September 20X6:

  Direct materials   £8,000
  Factory overheads   £12,000
  Direct labour   £10,000
  Increase in work-in-progress £4,000

  Prime cost is

  A £18,000
  B £26,000
  C £30,000
  D £34,000

2 An increase in the figure for work-in-progress will

  A Increase the prime cost
  B Decrease the prime cost
  C Increase the cost of goods sold
  D Decrease the factory cost of goods completed

3 Life membership fees payable to a club are usually dealt with by

  A Crediting the total received to a life membership fees account and transferring a proportion each year to the income and expenditure account

  B Crediting the total received to the income and expenditure account in the year in which these fees are received

  C Debiting the total received to a life membership fees account and transferring a proportion each year to the income and expenditure account

  D Debiting the total received to the income and expenditure account in the year in which these fees are received

4 A company has authorised capital of 50,000 5% preference shares of £2 each and 500,000 ordinary shares with a par value of 20p each. All of the preference shares have been issued, and 400,000 ordinary shares have been issued at a premium of 30p each. Interim dividends of 5p per ordinary share plus half the preference dividend have been paid during the current year. A final dividend of 15p per ordinary share is declared.

  The total of dividends payable for the year is

  A £82,500
  B £85,000
  C £102,500
  D £105,000

5   Your company auditor insists that it is necessary to record items of plant separately and to depreciate them over several years, but that items of office equipment, such as hand-held stapling machines, can be grouped together and written off against profits immediately.

The main reason for this difference in treatment between the two items is because

A   Treatment of the two items must be consistent with treatment in previous periods

B   Items of plant last for several years, whereas hand-held stapling machines last only for months

C   Hand-held stapling machines are not regarded as material items

D   Items of plant are revalued from time to time, whereas hand-held stapling machines are recorded at historical cost

6   The main purpose of an audit is to

A   Detect errors and fraud
B   Ensure that the accounts are accurate
C   Determine that the accounts show a true and fair view of the financial state of the organisation
D   Carry out compliance tests on the internal control system

7   You are given the following information for the year ended 31 October 20X7:

	£
Purchases of raw materials	112,000
Returns inwards	8,000
Decrease in stocks of raw materials	8,000
Direct wages	42,000
Carriage outwards	4,000
Carriage inwards	3,000
Production overheads	27,000
Increase in work-in-progress	10,000

The value of factory cost of goods completed is

A   £174,000
B   £182,000
C   £183,000
D   £202,000

8   The responsibility for ensuring that all accounting transactions are properly recorded and summarised in the final accounts lies with

A   The external auditors
B   The internal auditors
C   The shareholders
D   The directors

9   A club's membership fees account shows a debit balance of £150 and a credit balance of £90 at 1 June 20X7. During the year ending 31 May 20X8, subscriptions received amounted to £4,750. Subscriptions overdue from the year ended 31 May 20X7, of £40, are to be written off. At 31 May 20X8, subscriptions paid in advance amount to £75.

The amount to be transferred to the income and expenditure account for the year ending 31 May 20X8 is

A   £4,575
B   £4,655
C   £4,775
D   £4,875

MULTIPLE CHOICE QUESTIONS

10 The record of how the profit or loss of a company has been allocated to distributions and reserves is found in the

- A Capital account
- B Profit and loss account
- C Reserves account
- D Appropriation account

11 A fixed asset note includes

	At 31/12/X4	At 31/12/X3
Plant and machinery		
Cost	10,500	9,400
Depreciation	3,400	4,100
Motor vehicles		
Cost	12,600	10,500
Depreciation	4,100	3,600

Plant and machinery with a cost of £2,000 and a written down value of £1,200 was sold during the year.

In the cashflow statement what is the figure for payments to acquire fixed assets in the year to 31/12/X4?

- A £3,200
- B £4,400
- C £4,700
- D £5,200

12 A company had dividends payable of £35,000 at 31 December 20X1 and dividends payable of £45,000 at 31 December 20X2. The dividends in the profit and loss account for the year to 31 December 20X2 were £60,000.

What would appear in the cashflow statement for 'dividends paid'?

- A £10,000
- B £50,000
- C £60,000
- D £70,000

13 When comparing two balance sheets you notice that:

(i) Last year the company had included in current assets investments of £10,000. This year there are no investments in current assets.

(ii) Last year the company had an overdraft of £8,000, this year the overdraft is £4,000.

In the cash flow statement, the change in cash would be:

- A Increase £4,000
- B Decrease £4,000
- C Increase £6,000
- D Decrease £6,000

14 In a set of company accounts, which would normally increase administration expenses?

- A Reduction in the provision for doubtful debts
- B Depreciation of machinery in the factory
- C Payment of the audit fee
- D Payment of production director's salary

15. The difference between a receipts and payments account and an income and expenditure account is:

    A A receipts and payments account is prepared on an accruals basis and an income and expenditure account on a cash basis.
    B A receipts and payments account is prepared on a cash basis and an income and expenditure account on an accruals basis.
    C A receipts and payments account is prepared for a not for profit organisation and an income and expenditure account for a business.
    D A receipts and payments account for a manufacturing business and an income and expenditure account for a non-manufacturing business.

16. Which of these statements are true about the difference between a profit and loss account and a receipts and payments account?

    (i) A profit and loss account is prepared for a business and a receipts and payments account for a not-for-profit organisation.
    (ii) A profit and loss account is prepared for a manufacturing business and a receipts and payments account for a non-manufacturing business.

    A Both true
    B Both false
    C (i) true, (ii) false
    D (i) false, (ii) true

17. Which of the following statements is correct?

    A External auditors report to the directors
    B External auditors are appointed by the directors
    C External auditors are required to give a report to shareholders
    D External auditors correct errors in financial statements

18. What is an audit trail in a computerised accounting system?

    A A list of all the transactions in a period
    B A list of all the transactions in a ledger account in a period
    C A list of all the items checked by the auditor
    D A list of all the nominal ledger codes

19. Which is the following statements is *not* correct?

    A Internal auditors review value for money
    B Internal auditors should not liaise with external auditors
    C Internal audit is part of internal control
    D Internal audit should be independent of the activities it audits

20. Which of the following statements concerning the status of an external auditor is incorrect?

    A All companies must appoint external auditors
    B The duties of an auditor are defined by the Companies Act 1985
    C The auditor gives an opinion on the financial statements
    D The auditor reports to the members of the company

21. Which of the following is *not* an activity which internal auditors would normally carry out?

    A Fraud investigations
    B Value for money studies
    C Systems appraisal
    D The statutory audit

13 Final accounts and audit IV

1. Revenue reserves would decrease if a company

   A   Sets aside profits to pay future dividends
   B   Transfers amounts into 'general reserves'
   C   Issues shares at a premium
   D   Pays dividends

2. A receipts and payments account is similar to:

   A   An income and expenditure account
   B   A profit and loss account
   C   A trading account
   D   A cash book summary

3. Your firm has the following manufacturing figures.

	£
Prime cost	56,000
Factory overheads	4,500
Opening work in progress	6,200
Factory cost of goods completed	57,000

   Closing work-in-progress is

   A   £700
   B   £2,700
   C   £9,700
   D   £11,700

4. A major aim of the internal auditors is to

   A   Reduce the costs of the external auditors by carrying out some of their duties
   B   Support the work of the external auditors
   C   Prepare the financial accounts
   D   Report to shareholders on the accuracy of the accounts

5. The subscriptions receivable account of a club commenced the year with subscriptions in arrears of £50 and subscriptions in advance of £75. During the year, £12,450 was received in subscriptions, including all of the arrears and £120 for next year's subscriptions

   The amount to be taken to the income and expenditure account for the year is

   A   £12,205
   B   £12,355
   C   £12,545
   D   £12,595

6. The prime cost of goods manufactured is the total of

   A   All factory costs before adjusting for work-in progress
   B   All factory costs of goods completed
   C   All materials and labour
   D   Direct factory costs

7   Ensuring that the assets of a company are properly safeguarded and utilised efficiently and effectively is part of

    A   The stewardship function exercised by the directors
    B   The external auditor's responsibility
    C   The function of the financial accountant
    D   The internal auditor's responsibility

8   Which ONE of the following does NOT form part of the equity capital of a limited company?

    A   Preference share capital
    B   Share premium
    C   Revaluation reserve
    D   Ordinary share capital

9   A true and fair view is given by the accounts when:

    A   Assets are stated at their true values in the balance sheet
    B   They have been audited and found to be accurate
    C   They fairly reflect the financial position of an organisation, sufficient for users of the accounts to make proper judgements
    D   The auditors are able to certify that they contain no errors or omissions, and that no fraud has been committed

10 A sole trader has net assets of £19,000 at 30 April 20X0. During the year to 30 April 20X0, he introduced £9,800 additional capital into the business. Profits were £8,000, of which he withdrew £4,200. His capital at 1 May 20W9 was:

    A   £3,000
    B   £5,400
    C   £13,000
    D   £16,600

11 Which is the single most important attribute of an auditor (external or internal)?

    A   Professional skills and training
    B   Good communication skills
    C   Independence
    D   Accuracy

12 Which of the following is not a key difference between internal and external auditors?

    A   Reporting responsibilities
    B   Professionalism
    C   Appointment
    D   Objectives

13 Which of the following statements concerning the authorisation of journal entries is correct?

    A   All journal entries should be authorised by an appropriate person in writing
    B   The limits for authorisation should be specified and all journal entries should be signed by the originating and the authorising signatories
    C   There is no need to authorise low value journal entries
    D   Journal entries input to a computer system are impossible to authorise

MULTIPLE CHOICE QUESTIONS

14 What does the phrase 'proper cut-off procedures' mean in relation to the sale of goods?

    A   All goods are invoiced to customers.

    B   Stock records correctly record receipts and dispatches of goods for resale.

    C   Arrangements to ensure that all goods dispatched prior to the cut off point are either invoiced or accrued in the financial statements.

    D   Having place arrangements to check invoices prior to dispatch to customers.

15 An internal auditor identifies an internal control weakness in an accounting system. What action should now be taken?

    A   Consider the effect of the weakness and identify counter controls
    B   Report to management
    C   Instruct the operators of the system to change the procedures in use
    D   Do nothing

16 Which of the following internal control procedures will *not* help to detect fictitious employees on the payroll of a large company?

    A   Identification of employees by an independent official at the distribution of wages
    B   Paying employees by bank transfer
    C   Ensuring that all employees have contracts of employment prepared by the personnel department
    D   Ensuring that changes to the company payroll system (eg starters and leavers) are authorised

17 What do you understand by the term 'management fraud'?

    A   Theft by managers
    B   Fraud designed to improve the companies position or performance
    C   Using creative accounting
    D   Manipulating the company share price

18 The term 'audit trail' refers to?

    A   The ability to trace transactions through a processing system by reference to documentation
    B   The retention of documents
    C   Explaining how systems work to the company's auditors
    D   Designing systems so that controls operate efficiently

19 The primary reason for an external audit is to:

    A   Give an opinion on the financial statements
    B   Detect any major errors or frauds
    C   Aid decision making by management
    D   Aid decision making by shareholders

20 True and fair is determined by reference to:

    A   Compliance with company law
    B   Compliance with accounting standards
    C   Compliance with generally accepted accounting practice
    D   Compliance with previous financial statement

21 Who appoints external auditors?

    A   Directors
    B   Employees
    C   Managers
    D   Shareholders

14 Interpretation of accounts

1 Horsa's sales follow a seasonal pattern. Monthly sales in the final quarter of the year are twice as high as during other periods. He also benefits from a higher mark-up during the final quarter: an average of 25% on cost compared with 20% during the rest of the year.

Horsa's sales in 20X9 totalled £210,000. What was the amount of his gross profit?

    A   £36,750
    B   £37,800
    C   £39,667
    D   £46,200

2 Which one of the following formulae should be used to calculate the rate of stock turnover in a retail business?

    A   Sales divided by average stock
    B   Sales divided by year-end stock
    C   Purchases divided by year-end stock
    D   Cost of sales divided by average stock

3 A company's working capital was £43,200. Subsequently, the following transactions occurred.

    (a)   Creditors were paid £3,000 by cheque.
    (b)   A bad debt of £250 was written off.
    (c)   Stock valued at £100 was sold for £230 on credit.

Working capital is now

    A   £43,080
    B   £46,080
    C   £40,080
    D   £42,850

4 The formula for calculating the rate of stock turnover is

    A   Average stock at cost divided by cost of goods sold
    B   Sales divided by average stock at cost
    C   Sales divided by average stock at selling price
    D   Cost of goods sold divided by average stock at cost

5 Given a selling price of £350 and a gross profit mark-up of 40%, the cost price would be

    A   £100
    B   £140
    C   £210
    D   £250

MULTIPLE CHOICE QUESTIONS

6   Which of the following transactions would result in an increase in capital employed?

    A   Selling stocks at a profit
    B   Writing off a bad debt
    C   Paying a creditor in cash
    D   Increasing the bank overdraft to purchase a fixed asset

7   Sales are £110,000. Purchases are £80,000. Opening stock is £12,000. Closing stock is £10,000.

    The rate of stock turnover is

    A   7.27 times
    B   7.45 times
    C   8 times
    D   10 times

8   The rate of stock turnover is 6 times where

    A   Sales are £120,000 and average stock at selling price is £20,000
    B   Purchases are £240,000 and average stock at cost is £40,000
    C   Cost of goods sold is £180,000 and average stock at cost is £30,000
    D   Net purchases are £90,000 and closing stock at cost is £15,000

9   Working capital will reduce by £500 if

    A   Goods costing £3,000 are sold for £3,500 on credit
    B   Goods costing £3,000 are sold for £3,500 cash
    C   Fixed assets costing £500 are purchased on credit
    D   Fixed assets with a net book value of £750 are sold for £250 cash

10 From the following information regarding the year to 31 August 20X6, what is the creditors' payment period?

	£
Sales	43,000
Cost of sales	32,500
Opening stock	6,000
Closing stock	3,800
Creditors at 31 August 20X6	4,750

    A   40 days
    B   50 days
    C   53 days
    D   57 days

11 The draft balance sheet of B Ltd at 31 March 20X8 is set out below.

		£	£
Fixed assets			450
Current assets:	Stock	65	
	Debtors	110	
	Prepayments	30	
		205	
Current liabilities	Creditors	30	
	Bank overdraft (Note 1)	50	
		80	
			125
			575
Long-term liability: Loan			(75)
			500
Ordinary share capital			400
Profit and loss account			100
			500

Note 1: The bank overdraft first occurred on 30 September 20X7.

What is the gearing of the company?

- A 13%
- B 16%
- C 20%
- D 24%

12 Which of the following is not a ratio which is used to explain how well the operations of a business have been managed?

- A Asset turnover
- B Profit margin
- C Gearing
- D Return on capital employed

13 An increase in selling prices may lead to which of the following effects?

- A Asset turnover will increase
- B Profit margins will fall
- C Profit margins may increase subject to a fall in asset turnover
- D Return on capital employed will increase

14 Working capital is?

- A Fixed assets + net current assets
- B Current assets – current liabilities
- C Total assets – total liabilities
- D Liquid current assets – current liabilities

15 A firm buys materials on 2 months credit, they spend 2 months in stock and 0.5 months in production. Finished goods are normally retained for 3 months before sale and on average debtors take 3 months to pay. Calculate the time taken for cash to cycle through the business.

- A 6.5 months
- B 8.5 months
- C 3.5 months
- D 2.5 months

MULTIPLE CHOICE QUESTIONS

16   Arrange the following current assets in order of increasing liquidity (least to most liquid).

(A)   Stock
(B)   Cash
(C)   Debtors
(D)   Prepayments

A   B, D, C, A
B   A, B, C, D
C   A, C, D, B
D   D, B, C, A

15 Ratios

1   A business operates on a gross profit margin of 33¹/₃%. Gross profit on a sale was £800, and expenses were £680.

The net profit percentage is

A   3.75%
B   5%
C   11.25%
D   22.67%

2   During the year ended 31 October 20X7, your organisation made a gross profit of £60,000, which represented a mark-up of 50%. Opening stock was £12,000 and closing stock was £18,000.

The rate of stock turnover was

A   4 times
B   6.7 times
C   7.3 times
D   8 times

3   A business has the following trading account for the year ending 31 May 20X8:

	£	£
Sales turnover		45,000
Opening stock	4,000	
Purchases	26,500	
	30,500	
Less: closing stock	6,000	
		24,500
Gross profit		20,500

Its rate of stock turnover for the year is

A   4.9 times
B   5.3 times
C   7.5 times
D   9 times

4   A company's gearing ratio would rise if

A   A decrease in long-term loans is *less* than a decrease in shareholders' funds
B   A decrease in long-term loan is *more* than a decrease in shareholders' funds
C   Interest rates rose
D   Dividends were paid

5   A company has the following details extracted from its balance sheet:

	£'000
Stocks	1,900
Debtors	1,000
Bank overdraft	100
Creditors	1,000

Its liquidity position could be said to be

A   Very well-controlled because its current assets far outweigh its current liabilities
B   Poorly-controlled because its quick assets are less than its current liabilities
C   Poorly-controlled because its current ratio is significantly higher than the industry norm of 1.8
D   Poorly-controlled because it has a bank overdraft

6   The gross profit mark-up is 40% where

A   Sales are £120,000 and gross profit is £48,000
B   Sales are £120,000 and cost of sales is £72,000
C   Sales are £100,800 and cost of sales is £72,000
D   Sales are £100,800 and cost of sales is £60,480

7   A company has the following current assets and liabilities at 31 October 20X8:

		£'000
Current assets:	stock	970
	debtors	380
	bank	40
		1,390
Current liabilities	creditors	420

When measured against accepted 'norms', the company can be said to have:

A   a high current ratio and an ideal acid test ratio
B   an ideal current ratio and a low acid test ratio
C   a high current ratio and a low acid test ratio
D   ideal current and acid test ratios

8   Your company's profit and loss account for the year ended 30 September 20X8 showed the following:

	£'000
Net profit before interest and tax	1,200
Interest	200
	1,000
Corporation tax	400
Retained profit for the year	600

Its balance sheet at 30 September 20X7 showed the following capital:

	£'000
Share capital	8,000
Profit and loss account balance	1,200
	9,200
10% debenture	2,000
	11,200

Return on average capital employed for the year ended 30 September 20X8 is

MULTIPLE CHOICE QUESTIONS

    A   5.88%
    B   10.17%
    C   10.43%
    D   none of these

9   An increase in both debtors' and creditors' payment periods could result in:

    A   An increase in working capital
    B   A decrease in working capital
    C   An increase in current assets and current liabilities
    D   A decrease in current assets and current liabilities

10   The gearing ratio is often calculated as

    A   Long-term loans and current liabilities as a percentage of total shareholders' funds
    B   Current and long-term debt as a percentage of total net assets
    C   Long-term loans and preference shares as a percentage of total shareholders' funds
    D   Preference shares as a percentage of equity capital

11   What is the ideal current ratio for a business?

    A   1:1
    B   2:1
    C   It is the trend which is important.
    D   It does not matter provided the business can pay its way.

12   Which of the following factors would indicate a lowering of the current ratio? (Assume all other elements of working capital are unaffected for each option.)

    A   A decrease in the rate of stock turnover (measured as a multiple) ie 10 times pa to 6 times pa.
    B   An increasing bank overdraft
    C   A decrease in the bank overdraft
    D   An increase in the period of credit allowed to credit customers

13   A company has the following extract from its balance sheet: debentures £2.5 million, ordinary shares £1.5 million, preference shares £0.5 million, reserves £2.2 million, share premium account £0.2 million. Using a conventional approach calculate the gearing %.

    A   147%
    B   77%
    C   39%
    D   44%

MULTIPLE CHOICE QUESTIONS

Use these summarised accounts to answer Questions 14 to 19

Summarised Balance sheet at 31 December 20X4

		£'000	£'000
Fixed assets			4,700
Current assets:	Stock	1,200	
	Debtors	1,700	
	Cash	300	
		3,200	
Creditors amounts falling due within one year		(1,500)	1,700
			6,400
Creditors amounts falling due after more than one year: 20Y2 10% debentures			(3,000)
			3,400
Capital and reserves			
Ordinary £1 shares capital			2,000
Preference share capital			400
Profit and loss account			1,000
			3,400

Summarised Profit and Loss account at 31 December 20X4

	£'000
Turnover	12,000
Cost of sales	7,000
Gross profit	5,000
Operating expenses	(2,500)
Operating profit	2,500
Debenture interest	(300)
Profit before taxation	2,200
Taxation	(700)
	1,500
Preference dividend	(20)
	1,480

---

14 Return on capital employed is:

    A   34%
    B   39%
    C   65%
    D   73%

---

15 Asset turnover is:

    A   0.781 times
    B   1.875 times
    C   2.553 times
    D   3.529 times

---

16 The gross and net profit margins are:

	Gross	*Net*
A	21%	42%
B	71%	36%
C	42%	36%
D	42%	21%

MULTIPLE CHOICE QUESTIONS

17   Stock days and debtors days are:

	Stock days	Debtors days
A	36	52
B	36	88
C	62	52
D	62	88

18   The length of the cash cycle is:

- A   36 days
- B   68 days
- C   88 days
- D   192 days

19   The current ratio and the gearing ratio are:

	Current ratio	Gearing ratio
A	2.13	47%
B	2.13	53%
C	47%	2.13
D	68%	50%

Objective test questions

Conceptual and regulatory framework

16 It has been suggested that there are seven separate user groups of published accounting statements. These include owner/investors, loan creditors, analysts/advisors, business contacts, for example, customers and suppliers and the public. Which two are missing?

   1 ....

   2 ....

17 Dee has given you a piece of paper with two statements about accounting concepts.

   (a) A business continues in existence for the foreseeable future.
   (b) Revenues and expenses should be recognised in the period in which they are earned or incurred.

   Required

   Name the two accounting concepts described above.

   1 ....

   2 ....

18 The following statement describes an accounting concept. 'In conditions of uncertainty more confirmatory evidence is required about the existence of an asset or a gain than about the existence of a liability or a loss.'

   Which accounting concept is being described here? ....

19 A business has incurred the following expenses. You are to complete the table indicating whether the expenditure is capital expenditure or revenue expenditure.

	Capital expenditure	Revenue expenditure
Redecoration of factory		
New engine for machinery		
Cleaning of factory		
Purchase of delivery van		

20 Closing stocks are deducted from purchases and opening stocks in the profit and loss account in order to determine the cost of sales. Of which accounting concept is this an example?

   ....

21 Accounting standards are issued by the Financial Reporting Council.

   True or False?

Ledger accounting and books of prime entry

22 Your organisation sold goods to PQ Limited for £800 less trade discount of 20% and cash discount of 5% for payment within 14 days. The invoice was settled by cheque five days later. What is the double entry for the cash discount allowed?

Debit £	Credit £
....	....

OBJECTIVE TEST QUESTIONS

23 The following totals appear in the day books for March 20X8.

	Goods excluding VAT £	VAT £
Sales day book	40,000	7,000
Purchases day book	20,000	3,500
Returns inwards day book	2,000	350
Returns outward day book	4,000	700

Opening and closing stocks are both £3,000.

The gross profit for March 20X8 is ....

24 Diesel fuel in stock at 1 November 20X7 was £12,500, and there were invoices awaited for £1,700. During the year to 31 October 20X8, diesel fuel bills of £85,400 were paid, and a delivery worth £1,300 had yet to be invoiced. At 31 October 20X8, the stock of diesel fuel was valued at £9,800.

The diesel fuel to be charged to the profit and loss account for the year to 31 October 20X8 is

....

25 An increase in the provision for doubtful debts results in a decrease in .... and **increases/decreases** the profit for the year (circle as appropriate).

26 The petty cash imprest is restored to £100 at the end of each week. The following amounts are paid out of petty cash during week 23.

Stationery	£14.10 including VAT at 17.5%
Travelling costs	£25.50
Office refreshments	£12.90
Sundry creditors	£24.00 plus VAT at 17.5%

The amount required to restore the imprest to £100 is ....

27 A company's telephone bill consists of two elements. One is a quarterly rental charge, payable in advance; the other is a quarterly charge for calls made, payable in arrears. At 1 April 20X9, the previous bill dated 1 March 20X9 had included line rental of £90. Estimated call charges during March 20X9 were £80.

During the following 12 months, bills totalling £2,145 were received on 1 June, 1 September, 1 December 20X9 and 1 March 20Y0, each containing rental of £90 as well as call charges. Estimated call charges for March 20Y0 were £120.

The amount to be charged to the profit and loss account for the year ended 31 March 20Y0 is

....

The following data relates to questions 28-31

At 1 October 20X5, the following balances were brought forward in the ledger accounts of XY:

Rent payable account	Dr	£1,000
Electricity account	Cr	£800
Interest receivable account	Dr	£300
Provision for doubtful debts account	Cr	£4,800

You are told the following.

(a) Rent is payable quarterly in advance on the last day of November, February, May and August, at the rate of £6,000 per annum.

(b) Electricity is paid as follows.

   5 November 20X5   £1,000 (for the period to 31 October 20X5)
   10 February 20X6   £1,300 (for the period to 31 January 20X6)
   8 May 20X6   £1,500 (for the period to 30 April 20X6)
   7 August 20X6   £1,100 (for the period to 31 July 20X6)

   At 30 September 20X6, the electricity meter shows that £900 has been consumed since the last bill was received.

(c) Interest was received during the year as follows.

   2 October 20X5   £250 (for the six months to 30 September 20X5)
   3 April 20X6   £600 (for the six months to 31 March 20X6)

   You estimate that interest of £300 is accrued at 30 September 20X6.

(d) At 30 September 20X6, the balance of debtors amounts to £125,000. The provision for doubtful debts is to be amended to 5% of debtors.

28 The rent charge to the profit and loss account for the year is £ ....

29 The charge for electricity to the profit and loss account for the year is £ ....

30 The amount of interest receivable to appear in the profit and loss account for the year is

    £ ....

31 The charge or credit to the profit and loss account for doubtful debts is £ ....

    Charge/credit (circle as appropriate)

The following data relates to questions 32 to 37

Your organisation has recently employed a new accounts assistant who is unsure about the correct use of books of original entry and the need for adjustments to be made to the accounts at the end of the year. You have been asked to give the new assistant some guidance.

For each of the following examples of transactions to be recorded in the books of original entry complete the double entry posting sheet below.

32 Purchase of raw materials on credit from J Burgess, list price £27,000 less trade discount of 33 1/3 %, plus VAT of 17.5%.

33 Payment to a creditor, P Barton, by cheque in respect of a debt of £14,000, less cash discount of 2%.

34 Receipt of a piece of office equipment in payment of a debt of £2,500 from a debtor, J Smithers.

35 Write off a debt of £500 due from A Scholes.

36 Returns of goods sold to J Lockley, total invoice value of £470, including VAT of 17.5%.

OBJECTIVE TEST QUESTIONS

37 Purchase of a motor vehicle on credit from A Jackson, for £1,400, including road fund (vehicle licence) tax of £75.

DOUBLE ENTRY POSTING SHEET

ITEM	BOOK OF ORIGINAL ENTRY	DEBIT ENTRIES Account	£	CREDIT ENTRIES Account	£
(i)					
(ii)					
(iii)					
(iv)					
(v)					
(vi)					

The following data relates to questions 38 to 39

Business rates are paid annually on 1 April, to cover the following 12 months. The business rates for 20X1/X2 are £1,800, and for 20X2/20X3 are increased by 20%. Rent is paid quarterly on the first day of May, August, November and February, in arrears. The rent has been £1,200 per annum for some time, but increases to £1,600 per annum from 1 February 20X2.

38 The charge for business rates in the profit and loss account for the year ended 30 April 20X2 is

£ ....

39 The charge for rent in the profit and loss account for the year ended 30 April 20X2 is

£ ....

Stocks

40 SSAP 9 recognises two main ways of calculating cost of stocks. What are they? Complete the blanks below

1 ....

2 ....

The following data relates to questions 41 to 43

The trading account of T Ltd is set out below:

T Ltd
Trading Account for the year ended 30 April 20X1

	£'000	£'000
Turnover		1,000
Opening stock	200	
Purchases	_700_	
	900	
Closing stock	_300_	
Cost of goods sold		_600_
Gross profit		_400_

The opening and closing stock in T Ltd was valued on a FIFO basis. On a LIFO basis the opening and closing stock would have been valued at £180,000 and £270,000 respectively.

41 The gross profit if LIFO had been used for stock valuation would have been £ ....

42 What are the 'stock days', using average stock during the year, on the assumption that stock is valued on the FIFO basis?

43 What are the 'stock days', using the average method, on the assumption that stock is valued on the LIFO basis?

Fixed assets

44 A machine cost £9,000. It has an expected useful life of six years, and an expected residual value of £1,000. It is to be depreciated at 30% per annum on the reducing balance basis. A full year's depreciation is charged in the year of purchase, with none in the year of sale. During year 4, it is sold for £3,000.

The profit or loss on disposal is ....

45 The accounting concept which dictates that fixed assets should be valued at cost, less accumulated depreciation, rather than their enforced saleable value, is the .... concept.

46 A fixed asset was disposed of for £2,200 during the last accounting year. It had been purchased exactly three years earlier for £5,000, with an expected residual value of £500, and had been depreciated on the reducing balance basis, at 20% per annum.

The profit or loss on disposal was ....

47 By charging depreciation in the accounts, a business aims to ensure that the cost of fixed assets is spread .... which benefit from their use.

48 A machine was purchased in 20X6 for £64,000. It was expected to last for 5 years and to have a residual value of £2,000. Depreciation was charged at 50% per annum on the reducing balance method, with a full year's charge in the year of purchase. No depreciation is charged in the year of disposal. The company's year end is 31 December. The machine was sold on 3 April 20Y0 for £5,500. The profit or loss on sale is ....

The following data relates to questions 49 and 50

On 1 January 20X1 a business purchased a laser printer costing £1,800. The printer has an estimated life of 4 years after which it will have no residual value.

OBJECTIVE TEST QUESTIONS

49 Calculate the depreciation charge for 20X2 on the laser printer on the straight line basis:

....

....

50 Calculate the depreciation charge for 20X2 on the laser printer on the reducing balance basis at 60% per annum

....

....

Bank reconciliations

The following data relates to questions 51 and 52

On 10 January 20X9, Jane Smith received her monthly bank statement for December 20X8. The statement showed the following.

SOUTHERN BANK PLC

J Smith: Statement of Account

Date 20X8	Particulars	Debits £	Credits £	Balance £
Dec 1	Balance			1,862
Dec 5	417864	243		1,619
Dec 5	Dividend		26	1,645
Dec 5	Bank Giro Credit		212	1,857
Dec 8	417866	174		1,683
Dec 10	417867	17		1,666
Dec 11	Sundry Credit		185	1,851
Dec 14	Standing Order	32		1,819
Dec 20	417865	307		1,512
Dec 20	Bank Giro Credit		118	1,630
Dec 21	417868	95		1,535
Dec 21	417870	161		1,374
Dec 24	Bank charges	18		1,356
Dec 27	Bank Giro Credit		47	1,403
Dec 28	Direct Debit	88		1,315
Dec 29	417873	12		1,303
Dec 29	Bank Giro Credit		279	1,582
Dec 31	417871	25		1,557

Her cash book for the corresponding period showed:

CASH BOOK

20X8		£	20X8		Cheque no	£
Dec 1	Balance b/d	1,862	Dec 1	Electricity	864	243
Dec 4	J Shannon	212	Dec 2	P Simpson	865	307
Dec 9	M Lipton	185	Dec 5	D Underhill	866	174
Dec 19	G Hurst	118	Dec 6	A Young	867	17
Dec 26	M Evans	47	Dec 10	T Unwin	868	95
Dec 27	J Smith	279	Dec 14	B Oliver	869	71
Dec 29	V Owen	98	Dec 16	Rent	870	161
Dec 30	K Walters	134	Dec 20	M Peters	871	25
			Dec 21	L Philips	872	37
			Dec 22	W Hamilton	873	12
			Dec 31	Balance c/d		1,793
		2,935				2,935

51 Calculate the corrected cash book balance as at 31 December 20X8:

    ....

52 Fill in the missing words and figures.

    To reconcile the balance per the bank statement at 31 December 20X8 with the corrected cashbook balance at that date:

    - Add .... of £ .... ; and
    - Deduct .... of £ ....

The following data relates to question 53

Sandilands Ltd uses a computer package to maintain its accounting records. A printout of its cash book for the month of May 20X3 was extracted on 31 May and is summarised below.

	£		£
Opening balance	546	Payments	335,966
Receipts	336,293	Closing balance	873
	336,839		336,839

The company's chief accountant provides you with the following information.

(a) The company's bank statement for May was received on 1 June and showed an overdrawn balance of £1,444 at the end of May.

(b) Cheques paid to various creditors totalling £7,470 have not yet been presented to the bank.

(c) Cheques received by Sandilands Ltd totalling £6,816 were paid into the bank on 31 May but not credited by the bank until 2 June.

(d) Bank charges of £630 shown on the bank statement have not been entered in the company's cash book.

(e) Standing orders entered on the bank statement totalling £2,584 have not been recorded in the company's cash book.

(f) A cheque drawn by Sandilands Ltd for £693 and presented to the bank on 26 May has been incorrectly entered in the cash book as £936.

53 The corrected cash book balance at 31 May is £ ....

54 At 31 December 20X9 the cash book of a company shows a credit balance of £901. When the bank statement for the month of December was compared with the cash book, it was discovered that cheques totalling £2,468 had been drawn but not presented to the bank, and cheques received totalling £593 had not yet been credited by the bank.

    The balance on the bank statement at 31 December 20X9 was ....

Control accounts

55 An employee is paid at the rate of £3.50 per hour. Earnings of more than £75 a week are taxed at 20%. Employees' National Insurance is 7%, and Employer's National Insurance is 10%. During week 24, the employee works for 36 hours.

    The amounts to be charged to the profit and loss account and paid to the employee are:

    Profit and loss account   *Paid to employee*

    ....

OBJECTIVE TEST QUESTIONS

56 A sales ledger control account showed a debit balance of £37,642. The individual debtors' accounts in the sales ledger showed a total of £35,840. The difference could be due to entering cash discount allowed of .... on the debit side of the control account.

57 A business paid out £12,450 in net wages to its employees. In respect of these wages, the following amounts were shown in the balance sheet.

	£
Income tax creditor	2,480
National Insurance creditor – employees'	1,350
– employer's	1,500
Pension creditor for employees' contributions	900

Employees' gross wages, before deductions, were ....

58 A debit balance of £1,250 on X's account in the books of Y means that:

X .... Y

59 A business has the following transactions for the month of June 20X2:

Credit sales (including VAT at 17.5%)	164,500
Sales returns (including VAT at 17.5%)	6,200
Cheques from debtors	155,300
Discounts allowed to customers	5,100
Bad debts written off	2,600

The debtors balance at 30 June 20X2 was £8,300.

The debtors balance at 1 June 20X2 was £ ....

60 The following totals have been extracted from the books of a business at 30 September 20X2.

	£
Sales day book total	367,520
Purchases day book total	227,540
Returns inwards day book total	13,445
Returns outwards day book total	9,045
Discounts allowed	5,220
Discounts received	2,070
Cash receipts from debtors	361,200
Cash payments to creditors	210,040

The purchase ledger control account had a balance of £17,600 at 1 September 20X2. During the month a journal entry has recorded a contra entry between a debtors account and a creditors account of £940.

The balance on the purchase ledger control account at 30 September 20X2 is £ ....

Correction of errors and suspense accounts

61 An organisation restores its petty cash balance to £250 at the end of each month. During October, the total expenditure column in the petty cash book was calculated as being £210, and the imprest was restored by this amount. The analysis columns posted to the nominal ledger totalled only £200.

This error would result in the trial balance being £10 higher on the .... side.

62 A trial balance has an excess of debits over credits of £14,000 and a suspense account has been opened to make it balance. It is later discovered that:

(a) The discounts allowed balance of £3,000 and the discounts received balance of £7,000 have both been entered on the wrong side of the trial balance.

(b) The creditors control account balance of £233,786 had been included in the trial balance as £237,386.

(c) An item of £500 had been omitted from the sales records (ie from the sales day book).

(d) The balance on the current account with the senior partner's wife had been omitted from the trial balance. This item when corrected removes the suspense account altogether.

The balance on the current account with the senior partner's wife is £ ....

The following data relates to questions 63 to 71

After calculating net profit for the year ended 31 March 20X8, WL has the following trial balance.

	DR £	CR £
Land and buildings – cost	10,000	
Land and buildings – depreciation at 31 March 20X8		2,000
Plant – cost	12,000	
Plant – depreciation at 31 March 20X8		3,000
Stocks	2,500	
Debtors	1,500	
Bank	8,250	
Creditors		1,700
Rent prepaid	400	
Wages accrued		300
Capital account		19,400
Profit for the year ended 31 March 20X8		9,750
	34,650	36,150

A suspense account was opened for the difference in the trial balance.

Immediately after production of the above, the following errors were discovered:

(i) A creditor's account had been debited with a £300 sales invoice (which had been correctly recorded in the sales account).

(ii) The heat and light account had been credited with gas paid £150.

(iii) G Gordon had been credited with a cheque received from G Goldman for £800. Both are debtors.

(iv) The insurance account contained a credit entry for insurance prepaid of £500, but the balance had not been carried down and hence had been omitted from the above trial balance.

(v) Purchase returns had been over-cast by £700 when posting to the purchases returns account.

63 Prepare a journal entry to correct error (i).

	DR £	CR £
....	....	
....		....

OBJECTIVE TEST QUESTIONS

64 Prepare a journal entry to correct error (ii).

	DR £	CR £
....	....	
....		....

65 Prepare a journal entry to correct error (iii).

	DR £	CR £
....	....	
....		....

66 Prepare a journal entry to correct error (iv).

	DR £	CR £
....	....	
....		....

67 Prepare a journal entry to correct error (v).

	DR £	CR £
....	....	
....		....

68 The net profit for the year after correction of errors (i) to (v) is £ ....

69 The figure for debtors in the amended balance sheet is £ ....

70 The figure for prepayments in the amended balance sheet is £ ....

71 The figure for creditors in the amended balance sheet is £ ....

Final accounts and audit

The following data relates to questions 72 to 74

The following trial balance has been extracted from the ledger of Mr Yousef, a sole trader.

TRIAL BALANCE AS AT 31 MAY 20X6

	Dr £	Cr £
Sales		138,078
Purchases	82,350	
Carriage	5,144	
Drawings	7,800	
Rent, rates and insurance	6,622	
Postage and stationery	3,001	
Advertising	1,330	
Salaries and wages	26,420	
Bad debts	877	
Provision for doubtful debts		130
Debtors	12,120	
Creditors		6,471
Cash in hand	177	
Cash at bank	1,002	
Stock as at 1 June 20X5	11,927	
Equipment		
At cost	58,000	
Accumulated depreciation		19,000
Capital		53,091
	216,770	216,770

The following additional information as at 31 May 20X6 is available.

(a) Rent is accrued by £210.
(b) Rates have been prepaid by £880.
(c) £2,211 of carriage represents carriage inwards on purchases.
(d) Equipment is to be depreciated at 15% per annum using the straight line method.
(e) The provision for bad debts is to be increased by £40.
(f) Stock at the close of business has been valued at £13,551.

72 The gross profit for the year is £ ....

73 The rent, rates and insurance charge for the year is £ ....

74 Fill in the figures.

    Summarised balance sheet at 31 May 20X6

	£	£
Fixed assets		....
Current assets	....	
Less: Current liabilities	....	
Net current assets		....
Total assets less current liabilities		....

OBJECTIVE TEST QUESTIONS

75 At 1 November 20X8, a club's membership subscriptions account show a debit balance of £200 and a credit balance of £90. During the year ended 31 October 20X9, subscriptions received amounted to £4,800. At 31 October 20X9, subscriptions paid in advance amounted to £85 and subscriptions in arrears (expected to be collected) to £50.

The amount to be transferred to the income and expenditure account in respect of subscriptions for the year ended 31 October 20X9 is ....

76 The *accumulated fund* represents ....

....

The following data relates to questions 77 to 82

Miss Anne Teek runs a market stall selling old pictures, china, copper goods and curios of all descriptions. Most of her sales are for cash although regular customers are allowed credit. No double entry accounting records have been kept, but the following information is available.

SUMMARY OF NET ASSETS AT 31 MARCH 20X8

	£	£
Motor van		
Cost	3,000	
Depreciation	2,500	
Net book value		500
Current assets		
Stock	500	
Debtors	170	
Cash at bank	2,800	
Cash in hand	55	
	3,525	
Less current liabilities		
Creditors	230	
Net current assets		3,295
		3,795

Additional information

(a) Anne bought a new motor van in January 20X9 receiving a part exchange allowance of £1,800 for her old van. A full year's depreciation is to be provided on the new van, calculated at 20% on cost.

(b) Anne has taken £50 cash per week for her personal use. She also estimates that petrol for the van, paid in cash, averages £10 per week.

(c) Other items paid in cash were as follows.

Sundry expenses   £24
Repairs to stall canopy   £201

(d) Anne makes a gross profit of 40% on selling prices. She is certain that no goods have been stolen but remembers that she appropriated a set of glasses and some china for her own use. These items had a total selling price of £300.

(e) Trade debtors and creditors at 31 March 20X9 are £320 and £233 respectively, and cash in hand amounts to £39. No stock count has been made and there are no accrued or prepaid expenses.

A summary of bank statements for the twelve months in question shows the following.

Credits	£
Cash banked (all cash sales)	7,521
Cheques banked (all credit sales)	1,500
Dividend income	210
	9,231

Debits	£
Purchase of motor van	3,200
Road fund licence	80
Insurance on van	323
Creditors for purchases	7,777
Rent	970
Sundry	31
Accountancy fees (re current work)	75
Bank overdraft interest (six months to 1 October 20X8)	20
Returned cheque (bad debt)	29
	12,505

The bank statement for 1 April 20X9 shows an interest charge of £27.

Assume a 52 week year.

77 The cash sales for the year were £ ....

78 The credit sales for the year were £ ....

79 The purchases for the year to be included in the trading account were £ ....

80 The van depreciation charge for the year was £ ....

81 The profit or loss on disposal of the old van was £ ....

82 The van depreciation charge and the profit or loss on disposal of the old van must be taken into account in arriving at the net profit or loss for the year. What is the **total** of the **other expenses** that are deducted from gross profit to give the net profit for the year ended 31 March 20X9? ....

83 Opening stock is £1,000, purchases are £10,000 and sales are £15,000. The gross profit margin is 30%. Closing stock is £ ....

84 The following information is for the year ended 31 October 20X0.

	£
Purchases of raw materials	56,000
Returns inwards	4,000
Increase in stock of raw materials	1,700
Direct wages	21,000
Carriage inwards	2,500
Production overheads	14,000
Decrease in work-in-progress	5,000

The value of factory cost of goods completed is ....

OBJECTIVE TEST QUESTIONS

The following data relates to questions 85 and 86

Balances at 31 December 20X4

	£
Fixed assets (cost £60,000)	39,000
Stocks	
Raw materials	25,000
Work in progress, valued at prime cost	5,800
Finished goods	51,000

The following relevant transactions occurred during 20X5.

	£
Invoiced purchases of raw materials, less returns	80,000
Discounts received	1,700
Factory wages paid	34,000
Manufacturing expenses paid	61,900

Balances at 31 December 20X5

	£
Fixed assets (cost £90,000)	60,000
Stocks	
Raw materials	24,000
Work in progress	5,000
Finished goods	52,000

85   The prime cost of production for the year was £ ....

86   The total depreciation charge for the year was £ ....

87   At the beginning of the year in GHI Ltd, the opening work in progress was £240,000. During the year the following expenditure was incurred:

	£
Prime cost	720,000
Factory overheads	72,000

The closing work in progress was £350,000.

The factory cost of goods completed during the year was £ ....

88   At the start of the year a manufacturing company had stocks of raw materials of £18,000 and stocks of finished goods of £34,000. There was no work in progress.

During the year the following expenses were incurred:

	£
Raw materials purchased	163,000
Manufacturing expenses incurred	115,000

During the year sales of £365,000 were made. The stocks of raw materials at the year end were valued at £21,000 and the stocks of finished goods were valued at £38,000. There was no work in progress.

The gross profit for the year is £ ....

89   A company made a profit for the year of £18,750, after accounting for depreciation of £1,250. During the year, fixed assets were purchased for £8,000, debtors increased by £1,000, stock decreased by £1,800 and creditors increased by £350.

The increase in cash and bank balances during the year was ....

Interpretation of accounts

The following data relates to questions 90 and 91

KK Ltd has made a profit before tax of £445,000. There is to be a provision for corporation tax for the year of £111,000, a transfer to general reserve of £30,000 and a proposed final dividend of £60,000. During the year an interim dividend of £40,000 was paid. Trade creditors and accruals totalled £17,000.

90 The retained profit for the year was £ ....

91 The total creditors to be shown in the balance sheet were £ ....

The following data relates to questions 92 and 93

Given below are extracts from the trial balance of FG Ltd at 31 March 20X2 after preparation of the draft profit and loss account.

	£
Share capital (50 pence ordinary shares)	200,000
Share premium account	40,000
General reserve	20,000
Profit and loss account reserve at 31 March 20X2	84,000

Since preparation of the draft profit and loss account it has been discovered that three items had not been accounted for.

(i) On 1 April 20X1 the company issued 100,000 new ordinary shares at a price of 80 pence per share.
(ii) Closing stock had been over stated by £10,000.
(iii) The directors wished to make a transfer to the general reserve of £5,000.

92 The amended balance on the profit and loss account reserve at 31 March 20X2 was

£ ....

93 Fill in the figures below.

	£
Share capital	....
Share premium	....
General reserve	....

94 A company had the following gross profit calculation in its last accounting period.

	£
Sales	130,000
Cost of sales	60,000
Gross profit	70,000

Average stock during that period was £7,500.

In the next accounting period sales are expected to increase by 40%, and the rate of stock turnover is expected to double. If average stock remains at £7,500 the gross profit mark-up percentage will be

.... %.

OBJECTIVE TEST QUESTIONS

95 The gross profit mark-up is .... % where sales are £240,000 and cost of sales is £150,000.

The following data relates to questions 96 and 97

The following figures have been extracted from the published accounts of MBC plc, at 31 October 20X5.

	£m
Ordinary share capital	30
Share premium	3
Reserves	5
	38
6% debentures	10
	48

The net profit (after tax of £1m) for the year to 31 October 20X5 was £4m and dividends amounted to £0.5m.

96 Calculate the company's gearing ratio.

....

....

97 Calculate the company's return on average capital employed (ROCE).

....

....

The following data relates to questions 98 to 104

ARH plc has the following results for the last two years of trading.

ARH PLC
TRADING AND PROFIT AND LOSS ACCOUNT FOR THE YEAR ENDED

	31.12.X4	31.12.X5
	£'000	£'000
Sales	14,400	17,000
Less cost of sales	11,800	12,600
Gross profit	2,600	4,400
Less expenses	1,000	2,000
Less interest	200	–
Net profit for the year	1,400	2,400
Dividends proposed	520	780
Retained profit for the year	880	1,620

ARH PLC
BALANCE SHEET

	31 December 20X4		31 December 20X5	
	£'000	£'000	£'000	£'000
Fixed assts		2,500		4,000
Current assets				
Stocks	1,300		2,000	
Debtors	2,000		1,600	
Bank balances	2,400		820	
	5,700		4,420	
Less current liabilities				
Creditors	1,500		2,700	
Net current assets		4,200		1,720
		6,700		5,720
Less long term liabilities				
10% debentures		2,600		–
		4,100		5,720
Financed by:				
2.4 million ordinary shares of £1 each		2,400		2,400
Revaluation reserves		500		500
Retained profits		1,200		2,820
		4,100		5,720

98   The gross profit margin is

	20X4	20X5
	%	%
	....	....

99   The net profit margin is

	20X4	20X5
	%	%
	....	....

100 The return on capital employed is

	20X4	20X5
	....	....

101 The acid test ratio is

	20X4	20X5
	....	....

102 The asset turnover is

	20X4	20X5
	....	....

OBJECTIVE TEST QUESTIONS

103 The stock turnover period in days is

	20X4 Days	20X5 Days
	....	....

104 The gearing ratio is

	20X4 %	20X5 %
	....	....

Answers to Multiple choice questions

ANSWERS TO MULTIPLE CHOICE QUESTIONS

1 Conceptual and regulatory framework

1	A	Fails to take account of changing price levels over time.
2	B	Remember you were asked for the *main* aim.
3	D	Current purchasing power accounting.
4	C	Overstating profits and understating balance sheet asset values.
5	C	Assets less liabilities = opening capital plus profits less drawings.
		∴ Assets less liabilities less opening capital plus drawings = profit
6	D	Separate entity concept. A business is separate from its owner.
7	D	Improvements are capital expenditure, repairs and maintenance are not.
8	A	Accruals concept.
9	D	Once capital has been maintained, anything earned in excess is profit.
10	B	This is just a rewording of question 4, be careful with these in the exam.
11	C	The Accounting Standards Board.
12	C	Depreciation is an *application* of the accruals concept.
13	A	Shareholders and government are users of accounts.
14	D	Correct. This is not an objective from the statement of principles. Additional data is required to assess this.
	A	This is a primary objective.
	B	Again, a major objective.
	C	All classes of users require information for decision making.
15	A	Correct. This information is a need for the 'lender' group.
	B	This is an important need, particularly relative to other investment opportunities.
	C	A primary need.
	D	A major need for existing (and prospective) investors.
16	D	Correct. Not a member, although the sponsoring bodies of AAT are.
	A	A member of CCAB.
	B	A member of CCAB.
	C	Members of CCAB.
17	A	This is correct, the FRC also raises funds and controls the strategic direction of its subsidiary bodies such as the Accounting Standards Board.
	B	This is the role of the Accounting Standards Board.
	C	This is the role of the Financial Reporting Review Panel.
	D	Each professional body is essentially self regulatory. The only avenue for consultation is via the Consultative Committee of Accountancy Bodies.
18	C	In this way debtors are not overstated and accounts can be compared between periods.
19	C	Only realised profits can be included in the profit and loss account.
20	A	Depreciation allocates the cost of an asset to the periods expected to benefit from its use.

2 Double entry bookkeeping I

1. D   Gross profit – expenses = net profit.
2. C   Prepayment b/f £900 (9/12 × £1,200) + £1,600 – prepayment c/f £1,200 (9/12 × £1,600).
3. D   A decrease in the provision is written back to profit.
4. B   Accruals. The stationery must be charged to the period in which it was consumed.
5. A   Y is a creditor of X.
6. C   Trade discounts are not included in the cost of purchases.
7. C   Sales less returns inwards. Discounts allowed are shown as a deduction from gross profit.
8. D

CREDITORS CONTROL ACCOUNT

	£		£
Bank	542,300	Balance b/d	142,600
Discounts	13,200	∴ Purchases	578,200
Returns	27,500		
Balance c/d	137,800		
	720,800		720,800

9. D   £10,200 + £3,000 + £1,400 = £14,600.

10. C

	£
Opening stock	165
Purchases (1,350 – 80 + 70)	1,340
	1,505
Closing stock	140
Stationery in P&L	1,365

11. C   On a cash basis

	£
Sales	400
Purchases	200
Profit	200

On an accruals basis

	£
Sales	1,000
Purchases	500
Profit	500

Thus, the difference is £300.

12. B   Correct, invoices are listed on receipt.

    A   Incorrect, these are recorded in a memorandum column in the cash book prior to posting to creditors accounts and the discount received account.

    C   Incorrect, the supplier will deduct trade discounts prior to raising the invoice total.

    D   They would be recorded in the purchase returns day book in response to debit notes raised on suppliers.

13. D   Remember the debtors account is a memorandum account.

ANSWERS TO MULTIPLE CHOICE QUESTIONS

14 A The total of the cash paid column should be credited to the cash control account, and the total of the discounts received column to the credit of discounts received, and debited to the creditors control account.

15 D When cash is received by a business, a debit entry is made in the cashbook. A receipt of cash decreases an overdraft and increases a bank balance.

16 C

Electricity expense account

		1,000	b/d
		4,200	Profit and loss charge
Cash	4,000		
C/d	1,200		
	5,200	5,200	
		1,200	B/d

17 A £8,400 for 24 months is £350 per month. So, the charge for the year is 12 × £350, ie £4,200.

At 31/12/X2, rent has been prepaid to 31.12.X3 ie for 9 months which is 9 × £350 ie £3,150.

18 B

Rent received income account

B/d	1,000	5,000	Cash
Profit and loss account	4,500	500	C/d
	5,500	5,500	

19 A

Motor expenses account

Cash	4,000	1,500	B/d
		5,000	Profit and loss account
C/d	2,500		
	6,500	6,500	
		2,500	B/d

20 C

Debtors control account

B/d	2,500	10,600	Cash
		5,000	Contras
Sales	15,100	2,000	C/d
	17,600	17,600	

21 D The charge for the salary in the profit and loss account is the gross salary plus the employer's national insurance contribution. This is £1,000 plus £100 respectively, a total of £1,100.

22 D Businesses not registered for VAT still have to pay VAT.

23 C Correct, the VAT a/c is a personal a/c with HM Customs & Excise.

    A Incorrect, the VAT a/c has not been used to record the output tax charged.

    B Incorrect, the £200 represents the amount chargeable to VAT.

    D Incorrect, a complete reversal has occurred and the nominal account involved is incorrect (creditors record purchase ledger transactions).

… ANSWERS TO MULTIPLE CHOICE QUESTIONS

3 Double entry bookkeeping II

1 A Decrease = £400 + £1,200 – £250.

2 D A liability or a revenue.

3 C The sales ledger. This is posted from the sales day book and cash book.

4 C Ledger accounts are posted from books of prime entry.

5 D

	£
Opening stock	12,000
Purchases (bal. fig)	122,000
Purchase returns	(5,000)
Closing stock	(18,000)
Cost of goods sold	111,000

6 C Check against question 2 above.

7 D

	£
Assets	
Opening cash	1,000
Cash received £(1,000 + 175 VAT)	1,175
Closing cash	2,175
Stock £(800 – 400)	400
	2,575
Liabilities	
Opening liabilities	–
VAT creditor	175
Purchase stock	800
Closing liabilities	975
Capital	
Opening capital	1,000
Profit on sale of stock £(1,000 – 400)	600
Closing capital	1,600

8 B

	£
Opening capital	10,000
Capital introduced	4,000
Drawings	(8,000)
Loss (bal fig)	(1,500)
Closing capital	4,500

9 D As X is a creditor, only a return of goods would generate a credit entry.

10 A

MOTOR EXPENSES

	£			£
1.9 Prepayment b/d	80	1.9	Accrual b/d	95
Cash	95	30.9	Prepayment (80 ×3/4)	60
Cash	245		P&L c/d	385
30.9 Accrual c/d	120			
	540			540

ANSWERS TO MULTIPLE CHOICE QUESTIONS

11 A

Rent received income account

B/d	1,000	16,000	Cash
Profit and loss account	12,000		
C/d	3,000		
	16,000	16,000	
		3,000	B/d

12 C

	£
Purchases	10,000
Less purchase returns	(200)
	9,800
Add carriage inwards	1,500
Add opening stock	1,000
Less closing stock	(2,000)
Cost of sales	10,300

Note: £800 prompt payment discount received will appear as income in the profit and loss account. It is not deducted from cost of sales.

13 C The bad and doubtful debts account has already been debited.

14 C Correct. 10 × £120 less 20% = invoice price £960 less cash discount 2½% (£24).
    A This is list price less cash discount.
    B No discounts have been applied.
    D Cash discount not taken.

15 C Correct, the effect is double the amount concerned.

16 C Correct, an increase in the provision for bad debts will reduce profits and balance sheet debtors.
    D Incorrect, gross profit will not be affected since provisions for bad debts are dealt with in the P&L account.

17 D

Provision

		3,000	b/d
Bad debt expense	2,000		
Provision c/d	1,000		
	3,000	3,000	

Bad debts

Write off	1,000	800	Cash
Profit and loss	1,800	2,000	Provision written back
	2,800	2,800	

Total bad debt expense = £1,800 credit in the P & L account..

18 B

Provision A/c

		1,000	b/d
C/d	1,640	640	Movement
	1,640	1,640	

ANSWERS TO MULTIPLE CHOICE QUESTIONS

Provision

Specific	B	500
	F	800
General 2% (18,500 – 1,500)		340
		1,640

19 D Prudence. The provision prevents debtors being overstated.

20 C

Provision

		850	b/d
C/d	1,000	150	Expense
	1,000	1,000	

Bad debts expense

Provision	150		
Debtors	500	650	Profit and loss
	650	650	

21 D Both debtors and creditors are being reduced.

22 A Correct, debtors and creditors include VAT where applicable.

23 B Correct, all deductions will also be debited to wages control (and credited to deduction control a/c's) the balance on wages control then represents the gross wage expense.

   A The debit to P&L represents the gross pay costs including employers overheads.

   C Net wages will be credited to bank.

   D Incorrect.

24 D Correct. A margin of 20% on sales equates to a gross profit of 25% (mark up) on cost of sales. So total margin = 20% × 150,000 = 30,000. Cost of sales is 150,000 – 30,000 = 120,000. Purchases are 120,000 + 15,000 – 10,000 = £125,000.

   A Incorrect, you have reversed the opening and closing stock figures.

   B Incorrect, you have ignored the mark up entirely.

   C Incorrect, you have applied the mark up % to sales.

4 Stocks

1 B FIFO will treat stock on hand as the most recent purchases, which are the most expensive.

2 C Cost of sales is £1,300 understated and expenses £1,000 understated.

3 C Closing stock = 20 units @ £3 each = £60

4 D 2 @ £3.00 + 10 @ £3.50 = £41.00

ANSWERS TO MULTIPLE CHOICE QUESTIONS

5   C

	Units	Unit cost £	Total £	Average £
Opening stock	30	2	60	
5 August purchase	50	2.40	120	
	80		180	2.25
10 August issue	(40)	2.25	(90)	
	40		90	
18 August purchase	60	2.50	150	
	100		240	2.40
23 August issue	(25)	2.40	(60)	
	75		180	

6   B

		£	£
Sales			148,000
COS	Opening stock	34,000	
	Purchases	100,000	
		134,000	
	Closing stock (bal fig)	(26,000)	
			108,000
			40,000

7   C

	Quantity	Value £	
1 October (60 × £12)	60	720	
8 October (40 × £15)	100	1,320	
14 October (50 × £18)	150	2,220	(ie average cost £14.80)
21 October (75 × £14.80)	75	1,110	

8   B

Stock card	£	No	£	Average
6 @ £15	90	6	90	
10 @ £19.80	198	16	288	18.00
10 @ £18	(180)	6	108	18.00
20 @ £24.50	490	26	598	23.00
5 @ £23	(115)	21	483	

	£
Sales (15 @ £30)	450
Issues (10 @ £18 + 5 @ £23)	(295)
Profit	155

9   A   FIFO values stock at the latest prices.

10   C   SSAP 9 specifically discourages the use of LIFO and replacement costs.

11   B   Correct, £58,000 + £256,000 − £17,000 − £63,000 = £234,000.
      A   Incorrect, returns and stock changes must be allowed for.
      C   Incorrect, changes in stock levels must be allowed for.
      D   Incorrect, you have transposed opening and closing stocks.

12   B   Correct. This loss is not part of cost of sales.

      A   This is a reversal error.

      C   Incorrect; loss of stock is an expense, if the stock had been for proprietors own use then the drawings account would be used.

      D   Incorrect; the stock has disappeared, the debit to stock will increase stock!

ANSWERS TO MULTIPLE CHOICE QUESTIONS

13   B   Correct. The amount which can be realised, less any further expenses.
       A   Incorrect.
       C   Incorrect.
       D   Incorrect.

14   A   Correct, FIFO will produce the highest valuation of closing stock of the three methods, giving the higher profit figure.

       B   Incorrect, under LIFO costing closing stock will be valued at the earlier prices.

       C   Incorrect, LIFO is permissible under the Companies Act 1985 but not under SSAP 9.

       D   Incorrect, average cost will be recalculated after every new delivery into stock occurs.

15   C   Correct, the stock would be included at the lower of cost or NRV – assuming it was saleable at a profit the appropriate cost would be that relating to its finished goods state.

16   A   Carriage out will come under distribution costs in the profit and loss account.

17   B

	Quantity	Cost	Net realisable value (95% of sales price)	Valuation Per unit	total
Beads	2,000	£1.50	£1.4535	£1.4535	2,907
Buttons	1,500	£1.25	£1.33	£1.25	1,875
Bows	2,000	£1.60	£1.425	£1.425	2,850
					7,632

5 Fixed assets

1   A   It is **never** B as funds are not set aside; nor C, this is revaluation.

2   D   (£5,000 – £1,000)/4 = £1,000 depreciation per annum ∴ NBV = £2,000.

3   D

	£
Balance b/d	67,460
Less NBV of fixed asset sold	
15,000 – (15,000 – (4,000 + 1,250))	5,250
	62,210

4   A   If disposal proceeds were £15,000 and profit on disposal is £5,000, then net book value must be £10,000, the difference between the fixed asset register figure and the fixed asset account in the nominal ledger.

5   A   The stationery would appear as an asset rather than as an expense

6   C   Compare this with the answers to 1 above

7   C

	£
Profit	8,000
Add back: depreciation	12,000
Net cash inflow	20,000
Purchase of fixed assets for cash	(25,000)
Decrease in cash	5,000

8   A   We would need to know *either* sale proceeds *or* length of time in order to calculate the other.

ANSWERS TO MULTIPLE CHOICE QUESTIONS

9   A

Ledger accounts

	£
As at 1.1.X7	
Cost	60,000
Depreciation	15,000
	45,000

Fixed asset register

	£
At 1.1.X7	
Net book value	47,500
Disposal of asset which cost £(4,000 + 1,500)	(5,500)
	42,000

10   B

		£
Year 1	Purchase	2,400.00
Year 1	Depreciation	(480.00)
		1,920.00
Year 2	Depreciation	(384.00)
		1,536.00
Year 3	Depreciation	(307.20)
		1,228.80
Year 4	Sale proceeds	1,200.00
	Loss on disposal	(28.80)

11   A

	£	£
Net book value at 1st August 20X8		200,000
Less depreciation		(20,000)
Proceeds	25,000	
Loss	5,000	
Therefore net book value		(30,000)
		150,000

12   C   Correct, it is likely to be treated as capital expenditure.
       A   This is a repair, so it is revenue expenditure.
       B   This is a repair and renewal expense so it would be likely to be treated as a revenue item.
       D   Incorrect, these are unlikely to be sufficiently expensive to warrant treatment as capital expenditure.

13   C

		£
31/7/20X5	Cost	20,000
Year to 31/12/X5	Depreciation	4,000
Year to 31/12/X6	Depreciation	4,000
Year to 31/12/X7	Depreciation	4,000
Year to 31/12/X8	Depreciation	4,000
Net book value at date of sale		4,000
Sale proceeds		5,500
Profit on disposal		1,500

14   A   The assets has been depreciated for 4 years (X5, X6, X7 and X8).

	£
Sales proceeds	5,500
Profit on disposal	1,500
Net book value at disposal	4,000
Cost	20,000
Depreciation to date	16,000

ie £4,000 pa which is 20% of £20,000.

ANSWERS TO MULTIPLE CHOICE QUESTIONS

15 B

	£
Cost	15,000
1st year depreciation	(2,250)
Net book value	12,750
2nd year depreciation	1,913
Net book value	10,837

16 A The credit must go to a revaluation reserve.

17 D Shares would be included in investments.

6 Bank reconciliations

1 B £(565)o/d − £92 dishonoured cheque = £(657) o/d

2 D The question refers to the figure to be shown in the balance sheet.

	£	£
Balance per cash book		5,675
Reversal – Standing order entered twice	125	
Adjustment – Dishonoured cheque (450 × 2) entered in error as a debit		900
Bank overdraft	6,450	
	6,575	6,575

3 A

	£	£
Opening bank balance	2,500	
Payment (£1,000 − £200) × 90%		720
Receipt (£200 − £10)	190	
Closing bank balance		1,970
	2,690	2,690

4 B

	£	£
Balance per bank statement		800
Unpresented cheque		80
Dishonoured cheque *		–
Corrected balance	880	
	880	880

* This has already been deducted from the balance on the bank statement.

5 B

	£
Cash book balance	2,490
Adjustment re charges	(50)
Adjustment re dishonoured cheque	(140)
	2,300

ANSWERS TO MULTIPLE CHOICE QUESTIONS

6   B

	£	£
Bank statement balance b/d	13,400	
Dishonoured cheque	300	
Bank charges not in cash book	50	
Unpresented cheques		2,400
Uncleared bankings	1,000	
Adjustment re error (2 × 195)		390
Cash book balance c/d		11,960
	14,750	14,750
Cash book balance b/d	11,960	

Alternative approach:

	£	£
Cash book balance b/d	11,960	
Dishonoured cheque		300
Bank charges not in cash book		50
Unpresented cheques	2,400	
Uncleared bankings		1,000
Adjustment re error (2 × 195)	390	
Bank statement balance c/d		13,400
	14,750	14,750
Bank statement balance b/d	13,400	

7   A

	£	£
Cash book (the cash book has a credit balance)		1,240
Unpresented cheques	450	
Uncleared deposit		140
Bank charges		75
Bank overdraft	1,005	
	1,455	1,455

8   D   Provided that the cash receipts have been correctly posted to the cash book, then the fact that they have incorrectly been posted to creditors instead of cash sales or debtors will not affect the bank reconciliation.

9   D   All the other options would have the bank account £250 less than the cash book.

10 B

	£	£
Cash book		500
Unpresented cheques	6,000	
Uncleared deposit		5,000
Bank balance		500
	6,000	6,000

11 C   When funds are paid out of a bank account, a debit entry appears on a bank statements. A payment increases an overdraft and decreases a bank balance.

12 D

Balance per cash account	10,500 o/d
Less bank charges	175
Less transposition error	18
	10,693 o/d

ANSWERS TO MULTIPLE CHOICE QUESTIONS

13 B

Balance per cash account	10,500 o/d
Add bank charges	175
Add transposition error	18
Adjusted cash account	10,693
Less uncleared cheques	(1,050)
	9,643 o/d

14 B The only adjustment that should be made to the cash account is to record the bank charges. The cheques and lodgements will already have been recorded in the cash account.

15 B The £20 advance returned can be offset against the cash requirement.

16 D Correct.

	Cash £	Bank £	
Balance	500	(1,000)	
Receipts	12,600		
Contra	(5,500)	5,500	
Paid	(3,200)	(8,200)	
Drawings	(3,800)	(2,500)	(balancing figure) = total of £6,300
Balance	600	(6,200)	

    A Incorrect, you have recorded the contra entry incorrectly as cash withdrawn from the bank account.

    B Incorrect, you have treated the opening bank overdraft as an asset.

    C Incorrect, you have not included the contra entry in the bank workings.

7 Control accounts

1 C Credit sales = £80,000 − £10,000 + £9,000 = £79,000.

2 B All of the other options would lead to a *higher* balance in the supplier's records

3 C Debits total £32,750 + £125,000 + £1,300 = £159,050. Credits total £1,275 + £122,550 + £550 = £124,325. ∴ Net balance = £34,725 debit.

4 A The other options would make the credit side total £50 more than the debit side.

5 A £8,500 − (2 × £400) = £7,700.

6 B The trader cannot recover the VAT so it is included in purchases

	£
List price	2,000
Trade discount: 20%	400
	1,600
VAT at 17½%	280
	1,880

7 A

	£
Opening balance	34,500
Credit purchases	78,400
Discounts	(1,200)
Payments	(68,900)
Purchase returns	(4,700)
	38,100

8 B The VAT element of the invoices will go to the VAT account in the balance sheet.

9	B	The cost to the business consists of gross wage plus employer's NI.
10	B	

	£
Output VAT £27,612.50 × $\dfrac{17.5}{117.5}$	4,112.50
Input VAT £18,000 × $\dfrac{17.5}{100}$	3,150.00
∴ Balance on VAT a/c (credit)	962.50

11	C	The same error can still appear in the control account and the personal ledger.
12	A	Correct, if the day book was overcast, the total of the purchase invoices posted to the control account will be overstated.
	B	Incorrect, this would increase the difference by reducing the total of purchase ledger balances.
	C	Incorrect, again this would reduce the purchase ledger total.
	D	Incorrect, this would reduce the purchase ledger balance.
13	D	A credit balance treated as a debit must be subtracted twice (ie £300). An omitted debit balance must be added once. Thus, the required adjustment to the list of balances is subtract £180; no adjustment is required to the sales ledger control account.
14	A	Remember, daybook totals are posted to the control account. Individual invoices are posted to the individual accounts, so an error in a total does not affect the list of balances.
15	B	Goods returned reduce what customers owe.
16	C	Remember, daybook totals are posted to the control account. Individual invoices are posted to the individual accounts, so an error in a total does not affect the list of balances.
17	B	

Debtors control account

B/d	2,050	4,000	Sales return
Sales	90,000	72,300	Cash
		2,570	Discounts allowed
		13,180	C/d
	92,050	92,050	

| 18 | A | |

Debtors control account

B/d	2,050	10,000	Sales return
Sales	100,000	85,500	Cash
		1,550	Contra
		5,000	C/d
	102,050	102,050	

8 Errors and suspense accounts I

1 C

	£'000
Turnover (£1m + £10,000 − £20,000)	990
Cost of sales (£800,000 − £20,000)	780
Gross profit	210

ANSWERS TO MULTIPLE CHOICE QUESTIONS

Gross profit margin = $\frac{210}{990} \times 100 = 21.2\%$

2   A   Both errors will affect cost of sales and therefore gross profit, making a net effect of £40,000. Net profit will be further reduced by £10,000 missing from stationery stocks.

3   D   A and B will only affect the personal ledgers, C will cause an incorrect double entry.

4   D   In the other three cases only balance sheet accounts are affected and there is an equal and opposite debit and credit.

5   D   Remember these are **draft** accounts. No suspense account should remain in the final accounts.

6   C   An error of principle.

7   D   Debits will exceed credits by 2 × £48 = £96

8   B   A would give a debit balance of £130, C would have no effect and D would not cause a trial balance imbalance.

9   C   Think of the double entry. Bank has been credited by £420 but expenses only debited by £400.

10   D   An error of principle.

11   D   Both these errors affect both the debit and the credit in the nominal ledger and so do not stop the trial balance balancing.

12   B   Correct, carriage inwards should be treated as part of the cost of purchases in the trading account.

       A   There will be no effect on net profit.

13   B   Correct, the correcting journal would be

Dr	Suspense	£2,500	
Cr	Bank		£2,500

       A   Incorrect, this is a reversal error which would be corrected as:

Dr	Rates	£5,000	
Cr	Bank		£5,000

       C   Incorrect, an error of omission cannot create a TB difference.

       D   Incorrect, this is a reversal error.

14   A

Suspense account

B/d	450	2,500	Discounts allowed
Discounts received	2,050		
	2,500	2,500	

15   D   Discounts received should be a credit balance, but have recorded it as a debit. Thus, the suspense account is a credit of £4,100. So the required journal is:

Dr	suspense	£4,100	
Cr	discounts received		£4,100

16   B   When a debt previously written off is recovered, the correct entry is dr cash, cr bad debts expense. Thus the required journal entry is:

Dr	debtors control	£400	
Cr	suspense		£400

9 Errors and suspense accounts II

1   B   A and C are errors of commission, D is an error of original entry.

2   B   £9,000 is payable (P&L), but only £6,000 paid (April and July).

3   A

SUSPENSE ACCOUNT

	£		£
Balance b/d	210	Gas bill (420 – 240)	180
Interest	70	Discount (2 × 500)	100
	280		280

4   C   A is an error of omission, B is an error of principle, D is a transposition error.

5   B   The posting is correct, but the wrong amount has been used.

6   A

	£'000
Profit for the year	1,175
Add back depreciation	100
	1,275
Add: Issue of shares	1,000
Less: Repayment of debentures	(750)
Less: Purchase of fixed assets	(200)
	1,325
Less: Increase in working capital	(575)
Increase in bank balance	750

7   C

	£
Capital at 1.4.X7	6,500
Add: Profit (after drawings)	32,500
Less: VAT element	(70)
Capital at 31.3.X8	38,930

8   C   This is a posting made to the wrong class of account.

9   C   This will increase debtors but reduce cash.

10   D   Spread the net cost of the assets over their estimated useful life.

11   A   Closing stock is entered twice in an extended trial balance (once for the profit and loss account and once for the balance sheet). It is not included in a trial balance, which, of course, balanced without it!

12   B   Opening Stock is a debit balance.

13   B   The journal for this transaction is debit drawings and credit purchases. Thus, profit rises and net assets stay the same.

14   A   The journal for this correction is debit fixed assets, credit purchases. Thus, profit and net assets are increased.

15   D   Reclassifying a liability as long term rather than current, will increase net current assets, but has no effect on current assets or net assets.

16   D   This stock should be included at the lower of cost and net realisable value, causing profits to rise by £5,000.

10 Final accounts and audit I

1 C

	Total	Ordinary sales	Private drawings
	£	£	£
Cost of sales	144,000	142,200	1,800
Mark-up:			
12% on cost	216	–	216
20% on sales (= 25% on cost)	35,550	35,550	
Sales	179,766	177,750	2,016

2 A We need to calculate credit sales first in order to calculate cash sales.

DEBTORS

	£		£
Bal b/f	2,100	Bank	24,290
∴ Credit sales	23,065	Bal c/f	875
	25,165		25,165

CASH

	£		£
Balance b/f	240	Expenses	1,850
Cash sales		Bank	9,300
(41,250 – 23,065)	18,185	∴ Theft	7,275
	18,425		18,425

3 D

	£	£
Subscriptions received in 20X5		790
Less: amounts relating to 20X4	38	
amounts relating to 20X6	80	
		118
Cash received relating to 20X5		672
Add: subs paid in 20X4 relating to 20X5	72	
20X5 subs still to be paid	48	
		120
		792

Alternatively, in ledger account format:

SUBSCRIPTIONS

	£		£
Balance b/f	38	Balance b/f	72
∴ Income and expenditure a/c	792	Cash	790
Balance c/f	80	Balance c/f	48
	910		910

4 B

	£
Subscriptions received in 20X5	1,024
Less amounts relating to 20X6	58
	966
Add subs paid in 20X4 relating to 20X5	14
	980

Alternatively, in ledger account format:

SUBSCRIPTIONS

	£		£
∴ Income and expenditure a/c	980	Balance b/f	14
Balance c/f	58	Bank	1,024
	1,038		1,038

5   B

	£	£
Balance at 1 January		3,780
New enrolments		480
		4,260
Less release to income:		
1 × £80	80	
63 × £5	315	
4 × £6	24	
		419
		3,841

6   A   B and D are balance sheet items, C has not been deducted from operating profit.

7   C   (£120,000 ÷ 800,000)

8   B   The revenue cannot be recognised (or not) until 20X4 and the expenses should be in the same period.

9   B   Preference dividend proposed during the current year, but paid in the following year.

10   A

	£	£
Raw materials		
Opening stock	10,000	
Purchases	50,000	
Closing stock	11,000	
Cost of raw materials		49,000
Direct wages		40,000
Prime cost		89,000
Production overheads		60,000
		149,000
Increase in work in progress		
4,000 – 2,000		(2,000)
Cost of goods manufactured		147,000

11   B

	£
Net assets 31/12/X1	
2,000 + 500 + 300 – 50 + 200	2,950
Net assets 31/12/X2	
2,500 + 100 + 50 – 600 – 100 + 250	2,200
Decrease in net assets	750

From the accounting equation

Change in net assets = Capital + profit – drawings

$$-750 = \text{Profit} - \text{drawings (£1,000)}$$
$$-750 + 1{,}000 = \text{Profit}$$
$$250 = \text{Profit}$$

12   D   This is the accounting equation.

ANSWERS TO MULTIPLE CHOICE QUESTIONS

13	D	Reducing debtors will reduce current assets.
14	B	Drawings reduce capital, so they must be deducted.
15	A	Correct. 25% margin = $33^1/_3$% mark up. Cost of sales = 18,000 + 300,000 − 28,000 = 290,000. Mark up = 290,000 × $33^1/_3$% = £96,666, so sales = £386,666.
	B	Incorrect, you have applied the 25% margin to cost of sales.
	C	Incorrect because you have transposed the stock figures in the calculation of cost of sales.
	D	Incorrect you have applied a mark up to purchases without the stock adjustment.
16	D	Correct. £500,000 sales × 20% margin (25% mark up = 20% margin) = gross profit £100,000. Cost of sales = 400,000. Therefore closing stock = 420,000 − 400,000 + 15,000 = £35,000.
	A	This is opening stock.
	B	This is the difference between cost of sales and purchases ignoring stock changes.
	C	You have incorrectly applied the mark up to sales.
17	A	Correct, 25% mark up = 20% margin so gross profit = 500,000 × 20% = 100,000. Therefore cost of sales = 400,000. Opening stock was £10,000 and closing stock was £20,000. Therefore cost of sales should have been 10,000 + 450,000 − 20,000 = 440,000. So losses = 440,000 − 400,000 = 40,000.
	B	Incorrect, you have applied the mark up % to sales.
	C	Incorrect, you have transposed opening and closing stocks in the calculation of theoretic cost of goods sold.
	D	Incorrect, you have forgotten to include the value of the remaining closing stock and the original opening stock.
18	D	Correct, calculate purchases in the period = £6,000 + £37,000 − £4,000 = £39,000. Sales £5,000 × margin 20% = £10,000, therefore cost of goods sold is calculated as £40,000.

Opening stock 5,000 + purchases 39,000 =		£44,000 (theoretical cost of goods sold)
Cost of goods sold as calculated		£40,000
Stock loss		£ 4,000

	A	Creditors figures have been reversed in the calculation of purchases.
	B	Incorrect, creditors have been ignored.
	C	Incorrect, margin has been converted to a mark up in the calculation of cost of sales.
19	A	Correct, the debit balance represents a deficit for the year.
	B	Incorrect, the debit balance represents a surplus of expenditure over income not an asset.
	C	Surpluses would be added, deficits are deducted.
	D	Incorrect. the debit balance is not an asset.
20	D	Correct.

Subscriptions A/C

Balance b/d				
20 × £20	400			
I&E subscriptions				
200 × £200	4,000	Bad debts		
Balance c/d		3 × £20	60	60
5 × £20	100	Bank		4,440
	4,500			4,500

	A	Incorrect, you have recorded the opening subscriptions in arrears as prepaid.
	B	Incorrect, you have carried down the closing prepaid subscriptions as arrears.
	C	Incorrect, you have posted bad debts to the incorrect side of the account.
21	A	Correct.

Subscriptions A/C

	£		£
Arrears b/f	700	Prepaid b/f	1,500
I&E a/c (balance)	13,000	Bank	14,200
Prepaid c/f	3,200	Arrears c/f	1,200
	16,800		16,900

	B	Incorrect, this is the amount of cash received and the debtors and prepayments have been ignored.
	C	Incorrect, you have transposed the opening balances.
	D	Incorrect, you have transposed the closing balances.
22	C	Correct, the club members will have to decide upon an appropriate period for release to revenue.
	A	Incorrect, this contravenes the accruals concept.
	B	Incorrect, these are liabilities not assets.
	D	Incorrect, these are liabilities of the club.

11 Final accounts and audit II

1	D	Accumulated funds = net assets
2	A	A 'true and fair view' should enable users to make decisions based on the accounts.
3	C	

	£	£
Sales (10,000 × 220% × 50%)		11,000
Opening stock	–	
Purchases	10,000	
	10,000	
Closing stock	(5,000)	
Cost of goods sold		5,000
Gross profit		6,000
Less discount (5% × 11,000)		550
Net profit		5,450

4	C	It is similar to a profit and loss account and based on the accruals concept.
5	A	Accumulated and undistributed profits of a company
6	C	(£100,000 × 10) × 5p + £50,000 (100,000/50p) × 5% = £50,000 ordinary + £2,500 preference.
7	B	The total will be £260,000, of which £60,000 will be credited to share premium.
8	D	Because some of the WIP has been consumed to complete those goods.
9	B	£(485) o/d + £1,450 + £2,400 – £1,710 (£1,800 × 95%) – £250 = £1,405 debit balance.

ANSWERS TO MULTIPLE CHOICE QUESTIONS

10 B

	£
Subscriptions received	12,500
Add subscriptions in arrears c/f	250
	12,750
Deduct: subscriptions in arrears b/f	800
subscriptions in advance c/f	400
	11,550

11 A

	£	£	
Sales		25,500	(100%)
Opening stock	3,675		
Purchases	22,000		
Less closing stock	(4,000)		
Cost of sales		21,675	(85%)
Gross profit		3,825	(15%)

12 B

	£	£	
Sales		25,500	(120%)
Opening stock	5,250		
Purchases	26,000		
	31,250		
Closing stock	(10,000)		
Cost of sales		21,250	(100%)
Gross profit		4,250	(20%)

13 C

	£	£	
Sales		21,950	(100%)
Less cost of sales		17,560	(80%)
Gross profit		4,390	(20%)

Debtors

B/d	3,050	21,000	Cash
Sales	21,950	4,000	C/d
	25,000	25,000	

And purchases are £21,950 × 80% = £17,560

14 D

	£	
Sales	36,400	(130%)
Less cost of sales	28,000	(100%)
Gross profit	8,400	
Less expenses	(14,000)	
Net loss	5,600	

15 A Gross profit is £25,500 − £21,250 = £4,250, which is 16.67% of £25,500.

16 C Interest is classified as an expense; dividends are not.

17 D This is correct because proposed dividends are current liabilities (if proposed before the year end).
  A This is statutory reserve.
  B Otherwise known as the profit and loss reserve.
  C This is an unrealised reserve.

18	D	Correct, company will usually include this under distribution costs or administrative expenses.
	A	Incorrect, the contents of cost of sales are not defined by statute.
	B	Depreciation will be included under the relevant statutory expense heading. (eg office equipment depreciation will go into administrative expenses).
	C	Incorrect, net profit is calculated after interest.
19	A	Correct 15% × £500,000
	B	Incorrect, interest paid and accrued comprise the total expense for the year.
	C	Incorrect, only half a years interest is outstanding.
	D	Incorrect, this represents 18 months interest.
20	B	Correct.
	A	Incorrect, stock increases reduce cash, debtor decreases improve cash flow.
	C	Incorrect, a creditor increase improves cash flow.
	D	Incorrect, a creditor increase improves cash flow.
21	A	Correct. £515,000 + £230,000 + £315,000 − £200,000.
	B	Incorrect, you have not included the rights issue.
	C	Incorrect, you have included interest paid which is reported under 'returns on investment and servicing finance'.
	D	Incorrect, you have not included the share premium received.
22	B	Correct (£1,200,000 − 100,000) − £50,000
	A	Incorrect, you have added depreciation which is reported under 'operating cash flows'.
	C	Incorrect (£1,200,000 − 100,000) + (£500,000) = £1,100,000 outflow but you have ignored receipts and also included the leased assets. The cash flow effect of these is the interest and capital repaid in the lease payments.
	D	Incorrect, you have included the fixed asset creditor as a cash flow.

12 Final accounts and audit III

1	A	Prime cost is direct material plus direct labour. There are no *direct* expenses.
2	D	Cross-check this with the answer to 11.8.
3	A	These are funds received in advance so are treated as a liability, which diminishes over time.
4	B	

	£
Interim ordinary dividends 5p × 400,000	20,000
Preference dividend (50,000 × £2 × 5%)/2	2,500
Paid to date	22,500
Final ordinary dividend 15p × 400,000	60,000
Preference dividend (must be paid before final ordinary dividend)	2,500
	85,000

5	C	The materiality concept applies here.
6	C	This is the *main* purpose.

ANSWERS TO MULTIPLE CHOICE QUESTIONS

7 B

	£
Purchase of raw materials	112,000
Decrease in stock of raw materials	8,000
Carriage inwards	3,000
Raw materials used	123,000
Direct wages	42,000
Prime cost	165,000
Production overheads	27,000
Increase in WIP	(10,000)
Factory cost of finished goods	182,000

8 D This is part of their stewardship responsibilities.

9 B

SUBSCRIPTIONS ACCOUNT

		£			£
1.6.X7	Balance b/f	150	1.6.X7	Balance b/f	90
31.5.X8	Balance c/f	75		Bank	4,750
31.5.X8	Income and expenditure a/c	4,655*		Bad debts	40
		4,880			4,880

* ie balancing figure

10 D Appropriation account

11 D

	Plant and machinery £	Motor vehicles £
Increase in cost (from fixed asset note)	1,100	2,100
Sold asset cost	2,000	
Total cost of assets acquired	3,100 +	2,100

= 5,200

12 B

Dividends

			35,000	b/d
Paid	50,000			
Balance c/d	45,000		60,000	Profit and loss account
	95,000		95,000	

13 A The reduction in the overdraft is an increase in cash of £4,000.

The reduction in short term investments (of £10,000) would be included in movement in liquid resources (not cash!)

14 C A reduction in the provision for doubtful debts reduces admin expenses and depreciation of machinery and the production director's salary would increase cost of sales.

15 B Both are prepared for not-for-profit organisations.

16 C Profit and loss accounts are also prepared for non-manufacturing businesses.

17 C External auditors are responsible to the shareholders.

18 A A list of all the transactions in a period.

19 B Co-operation between internal and external auditors can be valuable.

ANSWERS TO MULTIPLE CHOICE QUESTIONS

20	A	Correct. Small limited companies and unincorporated businesses or partnerships need not have an external audit.
	B	Incorrect, the auditor has rights and duties under the Act.
21	D	Correct, the responsibility rests with the external auditors (although they do rely on internal audit to carry out some of the work at times).
	A	Often in conjunction with the external auditors or a regulatory body.
	B	Studies of efficiency, economy and effectiveness of operations a re commonly carried out.
	C	Appraising and suggesting improvements to systems is a key task for internal audit.

13 Final accounts and audit IV

1	D	This is a distribution of reserves.
2	D	It shows receipts and payments and is not based on accruals.
3	C	

	£
Prime cost	56,000
Factory overheads	4,500
Opening WIP	6,200
Factory cost of	(57,000)
Therefore closing WIP is	9,700

4	B	The others are not internal audit functions.
5	B	

SUBSCRIPTIONS ACCOUNT

	£		£
Balance b/f	50	Balance b/f	75
Balance c/f	120	Bank	12,450
Income and expenditure a/c	12,355		
	12,525		12,525

6	D	Only *direct* costs are included in prime cost.
7	A	The stewardship function exercised by the directors.
8	A	Equity capital is owned by *ordinary* shareholders.
9	C	They give users a 'true and fair' picture of the entity's financial position.
10	B	

	£
Opening capital (balancing figure)	5,400
Capital introduced	9,800
Profits	8,000
	23,200
Drawings	(4,200)
	19,000

11	C	Correct. Unless the auditor is independent from the company, the work or reports will lack credibility in the eyes of users.
	A	This is an important attribute.
	B	This is vital and is developed by adequate training and appropriate experience.
	D	This is obviously desirable as an attribute but is not the most important.

ANSWERS TO MULTIPLE CHOICE QUESTIONS

12	B	Correct. Both should be professionals.
	A	Internal auditors report (ideally) to the chief executive whereas external auditors report to the shareholders.
	C	Internal auditors are employees whereas external auditors are appointed by the shareholders.
	D	Management will determine the objectives of internal auditors, the Companies Act determines the objectives of an external auditor.
13	B	Correct, the limits should be reviewed regularly.
	A	It is usual for different levels of authorisation to apply to monetary values or classes of transactions eg writing off an asset requires a high level of authority.
	C	Incorrect, all journal entries must be authorised to retain control.
	D	Incorrect, some form of authorisation is always possible eg supervision or printing out journal entries input for authorisation prior to processing.
14	C	Correct. Under the accruals concept, all dispatches in a period must be invoiced or accrued so they can be matched with costs of sale. Goods dispatched must be deducted from stock records.
	A	This is a completeness control.
	B	This is an accuracy control.
	D	Again, this is an accuracy control.
15	A	Correct. The impact of the weakness upon control risk should be evaluated, there may be an effective counter control which could mitigate the effects of the weakness.
	B	This should not be done until the facts are checked and cost effective solutions devised.
	C	The auditor should not enforce system changes, this is the role of management on receipt of recommendations from management.
	D	This is not an option!
16	B	Correct. This will not prevent fraud, the necessity to create fictitious bank details may make the fraud more difficult to carry out.
	A	An effective, but time consuming control to operate.
	C	This will be an effective aid to internal control.
	D	A common way of committing a payroll fraud is the manipulation of starting and leaving dates, independent authorisation will help to prevent this.
17	B	Correct. Usually this is a characteristic, the fraud is often not performed for personal gain.
	A	Management fraud can be simply the theft of assets, but usually it is more complex.
	C	Not all creative accounting devices are necessarily fraudulent.
	D	This is an example of a sophisticated type of fraud.
18	A	Correct. The problem with many computerised systems is that it is often difficult to ascertain the audit trail and identify mistakes. This is less likely in a manual system.
	D	Controls should be present in manual and computer systems.
19	A	Give an opinion on the financial statements.
20	B	Compliance with accounting standards.
21	D	Shareholders, although the directors may make the appointment on their behalf.

ANSWERS TO MULTIPLE CHOICE QUESTIONS

14 Interpretation of accounts

1   B

	Total	Sales in first three quarters (9/15)	Sales in final quarter (6/15)
	£	£	£
Sales	210,000	126,000	84,000
Mark-up:			
25% on cost (= 20% on sales)	16,800		16,800
20% on cost (=16½ % on sales)	21,000	21,000	
	37,800		

2   D   Cost of sales tells us what stock has been *used*.

3   A   Transaction (a) would have no effect on working capital.

4   D   You will know this from question 2!

5   D $£350 \times \dfrac{100}{140} = £250$

6   A   Profit will be an addition to owner's capital (accounting equation!)

7   B   Stock turnover = $\dfrac{\text{Cost of sales}}{\text{Average stock}}$

Cost of sales = 12 + 80 − 10 = 82

Average stock = $\dfrac{12+10}{2}$ = 11

∴ Stock turnover = $\dfrac{82}{11}$ = 7.45 times

8   C   Check this against question 4.

9   C   Fixed assets are not part of working capital but will give rise to a creditor.

10   D   Purchases = £(32,500 − 6,000 + 3,800)
= £30,300

∴ Creditors' payment period = $\dfrac{4,750}{30,300} \times 365$ = 57 days

11   A   Gearing = $\dfrac{\text{debt}}{\text{debt} + \text{equity}} = \dfrac{75}{75+500} = 13\%$

12   C   Correct. This ratio is used to analyse the capital structure of a business.

13   C   Correct.

        A   Increased prices may result in reduced sales so asset turnover may fall.

        B   Selling price increases should increase margins.

        D   The effect of a price increase will be increased margins but reduced asset turnover, therefore effects on return on capital may be nil.

14   B   Correct. Current assets are normally stock, debtors, bank. Current liabilities are normally creditors, overdraft.

15	A	Correct. Stock holding 2 months + 0.5 months in WIP + 3 months in finished goods stock + 3 months debtor payment less 2 months credit from suppliers.
16	C	Correct, stock, debtors, prepayments, cash.
	A	Cash is the most liquid so the order is reversed.
	B	Incorrect, cash is more liquid than debtors.
	D	Incorrect.

15 Ratios

1   B

	%	£
Sales	100	2,400
Cost of sales	66 2/3	1,600
Gross profit	33 1/3	800
Expenses	28 1/3	680
Net profit	5	120

2   D

	%	£
Sales	150	180,000
COS	100	(120,000)
Gross profit	50	60,000

$$\therefore \text{Stock turnover} = \frac{120,000}{(12,000+18,000)/2} = 8 \text{ times}$$

3   A $\dfrac{\text{Cost of sales}}{\text{Average stock}} = \dfrac{£24,500}{(4,000+6,000)\div 2} = 4.9 \text{ times}$

4   A   Long-term loans raise gearing, shareholders funds reduce it.

5   C   Current ratio is 2,900 : 1,100 = 2.6: 1 ie high

               Acid test ratio is 1,000 : 1,100 = 0.9 ie acceptable

6   C

	£
Sales were	100,800
Cost of sales was	(72,000)
∴ Gross profit	28,800

Gross profit mark up = $\dfrac{£28,800}{£72,000} \times 100 = 40\%$

7   A   Current ratio = 1,390:420 = 3.3:1   (ie high)
               Acid test   = 420:420   = 1:1   (ie ideal)

8   C $\dfrac{\text{PBIT} \times 100}{\text{average capital}} = \dfrac{1,200 \times 100}{(11,200+11,800)/2} = 10.43\%$

9   C   Both debtors and creditors will increase.

10   C   Long-term loans and preference shares as a percentage of total shareholders funds.

11   C   Correct.

      A   This is the often quoted 'ideal' quick ratio but many businesses (such as large supermarket chains) operate on much lower ratios.

ANSWERS TO MULTIPLE CHOICE QUESTIONS

	B	This is the 'ideal' current ratio which is often quoted – however it may be inappropriate for a particular business.
	D	Incorrect, unless matters are monitored, the business may suddenly arrive at a funding crisis.
12	B	Correct. Increasing the bank overdraft will increase creditors, which will lower the current ratio.
	A	If stock turnover decreases, stock levels increase and relatively the current ratio will rise.
	C	This will reduce creditors and will therefore increase the current ratio.
	D	This will increase debtors and the current ratio is likely to increase.

13 D Correct: $\dfrac{2.5+0.5}{2.5+1.5+0.5+2.2+0.2} \times \dfrac{100}{1} = 44\%$

    A   This is debt ÷ ordinary shares + premium.

    B   This is the debt/equity ratio ie. $\dfrac{2.5+0.5}{2.2+1.5+0.2} = 77\%$

    C   You have ignored the effect of the preference shares as prior charge capital.

14 B Return on capital employed can be measured in many ways. Your examiner has stated that capital employed includes long term loans.

So ROCE $= \dfrac{\text{Profit before interest and tax}}{\text{Capital} + \text{reserves} + \text{debentures}} \times 100\%$

$= \dfrac{£2,500}{3,400+3,000} \times 100\%$

$= \dfrac{£2,500}{6,400} = 39\%$

    C   which is $\dfrac{\text{Profit before tax}}{\text{Capital and reserves}} = \dfrac{£2,200}{3,400} \times 100\%$ is sometimes used to calculate ROCE but is excluded by your examiner as it ignores long term debt, which is a source of capital employed.

15 B Asset turnover is $\dfrac{\text{Turnover}}{\text{Capital employed}} = \dfrac{£12,000}{£3,400+3,000} = \dfrac{£12,000}{£6,400} = 1.875$ times

16 D Gross profit margin $= \dfrac{\text{Gross profit}}{\text{turnover}} \times 100\% = \dfrac{£5,000}{£12,000} \times 100\%$

$= 42\%$

Net profit margin $= \dfrac{\text{Profit before interest and tax}}{\text{turnover}} \times 100\% = \dfrac{£2,500}{12,000}$

$= 21\%$

17 C Stock days are $\dfrac{\text{Stock}}{\text{Cost of sales}} \times 365 = \dfrac{1,200}{7,000} \times 365$

$= 62$ days

Debtor days are $\dfrac{\text{Debtors}}{\text{turnover}} \times 365 = \dfrac{1,700}{12,000} \times 365$

$= 52$ days

ANSWERS TO MULTIPLE CHOICE QUESTIONS

18   A   The cash cycle is stock days + debtor days less creditor days:

$$\text{Stock days} = \frac{\text{Stock}}{\text{Cost of sales}} \times 365 \quad = 62 \text{ days}$$

$$\text{Debtor days} = \frac{\text{Debtors}}{\text{turnover}} \times 365 \quad = 52 \text{ days}$$

$$\text{Creditor days} = \frac{\text{Creditors}}{\text{Cost of sales}} \times 365 \quad = \underline{(78 \text{ days})}$$

Cash cycle is $\underline{36 \text{ days}}$

19   B $\text{Current ratio} = \dfrac{\text{Current assets}}{\text{Current liabilities}} = \dfrac{£3,200}{£1,500} = 2.13$

$\text{Gearing ratio} = \dfrac{\text{Loan capital} + \text{preference shares}}{\text{Total capital employed}} = \dfrac{3,000 + 400}{2,000 + 400 + 1,000 + 3,000} = 53\%$

Answers to Objective test questions

ANSWERS TO OBJECTIVE TEST QUESTIONS

Conceptual and regulatory framework

16 1. Employees
    2. The government

17 1. Going concern
    2. Accruals

18 Prudence

19

	Capital expenditure	Revenue expenditure
Redecoration of factory		*
New engine for machinery	*	
Cleaning of factory		*
Purchase of delivery van	*	

20 The accruals concept

21 False. Accounting standards are issued by the Accounting Standards Board.

Ledger accounting and books of prime entry

22

	Dr £	Cr £
Discount allowed	32	
Debtors control account (PQ Ltd)		32

Sale price £800 − (20% × 800) = £640
Cash discount £640 × 5% = £32

23 The gross profit for March 20X8 is £22,000

Reconstruction of the trading account

	£	£
Sales		40,000
Returns inwards		(2,000)
		38,000
Opening stock	3,000	
Purchases	20,000	
Returns outwards	(4,000)	
Closing stock	(3,000)	
		(16,000)
Gross profit		22,000

24 Diesel fuel charge = £87,700

Diesel fuel creditor account   Cost of fuel used

	£		£
Balance b/fwd	(1,700)	Opening stock	12,500
Payments	85,400	Purchases	85,000
Balance c/fwd	1,300	Closing stock	(9,800)
Purchases	85,000	Transfer to P&L	87,700

25 A decrease in **debtors** and **decreases** the profit for the year.

ANSWERS TO OBJECTIVE TEST QUESTIONS

26 Amounts required to restore imprest = £80.70

	£
Stationery	14.10
Travel	25.50
Refreshments	12.90
Sundry creditors (£24 × 1.175)	28.20
	80.70

27 Telephone charge = £2,185

TELEPHONE ACCOUNT

		£			£
	Prepayment b/f (2/3 × £90)	60		Accrual b/f	80
	Bills paid	2,145		P&L account	2,185
	Accrual c/f	120		Prepayment c/f (2/3 × £90)	60
		2,325			2,325

28 Rent payable = £6,000.

RENT PAYABLE ACCOUNT

		£			£
1.10.X5	Bal b/fwd	1,000	30.9.X6	Charge to P&L a/c	6,000
30.11.X5	Bank	1,500	30.9.X6	Rent prepaid c/fwd	
29.2.X6	Bank	1,500		(1500 × 2/3)	1,000
31.5.X6	Bank	1,500			
31.8.X6	Bank	1,500			
		7,000			7,000
1.10.X6	Rent prepaid b/fwd	1,000			

Alternatively, as you are told that the rent is £6,000 per annum and there has been no increase or decrease this must be the annual charge.

29 Electricity charge = £5,000.

ELECTRICITY ACCOUNT

		£			£
5.11.X5	Bank	1,000	1.10.X5	Bal b/fwd	800
10.2.X6	Bank	1,300	30.9.X6	Charge to P&L a/c	5,000
8.5.X6	Bank	1,500			
7.8.X6	Bank	1,100			
30.9.X6	Accrual c/fwd	900			
		5,800			5,800
			1.10.X6	Balance b/fwd	900

30 Interest receivable = £850.

INTEREST RECEIVABLE ACCOUNT

		£			£
1.10.X5	Bal b/fwd	300	2.10.X5	Bank	250
30.9.X6	Transfer to P&L a/c	850	3.4.X6	Bank	600
			30.9.X6	Accrual c/fwd	300
		1,150			1,150
1.10.X6	Balance b/fwd	300			

ANSWERS TO OBJECTIVE TEST QUESTIONS

31   Provision for doubtful debts = £1,450 charge to profit and loss account.

PROVISION FOR DOUBTFUL DEBTS

		£			£
30.9.X6	Bal c/fwd		1.10.X5	Bal b/fwd	4,800
	(125,000 × 5%)	6,250	30.9.X6	Charge to P&L a/c	1,450
		6,250			6,250
			1.10.X6	Balance b/fwd	6,250

32

Book of original entry	Debit entries		Credit entries	
	Account	£	Account	£
Purchase day book	Purchases	18,000		
	VAT	3,150	J Burgess	21,150

33

Book of original entry	Debit entries		Credit entries	
	Account	£	Account	£
Cash book	P Barton	14,000	Bank	13,720
			Discount received	280

34

Book of original entry	Debit entries		Credit entries	
	Account	£	Account	£
Journal	Office equipment	2,500	J Smithers	2,500

35

Book of original entry	Debit entries		Credit entries	
	Account	£	Account	£
Journal	Bad debts	500	A Scholes	500

36

Book of original entry	Debit entries		Credit entries	
	Account	£	Account	£
Returns inwards day book	Returns inward	400	J Lockley	470
	VAT	70		

37

Book of original entry	Debit entries		Credit entries	
	Account	£	Account	£
Journal	Motor vehicle	1,325	A Jackson	1,400
	Motor expenses	75		

38   Rates payable = £1,830

RATES ACCOUNT

	£		£
1.5.X1 Balance b/f		30.4.X2 Profit and loss a/c	1,830
(1,800 × 11/12)	1,650		
1.4.X2 Rates paid	2,160	30.4.X2 Balance c/f (2,160 × 11/12)	1,980
	3,810		3,810

39 Rent payable = £1,300

RENT ACCOUNT

	£		£
1.5.X1 Rent paid	300	1.5.X1 Balance b/f	300
1.8.X1 Rent paid	300		
1.11.X1 Rent paid	300		
1.2.X2 Rent paid	300		
30.4/X2 Balance c/f (1,600/4)	400	30.4.X2 Profit and loss a/c	1,300
	1,600		1,600

An alternative calculation is:

	£
Rent payable 1.5.X1 to 31.1.X2 (1,200 × 9/12)	900
Rent payable 1.2.X2 to 30.4.X2 (1,600 × 3/12)	400
Total rent payable	1,300

Stocks

40 1. FIFO (first in, first out)
    2. Average cost

41 Gross profit: FIFO £400 + adjustment opening stock (£200 – £180) – adjustment closing stock (£270 – £300) = £390,000

42 FIFO $\dfrac{(200+300)/2}{600} \times 365$ days = 152 days

43 LIFO $\dfrac{(180+270)/2}{610} \times 365$ days = 135 days (But remember that SSAP 9 does not allow LIFO)

Fixed assets

44 Loss on disposal = £87

	£
9,000 × 0.7 × 0.7 × 0.7 =	3,087 (NBV)
Proceeds of sale	(3,000)
Loss on disposal	87

As this is the reducing balance method, the residual value is included in the 30% rate.

45 Going concern concept.

46 Loss on disposal = £360

	£
NBV (£5,000 × 0.8 × 0.8 × 0.8)*	2,560
Proceeds	(2,200)
Loss on disposal	360

* Remember this is the reducing balance method, the residual value is included in the 20% rate.

47 … over the accounting periods ….

ANSWERS TO OBJECTIVE TEST QUESTIONS

48   Profit on sale = £1,500

	£
NBV (£64,000 × 0.5 × 0.5 × 0.5 × 0.5)	4,000
Proceeds	(5,500)
Profit	1,500

As this is the reducing balance method, the residual value is included in the 50% rate.

49   20X2 depreciation charge = £450

$$\text{Annual depreciation} = \frac{\text{Cost minus residual value}}{\text{Estimated economic life}}$$

$$\text{Annual depreciation} = \frac{£1,800 - £0}{4 \text{ years}}$$

20X2 depreciation = £450

50   20X2 depreciation charge = £432

	£	
Cost at 1.1.20X1	1,800	
Depreciation 20X1	1,080	60% × £1,800
Book value 1.1.20X2	720	
Depreciation 20X2	432	60% × £720
Book value 1.1.20X3	288	

Bank reconciliations

51   Corrected cash book balance = £1,681 debit.

CASH BOOK

20X8		£	20X8		£
Dec 31	Balance b/d	1,793	Dec 31	Bank charges	18
Dec 31	Dividend	26	Dec 31	Standing order	32
			Dec 31	Direct debit	88
				Balance c/d	1,681
		1,819			1,819

52   Add **unrecorded lodgements** of £232

Deduct **unpresented cheques** of £108

BANK RECONCILIATION AS AT 31 DECEMBER 20X8

	£	£
Balance per bank statement		1,557
Add unrecorded lodgements:		
V Owen	98	
K Walters	134	
		232
Less unpresented cheques:		
B Oliver (869)	71	
L Philips (872)	37	
		(108)
Balance per cash book (corrected)		1,681

ANSWERS TO OBJECTIVE TEST QUESTIONS

53 Cash book balance = £2,098 overdrawn

CASH BOOK

		£			£
31.5.X3	Balance b/d	873	31.5.X3	Bank charges	630
	Error £(936 – 693)	243		Standing orders	2,584
31.5.X3	Balance c/d	2,098			
		3,214			3,214
			1.6.X3	Balance b/d	2,098

54 Balance per bank statement = £974 (in credit)

BANK RECONCILIATION

	£
Balance per cash book	(901)
Outstanding lodgements	(593)
Unpresented cheques	2,468
Balance per bank statement	974

Control accounts

55

	£
36 × £3.50	126.00
Employer's NI	12.60
Gross wages cost (P&L account)	138.60
36 × £3.50	126.00
Tax ((£126 – 75) × 20%)	(10.20)
Employees' NI	(8.82)
Paid to employee	106.98

56 £901

Cash discounts allowed should be credited. So a debit of £901 would result in an error of £1,802 between the ledger and the control account.

57

		£
Wages paid		12,450
Employee deductions	– tax	2,480
	– NI	1,350
	– pension	900
Gross wages		17,180

58 X is a debtor of Y or X owes Y.

59 Balance at 1 June 20X2 = £13,000

DEBTORS CONTROL ACCOUNT

	£		£
Opening balance (bal fig)	13,000	Sales returns	6,200
Sales	164,500	Bank	155,300
		Discounts allowed	5,100
		Bad debts written off	2,600
		Closing balance	8,300
	177,500		177,500

60 Closing balance = £23,045

PURCHASE LEDGER CONTROL ACCOUNT

	£		£
Returns outwards	9,045	Opening balance	17,600
Discounts received	2,070	Purchases	227,540
Bank	210,040		
Contra	940		
Closing balance	23,045		
	245,140		245,140

Correction of errors and suspense accounts

61 Credit

The entries are Dr Expenses £200, Cr Bank £210.

62 The balance on the current account is £9,600.

SUSPENSE ACCOUNT

	£		£
		Balance b/d	14,000
Discounts received	14,000	Discounts allowed	6,000
Current a/c – partner's wife	9,600	Creditors control a/c	3,600
	23,600		23,600

63

		£	£
DR	Debtor	300	
CR	Creditor		300

64

		£	£
DR	Heat & light	300	
CR	Suspense account		300

65

		£	£
DR	G Gordon	800	
CR	G Goldman		800

66

		£	£
DR	Insurance prepayment	500	
CR	Suspense account		500

67

		£	£
DR	Purchase returns	700	
CR	Suspense account		700

68 Corrected profit = £8,750

	£
First draft profit	9,750
Adjustment re heat and light	(300)
Adjustment re purchase returns	(700)
Revised net profit	8,750

69 Debtor = £1,800 (£1,500 + £300)

ANSWERS TO OBJECTIVE TEST QUESTIONS

70 Prepayments = £900 (£400 + £500)

71 Creditors = £2,000 (£1,700 + £300)

Final accounts and audit

72 Gross Profit = £55,141

	£	£
Sales		138,078
Opening stock	11,927	
Purchases (W)	84,561	
	96,488	
Less closing stock	13,551	
Cost of goods sold		82,937
Gross profit		55,141

Purchases

	£
Per trial balance	82,350
Add carriage inwards	2,211
Per P & L a/c	84,561

73 Rent, rates and insurance = £5,952

	£
Per trial balance	6,622
Add: rent accrual	210
Less: rates prepayment	(880)
	5,952

74 Summarised balance sheet at 31 May 20X6

	£	£
Fixed assets (58,000 − (19,000 + 15% × 58,000))		30,300
Current assets (W)	27,560	
Current liabilities (6,471 + 210)	(6,681)	
Net current assets		20,879
Total assets less current liabilities		51,179

WORKING

	£
Stock	13,551
Debtors (12,120 − 130 − 40)	11,950
Prepayment	880
Cash in hand	177
Cash at bank	1,002
	27,560

75 Subscription income = £4,655.

MEMBERSHIP SUBSCRIPTIONS

	£		£
Bal b/f	200	Bal b/f	90
∴ I&E	4,655	Received	4,800
Subs paid in advance c/f	85	Subs in arrears c/f	50
	4,940		4,940

76 The accumulated fund represents the book value of net assets in a not-for-profit organisation.

ANSWERS TO OBJECTIVE TEST QUESTIONS

77   Cash sales = £10,850

CASH BOOK

	Cash £		Cash £
Balance b/d	55	Drawings (52 × £50)	2,600
Cash takings (balancing figure)	10,850	Petrol (52 × £10)	520
		Sundry expenses	24
		Repairs to canopy	201
		Takings banked (contra entry)	7,521
		Balance c/d	39
	10,905		10,905
Balance b/d	39		

78   Credit sales = £1,650.

DEBTORS

	£		£
Balance b/d	170	Cash	1,500
Credit sales - balancing figure	1,650	Balance c/d	320
	1,820		1,820

79   Purchases = £7,600

CREDITORS

	£		£
Bank	7,777	Balance b/d	230
Balance c/d	233	Purchases (balancing figure)	7,780
	8,010		8,010

Goods taken as drawings

	£
Selling price (100%)	300
Gross profit (40%)	120
Cost (60%)	180

Therefore, purchases taken to the trading account = £7,780 − £180 = £7,600.

80   New van depreciation charge = £1,000

The bank statement shows that the cash paid for the new van was £3,200. Since there was a part exchange of £1,800 on the old van, the cost of the new van must be £5,000 with first year depreciation (20%) £1,000.

81   Profit on disposal = £1,300.

	£		£
Van at cost	3,000	Provision for depreciation at date of sale	2,500
Profit on disposal	1,300	Asset account (trade in value for new van)	1,800
	4,300		4,300

ANSWERS TO OBJECTIVE TEST QUESTIONS

82 Other expenses = £2,300

	£	£
Expenses:		
Rent	970	
Repairs to canopy	201	
Van running expenses (520 + 80 + 323)	923	
Sundry expenses (24 + 31)	55	
Bank interest	47	
Accounting fees	75	
Bad debts	29	
		2,300

83 Closing stock = £500.

	£
Sales (100%)	15,000
Gross profit (30%)	4,500
Cost of goods sold (70%)	10,500
Opening stock	1,000
Purchases (from previous question)	10,000
	11,000
Cost of goods sold	10,500
Closing stock (balancing figure)	500

84 Factory cost of goods completed = £96,800.

	£
Purchases of raw materials	56,000
Increase in stocks of raw materials	(1,700)
Direct wages	21,000
Carriage inwards	2,500
Production overheads	14,000
Decrease in work-in-progress	5,000
Factory cost of sales	96,800

Returns inwards are returns of sales and so do not form part of the factory cost of goods.

85 Prime cost = £115,000

	£
Opening stock	25,000
Purchases	80,000
	105,000
Less: closing stock	(24,000)
Raw materials used	81,000
Direct wages	34,000
Prime cost	115,000

86 Total depreciation charge = £9,000

	Fixed assets at cost £	Net book value £	Accumulated depreciation £
At 31 December 20X4	60,000	39,000	21,000
At 31 December 20X5	90,000	60,000	30,000
Depreciation charge for the year			9,000

87 The factory cost of goods completed during the year was £682,000

	£
Prime cost	720,000
Factory overheads	72,000
Add: Opening work in progress	240,000
Less: Closing work in progress	(350,000)
Factory cost of goods completed	682,000

88 The gross profit for the year is £94,000

	£
Opening stock of raw materials	18,000
Purchases	163,000
	181,000
Less: closing stock of raw materials	(21,000)
Raw materials used	160,000
Manufacturing expenses	115,000
Factory cost of goods produced	275,000

	£	£
Sales		365,000
Less: Cost of goods sold		
Opening finished goods stock	34,000	
Factory cost of goods produced	275,000	
	309,000	
Less: Closing stock of finished goods	(38,000)	
		271,000
Gross profit		94,000

89 Increase in cash and bank balances = £13,150

	£
Profit for the year	18,750
Add back depreciation	1,250
	20,000
Purchase of fixed assets	(8,000)
Increase in debtors	(1,000)
Decrease in stocks	1,800
Increase in creditors	350
∴ Increase in cash and bank	13,150

Interpretation of accounts

90 Retained profit = £204,000

	£	£
Profit before tax		445,000
Tax		111,000
Profit after tax		334,000
Transfer to general reserve	30,000	
Interim dividend	40,000	
Final proposed dividend	60,000	
		130,000
Retained profit		204,000

ANSWERS TO OBJECTIVE TEST QUESTIONS

91 Total creditors = £188,000

	£
Trade creditors and accruals	17,000
Corporation tax	111,000
Proposed dividend	60,000
	188,000

92 Amended profit and loss reserve = £69,000

	£
Draft profit and loss reserve	84,000
Adjustment for closing stock	(10,000)
Transfer to general reserve	(5,000)
	69,000

93

	£
Share capital (200,000 + 50,000)	250,000
Share premium (40,000 + 30,000)	70,000
General reserve (20,000 + 5,000)	25,000

94 Mark up = 51.67%

	£
Sales (£130,000 × 140%)	182,000
Cost of sales (2 × £60,000)	120,000
Gross profit	62,000

$$\text{Mark up} = \frac{62,000}{120,000} = 51.67\%$$

95 Mark up = 60%

	£
Sales (160% of cost of sales)	240,000
Cost of sales (£240,000/1.6)	150,000
Gross profit	90,000

$$\text{Mark up} = \frac{90,000}{150,000} = 60\%$$

96 $\text{Gearing} = \frac{\text{Prior charge capital}}{\text{Total capital}} \times 100\%$

$$= \frac{10}{48}$$

$$= 20.8\%$$

97 $\text{ROCE} = \frac{\text{Profit before interest and tax}}{\text{Average capital employed}} \times 100\%$

$$= \frac{5.6 \text{(W1)}}{46.25 \text{(W2)}} \times 100\%$$

$$= 12.1\%$$

Workings

1 *Profit before interest and tax*

	£m
Profit before interest and tax (bal. fig.)	5.6
Interest (10 × 6%)	0.6
Tax	1.0
Profit after tax	4.0

2 *Average capital employed*

	£m
Capital at end of year	48.0
Retained profit (4 − 0.5)	3.5
Capital at start of year	44.5

∴ Average capital employed = $\dfrac{48 + 44.5}{2}$ = £46.25m

98 The gross profit margin is

	20X4	20X5
2,600/14,400	18.1%	
4,400/17,000		25.9%

99 The net profit margin is

	20X4	20X5
1,400/14,400	9.7%	
2,400/17,000		14.1%

100 The return on capital employed is

	20X4	20X5
(2,600 − 1,000)/6,700	23.9%	
2,400/5,720		42.0%

101 The acid test ratio is

	20X4	20X5
(2,000 + 2,400)/1,500	2.9:1	
(1,600 + 820)/2,700		0.9:1

102 The asset turnover is

	20X4	20X5
14,400/6,700	2.1 times	
17,000/5,720		3.0 times

103 The stock turnover period in days is

	20X4	20X5
1,300/11,800 × 365	40 days	
2,000/12,600 × 365		58 days

104 The gearing ratio is

	20X4	20X5
2,600/6,700 × 100	38.9 %	0 %

Pre-assessment tests

Pre-assessment test 1

1. Which of the following does not describe the historical cost convention:

    A   Machinery is valued at depreciated original cost
    B   Stock is valued on the FIFO or weighted average cost method
    C   Properties are revalued to market value
    D   Stock is valued at the lower of cost and net realisable value

2. FRS 18 specifies *four* qualities that financial statements should have. These are: Relevance, Reliability, Comparability and ...

    A   Accuracy
    B   Consistency
    C   Understandability
    D   Materiality

3. The balance on a business's cash book at 31 March was a credit balance of £458.23. At that date there were unpresented cheques of £238.48 and outstanding lodgements of £331.66. What was the balance on the bank statement at 31 March?

    A   £365.05 in credit
    B   £365.05 overdrawn
    C   £551.41 in credit
    D   £551.41 overdrawn

4. During the quarter ending 30 June a business made sales of £288,909 inclusive of VAT and purchases of £165,000 exclusive of VAT. How much VAT is due to Customs and Excise at 30 June?

    A   £14,154
    B   £21,684
    C   £28,875
    D   £43,029

5. If an accountant encountered a situation where application of the materiality concept appeared to conflict with prudence, what course of action should he follow?

    A   Materiality takes precedence
    B   Prudence prevails
    C   Ignore both of them
    D   Make the financial information as 'neutral' as possible

6. At the start of May there was an accrual for telephone charges of £126.50 and the line rental had been prepaid by £30.00. At the end of May there were accruals for call charges of £152.78 and prepayment of line rental of £60.00. A bill for £462.52 was paid during the month. What is the telephone charge for the month of May in the profit and loss account?

    A   £273.24
    B   £458.80
    C   £466.24
    D   £651.80

PRE-ASSESSMENT TESTS

7 A business depreciates its machinery at 20% on cost on the straight line basis and its motor vehicles at 30% on the reducing balance basis. The relevant balances in the trial balance at 30 June are as follows:

	£
Machinery at cost	125,300
Motor vehicles at cost	73,450
Machinery – accumulated depreciation	62,400
Motor vehicles – accumulated depreciation	34,750

Depreciation for the year has not yet been charged.

What is the net book value of fixed assets that will appear in the balance sheet?

A £36,670
B £54,505
C £64,930
D £162,080

8 The following information is known about the three lines of stock that a business has at the end of its accounting year:

	Cost per unit £	Selling price per unit £	Selling costs per unit £	Units in stock
A	35.70	48.60	4.40	100
B	21.50	27.40	6.20	200
C	18.70	23.60	4.40	150

What is the value of stock in the balance sheet at the year end?

A £10,615
B £10,675
C £11,540
D £13,880

The following information relates to questions 9 and 10

A business has the following summarised accounts.

Profit and loss account for the year ended 30 September 20X2

	£
Sales	100,400
Cost of sales	63,200
Gross profit	37,200
Expenses	16,700
Profit before tax	20,500
Tax	4,100
Profit after tax	16,400

Included in cost of sales is depreciation of £15,900.

Balance sheet as at	30 September 20X2	30 September 20X1
Fixed assets	93,200	77,600
Current assets:		
Stock	10,400	8,300
Debtors	16,800	17,900
Bank	2,100	4,500
	29,300	30,700
Creditors: amounts falling due within one year	17,900	20,100
Net current assets	11,400	10,600
	104,600	88,200
Share capital	50,000	50,000
Share premium	10,000	10,000
Profit and loss account	44,600	28,200
	104,600	88,200

During the year fixed assets with a cost of £4,800 were sold for £3,000 at a profit of £200.

9 What is the cash flow from operating activities?

   A £33,000
   B £33,200
   C £39,400
   D £39,800

10 What was the cash outflow on expenditure on fixed assets?

   A £15,600
   B £18,400
   C £34,300
   D £37,100

Pre-assessment test 2

1. Which of the following would not be categorised as capital expenditure?

    A   Purchase of a new building at a cost of £100,000
    B   Legal fees of £5,000 relating to the purchase of the building
    C   Installation of new air-conditioning system in the building
    D   Re-decoration of the building

2. The 'bedrocks' of accounting per FRS 18 are:

    A   Prudence and accruals
    B   Accruals and going concern
    C   Going concern and prudence
    D   Accruals and consistency

3. A business has paid wages by cheque of £74,500 during the month. Deductions of £13,800 for PAYE and £10,400 for employee's National Insurance were made. The employer's National Insurance for the period was £11,200. What is the wages cost figure to appear in the profit and loss account for the month?

    A   £74,500
    B   £98,700
    C   £99,500
    D   £109,900

4. Which of these would not be considered a change of accounting policy?

    A   A change from straight line to reducing balance method of depreciation
    B   A change of stock valuation method from AVCO to FIFO
    C   A revaluation of freehold properties
    D   Depreciation had been shown as part of cost of sales, now it is being presented under administrative expenses

5. A business had debtors at 31 March 20X1 of £78,300. During the year to 31 March 20X2 credit sales totalled £485,600 and £490,300 was received from credit customers. A bad debt of £5,600 was written off during the year and the provision for doubtful debts is to remain at 2% of the debtors figure.

    What is the charge for bad and doubtful debts to the profit and loss account for the year ended 31 March 20X2?

    A   £5,394
    B   £5,600
    C   £5,806
    D   £6,960

6   A business had a balance on its suspense account which was caused by the two following errors in the double entry.

- discounts allowed of £480 had been entered into the wrong side of the discounts allowed account
- telephone expenses of £468 had been entered into the telephone account as £648

Once these two errors had been corrected there was no remaining balance on the suspense account.

What was the original balance on the suspense account?

A   £780 debit
B   £780 credit
C   £1,140 debit
D   £1,140 credit

7   Given below is an extract from the trial balance of a manufacturing company:

	£
Direct factory labour	355,400
Indirect factory labour	58,200
Factory supervisor's salary	16,800
Opening stock of raw materials	21,500
Heat, light and power	30,500
Purchases of raw materials	169,300
Depreciation charge for factory machinery	18,200
Factory cleaning costs	21,400
Closing stock of raw materials	19,800

What is the prime cost of production?

The following information relates to questions 8 to 10

Given below is a profit and loss account for a business for the year ended 30 June and a balance sheet at that date.

Profit and loss account

	£
Sales	258,300
Cost of sales	160,140
Gross profit	98,160
Operating expenses	51,660
Interest	6,600
Profit before tax	39,900
Tax	9,800
Profit after tax	30,100
Dividends	5,000
Retained profit	25,100

PRE-ASSESSMENT TESTS

Balance sheet

	£	£
Fixed assets		551,000
Current assets		
Stock	24,000	
Debtors	53,800	
Cash	4,200	
	82,000	
Creditors: amounts falling due within one year		
Trade creditors	28,400	
Tax	5,000	
	33,400	
Net current assets		48,600
		599,600
Creditors: amounts falling due after more than one year		
Long term loan		100,000
		499,600
Share capital		300,000
Share premium		80,000
Profit and loss account		119,600
		499,600

In the table below enter the relevant monetary amounts to calculate the following ratios:

8   Net profit percentage   = ... / .... × 100

                                                 = ...

9   Return on capital employed   = ... / .... × 100

                                                 = ...

10   Stock turnover days   = ... / .... × 365

                                                 = ...

Answers to Pre-assessment tests

Pre-assessment test 1

1   C   All of the others are concerned with valuation at cost.

2   C   Understandability

3   D

	£	
Cash book balance	458.23	overdrawn
Less: unpresented cheques	(238.48)	
Add: outstanding lodgements	331.66	
	551.41	overdrawn

4   A

	£
Output VAT (288,909 × 17.5/117.5)	43,029
Input VAT (165,000 × 17.5%)	(28,875)
VAT due	14,154

5   D   FRS 18 requires that financial information should be neutral, ie free from bias, and present a true and fair view.

6   B

Telephone expenses account

	£		£
Opening prepayment	30.00	Opening accrual	126.50
Cash paid	462.52	Profit and loss account	458.80
Closing accrual	152.78	Closing prepayment	60.00
	645.30		645.30

7   C

	£
Machinery – cost	125,300
Accumulated depreciation (62,400 + (125,300 × 20%))	87,460
NBV	37,840
Motor vehicles – cost	73,450
Accumulated depreciation (34,750 + (73,450 – 34,750) × 30%))	46,360
NBV	27,090
Total NBV (37,840 + 27,090)	64,930

8   A

	Cost	NRV	Quantity	Value
A	35.70	44.20	100	3,570
D	21.50	21.20	200	4,240
C	18.70	19.20	150	2,805
				10,615

9   A

	£
Operating profit	20,500
Add: depreciation	15,900
Less: profit on sale	(200)
Increase in stocks	(2,100)
Decrease in debtors	1,100
Decrease in creditors	(2,200)
Net cash flow from operating activities	33,000

PRE-ASSESSMENT TESTS: ANSWERS

10 C

	Fixed assets at NBV		
	£		£
Opening balance	77,600	Disposal (3,000 – 200)	2,800
		Depreciation	15,900
Additions (bal fig)	34,300	Closing balance	93,200
	111,900		111,900

Pre-assessment test 2

1. **D** All of the other three options are either part of the cost of buying the building or necessary to get it into operational condition.

2. **B** Accruals and going concern are the 'bedrocks'.

   The other concepts are 'desirable features'.

3. **D**

	£
Net wages	74,500
PAYE	13,800
Employee's NIC	10,400
Employer's NIC	11,200
	109,900

4. **A** This is a change of estimation technique.

   The others are all changes of measurement basis or presentation.

5. **A**

   Debtors control account

	£		£
		Bad debt written off	5,600
Opening balance	78,300	Cash received	490,300
Credit sales	485,600	Closing balance	68,000
	563,900		563,900

	£
Opening provision for doubtful debts (78,300 × 2%)	1,566
Closing provision for doubtful debts (68,000 × 2%)	1,360
Decrease in provision	206

   Bad debts expense

	£		£
Bad debt written off	5,600	Decrease in provision	206
		Profit and loss account	5,394
	5,600		5,600

6. **A** Double entry to correct errors:

		£	£
Debit	Discounts allowed (£480 × 2)	960	
Credit	Suspense		960
Debit	Suspense (648 – 468)	180	
Credit	Telephone		180

   Suspense account

	£		£
Telephone	180	Discounts	960
Opening balance (bal fig)	780		
	960		960

PRE-ASSESSMENT TESTS: ANSWERS

7   The prime cost of production is £526,400.

	£
Opening stock of raw materials	21,500
Purchases of raw materials	169,300
	190,800
Less: closing stock of raw materials	(19,800)
Direct materials used	171,000
Direct factory labour	355,400
Prime cost of production	526,400

8   Net profit percentage   = 46,500/258,300 × 100
    = 18.0%

9   Return on capital employed   = 46,500/599,600 × 100
    = 7.8%

10   Stock turnover days   = 24,000/160,140 × 365
    = 54.7 days

Mock assessments

CIMA
Paper C2 (Certificate)
Financial Accounting Fundamentals

Mock Assessment 1

Question Paper	
Time allowed	1½ hours
Answer ALL the questions	

DO NOT OPEN THIS PAPER UNTIL YOU ARE READY TO START UNDER EXAMINATION CONDITIONS

Answer ALL 40 questions

1   An imprest system is

    A   Accounting computer software
    B   An audit process
    C   Automatic agreement of the cash book and bank statement
    D   A method of controlling petty cash

2   Which ONE of the following is correct?

    A   All limited companies are required by law to have an external audit
    B   Only public limited companies are required by law to have an external audit
    C   Only limited companies above a certain size are required by law to have an external audit
    D   An external audit for a limited company is voluntary

3   At 31 March 20X1, accrued rent payable was £300. During the year ended 31 March 20X2, rent paid was £4,000, including an invoice for £1,200 for the quarter ended 30 April 20X2. What is the profit and loss account charge for rent payable for the year ended 31 March 20X2?

    A   £3,300
    B   £3,900
    C   £4,100
    D   £4,700

4   The responsibility for internal control rests with

    A   The internal auditors
    B   The external auditors
    C   The shareholders
    D   The directors

5   The annual insurance premium for S Ltd for the period 1 July 20X1 to 30 June 20X2 is £13,200, which is 10% more than the previous year. Insurance premiums are paid on 1 July.

    What is the profit and loss account charge for the year ended 31 December 20X1?

    A   £11,800
    B   £12,540
    C   £12,600
    D   £13,200

6   A bank reconciliation showed the following differences between the bank statement and the cash book.

    Unpresented cheques of   £750
    Outstanding deposits of   £500
    Bank charges of   £100

    If the balance on the bank statement is £1,000 overdrawn, what is the balance in the cash book before any adjustments?

    A   Debit £250
    B   Credit £1,150
    C   Credit £1,250
    D   Credit £1,500

7 Which ONE of the following expenses should be included in prime cost in a manufacturing account?

   A   Repairs to factory machinery
   B   Direct production wages
   C   Office salaries
   D   Factory insurance

8 The entries in a sales ledger control account are:

	£
Sales	250,000
Bank	225,000
Returns	2,500
Bad debts	3,000
Returned unpaid cheque	3,500
Contra purchase ledger account	4,000

   What is the balance on the sales ledger control account?

   A   £12,000
   B   £19,000
   C   £25,000
   D   £27,000

9 A Ltd has an item in stock which cost £1,000 and can be sold for £1,200. However, before it can be sold, it will require to be modified at a cost of £150. The expected selling costs of the item are an additional £100.

   How should this item be valued in stock?

   A   £950
   B   £1,000
   C   £1,050
   D   £1,100

10 A 'value for money' audit is:

   A   An external audit with limited scope.
   B   A review of expenditure to ensure effectiveness, efficiency and economy.
   C   A voluntary audit by an unregistered auditor.
   D   None of these.

11 Which ONE of the following statements regarding a fixed assets register is NOT correct?

   A   A fixed assets register enables reconciliation to be made with the nominal ledger
   B   A fixed assets register enables depreciation charges to be posted to the nominal ledger
   C   A fixed assets register agrees with the fixed asset nominal ledger account
   D   A fixed assets register records the physical location of an asset

12 B Ltd purchased a machine for £120,000 on 1 October 20X1. The estimated useful life is 4 years with a residual value of £4,000. B Ltd uses the straight-line method for depreciation and charges depreciation on a monthly basis.

   What is the charge for depreciation for the year ended 31 December 20X1?

   A   £7,250
   B   £7,500
   C   £29,000
   D   £30,000

13   In the quarter ended 31 March 20X2, C Ltd had VAT taxable outputs, net of VAT, of £90,000 and taxable inputs, net of VAT, of £72,000.

If the rate of VAT is 10%, how much VAT is due?

A   £1,800 receivable
B   £2,000 receivable
C   £1,800 payable
D   £2,000 payable

14   Which of the following statements concerning a 'true and fair view' is correct?

A   True and fair has a precise definition which is universally accepted
B   There can only be one true and fair view of a company's financial statements
C   True and fair means the financial statements are correct
D   True and fair is mainly determined by compliance with generally accepted accounting practice

15   The M Club discloses the following note to its Income and Expenditure Account:

'Subscriptions in arrears are accounted for when received; subscriptions in advance are accounted for on a matching basis.'

At 31 March 20X1, there were subscriptions owing of £1,000 and subscriptions in advance of £500. During the year ended 31 March 20X2, subscriptions of £10,000 were received, including subscriptions relating to the previous year of £800 and subscriptions in advance of £600.

What amount should be included for subscriptions in the year ended 31 March 20X2?

A   £8,100
B   £8,900
C   £9,100
D   £9,900

16   The total cost of salaries charged to the profit and loss account is:

A   The total gross salaries plus employer's national insurance contributions
B   The total gross salaries
C   The total net salaries
D   The total net salaries plus employer's national insurance contributions

17   The segregation of duties is

A   Delegation of duties by a manager
B   Two staff sharing one job
C   A feature of internal control
D   All of the above

18   The net profit percentage in a company is 12% and the asset turnover ratio is 2.

What is the return on capital employed?

A   6%
B   10%
C   14%
D   24%

MOCK ASSESSMENT 1: QUESTIONS

19 Which of the following are used in a coding system for accounting transactions?

   A   Department code
   B   Nominal ledger code
   C   Product code
   D   All of the above

20 APM Ltd provides the following note to fixed assets in its balance sheet.

   Plant and machinery

	Cost £'000	Depreciation £'000	Net book value £'000
Opening balance	25	12	13
Additions/charge	15	4	11
Disposals	(10)	(8)	(2)
Closing balance	30	8	22

   The additional machinery was purchased for cash. A machine was sold at a profit of £2,000.

   What is the net cash outflow for plant and machinery?

   A   £9,000
   B   £11,000
   C   £13,000
   D   £15,000

21 Which of the following errors will cause the trial balance totals to be unequal?

   A   Errors of transposition
   B   Errors of omission
   C   Errors of principle
   D   All of the above

22 Which ONE of the following is a record of prime entry?

   A   The nominal ledger
   B   The sales ledger
   C   The trial balance
   D   The sales day book

23 P is a sole proprietor whose accounting records are incomplete. All the sales are cash sales and during the year £50,000 was banked, including £5,000 from the sale of a business car. He paid £12,000 wages in cash from the till and withdrew £2,000 per month as drawings. The cash in the till at the beginning and end of the year was £300 and £400 respectively.

   What were the sales for the year?

   A   £80,900
   B   £81,000
   C   £81,100
   D   £86,100

24 Which of the following is NOT helpful in detecting an error?

   A   A bank reconciliation
   B   A sales ledger control account
   C   An imprest system
   D   A suspense account

25 Which ONE of the following is an appropriation by a limited company?

    A   Directors' salaries
    B   Dividends
    C   Donation to a charity
    D   Loan interest

26 At the year end of SED Ltd in December 20X0, a journal entry was raised to accrue for utility expenses of £3,600. This journal entry was reversed in January 20X1. During the year ended December 20X1, £30,000 was paid for utility expenses, of which £4,000 was prepaid at the year end.

The charge to the profit and loss account for utility expenses for the year ended December 20X1 was

£ ....

27 Z Ltd's cash book shows a credit balance of £2,200. A comparison with the bank statement showed the following:

(i) unpresented cheques totalling £600;

(ii) receipts of £1,200 not yet cleared by the bank;

(iii) bank charges of £300 not entered in the cash book;

(iv) a cheque from a customer for £400, which had been entered in the cash book when received, has now been returned by the bank as 'dishonoured'.

The overdraft balance on Z Ltd's bank statement is £ ....

The following data relates to questions 28 and 29

On the first day of Month 1, a business had prepaid insurance of £10,000. On the first day of Month 8, it paid in full the annual insurance invoice of £36,000, to cover the following year.

28 The amount charged in the profit and loss account for insurance for the year is £ ....

29 The amount shown in the balance sheet at the year end is £ ....

30 SSG Ltd bought a machine for £40,000 in January 19W8. The machine had an expected useful life of six years and an expected residual value of £10,000. The machine was depreciated on the straight-line basis. In December 20X1, the machine was sold for £15,000. The company has a policy in its internal accounts of combining the depreciation charge with the profit or loss on disposal of assets.

The total amount of depreciation and profit/loss charged to the internal profit and loss account over the life of the machine was £ ....

31 DEF plc has a supplier, M Ltd, and the balance on M Ltd's purchase ledger account at 31 July 20X2 was a credit balance of £2,000. On 5 August 20X2, DEF plc received the July statement from M Ltd showing a balance due of £3,000. The purchase ledger supervisor investigates the difference and discovers that:

(i) an invoice for £2,000 from M Ltd dated 31 July was not entered in the purchase ledger account until 3 August 20X2, but appears on M Ltd's July statement.

(ii) a cheque for £600 sent from DEF plc to M Ltd on 25 July 20X2 in payment of a July invoice does not appear on M Ltd's July statement. This cheque was presented by M Ltd on 31 July 20X2.

The purchase ledger supervisor at DEF plc contacts the sales ledger supervisor at M Ltd and correctly says that there is a difference between the ledger accounts of £ ....

32   On 1 October 20X2, the debtors' balance at G Ltd was £80,000. A summary of the transactions in the month of October is set out below.

	£
Cheques received	100,000
Contra creditors	6,000
Sales	90,000
Returns inwards	4,000
Discounts allowed	10,000

The debtors' balance at 31 October was £ ....

33   SAD plc paid £240,000 in net wages to its employees in August 20X2. Employees' tax was £24,000, employees' national insurance was £12,000 and employer's national insurance was £14,000. Employees had contributed £6,000 to a pension scheme and had voluntarily asked for £3,000 to be deducted for charitable giving.

The amount to be charged to the profit and loss account in August 20X2 for wages is

£ ....

34   At the beginning of Period 6, XYZ Ltd had opening stock of 20 units of product X valued at £4.00 each. During Period 6, the following stock movements occurred:

Day 5   Sold 15 items for £5.00 each
Day 10   Bought 8 items for £6.00 each
Day 14   Sold 12 items for £7.00 each

Using the FIFO method of stock valuation, the closing stock at the end of Period 6 was

£ ....

The following data relates to questions 35 to 37

The accounts for SPA plc are set out below.

Profit and loss account for the year ended 30 November 20X2

	£'000	£'000
Turnover		5,000
Opening stock	200	
Purchases	3,100	
Closing stock	(300)	
Cost of sales		(3,000)
Gross profit		2,000
Operating expenses		(500)
Operating profit		1,500

MOCK ASSESSMENT 1: QUESTIONS

Balance sheet at 30 November 20X2

	£'000	£'000
Fixed assets		3,000
Current assets		
Stock	300	
Debtors	900	
Bank	50	
	1,250	
Current liabilities		
Trade creditors	(250)	
		1,000
		4,000
Share capital		2,000
Profit and loss account		2,000
		4,000

35 The return on capital employed in SPA plc is ....

36 The fixed asset turnover ratio in SPA plc is ....

37 The quick ratio (acid test ratio) in SPA plc is ....

38 Tanwir commenced his business on 1 October 20X9, with capital in the bank of £20,000. During his first month of trading, his transactions were as follows.

1 October	Purchase stocks for £3,500 on credit from A Jones
3 October	Paid £1,200 rental of premises, by cheque
5 October	Paid £5,000 for office equipment, by cheque
10 October	Sold goods costing £1,000 for £1,750, on credit to P Duncan
15 October	Returned stocks costing £500 to A Jones
18 October	Purchased stocks for £2,400 on credit from A Jones
25 October	Paid A Jones for the net purchases of 1 October, by cheque
28 October	P Duncan paid £500 on account, by cheque

The balance on the account of A Jones at 31 October 20X9 was £ ....

The following data relates to questions 39 and 40

During his first year of trading, Tanwir brings his private car, valued at £6,000 into the business as well as his initial £20,000 of capital. The business made a net profit of £17,500 for the year, after deducting £650 for petrol which was paid out of his private funds. He has drawn £5,000 out of the business bank account for himself, as well as paying his home telephone bill of £450 from business funds.

39 Tanwir's capital at the end of his first year of trading was £ ....

40 State the accounting concept which has governed the treatment of the items which make up Tanwir's capital at the end of the year. ....

Mock assessment 1
Answers

DO NOT TURN THIS PAGE UNTIL YOU HAVE COMPLETED THE MOCK ASSESSMENT 1

MOCK ASSESSMENT 1: ANSWERS

1   D   A method of controlling petty cash.

2   C   Only limited companies above a certain size are required to have an external audit.

3   A

RENT PAYABLE

	£		£
Rent paid	4,000	Balance b/d – accrual	300
		Profit and loss charge	3,300
		Balance c/d – prepayment (1,200 × 1/3)	400
	4,000		4,000

4   D   This is part of their stewardship function.

5   C

	£
1 Jan – 30 June (12,000 × 6/12)	6,000
1 July – 31 Dec (13,200 × 6/12)	6,600
	12,600

6   B

	£
Bank statement balance	1,000 o/d
Less: bank charges	(100)
Add: unpresented cheques	750
Less: outstanding deposits	(500)
Balance per cash book	1,150 o/d

7   B   Only direct production costs are included in prime cost.

8   B

SALES LEDGER CONTROL ACCOUNT

	£		£
Sales	250,000	Bank	225,000
Unpaid cheque	3,500	Returns	2,500
		Bad debts	3,000
		Contra	4,000
		Balance c/d	19,000
	253,500		253,500

9   A

	£
Cost	1,000
Selling price	1,200
Less: modification costs	(150)
Less: selling costs	(100)
Net realisable value	950

10   B   This is normally carried out by internal auditors.

11   C   The fixed asset register should agree with the nominal ledger but will not necessarily always agree if there are either errors in the register or in the nominal ledger.

MOCK ASSESSMENT 1: ANSWERS

12   A   Annual depreciation $= \dfrac{£120{,}000 - 4{,}000}{4 \text{ years}}$

                       $= £29{,}000$

           Depreciation charge 1 Oct – 31 Dec $= £29{,}000 \times 3/12$
                                                                $= £7{,}250$

13   C

	£
Output VAT (£90,000 × 10%)	9,000
Input VAT (£72,000 × 10%)	(7,200)
	1,800 payable

14   D   True and fair is mainly determined by compliance with GAAP

15   D

SUBSCRIPTIONS ACCOUNT

	£		£
Income and expenditure a/c	9,900	Balance b/d – subs in advance	500
Balance c/d – subs in advance	600	Bank	10,000
	10,500		10,500

16   A   Employer's NI contributions are not deducted from gross salaries – they are an additional cost.

17   C   An internal control procedure designed to prevent certain types of fraud.

18   D   Return on capital employed   = Net profit % × asset turnover
                                                            = 12% × 2
                                                            = 24%

19   D   It is entirely possible that a coding system would identify the department and product to which the transaction relates as well as the nominal ledger code for posting. The department and product codes would be of most use for management accounting purposes.

20   B

FIXED ASSETS AT COST

	£'000		£'000
Balance b/d	25	Disposal	10
Additions (bal fig)	15	Balance c/d	30
	40		40

	£'000
Disposal – net book value	2
Profit on disposal	2
Proceeds	4

Net cash inflow   = £15,000 – 4,000
                         = £11,000

21   A   B and C will not give rise to any numerical imbalance.

22   D   The sales day book.

23	C					
			CASH ACCOUNT			
			£			£
		Balance b/d	300	Bankings (50,000 – 5,000)		45,000
				Wages		12,000
				Drawings		24,000
		Takings (bal fig)	81,100	Balance c/d		400
			81,400			81,400

24   D   A suspense account is a location where some accumulated errors may be recorded, but it is not a method of detecting errors.

25   B   Dividends are an appropriation. All of the others are expenses of the business.

26   £22,400

(£30,000 – £3,600 – £4,000)

27   £3,500

	£
Cash book balance	(2,200)
Bank charges	(300)
Dishonoured cheque	(400)
Amended cash book balance	(2,900)
Unpresented cheques	600
Outstanding lodgements	(1,200)
Bank statement balance	(3,500)

28   £25,000

£10,000 + (£36,000 × 5/12) = £25,000

29   £21,000

£36,000 × 7/12 = £21,000

30   £25,000

Annual depreciation $= \dfrac{£40,000 - £10,000}{6}$

$= £5,000$

4 years depreciation = £20,000

	£
Net book value in Dec 2001 = £40,000 – £20,000	20,000
Disposal proceeds	15,000
Loss on disposal	5,000

Total depreciation and loss on disposal = £20,000 + £5,000
= £25,000

31   £1,600

	£
DEF balance	2,000
Additional invoice	2,000
Amended balance	4,000
M Ltd balance	3,000
Less: cheque payment	(600)
	2,400

Difference remaining = £4,000 – £2,400
= £1,600

MOCK ASSESSMENT 1: ANSWERS

32 £50,000

Debtors account

	£		£
Opening balance	80,000	Contra	6,000
Sales	90,000	Cheques received	100,000
		Returns inwards	4,000
		Discounts allowed	10,000
		Closing balance	50,000
	170,000		170,000

33 £299,000

	£
Net wages	240,000
Employee's tax	24,000
Employee's NI	12,000
Pension scheme contributions	6,000
Charitable donations	3,000
Gross wages	285,000
Employer's NI	14,000
	299,000

34 £6.00

Opening stock	20 units @ £4.00
Day 5 sale	15 units costing £4.00
Remaining	5 units @ £4.00
Day 10 purchase	8 units @ £6.00
Day 14 sale	5 units @ £4.00
	7 units @ £6.00
Remaining	1 unit @ £6.00

35 37.5%

Return on capital employed $= \dfrac{\text{Operating profit}}{\text{Share captial} + \text{reserves}} \times 100$

$= \dfrac{1,500}{4,000} \times 100$

$= 37.5\%$

36 1.67 : 1

Fixed asset turnover ratio $= \dfrac{\text{Turnover}}{\text{Fixed assets}}$

$= \dfrac{5,000}{3,000}$

$= 1.67 : 1$

37 3.8 : 1

Quick ratio $= \dfrac{\text{Current assets} - \text{stock}}{\text{Current liabilities}}$

$= \dfrac{1,250 - 300}{250}$

$= 3.8 : 1$

38   Balance = £2,400

A JONES

	£			£
15.10 Returns	500	1.10	Purchases	3,500
25.10 Bank	3,000	18.10	Purchases	2,400
31.10 Balance c/d	2,400			
	5,900			5,900

39   Tanwir's capital = £38,700

	£
Cash introduced on 1 October 20X9	20,000
Car introduced	6,000
Profit for the year	17,500
Petrol paid for privately	650
Drawings	(5,000)
Home phone bill	(450)
Capital at the year end	38,700

40   The accounting concept which governs the treatment of capital is the entity concept. The entity concept ensures that the business is treated as a separate entity. Therefore every transaction made by Tanwir which affects the business must be recorded.

CIMA
Paper C2 (Certificate)
Financial Accounting Fundamentals

Mock Assessment 2

Question Paper	
Time allowed	1½ hours
Answer ALL the questions	

DO NOT OPEN THIS PAPER UNTIL YOU ARE READY TO START UNDER EXAMINATION CONDITIONS

MOCK ASSESSMENT 2: QUESTIONS

Answer ALL 40 questions

1 Which ONE of the following best describes the stewardship function?

   A   Ensuring high profits
   B   Managing cash
   C   Ensuring the recording, controlling and safeguarding of assets
   D   Ensuring high dividends to shareholders

2 External auditors are primarily responsible for

   A   writing a report to the shareholders expressing an opinion on the financial statements
   B   preparing the financial statements
   C   detecting errors and fraud
   D   ensuring that the accounts show a true and fair view

3 When preparing financial statements in periods of inflation, directors

   A   Must reduce asset values
   B   Must increase asset values
   C   Must reduce dividends
   D   Need make no adjustments

4 The following information relates to a bank reconciliation.

   (i)   The bank balance in the cashbook before taking the items below into account was £8,970 overdrawn.
   (ii)   Bank charges of £550 on the bank statement have not been entered in the cashbook.
   (iii) The bank has credited the account in error with £425 which belongs to another customer.
   (iv)   Cheque payments totalling £3,275 have been entered in the cashbook but have not been presented for payment.
   (v)   Cheques totalling £5,380 have been correctly entered on the debit side of the cashbook but have not been paid in at the bank.

   What was the balance as shown by the bank statement *before* taking the items above into account?

   A   £8,970 overdrawn
   B   £11,200 overdrawn
   C   £12,050 overdrawn
   D   £17,750 overdrawn

5 W Ltd bought a new printing machine from abroad. The cost of the machine was £80,000. The installation costs were £5,000 and the employees received specific training on how to use this particular machine, at a cost of £2,000. Before using the machine to print customers' orders, a test was undertaken and the paper and ink cost £1,000.

   What should be the cost of the machine in the company's balance sheet?

   A   £80,000
   B   £85,000
   C   £87,000
   D   £88,000

6   In a manual accounting system, the most important reason for extracting a trial balance prior to preparing financial statements is that

   A   it proves the arithmetical accuracy of the ledgers.
   B   it provides a summary of the financial statements.
   C   it proves the individual ledger accounts are correct.
   D   it reveals how errors have been made.

7   JSL Ltd operates the imprest system for its petty cash with a float of £750. At the end of July, the cashier prepared a spreadsheet for the petty cash expenses with a total column and analysis columns. A cash voucher for petrol for £50 was incorrectly entered as £5 in the total column and also in one of the analysis columns in the spreadsheet. The total column was posted to the cash account, the analysis columns were posted to the relevant nominal ledger accounts and cash was drawn from the bank for the total of the cash expenditure on the spreadsheet.

   The effect of this error would be

   A   a petty cash balance of £705.
   B   petrol expenses overstated by £45.
   C   an imbalance on the trial balance.
   D   a petty cash balance of £750.

8   The electricity account for the year ended 30 June 20X1 was as follows.

	£
Opening balance for electricity accrued at 1 July 20X0	300
Payments made during the year	
1 August 20X0 for three months to 31 July 20X0	600
1 November 20X0 for three months to 31 October 20X0	720
1 February 20X1 for three months to 31 January 20X1	900
30 June 20X1 for three months to 30 April 20X1	840

   Which of the following is the appropriate entry for electricity?

	Accrued At 30 June 20X1	Charge to profit and loss account year ended 30 June 20X1
A	£Nil	£3,060
B	£460	£3,320
C	£560	£3,320
D	£560	£3,420

9   The year end of M plc is 30 November 20X0. The company pays for its gas by a standing order of £600 per month. On 1 December 20W9, the statement from the gas supplier showed that M plc had overpaid by £200. M plc received gas bills for the four quarters commencing on 1 December 20W9 and ending on 30 November 20X0 for £1,300, £1,400, £2,100 and £2,000 respectively.

   Which of the following is the correct charge for gas in M plc's profit and loss account for the year ended 30 November 20X0?

   A   £6,800
   B   £7,000
   C   £7,200
   D   £7,400

10 S & Co. sell three products – Basic, Super and Luxury. The following information was available at the year end.

	Basic £ per unit	Super £ per unit	Luxury £ per unit
Original cost	6	9	18
Estimated selling price	9	12	15
Selling and distribution costs	1	4	5
	units	units	units
Units of stock	200	250	150

The value of stock at the year end should be

A £4,200
B £4,700
C £5,700
D £6,150

11 A car was purchased by a newsagent business in May 20X7 for:

	£
Cost	10,000
Road tax	150
Total	10,150

The business adopts a date of 31 December as its year end.

The car was traded in for a replacement vehicle in August 20Y0 at an agreed value of £5,000.

It has been depreciated at 25% per annum on the reducing-balance method, charging a full year's depreciation in the year of purchase and none in the year of sale.

What was the profit or loss on disposal of the vehicle during the year ended December 20Y0?

A Profit: £718
B Profit: £781
C Profit: £1,788
D Profit: £1,836

12 A summary of the balance sheet of M Ltd at 31 March 20X0 was as follows

	£'000
Total assets less current liabilities	120
Ordinary share capital	40
Share premium account	10
Profit and loss account	10
5% debentures 20Y0	60
	120

If the operating profit for the year ended 31 March 20X0 was £15,000, what is the return on capital employed?

A 12.5%
B 25%
C 30%
D 37.5%

MOCK ASSESSMENT 2: QUESTIONS

13 The annual sales of a company are £235,000 including VAT at 17.5%. Half of the sales are on credit terms; half are cash sales. The debtors in the balance sheet are £23,500.

What are the debtor days (to the nearest day)?

A   37 days
B   43 days
C   73 days
D   86 days

14 The concept of capital maintenance is important for

A   The sources of finance
B   The measurement of profit
C   The relationship of debt to equity
D   The purchase of fixed assets

15 Internal control includes 'detect' controls and 'prevent' controls. Which of the following is a detect control?

A   Signing overtime claim forms
B   Matching purchase invoices with goods received notes
C   Preparing bank reconciliations
D   Matching sales invoices with delivery notes

16 A stock record card shows the following details.

February 1   50 units in stock at a cost of £40 per unit
          7   100 units purchased at a cost of £45 per unit
         14   80 units sold
         21   50 units purchased at a cost of £50 per unit
         28   60 units sold

What is the value of stock at 28 February using the FIFO method?

A   £2,450
B   £2,700
C   £2,950
D   £3,000

17 The year end for ABC Ltd is July 20X2 and in that month a company car was stolen. The net book value of the company car was £8,000, but the company expects the insurance company to pay only £6,000. The correct journal entry to record this information was entered in the books in July 20X2. In August 20X2 the insurance company sent a cheque for £6,500.

The journal entry to record this is:

		Dr £	Cr £
A	Bank	6,500	
	Sundry debtor		6,500
B	Bank	6,500	
	Sundry debtor		6,000
	Disposal of fixed assets account		500
C	Bank	500	
	Disposal of fixed assets account		500
D	Bank	500	
	Sundry debtor		500

18 The trial balance of EHL plc does not balance and the debits exceed the credits by £2,300. The following errors are discovered:

- the single column manual cash book receipts column was undercast by £600;
- discount received of £400 had been debited to the interest payable account;
- the proceeds of £1,000 on the sale of a fixed asset had been credited to sales.

Following the correction of these errors, the balance on the suspense account would be

A   Cr £900
B   Cr £2,100
C   Cr £3,700
D   Dr £2,100

19 At the beginning of the year in GHI Ltd, the opening work-in-progress was £240,000. During the year, the following expenditure was incurred:

	£
Prime cost	720,000
Factory overheads	72,000
The closing work-in-progress was	350,000

The factory cost of goods completed during the year was

A   £538,000
B   £610,000
C   £682,000
D   £902,000

20 In July 20X2, a company sold goods at standard value added tax (VAT) rate with a net value of £200,000, goods exempt from VAT with a value of £50,000 and goods at zero VAT rate with a net value of £25,000. The purchases in July 20X2, which were all subject to VAT, were £161,000, including VAT. Assume that the rate of VAT is 15%.

The difference between VAT input tax and VAT output tax is

A   Dr £9,000
B   Cr £5,850
C   Cr £9,000
D   None of these

21 After the profit and loss account for Z Ltd had been prepared, it was found that accrued expenses of £1,500 had been omitted and that closing stock had been overvalued by £500.

The effect of these errors is an

A   overstatement of net profit of £1,000
B   overstatement of net profit of £2,000
C   understatement of net profit of £1,000
D   understatement of net profit of £2,000

MOCK ASSESSMENT 2: QUESTIONS

22 The cashier is reconciling his company's cash book with the bank statement at 31 March 20X3.

	£
The firm's cash book shows a debit balance of	12,350
The following information is available:	
Bank charges not entered in the cash book	170
Unpresented cheques	4,600
Direct debit payment on the bank statement not entered in the cash book	230
Sales receipts banked, but not credited by the bank	9,400
A cheque from a customer which had previously been entered in the cash book when received, has been returned by the bank as 'dishonoured, and this has not been recorded in the cash book	110

What should be stated as the bank balance in the company's balance sheet at 31 March 20X3?

A £11,840
B £12,060
C £12,860
D £16,640

23 D is preparing the accounts for A Ltd for the year ended 31 March 20X3. The most recent gas bill received by A Ltd was dated 6 February 20X3 and related to the quarter 1 November 20X2 to 31 January 20X3, and the amount of the bill was £2,100.

Which ONE of the following ledger entries should be made in A Ltd's books at 31 March 20X3?

		Debit		Credit
A	Accruals	Nil	Gas expense	Nil
B	Gas expense	£1,400	Accruals	£1,400
C	Accruals	£1,400	Gas expense	£1,400
D	Gas expense	£2,100	Accruals	£2,100

24 The following information related to Q plc for the year ended 28 February 20X3:

	£
Prime cost	122,000
Factory overheads	185,000
Opening work-in-progress at 1 March 20X2	40,000
Factory cost of goods completed	300,000

The closing work-in-progress at 28 February 20X3 was

A £33,000
B £40,000
C £47,000
D £54,000

25 N Ltd, which is registered for VAT, received an invoice from an advertising agency for £4,000 plus VAT. The rat of VAT on the goods was 17.5%. The correct ledger entries are:

		Debit £		Credit £
A	Advertising expense	4,000	Creditors	4,000
B	Advertising expense	4,700	Creditors	4,700
C	Advertising expense	4,700	Creditors	4,000
			VAT account	700
D	Advertising expense	4,000	Creditors	4,700
	VAT account	700		

26   E Ltd received an invoice for the purchase of fixed asset equipment which was credited to the correct supplier's ledger account, but debited to the equipment repairs account, instead of the equipment account.

The effect of not correcting this error on the financial statements would be:

A   Profit would be overstated and fixed assets would be understated.
B   Profit would be overstated and fixed assets would be overstated.
C   Profit would be understated and fixed assets would be overstated.
D   Profit would be understated and fixed assets would be understated.

27   H Ltd began trading on 1 July 20X1. The company is now preparing its accounts for the accounting year ended 30 June 20X2. Rates are charged for a tax year, which runs from 1 April to 31 March, and were £1,800 for the year ended 31 March 20X2 and £2,000 for the year ended 31 March 20X3. Rates are payable quarterly in advance, plus any arrears, on 1 March, 1 June, 1 September and 1 December.

The charge to H Ltd's profit and loss account for rates for the year ended 30 June 20X2 is

A   £1,650
B   £1,700
C   £1,850
D   £1,900

28   The return on capital employed for S plc is 24% and the net asset turnover ratio is 3 times.

What is the profit margin?

A   8%
B   28%
C   72%
D   It cannot be calculated

29   The total cost of salaries charged to a limited company's profit and loss account is

A   cash paid to employees
B   net pay earned by employees
C   gross pay earned by employees
D   gross pay earned by employees, plus employer's national insurance contributions

30   The following is the aged debtors analysis for J Ltd at 30 April 20X3:

Age of debt	Less than 1 month	1-2 months	2-3 months	Over 3 months
Amount (£)	12,000	24,000	8,000	6,000

The company provides for doubtful debts as follows:

Provision	0%	1%	10%	30%

The doubtful debt provision at 1 May 20X2 brought forward was £2,880.

The entry for doubtful debts in the profit and loss account for the year ended 30 April 20X3 and the net debtors figure in the balance sheet at that date should be:

	Profit and loss account	Balance sheet
A	£40 credit	£47,160
B	£40 debit	£47,160
C	£2,840 debit	£50,000
D	£2,840 credit	£47,160

31 The prime cost of goods manufactured is the total of

   A   raw materials consumed
   B   raw materials consumed and direct wages
   C   raw materials consumed, direct wages and direct expenses
   D   raw materials consumed, direct wages, direct expenses and production overheads

32 On 1 May 20X3, E Ltd owed a supplier £1,200. During the month of May, E Ltd:

   - purchased goods for £1,700 and the supplier offered a 5% discount for payment within the month
   - returned goods value at £100 which had been purchased in April 20X3
   - sent a cheque to the supplier for payment of the goods delivered in May

   The balance on the supplier's account at the end of May 20X3 is:

   A   £1,015
   B   £1,100
   C   £1,185
   D   £1,300

33 The main advantage of using a sales ledger control account is that

   A   double entry bookkeeping is not necessary
   B   it helps in detecting errors
   C   it helps with credit control
   D   it ensures that the trial balance will always balance

34 The following information relates to J Ltd for the year ended 30 April 20X3.

	£'000
Retained profit for the year	28,000
Net cash inflow from operating activities	26,000
Dividend paid	3,000
Profit on sale of fixed assets	1,000
Proceeds on sale of fixed assets	5,000
Taxation paid	2,000
Interest paid	4,000
Payments for fixed assets	8,000
Issue of debentures	6,000

   The cash flow statement will show

   A   a decrease in cash of £13,000
   B   an increase in cash of £14,000
   C   an increase in cash of £20,000
   D   an increase in cash of £22,000

35 Which of the following is an 'appropriation of profit' in a limited company?

   A   Interest paid
   B   Dividend paid
   C   Directors' remuneration
   D   Retained profit

36 N operates an imprest system for petty cash. On 1 February 20X3, the float was £300. It was decided that this should be increased to £375 at the end of February 20X3.

During February, the cashier paid £20 for window cleaning, £100 for stationery and £145 for coffee and biscuits. The cashier received £20 from staff for the private use of the photocopier and £60 for a miscellaneous cash sale.

What amount was drawn from the bank account for petty cash at the end of February 20X3?

- A £185
- B £260
- C £315
- D £375

37 The following are extracts from the financial statements for the year ended 31 January 20X3 of M plc:

	£'000
Issued ordinary shares of £1	200
Share premium account	50
Profit and loss account	25
Debenture	80
Profit before interest for the year ended 31 January 20X3	60

What is the return on total capital employed?

- A 17%
- B 22%
- C 24%
- D 30%

38 The following information was extracted from the balance sheets of Z Ltd at 31 December 20X2 and at 31 December 20X1:

	20X2 £'000	20X1 £'000
Stock	100	140
Debtors	150	130
Trade creditors	125	115
Other creditors	60	75

What figure should appear as part of the cash flow statement for the year ended 31 December 20X2?

- A £25,000 outflow
- B £15,000 outflow
- C £15,000 inflow
- D £25,000 inflow

39 In order to confirm that financial statements show a true and fair view, the external auditor should ensure that the financial statements comply with

- A company law
- B accounting standards
- C generally accepted accounting principles
- D all of the above

40   S Ltd purchased equipment for £80,000 on 1 July 20X2. The company's accounting year end is 31 December. It is S Ltd's policy to charge a full year's depreciation in the year of purchase. S Ltd depreciates its equipment on the reducing balance basis at 25% per annum.

The net book value of the equipment at 31 December 20X5 should be

A   Nil
B   £25,312
C   £29,531
D   £33,750

Mock assessment 2
Answers

**DO NOT TURN THIS PAGE UNTIL YOU HAVE
COMPLETED THE MOCK ASSESSMENT 2**

MOCK ASSESSMENT 2: ANSWERS

1   C   The directors main responsibility is to safeguard the assets of the business.

2   A   This is the auditors primary responsibility

3   D   Need make no adjustments

4   B   £11,200 overdrawn

Cash book	£	Bank statement	£
Balance	(8,970)	Balance	(11,200)
Bank charges	(550)	Credit in error	(425)
		Unpresented cheques	(3,275)
		Outstanding deposits	5,380
	(9,520)		(9,520)

5   D   £88,000

	£
Cost of machine	80,000
Installation	5,000
Training	2,000
Testing	1,000
	88,000

6   A   It proves the arithmetical accuracy of the ledgers.

7   A   The expenditure has been understated by £45 so the cash drawn from the bank will also be £45 short, giving a balance of £705

8   C   Accrued: £560; charge to P & L £3,320

Electricity account

		£		£
			Balance b/fwd	300
20X0				
1 August	Paid bank	600		
1 November	Paid bank	720		
20X1				
1 February	Paid bank	900		
30 June	Paid bank	840		
30 June	Accrual c/d			
(£840 × ²/₃)		560	Profit and loss account	3,320
		3,620		3,620

9   A   £6,800

Gas supplier account

	£			£
Balance b/fwd	200			
Bank £600 × 12	7,200	28 February	Invoice	1,300
		31 May	Invoice	1,400
		31 August	Invoice	2,100
		30 November	Invoice	2,000
		30 November	Balance c/d	600
	7,400			7,400

MOCK ASSESSMENT 2: ANSWERS

Gas account

			£		£
28 February	Invoice		1,300		
31 May	Invoice		1,400		
31 August	Invoice		2,100		
30 November	Invoice		2,000	30 November P&L account	6,800
			6,800		6,800

10   B   £4,700

	Cost £	Net realisable value £	Lower of cost & NRV £	Units	Value £
Basic	6	8	6	200	1,200
Super	9	8	8	250	2,000
Luxury	18	10	10	150	1,500
					4,700

11   B   Profit: £781

	£
Cost	10,000
20X7 Depreciation	2,500
	7,500
20X8 Depreciation	1,875
	5,625
20X9 Depreciation	1,406
	4,219
20Y0 Part exchange	5,000
Profit	781

12   A   12.5% $\dfrac{\text{Operating profit}}{\text{Capital employed}} = \dfrac{£15,000}{£120,000} \times 100 = 12.5\%$

13   C   73 days $\dfrac{\text{Debtors including VAT}}{\text{Credit sales including VAT}} = \dfrac{£23,500}{£117,500} \times 365 \text{ days} = 73 \text{ days}$

14   B   The measurement of profit

15   C   Preparing bank reconciliations

16   C   £2,950. 10 units at £45 plus 50 units at £50

17   B   This receipt will eliminate the insurance debtor and reduce the loss on disposal by 500.

18   B

Suspense account

		£		£	
DR	Discounts received	800	Opening balance	2,300	R
	Closing balance	2,100	Cash receipts	600	
		2,900		2,900	

Discount received should have been posted as a credit, so appears in the suspense account as DR 800

19   C

	£
Opening WIP	240,000
Prime cost	720,000
Overheads	72,000
Closing WIP	(350,000)
Factory cost of finished goods	682,000

MOCK ASSESSMENT 2: ANSWERS

20	C			
		Output tax 200,000 × 15%		(30,000)
		Input tax 161,000 × 15/115		21,000
		Payable		(9,000)

21	B		
		Missing accrual	1,500
		Closing stock overvalued – cost of sales understated	500
		Net profit overstated	2,000

22	A		
		Cash book balance	12,350
		Bank charges	(170)
		Direct debit	(230)
		Dishonoured cheque	(110)
			11,840

23	B	Gas charges for two months have to be accrued		
			DR	CR
		Gas expense	1,400	
		Accruals		1,400

24	C		
		Opening WIP	40,000
		Prime cost	122,000
		Overheads	185,000
		Factory cost of finished goods	(300,000)
		Closing WIP	47,000

25	D	£4,700 is payable. £700 goes to the VAT account in the balance sheet.

26	D	The cost of the equipment has been debited to the profit and loss account instead of fixed assets so both profit and fixed assets are understated.

27	C		
		1.7.20X1 – 31.3.20X2 1800 × 9/12 =	1,350
		1.4.20X2 – 30.6.20X2 2000 × 3/12 =	500
			1,850

28	A	Net profit margin = ROCE / Net asset turnover
		= 24%/3 = 8%

29	D	Remember, employers NI is an additional cost.

30	A			
		1-2 months	24,000 × 1%	240
		2-3 months	8,000 × 10%	800
		Over 3 months	6,000 × 30%	1,800
		Balance sheet total		2,840
		Provision b/f		(2,880)
		Credit profit and loss		(40)
		Total debtors	50,000	
		Less provision	(2,840)	
			47,160	

31	C	Prime cost includes all *direct* costs of production.

MOCK ASSESSMENT 2: ANSWERS

32 B

DR		Supplier account		CR
Returns	100	Balance b/f		1,200
Payment	1,615	Goods		1,700
Discount received	85			
Balance c/f	1,100			
	2,900			2,900

33 B It helps in detecting errors. It should agree to the sales ledger.

34 C

Net cash inflow from operating activities	26,000
Dividend paid	(3,000)
Proceeds of sale of fixed assets	5,000
Taxation paid	(2,000)
Interest paid	(4,000)
Payments for fixed assets	(8,000)
Issue of debentures	6,000
Net increase	20,000

35 B A and C are expenses. Dividends are paid out of retained profit.

36 B

Window cleaning	20
Stationery	100
Coffee etc.	145
Staff receipt	(20)
Cash sale proceeds	(60)
Increase in float	75
	260

37 A $\dfrac{\text{Profit before interest}}{\text{Capital}(200+50+25+80)}\% = \dfrac{60}{355}\% = 16.9\%$

38 C

	Inflow	Outflow
Reduction in stock	40,000	
Increase in debtors		20,000
Increase in trade creditors	10,000	
Reduction in other creditors		15,000
	50,000	35,000
Net inflow	15,000	

39 D Although GAAP is generally taken to include all of them.

40 B

		NBV
Purchase price		80,000
20X2	75%	60,000
20X3	75%	45,000
20X4	75%	33,750
20X5	75%	25,312

CIMA
Paper C2 (Certificate)
Financial Accounting Fundamentals

Mock Assessment 3

Question Paper	
Time allowed	1½ hours
Answer ALL the questions	

DO NOT OPEN THIS PAPER UNTIL YOU ARE READY TO START UNDER EXAMINATION CONDITIONS

Answer ALL 40 questions

1. A business is normally said to have earned revenue when

   A cash has been received
   B a customer is legally obliged to pay for goods delivered or services rendered
   C an order has been placed
   D goods have been manufactured and placed in stock

2. The role of the internal auditors is best described as

   A auditing the financial accounts
   B supporting the work of the external auditors
   C reporting to management on the accounting systems
   D ensuring value for money

3. The following information relates to C Limited at 30 June 20X3.

	£
Balance per cash book – credit balance	4,300
Unpresented cheques	1,500
Bank charges not entered in the cash book	300
Receipts not yet credited by the bank	2,600
Dishonoured cheques not yet recorded in the cash book	500

   What would be the balance shown on the bank statement at 30 June 20X3?

   A Overdraft £6,200
   B Overdraft £5,100
   C Overdraft £4,000
   D Favourable £2,400

4. Financial controls are primarily needed to

   A minimise the risk of fraud and error
   B comply with legal requirements
   C improve the efficiency of the business
   D reduce the expenses of the external auditors

5. The following information relates to NBV Limited for the year ended 31 July 20X3.

	£'000
Direct materials	160
Direct labour	200
Prime cost	360
Carriage outwards	880
Depreciation of delivery vehicles	30
Factory indirect overheads	450
Increase in work-in-progress stock	75
Decrease in stock of finished goods	55

   What should be the factory cost of goods completed for the year ended 31 July 20X3?

   A £735,000
   B £845,000
   C £885,000
   D £1,095,000

MOCK ASSESSMENT 3: QUESTIONS

6 The internal auditor at ILT plc has noticed that cheques from customers are being paid into the bank account approximately one month after the date on the cheque.

Should the internal auditor

- A instruct the cashier to pay cheques in more promptly?
- B disregard, because all cheques have been accounted for?
- C ask customers to pay more promptly?
- D inform senior management there may be a fraud?

7 Which of the following tests carried out by an external auditor is a compliance test?

- A Confirming authorisation of a reconciliation of the sales ledger control account
- B Checking unpresented cheques in a bank reconciliation
- C Checking a purchase invoice with the purchase day book
- D Inspecting physical existence of fixed assets

8 The following information relates to CFS plc:

	£'000
Machinery	
Cost at 1 January 20X2	80
Additions	20
Disposal	(10)
Cost at 31 December 20X2	90
Provision for depreciation at 1 January 20X2	15
Depreciation charge	8
Disposal	(6)
Provision for depreciation at 31 December 20X2	17

The proceeds on disposal of the machine were £1,000.

CFS plc is preparing the cash flow statement for the year ended 31 December 20X2. In relation to the items above, what should be the net adjustment to operating profit in order to determine the net cash flow from operating activities?

- A Deduct £11,000
- B Add back £3,000
- C Add back £5,000
- D Add back £11,000

9 Which ONE of the following attributes is the most important for any code to possess in order to be of use in an accounting system?

- A Easy to change the code number
- B Each code is a unique number
- C A combination of letters and digits to ensure input accuracy
- D Linked to assets, liabilities, income, expenditure and capital

10 The accountant at S Limited is preparing quarterly accounts for Quarter 3. In Quarter 2, he had accrued £1,600 for gas and this balance was carried forward to Quarter 3. In Quarter 3, a gas bill of £2,700 was paid. The accountant has accrued £2,400 for gas in Quarter 3.

What should be the charge for gas in the profit and loss account for Quarter 3?

- A £1,900
- B £2,400
- C £2,700
- D £3,500

11 Which of the following functions would most benefit from segregated duties of staff?

  A   Separate staff to maintain the sales and purchase ledgers
  B   Separate staff to maintain the personal and nominal ledger accounts
  C   Separate staff to deal with the bank reconciliation and the cash book
  D   Separate staff to deal with the trial balance and the preparation of accounts

12 D plc has a policy that all items of equipment which cost less than £1,000 are charged to an expense account, rather than a fixed asset account. This is an example of the application of the concept of

  A   going concern
  B   materiality
  C   money measurement
  D   prudence

13 Internal auditors report to

  A   the management
  B   the shareholders
  C   the external auditors
  D   the government

14 A Limited is preparing financial statements for the year ended 30 June 20X3. Rent is payable quarterly in advance on 1 February, 1 May, 1 August and 1 November. The annual charge for rent was £1,800 and £2,400 for the years ended 31 January 20X3 and 20X4 respectively.

  Which of the following ledger entries should be made in A Limited's accounts?

A	Rent expense	£2,000	Prepayment	£400
B	Rent expense	£2,050	Prepayment	£200
C	Rent expense	£2,050	Accrual	£200
D	Rent expense	£2,100	Prepayment/accrual	Nil

15 T Limited purchased a machine costing £14,000 on 1 August 19X9. The company estimated that the asset had a useful life of 4 years and an expected residual value of £2,000. The company uses the straight line method of depreciation. The company's financial year end is 30 November. It is the company's policy to charge a full year's depreciation in the year of purchase and none in the year of disposal. On 1 November 20X2, the asset was sold for £4,500.

  What should be the profit or loss on disposal in the year ended 30 November 20X2?

  A   Loss £500
  B   Loss £3,500
  C   Loss £9,500
  D   Profit £500

16 Which ONE of the following is true?

  A   External auditors normally check all purchase invoices
  B   External auditors should prepare the accounts
  C   External auditors must follow the audit procedures prepared by the internal auditors
  D   External auditors check the internal control system

17 The following information is an extract from the balance sheets of DCF plc.

	31 August 20X3 £'000	31 August 20X2 £'000
Stock	20	14
Trade debtors	16	18
Bank	12	10
	48	42
Trade creditors	(14)	(17)
	34	25

DCF plc is preparing the cash flow statement for the year end 31 August 20X3. In relation to the items above, what should be the net adjustment to operating profit in order to determine the net cash flow from operating activities?

A   Deduct £1,000
B   Deduct £2,000
C   Deduct £7,000
D   Add back £1,000

18 Which of the following entries would NOT affect the agreement of the totals in the trial balance?

(i)   An invoice for £300 for rent has been omitted from the ledgers

(ii)   A cash sale has been recorded as debit cash sales, credit cash

(iii)   An invoice for vehicle expenses has been charged to the vehicle fixed asset account

(iv)   A credit note for £500 for goods returned by a customer had been recorded in the correct ledgers, but as £5,000

A   (i) only
B   (i) and (ii) only
C   (i), (ii) and (iii) only
D   All of them

19 Which ONE of the following is NOT an intangible fixed asset?

A   Goodwill
B   Trademark
C   Investment
D   Patent

20 Which ONE of the following would NOT help detect errors in a computerised accounting system?

A   The use of coding systems
B   The use of batch processing
C   The use of passwords
D   The use of control accounts

21 E Ltd bought computer equipment on 1 January 20X0 for £24,000 and estimated that it would have a useful life of five years and a residual value of £2,000. E Ltd uses the straight line method of depreciation. On 31 December 20X1, it now considers that the remaining life is only two years and that the residual value will be nil.

What should be the annual depreciation charge for the years ended 31 December 20X2 and 20X3?

- A £2,800
- B £5,500
- C £6,600
- D £7,600

22 A company has a quick (acid test) ratio of 2:1. Current assets include stock of £10,000 and debtors of £6,000. Current liabilities are £4,000.

What is the bank balance?

- A Credit £4,000
- B Credit £2,000
- C Debit £2,000
- D Debit £4,000

23 Which of the following does NOT prevent fraud and errors?

- A Authorisation procedures
- B Organisation of staff
- C Suspense accounts
- D Reconciliations

24 Which ONE of the following statements is TRUE?

- A Internal auditors report to the directors
- B External auditors report to the directors
- C Internal auditors are employed by the shareholders
- D External auditors are employees of a company

25 The BMX cycling club started in January 20X1. The following fees were received in the years ended 31 December 20X1 and 20X2. There were no fees received in advance, or fees in arrears, at either year end.

	20X1 £	20X2 £
Joining fees	8,000	10,000
Annual fees	5,000	7,000
Life membership fees	4,000	6,000
	17,000	23,000

Joining fees are recognised over a period of 4 years and life membership fees are recognised over 10 years.

What should be the total amount of fees recognised in the income and expenditure account of the year ended 31 December 20X2?

- A £7,000
- B £11,500
- C £12,500
- D £23,000

26 ABC plc declared a final dividend of 5% for the year ended 28 February 20X3. The nominal value of the shares is 50 pence. X bought 1,000 shares at a price of £4 in December 20X2 and the shares were valued at a price of £3 on 28 February 20X2.

What should be the final dividend received by X?

A £25
B £50
C £150
D £200

27 The following information relates to companies Q and R plc, who are competitors selling widgets.

	Q plc	R plc
Gross profit percentage	30%	25%
Fixed asset turnover ratio	4	5

A director at Q plc believes that these ratios indicate that:

(i)   Q plc has a higher selling price
(ii) Q has lower purchasing costs
(iii) R plc has lower sales volume
(iv) R plc has fewer fixed assets

Which of the above are possibly true based on the information provided?

A (i) only
B (i) and (ii) only
C (i), (ii) and (iii) only
D (i), (ii), (iii) and (iv)

28 The internal accounts of E Ltd value stock at replacement cost. The warehouse manager has produced the following schedule for the values of the three items (X1, X2 and X3) in stock at the year end.

	First in/first out £'000	Net realisable value £'000	Replacement cost £'000
X1	10	20	30
X2	15	11	8
X3	12	14	13
	37	45	51

At what value should the stock be stated in the statutory financial statements?

A £33,000
B £37,000
C £45,000
D £51,000

29 The job descriptions of staff in the credit control department are normally segregated because

A lower salaries can be paid
B work is completed more efficiently
C control is facilitated
D staff are less likely to become bored

30 The style of management accounts within an enterprise is determined by

    A   company law
    B   company law and accounting standards
    C   the shareholders
    D   the directors

31 Which of the following is the best description of current purchasing power accounting?

    A   A method of accounting which considers the effects of changing price levels by reference to the retail price index
    B   A method of adjusting historical cost accounts for the effects of changing price levels by using indices specific to the enterprise
    C   A method of accounting which uses market values
    D   A method of accounting which uses economic values (value in use)

32 The following information relates to P Ltd at 30 September.

	20X3 £'000	20X2 £'000
Stock of raw materials	60	40
Work-in-progress stock	50	85
Stock of finished goods	20	28

    For the year ended 30 September 20X3:

	20X3 £'000
Purchases of raw materials	710
Manufacturing wages	42
Factory overheads	360

    The prime cost of production in the manufacturing account for the year ended 30 September 20X3 is

    A   £690,000
    B   £732,000
    C   £1,092,000
    D   £1,135,000

33 The following information was extracted from the pay slip of J, who received her net salary in cash for the month ended 31 March 20X3.

	£
Gross salary	3,000
Tax deducted	450
Employer's national insurance	300
Employee's national insurance	250
Employer's contribution to pension fund	210
Employee's contribution to pension fund	180
Voluntary deduction for payment to charity	20

    The charge to the profit and loss account, the balance on the payroll control account and the net pay for J's salary for March was

	Charge to profit and loss account	Balance on payroll control account	Net pay
A	£2,100	£1,410	£2,100
B	£3,510	£700	£2,300
C	£3,000	£1,000	£1,590
D	£3,510	£1,410	£2,100

34 An audit trail in a computerised accounting system is

- A information regarding all transactions in a period
- B a history of all transactions on a ledger account
- C a list of all transactions checked by the internal auditor
- D a list of all transactions automatically posted from day books to ledgers

35 Which of the following are normally produced in the month-end routine of a computerised accounting system?

(i)   Balances on all ledger accounts at the end of the month

(ii) Balances on the debtors' and creditors' personal ledgers and the debtors' and creditors' control accounts

(iii) Balance on stock (inventory)

(iv) The profit and loss account and balance sheet

- A (i) only
- B (i) and (ii) only
- C (i), (ii) and (iii) only
- D All of them

36 The entity concept means that:

- A The business is considered to be the same entity as its owner
- B There is a distinction between the owner and the business
- C A business's records must show all the owner's personal transactions as if he were part of the business
- D Records must be prepared using the same accounting policies as other businesses of a similar nature and size

37 W Ltd did not reverse a prepayment brought forward at the beginning of the accounting period. This contravenes which accounting concept?

- A prudence
- B accruals
- C consistency
- D going concern

38 Which of the following sets of items all appear on the same side of the trial balance?

- A Sales; interest received; accruals
- B Debtors; drawings; discount received
- C Capital; trade creditors; sundry expenses
- D Rent payable; prepayments; retained profits

39 Which of the following accounting treatments is an example of the application of the accruals concept?

- A Revaluation of fixed assets
- B Valuation of stock at the lower of cost and net realisable value
- C Depreciation of fixed assets
- D Provision for doubtful debts

40 A business has installed a new computer system and has treated the costs incorrectly as a revenue expense. Which statement correctly describes the effect of this error?

   A   Fixed assets overstated, net profit understated
   B   Fixed assets understated, net profit understated
   C   Fixed assets overstated, gross profit understated
   D   Fixed assets understated, expenses understated

Mock assessment 3
Answers

DO NOT TURN THIS PAGE UNTIL YOU HAVE
COMPLETED THE MOCK ASSESSMENT 3

MOCK ASSESSMENT 3: ANSWERS

1 B A business is normally said to have earned revenue when the customer becomes legally obliged to pay for goods and services. Cash can be received in advance, in which case the revenue has not yet been earned.

2 C Internal auditors may also undertake value-for-money audits and support the external auditors, but their main job is to report to management on the accounting system

3 A

	£
Balance per cash book	(4,300)
Unpresented cheques	1,500
Bank charges not entered in the cash book	(300)
Receipts not yet credited by the bank	(2,600)
Dishonoured cheques not yet recorded in the cash book	(500)
Balance per bank statement	(6,200)

4 A While financial controls are of use in all of these areas, their **primary** function is to minimise the risk of fraud and error.

5 A

	£'000
Prime cost	360
Factory indirect overheads	450
Increase in stock – work in progress	(75)
Factory cost of goods completed	735

6 D Late payment of customer cheques suggests that a fraud such as 'teeming and lading' could be taking place.

7 A This is a compliance test. The others are substantive tests.

8 D

	£'000	£'000
Loss on sale of machinery		
Net book value (10 – 6)	4	
Disposal proceeds	(1)	
Loss on disposal		3
Depreciation charge for the year		8
Total to add back to operating profit		11

9 B Each code number <u>must</u> be unique or the system will be inoperable.

10 D

	£
Accrual for Quarter 2 reversed	(1,600)
Gas bill paid	2,700
Accrual Quarter 3	2,400
Charge to profit and loss Quarter 3	3,500

11 C The bank reconciliation is an external check on the accuracy of the cash book entries, so it would be good security to have these two functions segregated.

12 B Items costing less than £1,000 are considered insufficiently <u>material</u> to capitalise.

13 A Internal auditors are employed by management and report to them.

14 B *Rent expense*

7 months (July X2 – Jan X3) @ 1,800	1,050
5 months (Feb X3 – June X3) @ 2,400	1,000
Expense for 12 months to 30 June 20X3	2,050

Prepayment

	£
Quarterly payment made 1 May 20X3	600
Prepayment for July 20X3	200

15 A Annual depreciation on the machine : Depreciable amount (14,000 − 2,000)/4 = 12,000/4 = **3,000**

	£
Cost	14,000
Depreciation – 3 years	9,000
Net book value	5,000
Proceeds of sale	(4,500)
Loss on disposal	500

16 D Part of an external audit will always be a check on the internal control system.

17 C

Increase in stock	(6,000)
Decrease in debtors	2,000
Decrease in creditors	(3,000)
Net adjustment	(7,000)

18 D All of these entries, or lack of entries, have equal postings to debit and credit, so the errors will not be detected by taking out a trial balance.

19 C An investment is classified as a tangible fixed asset.

20 C Passwords will prevent, and maybe even detect, unauthorised access to the **computer** system, but would have no effect on the accounting system

21 D

	£	£
Original cost	24,000	
Residual value	(2,000)	
	22,000	
Annual depreciation (22,000 / 5)		4,400
31 December 20X1		
Original cost	24,000	
2 years depreciation	(8,800)	
	15,200	
Annual depreciation (15,200 / 2)		7,600

22 C

Debtors	6,000
Bank	2,000
Quick assets	8,000
Current liabilities	4,000
Ratio:	2 : 1

23 C Suspense accounts are an aid to investigating and correcting fraud and error, but will not prevent them from occurring.

24 A Internal auditors are employees of the company and report to the directors. External auditors are employed by the shareholders and report to them.

25 C

	£
Annual fees	7,000
Joining fees (8,000 + 10,000 / 4)	4,500
Life membership fees (4,000 + 6,000 / 10)	1,000
Total recognised for the year	12,500

MOCK ASSESSMENT 3: ANSWERS

26   A.   1,000 shares at 50p nominal value = £500 Dividend @ 5% = £25. Note that the market price of the shares is irrelevant.

27   B   Q has a higher GP% than R. This must be due to either higher selling price or lower purchase costs, or a combination of both. As R has a lower GP%, we would expect it to have a higher turnover, not a lower turnover as in (iii). A higher turnover will account for the higher fixed asset turnover ratio, so there is no reason to suspect fewer fixed assets as in (iv).

28   A

X1	10,000
X2	11,000
X3	12,000
	33,000

Remember: lower of cost and NRV

29   C   Segregation of duties is a valuable control in accounts departments.

30   D   Management accounts are produced for internal purposes. They are not regulated by law or accounting standards.

31   A   Current purchasing power is based upon the overall retail price index, not indices specific to the business.

32   B

Purchases of raw materials	710,000
Increase in stock of raw materials	(20,000)
Manufacturing wages	42,000
Prime cost	732,000

33   D

	Profit & loss A/C	Payroll control	Net pay
Gross salary	3,000		3,000
Tax deducted		450	(450)
Employer's national insurance	300	300	
Employee's national insurance		250	(250)
ER's contribution to pension	210	210	
EE's contribution to pension		180	(180)
Charitable deduction		20	(20)
Total	3,510	1,410	2,100

Note that the balance remaining in payroll control will be the charge to profit and loss account less net pay. This balance will be paid to the tax authorities, the pension fund and the charity.

34   A   The auditors must have access to information regarding **all** transactions in the period. This is described as the audit trail.

35   D   The month-end routine has to produce a profit and loss and balance sheet. Therefore it has to produce a trial balance, which requires balances on all of the ledger accounts.

36   B   Under the entity concept, the business is considered to be a separate entity from the owner, even if he is a sole proprietor. So transactions between the owner and the business are recorded and accounted for.

37   B   Prepayments are an application of the accruals concept.

38   A   Sales, interest received and accruals will all be credit balances.

39   C   Depreciation is an application of accruals – it spreads the cost of an asset over the periods expected to benefit from its use.

MOCK ASSESSMENT 3: ANSWERS

40   B   The computer system should have been debited to fixed assets, so fixed assets are understated. The cost has been shown as a revenue expense, so reducing net profit.

Review Form & Free Prize Draw – Paper C1 Financial Accounting Fundamentals

All original review forms from the entire BPP range, completed with genuine comments, will be entered into one of two draws on 31 July 2005 and 31 January 2006. The names on the first four forms picked out on each occasion will be sent a cheque for £50.

Name: _____   Address: _____

How have you used this Kit?
(Tick one box only)

☐ Home study (book only)
☐ On a course: college _____
☐ With 'correspondence' package
☐ Other _____

Why did you decide to purchase this Kit?
(Tick one box only)

☐ Have used the complementary Study text
☐ Have used other BPP products in the past
☐ Recommendation by friend/colleague
☐ Recommendation by a lecturer at college
☐ Saw advertising
☐ Other _____

During the past six months do you recall seeing/receiving any of the following?
(Tick as many boxes as are relevant)

☐ Our advertisement in *CIMA Insider*
☐ Our advertisement in *Financial Management*
☐ Our advertisement in *Pass*
☐ Our brochure with a letter through the post
☐ Our website www.bpp.com

Which (if any) aspects of our advertising do you find useful?
(Tick as many boxes as are relevant)

☐ Prices and publication dates of new editions
☐ Information on product content
☐ Facility to order books off-the-page
☐ None of the above

Which BPP products have you used?

Text	☐	Kit	☑	i-Pass	☐
Passcard	☐	CD	☐		
Big Picture Poster	☐	Virtual Campus	☐		

Your ratings, comments and suggestions would be appreciated on the following areas.

	Very useful	Useful	Not useful
Effective revision	☐	☐	☐
Exam guidance	☐	☐	☐
Multiple choice questions	☐	☐	☐
Objective test questions	☐	☐	☐
Guidance in answers	☐	☐	☐
Content and structure of answers	☐	☐	☐
Mock assessments	☐	☐	☐
Mock assessment answers	☐	☐	☐

Overall opinion of this Kit   Excellent ☐   Good ☐   Adequate ☐   Poor ☐

Do you intend to continue using BPP products?   Yes ☐   No ☐

The BPP author of this edition can be e-mailed at: marymaclean@bpp.com

Please return this form to: Nick Weller, CIMA Range Manager, BPP Professional Education, FREEPOST, London, W12 8BR

Review Form & Free Prize Draw (continued)

TELL US WHAT YOU THINK

Please note any comments and suggestions/errors below

Free Prize Draw Rules

1 Closing date for 31 July 2005 draw is 30 June 2005. Closing date for 31 January 2006 draw is 31 December 2005.

2 Restricted to entries with UK and Eire addresses only. BPP employees, their families and business associates are excluded.

3 No purchase necessary. Entry forms are available upon request from BPP Professional Education. No more than one entry per title, per person. Draw restricted to persons aged 16 and over.

4 Winners will be notified by post and receive their cheques not later than 6 weeks after the relevant draw date.

5 The decision of the promoter in all matters is final and binding. No correspondence will be entered into.

See overleaf for information on other
BPP products and how to order

CIMA Order

To BPP Professional Education, Aldine Place, London W12 8AW
Tel: 020 8740 2211　Fax: 020 8740 1184
email: publishing@bpp.com
Order online www.bpp.com

Occasionally we may wish to email you relevant offers and information about courses and products. Please tick to opt into this service. ☐

POSTAGE & PACKING

Study Texts and Kits

	First	Each extra	Online
UK	£5.00	£2.00	£2.00
Europe*	£6.00	£4.00	£4.00
Rest of world	£20.00	£10.00	£10.00

Passcards/Success CDs/Posters

	First	Each extra	Online
UK	£2.00	£1.00	£1.00
Europe*	£3.00	£2.00	£2.00
Rest of world	£8.00	£8.00	£8.00

Grand Total (incl. Postage) £ _____

I enclose a cheque for _____
(Cheques to *BPP Professional Education*)

Or charge to Visa/Mastercard/Switch

Card Number ☐☐☐☐ ☐☐☐☐ ☐☐☐☐ ☐☐☐☐

Expiry date ☐☐☐☐　Start Date ☐☐☐☐

Issue Number (Switch Only) ☐

Signature _____

Mr/Mrs/Ms (Full name) _____
Daytime delivery address _____
Postcode _____
Daytime Tel _____
Email _____
Date of exam (month/year) _____

		6/04 Texts	1/05 Kits	1/05 Passcards	Big Picture Posters	Success CDs	Virtual Campus	i-Pass	i-Learn
CERTIFICATE									
C1	Management Accounting Fundamentals	£24.95 ☐	£12.95 ☐	£9.95 ☐	£6.95 ☐	£14.95 ☐	£50 ☐	£24.95 ☐	
C2	Financial Accounting Fundamentals	£24.95 ☐	£12.95 ☐	£9.95 ☐	£6.95 ☐	£14.95 ☐	£50 ☐	£24.95 ☐	
C3	Business Mathematics	£24.95 ☐	£12.95 ☐	£9.95 ☐	£6.95 ☐	£14.95 ☐	£50 ☐	£24.95 ☐	
C4	Economics for Business	£24.95 ☐	£12.95 ☐	£9.95 ☐	£6.95 ☐	£14.95 ☐	£50 ☐	£24.95 ☐	
C5	Business Law	£24.95 ☐	£12.95 ☐	£9.95 ☐	£6.95 ☐	£14.95 ☐	£50 ☐	£24.95 ☐	
MANAGERIAL		7/04 Texts							
P1	Management Accounting - Performance Evaluation	£24.95 ☐	£12.95 ☐	£9.95 ☐	£6.95 ☐	£14.95 ☐	£90 ☐	£24.95 ☐	£34.95 ☐
P2	Management Accounting - Decision Management	£24.95 ☐	£12.95 ☐	£9.95 ☐	£6.95 ☐	£14.95 ☐	£90 ☐	£24.95 ☐	£34.95 ☐
P4	Organisational Management and Information Systems	£24.95 ☐	£12.95 ☐	£9.95 ☐	£6.95 ☐	£14.95 ☐	£90 ☐	£24.95 ☐	£34.95 ☐
P5	Integrated Management	£24.95 ☐	£12.95 ☐	£9.95 ☐	£6.95 ☐	£14.95 ☐	£90 ☐	£24.95 ☐	£34.95 ☐
P7	Financial Accounting and Tax Principles	£24.95 ☐	£12.95 ☐	£9.95 ☐	£6.95 ☐	£14.95 ☐	£90 ☐	£24.95 ☐	£34.95 ☐
P8	Financial Analysis	£24.95 ☐	£12.95 ☐	£9.95 ☐	£6.95 ☐	£14.95 ☐	£90 ☐	£24.95 ☐	£34.95 ☐
STRATEGIC		7/04 Texts							
P3	Management Accounting - Risk and Control Strategy	£24.95 ☐	£12.95 ☐	£9.95 ☐	£6.95 ☐	£14.95 ☐		£24.95 ☐	
P6	Management Accounting - Business Strategy	£24.95 ☐	£12.95 ☐	£9.95 ☐	£6.95 ☐	£14.95 ☐		£24.95 ☐	
P9	Management Accounting - Financial Strategy	£24.95 ☐	£12.95 ☐	£9.95 ☐	£6.95 ☐	£14.95 ☐		£24.95 ☐	
P10	Test of Professional Competence in Management Accounting (TOPCIMA)	£24.95 ☐ (For 5/05: available 3/05)							
Toolkit		£24.95 ☐							
Learning to Learn Accountancy (7/02)		£9.95 ☐							

Total _____

We aim to deliver to all UK addresses inside 5 working days. A signature will be required. Orders to all EU addresses should be delivered within 8 working days. *Europe includes the Republic of Ireland and the Channel Islands. All other orders to overseas addresses should be delivered within 6 working days.

1

The Cosmetic Use of Botulinum A Exotoxin

Alastair Carruthers and Jean Carruthers

This chapter is designed to be a guide to the cosmetic use of Botulinum A Exotoxin (BTX-A). It is hoped that the combination of text and illustrations will make this simple and straightforward.

From the dermatologic point of view, there are two important blocks to the use of BTX-A. First, dermatologists do not commonly deal with striated muscle. We do not understand its anatomy, function, or innervation, and we may not have thought about the effects produced by its contraction for some years. Second, BTX-A is the most potent toxin known (1). This will give both physician and patient cause for reflection.

This chapter therefore begins with a brief review of the important background information that is necessary to understand the method of action and the safety of BTX-A therapy. It includes a discussion of the consent process. A step-by-step description of the method of BTX-A injection follows, covering storage, dilution, and handling. This is followed by its use in relatively straightforward areas such as the glabella and crow's-feet, and then areas such as the brow. The use of electromyography is described. The chapter concludes with a discussion of the anticipated effects and the side effects of BTX-A therapy.

The authors' clinical experience is with BOTOX (Allergan Inc., Irvine, CA), and so throughout the text, units given are of BOTOX unless specifically stated otherwise.

BACKGROUND

How Does Botulinum A Exotoxin Work?

BTX-A produces its effect by preventing the release of acetylcholine (ACh) from the presynaptic neuron of the neuromuscular junction (NMJ) (2). Specific receptors on the presynaptic neuron bind the toxin rapidly and irreversibly. *In vitro,* this appears to occur in 32 to 64 minutes (3). This is important since it is during this time that the effect of the toxin can be spread from the site of injection. Thereafter, it will be stably bound. Subsequently, the toxin is internalized and released into the cytosol, where it interferes in the function of proteins necessary for ACh release (4–6). BTX-A is an enzyme, acting as a zinc-dependent endoprotease. In consequence, a small amount of toxin can produce a significant effect. The larger the dose of toxin, the more rapid will be the onset of its effect (as soon as 6 hours in some cases of clinical botulism), whereas a very small dose may produce an effect that is clinically undetectable or may not be observed for 1 to 2 weeks. For example, unintended spread to the extraocular muscles from injection into orbicularis oculi for benign essential blepharospasm may not produce diplopia for 1 to 2 weeks after injection. The clinical consequence is that precautions must be taken to reduce spread of the toxin for 2 to 3 hours after injection; its effect will usually be observed at 24 to 72 hours and will be maximal at 2 weeks. Complete paralysis of the injected area is usually seen by 3 to 4 days.

It will be understood from the previous that the dose of BTX-A required to produce a clinical effect is extremely small (1 mouse unit is 3×10^7 molecules [1]). As a result, the toxin must be extremely specific and extremely effective. It is unlikely to produce effects other than those related to its function.

Immunology

BTX-A is an immunogenic protein in appropriate circumstances. As a toxoid, it is used to raise an antibody response both in humans who are occupationally exposed to the toxin and also in animals for production of serum containing antibodies. In individuals who have developed antibodies, injecting the toxin has no effect. This is seen very occasionally in an individual who has no response to an initial injection of BTX-A. Of greater significance is the development of antibodies in individuals who are being treated with the toxin. This is relatively common in neurological patients who are treated with doses of 100 to 200 units (BOTOX) per session or greater. Ten percent to 20% or more of these patients will develop antibodies to BTX-A over time. BTX-B and BTX-F are under investigation as alternatives to BTX-A in these individuals, since there is not immunologic cross-reactivity (7,8). In a 13-year experience with BTX-A and over 10,000 injection sessions, the authors have not seen an individual develop resistance to BTX-A. There has not, to our knowledge, been reported a case of an individual developing resistance to BTX-A as a result of antibody formation at a dose of less than 100 units per session.

Toxicity

As discussed previously, the BTX-A molecule is extremely powerful. At the low dilutions necessary for clinical use, the molecule is also unstable. In consequence, bioassay, rather than a nonbiologic method, is necessary to give a clinically relevant assessment of toxicity. The mouse bioassay has long been the standard for BTX-A. An appropriately prepared specimen is injected intraperitoneally into a group of mice. It is injected alone, after heating (which destroys the toxin), and in combination with known BTX antibodies. This method provides a qualitative assessment of whether a particular BTX neurotoxin is present in the sample. If the animal model is standardized (usually an 18- to 22-g female Swiss-Webster mouse) and serial dilutions of the specimen are injected in a group of mice, then *quantitative* assay is possible. The LD_{50} for this mouse model is the mouse unit used clinically and commercially. Despite the straightforward nature of this assay, there is a significant difference in results between laboratories (9). Fortunately, in clinical use, it is not possible to pick up small dose differences (10).

Of greater concern is the difference between the bioassays of the two commercially available neurotoxins (BOTOX and Dysport, Speywood, Maidenhead, United Kingdom). BOTOX is produced by a multiple precipitation technique, whereas Dysport is produced by column-based methods. This difference in production methods produces a differential between the effects on humans and mice. In particular, the dose (in mouse units) of Dysport required to produce a given effect is 3 to 4 times greater than the dose of BOTOX (11).

Work in primates, in conjunction with estimates derived from accidental botulism, suggests a human LD_{50} of approximately 40 U/kg if the toxin is delivered systemically (12–14). Oral ingestion would require a dose several orders of magnitude greater.

A number of other bioassays are in use, including the mouse hemidiaphragm model and methods utilizing the development of a flaccid limb. ELISA assays of antibodies to BTX-A have not shown good clinical correlation (15–17).

CLINICAL USE OF BOTULINUM A EXOTOXIN

Consent

Despite the simplicity and excellent safety profile of BTX-A, it is important, as always, to obtain properly informed consent prior to treatment. Figure 1 is a copy of our current consent form, which is a relatively simple document reflecting our current comfort level with this modality. We believe it is important that individuals contemplating this treatment should understand the mechanism of action of BTX-A, the delay in onset of its effect, and the inevitable disappearance of that effect. They should also understand that, barring extremely rare events, all the side effects of treatment are related to the clinical effect of the toxin. These points should be amplified by the physician with particular relevance to the individual being treated and the areas being treated. Finally, depending on the jurisdiction, the individual should be informed of the regulatory position of BTX-A. For example, in the United States, BOTOX is not approved by the Food and Drug Administration (FDA) for cosmetic use. The FDA has repeatedly denounced the *promotion* of the cosmetic use of BTX-A (18). However, in a position paper from the Device and Technique Assessment Committee of the American Society of Plastic and Reconstructive Surgeons, it was concluded that " . . . BOTOX is a safe and effective, although temporary, treatment for [cosmetic] problems" (19).

BOTOX should not be used during pregnancy or lactation.

Storage, Dilution, and Handling

BOTOX should be stored at −4°C (25°F) or lower, and Dysport at 2°C to 8°C (35°F to 45°F), and the expiration date is indicated on the package. This is usually a month or more ahead. Brief warmer temperatures (for example, in shipment) do not seem to affect this.

The BOTOX vial (Fig. 2) contains 100 units; the Dysport vial, 500 units. According to the manufacturer's instructions, this should be diluted with preservative-free saline 0.9%. A recent publication (20) has suggested that saline with preservative (0.9% benzyl alcohol) is equally effective. However, there are as yet no data on the stability of the toxin when diluted with preserved saline, nor on whether the preservative retains its efficacy.

The manufacturer's instructions are that the contents of the reconstituted vial should be used within 4 hours. Gartland and Hoffman (21) reported a significant loss of toxicity at 12 hours, although others (20) have not demonstrated this clinically and have suggested that the toxin is stable for a month or longer. Other evidence is beginning to accumulate to support the extended stability of the toxin, but at the present time, it would be wise to "batch" patients, to use the vial contents within a few days, and to observe strict sterile technique when diluting the toxin.

The dilution of the toxin (i.e., the dose per unit volume) will vary with the area to be treated. In general, a higher dilution (50 or 100 u/ml) will allow for more accurate placement and therefore greater longevity and fewer side effects. Lower dilutions (5 to 25 u/ml) will encourage the spread of the toxin, perhaps creating a smoother effect. In addition, the toxin "lost" in the vial and syringes will be minimized. Suggestions, both from the literature and the authors' experience, will be made

Jean D.A. Carruthers, FRCSC   Alastair Carruthers, FRCPC

CONSENT TO BOTULINUM TOXIN TREATMENT FOR FACIAL WRINKLES

Rationale

I am aware that when a small amount of purified botulinum toxin (BOTOX) is injected into a muscle it causes weakness or paralysis of that muscle. This appears in 3 - 4 days and usually lasts 4 months but can be shorter or longer.

Frown lines between the eyebrows are due to contraction of small muscles around them between the eyebrows. Injecting BOTOX into this area will paralyze or weaken these muscles causing temporary improvement or disappearance of the frown lines. Similarly, crow's feet and horizontal forehead lines can also be improved by the injection of BOTOX into this area which will weaken the muscles and cause improvement in wrinkles in this area.

Results and Postoperative Care

(1) I understand that I will not be able to "frown" while injection into this area is effective but that this will reverse itself after a period of months at which time retreatment is appropriate.

(2) I understand that I must stay in the erect posture and that I must not manipulate the area of the injection for 3 - 4 hours post-injection.

(3) I understand that it would be advantageous for me to forcibly and repeatedly use the treated muscles in the 3-4 hours post-injection to get a better result.

Risks and Complications

BOTOX treatment of frown lines can cause minor temporary droop of one eyelid in less than 3% of injections. This usually lasts 2 - 4 weeks. Occasional numbness of a small area on the forehead lasting 2 - 3 weeks, bruising and transient headache have also occurred.

In a very small number of individuals the injection does not work as satisfactorily or for as long as usual.

Photographs

I authorize the taking of clinical photographs and their use for scientific purposes both in publications and presentations. I understand my identity will be protected.

Pregnancy and Neurologic Disease

I am not aware that I am pregnant nor that I have any significant neurologic disease.

Payment

I understand that this procedure is cosmetic and that payment is my responsibility.

I have read the above and understand it. My questions have been answered satisfactorily by the doctor. I accept the risks and complications of this procedure.

_____   _____
Signed   Date

_____   _____
Name   Witness

FIG. 1. Cosmetic use of BOTOX consent form.

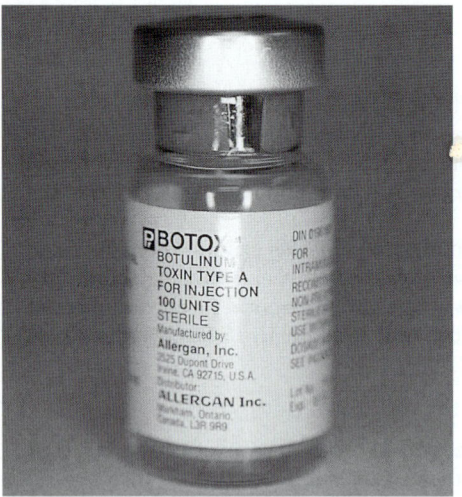

FIG. 2. BOTOX vial (Allergan Inc., Markham, Ontario, Canada).

in the following sections, and these should be modified by the physician's experience. However, it can be said that there are two broadly differing views of the toxin use. The "Fulton" view (20) uses large volumes of low-dose toxin to smooth the crow's-feet and brow area by weakening and not paralyzing the underlying muscles. Unfortunately, this study does not present longevity data. The other view, as initially presented by the authors (22) and subsequently by others, was that low-volume, concentrated toxin could be used to paralyze specific muscles to create a desired effect—paralysis of the glabellar area being the best example. These views should not be regarded as opposing but rather as exemplifying different uses of the toxin for esthetic reasons. They emphasize the importance of individualizing the treatment to each person rather than using a standardized approach.

GLABELLA

Vertical lines between the eyebrows—glabellar frown lines—are associated with anger, anxiety, worry, and fear—all negative emotions. They are also associated with compassion, as seen in many of the portraits of famous statesmen. However, many individuals develop frown lines inappropriately, frowning when they are concentrating or even in their sleep (Fig. 3). For these individuals, *paralysis* of the glabella will correct this inappropriate use of the facial muscles, allowing them to express themselves more accurately. In addition, it will relieve the frontal tension that many of these individuals experience. Other individuals, especially those with type 2 Glogau wrinkles (23) (Fig. 4), do not like the slowly increasing wrinkles in the glabellar area,

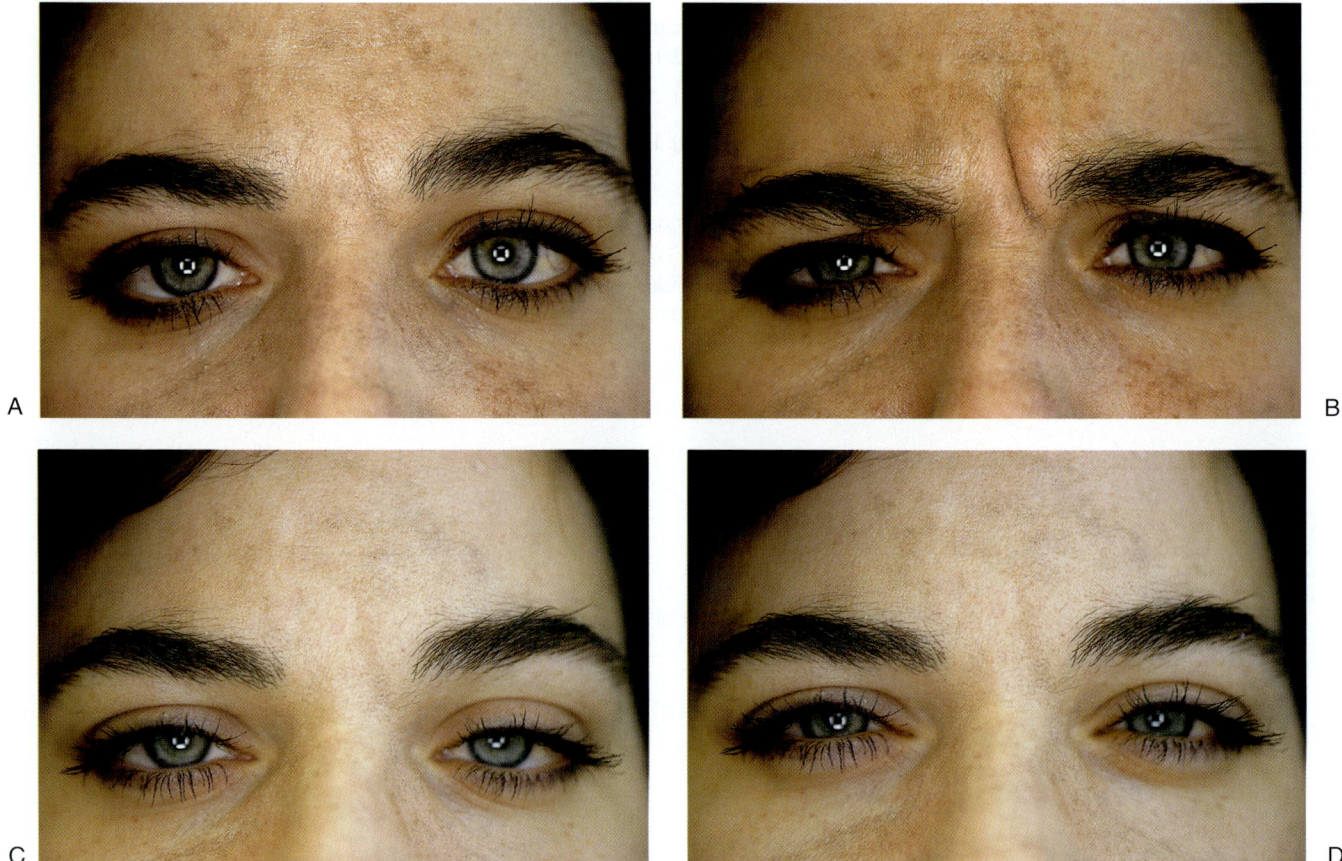

FIG. 3. Patient with horizontal type eyebrows before BOTOX injection, at rest **(A)** and frowning **(B)**, and after BOTOX injection, at rest **(C)** and frowning **(D)**.

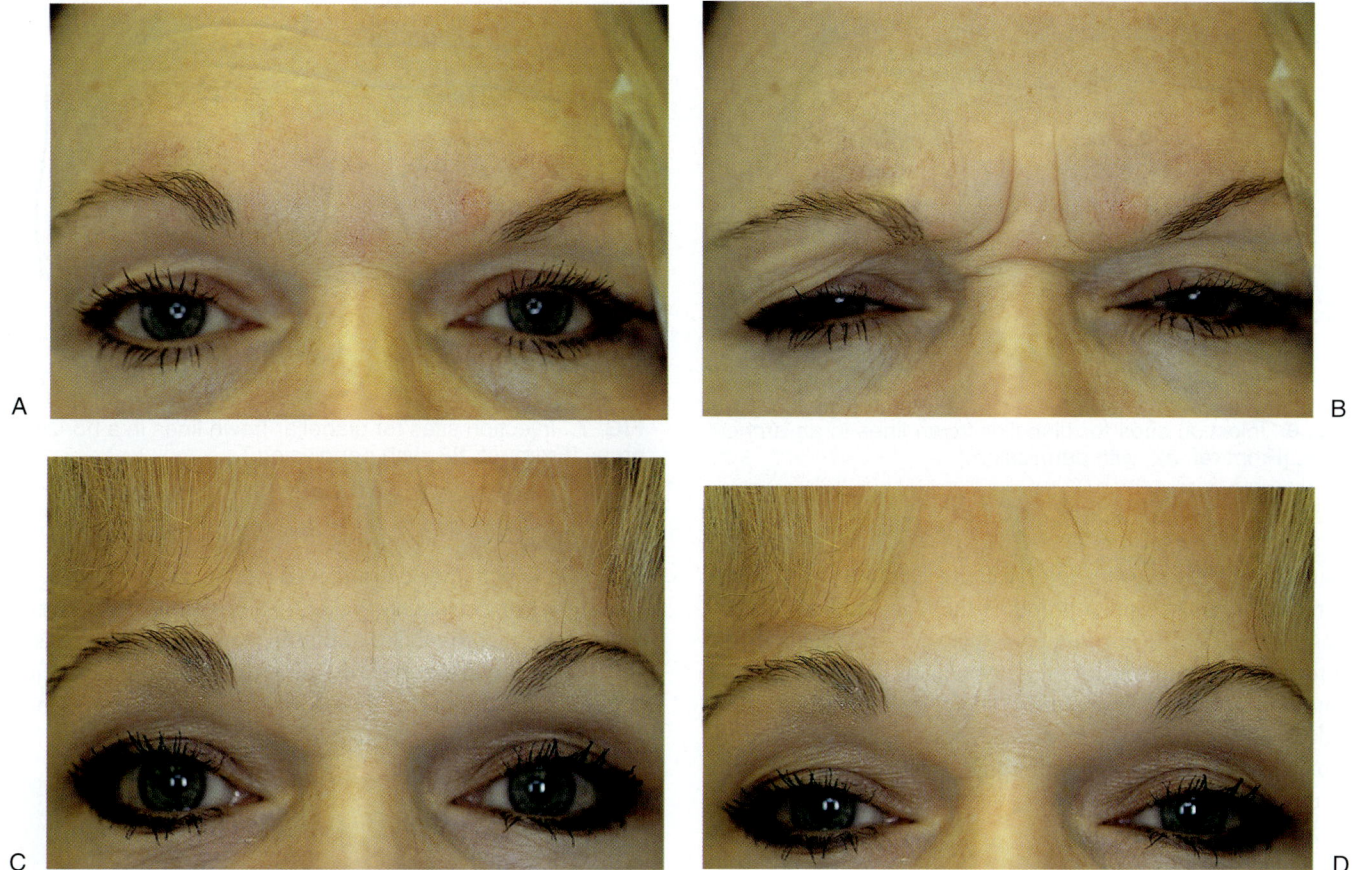

FIG. 4. Glogau type 2 patient before BOTOX injection, at rest **(A)** and frowning **(B)**, and after BOTOX injection, at rest **(C)** and frowning **(D)**.

can do without the negative emotions expressed by this area, and like the "open-eyed" look that unopposed action of central frontalis produces. In these individuals, paralysis is less important than significant weakening of the area, so they may be more tolerant of minimal residual muscle function.

Anatomy

The muscular anatomy of the brow is complex (Fig. 5). The corrugator moves the brow inferomedially, the orbicularis moves it medially. The procerus and depressor super-

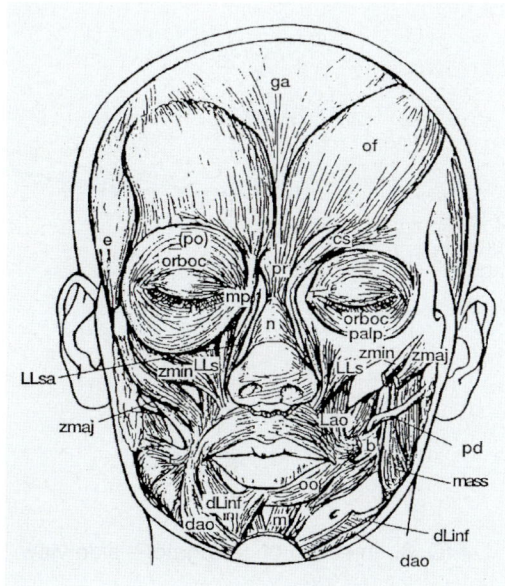

FIG. 5. Anatomy of the muscles of facial expression, frontal view. ga, galea aponeurotica; of, frontal belly, occipitofrontalis muscle; cs, corrugator supercilii; pr, procerus; orboc, orbicularis oculi; orboc palp, orbicularis oculi, palpebral part; e, epicranius (temporoparietalis muscle); n, nasalis muscle; LLs, levator labii superioris; LLsa, levator labii superioris alaeque nasi; zmin, zygomaticus minor; zmaj, zygomaticus major; pd, parotid duct; Lao, levator anguli oris; b, buccinator; mass, masseter; oor, orbicularis oris; dLinf, depressor labii inferioris; dao, depressor anguli oris; m, mentalis muscle. [From ref. 24, with permission.]

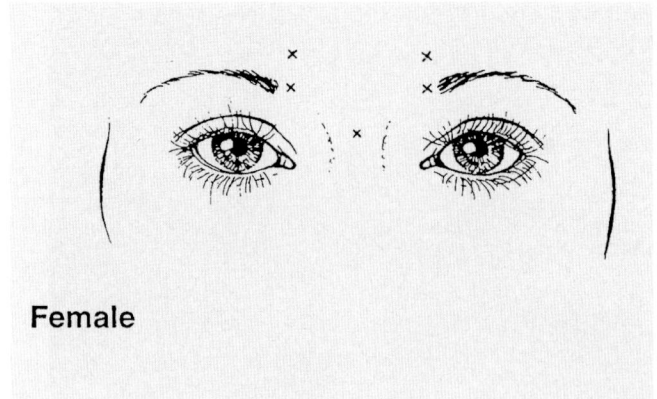

FIG. 6. Injection sites for glabellar frown lines in an arched brow. [From ref. 32, with permission.]

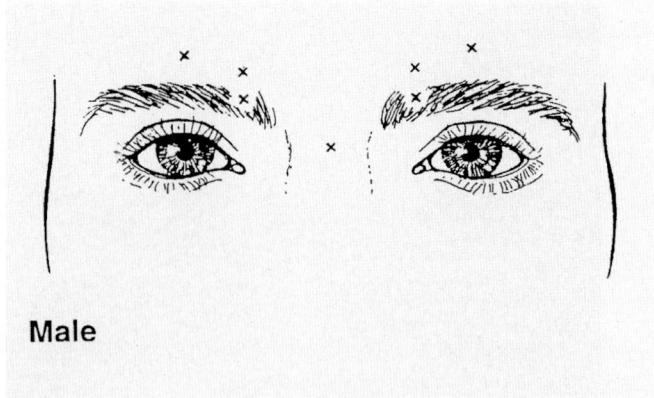

FIG. 7. Injection sites for glabellar frown lines in a horizontal brow. [From ref. 22, with permission.]

cilii both pull the brow inferiorly. It is the combination of action of these muscles that produces the frown rather than the single action of the corrugator. However, individuals differ both in their anatomy and their consequent function, so it is important to tailor the treatment of frown lines to the individual. For example, the medial extent of the cilia of the eyebrows may extend from the midline to lateral to the medial insertion of corrugator.

Technique

A number of studies have reported on injection technique for the glabella (20,22,24–38). The authors' technique, which has evolved over several hundred glabellar injection sessions, is effective and has a low incidence of side effects. This description is slightly different from those that have previously been published (22,24,32).

The first part of the treatment is assessment of the individual, with particular regard to the position of the brow—is it an arched (female-type) brow or a horizontal (male-type) brow? Is the brow ptotic—that is, does it cross the orbital rim? At the same time, asymmetry of the brow and also of the eyelids should be noted. Photographs should be taken at rest and on maximal frown. It is useful to prechill the area with an ice pack to reduce the mild stinging that is felt on BTX-A injection.

Figures 6 and 7 show the sites where the toxin will be deposited in both female- and male-type brows. We prefer to approach the corrugator behind the medial brow from an insertion point slightly above the brow. This is a vascular area, with the supratrochlear vessels immediately lateral to the site of injection. Minor bleeding is fairly common, so it is better to select an insertion point where pressure can be safely applied after the injection.

The appropriate dose is drawn up into a tuberculin syringe, for example, 25 units in 0.5 ml to treat the glabella. With this dilution, 1 unit is present in each 0.02 ml. A 30-gauge half-inch needle is attached and the air expressed. The individual is treated in the sitting position, head slightly lower than the physician and chin down. The needle is inserted just above the eyebrow directly above the caruncle of the inner canthus. The thumb of the contralateral hand is

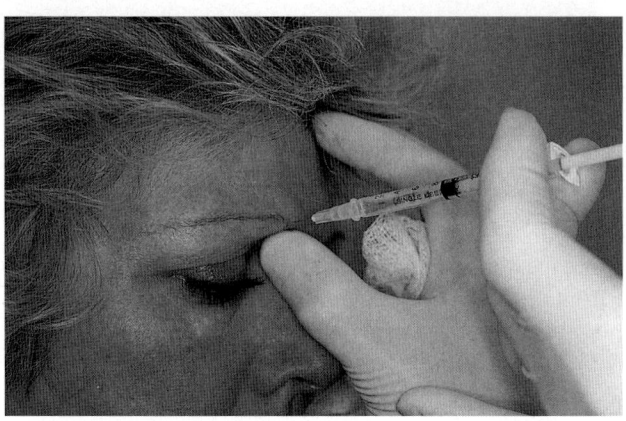

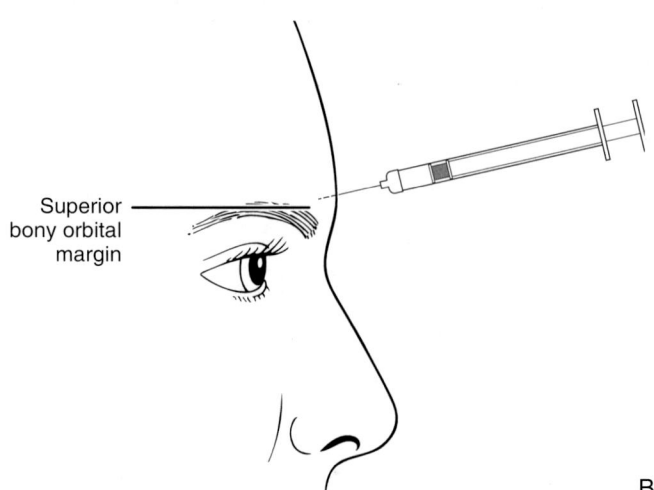

FIG. 8. Injection of corrugator—side view.

1/Botulinum A Exotoxin · 7

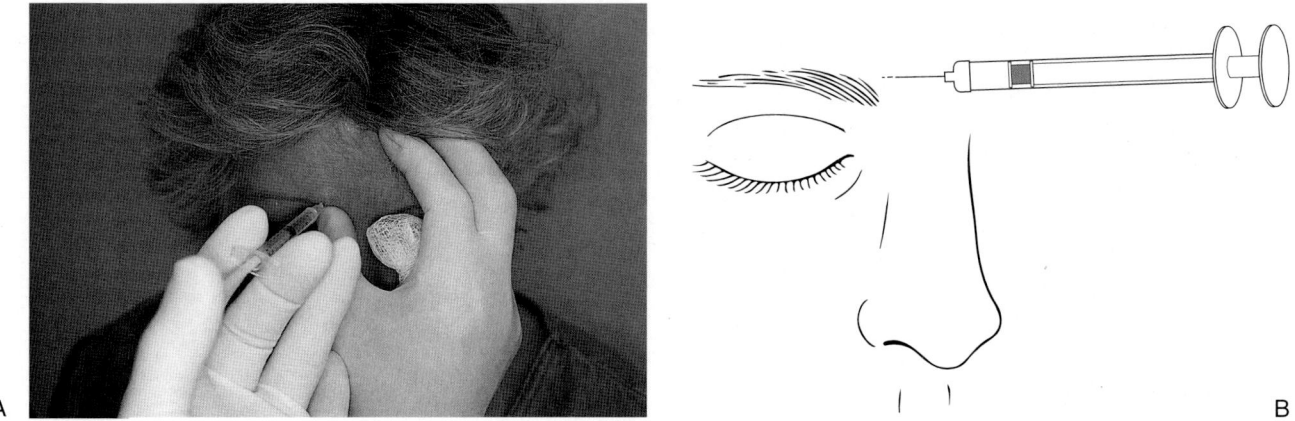

FIG. 9. Physician's view of injection into the corrugator showing the units on the syringe.

used to feel the position of the supraorbital ridge by comparison with the eyebrow. The injection should be above the supraorbital ridge whatever the position of the eyebrow. The needle is angled slightly downward and posteriorly to approximately half its length. Three to 5 units is injected at this point (Figs. 8, 9).

The needle is withdrawn *almost* completely and is then advanced superiorly such that the tip is at least 1 cm above the previous injection site in the orbicularis oculi. The orbicularis oculi is superficial to the frontalis in this location, and this injection should therefore be relatively superficial. A further 4 to 5 units is injected (Figs. 10, 11). This procedure is then repeated on the opposite side. Three to 5 units is injected into the procerus in the midline at a point below a line joining the brows and above the crossing point of the X formed by joining the medial eyebrow to the contralateral inner canthus (Fig. 12). Finally, in many individuals but particularly those with a horizontal brow, we inject 2 to 5 units into a point 1 cm above the supraorbital rim in the mid-pupillary line (Fig. 13). Again, it is important to check that excessive eyebrow ptosis is not present by feeling the supraorbital rim with the thumb of the other hand.

The treated individual is then encouraged to sit for a few moments (while the physician makes notes of the procedure—see later) and to gently wipe any blood off the treated area with a damp gauze and mirror. They are instructed not

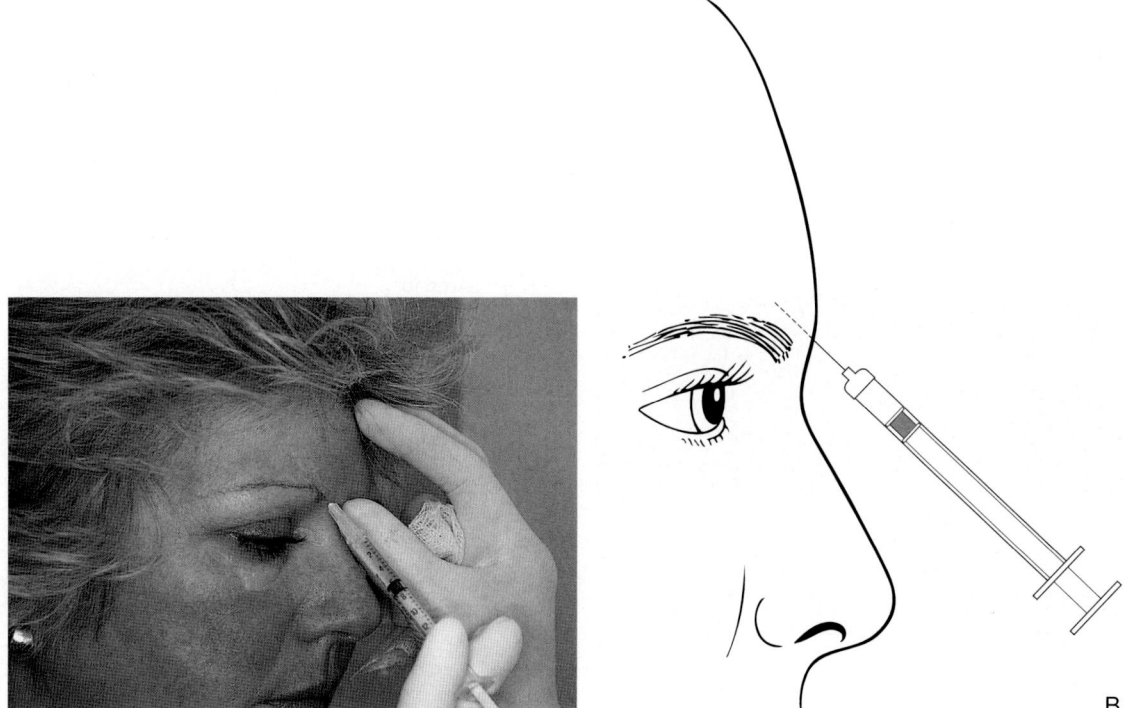

FIG. 10. Side view of injection into the orbicularis above the medial brow.

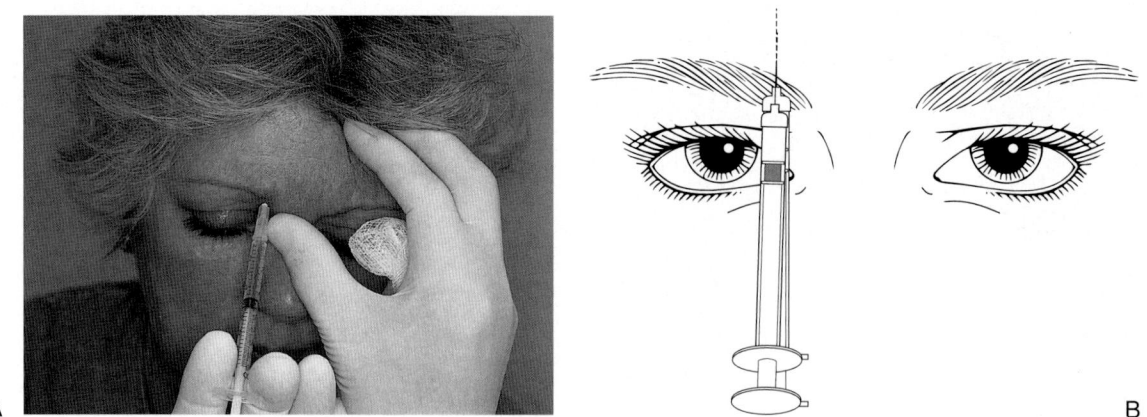

FIG. 11. Physician's view of the injection into orbicularis above the medial brow.

to press or manipulate the area, to stay vertical, and to frown as much as possible for the next 2 to 3 hours until binding has occurred (Fig. 14).

Charting

Figure 15 shows our typical method of recording our BTX-A procedures in the patient's record. We believe it is important to note the anatomic site of each injection, together with the dose delivered to that site in units. In addition, we note the lot number of the vial, how fresh that toxin is (usually very fresh, which is within 4 hours), the dilution used, the total dose administered, and whether there were any unusual occurrences during the procedure.

Follow-Up

We often ask treated individuals to return in 4 to 6 weeks so that we can assess their response and take further photographs. Our preference for individuals with deep glabellar frown lines is to keep them nonfrowning for a year or more by injections at 3-month intervals. Thereafter, they return when they consider they need retreatment.

All individuals are instructed to contact their physician if anything unexpected occurs.

Touch-up injections are uncommon in our practice. However, if touch-up is necessary, it should not be performed prior to 4 weeks because of the possibility of inducing antibody formation. Touch-up prior to 2 weeks is definitely contraindicated since the full effect of the initial injection will not have occurred until that time.

Complications

Complications of BTX-A treatment can be divided into those that are unrelated to the action of the toxin and those that are so related. The first category would include pain during injection, headache in the few hours afterwards, bruising

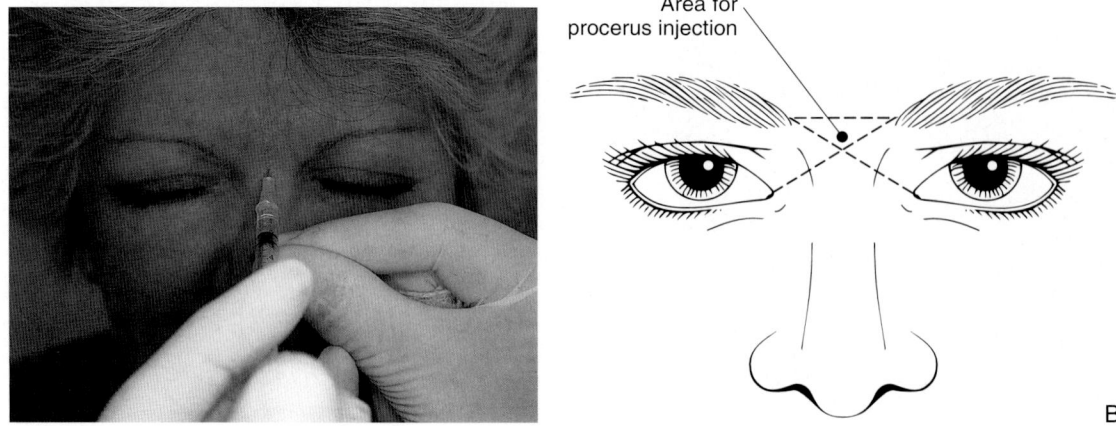

FIG. 12. Injection site for the procerus.

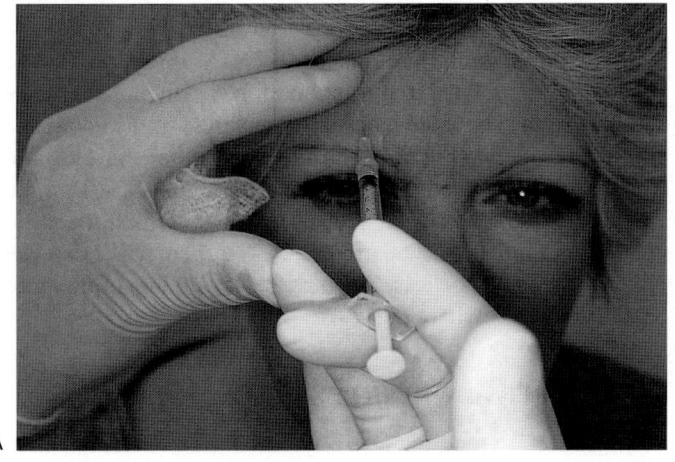
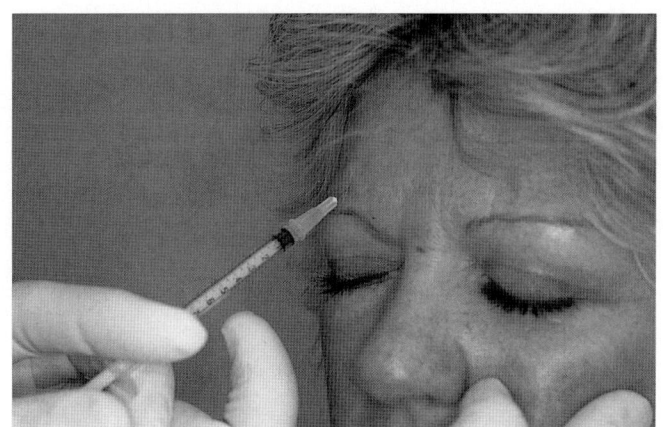
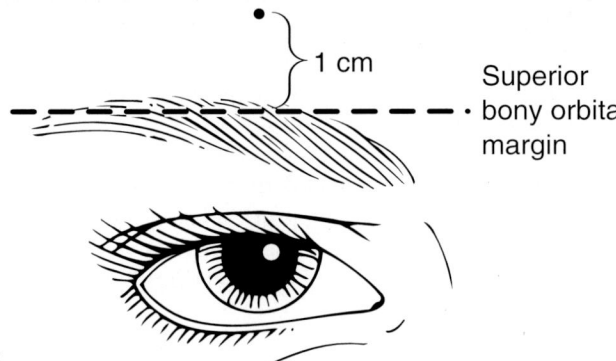

FIG. 13. Injection site in the mid-pupillary line: surgeon's view **(A)**; side view **(B)**; diagram **(C)**.

(1) Avoid massage or manipulation of the treated area for 3 to 4 hours.

(2) Maintain vertical posture---walking, sitting, etc.---but no reclining.

(3) Use the treated muscles (e.g., forceful frowning) repeatedly in the 2 to 4 hours after injection. The medication works better in actively contracted muscles.

FIG. 14. Postinjection instructions.

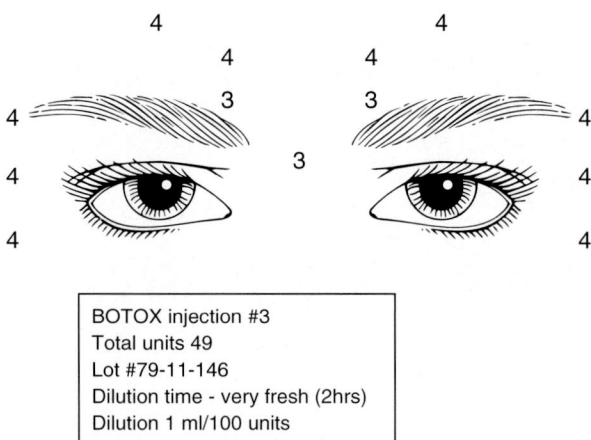

FIG. 15. Sample of cosmetic BTX-A therapy charting.

at the injection site, and paresthesia at the injection site, all of which occur but are not of great importance (24). It is important to note that we have not observed any significant complications related to the systemic effect of the toxin during approximately 10,000 injection sessions, over 13 years of use in doses ranging from 2.5 to 100 units per injection session but averaging 25 units (39). Neurologists using doses greater than 100 units per session report that a significant proportion of individuals develop antibody-related resistance to the effect of the toxin. They also report rare "allergic" effects such as rashes. Based on our experience, these must be extremely unusual in the doses used cosmetically. Finally, because the toxin is extremely dilute, because it is nonparticulate, and considering its mode of action, it would not be expected to cause any effects if injected intravenously, for example into the retinal circulation. Indeed, no such effects have so far been reported to our knowledge.

Ptosis and Diplopia

Unwanted complications of BTX-A injection in the glabellar area related to the action of the toxin include ptosis and diplopia. These are caused by weakness of the levator of the upper eyelid (Fig. 16) and the extraocular muscles and are caused by spread of the toxin to these muscles from the injection site. Careful adherence to the described injection technique and to the postinjection regimen will keep the ptosis rate to 3% or less. We have reviewed this topic more extensively elsewhere (37).

PERIORBITAL WRINKLES

Wrinkles extending laterally from the periorbital area ("crow's-feet") are viewed as indicative of aging and, in particular, photoaging. Correction of these wrinkles is commonly requested as part of facial rejuvenation. The wrinkles are produced by a combination of intrinsic and extrinsic aging of the skin combined with the action of the underlying muscles of facial expression. However, the wrinkles are *produced* by the action of the underlying muscles in the majority of individuals. Weakening or "relaxing" these muscles will significantly improve these wrinkles even in severely photoaged skin (Glogau type IV [23]) (Fig. 17).

Anatomy

The muscles of facial expression in the lateral periorbital area are considerably more straightforward than in the medial brow. The orbicularis oculi rings the orbit and produces forceful closure of the eyelids. Wrinkles laterally radiate from the area of the lateral canthus (Fig. 18). However, because of individual variation in the anatomy and use of these muscles, we recognize different patterns of lateral orbital wrinkles (Fig. 19).

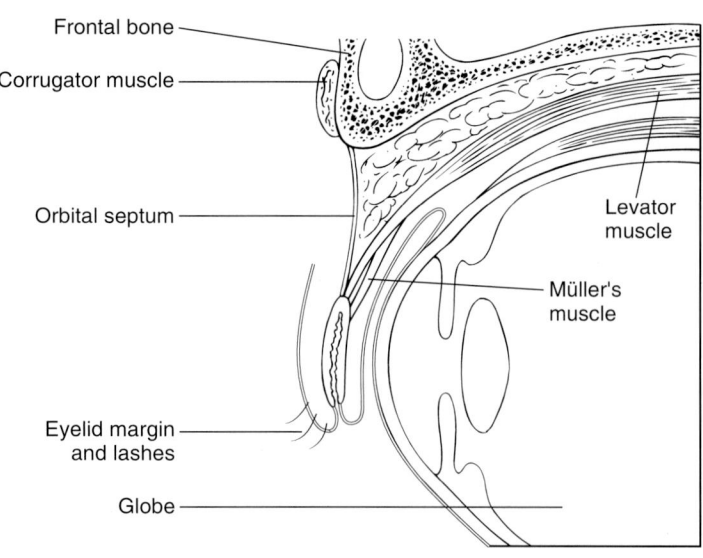

FIG. 16. Lateral view of orbital anatomy showing upper eyelid levators.

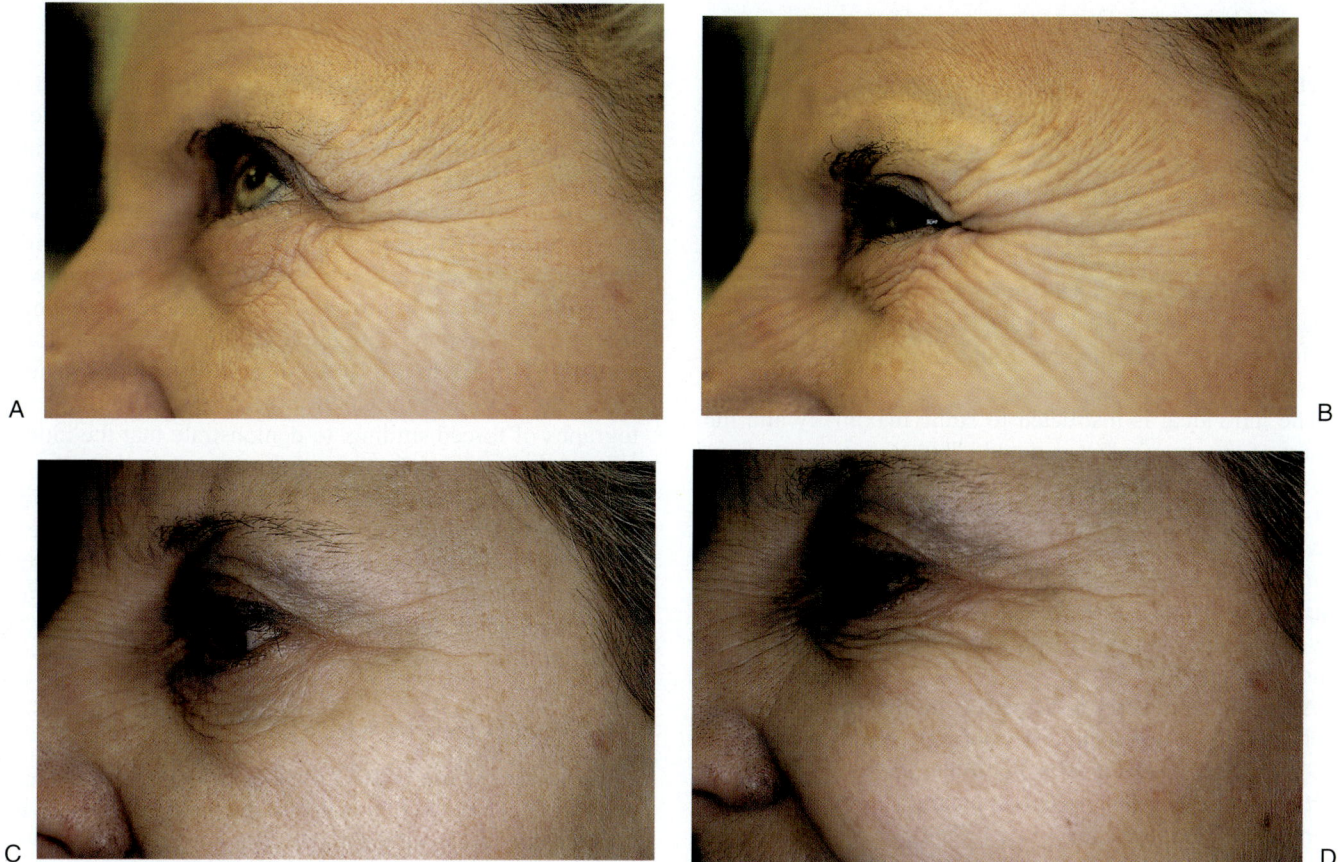

FIG. 17. Glogau type IV crow's-feet before BOTOX injection, at rest **(A)** and smiling **(B)**, and after BOTOX injection, at rest **(C)** and smiling **(D)**.

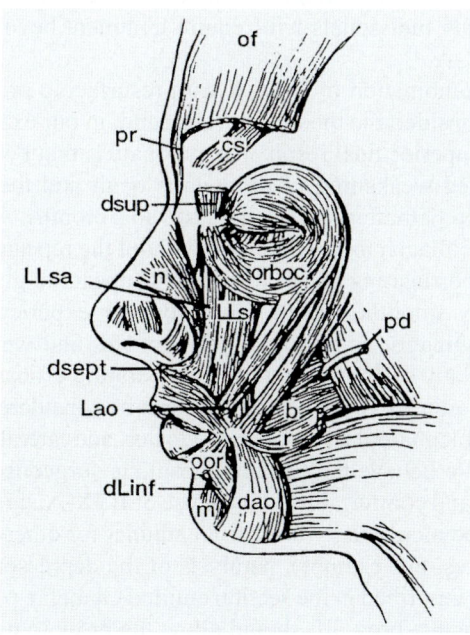

FIG. 18. Anatomy of the lateral face. of, frontal belly, occipitofrontalis muscle; cs, corrugator supercilii; pr, procerus; dsup; depressor supercilii; orboc, orbicularis oculi; n, nasalis muscle; LLs, levator labii superioris; LLsa, levator labii superioris alaeque nasi; pd, parotid duct; dsept, depressor septi; Lao, levator anguli oris; b, buccinator; r, risorius muscle; oor, orbicularis oris; dLinf, depressor labii inferioris; dao, depressor anguli oris; m, mentalis muscle. [From ref. 24, with permission.]

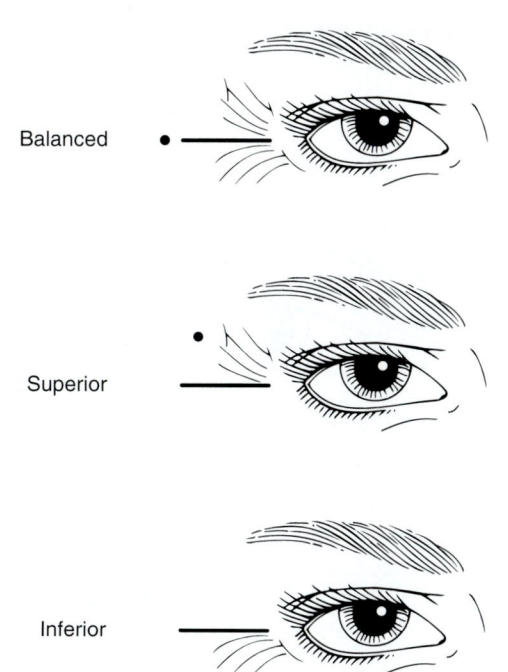

FIG. 19. Different patterns of crow's-feet lines.

Technique

A number of authors have described injections into the lateral orbital area (20,24,25,27–29,32,34–40). The dose per side ranges from 5 to 15 units and the dilution from 100 U/ml to 5 U/ml. It is our practice to begin with a total of 6 units per side (at a concentration of 50 to 100 U/ml) and to increase this to 15 units per side depending on the degree and longevity of the response. The dose is delivered into these injection sites in approximately equal doses (i.e., 2 to 5 units per site).

The individual is instructed to smile maximally and the center of the crow's-feet is noted. This area is injected approximately 1 cm lateral to the lateral orbital rim. The other two injections are approximately 1 to 1.5 cm above and below the first injection (Fig. 20). Careful observation of a number of individuals will show that some have crow's-feet equally above *and* below the lateral canthus, whereas others have them almost exclusively above *or* below the lateral canthus (see Fig. 19).

As we have already indicated, it is important to assess each individual and to treat accordingly, rather than using predetermined injection sites. For individuals whose crow's-feet are mainly below the lateral canthus, using the assessment and injection technique described here will produce a line of injections sites that are angled from anteroinferior to superoposterior (see Fig. 19). Nonetheless, the most anterior injection should still be lateral to a line drawn vertically from the lateral canthus.

Complications

Injection in the lateral orbital area is extremely safe, with very few reported complications. The skin is thinner and blood vessels more superficial in this area, so bruising is more common. Pain tends to be less than in the glabella. Keen et al. (40) described a slight droop of the lateral lower eyelid in 5% of individuals, but avoiding injecting medial to the lateral canthus prevented this. Ascher et al. (29) reported a worsening of preexisting fat herniations. We have noted two problems. First, preexisting problems that the individual had not noted previously may become more apparent when the crow's-feet are improved. This emphasizes the importance of preinjection photographs both at rest and on forced smiling. Dr. Michael Carney (unpublished observation, 1996) stresses the importance of including the mouth in photographs of forced smiling, to demonstrate that the individual is indeed attempting to contract the area maximally.

The other problem we have encountered is that some individuals appear to use the orbicularis oculi to distribute redundant skin in the lateral orbital area. Relaxing these muscles may allow the skin to drape itself beneath the lateral lower eyelid. Adjunctive procedures are indicated for this problem.

ADJUNCTIVE PROCEDURES

The cosmetic use of BTX-A should be part of an overall plan for facial rejuvenation rather than an end in itself. It is our practice to encourage all the individuals we treat to use sun protection and daily sunscreens as well as a topical retinoid and an alpha hydroxy acid. This is of particular relevance in the lateral orbital area, which can be significantly improved by such techniques with or without BTX-A. However, many individuals will require treatment beyond these and BTX-A.

The combination of BTX-A with resurfacing procedures makes considerable theoretical sense and, in our experience, gives a superior final result. The rationale is that both BTX-A–induced weakening of orbicularis oculi and the dermal collagen repair after resurfacing last 3 to 4 months. Allowing the new collagen to be laid down without the repeated pleating and corrugating due to orbicularis appears to give a significantly smoother result. However, our experience with this combination is still relatively limited, and we are unaware of any scientific studies demonstrating efficacy.

Other adjunctive procedures that can be considered in this area are blepharoplasty, upper and lower, and lateral canthoplasty. We believe that as more cosmetic surgeons become familiar and comfortable with the use of BTX-A, this modality will be increasingly used as an adjunct for other surgical procedures. For example, paralysis of the depressors of the brow (as described in the section entitled Glabella, p. 4) prior to endoscopic brow lift should allow the brow to heal in its new non-ptotic position and perhaps allow surgeons to avoid some of the traumatic suspension devices, such as screws in the cranium, that have been described.

HORIZONTAL FOREHEAD LINES

Treatment of the forehead requires much more delicacy than that of the previously discussed areas, and we advise caution. The reason for this is that brow ptosis is a significant

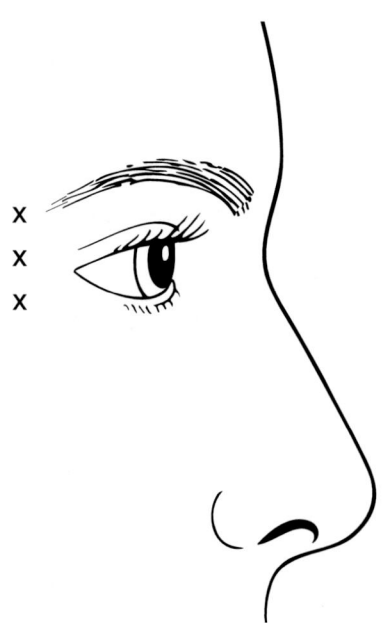

FIG. 20. Approximate injection sites for crow's-feet. (Courtesy of Mosby.)

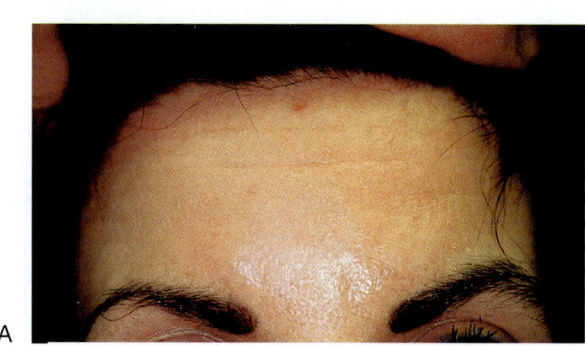 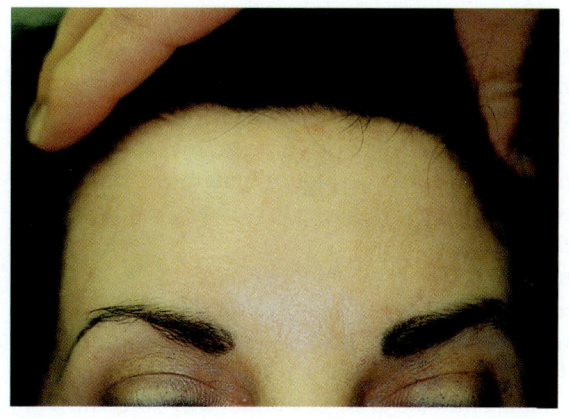

FIG. 21. Patient with one line on the forehead: before (A) and after (B) BTX-A injection.

problem if the frontalis is significantly weakened. In addition, if the frontalis is weakened and the depressors of the brow are not, unopposed action of the depressors will lower the brow, producing shadowing of the eyes and an angry appearance. In consequence, the preinjection assessment is extremely important in this area, the individual should be carefully informed about the anticipated results, and an attempt should be made to leave some functional areas of the frontalis to allow brow elevation.

Anatomy

The frontalis is a large muscle that is inserted into the galea aponeurotica superiorly and into the brow area inferiorly. There is a variable gap between the two bellies of the frontalis medially (see Fig. 5).

Technique

Distinction should be made between those individuals who have one or perhaps two deep horizontal forehead lines and those who have numerous lines across the forehead (Figs. 21, 22). The former can be treated with approximately 10 to 15 units of BTX-A in approximately 1-unit doses injected along both sides of the line at 1- to 2-cm intervals (Fig. 23). This technique should not significantly weaken the frontalis overall, so, as long as the injections are kept at least 1 cm above the brow, the likelihood of brow ptosis is low.

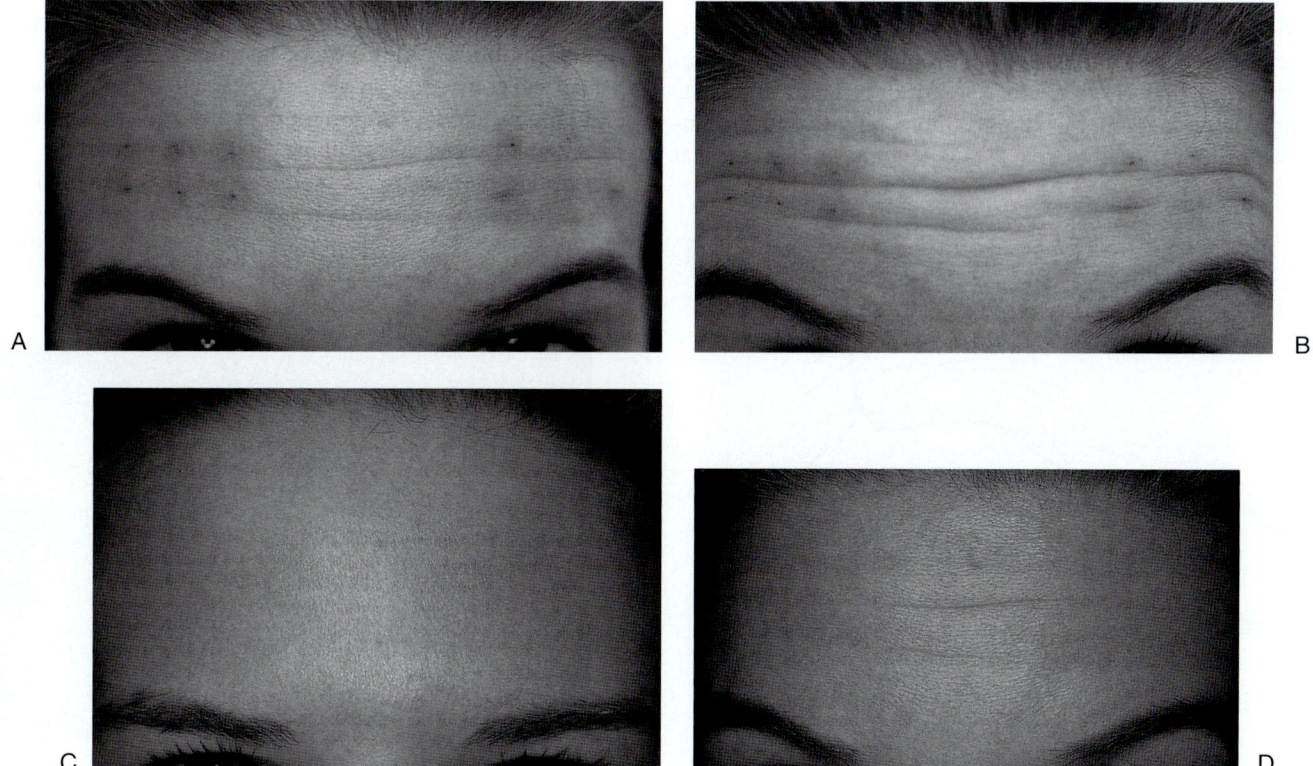

FIG. 22. Patient with multiple lines on the forehead. Immediately after injection, at rest (A) and on brow elevation (B). After BOTOX has had an effect, at rest (C) and on attempted brow elevation (D).

For individuals who have a number of forehead lines, the aim of treatment is to functionally weaken the frontalis to soften the lines. Again, careful preinjection assessment and photography are important to distinguish those individuals who are using the frontalis to keep their brow and eyelids at an acceptable level (i.e., non-ptotic) from those whose brow is in a good position but who tend to overuse the frontalis expressively.

A number of different techniques (20,25,28,29,32,35–38) have been described for this clinical problem. Keen et al. (28) used 16 injection sites with a total of 20 units and a dilution of 2.5 to 5 U/ml. Garcia and Fulton (20) appear to inject 6 to 8 units into the brow at a dilution of 10 U/ml. They avoid the upper central brow, concentrating on the area above the lateral and mid eyebrow but avoiding the 1 cm above the eyebrow. Ascher et al. (29) used 40 to 50 units of Dysport for the forehead. Klein (36) uses 18 units divided into six injection sites in a grid across the forehead. He avoids the area immediately above the eyebrow and also the area above the lateral eyebrow. He points out that much of the expressivity of the forehead lies in the lateral forehead, so that retention of function in this area will allow retention of expressivity. In addition, the majority of individuals object to the line centrally more than laterally.

Finally, Dr. Richard Glogau has recently described an elegant solution to the problems described above (unpublished observation, 1996) (Fig. 24). He draws a line from the glabella to the hairline at the junction of the forehead and temple on each side. He injects a total of 15 to 20 units at 1- to 2-cm intervals along these lines. Theoretically, this will allow retention of frontalis action in the upper central brow and above the lateral eyebrow but will cross all the forehead lines as well as all the fibers of frontalis. It should be remembered that BTX-A can spread significant distances along individual muscles. For example, only two to four injection sites are used to treat sternocleidomastoid in cervical dystonia (spasmodic torticollis). In a woman with fine tissues, the technique described by Glogau might paralyze the entire frontalis, whereas in a large man with abundant facial musculature, it might not be adequate. Adjustment of the dose and concentration of toxin used will be crucial with this technique, and it is important to explain this to the individuals being treated and to enlist their assistance in the assessment and monitoring of the response. It is better to underdose than to overdose foreheads.

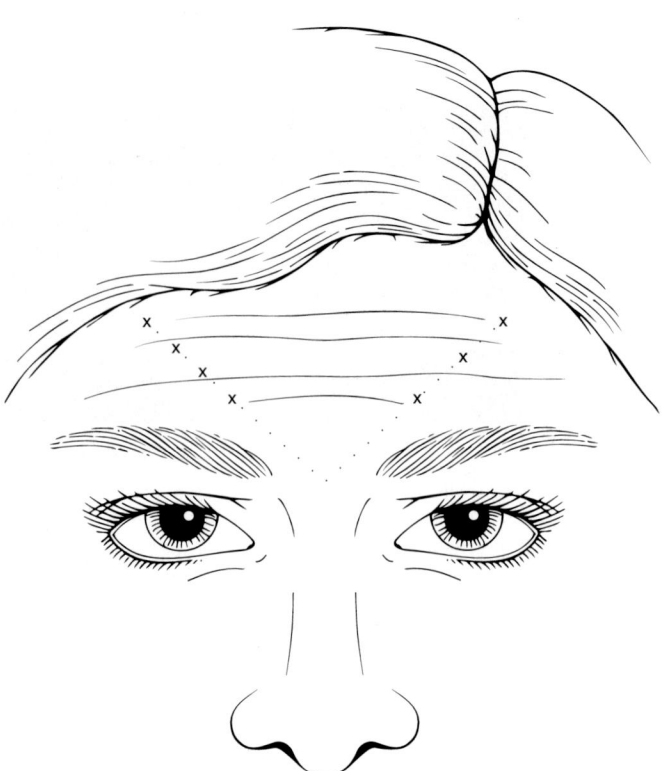

FIG. 24. Glogau injection technique for horizontal forehead lines.

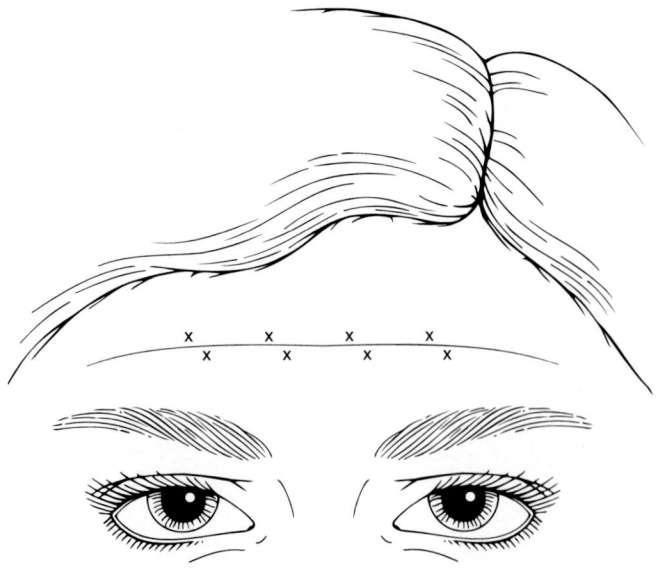

FIG. 23. Injection technique for Figure 21.

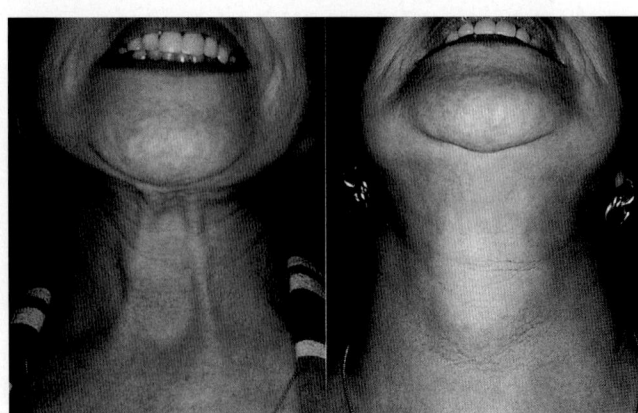

FIG. 25. Platysmal bands before *(left)* and after *(right)* treatment with BTX-A. (Courtesy of Dr. Michael Carney.)

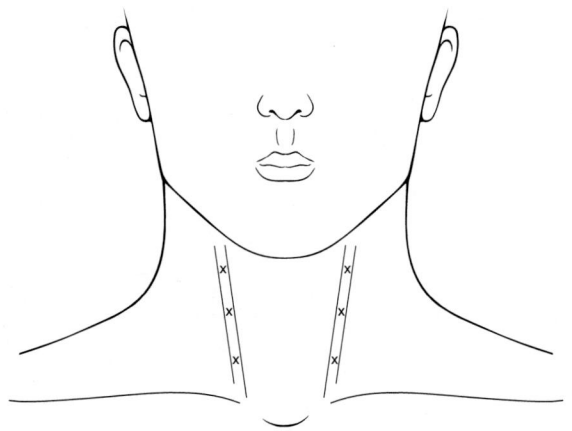

FIG. 26. Injection sites for platysmal bands.

Complications

Ptosis of the eyebrows is the most significant complication of treatment of the forehead, and avoidance of this has already been discussed. Bruising and pain are unusual in this area.

OTHER AREAS

Platysma

BTX-A is ineffective in the treatment of redundant skin in the neck, which requires a rhytidectomy procedure. However, some individuals use their platysma as a muscle of expression with unacceptable banding in the neck on contraction of platysma. This can be seen without or after rhytidectomy. In addition, these bands may draw attention to an aging neck. Dr. Carney has described treating these bands with 15 units per band divided into three doses of 5 units each, equally spaced along the band (Figs. 25, 26).

Nasalis

Some individuals are concerned about the "flare" of their nostrils producing a degree of columellar show. We have a number of individuals in whom 5 units injected into the most active area of muscular contraction on each side of the nose produces a satisfactory improvement in this flaring for 3 to 4 months (Fig. 27).

Mentalis

Most people have a smooth chin protuberance. However, in some, insertion of muscle fibers produces a "dimpling" of this normally smooth area on contraction of the mentalis. Injection of 5 to 10 units into the point of the chin will improve this, although caution must be taken to avoid injection too close to the mental fold, which may produce an incompetent mouth.

Melolabial Folds

Melolabial folds are a difficult problem cosmetically. They are undoubtedly caused by muscular contraction, so use of BTX-A is attractive. Blitzer and co-workers (25) reported improvement in melolabial folds with BTX-A therapy, but we remain unimpressed with our results in this area. Any attempt to inject in the area of the fold is likely to produce an asymmetric smile, an incomplete result, or a flaccid cheek. We occasionally inject 2 to 3 units into the levator labii superioris alaeque nasi (see Fig. 5) using electromyography (EMG) control, with some improvement. However, although this will produce some softening of the medial melolabial fold, it may also produce lengthening of the upper lip (Fig. 28). We prefer alternative methods for the treatment of this area.

The area around the mouth, including the melolabial folds, should generally be avoided in the cosmetic use of BTX-A (Fig. 29).

Facial Asymmetry

An important cosmetic use of BTX-A is the correction of facial asymmetry. Commonly treated areas are asymmetric

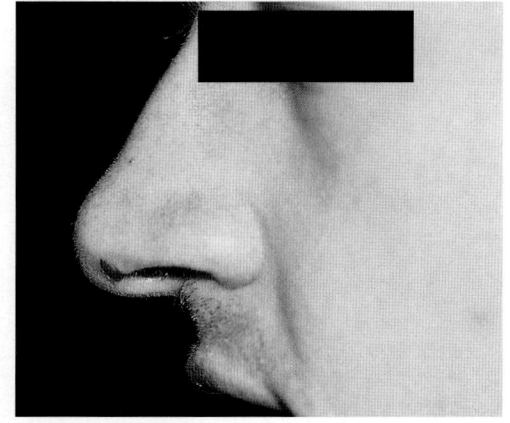
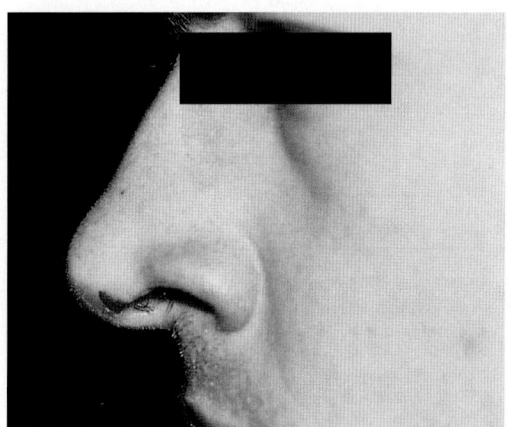

FIG. 27. Patient with nasal flare and columellar show: at rest **(A)** and contracting the nasalis **(B)**. [From ref. 32, with permission.]

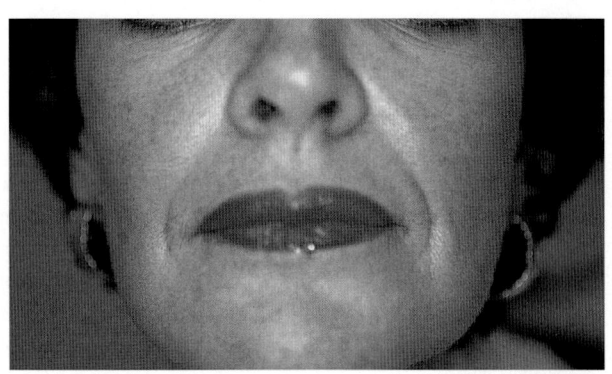 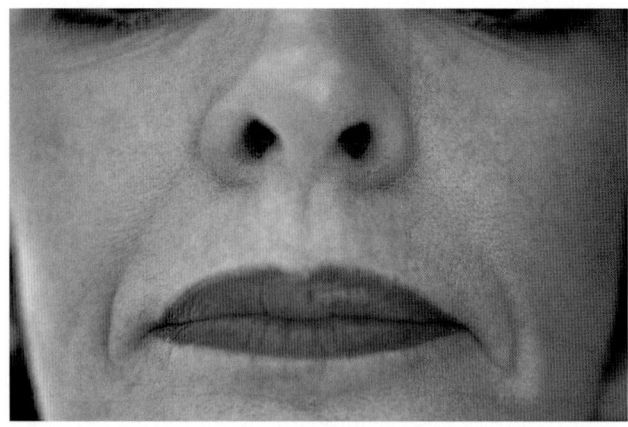

FIG. 28. Patient with marked melolabial folds before **(A)** and after **(B)** BTX-A injection, showing some softening of the upper melolabial fold and lengthening of the upper lip.

brows after surgery, asymmetric faces after Bell's palsy, and face-lift as well as hemifacial spasm.

ELECTROMYOGRAPHY

Use of an EMG device is common for some uses of BTX-A such as in strabismus and laryngeal dystonia. It is less commonly used in blepharospasm treatment, and one of us (JC) in over 5000 injection sessions for blepharospasm over 13 years has not used an EMG for this indication.

Some authors have found that an EMG device is preferable for cosmetic indications (25,28,30,33,35,36,40), whereas others including ourselves do not (20,22,24,26,27,29,32,34, 37–39). EMG is of value to accurately localize small muscles such as levator labii superioris alaeque nasi. It is an excellent teaching tool for localizing the muscles being treated when beginning to use BTX-A cosmetically. In addition, it is useful for demonstrating to the patient that the needle is in the muscle that causes the expression that needs to be relaxed. This encourages, educates, and involves the patient in the therapeutic modality. However, the EMG device and the Teflon-coated needle that is used as a monopolar electrode are expensive. The needle is 27 gauge and therefore more painful for the patient and more likely to produce postprocedure pain and bruising. It certainly makes the procedure significantly more cumbersome and lengthy.

The EMG device sold by Allergan Inc. (Irvine, CA) is shown in Figure 30. It is a small, battery-powered amplifier that converts the signal from the muscle to a sound from a small loudspeaker. A gain control allows adjustment of the volume of the signal. The Teflon-coated needles (Fig. 31), also supplied by Allergan Inc., have a lead attached to their hub that connects with the lead to the EMG device. All but the needle tip is covered with Teflon, so that only signals picked up by the needle tip will be heard. An alternative is to use an adaptor attached to a metal-hub, noncoated, 30-gauge needle. This needle is dramatically less costly than the Teflon-coated needle, as well as being finer and therefore less painful for the patient. However, signal will be received from the whole length of the needle and multiple punctures are necessary, rather than "threading" the needle through muscles, to be certain that the tip of the needle is in the desired muscle. The metal-hub, 30-gauge needles are less sharp

FIG. 29. Danger zones for injection of BTX-A.

FIG. 30. Electromyographic device (Allergan Inc., Irvine, CA).

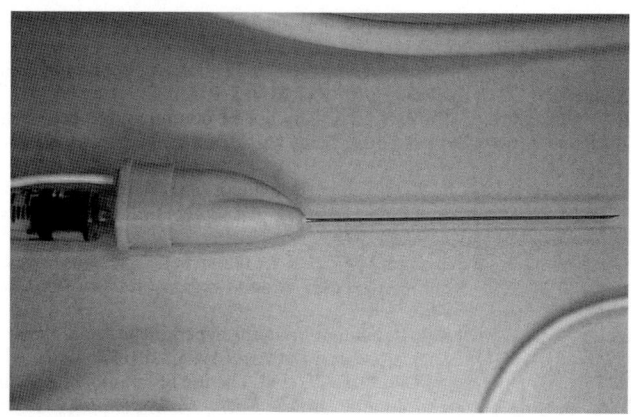

FIG. 31. Teflon-coated electromyography needle (Allergen Inc., Irvine, CA).

than the 30-gauge, plastic-hub needles we commonly use and are therefore more painful.

Technique

The Teflon-coated needle is connected to the syringe and the EMG device. A neutral electrode is attached to the patient's skin off the face. To inject the glabellar area, the technique just described can be used, with the addition of instructions to the patient to frown or relax as necessary to ascertain accurate placement of the needle tip. However, because of the greater size of the needle, it is kinder to use a "threading" technique as follows (Fig. 32): The needle is inserted through a single puncture site above the eyebrows in the midline. It can then be gently threaded into the corrugator, the orbicularis, and the procerus, starting on one side and gradually working around fanwise to the opposite side. The needle must be almost completely withdrawn on each occasion prior to repositioning. Leaving it in muscle and accidentally dragging the muscle to a new location is very painful. We recommend icing prior to and after this technique to reduce pain and bruising.

RESULTS

This chapter is designed as a practical description of the use of BTX-A. We have previously summarized our published reports and those of others (32,37). The results of BTX-A injection are variable. Some patients will have a response that is disappointing in that it lasts only a few weeks. The majority will notice some function starting to return at 3 to 4 months but will not have full function back for 6 months or longer. Approximately 25% of individuals will have a response for 5 months to a year or even longer. This last group may have an extended response because of retraining of their facial expressions.

CONCLUSIONS

We hope that this chapter has served as a practical introduction to the cosmetic use of BTX-A as well as being an interesting discussion of alternative techniques for those already using this therapy. BTX-A–treated individuals are singularly enthusiastic about this form of therapy, which is extremely gratifying for their physicians!

However, this chapter is not intended as a complete training course in the cosmetic use of BTX-A. We strongly recommend that physicians take a course with both didactic training and demonstration of the use of BTX-A on patients.

BTX-A is a useful addition to the therapeutic armamentarium of all physicians interested in cosmetic management. We have indicated the areas where it is now commonly used and some of those areas where we can see that there is potential for expansion of its use. Undoubtedly, this list will expand over the next few years as the cosmetic use of BTX-A grows in acceptance.

REFERENCES

1. Middlebrook JL. Cell surface receptors for protein toxins. In: Simpson LL, ed. *Botulinum neurotoxin and tetanus toxin.* San Diego: Academic Press, 1989;95–119.
2. Simpson LL. Peripheral actions of the botulinum toxins. In: Simpson LL, ed. *Botulinum neurotoxin and tetanus toxin.* San Diego: Academic Press, 1989;153–178.
3. Simpson LL. Kinetic studies on the interaction between botulinum type A and the cholinergic neuromuscular junction. *J Pharmacol Exp Ther* 1980;212:16–21.
4. Simpson LL. The structure and mechanism of action of botulinum toxin [abstract]. *Mov Disord* 1995;10:362.
5. de Paiva A, Ashton AC, Foran P, et al. Botulinum A like type B and tetanus toxins fulfils criteria for being a zinc-dependent protease. *J Neurochem* 1993;61:2338–2341.
6. Schiavo G, Rossetto O, Benfenati F, et al. Tetanus and botulinum neurotoxins are zinc proteases specific for components of the neuroexocytosis apparatus. *Ann N Y Acad Sci* 1994;710:65–75.
7. Moyer E, Setler PE. Botulinum toxin type B: experimental & clinical experience. In: Jankovic J, Hallett M, eds. *Therapy with botulinum toxin.* New York: Marcel Dekker, 1994;71–85.

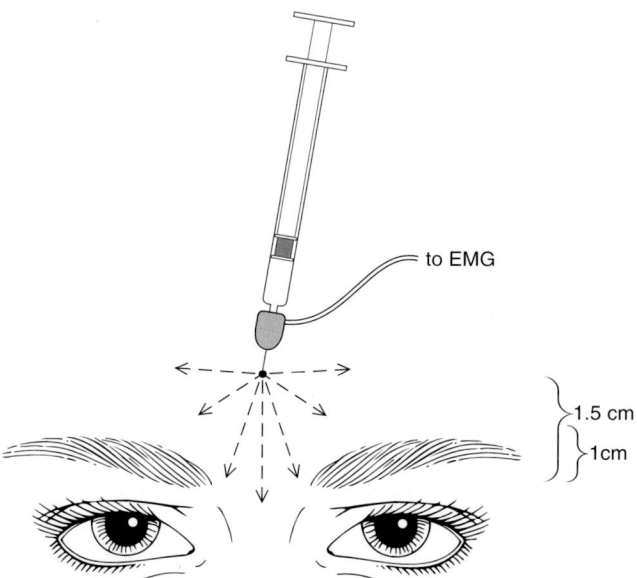

FIG. 32. Diagram of electromyography-guided injection into the area using a fanwise injection technique.

8. Rhew K, Ludlow CL, Karp B, et al. Clinical experience with botulinum toxin F. In: Jankovic J, Hallett M, eds. *Therapy with botulinum toxin.* New York: Marcel Dekker, 1994;323–328.
9. Schantz EJ, Kautter DA. Microbiological methods: standardized assay for *Clostridium botulinum* toxins. *J Assoc Analyt Chem* 1977;61:96–99.
10. Greene P. Clinical trials for cervical dystonia II. In: *National Institutes of Health Consensus Development Conference on Clinical Use of Botulinum Toxin Program.* Bethesda, MD: National Institues of Health 1990;53–56.
11. Pearce LB, Borodic GE, First ER, et al. Measurement of botulinum toxin activity: evaluation of the lethality assay. *Toxicol Appl Pharmacol* 1994;128:69–77.
12. Scott AB, Suzuki D. Systemic toxicity of botulinum toxin by intramuscular injection in the monkey. *Mov Disord* 1988;3:333–335.
13. Meyer KF, Eddie B. Perspectives concerning botulism. *Z Hyg Infect Krankh* 1951;133:255–263.
14. Lamanna C, Hillowalla RA, Alling CC. Buccal exposure to botulinal toxin. *J Infect Dis* 1967;117:327–331.
15. Tsui JK, Wong NLM, Wong E, et al. Production of circulating antibodies to botulinum-A toxin in patients receiving repeated injections for dystonia [abstract]. *Ann Neurol* 1988;23:181.
16. Dezfulian M, Bitar R, Bartlett J. Kinetics study of immunological response to *Clostridium botulinum* toxin. *J Clin Microbiol* 1987;25:1336–1337.
17. Clarke CE. Therapeutic potential of botulinum toxin in neurological disorders. *Q J Med* 1992;299:197–205.
18. Not for wrinkles. *FDA Consumer,* Dec. 1995;29:19.
19. Garner W. Review of the use of botulinum toxin for esthetic improvement. *Ann Plast Surg* 1996;36:192.
20. Garcia A, Fulton JE. Cosmetic denervation of the muscles of facial expression with botulinum toxin. *Dermatol Surg* 1996;22:39–43.
21. Gartland MG, Hoffman HT. Crystalline preparation of botulinum toxin type A (BOTOX): degradation impotency with storage. *Otolaryngol Head Neck Surg* 1993;108:135–140.
22. Carruthers JDA, Carruthers JA. Treatment of glabellar frown lines with C. botulinum-A exotoxin. *J Dermatol Surg Oncol* 1992;18:17–21.
23. Glogau R. Chemical peeling in aging skin. *J Geriatr Dermatol* 1994; 2:30–35.
24. Carruthers A, Carruthers JDA. Botulinum toxin in the treatment of glabellar frown lines and other facial wrinkles. In: Jankovic J, Hallett M, eds. *Therapy with botulinum toxin.* New York: Marcel Dekker, 1994;577–595.
25. Blitzer A, Brin MF, Keen MF, et al. Botulinum toxin for the treatment of hyperfunctional lines of the face. *Arch Otolaryngol Head Neck Surg* 1993;119:1018–1022.
26. Guyuron B, Huddleston SW. Aesthetic indications for botulinum toxin injection. *Plast Reconstr Surg* 1994;93:913–918.
27. Carruthers A, Carruthers JDA. The use of botulinum toxin to treat glabellar frown lines and other facial wrinkles. *Cosmet Dermatol* 1994; 7:11–15.
28. Keen M, Blitzer A, Aviv J, et al. Botulinum toxin A for hyperkinetic facial lines: results of a double-blind, placebo-controlled study. *Plast Reconstr Surg* 1994;94:94–99.
29. Ascher B, Klap P, Marion M-H, et al. La toxine botulique dans le traitement des rides fronto-glabellaires et de al region orbitair. *Ann Chir Plast Esthet* 1995;40:67–76.
30. Low MJ, Wieder JM. Botulinum toxin for hyperkinetic facial lines: a placebo-controlled study. *Cosmet Dermatol* 1995;8:46–47.
31. Foster JA, Barnhorst DA, Papay F, et al. The use of botulinum A toxin to ameliorate facial kinetic frown lines. *Ophthalmology* 1996; 103:618–622.
32. Carruthers A, Kiene K, Carruthers J. Botulinum A exotoxin use in clinical dermatology. *J Am Acad Dermatol* 1996;34:788–797.
33. Lowe NJ, Wieder JM, Maxwell A, et al. Botulinum A exotoxin for glabellar folds: a double blind placebo controlled study using an electromyographic injection technique. *J Am Acad Dermatol* 1996; 35:569–572.
34. Carruthers A, Carruthers J. Cosmetic uses of botulinum toxin. In: Coleman WP, Hanke W, Alt T, eds. *Cosmetic surgery of the skin.* New York: Mosby Year Book, 1997;231–235.
35. Blitzer A, Binder WJ, Aviv JE. The management of hyperfunctional facial lines with botulinum toxin: a collaborative study of 210 injection sites in 162 patients. *Arch Otolaryngol Head Neck Surg* 1997; 123:389–392.
36. Klein AW. Cosmetic therapy with botulinum toxin: anecdotal memoirs. *Dermatol Surg* 1996;22:757–759.
37. Carruthers J, Carruthers A. Cosmetic uses of botulinum A exotoxin. In: Dzubow L, ed. *Adv Dermatol* 1996;12:280–303.
38. Carruthers J, Carruthers A. Combining botulinum toxin injection and laser resurfacing for facial rhytides. In: Coleman WP, Lawrence N, eds. *Skin resurfacing.* Baltimore: Williams & Wilkins, 1997;235–243.
39. Carruthers J, Carruthers A. BTX-A in clinical ophthalmology. *Can J Ophthalmol* 1996;31:389–399.
40. Keen M, Kopelman JE, Aviv JE, et al. Botulinum toxin: a novel method to remove periorbital wrinkles. *Facial Plast Surg* 1994;10:141–146.

2

Injectable Collagen: A Tutorial

Arnold William Klein

The use of injectable bovine collagen for soft-tissue augmentation has been in clinical practice for over 16 years. However, the product(s) and associated implantation techniques continue to evolve. What follows is my present approach to treating patients with these xenogeneic substances. Clearly, the successful use of these substances will be determined less by their properties than by the skill one develops in their application. This chapter is not meant for physicians who plan to use these products occasionally in their practice, because occasional use will not allow them to develop the skill necessary to produce the pleasing, predictable results that these products can and do offer. Indeed, some physicians have labeled the use of injectable collagen a "no-brainer," and I am certain there are those who can inject an entire face in 10 minutes. Nevertheless, I am certain these patients never return for further therapy; they will seek out another physician skilled in the application of injectable collagen or give up collagen implantation altogether.

THE CONSULTATION

Mrs. C. has come to see me 2½ months before her son's wedding. She is a 62-year-old successful businesswoman who feels she looks "tired." She had a rhytidectomy and upper and lower blepharoplasty about 6 months prior to her visit, performed by a local plastic surgeon, and she is less then pleased with the results (Fig. 1). She certainly is not the ideal candidate for collagen therapy, but she wants to know if there is "anything" that I can do to improve her appearance. Her friends have had great success with "collagen treatments" and she would like to try it. She has no contraindications to treatment, no history of allergy to local anesthetics, no history of anaphylaxis, and no history of prior allergy to injectable collagen, and she is not undergoing or planning to undergo desensitization to beef products. First, I ask Mrs. C. what bothers her most about her face. She hates the area above her lip as it is very lined, and her upper lip, while never large, seems to have disappeared altogether (Fig. 2). She also finds that her lower lip has assumed an accordion-like appearance. She is bothered by the redundant skin at her jaw line that she expected to disappear with the surgery and hates the "drool groove" that descends from the corner of her mouth (Fig. 3). In regard to her mid face, she thinks her nasolabial folds make her look old and haggard. On her upper face, she is bothered by the hollows under her eyes, her crow's-feet, and the generally tired look of her eyes (Fig. 4). She demonstrates a significant amount of scleral show secondary to her lower lid blepharoplasty, which does not seem to concern her. Finally, she is bothered by the horizontal forehead lines and frown lines (Fig. 5). She provides this information in a very organized manner and has brought notes along to remind her of the areas she wishes to discuss. I sit and listen till she has completed her assessment.

When she arrived at my office, she was provided reprints of multiple articles that I have published on collagen therapy as well as brochures provided by the company. Although patients usually have a 30-minute wait in my office prior to their consultation, they rarely review the provided literature. She now asks if I can help her. First, I tell her that I don't have miracles or magic wands. While I know I can improve most of the areas, it will be expensive and require at least one and possibly two treatment sessions. She has already investigated laser resurfacing but is frightened because of her time constraints and the inability of that technique to address the size of her lips and the mesolabial area. I leave the consultation room and have my nurse discuss with her the amount of material that will be necessary to obtain full correction and the associated cost. Often, patients feel that all that is required is one syringe to address all of their areas. Because I tend to underestimate the amount of material that is required, I find my nurses do a much better job in determining treatment amounts and associated costs.

Mrs. C. decides to proceed with treatment. I explain that she must be tested twice, not simply once. In that most treatment-associated reactions occur shortly after the first treatment, a second test reduces this most undesirable sequela.

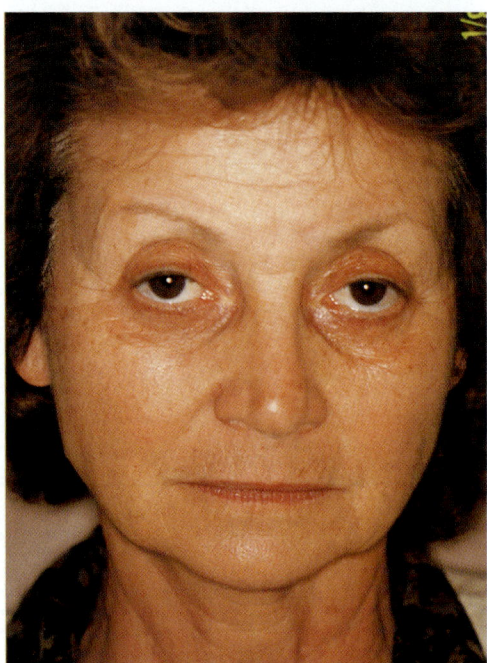

FIG. 1. Full face before implantation.

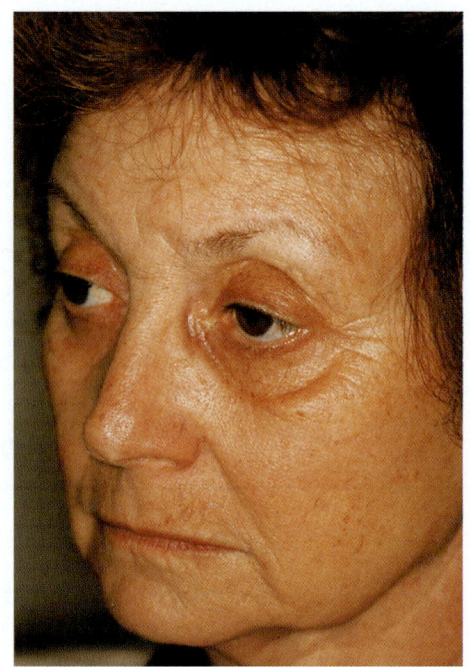

FIG. 3. Drool groove and corner of mouth before implantation.

Additionally, I explain the possible downsides of collagen therapy: allergenicity, intermittent swelling, vascular and necrotic events, and the like. I also stress that she must have realistic expectations. I can and will improve her appearance, but I cannot make every line go away. The changes will be subtle. Also, I cannot address the redundant skin of her jaw—collagen therapy cannot reduce the redundant skin. She decides to undergo skin testing and one third of the 0.3-ml test syringe is placed in a tuberculin manner in the volar surface of her right forearm. She is asked not to consume alcohol that day, nor to exercise. Anecdotal experience has shown that patients occasionally have some swelling at the test site with these two activities. The test site is evaluated at 48 hours and again at 4 weeks. She is cautioned that any redness, swelling, tenderness, induration, and/or pruritis occurring at the site 6 to 8 hours after testing or present at 1 month is considered a positive test and she cannot and should not have collagen therapy, no matter how motivated she is.

Mrs. C. returns to the office 4 weeks later for her second test. First, the initial test site in the volar forearm is evaluated for any signs of allergenicity. She is questioned as to whether or not the site has swelled, gotten red, or itched. All being negative, a second test is administered at the right hairline and the same caveats are given regarding exercise and alcohol. Her treatment session is scheduled 2 weeks after her second test. She is again told the estimated amount of material

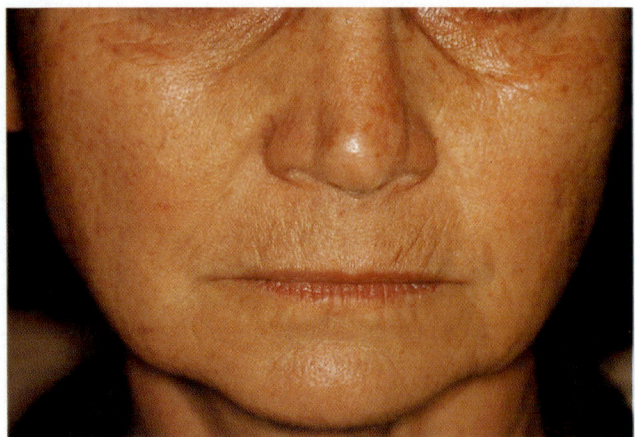

FIG. 2. Lips and perioral area prior to implantation.

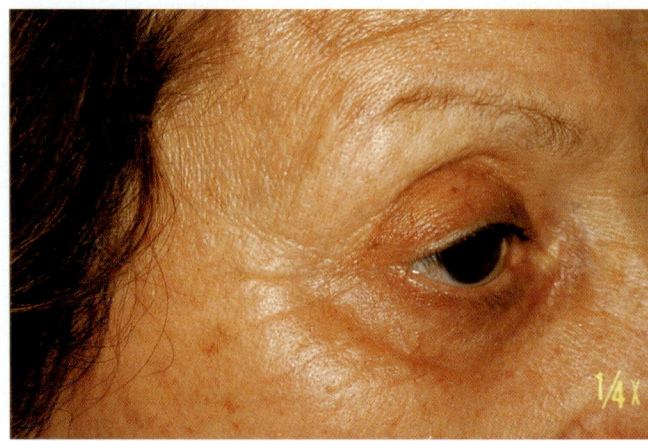

FIG. 4. Eye and periorbital crow's-feet before implantation.

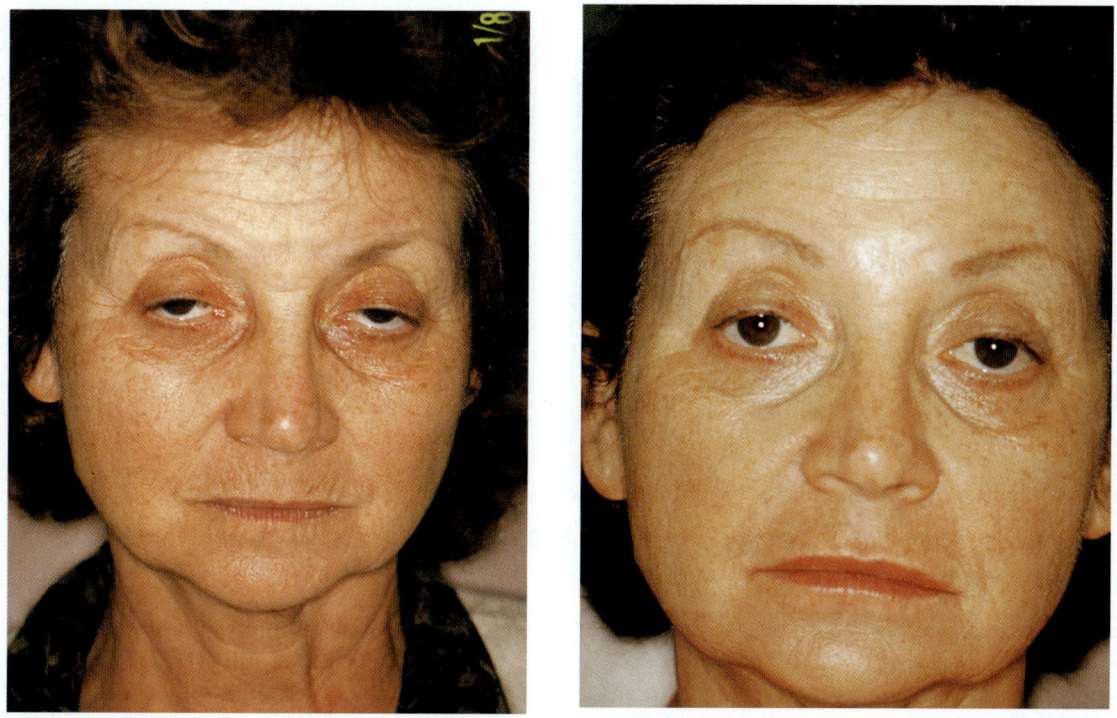

FIG. 56. A: Full face before implantation. **B:** Full face 3 weeks after implantation.

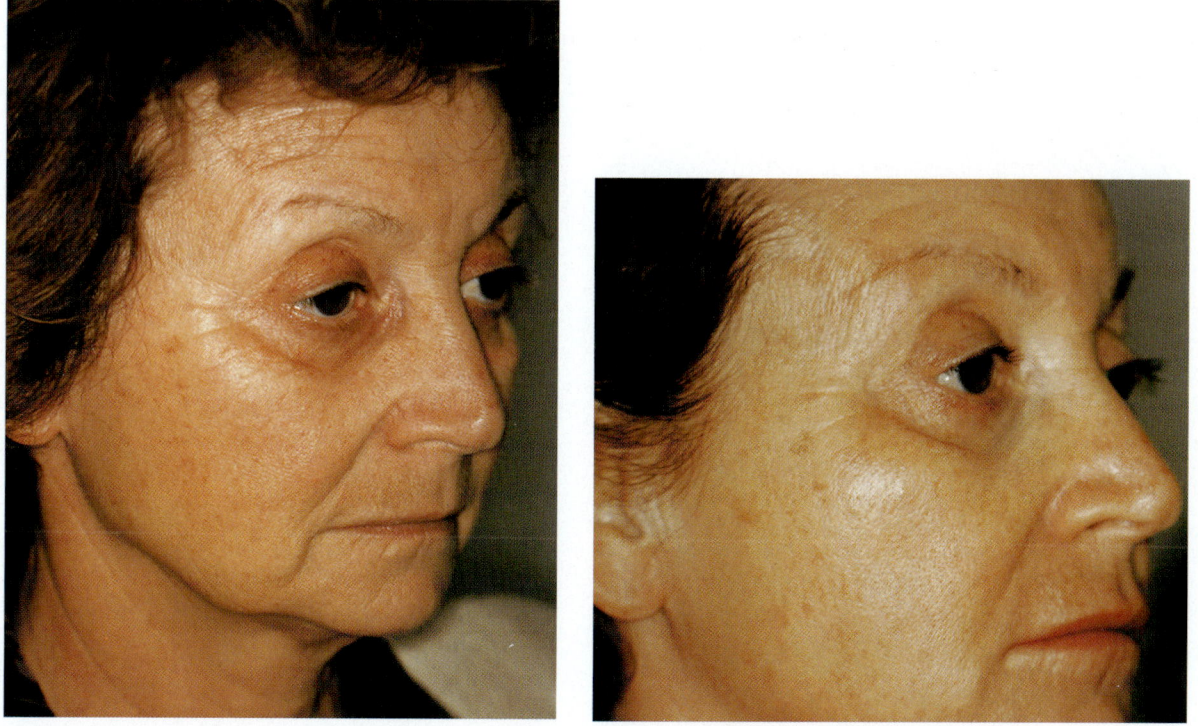

FIG. 57. A: Side view before implantation. **B:** Side view 3 weeks after implantation.

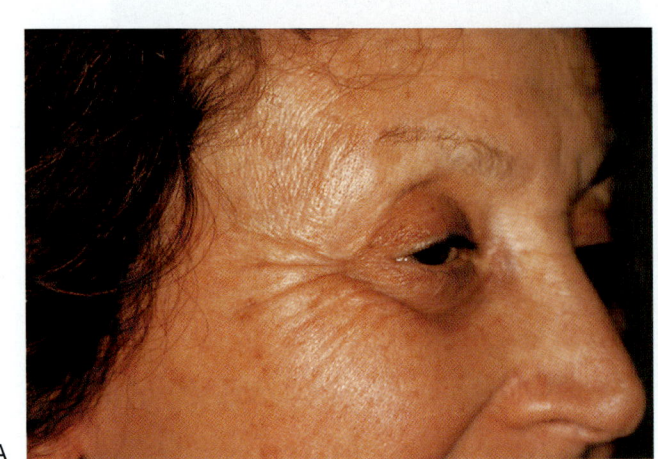 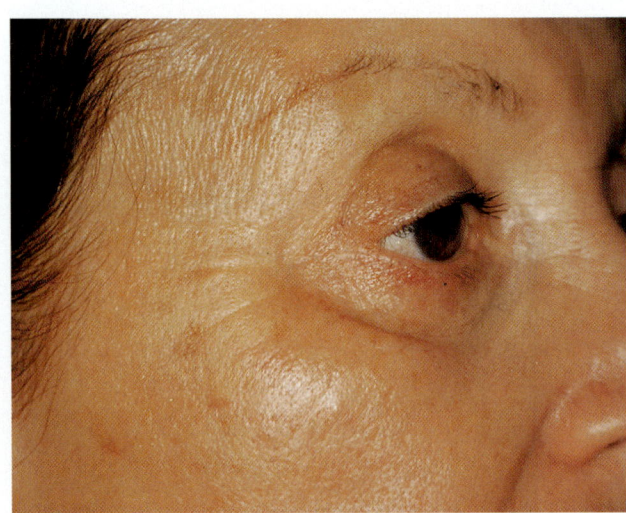

FIG. 58. **A:** Periorbital area before implantation. **B:** Periorbital area 3 weeks after implantation.

tween her eyebrows and forehead contribute to the rested look.

The preceding narrative should serve as a simple framework for my implantation techniques. I am sure other individuals have different techniques that provide equally pleasing and persistent results. Although the Collagen Corporation offers an injection-assist device called the Adjustable Depth Gauge, I still prefer to inject "freehand," but I am certain others find this device most helpful. If you do indeed become a fellow collagen injector, I think you will find the Collagen Corporation responsive to your needs both clinically and academically.

3

Fibrel: Soft-Tissue Augmentation

Gary D. Monheit

The search for the ideal dermal filler has challenged investigators who experiment with wound healing and collagen synthesis. The ideal implant should be (a) physiologic, (b) safe, (c) permanent, and (d) easily administered. Investigators searched for methods to stimulate collagen synthesis in scars, in skin contour defects, and under rhytides. They have used substances such as oils and paraffins to create inflammation with resultant laying down of new collagen, stimulating wound healing. Problems, though, developed, such as prolonged inflammation and then scarring (1,2). Silicone usage in microdroplet technique is designed to stimulate an encapsulating ring of collagen that elevates depressed scars and rhytides. Zyderm collagen implants were first thought to stimulate native collagen production, but later usage proved this theory wrong. Fibrel also is a method to stimulate production through reinjury and inflammation. Each of these techniques has attempted to re-create the body's own methods of repair for collagen synthesis and soft-tissue augmentation.

The safety of implants is an important yet controversial subject: many of the implant materials are under investigation for potential side effects and complications. Granulomatous reactions with scarring, allergy, infarction with tissue necrosis, and potential systemic disease have all been reported with implant material. Recently, reports by the lay press have indicted implant material with little solid scientific data to back up the allegations (3).

None of the implant materials are permanent, and each has a particular longevity based on material used, location, and defect treated. A thorough understanding of each of these variables is necessary to master the use of these materials for skin contour correction (Fig. 1).

FIBREL

The attempt to discover the ideal filling material has intrigued researchers, and as early as 1944, Bailey and Ingraham published their results on the use of fibrin from pooled plasma to elevate cutaneous scars. Based on the mechanism of wound healing, the fibrin was injected under depressed scars with clot formation, initiating the clotting cascade, to stimulate collagen synthesis. The investigators theorized that the chemical agents in plasma initiated healing in collagen synthesis. It was the attempt to produce excessive collagen under depressed scars and wrinkles by this mechanism that led to the development of Fibrel.

Mechanism of Action

Fibrel utilizes the mechanisms of wound healing to re-create the necessary events for the production of collagen in a specific area. In wound healing, an injury to the skin damages tissue with the consequent release of platelets and thromboplastic and thrombolytic factors. Fibrinogen, through the release of thrombin, is changed to fibrin, which then stimulates fibroblasts in and near capillaries to produce collagen (4). During this same event, plasma profibrinolysin is produced in the resultant clot, producing fibrinolysin, which inhibits or destroys the fibrin clot, thus curtailing further collagen production (see Fig. 1).

Fibrel provides the necessary ingredients to re-create this healing mechanism under scars and wrinkles. The absorbable gelatin powder provides a framework for the clot to form on, and it remains stable under the scar. Plasma provides the necessary ingredients for collagen synthesis, and epsilon-aminocaproic acid (EACA) inhibits the production of fibrinolysin, allowing excessive collagen to be produced within the clot (5). Thus, the treatment of skin depressions through Fibrel implantation will elevate the scar and produce a fibrin clot in which new collagen will be created that will give lasting elevation of the scar (Fig. 2).

The gelatin powder is a porcine derivative used widely as a hemostatic agent; it has low immunogenicity. It elevates the depression and provides a matrix to trap clotting factors for the deposition of new collagen.

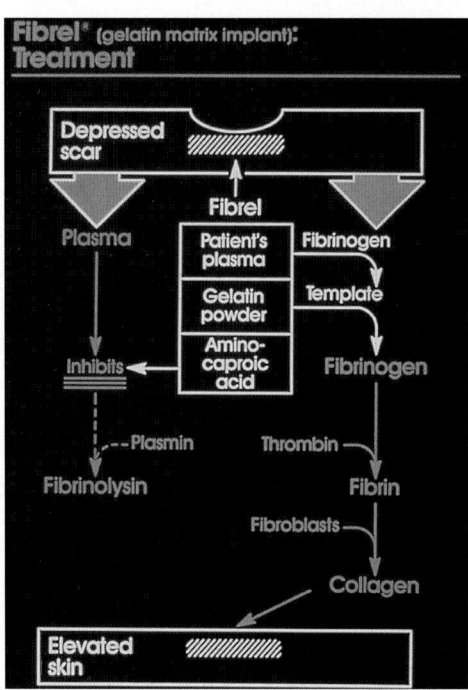

FIG. 1. Fibrel mechanism.

The Product

Fibrel is composed of a lyophilized mixture of 100 mg of absorbable gelatin powder with 125 of mg EACA. EACA has been shown to enhance collagen synthesis through a blockade of the fibrinolytic system (6). Both the gelatin and EACA used in Fibrel are used routinely as hemostatic agents. Blood plasma provides a supplemental source of fibrinogen and other clotting factors that enhance the collagen matrix and add to the efficacy of Fibrel. Unlike collagen or silicone, which remain as foreign implants beneath the skin surface, the clot matrix of Fibrel is absorbed as the new collagen is gradually incorporated into the skin. The gelatin substance in Fibrel thus provides a temporary framework in which new tissue may grow. Histologic and preclinical data suggest that within 90 days, the implant is colonized by the patient's own normal connective tissue as cells and blood vessels grow into the Fibrel implant (9). Theoretically, Fibrel should be a physiologic implant with little chance of allergenicity, or foreign body reaction. The gelatin powder elevates the depression and provides a matrix to enhance blood clotting by entrapping the necessary clotting factors and serve as a template for subsequent deposition of new extracellular matrix essential for wound healing. The antifibrinolytic action of EACA has a fibrin-stabilizing effect. In an-

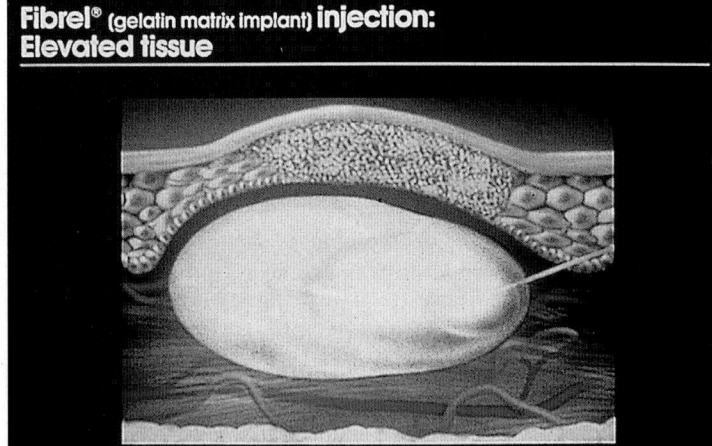

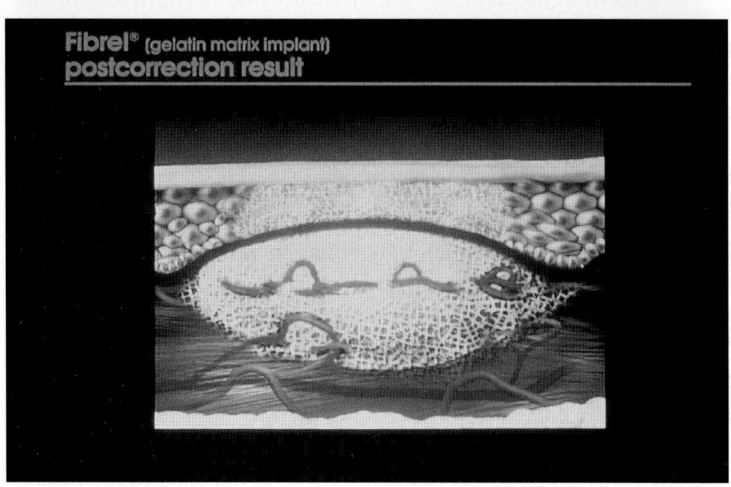

FIG. 2. Slide diagnostics. **A:** Injection with elevation. **B:** Healed, elevated.

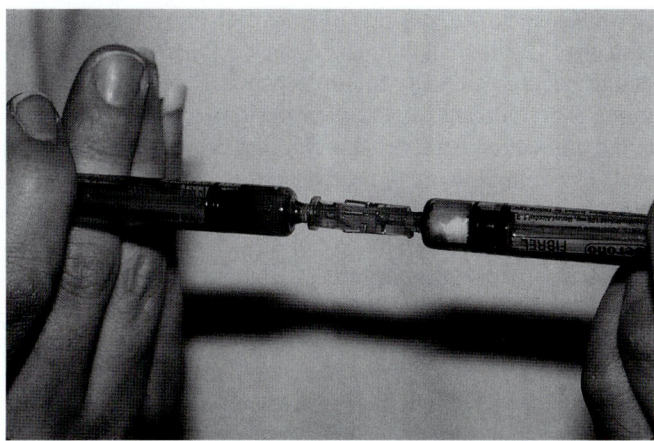

FIG. 3. Reconstitution of Fibrel.

imals, it has been shown to enhance new collagen synthesis through blockage of the fibrinolytic system (6).

Commercial Fibrel comes in a kit. It is sterile, does not require refrigeration, and has a long shelf life. The kit contains everything needed for treatment. The mixture of lyophilized gelatin powder and EACA is provided in a syringe and is reconstituted with 0.5 ml of the patient's serum and 0.5 ml of normal saline (0.9%) (Fig. 3), as will be described in the next section (6).

INDICATIONS AND TECHNIQUE

Fibrel is indicated as a dermal implant for the correction of depressed cutaneous scars and wrinkles. A thorough consultation and examination of the patient's defects should be performed prior to treatment. Those scars or wrinkles that will respond to filler substance are outlined. This is determined by minimally stretching the skin with the patient in a semivertical position. Distensible scars that flatten out with stretching are amenable to elevation with Fibrel. Bound down, fibrotic scars or ice pick scars will not flatten with distention and are thus not treatable with injectable filling material. A skin test is performed by diluting 0.5 ml of the Fibrel suspension, 1 in 1000 with saline, and placing it on the patient's arm. A 6-week period is allowed to ensure that the patient is not allergic to the implant. Potentially antigenic materials include the porcine gelatin protein and the EACA. Of the 321 patients evaluated in the multicenter Fibrel study, only 6 developed a positive skin test reaction, or 1.9% (7). A positive reaction would be induration and erythema that persists longer than 24 to 48 hours. None of the patients in the study with a negative skin test had an adverse allergic reaction to Fibrel treatment (7).

Fibrel is used for depressed cutaneous scars that can be elevated by stretching the skin at the edges of the scar. The more fibrotic scars or ice pick scars do not elevate well and require special treatment for elevation. Deeper creases, furrows, and grooves may also be treated with Fibrel as a dermal implant for elevation. Fine creases on eyelids and lips, and photoaging rhytides on facial skin do not respond as well to Fibrel injections because of the viscosity of the implant and the associated inflammation. During the consultation, lesions that will respond to the implant are identified and a thorough explanation of the treatment technique, and of potential side effects, morbidity, and complications are explained to the patient. Particular emphasis must be placed on the differences between this filling agent and Zyderm collagen. Because Fibrel uses a mechanism to create collagen through wound healing, an inflammatory reaction is a necessary component of the treatment. The patient should develop postoperative erythema, induration, and swelling, which may last as long as 5 days. The patient must schedule the necessary postoperative recovery time, being fully informed of the morbidity during healing.

Final collagen synthesis may take 6 weeks to 2 months. Patients must be informed of these differences so they will understand the nature of healing and implant formation. Patients who should be excluded from Fibrel treatment are those with (a) a history of keloid formation, (b) a sensitivity to gelatin or aminocaproic acid, (c) bleeding disorders, (d) a history of cardiac, renal, or herpetic disease, (e) a history of autoimmune disease, or (f) pregnancy or lactation.

One month after the skin test, the patient presents for skin test evaluation; if the test is negative, treatment can begin.

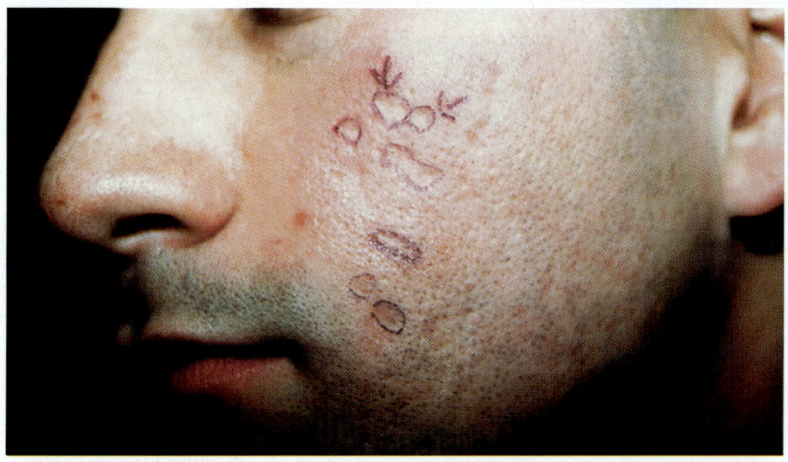

FIG. 4. Scars for Fibrel treatment, distensible and fibrotic.

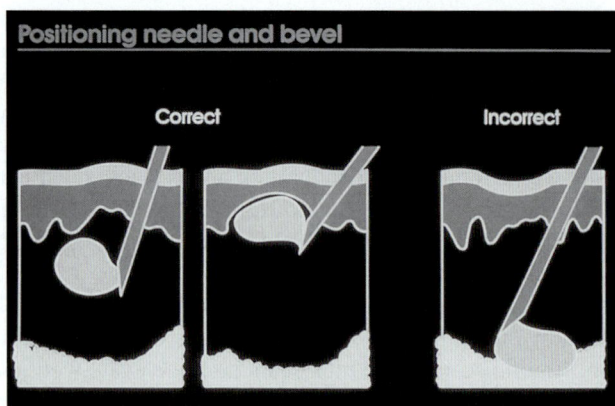

FIG. 5. Placement of scar: mid to upper dermis.

The scar or wrinkle is again outlined, and phlebotomy is performed to remove approximately 10 ml of the patient's blood. This is centrifuged for 10 to 15 minutes, and the clear plasma is drawn into the mixing syringe. This is connected to the syringe with lyophilized gelatin powder and EACA. The two syringes are mixed with 10 to 12 horizontal exchanges, performed slowly to avoid bubbling and frothing. The process is concluded by drawing the Fibrel mixture into the delivery syringe and expressing the air bubbles. The patient then is ready for injection.

The patient's scars are categorized into those that are distensible and those that are fibrotic and more bound down (Fig. 4). The distensible scars can be injected with a 30-gauge needle using the multiple puncture or fanning technique. These do not require preinjections of local anesthesia and the injection is placed directly into the mid to upper dermis. The technique includes spreading the skin and entry of the needle at a 35-degree angle. The implant injection produces a *peau d'orange* texture and blanching. A correction of 150% is necessary because of equalization of serum and fluids during clot resorption. Care must be taken to avoid implant extrusion through pores or around the needle orifice, and to avoid injection into the subcutaneous tissue. The direct puncture technique places the needle at the edge of the scar, advancing into the scar, and injection is made into the middle of the scar. The fanning technique, which is an adaptation of the single puncture, advances the needle in a circumferential pattern throughout the scar, introducing the filler substance within the mid and upper dermis of the entire scar. Common to all of these techniques is the placement of Fibrel within the mid to upper dermis and within the scar (Fig. 5). The physician monitors scar elevation during the treatment.

The approach to fibrotic scars utilizes a custom undermining needle available in the Fibrel kit. This device allows the cosmetic surgeon to create a dermal pocket for the injection of the filler substance. The 18-gauge needle with a special cutting surface will loosen the scar bonds, holding the scar

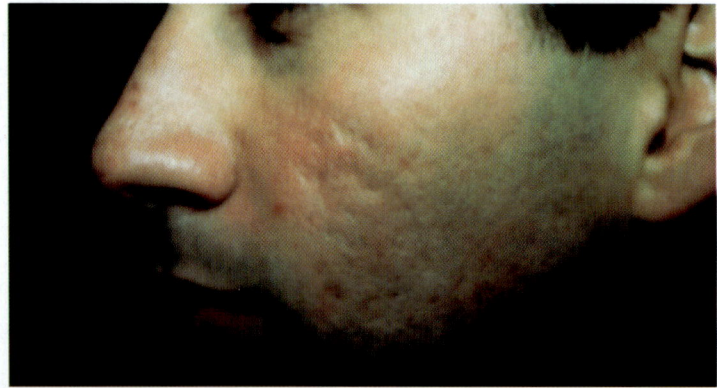

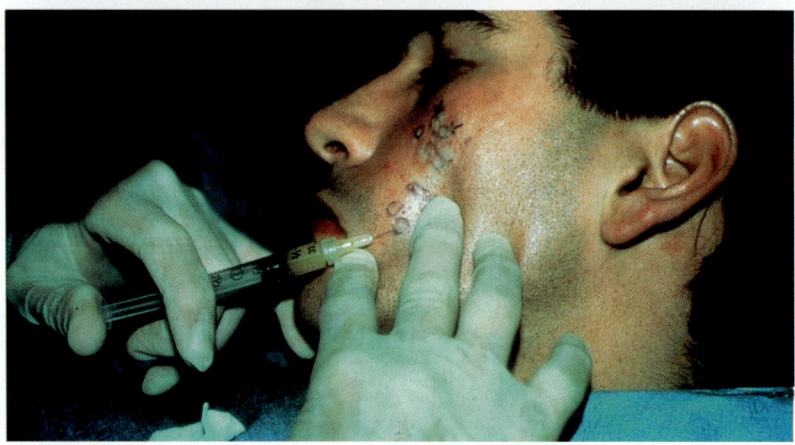

FIG. 6. Patient demonstration. **A:** Preoperative. **B:** Injection technique.

4

Glycolic Acid Peels

Chérie M. Ditre

Glycolic acid has been recently popularized as a chemexfoliant or chemical peeling agent. Both physicians and patients have found glycolic acid peels favorable as (a) a baseline cosmetic procedure for the less photoaged, or an introduction to cosmetic procedures for the less aggressive patient; (b) a penetration enhancer when combined with other peeling agents; (c) a solo or adjunctive treatment of benign and premalignant skin conditions; and (d) a pulse therapy when applied at regular intervals and used in conjunction with a daily home maintenance routine.

The public has designated glycolic acid peels "lunchtime peels" because of the quick recovery time and the minimally apparent disfigurement immediately after the procedure. These are possible because the glycolic acid peels mainly target the epidermis, and therefore they are considered superficial peeling agents. Despite efforts to standardize the peel technique for physicians, confusion still exists over the formulations of glycolic acid in the peel, the methodology, the application, and the indications for their use. This chapter addresses these practical considerations for the use of glycolic acid peels in a cosmetic and general dermatologic practice.

CHOOSING A GLYCOLIC ACID PEEL FORMULATION

Commercially made glycolic acid peels vary: they are classified as partially neutralized, buffered, esterified, or free acid formulations. Bioavailability may be affected by these various formulations.

Partial neutralization refers to the combination of glycolic acid with a base such as ammonium hydroxide to yield a salt such as ammonium glycolate. The pH of the resultant solution is raised (mean pH, 3.8) from that of glycolic acid. These glycolic acid peels may be preferred by physicians who delegate execution of the peel procedure to their nurse or aesthetician.

A buffered glycolic acid peel refers to a solution that resists pH changes when additional acid or base is added. An effective glycolic acid peel solution is one in which there are equal moles of glycolic acid and sodium glycolate. This means that in the pH range of 2.8 to 4.8, glycolic acid solution is stabilized against the addition of an external strong acid such as hydrochloric acid. The role of buffered glycolic acid peels does not have practical application in office use, as it does not appear to offer any biologic benefit. It is this author's belief that the term *buffered solution* has been confused with partially neutralized formulations. Esterified glycolic acid peel solution refers to a "glyco-citrate" solution, with an ester bond formed between the carboxyl group of glycolic acid and the hydroxyl group of citric acid. It has been claimed that admixture of the two alpha-hydroxyl acids attenuates the irritability of the glycolic acid[1]. The stability of the postulated dimer (glycolyl citrate or citryl glycolate) needs to be substantiated.

Last, free glycolic acid solution refers to a non-neutralized solution in which glycolic acid exists in an acidic pH ranging between 0.6 and 1.7 in an aqueous vehicle. The free glycolic acid is believed to allow greater bioavailability and reactivity when applied to the skin. Epidermolysis can result if there is any perturbation in the skin barrier function prior to the application of the free glycolic acid peel. For this reason, this peel is best handled by a skilled operator. In a recent communication in *Skin and Allergy News* (Sept. 1996), Dr. Glenn (Lac-King-Drew Medical Center, Los Angeles, CA) reported her study results showing that the free glycolic acid peel worked better than partially neutralized formulations for dark-complexioned patients with dyschromia. The risks and benefits of the aforementioned types of glycolic acid peel formulations merit further exploration.

---

[1] Klein M. Issues and perspectives of AHAs. *Cosmetic Dermatol* 1994(suppl):1–2.

PRACTICAL CONSIDERATIONS IN PERFORMING A GLYCOLIC ACID PEEL: PRE-PEEL CONSULTATION INDENTIFYING PATIENT/PHYSICIAN GOALS

It is important for the physician to first understand the skin conditions that can realistically be treated with glycolic acid peels. Patients who are looking to simply improve their skin tone and are seeking a freshened appearance for their skin are ideally suited for glycolic acid peels. Aesthetic improvement of fine lines, sallow complexions, dyspigmentation, lentigines, ephilides, and rough-textured skin can be achieved. The physician must explain to the patient that (a) these goals may be accomplished only with a *series* of treatments, and (b) this process requires at least monthly treatments until the goals are met. The number of treatment months will vary with the particular condition being addressed, but the patient will generally see cosmetic improvement after 4 to 6 months.

Deeper lines and wrinkles such as rhytides, glabellar creases, and marionette chin creases should be addressed with other techniques: a glycolic acid peel will not sufficiently treat these conditions. Patients who are ideally selected for glycolic acid peels are those interested in minimal recovery time and no interruption of work or social schedules. However, those patients who are interested in a one-treatment resolution of their conditions, and who are amenable to a lengthier recovery time, are best advised to seek other, greater-depth chemical peeling agents or laser surgery.

Other conditions treated adjunctively with glycolic acid peels and other topical or oral modalities are melasma, postinflammatory hyperpigmentation, acne, shallow acne scars, rosacea, seborrheic and actinic keratoses, keratosis pilaris, and warts. Similarly, the physician must instruct the patient on the need for repeated treatments.

The next area to address with the patient is the cosmetic unit or area of the body the patient is seeking to improve. In general, any cosmetic unit can be treated with glycolic acid peels, such as the face, neck, chest, back, hands, arms, and legs. It should be noted that the neck is the most sensitive area, so the concentration of the acid, and the time it is in contact with the neck, should be lowered. In contrast, the hands, arms, legs, chest, and back seem to tolerate higher concentrations more favorably.

Last, the glycolic acid peels can be used on patients with Fitzpatrick skin types I to VI, on men and women, and on teens and adults. The most sensitive population has appeared to be Asian patients, whose tolerance for the peel seems to be limited to lower concentrations (20% to 35%).

MEDICAL HISTORY AND EXAMINATION

On the initial pre-peel consultation, the physician should obtain a detailed medical and skin history (a sample patient record is shown in Fig. 1). Particular regard to any prior history of viral infections, such as chronic or recurrent herpes simplex; active dermatoses, such as atopic, seborrheic, or eczematous types; and medications, such as oral or topical retinoids, must be identified. If the patient has a history of herpes, he or she must be treated prophylactically with an antiviral agent such as Zovirax at least 6 hours before the glycolic acid peel, and treatment must be continued for a routine course of therapy. If the patient presents to the office with active symptoms or lesions of herpes simplex in the area to be treated, the physician is best advised to postpone the peel.

Medications causing disruption of the stratum corneum may enhance the depth of penetration of the glycolic acid peel. Patients on retinoids, either oral (Accutane/13-*cis*-retinoic acid) or topical (Retin-A/all-*trans*-retinoic acid), may have increased reactivity to the glycolic acid peel. Therefore, it is recommended that patients discontinue use of topical tretinoin at least 7 days prior to the scheduled peel. The use of deeper chemical peeling agents with patients who are on Accutane therapy remains controversial because of questions regarding healing; therefore, it is best left to the physician's expertise when to undertake the more superficial glycolic acid peels.

Other medications that may affect peel penetration are topical Efudex (5-fluorouracil). Efudex will disrupt actinic keratoses, and therefore glycolic acid peels may cause epidermolysis of these treated areas. This is, however, a favorable effect in the destruction of these premalignant conditions. Nevertheless, the patient must be cautioned on the increased potential for causing a deeper chemical peel of these involved areas. Likewise, patients using antiplatelet agents such as coumadin and heparin should be cautioned regarding the risk of bleeding and eventual development of a thicker eschar.

Patients using photosensitizing agents such as oral contraceptives or tetracycline must be *strongly* advised to adhere to postpeel instructions regarding sunscreen use and photoprotective devices.

Those patients with a history of sensitive skin, atopic dermatitis, or other dry skin complaints may be less tolerant of the peel. It is for this reason that a home-use glycolic acid preparation should be applied daily beginning 2 weeks prior to the peel. This will help determine if the patient has any unusual sensitivity to glycolic acid prior to the peel. If dermabrasion, laser or other surgery, or other chemical peels have been recently performed, the patient should be advised to wait at least 6 to 12 months to heal before engaging in the glycolic acid peel.

Relative Exclusions

Relative exclusions to the glycolic acid peels are, as mentioned, active herpes simplex and facial warts. The concern here is the potential to spread the herpes virus to areas desquamated by the glycolic acid peel. Similarly, with the potential to spread molluscum contagiosum or facial planar warts by glycolic acid peeling, it may be wise to treat these conditions first, and then, after healing has taken place, to begin glycolic acid peels.

Patient Record: Glycolic Acid Peel

NAME: _____

ADDRESS: _____
_____

TELEPHONE NUMBER: _____

DATE							
Acid Concentration (%)							
Time In Minutes							
Erythema (0,1,2,3) *							
Discomfort (0 = None, 10 = Highest)							
Frosting (0,1,2,3) *							
Others							

* 0 = None, 1 = Mild, 2 = Moderate, 3 = Severe

HISTORY:
[ ] Prior Sensitivity [ ] Allergies [ ] Atopic Skin Reactions [ ] Eczema
[ ] Seborrheic Dermatitis [ ] Collagen Disease [ ] Autoimmune Disease [ ] Viral Infections
[ ] Medication Used _____

PRODUCTS/TREATMENT BEING USED:
[ ] Electrolysis [ ] Waxing [ ] Depilatories [ ] Masks
[ ] Prior Peel Dermabrasion [ ] Hair Dying Treatments [ ] Permanent Wave or Straightening Treatments
[ ] Tretinoin [ ] Loofa or other types of exfoliating sponge
Comments/Others: _____

EXCLUSIONS TO PEELS:
[ ] Active Herpes Simplex [ ] Recent Surgery (healing wounds)
[ ] Recent Radiation Treatment [ ] History of Hypertrophic or Keloidal Scarring
[ ] Warts [ ] Cryotherapy/Cryosurgery (within 1 month)
Comments/Others: _____

INDICATIONS FOR TREATMENT:
[ ] Skin Texture [ ] Skin Brilliance [ ] Mild Photodamage [ ] Skin Tone
[ ] Fine Wrinkles [ ] Pore Size [ ] Acne Scars [ ] Melasma
[ ] Surface Laxness [ ] Hyperpigmentation [ ] Benign Lentigines
[ ] Periorbital Solar Comedones [ ] Acne Adjunct To Acne Therapy
Other: _____

AREAS OF FACE THAT NEED IMPROVEMENT:
[ ] Forehead [ ] Cheeks [ ] Browline [ ] Mouth Lines [ ] Crows Feet
[ ] Chin
Other: _____

SPEED OF IMPROVEMENT NEEDED OR WANTED (TIME):
[ ] Within a month [ ] Within a few months [ ] Within six months
Comments: _____

AMOUNT OF TIME OUT OF CIRCULATION POSSIBLE
[ ] No time/back in your routine the day after the peel [ ] A few days, up to a week
Comments: _____

FIG. 1.

Other cosmetic treatment such as electrolysis, depilatories, hair removal and bleaching agents, waxing, masks, exfoliants, and loofahs should be discontinued 1 week prior to the peel for fear of disrupting the epidermal barrier. Those patients who are not dedicated to photoprotective behavior and reduction of photodamage should also be excluded from treatment.

PRE-PEEL INSTRUCTIONS AND PATIENT PREPARATION

After the patient has been screened and is thus a candidate for glycolic acid peels, he or she should be placed on a daily home glycolic acid preparation and the pre-peel instructions reviewed (Table 1). The glycolic acid pre-peel products are generally available from most companies in an 8% to 15% concentration. Initially, an 8% to 10% product can be used on the younger, less wrinkled, and less photoaged patient, whereas the 15% products may be given to the more wrinkled, more photoaged individual. Cream formulations are generally preferred by the older, dryer-skinned patient, while lotion formulations are preferred by a younger, less photoaged patient. Gel formulations are well accepted by oilier skin types. The product can be started nightly for the first week, then increased to twice daily as tolerated. If the patient has any unusual sensitivity to the glycolic acid, he or she should notify the physician. This prior preparation allows preliminary desquamation, which the patient may recognize as a fine flaking of the skin. Although rare, those few patients who are uncomfortable with the appearance of the desquamation should be dissuaded from the peel because of the potential for enhancement of this mild desquamation. In this author's experience, unusual sensitivity of the face to glycolic acid is rare.

Whenever possible, it is best to show the patient a series of photographs of other patients before, during, and after the procedure, demonstrating varying degrees of peeling. Some of the photographs can be obtained via the various glycolic acid peel manufacturers, but the physician is encouraged to collect his or her own photographs for the purpose of documentation. It is important to emphasize to the patient that the peel process is gradual and should be repeated at least monthly. In addition, the patient must be compliant with their use of the home glycolic acid products.

Upon completion of the pre-peel preparation, the patient should be instructed to arrive on the day of the peel with a clean face. Female patients should remove all cosmetics from their skin. Male patients should abstain from shaving on the peel day. A consent form should be signed and witnessed in the office before the actual procedure is undertaken. An example of such a consent form is provided (Fig. 2).

Peel Procedure: Materials and Preparation

The materials needed for a glycolic acid peel include 60-inch drape sheets; a fan-shaped brush, 2×2-inch gauze sponges, or a cotton-tipped swab or applicator; premoistened and frozen 4×4-inch gauze sponges; a small fan; a timer; a nylon bib; a shower cap or hair clips; dispensing cups; and ice water in a bowl or a water spray bottle. The patient should be instructed to remove his or her contact lenses before draping. The nylon bib should be placed around the patient's neck, the shower cap secured on the head, and the drape sheets wrapped around the neck. The patient should lie back on the table with the head slightly elevated (Fig. 3). The skin should first be cleansed thoroughly. The physician should do an overall inspection of the areas to be peeled, noting any abrasions, areas of dry skin, or possible irritation. Petrolatum should then be applied sparingly to the lateral and medial canthi of the eyes, the nasal alae, the nasolabial creases, the outer commissures of the lips, and also the lips themselves (Fig. 4). This is done to protect potential pooling sites from extra glycolic acid solution. The fan should be turned on and directed at the patient's face to keep the area being treated cool. The patient may also be offered a hand-held fan so they may assist in this process.

TABLE 1. *Pre–glycolic acid peel instructions*

1. Avoid extensive sun exposure. Apply sunscreen as part of your daily skin care regimen before routine exposure to daylight.
2. Two weeks prior to your peel you should begin your regimen of glycolic acid product used twice a day.
3. For one week prior to the peel, please STOP using the following treatments and products:
   Electrolysis
   Waxing
   Depilatories
   Masks
   Other peels for dermabrasion
   Hair dyeing treatments
   Permanent wave or straightening treatments
   Tretinoin (Retin-A)
   Loofah or other types of sponges
   The use of these products/treatments prior to your peel may increase the reactivity of the skin to glycolic acid.
4. We have reviewed your medical history and discussed the following areas:
   Allergies
   Collagen disease/autoimmune disease
   Viral infections
   History of atopic skin reactions, eczema
   Medications used
   Tobacco use
   Sun sensitivity
   Seborrheic dermatitis
   If there is any additional information in these areas that has not been discussed, please contract me prior to your peel. As a reminder, if you do have a history of herpes simplex (cold sores), you should be on preventative medication. The peel procedure can induce an episode of herpes lesions in patients who have had them previously.
5. On the day of the peel, please come to the office with a fully *cleaned* face. If possible, no makeup, cologne, or aftershave should be applied. Additionally, you should avoid shaving on the day of the peel if possible.

I, _____, consent to the treatment known as a glycolic acid chemical peel. The treatment has been explained to me, and I have had the opportunity to ask questions. The procedure may cause swelling of my face or _____ (body site treated) that may be uncomfortable. The procedure may cause my skin to appear red and peel like a sunburn. During and after the procedure, the following may be experienced: stinging, itching, burning, mild pain, tightness, peeling, and scabbing of the superficial layer of the skin. These sensations will gradually diminish over the course of 1 week as the skin returns to its normal appearance. However, some patients may react differently. For example, in some cases, the skin may be uncomfortable and look like a very bad sunburn. The peeling usually lasts about 3 to 7 days, although it may last longer.

I understand that there is a risk (although small) of developing a temporary or permanent pigment (color) change in the skin. There is a small incidence of the reactivation of "cold sores" (herpes infection) in patients with a prior history of herpes. There also is a rare incidence of a flare of acne-like lesions after the peel. There is a rare incidence of scarring. I have been given a copy of the post---glycolic acid peel instructions and have reviewed them.

_____   _____
Patient's Signature (or Guardian)   Date

_____
Patient's Name (please print)

_____
Witness

FIG. 2.

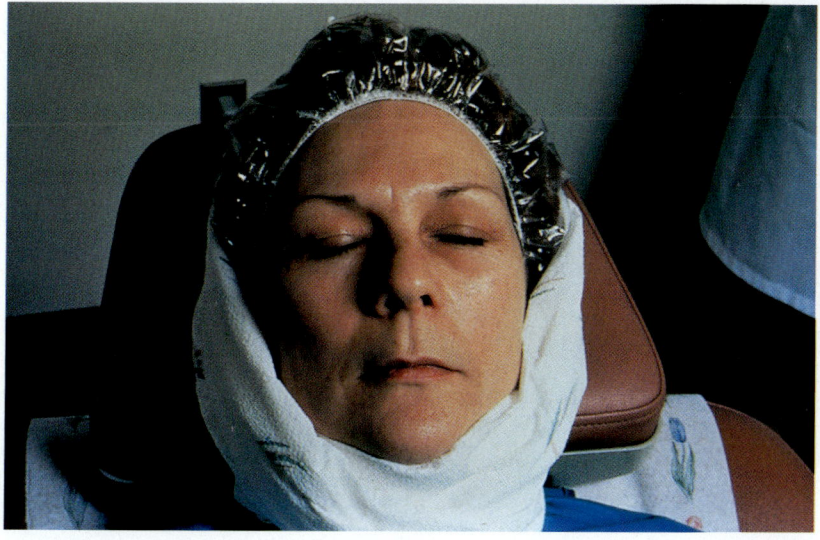

FIG. 3.

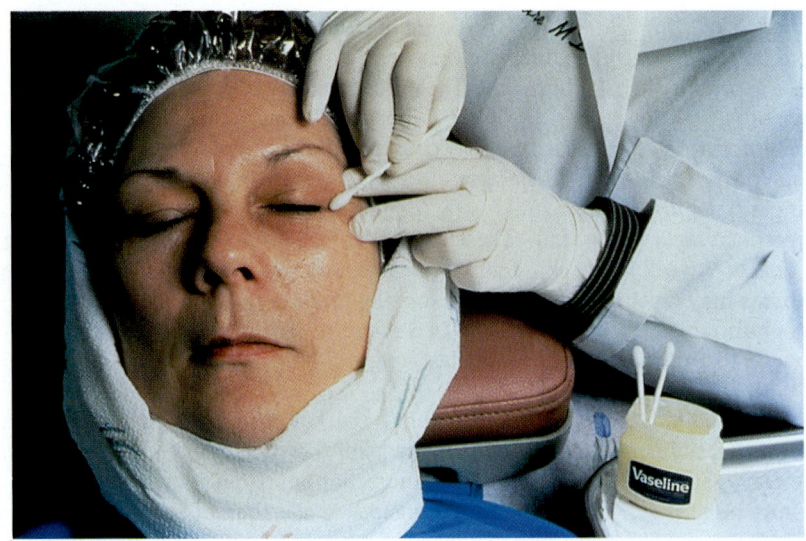

FIG. 4.

THE PEEL PROCEDURE

The physician should always start the patient on a 20% glycolic acid preparation. This peel may be thought of as a diagnostic, baseline peel. Approximately 2 ml of the glycolic acid solution is transferred into a small dispensing cup. The glycolic acid solution may be applied with a fan-shaped brush, with a cotton-tipped swab or applicator, with a gauze sponge, or by finger massage with a gloved hand (Figs. 5–7). As soon as the glycolic acid touches the skin, the timer is turned on. The entire application should take place within a 30-second interval. The acid is then allowed to remain in contact with the skin until erythema erupts abruptly. The duration of the first peel should be approximately 2 to 5 minutes while watching for this erythema. This time interval may be decreased or extended, depending on the patient's reaction and comfort level during the procedure, which may be assessed by asking him or her to rate the discomfort on a scale of 0 to 10 (10 being the greatest degree of discomfort). If the patient verbalizes a level of 8 to 10 at any time during the procedure, the peel should be terminated immediately. In addition, if at any time during the peel blanching is noticed (epidermolysis), the glycolic acid should be neutralized and rinsed off with cool water.

Applications should be started at the forehead and continued to the cheeks, the chin, and then the nose. Patients should keep their eyes closed throughout the entire procedure. The solution must be carefully applied around the upper lip to avoid drippage into the nasal cavity. Continuous reapplication of the acid can be performed without fear of enhanced penetration. The solution should be applied sparingly around the closed eyes. If the solution should enter the eye, immedi-

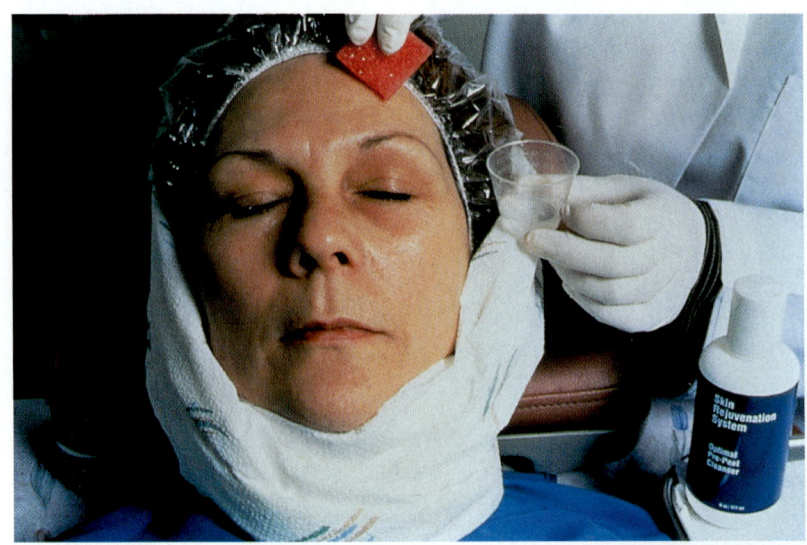

FIG. 5.

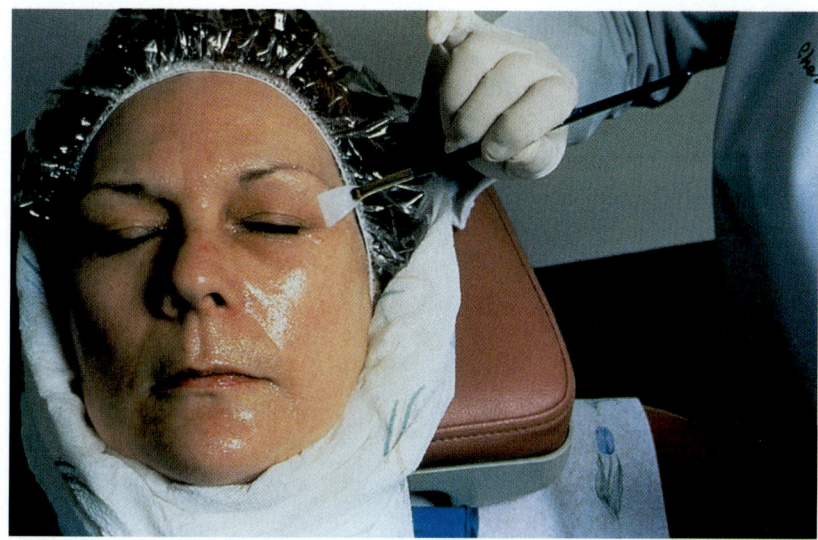

FIG. 6.

ate flushing with water is recommended. The sensation of glycolic acid in the eye is akin to lemon juice in the same location. To date, no untoward effect has been report with this occurrence. Nevertheless, the flushing with water does quell this sensation.

The endpoint of the glycolic acid peel is a resultant even erythema throughout the areas treated. The onset of epidermolysis or frosting or blanching should be noted and the reaction stopped. If the 20% concentration is tolerated on the skin for 5 minutes, then a subsequent peel should begin with the next higher concentration, but then a shorter time of exposure is recommended. Once this concentration is maximized at 5 minutes, the next higher concentration is chosen for the subsequent peel.

To initiate termination of the procedure, the closed eyes should be covered with damp 2×2-inch gauze sponges (Fig. 8). The glycolic acid can be neutralized with a bicarbonated solution, which abruptly ends further action of any remaining free acid. A noticeable foaming reaction occurs when the bicarbonate neutralizer hits the acidified skin. Patient may at this time verbalize that their pain or discomfort level has been enhanced; this lasts for approximately 15 seconds, and it can be quelled with chilled water sprayed onto the skin. When the foaming ceases, neutralization is complete. The treated area may then be covered with prefrozen 4×4-inch gauze sponges (Fig. 9). This provides additional relief from any residual sensations of burning, stinging, or discomfort. The patient will usually feel comfortable within 1 minute of such application. At this point, the sponges can be removed, the petrolatum wiped off, and the face or cosmetic unit dried

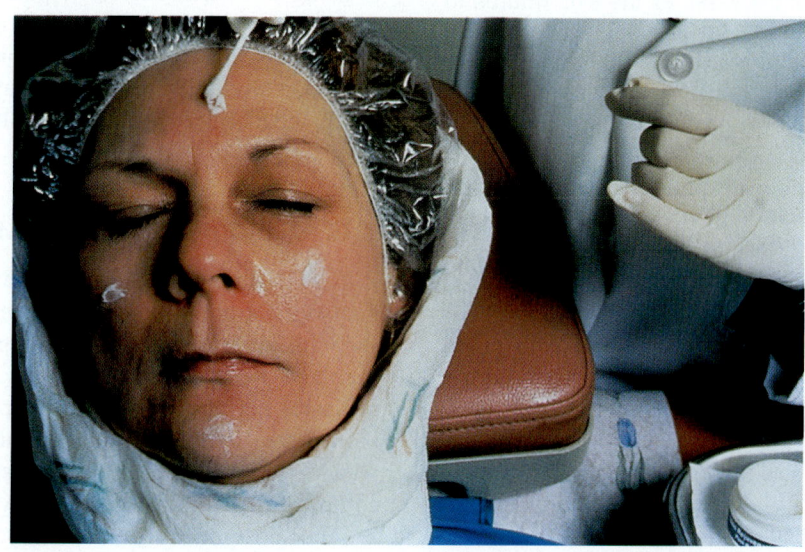

FIG. 7.

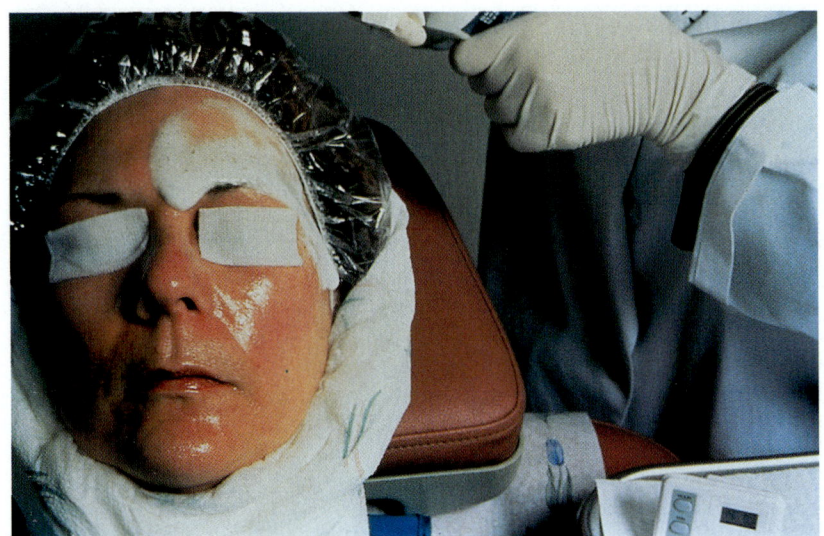

FIG. 8.

with the drape sheet. If the patient reports any continued areas of burning or stinging, the bicarbonated neutralizer may be sprayed again until the sensation has ceased.

POSTPEEL TREATMENT AND INSTRUCTIONS

A postpeel, glycolic acid–free moisturizer is then applied. It is recommended that the home glycolic acid preparations be avoided until the skin returns to normal appearance. This may take 3 to 7 days after the procedure, and for that period only the glycolic acid–free moisturizer is to be used. The patient is also instructed not to use any retinoids on the skin during this recovery period. The patient is told to expect postpeel tightness in the first 24 hours and possibly some degree of erythema. The patient should be instructed not to apply makeup for the first 24 hours and to avoid sun exposure. If edema, stinging, tingling, burning, itching, or persistent erythema is experienced, the patient is instructed to apply cool or ice-water compresses over the next 24 to 48 hours until these sensations subside. If epidermolysis has occurred during the procedure, the patient is told that the skin will scab within 7 to 10 days. It is usually unnecessary to use topical hydrocortisone after the peel unless edema or epidermolysis has occurred. At this time, the patient should be given the postpeel instructions (Table 2). In addition, sunscreens may be used, and they are encouraged if the patient is going to be outdoors. The patient is admonished not to peel, pick, or exfoliate the skin in any way. If the patient is having any significant discomfort, it is advised that the physician monitor the patient at that time. The patient is then instructed to schedule a return for the subsequent peel within 4 weeks.

TABLE 2. *Post–glycolic acid peel instructions*

It may take up to 1 week for the appearance of your skin to return to normal. During the repair/renewal period, you may or may not experience some of the following: stinging, itching, burning, mild pain, tightness, and peeling and scabbing of the superficial layer of the skin. These sensations will gradually diminish over the course of the week as the skin returns to its normal appearance. If swelling occurs, use ice-water compresses intermittently for 24–48 hours, as needed.

Following these guidelines will help accelerate the renewal process:
1. Apply the postpeel emollient twice daily for 3–7 days until the skin returns to its normal appearance. Then restart your maintenance regimen of glycolic acid.
2. Wash the treated area very gently.
3. Do not use abrasive or exfoliating sponges on the treated area.
4. Avoid extensive sun exposure.
5. Continue to apply sunscreen, as tolerated, beginning the day after the procedure.
6. To avoid possibility of scarring, please DO NOT:
   Peel the skin
   Pick the skin
   Scrape the skin
   Scratch the skin
   Use a mask on the skin
7. Please call if you have any questions or comments.

THE ROLE OF THE NURSE/AESTHETICIAN

The nurse or aesthetician can maximize the use of the dermatologist's time in a cosmetic dermatologic practice. The assistant can be responsible for preparation by properly draping the patient, cleansing the skin, and protecting potential occlusion sites as mentioned with petrolatum. The physician is then free to perform the peel and neutralize the process when the peel is completed. The assistant can apply the cold compresses and moisturizer to advance the patient's recovery. The postpeel instructions may then be reinforced by the assistant.

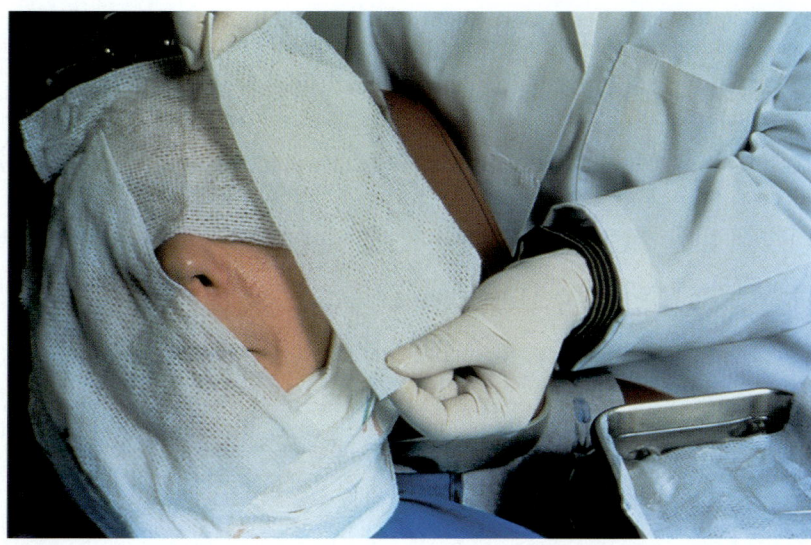
FIG. 9.

PITFALLS AND ADVERSE REACTIONS

If a patient has not discontinued the use of all topical retinoids before the peel, there is a risk of enhanced penetration of the glycolic acid. This can result in unexpected epidermolysis, and it therefore increases the postpeel recovery time by 7 to 10 days. The patient must be instructed regarding this event and informed that a deeper peel and scabbing can occur. If this does happen, the physician should encourage the patient to prolong the use of a glycolic acid–free moisturizer. The physician may recommend topical hydrocortisone, and, in cases when periocular and perioral edema is severe, oral steroids may be needed. It may also be necessary to begin the patient on oral antiviral agents as well as oral antibiotics, particularly in patients with a history of recurrent herpes simplex. In general, severe edema and erythema are quelled by the use of oral steroids if given early.

Another adverse reaction of a peel may occur if a vigorous rubbing or abrasive technique is used to apply the glycolic acid to the skin. If this should happen, then the same reactions may occur, including enhanced erythema and edema. The same postpeel instructions would be applicable as mentioned. The risk here is of hypo- or hyperpigmentation occurring in the scrubbed sites, and this must be monitored by careful follow-up. Another possible risk is the eruption of acneiform papules periorally and in particular on the chin. This perioral dermatitis has been observed in a few patients, and it is resolved with topical or oral antibiotics. If the chin/perioral area is protected, a glycolic acid peel may be performed on these patients in the other cosmetic units such as the cheeks, nose, and forehead. Although rare, a physical urticaria has been seen immediately after the peel on the treated sites. This generally resolves within 24 hours without additional treatment.

CONCLUSION

Glycolic acid, although used over the past two decades, has only recently become popular. The benefits of glycolic acid peels are finding broader application not only in cosmetic improvement of the skin, but also in improvement of skin disorders such as acne, rosacea, melasma, and keratosis pilaris, as well as others mentioned earlier. This chapter has outlined a method by which glycolic acid peels may be performed, the indications, applications, and various formulations that are available today. It is expected that further uses of glycolic acid peels will be developed, and so it is hoped that this fundamental information is useful to the reader. The usefulness of this technique for alleviating the signs of photoaging, as well as other potential benefits for skin disorders, makes the future of glycolic acid peels exciting.

SUGGESTED READINGS

Bartolone J, Santhanam U, Penska C, Lang B, Anthony J. Alpha hydroxy acids modulate skin cell biology. *Poster presentation, SID,* Chicago, IL, May 1996.

Bernstein EF, Van Scott EJ, Yu RJ, Lakkakorpi J, Ditre CM, Uitto JJ. A pilot investigation of the effects of citric acid on viable epidermal thickness and dermal glycosaminoglycans. *Poster presentation, SID,* Chicago, IL, May 18–24, 1996.

Briden ME, Kakita LS, Petratos MA, Rendon-Pellerano MI. Treatment of acne with glycolic acid. *J Geriatr Dermatol* 1996;4:22–27.

Briden ME, Rendon-Pellerano MI. Treatment of rosacea with glycolic acid. *J Geriatr Dermatol* 1996;4:17–21.

Clark CP. Alpha hydroxy acids in skin care. *Clin Plast Surg* 1996;23: 49–56.

Costello EJ, Filchone EM. Preparation and properties of pure ammonium DL lactate. *J Am Chem Soc* 1953;75:1242–1422.

Ditre CM, Griffin TD, Murphy GF et al. The effects of alpha-hydroxy acids on photoaged skin: a pilot histological and ultrastructural study. *J Am Acad Dermatol* 1996;34:187–195.

Ditre CM, et al. Introduction: practical use of glycolic acid as a chemical peeling agent. *J Geriatr Dermatol* 1996;4:2–7.

Greaves MW. Topical alpha-hydroxy acid derivatives for relieving dry itching skin. *Cosmetic Toil* 1991;105:61.

Griffin TD, Van Scott EJ. Case of pyruvic acid in the treatment of actinic keratoses: a clinical and histopathological study. *Cutis* 1991;47: 325–329.

Kakita LS, Petratos MA. The use of glycolic acid in Asian and darker skin types. *J Geriatr Dermatol* 1996;4:8–11.

Keenan WF. Comparative efficacy of two different formulations on xerosis [letter]. *J Am Acad Dermatol* 1990;23:769–770.

Klaus MV, Wehy RF, Rogers RS 3rd et al. Evaluation of ammonium lactate in the treatment of seborrheic keratoses. *J Am Acad Dermatol* 1990;22:199–203.

Lavker RM, Kaidbey K, Leyden JJ. Effects of topical ammonium lactate on cutaneous atrophy from a potent topical corticosteroid. *J Am Acad Dermatol* 1992;25:535–544.

MacEachern L, Rensjers K, Dickens M. The percutaneous absorption of glycolic acid in human skin. *Poster presentation, SID*, Chicago, IL, May 1996.

Perricone NV. An alpha hydroxy acid acts as an antioxidant. *J Geriatr Dermatol* 1993;1:101–104.

Piacquadio D, Dobry M, Hunt S et al. Short contact 70% glycolic acid peels as a treatment for photodamaged skin. A pilot study. *J Dermatol Surg* 1996;22:449–452.

Rendon-Pellerano MI, Bernstein EF. The use of glycolic acid in the management of xerosis and photoaging. *J Geriatr Dermatol* 1996;4:12–16.

Ridge JM, Siegle RJ, Zuckerman J. Use of alpha hydroxy acids in the therapy for 'photoaged' skin. *J Am Acad Dermatol* 1990;23:932.

Sakaki S, et al. Application of MTT test for screening of cell growth activators. Evaluation of alpha-hydroxy acids. *J Soc Cosmetic Chem* 1993;27:116–119.

Siskin SB, Quinlan PJ, Finkelstein MS et al. The effects of ammonium lactate 12% lotion vs. no therapy in the treatment of dry skin of the heels. *Int J Dermatol* 1993;32:905–907.

Smith HF, et al. *J Individ Hyg Toxicol* 1941;23:259.

Smith W. Hydroxy acids and skin aging. *Soap Cosm Chem Spec* 1993;9:55–76.

Stern EC. Topical application of lactic acid in the treatment and prevention of certain disorders of the skin. *Urol Cutan Rev* 1946;50:106–107.

Stiller MJ, Bartolone J, Stern R et al. Topical 8% glycolic acid and 8% lactic acid reams for the treatment of photodamaged skin: a double-blind vehicle-controlled clinical trial. *Arch Dermatol* 1996;132:631–636.

Takahashi M, et al. The influence of hydroxy acids on the theological properties of stratum corneum. *J Soc Cosmetic Chem* 1985;36:177–187.

Van Scott EJ. The unfolding therapeutic uses of the alpha hydroxy acids. *Mediguide to Dermatology* 1988;3:1–5.

Van Scott EJ. Alpha hydroxy acids: procedures for use in clinical practice. *Cutis* 1989;43:222–228.

Van Scott EJ, Yu RJ. Control of keratinization with α-hydroxy acids and related compounds. I. Topical treatment of ichthyotic disorders. *Arch Dermatol* 1974;110:586–590.

Van Scott EJ, Yu RJ. Modulation of keratinization with alpha hydroxy acids and related compounds. In: Frost P, Comez EC, Zaias N, eds. *Recent advances in dermatopharmacology*. New York: Spectrum, 1978:211–217.

Van Scott EJ, Yu RJ. Substances that modify the stratum corneum by modulating its formation. In: Frost P, Horwitz SN, eds. *Principles of cosmetics for the dermatologist*. St. Louis: CV Mosby, 1982:7–74.

Van Scott EJ, Yu RJ. Hyperkeratinization, corneocyte cohesion and alpha hydroxy acids. *J Am Acad Dermatol* 1984;11:867–879.

Van Scott EJ, Yu RJ. Alpha hydroxy acids: therapeutic potentials. *Can J Dermatol* 1989;1:108–112.

Van Scott EJ, Yu RJ. Alpha hydroxy acids: science and therapeutic use. *Cosmet Dermatol* 1994;7(10S):12–20.

5

Medium-Depth Chemical Peeling with TCA, Optionally Preceded by Solid CO_2

Harold J. Brody

The evolution of the medium-depth peel with trichloroacetic acid (TCA) has evolved over the last 50 years in dermatologic surgery. In the past 10 years, combinations of superficial agents have made high-strength TCA peeling unnecessary. The deepest of these combinations is easy to perform and illustrated in this chapter.

Medium-depth chemical peeling or chemical resurfacing is defined as the application of a wounding agent, or agents, to produce an initial dermal wound, usually in the upper reticular dermis. The application is usually performed as a single procedure to achieve one or two of four goals: the removal of actinic keratoses or mild actinic rhytides, the resolution of pigmentary dyschromias, and the flattening of depressed scars. They may be repeated approximately every 6 to 12 months, based on the amount of actinic damage still remaining or recurring after the peel, or for continued scar effacement. Traditionally, the classic peel for this depth category was the 50% TCA peel, used extensively for three decades as the classic peel for the patient who did not warrant, tolerate, or desire a "phenol peel." The Baker-Gordon phenol peel penetrates deeper than the classic 50% TCA peel. TCA, however, is an agent that is likely to produce increased scarring with higher concentrations. Insulting the epidermis with a refrigerant allows a less potent concentration of TCA, such as 35%, to penetrate to the depth of a higher-strength 50% solution, but with a greater degree of safety.

If one wishes to penetrate only through the epidermis to the upper papillary dermis, a more superficial 35% TCA peel alone may be performed. Though this example illustrates the deeper combination peel, the application and defatting technique for the single-agent peel is the same.

Solid carbon dioxide (CO_2), or dry ice, at a temperature of −78.5°C, does not usually induce scarring or hypopigmentation and therefore has a wider margin of safety than liquid nitrogen when combined with TCA. With a long history of safety as a single agent in the last 75 years, this freezing agent is a reliable modality to use with TCA for combination medium-depth chemical resurfacing. Over 4000 combination peels using CO_2 and TCA confirm its safety.

PREOPERATIVE EVALUATION

Before a wounding agent or technique is selected, patients should sign a consent form. Informed consent rests on good communication and joint decision-making between physician and patient. The consent should tell the patient about the postoperative course and the risks of pigmentary change, scarring, herpes simplex, bacterial infection, and the onset of postpeel acne. Patients should understand that results cannot be guaranteed and that they must avoid direct sun as much as possible after peeling. They should be judged to have reasonable expectations and to be mentally stable to withstand the peel and the postoperative period. The patient should not have had cosmetic undermining surgery within 3 months of the peel. Pregnancy and oral contraceptives may increase the risk of pigmentary return after peeling. A history of herpes simplex needs prophylactic acyclovir or valacyclovir beginning on the day of the peel.

Fitzpatrick's skin classification gives a measure of pigmentary responsiveness of the skin to ultraviolet light and, many times, an ethnic origin. Skin types I to III are ideal for peeling of all varieties, but type IV skin can be peeled also. If the patient has an eye color other than brown, for example, green, light brown, or blue, the likelihood of postinflammatory pigmentation is less. Types V and VI can also be peeled with TCA alone, but the combination of CO_2 and TCA is not indicated for these skin types. We perform test spots at the hairline on patients who are at greatest risk (skin types V and VI), but this is no assurance that the remainder of the face will respond identically.

Assessment of the degree of sun damage is essential to the

examination and evaluation prior to peeling. Glogau has developed a classification of photoaging that is helpful in assessing sun damage in patients with and without a history of sebaceous gland activity or acne. One cannot generalize, treating groups I and II, neither of which contain wrinkles at rest, with superficial or medium-depth peels, and treating groups III and IV, which contain moderate and severe wrinkles, respectively, with medium-depth or deep peels. Some patients have scarring in the absence of sun damage or sun damage in the absence of scarring, and this may affect the choice of the type of medium-depth peel procedure. Every cosmetic unit of the skin (the perioral, periorbital, cheek, forehead, and nasal areas) should be individually assessed to determine which peeling agent or procedure is necessary for best correction of the area without undue risk.

The woman in Figures 1 and 2 has a Fitzpatrick III, Glogau Photoaging II skin type. Her chief problem is melasma and sun-induced splotchy pigmentation on the cheeks and forehead. She was peeled previously with two coats of Jessner's solution twice on a monthly basis and treated with 4% hydroquinone gel and tretinoin without success. Because of this darker skin type, her melasma will return after peeling without proper sunscreens and proper prescriptive cream application after the procedure. A sunscreen with a sun protection factor (SPF) of 15 is adequate for use in the morning on a daily basis. Purpose (SPF 15, Johnson and Johnson) is ideal. A compounded bleach formula (Table 1) will be helpful. There is no evidence that application of bleach prior to the peel will make a difference in the return of pigment afterwards. It will, however, be easier for the patient to return to a cream that she has used before and that she knows her skin will tolerate.

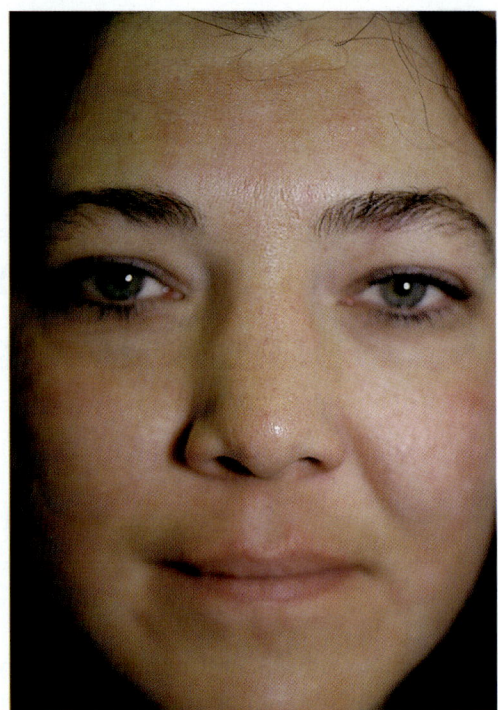

FIG. 2.

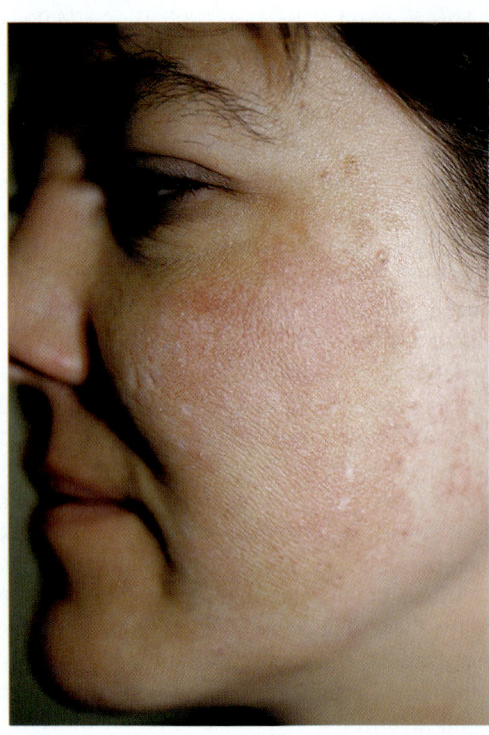

FIG. 1.

This bleach for darker skin types contains tretinoin (all-*trans*-retinoic acid) which promotes faster healing in the immediate postpeel period if used for about a month prior to peeling. Topical tretinoin also potentiates the action of hydroquinone. Tretinoin application before and after TCA does not significantly enhance the efficacy of the peel.

Hydroquinone affects the melanocyte system by decreasing the formation and increasing the degradation of melanosomes. It also inhibits tyrosinase. Hydroquinone interferes only with the formation of new melanin. The production of melanin is resumed when treatment with the drug is discontinued. Resumption of usage as soon as tolerable after reepi-

TABLE 1. *Bleaching formula for darker skin types*

Hydroquinone	6%
Ascorbic acid	0.05%
Retinoic acid	0.1%
Propylene glycol	4%
Hytone cream	2.5%, 30 g

Dissolve the crystals in propylene glycol, mix with the cream, and apply twice a day.

The initial concentration of hydroquinone is 6%. This may be increased if pigmentation returns after peeling. Ascorbic acid prevents the hydroquinone from oxidizing. Hytone (hydrocortisone) cream (Dermik) is paraben-free. Creams with higher concentrations of hydroquinone should be discontinued as soon as the appropriate amount of pigment loss is achieved to avoid paradoxical hypopigmentation.

This cream may be ordered from Medical Center Pharmacy, Tampa, FL. Its potency decreases after 2 months.

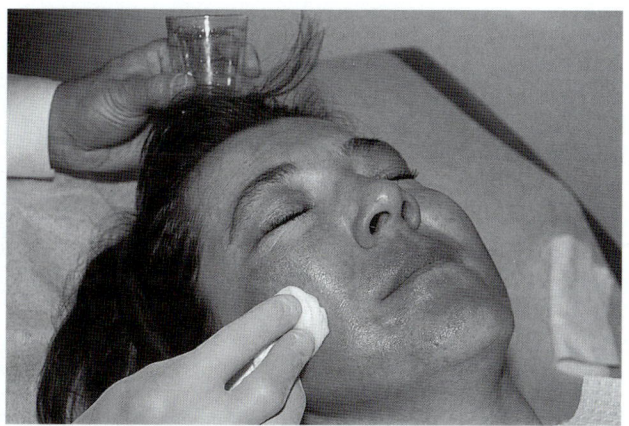

FIG. 19.

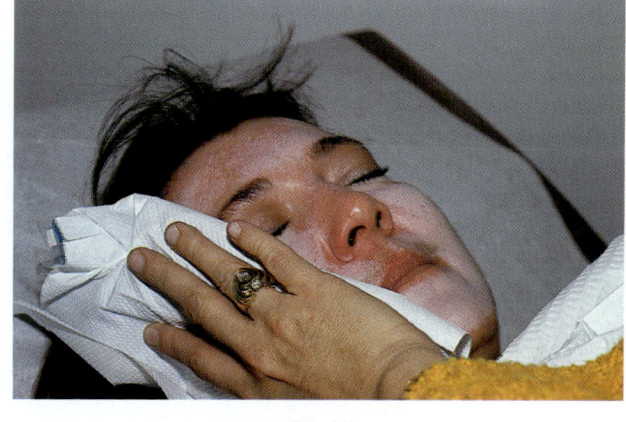

FIG. 22.

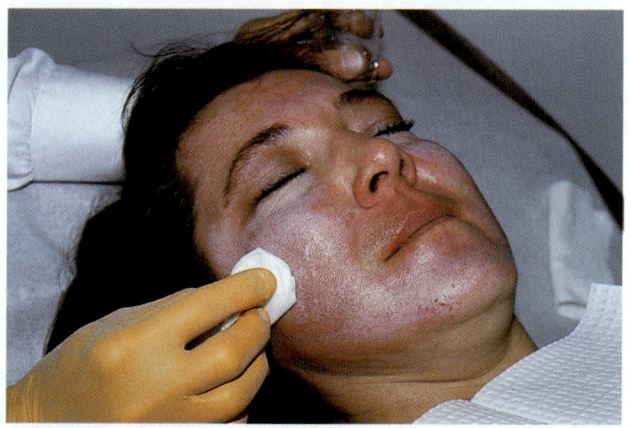

FIG. 20.

est ease for the physician and the best tolerance for the patient, because of the inevitable progressive squirming for 1 to 2 minutes while frosting is occurring (Fig. 20). Peeling does not affect hair follicles or hair growth. Careful application of the solution into the hairline and around the angle of the mandible conceals the line of demarcation between nonpeeled and peeled skin.

Gel icepacks covered with a paper towel can be applied to ease the patient's discomfort as soon as frosting has resulted in a light white color of the skin (Fig. 21). The patient can assist in holding these in place (Fig. 22). Many times, the sebaceous nature of the hairline requires continual application and rubbing to achieve whitening (Fig. 23). The fan is still helpful for patient tolerance (Figs. 24, 25). Earlobes should be peeled to maximize visual results (Fig. 26). If any areas were inadvertently left uncoated, they may be inspected and treated (Fig. 27). Fifty percent TCA can be applied to treat individual scar rims (Fig. 28). Having the patient sit up as promptly as possible breaks the reclining position that the patient identifies with the most pain and signifies a conclusion to the procedure as part of a continual soothing and reassuring "talkesthesia" (Fig. 29).

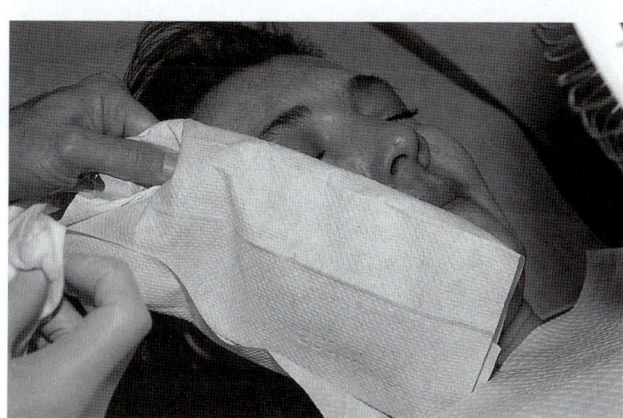

FIG. 21.

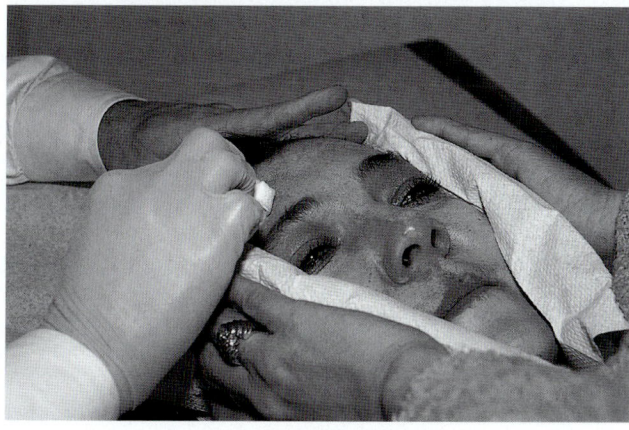

FIG. 23.

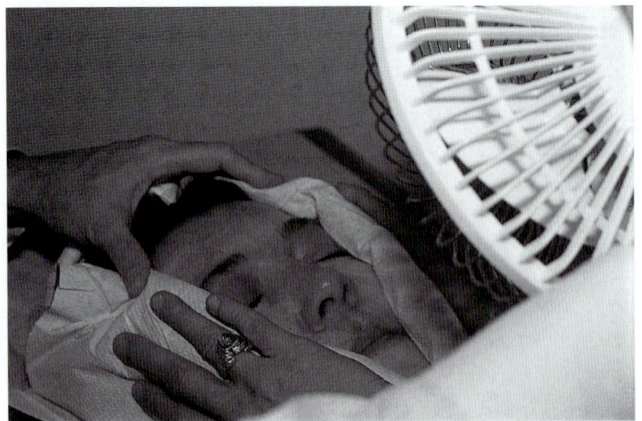

FIG. 24.

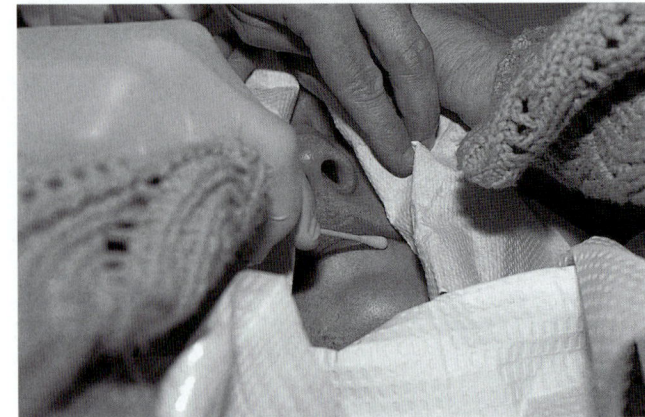

FIG. 27.

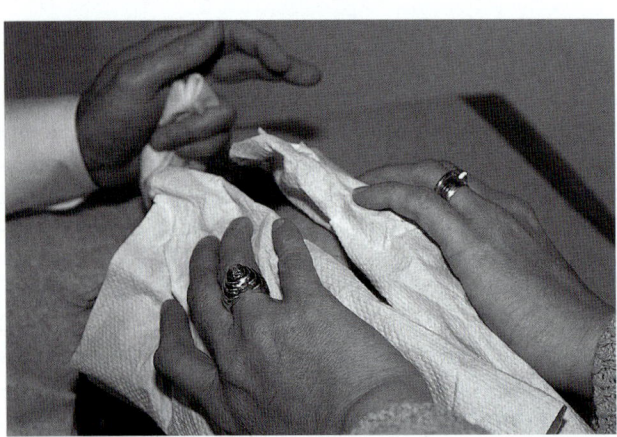

FIG. 25.

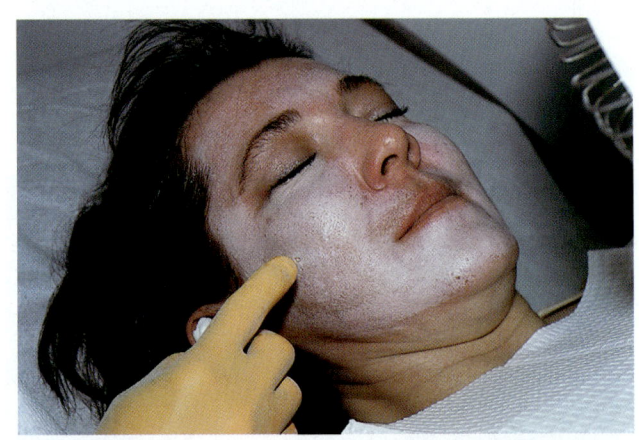

FIG. 28.

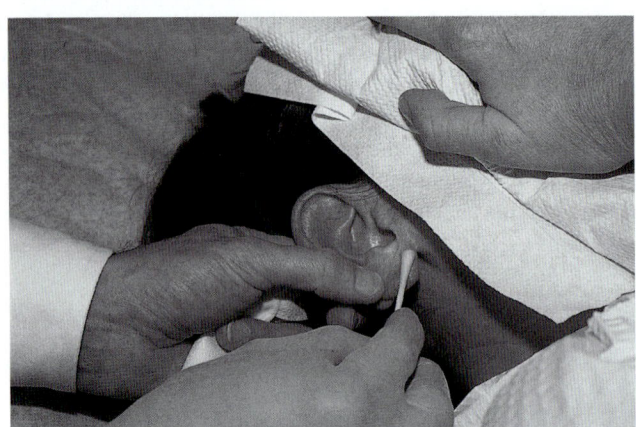

FIG. 26.

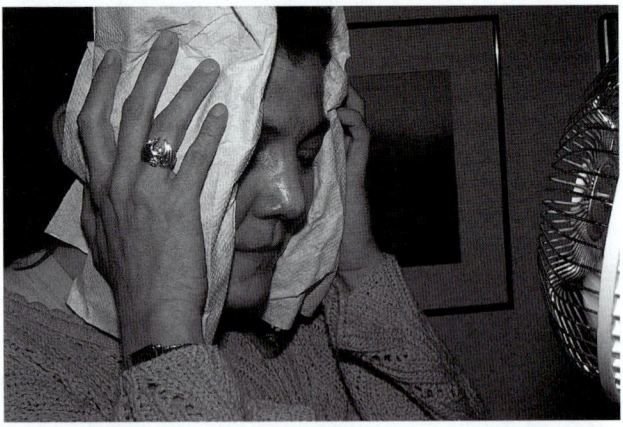

FIG. 29.

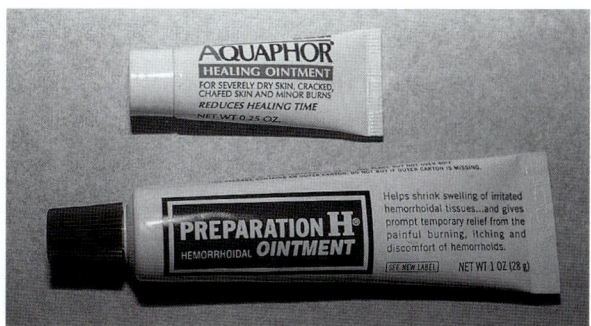

FIG. 30.

The burning sensation that accompanies the application of the TCA not only is lessened by the pretreatment with CO_2, but it also can be minimized by the immediate application of an ice pack or cold gel pack (3M) after adequate frosting has occurred. Most patients are uncomfortable for 3 minutes or less, no longer. No aqueous solutions are applied, to avoid inadvertent dilution, and after 5 minutes, a soothing petrolatum-based emollient such as Vaseline, Aquaphor, or Preparation H (Fig. 30) can be utilized. The nurse initially applies it to the patient's skin (Fig. 31).

There are important things to notice about the frost. The endpoint (solid white frost) is associated histologically with penetration into the papillary dermis. The skin turns progressively *thin pale white*, then *white*, and then *solid white*. A predictable exact estimation of depth cannot be appreciated from the color or from palpation, although the progression to stronger colors may certainly indicate increasing penetration. If an exact judgment were possible, scarring might be reduced or eliminated. If several shades of white remain in the skin after 5 to 10 minutes, the decision may be made to return to the light white areas and reapply TCA. This results in increased protein coagulation and wounding. If the assumption is made that initial solution application did occur in these lighter areas, reapplication is usually not necessary, and the clinical result will be typically even and excellent as expected for this generally safe wounding agent. Forcing uptake by continued reapplication in an area of increased photodamage is acceptable in the treatment of actinic keratoses or scarring, for example, but for photopigmentation or rhytides, reapplication may engender greater risk of complications. As a general rule, the production of the typical very white frost of 35% TCA is not associated with long-term complications.

Frosting by TCA depends on the preexisting photodamaged status of the skin, the choice of applicator, and the adequacy of defatting. TCA exhibits a distinctive white frost unique to the chemical. Observation of the frost itself as a measure of depth is not as valuable as the actual selection of proper wounding technique or wounding agent. The appearance of the frost does give an index of how evenly the agent has been applied. If the skin is treated first with tretinoin or AHAs, or if the corneal layer has been stripped with acetone or alcohol, the frosting and uniformity of application will be faster. If not, the frosting or penetration will be slower and more variable. Either way, absorption will occur because photodamage itself is not a barrier to wounding agents.

Continual application or overcoating of solution after the color endpoint has been reached will result in deeper penetration and increased risk of complications. Cessation of application before the frosting endpoint is reached is quite acceptable and may be desired especially if a "freshening peel" concept is desired with superficial or medium-depth agents.

The old concept of "neutralization" of TCA with alcohol or water immediately after frosting is useless to reverse the immediate effect of the application of the wounding agent. Once frosting has occurred, penetration is already achieved. Adding water to an aqueous wounding agent on the skin prior to frosting is actually dilution and will affect the concentration and reproducibility of the peel. "Neutralizing" TCA is outdated, and the term is a misnomer.

After 10 minutes when the patient is again comfortable, the entire face or local areas may be electively retreated with 35% TCA if actinic keratoses or local acne-scarred areas are considerable. Medium-depth neck peeling is unpredictable and may not yield consistently good results. Multiple superficial repetitive 20% to 35% TCA peelings, without CO_2, monthly or every several months is a more consistently reliable treatment for mobile areas such as the neck that can easily scar.

The patient should be given postpeel instructions that informs him or her not to pick at the peeling skin (Table 2). Soaking in the shower or over the sink with water, optionally mixed with a dilute solution of povidone-iodine skin cleanser, followed by the application of a soothing ointment

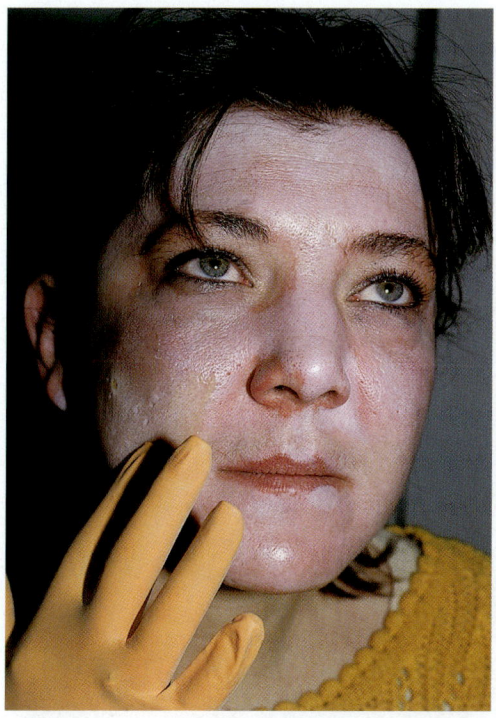

FIG. 31.

TABLE 2. *Postpeel instructions*

You have been peeled with chemicals that may cause water blisters that may break, crust, turn brown and peel off over a period of a week.

Washing with a mild soap (e.g., Dove) and generic povidone-iodine skin cleanser at least twice daily is necessary to prevent any infection. Use your fingertips and not a Buf-Puf, since the skin is very sensitive at this time. Vaseline, Aquaphor, Preparation H, or another moisturizer suggested by your physician should be used during this week all over the face after washing and soaking. Do not pick at the peeled skin.

Three aspirin or ibuprofen are to be taken 3 to 4 times daily to reduce swelling.

Total sunblock and a hat should be used to prevent hyperpigmentation immediately after healing.

Your prescription creams can be applied after the first week, but your skin will be more sensitive than usual.

If pain begins, which may signal a fever blister, call us immediately.

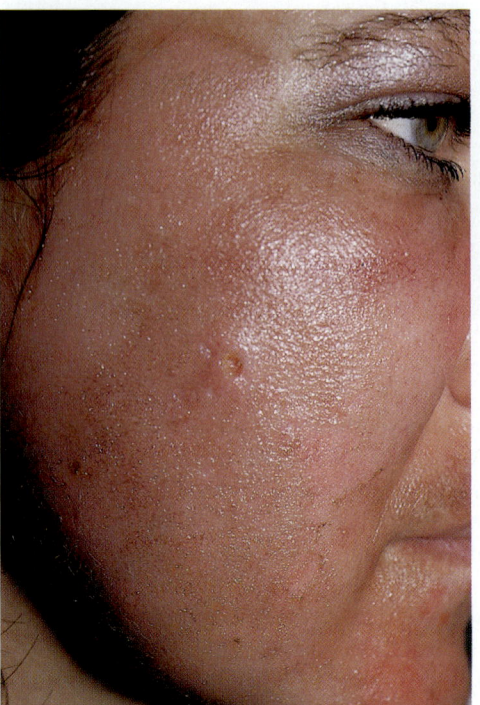

FIG. 33.

at least three times daily is required. Overgreasing may produce acne lesions during healing and should dictate a change in ointment. However, healing is more rapid if under an ointment base from the onset.

Aspirin or ibuprofen can be taken three to four times daily to reduce swelling. If pain is experienced, we suspect herpes unless proven otherwise, and the patient should contact the physician.

An hour after the original frost, erythema appears and changes to a brownish hue. Considerable edema is present during the first 48 hours (Fig. 32). Vesiculation is especially noticed around the scar on the right cheek (Fig. 33). Discomfort is relatively mild to minimal. After several days when the edema partially resolves, a crust forms. Crust separation generally begins between the 4th and 8th postoperative days and is completed usually by day 8. At day 6 after peeling, the crust on the patient in Figure 34 has not completely separated from the entire face, but it will do so by day 9. The patient is encouraged to minimize crusting by washing twice daily with antiseptic compresses and then applying the soothing Aquaphor ointment.

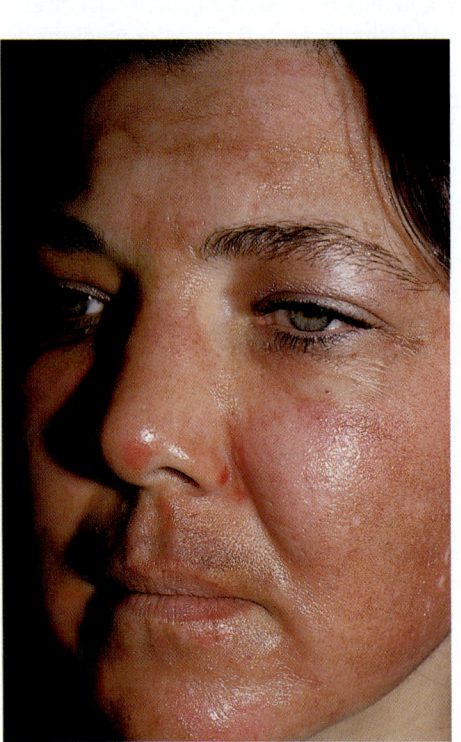

FIG. 32.

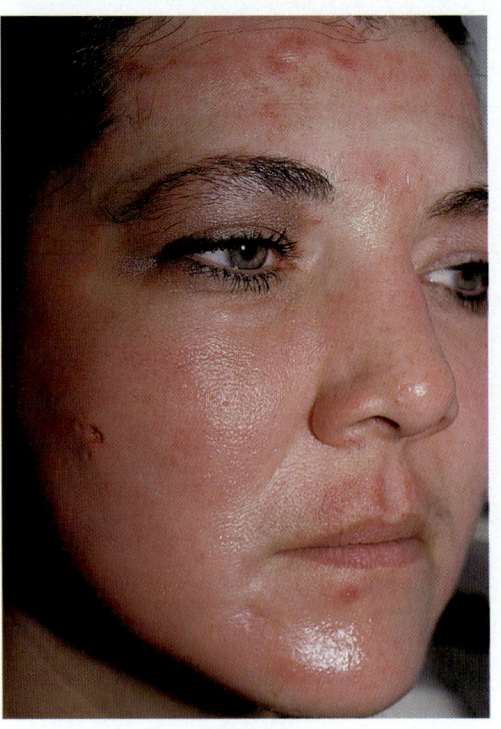

FIG. 34.

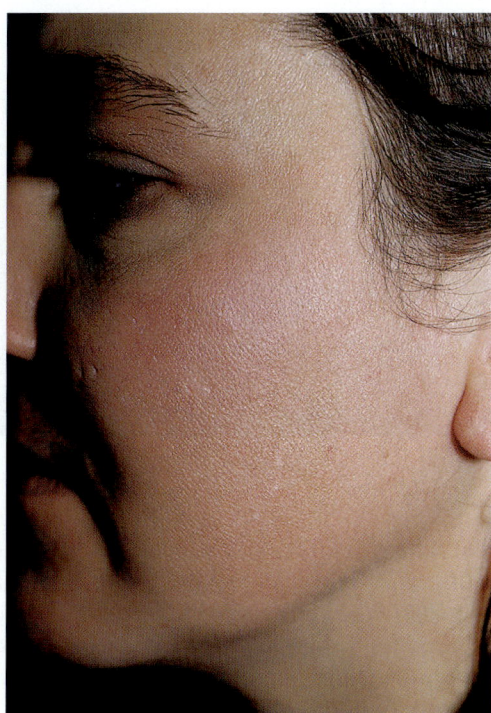

FIG. 35.

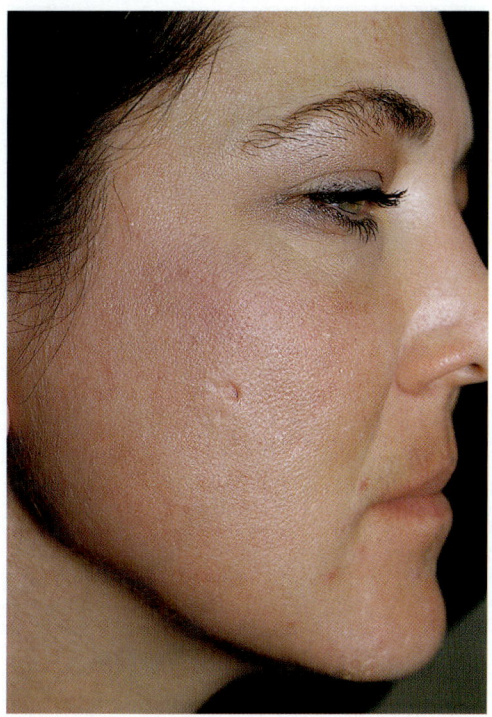

FIG. 37.

Slight erythema persists for 30 to 60 days, and solar restriction is imperative until the erythema has resolved (Figs. 35–37). Sunscreens and the bleaching formula in the regimen are reinstituted as soon as the patient can tolerate them after reepithelialization. Ideally, protection should continue indefinitely. Makeup can be applied at any time to any area that has resurfaced during the healing course. At 6 weeks, the patient shows a slight hint of pigmentation returning on the forehead (Fig. 38). The bleaching formula is increased to 8% hydroquinone at this time.

Four months after peeling, reexamination of the patient reveals almost complete resolution of her melasma (Fig. 39). The acne scarring has been blended on both sides of her face. The largest scar on the right cheek has the edge blunted and

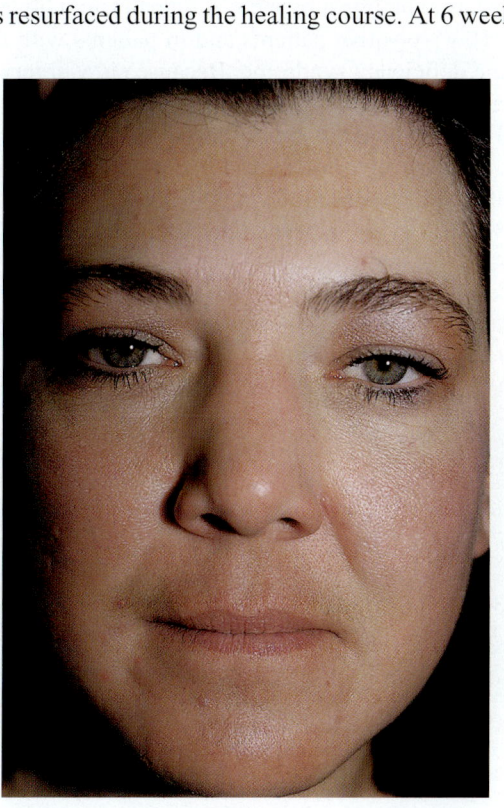

FIG. 36.

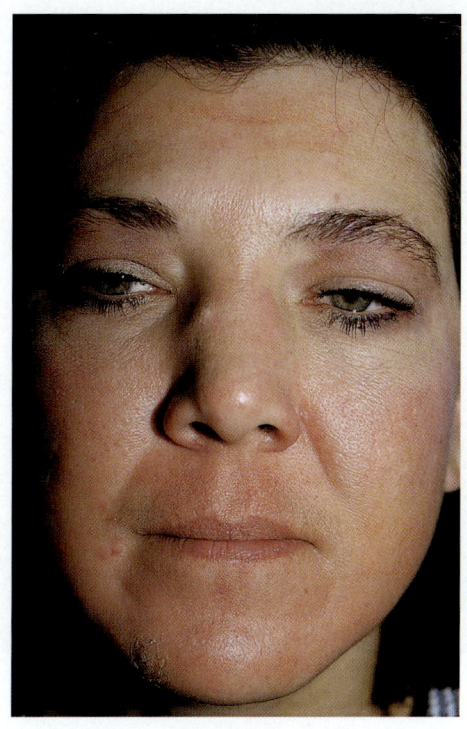

FIG. 38.

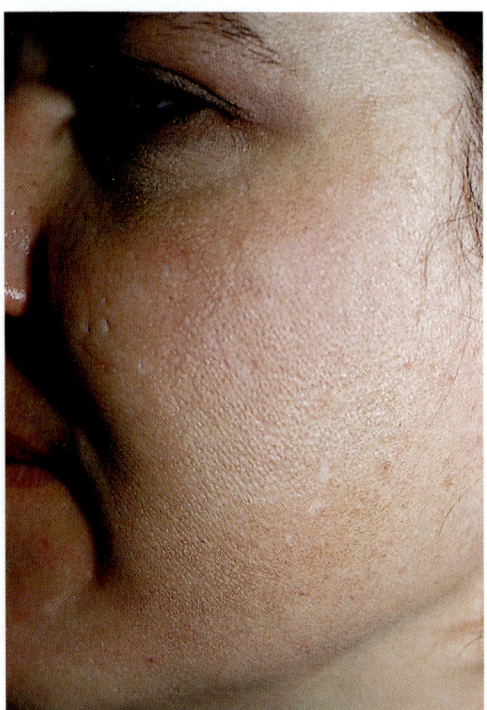

FIG. 39.

effaced but still needs excision (Fig. 40). Compare with Figures 1 and 3 that show before peeling. The patient will taper the bleaching cream over the winter so that ideally she is only using it several times a week during her premenopausal years.

Medium-depth peels may be repeated in around 6 months if there are skip areas or if repeeling *in toto* or in part would

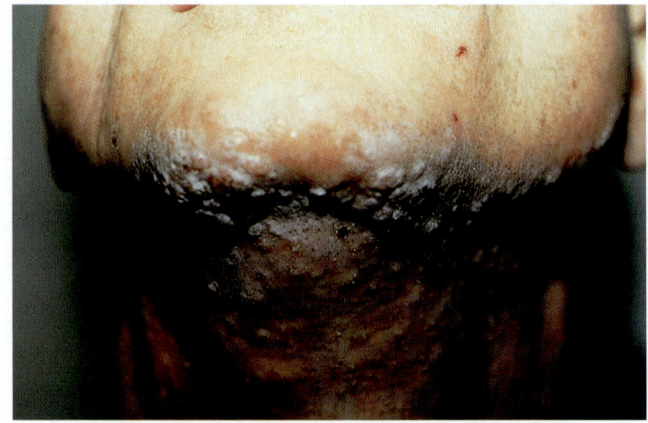

FIG. 41.

benefit the patient. If all erythema and edema have subsided, the patient can be repeeled sooner, possibly with a lower concentration of wounding agent, but not before 90 days. In a patient peeled too soon with another peel of equal depth while erythema is still present, we have seen resultant scarring because the dermal collagen has not completely reorganized. This is not a risk in superficial peeling, where it is acceptable to repeel erythematous skin with continual epidermal sloughs, incurring little or no risk of scarring.

Satisfying clinical results can be obtained with combination peels not only with pigmentation or scars, as in this patient, but also in correcting mild-to-moderate actinic keratoses and in improving fine rhytides.

We have used this peel in an attempt to peel extensive molluscum contagiosum seen in human immunodeficiency virus (HIV)–positive patients and in patients with the autoimmune deficiency syndrome. Because cryosurgery is often used alone to treat molluscum, combined CO_2 plus TCA is useful to debulk large clumps of virus. Figures 41 and 42 show, respectively, before and 1 month after peeling with CO_2 and hard pressure followed by 35% TCA. Peels of 35% to 50% TCA alone appear to be safe and do not induce le-

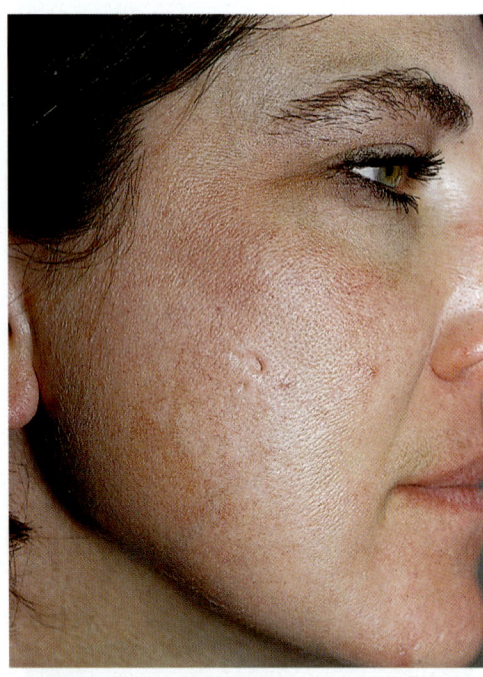

FIG. 40.

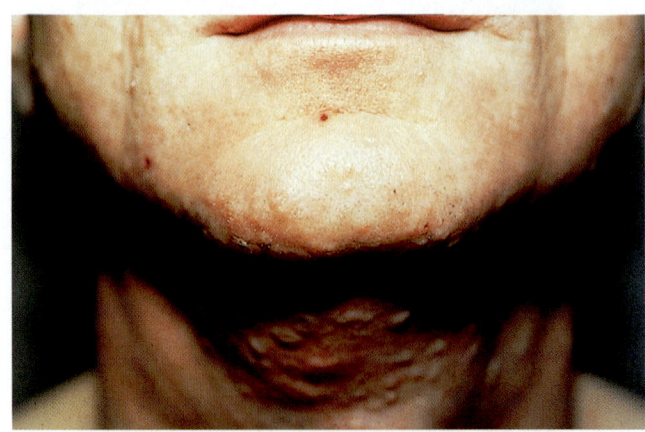

FIG. 42.

sional spread. Local application to the molluscum of 75% to 100% TCA has been reported by Sadick to be of value in this setting. This is not truly a peel but illustrates the destructive use of high-strength TCA.

ADDITIONAL DISCUSSION

Combination Peels

There are three combination peels histologically proven to penetrate through the papillary dermis. In addition to solid CO_2 followed by TCA, Jessner's solution (JS) followed by TCA and glycolic acid followed by TCA also can be used. They are all technique dependent. While all three combination peels are used for photodamage, their pros and cons make knowledge of all peels desirable for maximal correction depending on the patient's needs. Consider the preliminary and procedural differences between the different types of medium-depth peels:

Fitzpatrick Skin Type. JS plus TCA and glycolic acid plus TCA may be performed on any skin type for pigmentary dyschromias, including darker skin types with the usual caution. CO_2 plus TCA is intended only for skin types I to III and type IV using CO_2, mild only.

Lesion Debridement. First, only the CO_2-plus-TCA peel provides inherent debridement of lesions within the peel as does cryosurgery. The identification and removal of any exophytic actinic or seborrheic keratosis is required prior to peeling. This may be done by traditional dermatologic surgery with curettage, cryosurgery, or electrosurgery, and biopsy can be submitted if indicated. Subsequent peeling with 35% TCA over these areas is not harmful and will not usually result in hypopigmentation if carefully performed. Cryosurgery with liquid nitrogen, twice as cold as CO_2, can be the exception, and aggressive overfreezing of keratoses will result in depigmented macules with or without peeling with TCA. Extra coating with JS, glycolic acid, or repeated TCA coats on these individual hypertrophic lesions may not result in total ablation. CO_2 application eliminates this extra step.

Wound Depth and Histologic Correction. CO_2 plus TCA has the greatest wound depth and histologic correction of elastotic changes with the widest papillary dermal Grenz zone. JS plus TCA or glycolic acid plus TCA are generally more superficial in penetration but are technique sensitive and can be roughly equivalent in depth.

Indications

Scarring. CO_2 is a physical modality, and it can be combined with electrosurgery around depressed scars prior to TCA application. It is the only peel to predictably efface depressed scarring. Hard 15- to 20-second application of dry ice to efface the rims or the edges of depressed scars before the immediate repetitive application of 35% to 50% TCA afterward to these rims has resulted in substantial improvement. Pitted scars will not respond to peeling, nor will deep scars with severe atrophy of both the dermis and fat. These are best removed by punch grafting or excision 4 to 6 weeks prior to dermabrasion, peeling, or laser.

Actinic Keratoses. These are improved by all three peels. However, more progressive keratoses exhibit more mucinous change in the dermis. Depth of peel has an important effect on length of remission.

Melasma and Postinflammatory Hyperpigmentation. All three peels are effective, but CO_2 cannot be used on people with darker skin types. Risk of rebound pigmentation exists in all peels without use of bleaching agents.

Rhytides. Fine rhytides are improved by all medium-depth peels and are a reflection of changes in papillary and reticular dermal quality. Coarse rhytides may be softened but not removed by any medium-depth combination.

Molluscum Contagiosum. As cryosurgery alone is effective for molluscum contagiosum in patients with HIV, CO_2 plus TCA is deepest and most effective as a peel. The local destructive effect of high-strength TCA alone has application here as long as the patient realizes that postinflammatory hyperpigmentation may occur for an undetermined time.

Complications

Complications must be considered when peeling with TCA. In medium-depth peeling, the risk of scarring is small. In a series of more than 3000 patients treated with dry ice followed by 35% TCA with rare local 50% TCA application to scars or individual rhytides, the incidence of hypertrophic scarring was less than 1%.

Transient hyperpigmentation can occur in darker skin types with 35% TCA alone or CO_2 plus TCA. Proper management with bleaching regimens and a good patient–physician relationship usually promotes slow but total resolution. Hypopigmentation is not the rule and is very rare. Bacterial infection with impetigo, readily treated with antibiotics, is not a serious complication unless it causes deeper injury and a scar. Herpes simplex infections are readily treated with acyclovir or valacyclovir and usually do not produce permanent sequelae. The drugs seem very effective for recurrent herpes even if begun at the first sign of the attack during reepithelialization. Primary herpes attacks during the healing time are devastating. Prolonged erythema resolves with time, but local persistent erythema should be carefully evaluated and not allowed to progress to scar formation. Topical or intralesional steroids, silicone gel sheeting, or the flash-lamp-pumped pulsed dye laser can be instituted promptly to thwart the formation of hypertrophic scars.

Medium-Depth Peels Combined with Deeper Methods

Combinations of various medium-depth chemical resurfacing peels to effectively blend cosmetic units with deeper methods are effective and useful. One may choose to use a deep resurfacing agent on the upper lip only, and a medium-

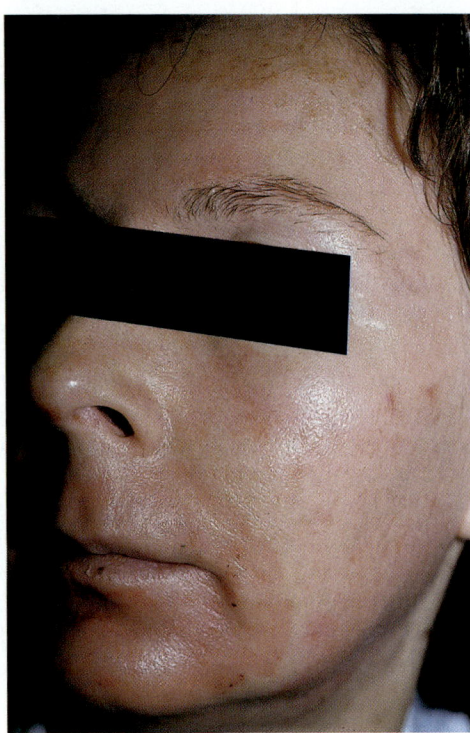

FIG. 43.

depth agent on the remainder of the face. If the elastotic changes in the forms of wrinkling and actinic keratoses in the skin are properly assessed, the pigmentary discrepancy between areas after the procedure will be practically undetectable. An example is the CO_2 laser, dermabrasion, or the Baker-Gordon formula in the perioral area for wrinkles, and the solid CO_2 plus TCA peel elsewhere on the face for minimally wrinkled areas. The appearance of the face 1 week after perioral laser resurfacing and CO_2 plus 35% TCA chemical resurfacing to the remainder of the face is illustrated in Figure 43. The healing time and erythema from the laser are more prolonged than those from the peel, but blending of areas is successful after 4 to 6 months when all the erythema has resolved.

Histologic Depth Studies

Histologic depth studies on medium-depth peeling with the combination of dry ice followed by 35% TCA have demonstrated a peel depth slightly greater than that obtained with 60% TCA alone. The combination of the two agents on a human model seems to produce a wound of similar thickness to full-strength phenol. With 60% TCA alone, the dermal elastotic band was the most weakly staining of all wounding agents. Unoccluded CO_2-plus-TCA–treated skin stained with ease, however, and showed an obvious elastic-staining dermal band. This confirmed CO_2 plus 35% TCA to be a greater wounding agent than 60% TCA alone, although still not as potent as the Baker-Gordon phenol solution.

Solid CO_2 (hard pressure, 15- to 20-second application) plus 35% has been histologically compared to JS (four coats applied with two cotton-tipped applicators) plus 35% TCA in the human model. When measurements in wound depth, the time to return to normal epidermal thickness, depth of the Grenz zone, and thickness of the dermal elastotic band were compared, the wound depth was greater for CO_2 plus TCA than for JS plus TCA 90 days after peeling. The difference is probably not a significant depth difference, and both peels are capable of penetrating through and remodeling the papillary dermis.

Reapplication of TCA 10 minutes after frosting will substantially increase the wound depth. This concept of multiple reapplications is especially helpful in selected sun-damaged areas with impaired penetration such as in areas with actinic keratoses or scarring, or in areas where increased penetration is desired with less risk of skin texture change. It is not recommended to try to remove thick rhytides.

SUMMARY

The results with 35% TCA alone or in combinations can be very gratifying for patient and physician. Each cosmetic unit must be evaluated for use, and TCA may not be the appropriate choice. When it is, however, combining it with solid CO_2 permits a superlative method of resurfacing and rejuvenation. The physician must adhere to the following rules:

1. Be certain that the proper indications for peeling are actually present on the skin.
2. Perform a proper history and physical to evaluate for contraindications.
3. Choose the proper peel for the individual cosmetic unit. Be sure that the entire face does warrant the same process on each unit. If it does not, perform a combined chemical or physical resurfacing procedure with varying techniques on different cosmetic units.
4. Observe and record factors during peeling that tell how the TCA was applied and therefore determine the peel depth.
5. Be thoroughly familiar with complications and their treatment.
6. Be sure the patient is confident that he or she will be certain to receive priority attention during and after the recovery period.

6

The Combination Jessner's-Trichloroacetic Acid Peel: An Enhanced Medium-Depth Chemical Peel

Gary D. Monheit

Chem-exfoliation involves the application of a chemical agent to wound the dermis for the removal of superficial skin lesions and for improvement of the texture of damaged skin. Various acidic and basic chemical agents have been used to produce the effects of light, medium, or deep chemical peels, by differences in their abilities to destroy skin. The depth of destruction caused by a resurfacing procedure can be related to the following factors:

1. Strength of agent applied
2. Preparation of skin prior to procedure
3. Defatting procedure
4. Technique or quantity of application
5. Patient skin type

These variables must be taken into account when a physician evaluates the patient to determine which procedure is best. These indications will be discussed with the basic peel technique. Medium-depth peeling is defined as the application of a chemical agent to produce a dermal wound to the level of the papillary dermis. The procedure is performed to remove actinic keratoses, moderate photoaging of the skin (including superficial rhytides), and pigmentary dyschromias, for improvement of depressed scars, and as a blending technique for localized deeper peels or laser resurfacing. The medium peel is a single procedure, but it can be repeated after 9 months based on the amount of photodamage that remains after the peel. The concentration of trichloroacetic acid (TCA) has been found to correspond to the depth of the peel and, thus, the efficacy of the procedure. TCA to 25% represents a superficial peel, 25% to 40% is the range for medium-depth peeling, and above 45% is a deep chemical peel.

Although the results of the peel for photoaging skin are better with the higher concentrations of peel solution, the incidence of complications is increased greatly with TCA concentrations over 50% (1). In an attempt to reduce the morbidity of deeper pealing techniques, combinations of products have been used to reduce the toxicity of any one agent. A combination of carbon dioxide freeze and TCA has been found by Brody (see Chapter 5) to produce superior results for acne scars and photoaging skin (2). The author has found the use of Jessner's solution (Table 1) prior to a 35% TCA peel to increase the efficacy of this concentration with little risk of the complications of higher concentrations (3). This peel is a pushed medium-depth chemical peel with results similar to a 50% TCA or an 89% phenol solution (3).

METHOD

The combination medium-depth peel includes use of Jessner's solution as a keratolytic agent to further the absorption and penetration of a 35% TCA peel. The technique is used for moderate photoaging effects, including pigmentary changes, lentigenes, epidermal growths, dyschromias, and superficial rhytides. It is a single procedure with healing in 7 to 10 days. It also in used therapeutically to remove diffuse actinic keratoses as an alternative to topical chem-exfoliation with topical 5-fluorouracil (5-FU) chemotherapy (3). It can be used as a therapeutic chemical peel to remove actinic keratoses and prevent skin cancer.

During the preliminary consultation, the patient should be informed of the procedure including a realistic description of the results and morbidity of the procedure. The resultant erythema, swelling, and peeling will keep the patient homebound for approximately 1 week and maybe longer. The patient should understand that the procedure will not remove lines of expression or deeper folds or wrinkles. The surgeon cannot promise the eradication of every actinic keratosis or epidermal growth. As a cosmetic procedure, it is best used

TABLE 1. *The Jessner's solution formula*

Resorcinol	14 g
Salicylic acid	14 g
Lactic acid	14 ml
QS Ethanol	100 ml

for the fine rhytides of facial skin resulting from photodamage and not for the deeper grooves or wrinkles associated with expression lines, gravitational furrows, or sleep lines. This is most consistent with Glogau type III or IV photoaging skin, or sun damage of a moderate degree. The patient, thus, should have a preoperative understanding of what results are expected. Many patients are able to return to work in 7 days. The procedure is divided into preoperative preparation, sedation, cleansing, absorbing agent, peeling agent, and recovery.

Preoperative Preparation

Preparation for the peel includes use of the following agents for 3 to 6 weeks prior to the peel procedure:

1. Sunscreen—SPF 15 or above
2. Tretinoin—retinoic acid (0.05%) applied nightly as tolerated
3. Hydroxy acid preparation—5% to 7% as indicated
4. Bleaching preparation—4% to 8% hydroquinone for type III through VI Fitzpatrick pigmentation, or for treatment of pigmentary dyschromias
5. Antiviral agents, if indicated

Sedation

The pocedure is usually performed with sedation and nonsteroidal anti-inflammatory agents. The patient is informed that the peeling agent will sting and burn temporarily, and aspirin is given prior to peeling and continued through the first 24 hours if the patient can tolerate the medication. Its anti-inflammatory effect is especially helpful in reducing swelling and relieving pain. For full-face peels, it is useful to give preoperative sedation (diazepam, 5 to 10 mg by mouth) and mild analgesia (meperidine 25 mg, hydroxyzine HCl 25 mg intramuscularly). The discomfort from this peel is not long lasting, so short-acting sedation and analgesia are all that are necessary. Most patients are comfortable at the conclusion of the procedure.

Cleansing

Vigorous cleansing and degreasing is necessary for even penetration of the solution. The face is gently scrubbed with Septisol using 4×4-inch gauze and water, then rinsed and dried. Next, an acetone preparation is applied to remove residual oils and debris. The skin is essentially debrided of sebum, stratum corneum, and excessive scale. The necessity for thorough degreasing cannot be overemphasized for an even, fully penetrant peel (4). The physician should feel the dry cleansed skin to check the completeness of degreasing. If oil is felt, degreasing should be repeated. A splotchy peel is usually the result of uneven penetration of peel solution due to residual oil or stratum corneum from inadequate degreasing. Such aggressive degreasing is usually not a part of resurfacing procedures such as glycolic acid peels or laser resurfacing, but it is a vital component of this peel.

Absorbing Agent

The Jessner's solution is then applied with either cotton tip applicators or 2×2-inch gauze. It is applied evenly with usually one coat to achieve a light but even frosting. The frosting achieved with Jessner's solution is much lighter than that produced with TCA, and the patient is usually not uncomfortable. An erythema appears with a faint tinge of frost that is blotchy on the face. Even strokes are used to apply the solution to the unit areas covering the forehead to the cheeks to the nose and chin. The eyelids are treated last, creating the same erythema with blotchy frosting. The Jessner's solution not only aids in the penetration of the TCA but creates a more even peel over the face without "hot spots" of deeper TCA penetration.

Peeling Agent

The TCA is then applied evenly with one to four cotton tip applicators, or it can be applied with a single 2×2-inch gauze pad if heavier applications are desired in any one area or in all areas. Cotton tip applicators are useful to quantitate the amount of peel solution to be applied. Three or four cotton tip applicators are used for broad surface areas such as forehead and cheeks, two for the mouth and nose, and one, slightly dry, for the eyelids.

The white frost from the TCA application appears on the treated area in a few moments. Even applications should eliminate the need to go over areas a second or third time, but if frosting is incomplete or uneven, the solution should be reapplied. TCA takes longer to frost than Baker's formula or straight phenol, and the surgeon should wait at least 3 or 4 minutes before determining the evenness of frosting. Areas of poor frosting should be retreated carefully with a thin application of TCA. Anatomic areas of the face are peeled sequentially from forehead to temple to cheeks and finally to the lips and eyelids. The white frosting indicates keratocoagulation, and at that point the reaction is completed. Careful feathering of the solution into the hairline and around the rim of the jaw and brow conceals the line of demarcation between peeled and nonpeeled areas. The perioral area has rhytides that require a complete and even application of solution over the lip skin and the vermilion line. This is best accomplished by an assistant stretching and fixating the upper and lower lips while the peel solution is applied.

Certain areas and skin lesions require special attention. Thicker keratoses do not frost evenly and thus do not pick up peel solution. Additional applications rubbed vigorously into the lesions may be needed for peel solution penetration. Wrinkled skin should be stretched to allow an even coating of solution into the folds and troughs. Oral rhytides require peel solution to be applied with the wood portion of a cotton tip applicator and extended into the vermilion of the lip. Deeper furrows such as expression lines will not be eradicated by peel solutions and thus should be treated like the remaining skin. The more severe actinically damaged skin requires a greater layer of peel solution for adequate frosting and penetration.

Eyelid skin must be treated delicately and carefully. A semi-dry applicator should be used to carry the solution within 2 to 3 mm of the lid margin. The patient should be positioned with the head elevated at 30° and the eyelids closed. Excess peel solution on the cotton tip should be gently drained on the bottom before application. It is then rolled gently on the lids and the periorbital skin. Never leave excess peel solution on the lids, because the solution can then roll into the eyes. Keep tears dry with a cotton tip applicator during peeling, as they may pull peel solution to the puncta and eye by capillary attraction. The solution is diluted immediately with cool saline compresses at the conclusion of the peel. This relieves the stinging, but it does not neutralize the reaction, which is completed with the appearance of white frosting.

There is an immediate burning sensation as the peel solution is applied, but this subsides as frosting is completed. Cool saline compresses offer symptomatic relief for a peeled area as the solution is applied to other areas. The compresses are placed over the face for 5 to 10 minutes after the peel until the patient is comfortable. The burning subsides fully when the patient is ready to be discharged. At that time, most of the frosting has faded and a brawny desquamation is evident.

Recovery

Postoperatively, there is expected edema, erythema, and desquamation. With periorbital peels and even forehead peels, eyelid edema can be severe enough to close the lids. For the first 72 hours, the patient is instructed to soak four times a day with a 0.25% acetic acid compress: 1 tablespoon white vinegar in 1 pint of warm water. A bland emollient is applied to the desquamating areas after soaks. After 24 hours, the patient can shower and gently cleanse with a mild nondetergent cleanser. The erythema intensifies as desquamation completes itself within 5 to 7 days. Healing is thus completed within 1 week to 10 days. At the end of 1 week, the bright red color has faded to pink and has the appearance of a sunburn. This can be covered by cosmetics and will fade fully within 2 to 3 weeks.

The Jessner-TCA peel will give significant improvement to moderately photodamaged skin, but more severely aged skin may not respond as well. Oral, vertical rhytides on the lips and eyelid wrinkles respond very little to this peel, but they do respond well to the deep peel solution, Baker's phenol. A combined peel using Baker's phenol on the lips or lids, and Jessner's TCA on the remainder of the face will blend the deeper results with the rest of the facial skin. In this way, the strength of the peel is customized to the needs in each area of the face.

PATIENT PRESENTATION AND RESULTS

Actinic keratoses respond to chem-exfoliation, and indications for the peel are virtually the same as for topical chemotherapy with 5-FU. Advantages of using the peel rather than 5-FU include the single application of therapeutic agent and the rapid recovery period. Topical 5-FU must be applied for 3 weeks, and the healing then takes an additional 3 weeks. The Jessner's-TCA peel will be healed within 1 week after a single office application. The morbidity of topical chemotherapy, which includes scabbing, crusting, and discomfort, is greatly reduced with the peel program, resulting in less time off work for recuperation. Many keratoses though are too thick to respond to the peel alone and should be identified preoperatively and treated with either extra peel solution or cryosurgery before the peel. The peel may be performed on the forehead, temples, and cheeks alone, rather than the entire face, if these are the only areas with keratoses. The peel can be continued to the scalp, neck, and even hands and arms, but care must be taken to use less peel solution in these areas with a reduced capacity for healing.

Case 1

Patient 1 is a 45-year-old man with a history of actinic keratoses requiring repeated treatments over the past 5 years. His profession has made it impossible to tolerate a 6-week course of 5-FU therapy, and sequential cryosurgical treatment sessions have not been effective in controlling the new lesions. The patient had a combination Jessner's-35% TCA peel performed regionally over the temples and forehead. He was healed within 10 days and returned to work. Notice the resolution of pigmentary changes, improvement of rhytides, and general improvement of skin texture. The patient has been followed for over 4 years and encouraged to use sunscreen and retinoic acid to sustain the results (Fig. 1).

Case 2

The medium-depth chemical peel is effective for improving moderate photoaging effects including fine rhytides, cross hatching, and lentigenes found with moderate photoaging skin. Patient 2 is a 46-year-old Caucasian woman

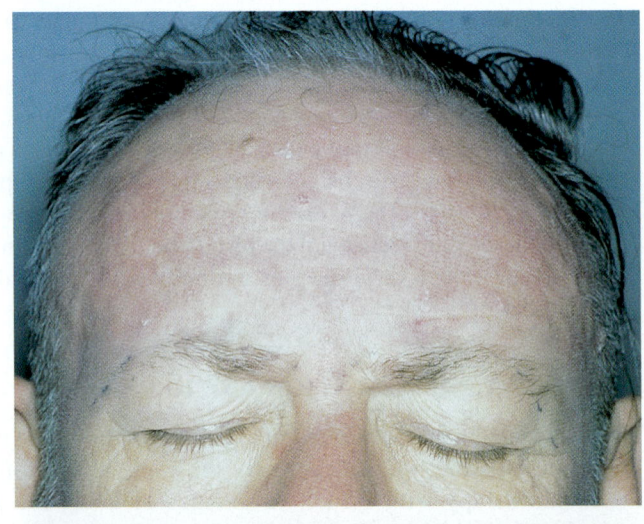
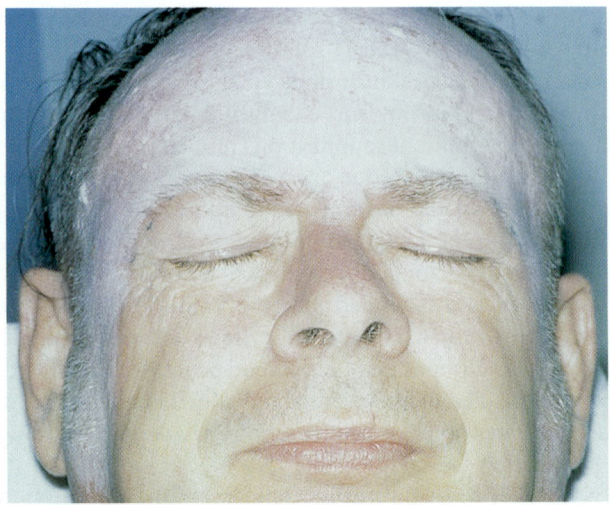
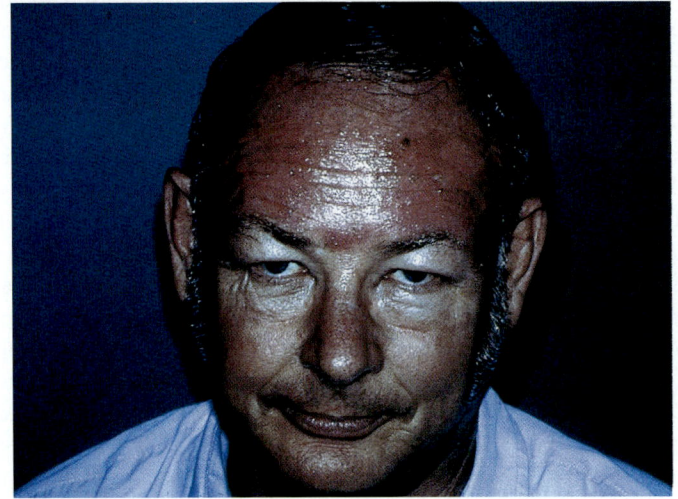
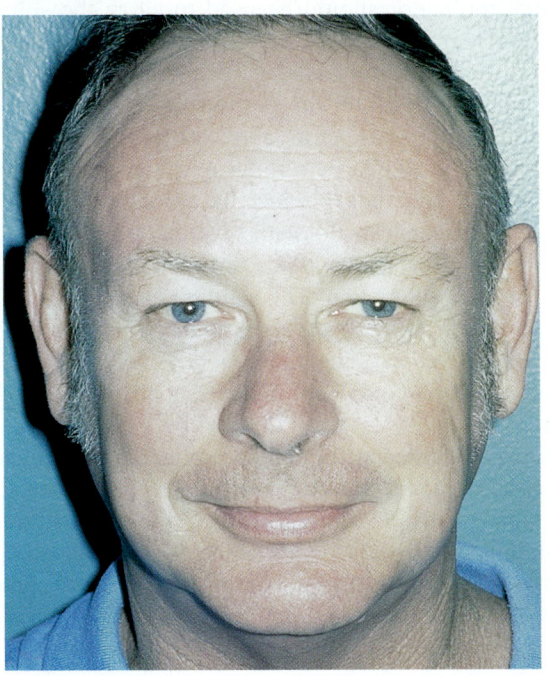

FIG. 1. Chemical peeling for actinic keratoses. **A:** Preoperative appearance for multiple actinic keratoses. **B:** Application of TCA 35% after Jessner's solution to the forehead. **C:** Erythema and peeling, 4 days later.

with skin problems associated with Glogau type III photoaging skin. This includes epidermal growths, pigmentary changes, and dermal defects such as wrinkled and weathered skin. A full-face combination Jessner's-35% TCA peel was performed after adequate preoperative skin preparation, including sunscreen, glycolic acid lotion every morning, and retinoic acid at bedtime. To achieve the dermal penetration required, the TCA was layered more heavily over the wrinkled areas. The patient healed fully within 2 weeks and demonstrates predicted results after 3 months (Fig. 2).

Case 3

Patient 3 developed melasma that was not responsive to topical treatment alone. For this reason, the combination peel was recommended to remove the epidermis fully with its pigmentary changes. To prevent recurrence of the pigment, the patient was begun on the following topical therapy 6 weeks prior to the procedure:

1. Sunscreen SPF 15
2. Hydroquinone, 8% applied twice a day
3. Retinoic acid, 0.05% at bedtime
4. Hydrocortisone, 1% every morning

The patient healed fully within 10 days and was begun on topical therapy again within 1 month. The bleach was reduced to 4% within 2 months and eliminated in 6 months. She has been followed over 2 years and did not develop a recurrence of the pigmentary condition (Fig. 3).

In some patients, cosmetic areas have different degrees of

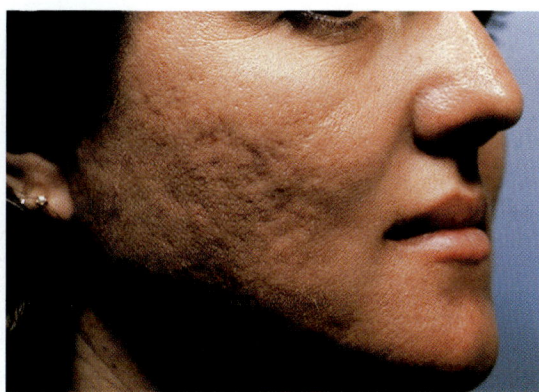

FIG. 9. This 39-year-old woman has moderately extensive postacne scarring.

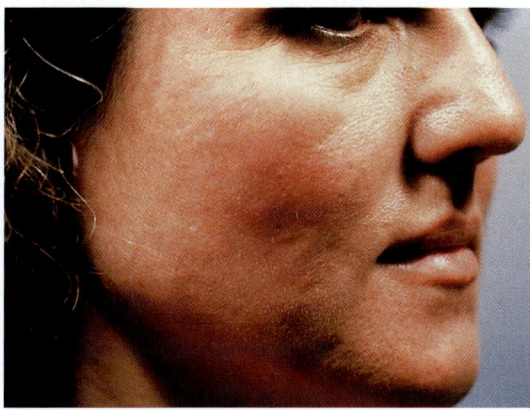

FIG. 10. Same patient as Figure 9, 4 months after a dermabrasion using a diamond fraise. The patient felt that the improvement was between 85% and 90%. Despite the patient's pigmentation being a Fitzpatrick class III, there is no evidence of hyperpigmentation or hypopigmentation.

Scarring

Scarring can be definitively improved by a dermabrasion. This technique cannot improve all of the characteristics of a scar. Although I have never heard or read a discussion on the characteristics of scars, I have concluded that there are four essential characteristics. They consist of the following: (a) contour irregularities, (b) consistency changes, (c) color alterations, and (d) texture changes. The contour changes can be evident when a depression is present in an atrophic scar or when an elevation is present in a hypertrophic or keloidal scar. Consistency changes are felt when the scars undergo tactile examination. Atrophic scars will have decreased consistency and hypertrophic and keloidal scars will have increased consistency over that which is normal. Color changes are represented by hypopigmentation or hyperpigmentation. The last characteristic is changes in texture, which I refer to as the visual changes of the skin. More specifically, I refer to the loss of epidermal appendages as seen by the absence of pores and normal epidermal structures. The texture in an atrophic scar is altered, producing shiny skin with no poral openings. Dermabrasion can improve contour defects and in the instance of hypertrophic and keloidal scars can improve the consistency that preexisted. However, the consistency of a thinned atrophic scar is not improved. Color changes can improve if hyperpigmentation is present as seen in melasma, but dermabrasion will not replace the melanocytes that are absent in areas of permanent hypopigmentation. Texture changes are associated with atrophy and cannot be improved with dermabrasion. As a consequence, dermabrasion is most effective in contour defects and is effective in some instances of consistency or color changes. Textural changes are unchanged. The surgeon must evaluate these characteristics, understand their relationship to the possible results following dermabrasion, and be able to articulate these facts to the prospective patients.

Postacne Scarring

The most common indication for facial dermabrasion is to improve postacne scars. Facial scarring represents a significant deformity that is often hard to disguise. Some patients decide to pursue temporary, but relatively easy, approaches such as the use of filler substances, such as Zyderm (Collagen Biomedical, Palo Alto, CA), Fibrel (Mentor Corporation, Goleta, CA), or lipotransfer. Dermabrasion requires greater commitment and a significant recovery period but does provide permanent improvement. Zyderm and Fibrel are indicated for temporary improvement of scars that have indistinct borders and are small in number. Lipotransfer is beneficial when cystic acne has created an inflammatory response resulting in atrophy of the deep dermis and subcutaneous fat. None of the filling substances provide excellent results when the borders of the acne scars are sharply defined.

Dermabrasion is effective on well-defined scars with distinct borders (Figs. 9, 10) and broad-based scars with ill-defined borders (Figs. 11–16). It is effective for both shallow and medium-depth scars and can be used to bevel and modify the borders of deep scars. Icepick scars that are small in diameter but quite deep do not improve significantly after dermabrasion (Figs. 17–19) (15,22,37,38). Punch graft re-

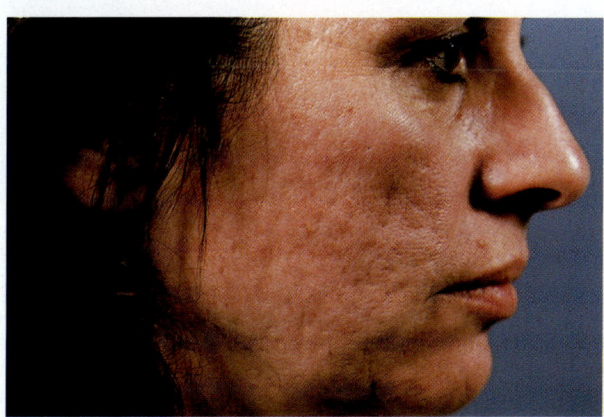

FIG. 11. This 43-year-old woman has severe scarring from cystic acne involving all areas of her face.

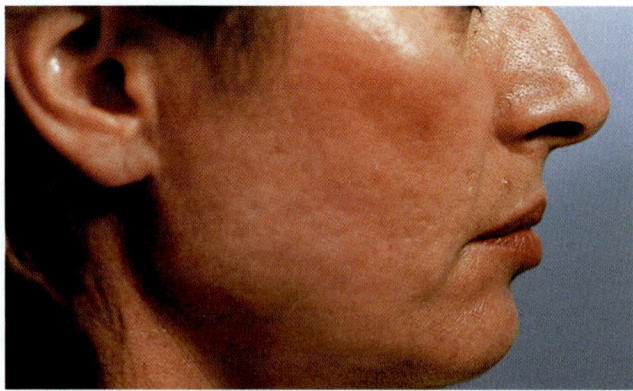

FIG. 12. Same patient as Figure 11, 4 months following a dermabrasion using the coarse diamond fraise. This patient evaluated her improvement as 85%. Color blending is excellent.

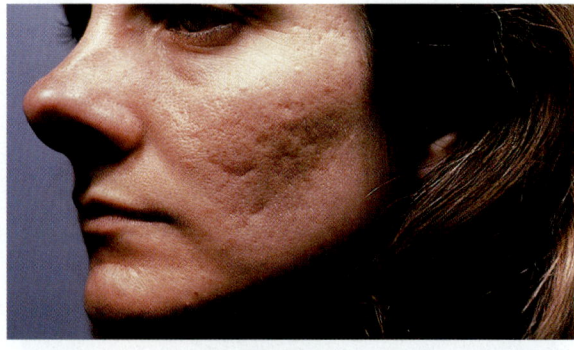

FIG. 15. This is a 31-year-old female patient with preexisting cystic acne resulting in extensive scarring of her cheeks. There is both dermal and subcutaneous atrophy.

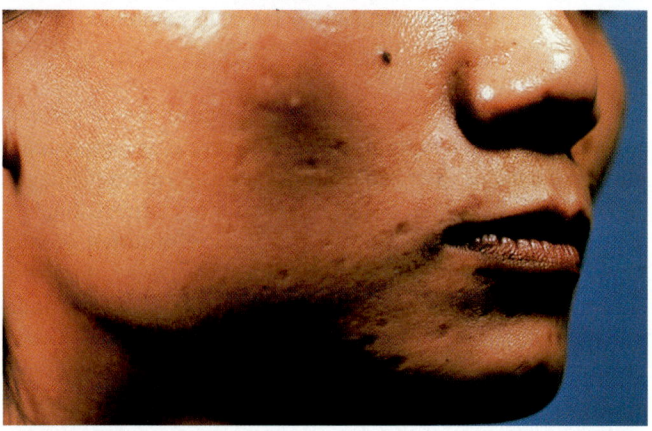

FIG. 13. This is a 34-year-old Korean woman with extensive scarring resulting from childhood smallpox. The scars are large in size with well-defined borders and moderate to severe hyperpigmentation.

FIG. 16. Same patient as in Figure 15, 5 months following a full facial dermabrasion using a coarse diamond fraise. The patient stated her improvement as 75% to 80%. There is excellent blending of facial color with the exception of a small area on her right central cheek, which subsequently regained normal pigmentation.

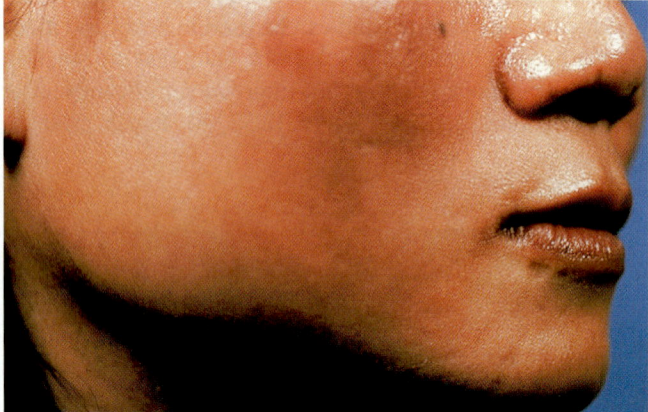

FIG. 14. Same patient as Figure 13, 3 months after a dermabrasion using the coarse diamond fraise. All preexisting scarring is significantly improved, with nearly complete clearing of almost all scars. Overall, there is improvement of her pigmentation with marked decrease in the hyperpigmented areas concentrated in the individual smallpox scars. Note the line of demarcation at the mandibular angle where the dermabraded area meets the nondermabraded area. This improved over the ensuing year.

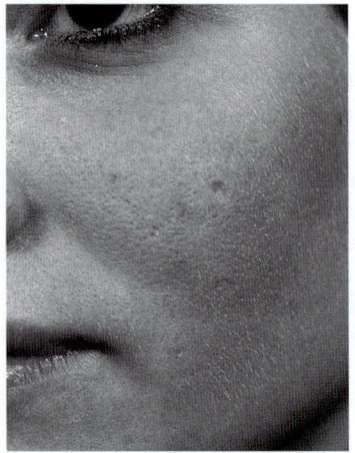

FIG. 17. This is a 22-year-old female patient with mild scarring of her central cheeks with several icepick scars and one large, deep, well-defined scar in the malar area.

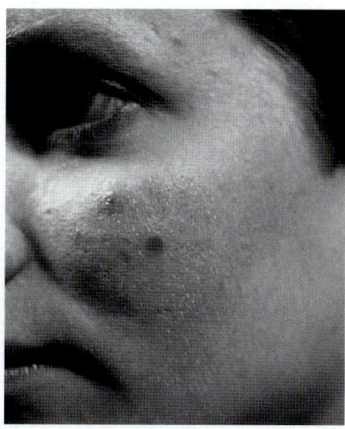

FIG. 18. This is the same patient as Figure 17. This photograph was taken 1 week after two punch grafts were performed on the deeper scars of her left central cheek. Four to 8 weeks after grafting is the ideal time to dermabrade.

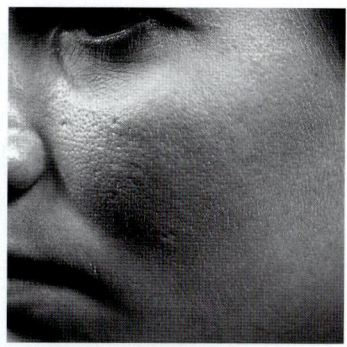

FIG. 19. Same patient as in Figure 18. This photograph was taken 4 months postoperatively after a facial dermabrasion using an extra-coarse diamond fraise. There is marked improvement of the preexisting icepick scars in addition to the scars that were treated with transfer grafts. One small icepick scar that was not treated can be seen immediate to the upper graft. This would have been better treated with a small transfer graft. The patient was satisfied with her results.

placement performed 4 to 8 weeks prior to the dermabrasion gives the best results. I have not been impressed with either the punch elevation technique or scar excision combined with primary closure. Deep broad-based scars are the result of tissue damage of the epidermal and dermal layers and atrophy of the underlying fatty tissue. Dermabrasion is helpful but is not as effective in these scars (Figs. 20, 21).

Compulsive excoriation can be seen in patients with or without acne. Although this exemplifies the patient's neurotic tendencies, these patients generally respond exceedingly well to dermabrasion. I have found that most patients permanently cease their excoriating (Figs. 22–33).

Patients must understand that dermabrasion does not provide flawless skin. Superficial scars usually disappear, and medium to deep scars are improved. I cannot predict preoperatively the extent of improvement in patients who undergo facial dermabrasion. Using the method that I have developed over the past 25 years, my average cosmetic improvement ranges between 75% and 85% as judged by the patient and our medical staff. In my experience, the need for a second dermabrasion is less than 3%. This contrasts to the advice given to patients by general plastic surgeons, who frequently state that their usual improvement is 30% to 40%, requiring two or three dermabrasions to achieve an adequate result.

If indicated, I delay a repeat dermabrasion for at least 6 months. Because residual inflammation and edema persist for 3 to 4 months after the dermabrasion, I delay use of filler substances and lipotransfer for 6 months. Unfortunately, liquid silicone is no longer available for improvement of these residual scars. Although silicone used for these purposes is not approved, when used properly, I feel its use was a safe, effective, and permanent improvement for residual scars.

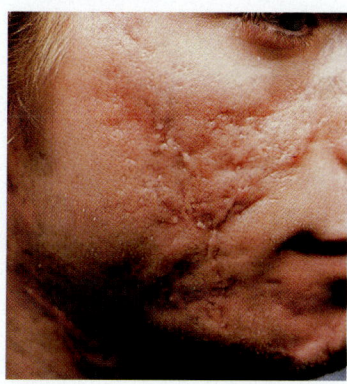

FIG. 20. This is a 20-year-old man with severe hypertrophic scarring and marked bridging secondary to severe cystic acne. This patient had been told by three plastic surgeons that his case was too severe to respond to dermabrasion.

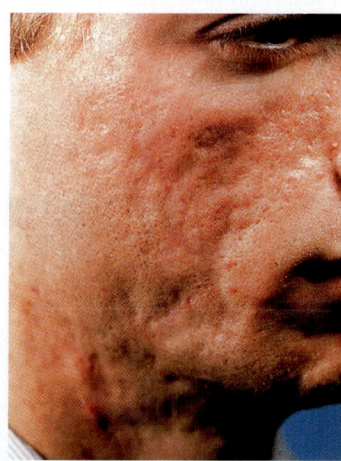

FIG. 21. Same patient as Figure 20, 11 months following a dermabrasion using a coarse diamond fraise. There is marked improvement of the preexisting scarring with complete absence of the bridging defects. This patient's attitude and self-image were markedly improved. He chose to undergo a second dermabrasion that provided additional significant improvement. Fat transfer would probably be helpful to improve the subcutaneous atrophy.

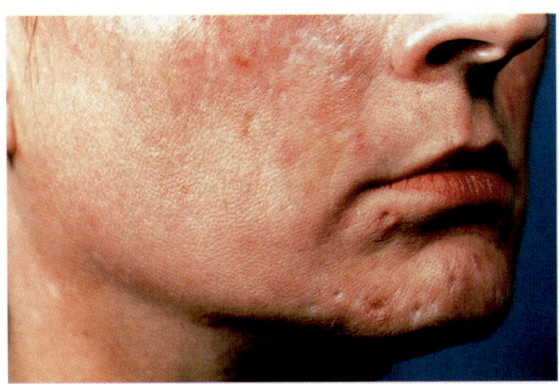

FIG. 22. This is a 40-year-old female patient who had extensive scarring from compulsive excoriation. Scars of her chin and cheeks are broad based and deep.

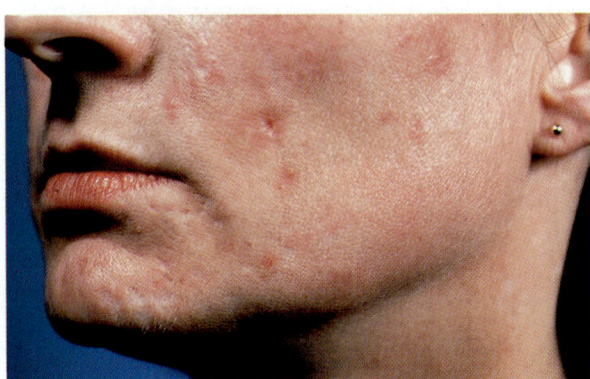

FIG. 23. Same patient as Figure 22, showing scars that are characteristic of compulsive excoriation. They have well-defined borders and usually have significant hypopigmentation.

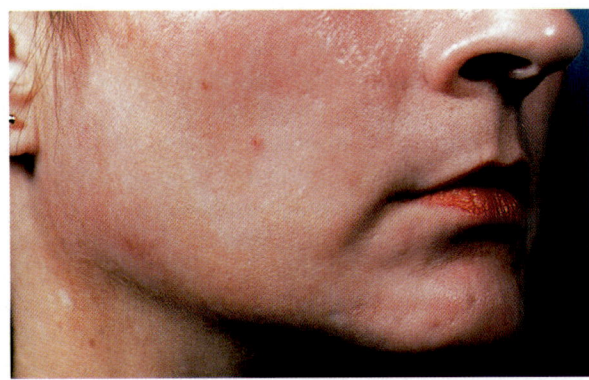

FIG. 24. Same patient as Figure 22. This photograph was taken 4½ months after a facial dermabrasion performed with a coarse diamond fraise. Her preexisting scarring is almost completely resolved, with only subtle defects are present on her chin. She is no longer excoriating.

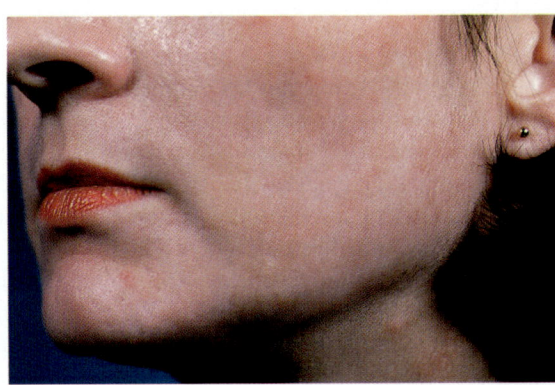

FIG. 25. This is the same patient as Figure 23. There is apparent hypopigmentation of the patient's entire face secondary to the dermabrasion. This hypopigmentation was permanent and is the only significant case of permanent hypopigmentation that I have experienced in over 25 years of performing facial dermabrasion.

FIG. 26. This 33-year-old female patient has scarring from compulsive excoriation. Her scars are well defined, broad based, moderately deep, and hypopigmented.

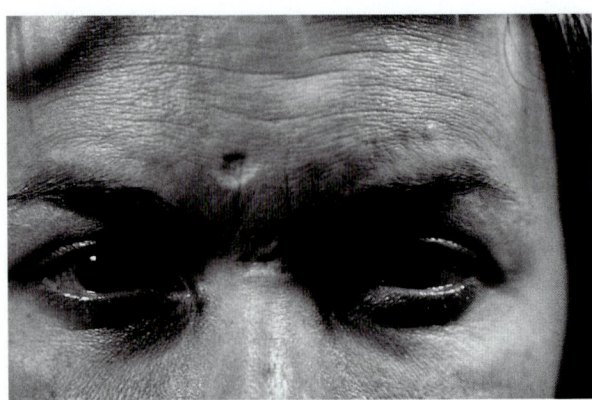

FIG. 27. Same patient as Figure 26, showing well-defined, deep scarring of her glabella and nasal root secondary to compulsive excoriation. The scar of her glabella is an obvious cosmetic defect.

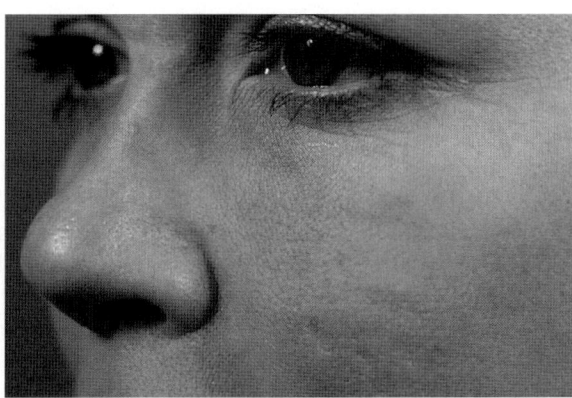

FIG. 28. Same patient as Figure 26, 10 months after a facial dermabrasion using an extra-coarse diamond fraise. The patient evaluated the improvement of her left cheek as 85% to 90%.

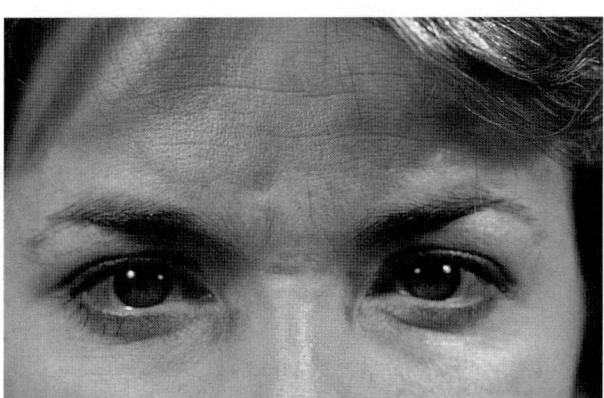

FIG. 29. Same patient as Figure 27, 10 months following a facial dermabrasion with improvement of the deep glabella scar considered to be 50% to 60%.

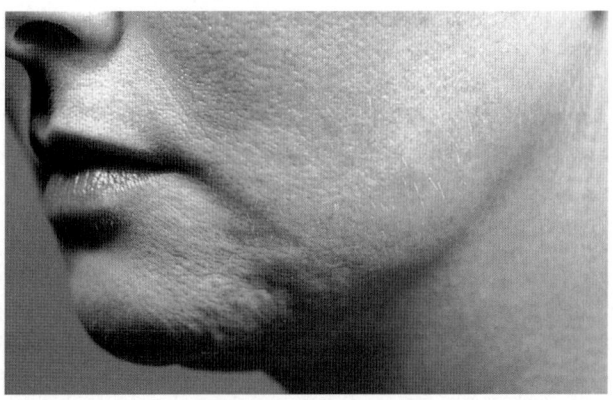

FIG. 30. This is a 39-year-old patient with scarring of her chin secondary to compulsive excoriation.

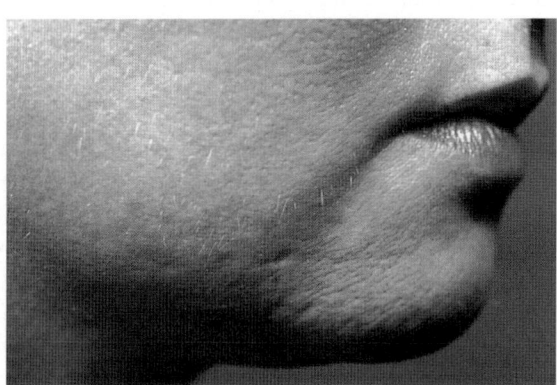

FIG. 31. Same patient as Figure 30, showing the right side of her chin. This patient had earlier undergone a dermabrasion performed by a plastic surgeon, with no significant improvement.

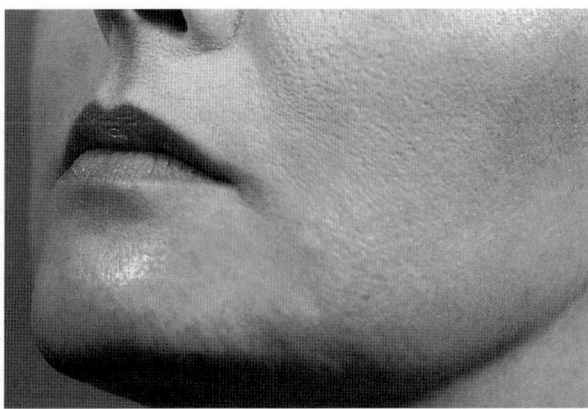

FIG. 32. Same patient as Figure 30, 3 months following a dermabrasion using a coarse diamond fraise. Improvement is estimated at 85%.

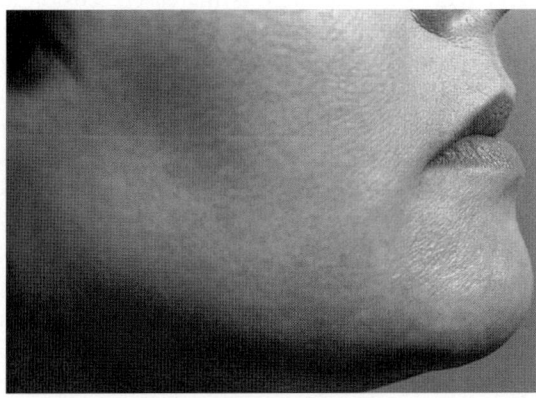

FIG. 33. The right side of the patient seen in Figures 30 to 32, 3 months following a dermabrasion. There are no apparent scars seen. The patient discontinued any further excoriating.

Traumatic Scars

Cutaneous scars caused by traumatic injury respond well to dermabrasion. Yarborough has shown that intervention is most effective when the scars are 4 to 6 weeks postinjury (21). This treatment is effective not only for lacerations that were not sutured but also for those that were closed at the time of injury. Yarborough warns that an appropriate delay must occur before a second dermabrasion is used for improvement of a traumatic scar. He cites a patient who developed a postdermabrasion scar when a second dermabrasion was employed 6 weeks following the primary dermabrasion. He recommends a delay of 6 months between dermabrasions. After accidents in which glass, road debris, gunpowder, or similar foreign objects are superficially embedded in the skin, some surgeons use dermabrasion to debride the affected area. Although I have limited experience with these circumstances, the use of a BufPuf (3M Personal Care Products, St. Paul, MN) abrasive sponge, a surgical scrub brush, or a curette with local anesthesia can be equally effective as, technically easier than, and less expensive than dermabrasion.

Postsurgical Scars

Dermabrasion is highly recommended and is particularly helpful for improving scars following surgery, particularly those of the face. When a patient is fair-skinned and exhibits very little or no actinic damage, a spot dermabrasion may be performed over and around the scar. In patients with visible sun damage or in dark-complected patients, spot dermabrasion will probably result in a visible difference of skin color. As a caution, I would dermabrade an entire cosmetic segment.

When using skin flaps for reconstruction, the dermabrasion is particularly effective in blending the scar, particularly if it is on the nose. If the flap procedure has been used for eradication of a carcinoma, dermabrasion of the entire nose provides the additional benefit of eliminating surrounding actinic damage, which reduces the potential for subsequent new cancers.

Excisional surgical scars are frequently more fragile that traumatic scars because there is increased tension across these wounds. Premature dermabrasion may result in wound dehiscence. Katz and Oca conducted a controlled study of the effectiveness of spot dermabrasion (scar-abrasion) on the appearance of surgical scars (28). They obtained the best cosmetic result when delaying the dermabrasion for 8 weeks following the surgical excision.

Skin grafts often produce an imperfect match between the graft and recipient tissues. There is a contrast in texture, color, and thickness of the skin, which may lead to an obvious defect. Dermabrasion performed 6 weeks after grafting will often help blend a full-thickness graft. Since the graft has a limited number of follicles and sweat glands, the dermabrasion is best confined to the junction of the graft and the surrounding tissues. Although it may be possible to lightly dermabrade over the graft, deep dermabrasion may lead to loss of the graft.

Actinic Damage

Field has extensively reviewed the therapeutic value of dermabrasion on actinically damaged skin (39). He showed that dermabrasion heals more rapidly, is considerably more effective, and is not associated with the severe dermatitis and occasional allergic reactions that are found with 5-flurouracil (5-FU). Many individuals with severe sun damage will regularly develop actinic keratoses requiring frequent treatment with liquid nitrogen. This often leads to a mottled irregular appearance where the hypopigmented treated areas contrast with the normally pigmented untreated areas. Additionally, these patients have a constant risk of deterioration of these keratoses into squamous cell carcinomas. Dermabrasion of actinically damaged skin provides an even, smooth appearance with a dramatic decrease of actinic keratoses, ephelides, and wrinkling (17,39,40). Often, these patients will have years free of any actinic lesions following dermabrasion. The prevention of cutaneous cancer is an obvious therapeutic effect. Dermabrasion easily surpasses the use of 5-FU, which results in slow healing over a 6- to 8-week period and may mask carcinomas, with resultant occult growth before clinical reappearance. Field reports reepithelialization after dermabrasion usually being complete after 10 days, with the reappearance of occult carcinomas not having occurred in his large series (39).

When treating actinic damage, it is best to dermabrade an entire cosmetic unit if a full face dermabrasion is not required. Segmental dermabrasion of the anterior scalp is appropriate in prematurely balding men exhibiting significant actinic damage. To avoid changes in pigmentation between the treated and nontreated skin, the dermabrasion can be extended inferiorly to the level of the eyebrows. The upper lip or nose can be individually abraded, but dermabrasion of the chin should be extended to include the cheeks to avoid obvious demarcation. Benedetto et al. have demonstrated that clinical and histologic improvement of photodamaged skin will persist after dermabrasion (29). They emphasize that this eliminates the necessity for continued treatment of premalignant and neoplastic changes.

Rhytides

Dermabrasion has been used extensively for improvement of rhytides. In most individuals, this wrinkling is due to actinic damage, referred to as extrinsic aging. The wrinkling resulting from degeneration of dermal collagen is referred to as intrinsic aging.

Fine wrinkles and cutaneous laxity are frequently apparent in older individuals even when sun exposure has been limited. The wrinkling in expression lines are the result of muscular movement, particularly around the eyes and mouth. These wrinkles may temporarily improve with dermabrasion but will reappear with continued muscle movement as postoperative edema subsides. Sleep creases result from the skin folding during sleep (41). They un-

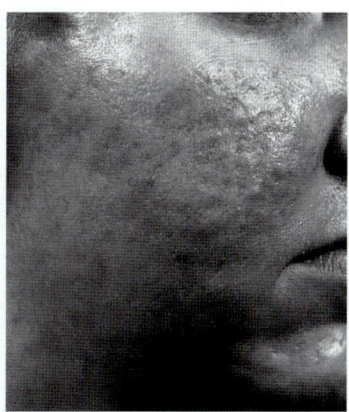

FIG. 50. Same patient as in Figures 47 to 49. The patient is 10 months postdermabrasion, showing flattening of the hypertrophic scars in her central cheeks following the use of topical steroid therapy. This patient shows that the effects of Accutane can persist for years following its cessation.

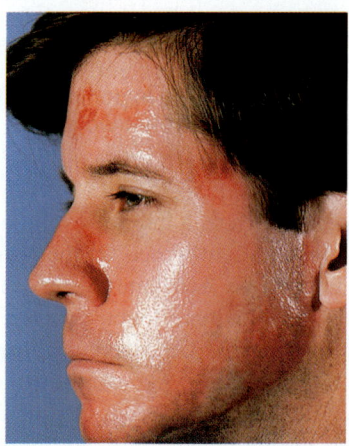

FIG. 51. This is a 38-year-old man, 6 weeks following a facial dermabrasion with a coarse diamond fraise. He is 15 months post–Accutane therapy. There is persistent, mottled erythema present on his forehead and areas of his cheeks and chin.

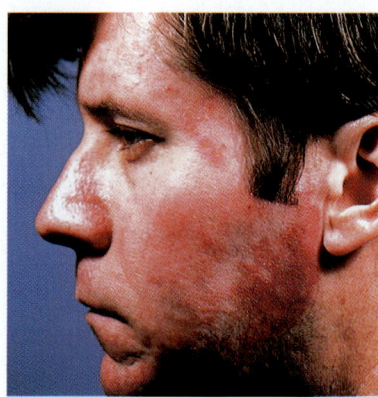

FIG. 52. Same patient as Figure 51 now shown at 4 months postdermabrasion. There is persistent erythema, elevation, and induration present in the areas noted. There is a linear fashion to the scars of his left mandibular area, which does not follow the direction of the strokes that I use while the dermabrasion is being performed.

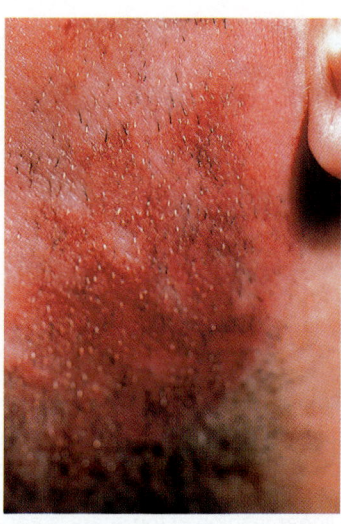

FIG. 53. Same patient as Figure 51. This photograph clearly shows the growth of whisker hair throughout the entire area affected by the persistent erythema, induration, and isolated hypertrophic scars. The presence of facial hair proves that the dermabrasion was not performed too deeply.

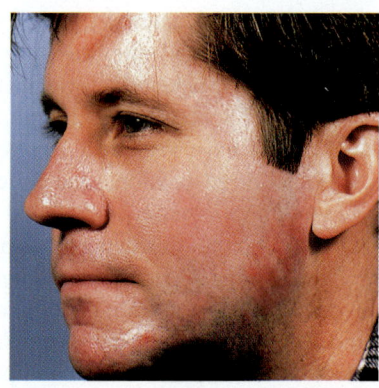

FIG. 54. Same patient as Figure 51, presently at 7 months postdermabrasion. The areas of erythema are more subtle but the hypertrophic scarring in the left preauricular area has become more extensive in size and height.

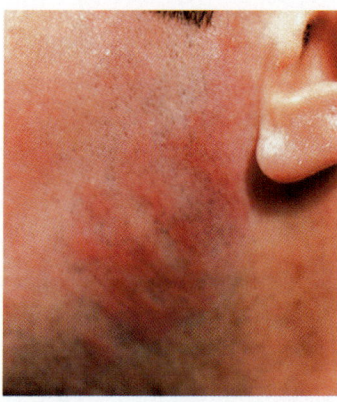

FIG. 55. Same patient as Figure 51, at 7 months postdermabrasion. It is obvious that the area of persistent erythema and induration as seen in Figure 51 has now progressed to hypertrophic scarring.

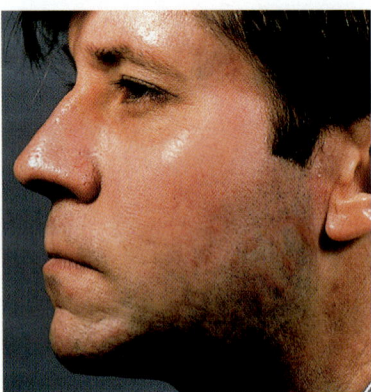

FIG. 56. Same patient as Figure 51, now at 8 months postdermabrasion. Steroid therapy used systemically, topically, and intralesionally has improved the hypertrophic scars on the left cheek. The linear fashion of the scars is apparent. Their direction is approximately 90° from the angle at which the strokes are made during the performance of the dermabrasion.

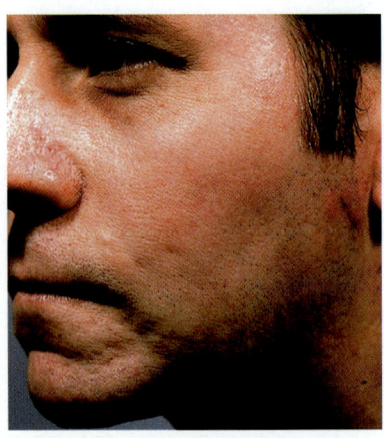

FIG. 58. Same patient as in Figure 51, now 11 months postdermabrasion. Only a small 1-cm hypertrophic scar persists in the preauricular area. The other scars have responded to the previously outlined steroid therapy. This patient had completed one course of Accutane therapy 14 months prior to his facial dermabrasion. He was completely reepithelialized without incident on the 12th day following his dermabrasion. This is the expected time of reepithelialization seen in normal healing. The erythema did not become intense until 2 months into his postoperative phase. All hypertrophic scars resolved, leaving subtle atrophic hypopigmented skin.

Areas over the bony prominences, which are the classic zones susceptible to postoperative dermabrasion scarring, healed normally. These patients were eventually treated successfully using topical corticosteroids and intramuscular betamethasone sodium phosphate and betamethasone acetate suspension (Celestone Soluspan, Schering, Kenilworth, NJ).

In unpublished data, I have reviewed 100 personal consecutive cases of facial dermabrasion. One patient who had never undergone isotretinoin therapy developed atrophic facial scarring. It was found that this patient was a vegetarian. I have found that vegetarians or patients who have bulimia or anorexia can develop postoperative dehiscence after rhytidectomy and atrophic or hypertrophic scarring after dermabrasion or medium-to-deep facial chemical peels. My review of the literature led me to believe that these forms of abnormal healing result from a lack of essential amino acids being present in the patient's diet. Of the remaining 99 patients, 26 had undergone Accutane therapy and 73 patients had never received Accutane therapy. None of this latter group of 73 patients developed delayed healing or abnormal scarring. In the group of 36 Accutane-treated patients, 14 showed delayed healing that was not complete at 15 days or more following the dermabrasion. The longest period for reepithelialization was 28 days. Ten patients developed atrophic or hypertrophic scarring, in many cases not apparent

Text continues on page 95

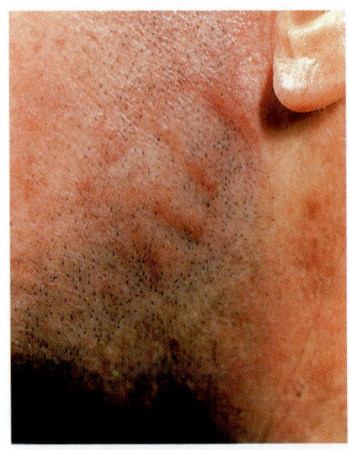

FIG. 57. This is the same patient as Figure 51, now at 8 months postdermabrasion. With the use of systemic topical and intralesional steroid therapy, the hypertrophic scars on his left cheek are now smaller in size and decreased in consistency.

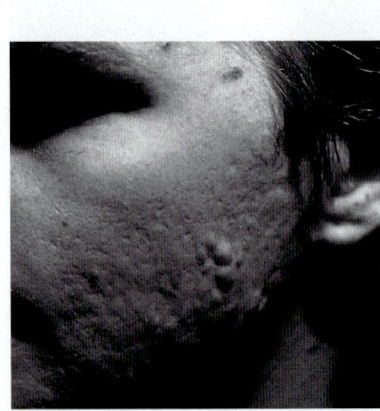

FIG. 59. This is a 22-year-old male patient with hypertrophic scarring from preexisting severe cystic acne. This patient had completed one course of Accutane therapy 6 months prior to the facial dermabrasion using the Schumann Derma III high-speed machine.

FIG. 60. Same patient as seen in Figure 59. This photograph was taken at 8 weeks and shows some erythema present in the region of the preexisting hypertrophic scars. The skin contour is flat and there is no suggestion of induration or the recurrence of hypertrophic scarring.

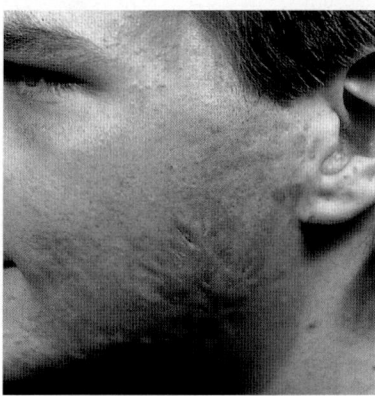

FIG. 61. Same patient as Figure 59. The patient is now 6 months postdermabrasion and extensive hypertrophic scarring of the entire posterolateral cheek has occurred. These scars are more extensive than the original scars that existed prior to the dermabrasion. This patient had not returned for the routine follow-up care, his last visit being at 8 weeks as seen in Figure 60.

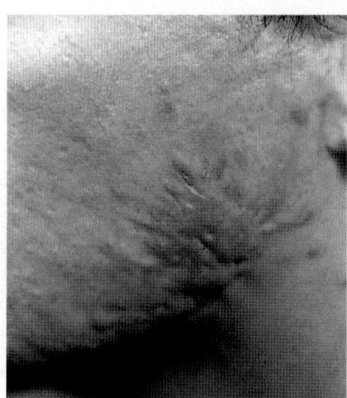

FIG. 62. Same patient as Figure 59. The patient is now 9 months postdermabrasion and shows persistent scarring of the mandibular angle and left cheek. Because of the age and extensive nature of these scars, they were unresponsive to systemic, topical, and intralesional steroids that were combined with external pressure dressings. The importance of early intervention cannot be overemphasized.

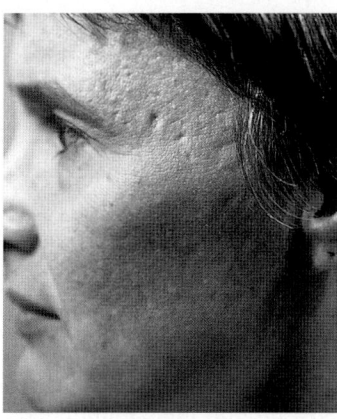

FIG. 63. This 46-year-old female patient had undergone one course of Accutane approximately 2 months in duration 8 years prior to the facial dermabrasion. There are deep scars of her left temple and preauricular areas. A minimal number of milia are present. Scars are present on her anterior central cheek but are not obvious on this photograph.

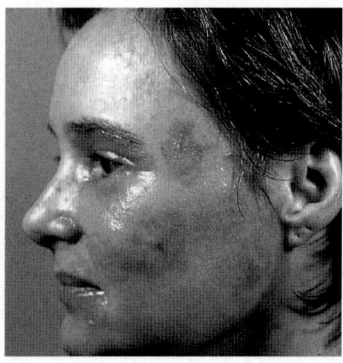

FIG. 64. Same patient as Figure 63 at 12 days postdermabrasion. Only three areas have not completely reepithelialized, on her temple and left central cheek where the acne preexisting scars were concentrated. The mandibular angle is a danger area because it overlies bone and because rapid freezing will dermabrade more efficiently. Reepithelialization was complete in the normal time period of 14 days.

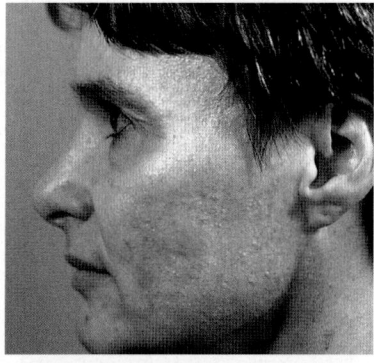

FIG. 65. Same patient as Figure 63 at 8 months postdermabrasion. The three areas that were last to reepithelialize show no evidence of persistent erythema, induration, or postoperative scarring. There is evidence of hypertrophic scarring in the central cheek that is separate and inferior and posterior to the last area to reepithelialize as shown in Figure 64.

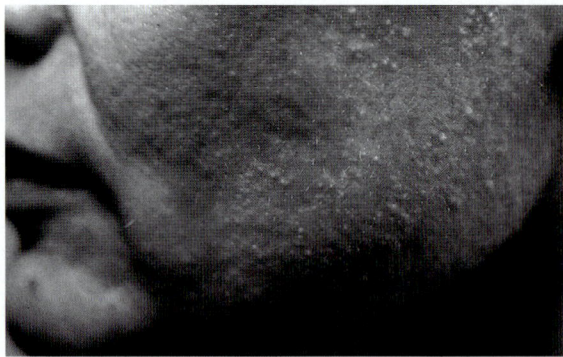

FIG. 66. Same patient as Figure 63 at 8 months postdermabrasion. This close up photograph of the affected area seen in Figure 65 shows that hypertrophic scarring is present over an extensive area in the central cheek. There is also atrophic scarring posterolateral to the nasolabial fold and oral commissure. These areas were reepithelialized prior to 12 days as seen in Figure 64. More milia are present at this stage than were present, as seen in her preoperative photograph in Figure 63.

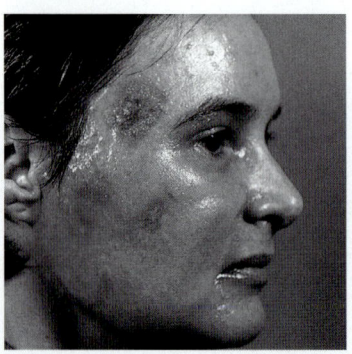

FIG. 69. Same patient as Figure 68 at 12 days postdermabrasion. The areas of greatest scarring were dermabraded more deeply and have not completely reepithelialized. A small area over the midportion of the mandible is not completely reepithelialized resulting from a deeper dermabrasion because this area represents a danger zone.

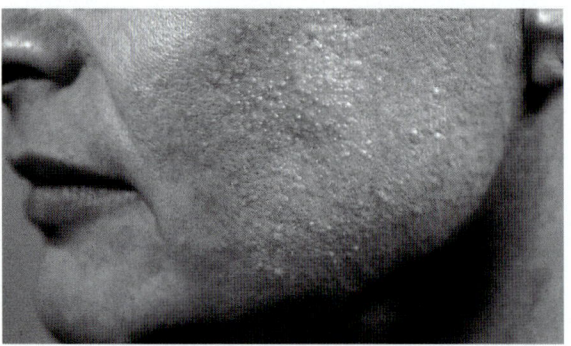

FIG. 67. Same patient as Figure 63 at 14 months postdermabrasion. Aggressive systemic and topical steroid therapy had been initiated 3 months postdermabrasion at the onset of the scarring. Her skin is hypopigmented and atrophic in most areas. The hypertrophic scar of her central cheek is now minimized but remains. This type of scarring has been seen only in post-Accutane patients.

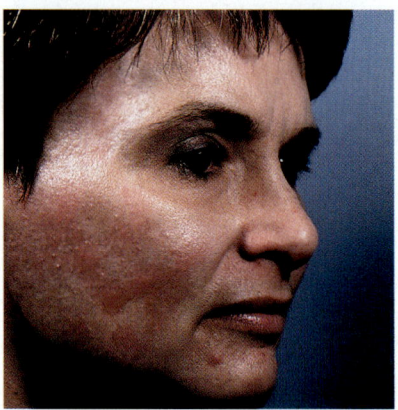

FIG. 70. Same patient as Figure 68 at 8 months postdermabrasion. Hypertrophic scars are present in the mid cheek in areas that were reepithelialized prior to 12 days as seen in Figure 69. The V-shaped pattern of these scars does not correspond to the strokes that are made during dermabrasion. Note that the three areas that were dermabraded to the deepest level are not affected by the scarring. The area over the midportion of the mandible shows some erythema suggestive of an incipient scar.

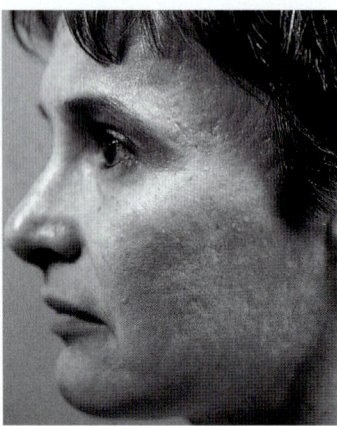

FIG. 68. This is the same patient as Figures 63 to 67. Her significant scarring is in the temple, preauricular, and central cheek areas. Scars in these areas are moderately deep and will require an aggressive dermabrasion using the extra-coarse diamond fraise.

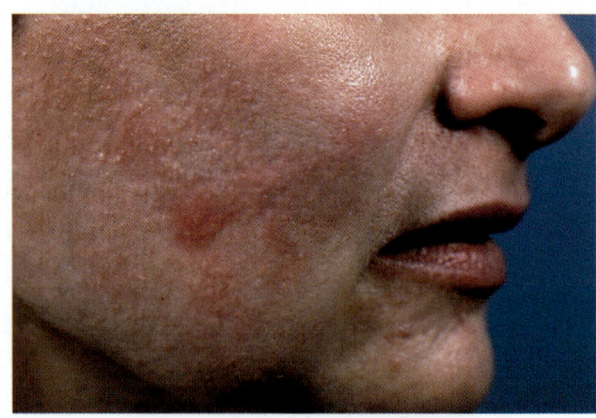

FIG. 71. Same patient as Figure 68 at 9 months postdermabrasion. The V-shaped hypertrophic scar of the central cheek is somewhat diminished but continues to be an obvious cosmetic defect. The point of greatest scarring is the midpoint of the central cheek area. Aggressive systemic and topical therapy does not resolve this complication. The incipient scar at the midportion of the mandible is now resolved. Overall, the remaining skin of her cheek is hypopigmented and appears atrophic.

until 4 to 6 months following reepithelialization. Not all of the patients developing scars had experienced delayed healing. When combining the incidence of delayed healing and postoperative scarring, 19 post-Accutane patients had experienced complications. This represented a 73% complication rate in isotretinoin-treated patients.

I believe that the complications of delayed healing and postoperative scarring are much more likely in Accutane-treated patients than most surgeons are willing to accept. In my 25 years of clinical experience in performing facial dermabrasion, I recall patients developing postoperative scarring in the early years of my career, probably the result of inexperience. The absence of any of my patients developing postoperative scars during the period of at least 10 years preceding the introduction of Accutane is significant. The fact that 65 of the 66 patients who had never received Accutane had no delayed healing or postoperative scarring in this series is also significant. Although statistical analysis has not been done on this unreported series, it is obvious that there is a cause-and-effect relationship between Accutane treatment and the occurrence of delayed healing and/or postoperative scarring.

It is difficult to establish criteria to identify the post–Accutane patients who are susceptible to abnormal healing. As a general rule, I believe that the greater the elapsed time from the cessation of isotretinoin therapy, the less likelihood there is of developing postoperative complications. Obviously, a delay of 6 months after Accutane cessation is inadequate. One of my most severely affected patients had been off for 6 months. He developed severe and extensive keloidal scars of the cheeks (see Figs. 59–62). Unfortunately, another one of my most severely affected cases is a patient who had been off Accutane for 8 years (see Figs. 63–71). Thus, the elapsed time cannot ensure freedom from complications. The dosage of Accutane and the length of therapy also do not appear to be directly related to these postoperative complications. In fact, many patients who have undergone two and occasionally three courses of Accutane treatment had no complications. This led me to conclude that patients who fail to respond to Accutane therapy are better candidates than those who experience an effective and long-lasting response. Patients who persist in having clinical acne prove that there is an existing population of pilosebaceous glands present. I am more concerned with patients who have experienced a profound effect during and after their Accutane therapy. Those patients who have no ongoing acne and those who have a marked decrease in sebum production are those who I consider to be at higher risk. At this point, I cannot identify specific criteria that will reliably predict post-Accutane patients who are susceptible to these complications.

In my personal experience, I have observed that a higher percentage of post-Accutane patients who undergo dermabrasion during the first 2 years following Accutane therapy will develop abnormal healing. These patients have more severe hypertrophic scarring than those off Accutane for more than 24 months. Therefore, I delay any dermabrasion or chemical peel for a minimum of 24 months after ces-

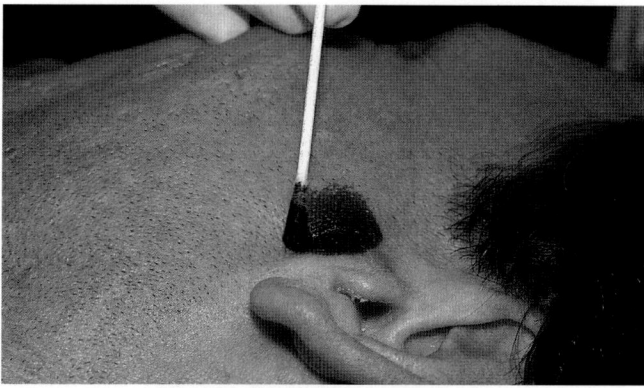

FIG. 72. When a patient has undergone Accutane therapy, it is advisable to determine the numbers and size of existing sebaceous glands by skin biopsy. If this is normal, a spot dermabrasion of 1.5 to 2.0 cm is performed in the preauricular area.

sation of Accutane. After 21 months, a 3-mm punch biopsy is performed in the preauricular area. The histopathology laboratory is instructed to make horizontal cuts through the specimen, parallel to the skin surface, rather than the usual method of cutting slices perpendicular to the skin surface. This allows the pathologist to easily count the number of pilosebaceous glands in the 3 mm specimen. The pathologist is instructed to evaluate the size of the sebaceous glands and to report if they are smaller than usual. When there is evidence of a diminution in either the number of glands or the size of glands, the specimen is considered abnormal and the patient is advised against undergoing dermabrasion or chemical peeling at that time. I have provided the pathologist with skin specimens from normal patients who have preauricular skin excised during the process of rhytidectomy to be used as a baseline reference. If the patient's biopsy is normal, a 1.5-cm circular dermabrasion is performed on the contralateral preauricular area (Figs. 72–77). The patient is examined on the 7th and 14th postoperative days to evaluate reepithelialization, which should be completed between the 9th and 12th

FIG. 73. To limit the skin damage caused by the frostbite from the cryospray, the cardboard backing of a prescription pad is cut to provide a small circular hole about 2 cm in size.

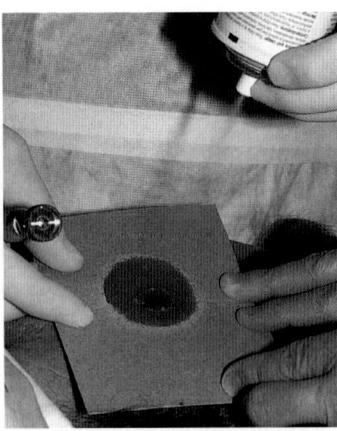

FIG. 74. An assistant holds the cardboard template on the preauricular area and the cryospray is applied until the skin is frozen firmly.

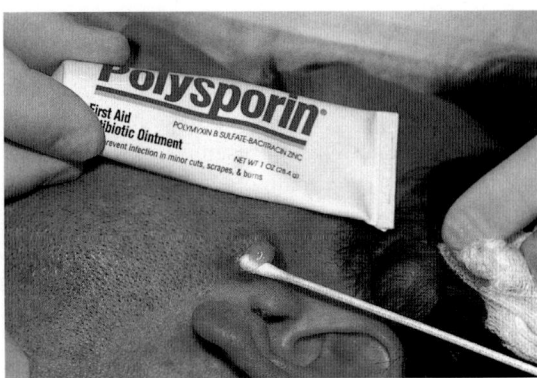

FIG. 76. Polysporin ointment is applied to the dermabraded site and it is then covered with Telfa.

days in normal patients. If reepithelialization occurs on the 15th day or later, the test dermabrasion is considered abnormal and the patient is advised against undergoing dermabrasion or chemical peeling.

I discuss in detail with every post-Accutane patient the possibility of these complications. A definitive note is written into the patient's chart documenting the discussion and confirming that the patient understood the possible risks. A special release outlining the possibility of these complications is used for the spot dermabrasion and the facial dermabrasion, if performed. Since scarring may be delayed for weeks after the reepithelialization is complete I usually delay the dermabrasion until 8 to 12 weeks have elapsed. If the site of the spot dermabrasion is supple, has normal texture and contour, and is free of erythema or induration, I advise that there is no apparent abnormal healing and the patient may choose to proceed with a full face dermabrasion or chemical peel. As noted earlier, despite these tests appearing normal, I cannot guarantee to the patient that the surgery will be free of complications.

In post-Accutane patients who develop hypertrophic scarring, there are frequently common clinical findings. The normally expected erythema that usually lasts for 2 or 5 months is replaced by a more intense and persistent erythema. In some cases, the erythema will have a reticulated appearance (see Fig. 51). This persistent erythema will invariably be associated with the onset of subtle underlying induration. The two signs of persistent erythema and subtle induration should always alert the surgeon that an incipient scar is forming. As scar formation progresses, the affected areas will become raised and sometimes nodular (see Figs. 52, 53, 65, 66). I have seen scars that are linear and, as in two patients, the pattern was perpendicular to the direction of stroke used during the dermabrasion (see Figs. 56, 57, 70, 71). In addition to hypertrophic scars, patients may develop areas of atrophy, sometimes encompassing an entire cheek and temple (see Figs. 66, 67, 71).

It is of greatest interest that these Accutane scars usually involve the central cheeks and adjoining areas. This is not the area in which scars occur because the dermabrasion has been performed too deeply. These classic danger areas, to be described later, which result from deep dermabrasion, occur

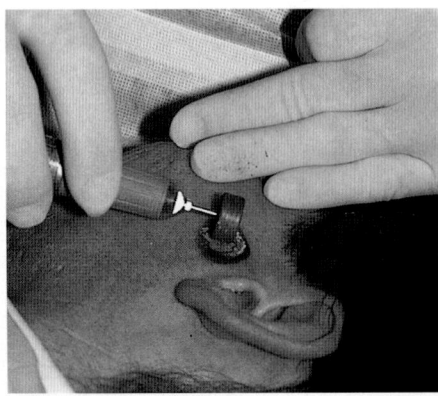

FIG. 75. The area is then dermabraded until the gentian violet is eliminated. The dermabrasion should be deep enough to provide a medium-depth injury.

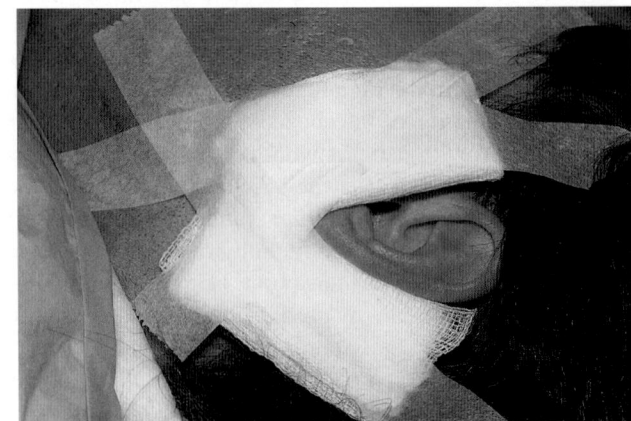

FIG. 77. Several pieces of sterile gauze may be placed over the dermabraded site to absorb any exudate that will occur during the first several days. Often, this is necessary only overnight, followed by the use of a Band-Aid and Polysporin.

over bony prominences. I have never seen a scar of the central cheek except in Accutane patients.

The surgeon should also avoid using Accutane for 6 months after a dermabrasion or chemical peel. Katz has reported a patient who developed scarring of the central cheek that appeared 6 weeks after the institution of Accutane therapy (54). Fourteen weeks earlier, a facial dermabrasion had been performed. Other retinoids such as etretinate (Tegison, Roche Laboratories, Nutley, NJ) are now used for psoriasis. It is stored for a much longer time than Accutane and may have cutaneous effects for several years after discontinuation of therapy (55). These patients may also be susceptible to the abnormal healing seen following Accutane therapy.

Hypertrophic and Keloidal Scars

Some patients will develop hypertrophic scars or keloids during the active phase of severe acne. Dermatologists know this as acne keloidalis. Although I have never seen this in 25 years of practice, I would recommend that dermabrasion be delayed until this phase of scarring is quiescent. When all scars are mature and no new scars have developed, the dermabrasion may be performed. It is an accepted surgical dogma that patients with previous hypertrophic scars or keloids have an inherent ability to form these abnormal types of scars following surgical procedures (56). Sculpting of hypertrophic scars using dermabrasion is usually beneficial and generally does not result in the recurrence of hypertrophic scars in cases that are uncomplicated by others factors such as patient manipulation, previous Accutane therapy, or infection.

Cryoglobulinemia

I believe that cryoglobulinemia is a contraindication to dermabrasion when topical refrigerants are used. These patients should not be treated with freezing agents. Tests evaluating the quantitative cryoglobulins present should be performed if the qualitative screening test is positive. I have successfully performed dermabrasions without complications on patients who demonstrated only a trace amount of cryoglobulin on the quantitative test. The alternative use of tumescent anesthesia may be appropriate in this situation (32,33). Although I have considered cryofibrinogenemia to be a contraindication to dermabrasion using cryoanesthesia, extensive discussions with an expert in the condition revealed that this concern was unfounded. As a consequence, preoperative laboratory evaluation for serum cryofibrinogen is no longer ordered.

Vitiligo

Vitiligo is not a contraindication for dermabrasion. In 1979, Burks stated that dermabrasion was the most satisfactory treatment for the improvement of vitiligo (36). Other surgeons with whom I have discussed this topic have had results confirming those of Burks. Although the melanocyte is susceptible to the cryogenic injury of liquid nitrogen, the higher temperature of Frigiderm and Fluoro Ethyl does not appear to affect the production of melanin. In my limited experience with vitiligo patients, none have had permanent depigmentation in the areas treated with cryoanesthesia and dermabrasion. Recently, studies on vitiligo treatment show that melanocytes transplanted in epithelial sheet grafting had the best survival when the recipient site was prepared using dermabrasion (57,58).

Pigmentary States

Light-skinned black patients, mulattos, Asians, and brunette whites are more susceptible to pigmentary changes following dermabrasion. Postoperative hyperpigmentation is a strong possibility. If these patients fully understand this possibility, they may be offered the procedure. Hypopigmentation can be permanent but hyperpigmentation is usually temporary. The use of bleaching agents and superficial chemical peels initiated at the first evidence of hyperpigmentation will usually control this problem promptly. Strict avoidance of sun exposure and the regular use of a high-SPF (i.e., over 15) sunscreen are mandatory. In areas of high sunlight exposure, such as the southern United States, the continued use of sunscreens and bleaches may be required for several months or longer postoperatively. Deeply pigmented black patients usually do well after dermabrasion, although they must be forewarned that there will be temporary postoperative hypopigmentation (59). The normal color usually returns in 4 to 6 weeks following dermabrasion.

THE CONSULTATION

The selection of appropriate candidates for dermabrasion is the central part of the procedure. This requires a thorough and organized approach. Each surgeon will develop an individual style that best suits the mode and character of their individual practice. I favor the following approach. An experienced surgical nurse or trained consultant interviews the preoperative candidates. Preoperative and postoperative photographs of patients on whom I have performed a facial dermabrasion are shown. This will include therapeutic procedures for active acne and reconstructive procedures for postacne scarring. The procedure and its postoperative phase are discussed by the consultant, and the patient is given an opportunity to ask questions. A period of 30 minutes is allowed for this session. The patient is then examined by me either immediately following this session or at a time arranged at a later date.

An extensive written past history is completed by the patient and evaluated by the consultant and surgeon. Usually, the first question I ask relating to the dermabrasion is, "How may I help you?" This allows the patient to identify his or her needs and goals. I then ask the patient to specifically identify the percentage of improvement envisioned. Three questions are posed: "How much improvement do you hope for?"

"How much improvement do you think is reasonable?" and "What is the minimum percentage of improvement you would accept?" The answers to these questions will give you an insight into the patient's concept of possible goals and results in his or her individual case. Patients are told before answering the first question that a 100% improvement is impossible and they should consider the goal to be improvement, not perfection. Many patients have definitive ideas about the maximum obtainable goal, some of which are realistic and some of which are totally unrealistic. This is not an opportunity for you to criticize the patient for unrealistic goals but rather an opportunity to educate a patient about the possible outcome. When answering the second question about what percentage of improvement is considered reasonable, you should remember that patients have no idea what the usual percentage of improvement is. I tell the patient that I recognize this, but that an answer provides me with insight into their concept of dermabrasion. In my personal experience, most physicians in the Midwest will state that a patient can expect a 30% to 40% improvement and that two or three dermabrasions will be necessary for an adequate result. This percentage of improvement seems to be appropriate nationwide, both from personal communication and review of the literature. The last question, which addresses the minimal acceptable improvement, reveals to you the patient's motivation to undergo the surgery. Most patients will respond, "Any improvement at all." This shows high motivation. When patients state that their minimum acceptable percentage is 75%, I reiterate to them that the national average is only 30% to 40%. I will not accept any patient whose minimum percentage of improvement is over 50%. This discussion is an opportunity for you to understand the patient's concept and goals of dermabrasion and to educate them about an appropriate perspective of this procedure. Unreasonable expectations based on fantasy or sensational results seen in advertisements or in the lay press are addressed. Most patients who seek consultation after disappointing results at the hands of another surgeon, do so because of inadequate education on the limitations of the procedure. The predictable results of the surgery must be within the realm of the patient's goal. This phase of the evaluation will require time and patience but virtually eliminates postoperative dissatisfaction since the patient has been given a clear explanation of realistic results. Although the vast majority of my patients obtain a 75% to 85% improvement following a single dermabrasion, I emphasize to the patient that no reliable percentage of improvement can be predicted. Because individuals usually gain greater self-esteem and self-confidence, even limited cosmetic improvement will be helpful. Realistically, since dermabrasion is time consuming, involves risk, and is relatively expensive, the goal of "any improvement at all" is unrealistic. Because most dermabrasion candidates are highly motivated, they will accept an improvement that may be less than what their family and friends, and you, as the surgeon, had hoped for. It is important for friends and relatives to understand that patients undergo this procedure as a method of self-improvement. They are seeking personal benefits and should not be negatively influenced by family or friends. Occasionally, family members will actively discourage the patient from undergoing dermabrasion, expressing that they think the patient looks fine. Families frequently forget that it is the patient who must suffer from the scarring, not the family. It is the patient, not the family, who suffers daily from disfigurement of the scarring. It is important for friends and the family to be supportive and to allow the patient to arrive at a decision that is best for him or her personally.

During the next phase of the evaluation, I have the patients stand in front of a large mirror. Their face is illuminated by soft overhead light. They are asked to identify scars that they want improved. Occasionally, their assessment of scar severity contrasts significantly from mine. I then carefully examine and verbally describe the scars that the patient wishes to improve. What I may perceive as a surgical need may not at all be the areas that are important to the patient. On some occasions, patients have not identified the most severely affected area of scarring as important. This is especially true if this particular scar was sustained during childhood and the individual has become accustomed to it despite its obvious cosmetic defect. It is my obligation to properly assess and treat the defects that are important to the patient.

The above phase of scar evaluation is done in front of a large mirror using oblique overhead light. Since sunlight emanates from above and most indoor lighting is mounted in the ceiling, the use of overhead light best approximates the shadows that are most commonly seen by the patient. A detailed description of the scars, including their size, depth, and location, is noted in the chart and read to the patient as it is entered. This allows the patient to understand the severity and extent of the scars. Some patients with extensive and severe scarring will verbalize that they are only modestly affected. This misconception should be delicately corrected. I also ask the patient questions and examine the patient for evidence of vitiligo, chloasma, pseudofolliculitis, herpetic scarring, verrucae plana, and evidence of cold allergy or cryoglobulinemia. Vaccination scars and other surgical or traumatic scars are examined for evidence of hypertrophic or keloidal scars, hypopigmentation, or atrophic changes. The absence of each item is noted specifically and any abnormality is recorded in the chart.

Following the physical examination, I discuss the usual events, including the preoperative, operative, and postoperative phases. The usual events of erythema, edema, exudation, discomfort, crust formation, milia, acne exacerbation, and vascular flushing are reviewed. Side effects such as purpura, permanent hypopigmentation, and temporary postinflammatory hyperpigmentation are discussed. Complications including infection and scar formation are reviewed in detail. I also ask what guarantees they believe will be provided preoperatively. Most understand that no guarantee is given or implied. If they do not, a further discussion will clarify this point. A list of each discussion topic is included on my consultation sheet, and as each subject is discussed a checkmark is made so that there is evidence that the patient has received this information. The discussion of these conditions is done in lay terms to avoid the confusion and misunderstanding if medical terms were used. The patient is then asked if he or she understands the information and if there are any questions. I give an extensive typewritten list of postoperative instructions to the patient to clarify, support, and amplify the information that I have given verbally. The duration of surgery, the areas to be dermabraded, and the charges to be made are recorded in the chart by me and outlined to the patient. I then ask patients if they are prepared to make a decision. A significant number of patients schedule the operation a the time of the consultation and evaluation, since they have considered the surgery for several years. A copy of the postoperative instructions is given to the patients at the conclusion of the evaluation. They are told to review them carefully so they are familiar with their postoperative responsibilities.

My portion of the evaluation usually requires 30 to 35 minutes. Some patients require more than the allotted time. They are asked to return for a second appointment if adequate time is not available. Patients who are inappropriate in their actions, those who fail to understand the information provided, or those who are mismatched with my personality or approach are told in a gentle and understanding manner that I prefer to defer their surgery or refer them to another surgeon. With patients who are manipulative or aggressive, I simply state that the relationship is uncomfortable and that I feel we will be unable to achieve the type of relationship that is important for the success of the procedure. Names of several other physicians are then offered. Those patients who are emotionally incapable of proceeding with the surgery are assessed in a compassionate and understanding way. Patients who are not yet emotionally prepared to undergo the rigors of the procedure but who demonstrate anatomic defects amenable to dermabrasion are told that the surgery can be performed when they are in a more stable condition. Patients will surprisingly accept this approach. In this way, I have not denied patients the opportunity to achieve the improvement that they so desire; the goal has merely been delayed. It is also helpful if I encourage the establishment of a treatment program conducted by a psychologist or psychiatrist, so that the patient will progress toward improved emotional stability.

If I am aware that the patient has had periods of depression or psychotic episodes, I personally review the details with the treating psychiatrist or psychologist. Most consultants in the field of mental health have little understanding of the magnitude of the dermabrasion procedure. In these circumstances, I will write a letter extensively outlining the procedure, its postoperative care, and its emotional stress, and I express my concerns over this particular patient. This letter and a copy of the eight-page single-spaced postoperative orders are sent to the treating mental health consultant. Often, a call is made to the consultant to further explain the procedure and its results. This allows the consultant to provide a candid and informed decision concerning the patient's ability to undergo the surgery now or in the near future. I require a written letter from the consultant stating that the surgery is an appropriate procedure to be performed at this time. If the consultant's letter is vague, a call is made and a letter of explanation providing a more definitive answer is requested. If this is not forthcoming, I will not agree to perform the surgery. I caution that in a court of law the jury would presume that the psychologist or psychiatrist would be the expert in determining the mental status of the patient. A surgeon who decides to go against the advice of a mental health consultant is begging for emotional and possibly legal complications. A variety of psychologically abnormal patients pose potential problems for the dermatologic surgeon. Evaluating and understanding the emotional makeup of patients is essential to the success of the procedure. The surgeon performing dermabrasion is strongly advised to read the literature by Wright (43,44).

PREOPERATIVE PREPARATIONS

Preoperative laboratory examination will include a complete blood count (CBC); tests for qualitative serum cryoglobulins, HIV, and hepatitis B surface antigen; and, in all female patients of child-bearing capability, a pregnancy test. The letter instructs the laboratory to request photographic identification such as a driver's license to prevent a surrogate from providing blood for this preoperative evaluation. Patients who refuse to undergo this preoperative laboratory testing are noncompliant and the surgeon has the right to refuse to perform the surgery. A standardized series of preoperative photographs are taken using color-slide film (Ektachrome Tungsten, ET 135-36, ISO 160) and photoflood illumination, Kelvin 3200° (Fig. 78). These pictures are taken in sufficient time so that the film may be developed and returned to the office prior to the day of surgery. This allows for a repeat photographic session if the film is lost or the results inadequate. At the initial photographic session, which

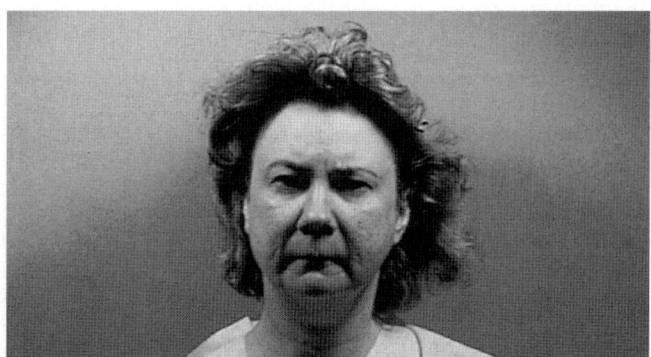

FIG. 78. Photographs taken preoperatively to document the extent and nature of the cutaneous defects are strongly advised. I use photo floodlamps that provide oblique light simulating that seen with sunlight exposure and overhead indoor light. This oblique light produces shadows, which makes the defects most noticeable. Physicians using an electronic flash attached to the camera are creating flat light that minimizes the shadowing and often will obscure the preoperative defects.

is usually no later than 2 weeks prior to the surgery, a written set of postoperative instructions is reviewed in detail by a nurse experienced in the dermabrasion technique. It is helpful if the patient is accompanied by the adult who will assist him or her during the immediate postoperative phase so that both can review the instructions.

Equipment for Dermabrasion

I use two different power units. The commonly used unit is the Bell International Hand Engine (Robbins Instrument Co.). This hand-held electric engine is attached to a small console by a coiled electrical cord that allows maximum flexibility with little drag (Figs. 79, 80). The unit is offered in several rpm ranges, with my preference being model 38-L, which provides 1500 to 33,000 rpm. In addition to providing higher rpm than model 5-D and 25-D (600 to 18,000 rpm), the model 38-L provides greater torque. Only diamond fraises can be used with the higher rpm unit, since they can be adequately balanced. The wire brush is not capable of this precise balance and must be restricted to speeds less than 20,000 rpm to prevent fatigue of the shaft that can result in its bending or rupturing during use.

An accessory offered by Robbins Instrument Co. is a protective fender that clips onto the handpiece to reduce spray (Fig. 81). I strongly recommend against its use because it can vibrate loose and fall into the fraise, creating a potentially dangerous situation.

Because these machines are electric, the motor must be gas sterilized rather than steam autoclaved. A compact and economical gas sterilizer is the Anprolene gas sterilizing agent (H. W. Anderson Products, Oyster Bay, NY) (Fig. 82). The use of alcohol or ether as a wipe has been shown by the Centers for Disease Control to be inadequate as a sterilizer. A plastic sleeve placed over the hand engine, in my opinion, does not sufficiently protect from blood contamination. It also restricts air movement over the electrical winding and magnets necessary to cool the hand engine. Shelton and Grekin have evaluated the necessity of sterilizing the entire hand engine (60). They point out that the chuck may be removed from the electrical housing, allowing it to be steam autoclaved. They do not feel that sterilization of the electrical portion of the handpiece is necessary. I feel that it is prudent to sterilize the entire handpiece and electrical cord to avoid cross-contamination.

The second unit I use is the high-speed Derma III Dermabrader produced by A. Schumann of Dusseldorf, Germany (Fig. 83). This unit provides extremely high torque with a range from 15,000 to 60,000 rpm. It allows the experienced operator to decrease the operative time by approximately 25%. The additional torque is particularly helpful for firm, hypertrophic scars. The manufacturer provides specially designed high-speed diamond fraises of medium and coarse grit to withstand the high rpm. These fraises have a much thicker shaft than those used in the Bell hand engine and, therefore, are not interchangeable (Fig. 84).

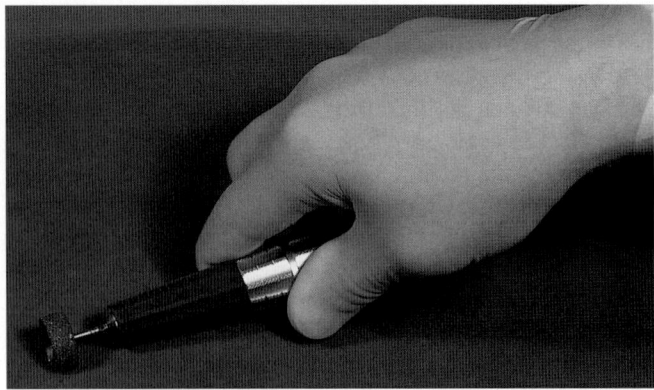

FIG. 80. The Bell Hand Engine is easily grasped with the surgeon's hand, creating a fulcrum that originates at the middle of the surgeon's hand and extends to the cutting edge of the fraise. In this photograph, the fulcrum is approximately 10 cm. The handpiece is balanced on the thumb. No pressure is applied to the fraise. The cutting action is based on the abrasiveness of the cutting surface, not pressure applied to the fraise.

FIG. 79. The Bell Hand Engine is a lightweight high-speed electrical engine capable of providing high torque. It is attached by a removable coiled electric cord to a small console that controls the direction of rotation and the speed of the fraise or wire brush. I prefer a handpiece that provides at least 30,000 rpm, such as the 38-L model shown here.

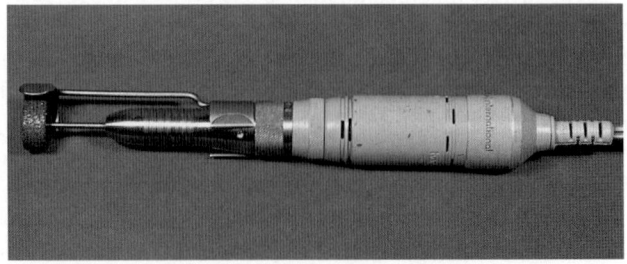

FIG. 81. The Bell Hand Engine can be supplied with a protective fender that is attached to the handpiece. This is a potentially dangerous accessory since it is not permanently attached to the handpiece. I have found that with vibration, the fender can shake loose and be drawn into the rotating fraise, causing a dangerous situation. Also the fender is large and creates a visual obstruction of the surgical field.

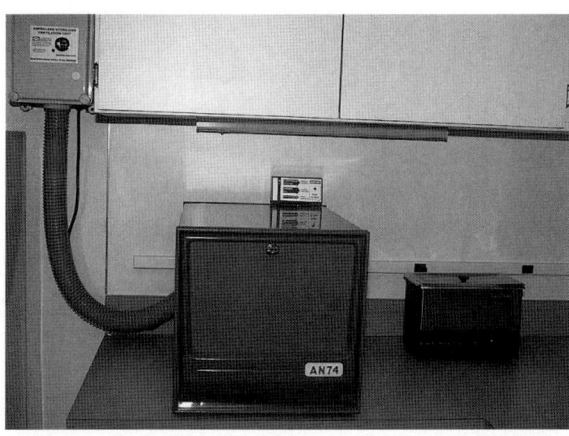

FIG. 82. The Anprolene gas sterilizing system provides adequate sterilization without damaging the electric motor or dulling sharp surfaces. The unit should be vented to the outside atmosphere since its fumes are harmful. Smaller units are available.

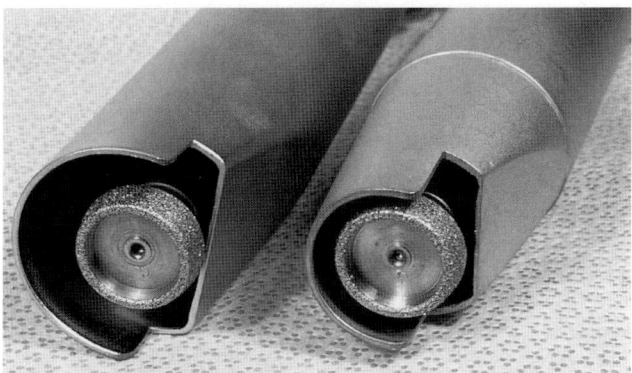

FIG. 84. The Schumann Derma III Dermabrader is supplied with custom high-speed fraises of varying sizes, the largest of which is the most practical. Two protective sleeves are provided, with the smaller sleeve, as seen on the right, being the more appropriate.

The Schumann machine has several disadvantages. The handpiece is larger in diameter and weighs almost 19 ounces compared to the 6½ ounces for the Bell handpiece (Fig. 85). The electrical cord exits from the inferior portion of the handpiece and can drag on the patient while being used. The handpiece can be modified by tapping an additional screw hole at a 120° angle from the original position. Another disadvantage of the Schumann unit is its 14-pound foot-pedal, which is impossible to move without assistance (see Fig. 83). This is attached to a large control console that is placed on a movable stand. This requires significantly more storage space than the Bell hand engine. The greatest disadvantage of the Schumann unit is its cost: it presently is retailing at four times the cost of the Bell hand engine.

Because of the superior abrasive ability of the high-speed fraise and the additional weight of this handpiece, the skin is abraded very rapidly, which can create ridging. I use the Schumann unit on patients with severe scarring who have thick, seborrheic skin. The skin is first abraded with the Schumann machine and then, prior to the unit of skin losing an adequate freeze, each site undergoes fine contouring using the Bell hand engine. The combination of these machines provides an excellent means for an efficient and rapid dermabrasion. I do not recommend the Schumann unit for shallow scarring, over the bony prominences (danger areas), or on the nose.

The abrasive surfaces used in dermabrasion consist of diamond fraises, stiff wire brushes, and serrated wheels (Figs. 86–89). I prefer the diamond fraise and recommend it over the wire brush for all surgeons. For inexperienced surgeons, the fraise is the better choice because it does not catch on soft skin or ricochet as readily as the wire brush. Varying grits available in diamond fraises allow the inexperienced surgeon to use less abrasive fraises, which provides a greater margin of safety. Although Kurtin and Robbins originally designed the wire brush in three widths, 3.0, 6.0, and 12.0 mm, only the 3.0- and 6.0-mm sizes are presently produced. As the width of the brush increases, so does the weight, thus the maximum rpm of the machine must decrease to avoid ex-

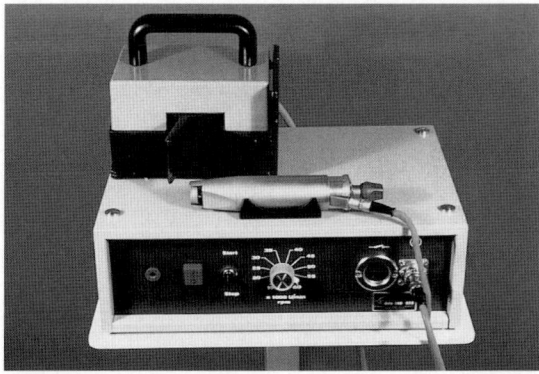

FIG. 83. The Schumann Derma III Dermabrader is a high-speed electrically driven machine capable of producing 60,000 rpm. The console is four times larger than the Bell Hand Engine, which is a distinct disadvantage. The 14-pound footpedal on top of the console is considerably larger than the footpiece of the Bell Hand Engine.

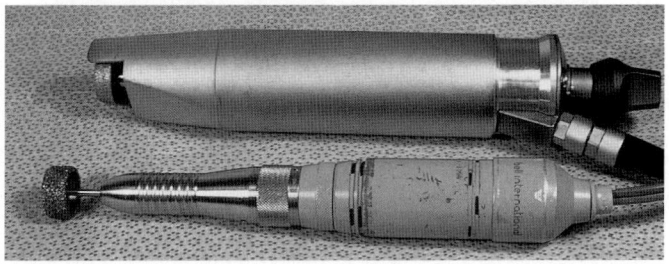

FIG. 85. The Schumann Derma III Dermabrader *(top)* is larger in diameter and weighs 19 ounces as compared to the Bell Hand Engine *(bottom)*, which weighs 8½ ounces. The latter has a much smaller diameter, which is more comfortable in the surgeon's hand.

FIG. 86. The diamond fraises used in the Bell Hand Engine have several different abrasive grits. The three pictured fraises are 16 mm in diameter and 6 mm in width. Three different grits can be provided in fraises: extra-coarse *(left)*, coarse *(middle)*, and standard *(right)*.

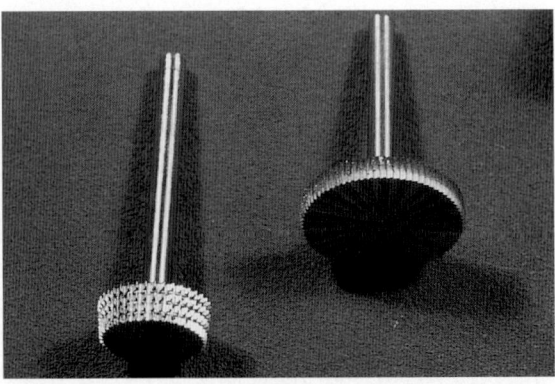

FIG. 88. Serrated wheels that were introduced by Kromayer at the turn of the century are now rarely used in modern dermabrasion. They are provided in varying widths, diameters, and designs.

ceeding the safe rotational speed. Only one diameter, 17 mm, is available in wire brushes. Although the 3-mm wire brush is available in three different wire calibers, the more popular 6-mm brushes are made of only medium caliber wire measuring 0.003 inch. Since wire brushes are limited to width, diameter, and grit, the surgeon must alter the technique and rpm to achieve the desired result.

Diamond fraises come in a wide variety of diameters (10.0 to 17.0 mm) and widths (2.5 to 10.5 mm). Abrasive grits are now available in three types: standard, coarse, and extra-coarse (see Fig. 86). Several manufacturers produce fraises, and there is some variation in diameter, width, grit, and identification between suppliers. A fraise with a greater width is more efficient because of its larger abrasive surface. This greater width gives it less tendency to gouge. The neophyte is advised to start with a wide fraise with a standard grit at a moderate rpm using the Bell hand engine.

When dermabrading skin over bony prominences, freezing will be more efficient because bone is relatively avascular. Dermabrading on firmly frozen skin provides maximum effectiveness. Even the experienced surgeon may choose the less abrasive standard or coarse grit over the extra-coarse grit to limit the depth of the abrasion over these danger areas. Decreasing the diameter of the diamond fraise and lowering the rpm will also decrease the efficiency of the dermabrasion. Diamond fraises can be produced in many shapes (see Fig. 89). The pear-shaped fraise can be used to feather around the alar rim, the tragus, and the root of the nose. It is also quite effective when feathering the edges of exceedingly deep scars or deep anatomic cavities such as the cleft of the chin or the philtrum. The bullet-shaped Pinski fraise can be used both for flat areas and for feathering (see Fig. 89). Because of its construction, the wire brush is not available in these shapes.

When fraises of equal grit are used, instruments of a smaller diameter will be less efficient than those with a

FIG. 87. The wire brush is constructed in three varying widths of 3 mm to 12 mm with a diameter of 17 mm. Three calibers of wire (fine, medium, and coarse) are available but are offered only in the 3-mm-width brush. The brushes of 6 mm and 12 mm are supplied only with medium-caliber wire.

FIG. 89. Special fraises have been designed for special uses. The pear fraise *(top)* can be used for contouring small defects, particularly the alar flare, the tragus, and the philtrum. The Pinski bullet fraise is used in highly contoured areas. Because of its larger size, it is more efficient than the pear fraise. Both shapes come in varying grits.

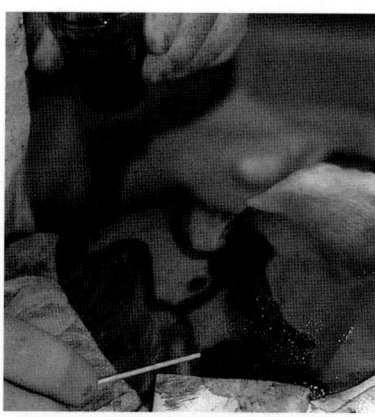

FIG. 139. The chin, central cheek, infraorbital area, and mandibular body have been completed. Additional gentian violet is painted on the unaffected or less scarred facial skin of the lateral posterior cheek.

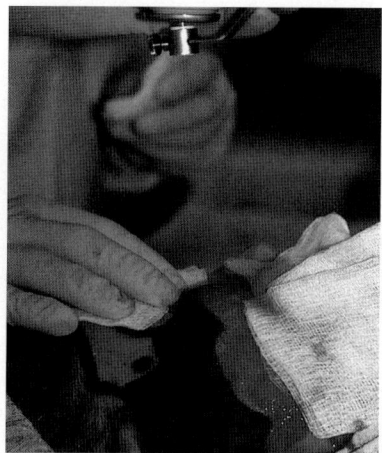

FIG. 140. Because there is less scarring in this area, the freeze can be more superficial, or the operator may choose to use a less aggressive fraise (i.e., the coarse or standard grit) to decrease the effectiveness of the dermabrasion. Since the purpose of the abrasion in this area is to maintain an even color over the face, the depth of abrasion does not have to be as deep as that which is necessary in the scarred areas of the central cheek.

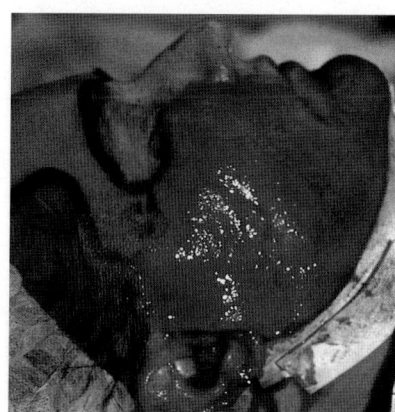

FIG. 141. The entire right cheek and chin have been completed. There is minimal bleeding and essentially no discomfort. A sensation of stinging is usually present.

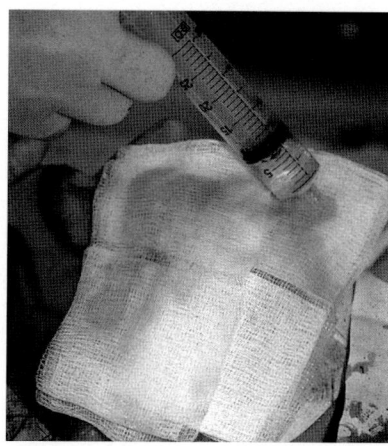

FIG. 142. Sterile gauze is opened and applied to the abraded area. One percent Xylocaine anesthetic liquid used for local infiltration anesthesia is applied to the cotton gauze. Since the nerve endings are exposed, this may decrease the postoperative stinging sensation.

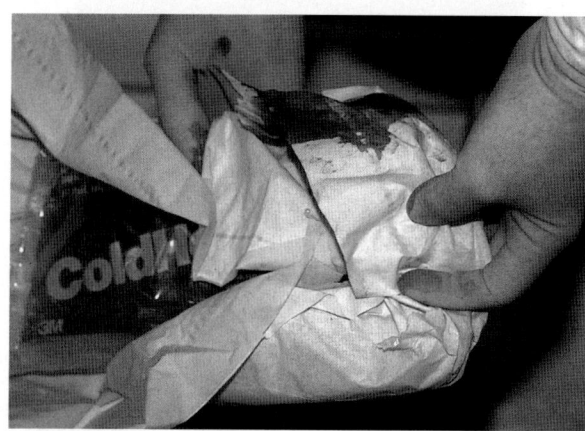

FIG. 143. The ColdHot Pack is removed from the paper towel that has been applied to the left cheek during the period of abrasion to the right cheek. The right side has taken approximately 30 minutes to complete.

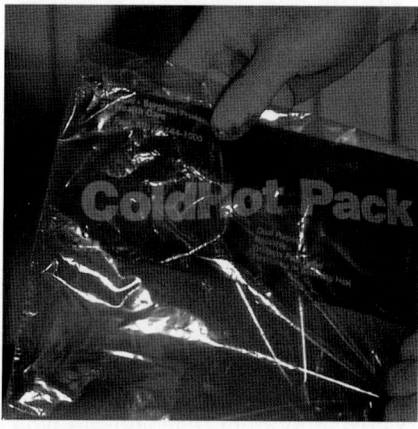

FIG. 144. Underneath the paper towel, the ColdHot Pack is enclosed in a Ziploc bag.

114 · COSMETIC DERMATOLOGIC SURGERY

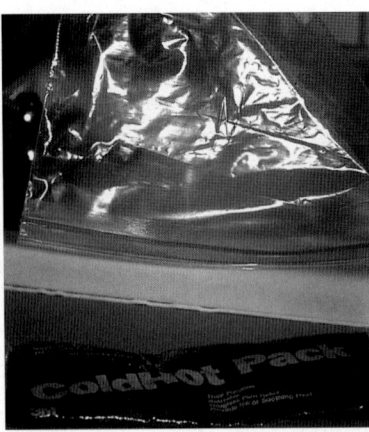

FIG. 145. Because only the paper towel and Ziploc bag have the potential of becoming contaminated, it is not necessary to sterilize the ColdHot Pack between cases to avoid cross-contamination.

FIG. 146. After the right cheek and chin have been completed, the abrasion begins on the left side. The previously marked Xs identify the areas of significant scarring. I will dermabrade these areas first to attain maximum benefit from the intervening prechill.

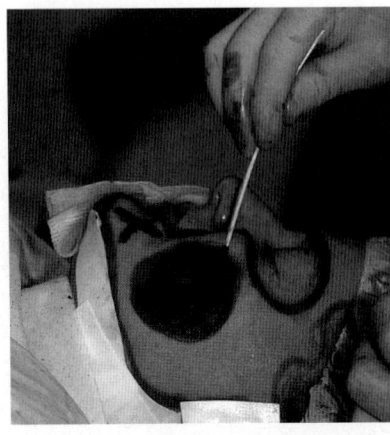

FIG. 147. The areas marked with Xs are painted with gentian violet. Note the Microfoam tape over the external ear used to prevent the cryospray from reaching the tympanic membrane.

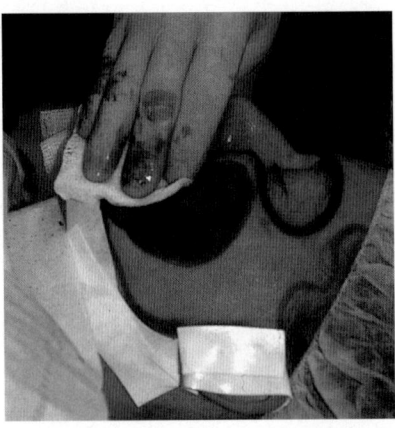

FIG. 148. Any gentian violet that has not dried is blotted with a sterile gauze, because excessive gentian violet will become embeded into the surface of the fraise, decreasing its effectiveness.

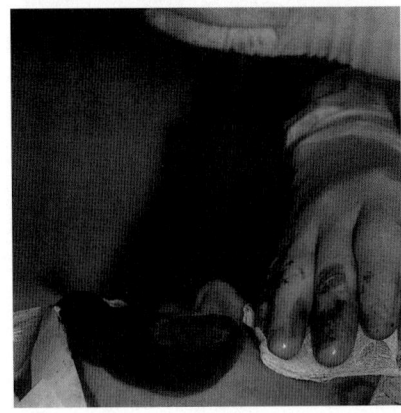

FIG. 149. Multiple bursts of cryospray are applied to the left cheek in a manner similar to that done on the right cheek. Multiple short bursts of 4 to 6 seconds is tolerated much better than a single burst of 30 seconds.

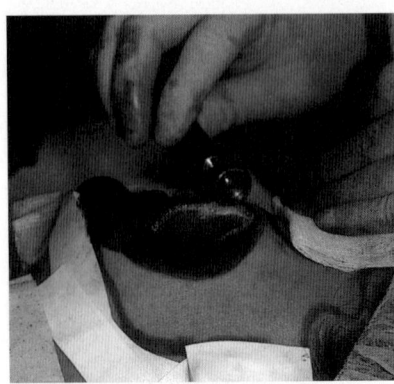

FIG. 150. The abrasion then continues in a similar fashion to that described for the right side.

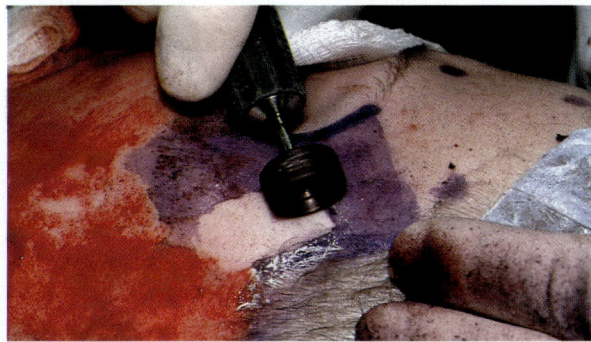

FIG. 151. The skin should be dermabraded so that the debris is not left on the abrasion site. In this photo, the abrasion is progressing from the left to the right, or from the inferior portion of the temple to the superior portion. Though debris is left on the abrasion site because the fraise is turning a counterclockwise direction as we look at the end of the fraise. Because of this counterclockwise motion the debris is pushed ahead of the fraise and on to the unabraded skin.

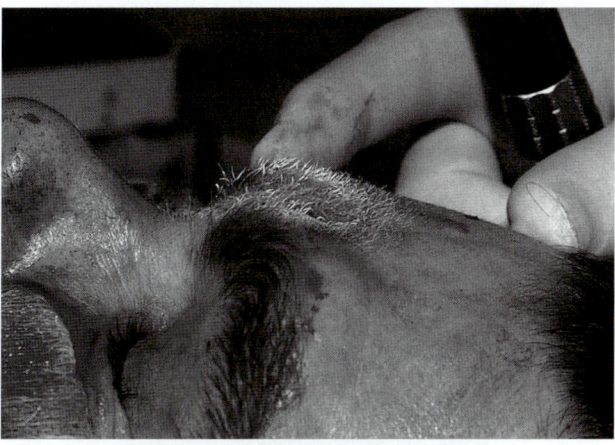

FIG. 154. When frozen, the glabellar area is very painful if not blocked with local anesthesia. With the use of anesthesia, the pain, which is similar to that which occurs when eating ice cream too rapidly, can be completely eliminated.

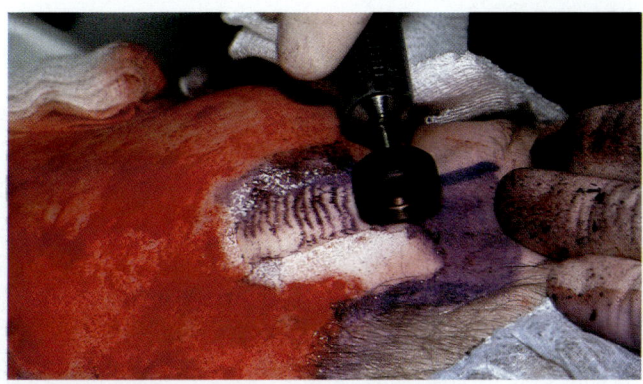

FIG. 152. In this instance, the fraise has been reversed and is now operating in a clockwise motion. The dermabrasion is progressing from the left to the right, or from the inferior portion of the temple to the superior portion, exactly the same direction as seen in Figure 151. In this instance, the debris has been deposited on the abraded site as each stoke has been made. This obscures the newly abraded skin. The rule for the surgeon to remember is that the fraise should turn counterclockwise if the instrument is advancing toward the surgeon and should be used in the clockwise rotation if the handpiece and fraise are moving away from the surgeon.

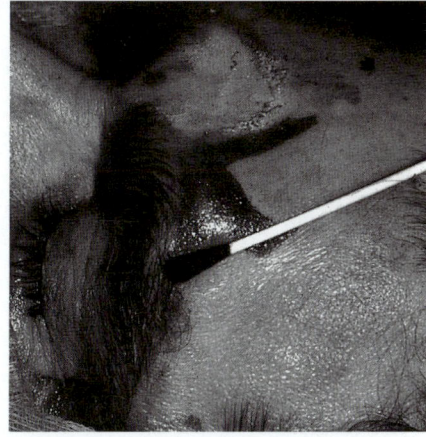

FIG. 155. After the glabella has been dermabraded, the remaining portion of the forehead is painted with 1% gentian violet. The scarred areas should be identified, painted with gentian violet and treated first to ensure that a dermabrasion of sufficient depth is performed.

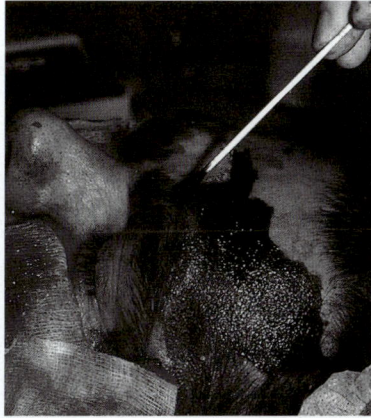

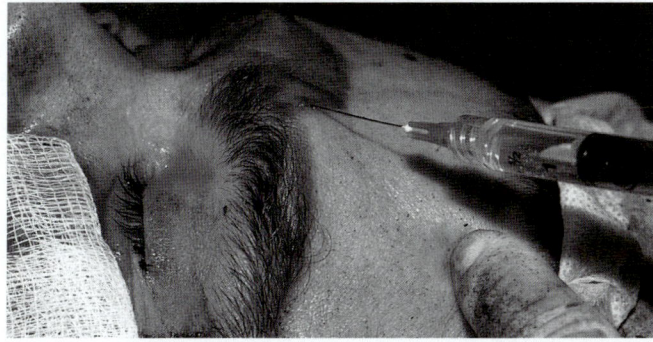

FIG. 153. The supratrochlear and supraorbital nerves are blocked using 2% Xylocaine without epinephrine. I prefer not to use epinephrine because of its vasoconstrictive ability, since I fear that this may increase the depth of freeze from the cryospray.

FIG. 156. Because the gentian violet is painted to the edge of the abraded area, some of the blue pigment will be painted onto the abraded skin. Gentian violet is a water-soluble substance and will not cause a permanent tattoo. Although the blue pigment will be absorbed by the abraded skin, the surgeon should not be fearful that this pigment will be permanently incorporated into the skin.

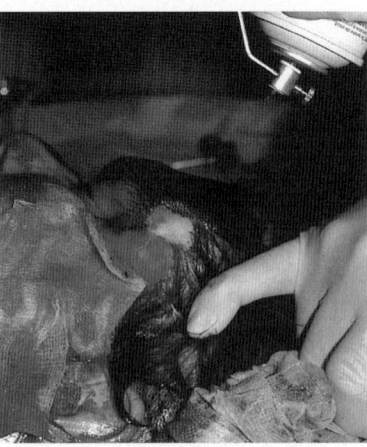

FIG. 157. The forehead is frozen using Fluoro Ethyl in a manner similar to that used on the cheeks. A prechill is not necessary on the forehead, because the relatively avascular underlying bone will allow the cryospray to freeze the skin very effectively.

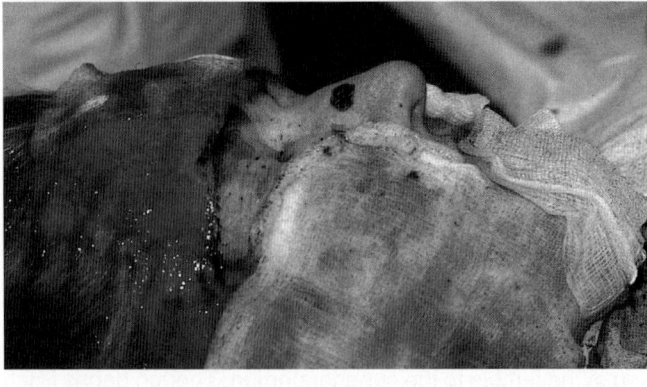

FIG. 160. In this patient, there is a scar on the right side of her nose, which is marked with gentian violet. It is not necessary to treat the entire nose, which has many contours and is susceptible to scarring. As an alternative, a small spot dermabrasion will be performed.

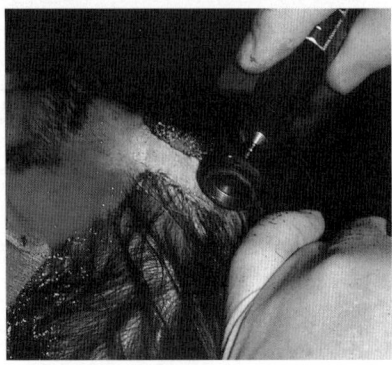

FIG. 158. The left hand holds the hair away from the forehead. The fraise is turning so that the abrasive surface will push the hair upward in a cephalad direction. If the rotation of the fraise is downward, hairs will be pushed onto the forehead, which obstructs the view.

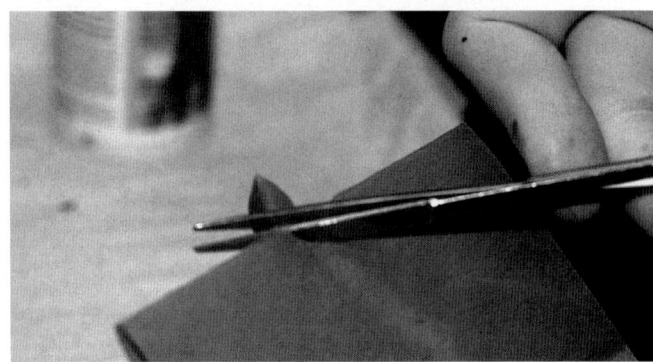

FIG. 161. The cardboard backing from a prescription pad is removed and folded. A scissors is used to cut a small circular hole through which the Fluoro Ethyl can be sprayed.

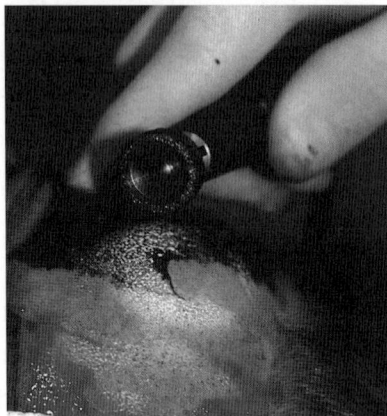

FIG. 159. Note that the width of the stroke, in both this figure and the preceding figure, is very short, less than 1.5 cm. Because the forehead is curved, a long stroke would require the surgeon to move the handpiece in an arc, which may potentially cause gouging. Short strokes eliminate this possibility.

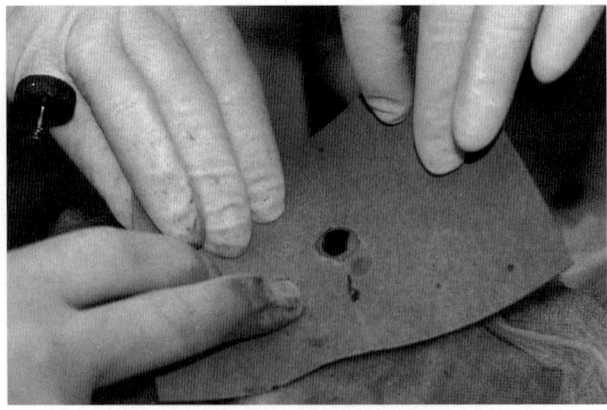

FIG. 162. The hole in the cardboard is placed on the skin at the site of the scar. Pressure may be placed on the cardboard so that the skin is elevated above its natural contour. This will automatically provide the proper amount of beveling to the edges of the dermabraded site.

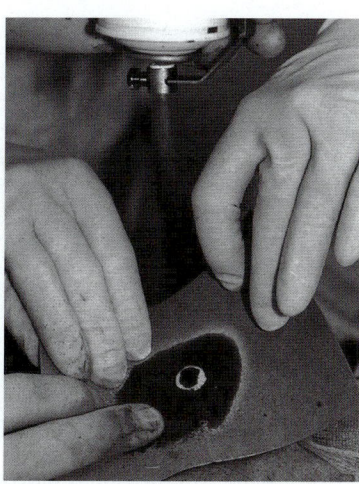

FIG. 163. The area is sprayed in the same manner as described for the cheeks. Multiple blasts of the cryospray are used to provide for a firm, frozen base.

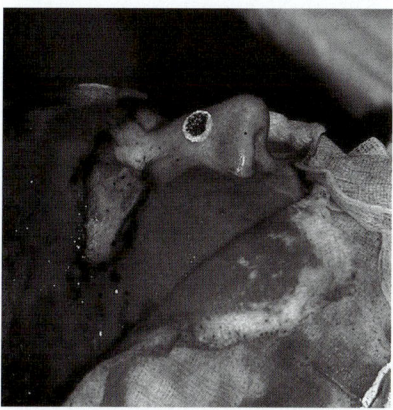

FIG. 164. The cardboard may be either removed or left in place since the skin has been frozen to a firm state. Note that a small area of frozen skin exists beyond the point that has been treated with gentian violet.

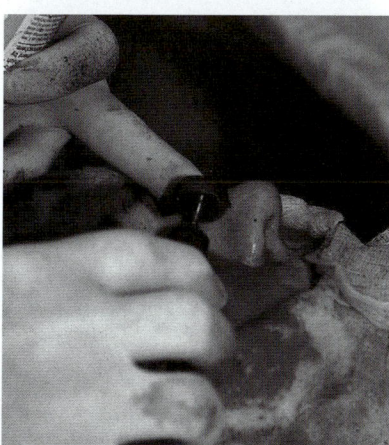

FIG. 165. The affected area is dermabraded to the base of the scar. If additional cycles of freezing and dermabrasion are necessary, the cardboard template is again placed over the surgical site to limit the extent of spray.

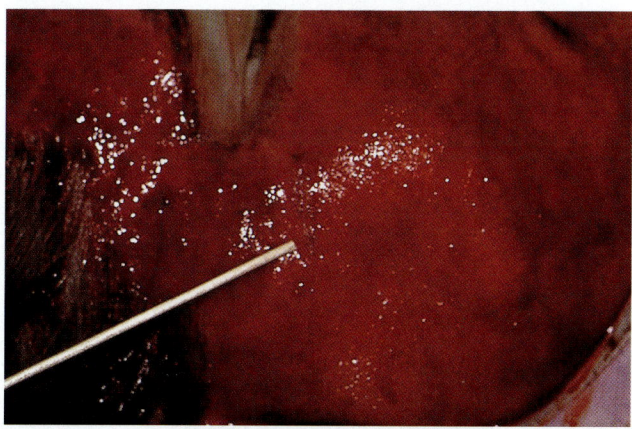

FIG. 166. After all areas have been dermabraded and cleaned with half-strength hydrogen peroxide and warm tap water, the surgical sites should be carefully examined for skip areas. The wooden stick shows an area over the right zygomatic arch that has not been dermabraded to a sufficient depth.

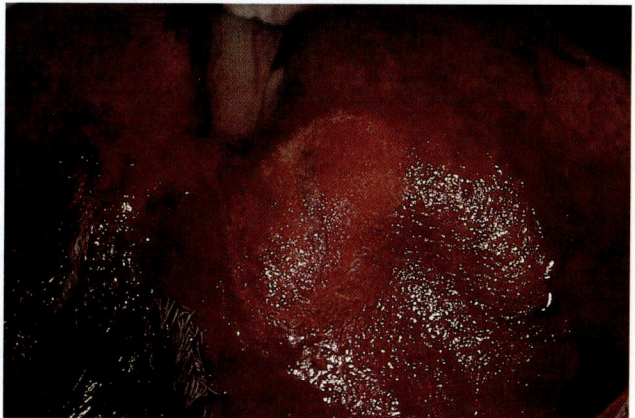

FIG. 167. Although the insufficiently abraded skin is erythematous, the depth of the dermabrasion has not reached the capillary loops and no bleeding is present. When the affected area is refrozen, the inadequately abraded skin will have a white cast compared to the red color of the adequately abraded skin.

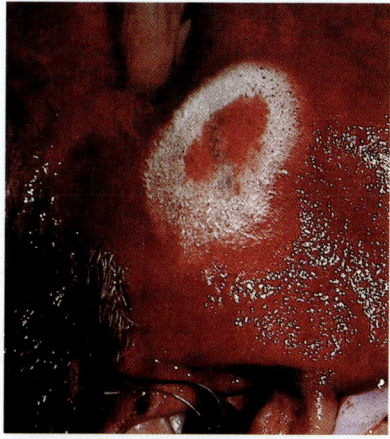

FIG. 168. Because the skin has thawed and the vascular tree has attained maximum vasodilatation, it is difficult to refreeze any area that has previously thawed. Without a firm freeze, the abrasion is inefficient and the depth of surgical injury is shallow.

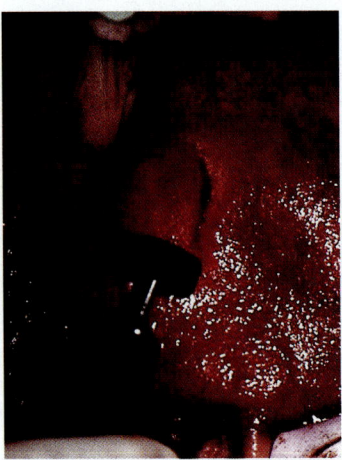

FIG. 169. The area is dermabraded primarily to accomplish adequate blending. Redermabrading an area after it is completely thawed should not be used to treat the deep scars as recommended by Stegman and Tromovich (62). If these skip areas are not identified and dermabraded, they will usually appear as a linear hyperpigmented zone after reepithelialization is completed.

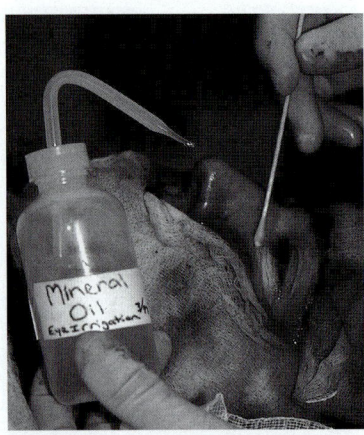

FIG. 171. With the patient's head slightly elevated and turned so that any tears will run down the lateral cheek, the phenol solution is applied with a damp cotton stick applicator. Care should be taken not to soak the cotton tip, which would provide too much chemical to the eyelid, potentially causing the excess liquid to run into the conjunctival sac. Mineral oil is used to flush the conjunctival sac if this should occur. Water should not be used, since it makes the phenol more potent.

Thirty minutes prior to the surgery, an injection of 50 mg of hydroxyzine hydrochloride (Vistaril, Roerig, New York, NY) and 75 to 100 mg of meperidine hydrochloride (Demerol, Winthrop-Breon Lab, New York, NY) is given intramuscularly. The patient should be adequately sedated and at ease during the surgical procedure. General anesthesia is not necessary for this procedure. The use of preoperative and intraoperative analgesics combined with the anesthetic effect of the refrigerant spray is the safest, most efficient, and most economical method of performing facial dermabrasion. Of the thousands of patients I have treated using this method, only a few can be cited as having experienced significant discomfort. Some surgeons prefer to also use regional anesthetic blocks with cryoanesthesia (62–65).

The patient holds a ColdHot Pack (3M ColdHot Pack, 3M Medical-Surgical Division, St. Paul, MN) against the right cheek (see Fig. 108). The Cold/Hot Pack is placed into a polyethylene bag (Ziploc, Dow Brand, Indianapolis, IN) which is encased in a folded paper towel. Both the polyethylene bag and the paper towel are discarded at the end of surgery, preventing contamination of the ColdHot Pack by the patient's blood. This eliminates the need for sterilization of the ColdHot Pack. This pack has been chilled overnight in the freezer section of a standard refrigerator. The paper toweling wrapped around the polyethylene bag provides insulation for the patient's hand. This prechill is maintained on the right cheek for 20 to 30 minutes immediately prior to dermabrasion. I have seen no ill effect from this method of prechill, with the exception of one patient, age 69, who de-

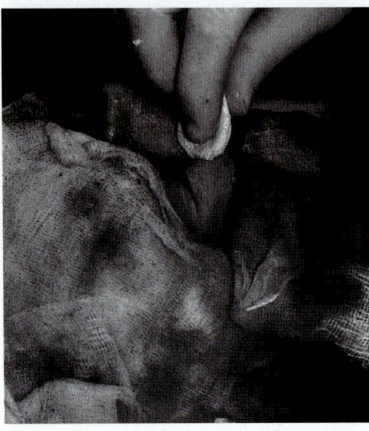

FIG. 170. If the patient has periorbital hyperpigmentation, I generally will perform a chemical peel using 88% phenol or the Baker's phenol solution. The area is cleaned with acetone as a degreaser prior to the application of the chemical.

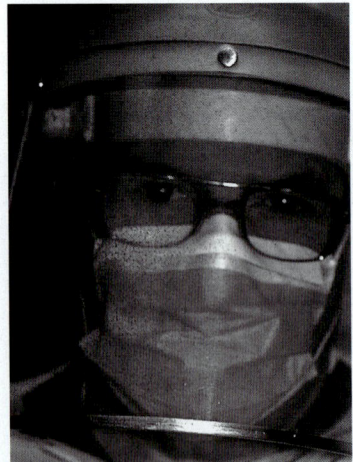

FIG. 172. This photograph shows the protective guard that has been used throughout the preceding full-face dermabrasion. Note that there is essentially no splatter of blood on the plastic guard. This is because the skin has been frozen firmly, which eliminates the spray of blood that can obstruct the surgeon's vision.

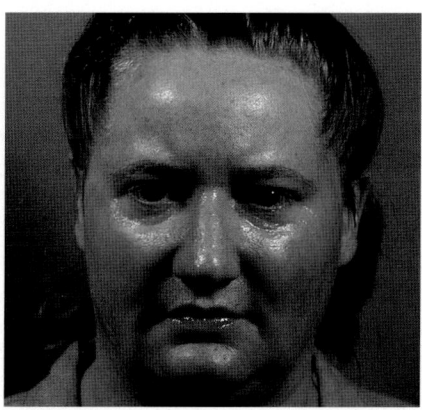

FIG. 218. The patient is 32 days postoperative and has complete reepithelialization. She has regained an almost normal skin color. Although residual edema exists, the patient appears normal.

quate. Another effective method of removing the fibrin crust is to stand in the shower, allowing the water to flow over the scalp onto the face. Wet gauze is used to dislodge the crust. Showers should be encouraged 2 to 4 times per day. When wetpacking is not being performed, the patient is instructed to apply Vaseline petroleum jelly covered by Saran Wrap to avoid drying of the treated areas (see Figs. 202, 203). If the crust becomes too thick, infection and scarring can occur. Manual removal using a blunt curette is occasionally indicated (see Fig. 208).

Patients usually undergo the dermabrasion on Monday and are seen each day during the first week to monitor progress and provide advice on wetpacking. By the ninth day, patients are usually wetpacking on a prn basis, if any crust occurs. Saran Wrap and Vaseline are used only on the areas that are not fully reepithelialized.

Most patients will obtain complete reepithelialization between the 11th and 13th postoperative day. The surgeon should expect the healing to be delayed in areas of dimin-

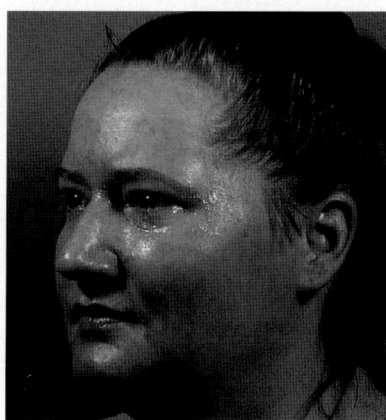

FIG. 219. A side view of the patient at 32 days postoperative. There is good blending of the color along the mandibular line. Mild erythema persists and the residual edema that is present will prevent adequate evaluation of therapeutic and cosmetic improvement until 4 months has passed.

ished vascularity, such as preexisting atrophic, hypertrophic, or keloidal scars. Rarely, a patient may take longer to have normal reepithelialization. During the second week, the patient is seen on Monday, Wednesday, and Friday. Since the length required for complete reepithelialization is related to the depth of the dermabrasion, I have observed that patients who reepithelialize in less than 7 days will frequently have no significant anatomic change, a fact that is commonly reported by patients who have undergone dermabrasion without the use of cryoanesthesia to solidify the skin. As a consequence, they find that they have little or no cosmetic improvement. This can also occur when a cryospray is used if the surgeon is too timid to freeze the skin rock hard.

Every patient who has recently undergone dermabrasion or facial chemical peeling is scheduled for an office visit at the same time, thus forming a peer support group. Patients who have progressed further in the recuperative phase are able to advise and encourage those who have recently undergone their procedures. Patients are advised that any recurrence of herpes simplex, which is represented by grouped erosions rather than epidermal vesicles, should be brought to the attention of the nursing staff prior to being placed in the examination room with other recuperating patients.

Patients who have completely reepithelialized at the conclusion of 2 weeks may return to work. They should avoid sun exposure as long as there is any residual erythema, to avoid postinflammatory hyperpigmentation. At the beginning of the 4th week, a small area in the preauricular zone is tested with a sunscreen. An SPF of 15 or higher is recommended. If no allergic or irritant reaction occurs after 7 days of limited use, the patient is instructed to apply the sun screen twice daily when sun exposure is anticipated. A 2.5% hydrocortisone cream (Hytone, Dermik Lab, Fort Washington, PA) is applied two to four times per day to provide lubrication, minimize pruritus, and decrease erythema. Noncomedogenic water-based cosmetics such as Allercreme or Almay are used during the next 3-month period by female patients. Heavy lifting or strenuous exercise is avoided during the first 6 postoperative weeks. If this is not followed, some patients will experience transitory petechiae. Patients are asked to return on a biweekly or monthly schedule until all the erythema subsides and the skin has returned to its normal color. This is usually accomplished before the 12th postoperative week.

Biologic Dressings

Moist or occlusive dressings applied to the treated area improve wound healing. For over 30 years, dermatologists have known that occlusive dressings are more effective in promoting reepithelialization than is air exposure (67–69). Biologic dressings that provide occlusion and moisture have been available on the market for over a decade. Many surgeons prefer Vigilon, the product that I use. Vigilon retains a large amount of exudate and, because of this, must be changed on a daily basis to avoid infection. This usually requires medical supervision. Vigilon is placed directly on the abraded sites (see Figs. 173–176). Each side of the Vigilon is laminated with a polyethylene film. One side of this film is removed from the Vigilon before it is applied to the abraded skin (see Fig. 173). The remaining polyethylene film forms an exterior barrier, trapping the moisture between it and the abraded skin. To prevent movement of the Vigilon, it may be secured with tape or cotton mesh placed over the patient's head (70). Some surgeons prefer to apply Vigilon over petrolatum or antibiotic ointment followed by a Telfa dressing (Kendall Company, Boston, MA) onto which sterile gauze pads are applied to absorb additional exudate. Coban dressing (3M Medical-Surgical Division, St. Paul, MN) may be applied to secure the outer dressing (59). After 2 to 4 days, biologic dressings may be discontinued and a film of petrolatum or antibiotic ointment is applied to maintain a moist surface. Until reepithelialization is complete, frequent showers and dilute boric acid wetpacks are helpful. Mild soaps may be introduced after 5 or 6 days. Even with the use of occlusive biologic dressings, crust formation may continue to occur after the 4th postoperative day. Wetpacks should be used if any crust appears.

BioBrane II, (Dow Hickam Pharmaceutical, a division of Mylan Laboratories, Sugarland, TX), another biosynthetic membrane, is composed of a semipermeable silicone membrane that is bonded to a flexible, knitted nylon material. Peptides derived from porcine collagen are bonded to this elastic membrane, which provides a biocompatible hydrophilic, hypoallergenic, nontoxic, semipermeable membrane. This membrane controls evaporation and flexes with the movement of the skin. BioBrane II comes in varying porosities, with the most porous type being favored (26). Following dermabrasion, a large sheet of BioBrane II is applied to the wound, cutting out holes for the mouth, nose, and eyes. The dressing is immobilized with a cloth mask that is removed the following day, since BioBrane becomes fixed by fibrin. Exudate is produced for the first 24 to 36 hours, after which the dressing becomes dry. The patient may wet the dressing after 2 days. Separation occurs when reepithelialization is complete. As healing progresses at the periphery, the loose edges may be cut free. The advantage of BioBrane II is that it does not require medical supervision or nursing personnel to change it as does Vigilon. But BioBrane II does not provide a moist barrier as does Vigilon.

Omniderm (Omniderm, Montreal, Quebec, Canada) is another wound dressing. The surgeon must order the mesh version that allows blood and serum to ooze through. As with BioBrane II, this material is not removed and is allowed to spontaneously separate. Antibacterial ointments may be applied directly over this dressing, giving it the advantages of a moist dressing.

It is believed that biologic dressings reduce the formation of milia and postoperative discomfort. It is also claimed to reduce the reepithelialization time as compared to wetpacking (25). I have not found this latter claim to be true.

TRANSFER GRAFTING

In patients who have deep icepick scars, the dermabrasion is incapable of reaching the depth of the scar to eliminate the cosmetic defect (Fig. 220). This can be corrected by performing transfer grafting (Figs. 221–229). A cylindrical piece of skin encompassing the icepick scar is removed and replaced with normal skin from a facial donor site, usually the postauricular sulcus. The icepick scars are removed using hair transplant punches of varying size. These sizes are carefully documented so that larger grafts can be cut from the donor site to fit snugly into the recipient areas (see Fig. 222). Because of the elastic quality of skin, the recipient hole will enlarge slightly and the donor graft will contract slightly. This is why a larger hair transplant punch must be used in the donor site than the size punch that was used to excise the icepick scar at the recipient site. The donor grafts are placed into the surgical defect at the site of the preexisting icepick scars (see Fig. 223). Patients are given a mirror and approve or disapprove each fit. In so doing, they are allowed to participate in their care, and if the result after healing is not completely satisfactory, they recognize that they shared the responsibility when the final fit was determined. Sterile Clearon tapes (Ethicon, Somerville, NJ) are placed over the grafts (see Fig. 224). The tape may be removed between the 5th and 7th postoperative day. With the action of facial motion and sebum production, these tapes may become dislodged at an earlier time.

The donor skin should be selected from an area that will not produce a postoperative cosmetic defect. Also of importance is the selection of a donor site that closely matches the color and texture of the skin from which the icepick scars will be removed. In most instances, the skin of the postauricular sulcus will serve this purpose well (see Fig. 225). After the donor grafts are harvested, the sites are closed with interrupted sutures that are removed in 1 week (see Fig. 226).

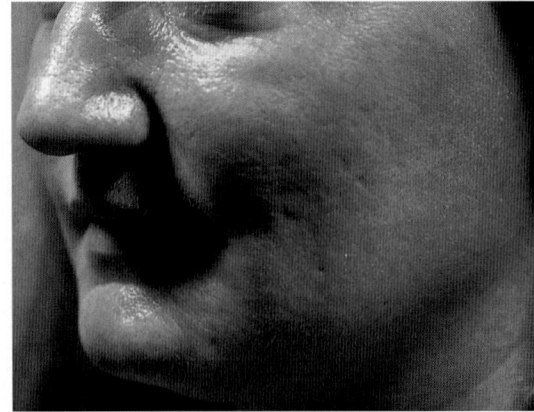

FIG. 220. In patients where deep icepick scars are present, removal of the scars with use of transfer grafts can remarkably improve the postoperative results. This is the same patient as seen in the operative and postoperative series (see Figs. 109 to 219).

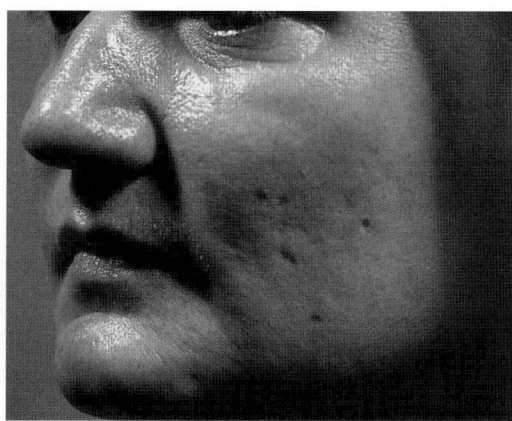

FIG. 221. The skin has been prepped with Technicare and the icepick scars have been identified with a sterile gentian violet pen.

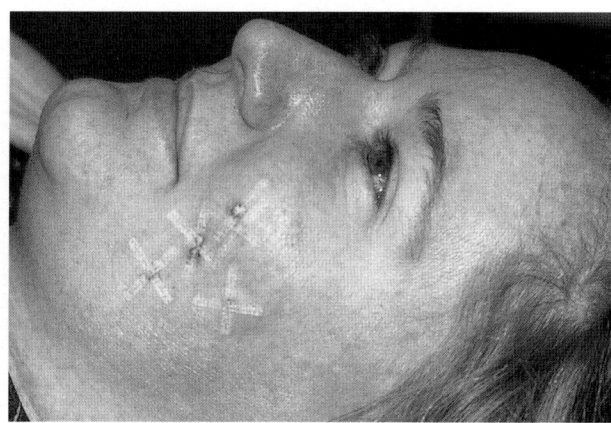

FIG. 224. The transfer grafts have been placed into the surgical defect of the preexisting icepick scars. The patient is given a mirror and approves or disapproves of each fit. Sterile Claron tapes are placed over the grafts and will remain in position for 5 to 7 days.

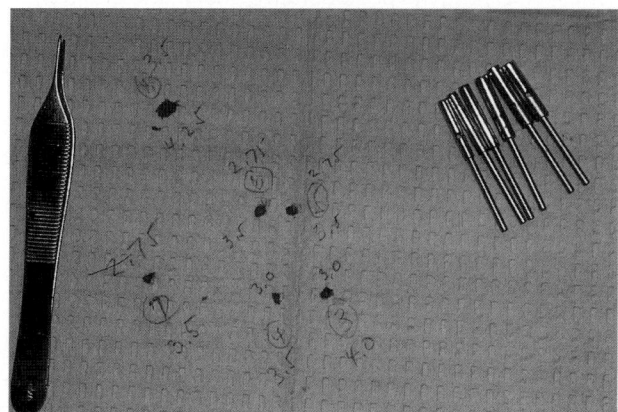

FIG. 222. The sizes of the grafts are documented on a sterile paper drape for recording in the chart. Hair transplant punches of varying sizes are available to accommodate the different sizes of the icepick scars and the subsequent transfer grafts.

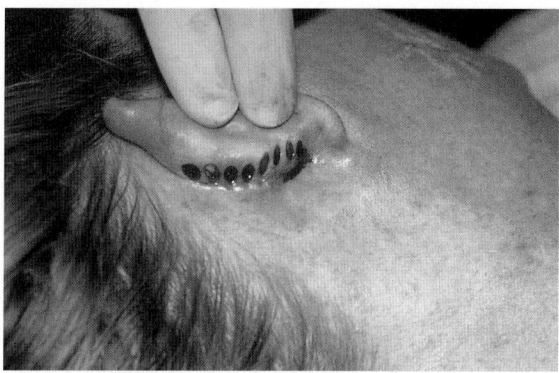

FIG. 225. The transfer grafts are harvested from the postauricular sulcus. Since this is facial skin, the texture match is excellent. The color match may not appear excellent at the time of transfer because the donor skin has only minimal sun damage. Since dermabrasion rejuvenates the skin, the treated sun-damaged cheek skin will be lighter in color and blend well with the postauricular skin.

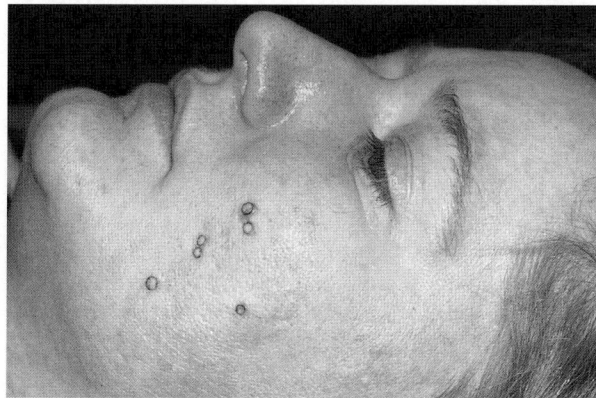

FIG. 223. The existing scars have been removed with hair transplant punches of varying sizes. The donor grafts have been harvested from the postauricular sulcus in sizes slightly larger than the defects made during the removal of the icepick scars. The donor grafts have been inserted.

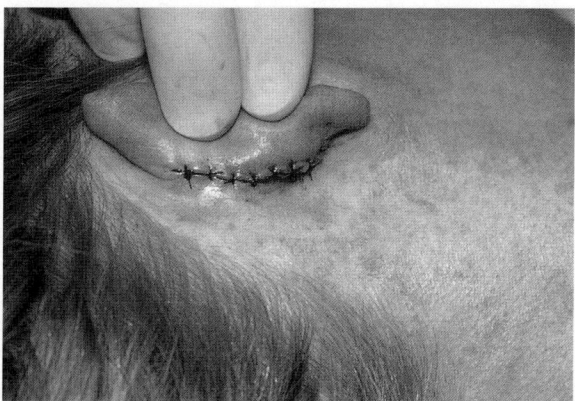

FIG. 226. The graft sites are closed with interrupted sutures, which are removed in 1 week. This donor site is excellent since it is not obvious. Frequently, the scars are imperceptible even on close examination.

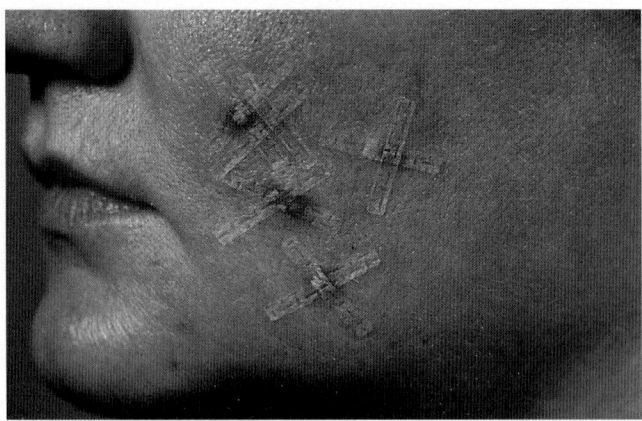

FIG. 227. This is a close-up picture of the grafts on the day of insertion. Slight bulging of the grafts is acceptable because the dermabrasion will flatten the contour. If the grafts are depressed and below the level of the adjacent skin, it will be more difficult to obtain a flat contour at the time of dermabrasion.

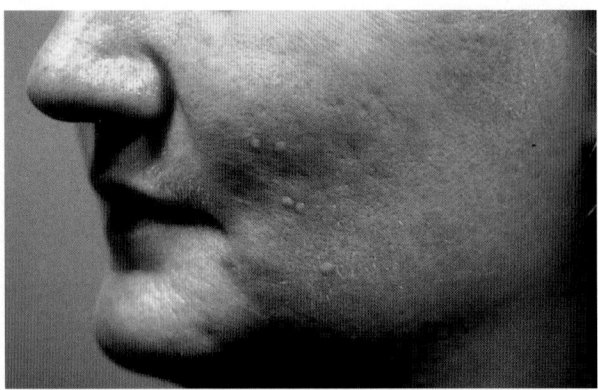

FIG. 229. A 4- to 8-week delay between the placement of transfer grafts and the dermabrasion is ideal. This patient was delayed in having her dermabrasion completed. At 3 months, there is still some bulging of the grafts, but the erythema has subsided, showing that the grafts have taken well. These grafts will be planed perfectly flat and level with the adjacent skin. During the postoperative phase, the grafts will be edematous and elevated for up to 6 weeks. They usually become flat and imperceptible, providing a superb cosmetic result.

When the grafts are inserted into the recipient defect, slight bulging of the donor skin is acceptable because dermabrasion will flatten the contour. If grafts are depressed and below the level of the adjacent skin, it will be more difficult to obtain a flat contour at the time of dermabrasion. When the tape is removed between the 5th and 7th day, the graft sites will be apparent, usually showing some elevation above the adjacent normal skin (see Fig. 228). Erythema will be present, which is the usual finding in a full-thickness graft. The grafts should be dermabraded 4 to 8 weeks after their insertion to obtain maximum cosmetic results. Some elevation of the graft due to normal scar contraction is usually apparent at the time of dermabrasion (see Fig. 229). When the dermabrasion is performed, these grafts will be planed perfectly flat with the adjacent skin. During the postdermabrasion phase, the grafts may become edematous and elevated for up to 6 weeks. They usually flatten and become imperceptible, providing a superb cosmetic result.

USUAL COURSE, SIDE EFFECTS, AND COMPLICATIONS

The predictable and expected reactions occurring during the normal course of postoperative care are listed in Table 3. Edema, erythema, crust formation, and mild discomfort are experienced by all patients. These symptoms are minimized by wetpacks and biologic dressings. Excessive crust formation may be removed by the gentle use of gauze while showering. Severe crust formation can be removed by curettage (see Fig. 208). Discomfort is mild and usually does not require analgesic medication, although meperidine is prescribed for the first 2 postoperative days. Most patients use a mild hypnotic prescription to help with sleeping for the first 2 or 3 postoperative nights.

After crusting has subsided and reepithelialization has been completed, a moderate to intense erythema is normal. Female patients may choose to disguise this redness by using a green or blue toner beneath their foundation. Moisturization with bland lotions are helpful. Facial washing is usually necessary only twice a day at this point, because the skin will be dry. The patient should totally avoid sun until a sunscreen lotion can be tolerated. Even then, unnecessary sun exposure should be avoided for 6 to 12 weeks.

By the 4th to 6th postoperative week, erythema begins to fade, usually in a patchy fashion. If erythema persists, it should be closely examined for induration. Persistent erythema over an area of induration are the cardinal signs of an incipient scar. Weak corticosteroid lotions or creams usually help resolve these areas rapidly. If focal areas continue to redden or begin to thicken, the early use of Cordran Tape (Eli

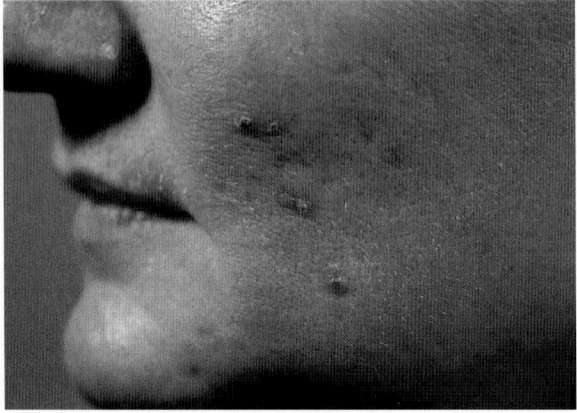

FIG. 228. The patient is now 9 days after grafting for icepick scars. The tapes can be removed between the 5th and 7th day. The graft sites are apparent, showing some elevation above the adjacent normal skin, and erythema is present, an expected finding in a full-thickness graft.

TABLE 3. *Related events following dermabrasion*

Usual events
  During reepithelialization
    Edema
    Exudate
    Discomfort
    Crust formation
  Following reepithelialization
    Erythema
    Pruritus
    Milia
    Pustules
    Flushing (cold, alcohol, exercise)
  Side effects
    Purpura
    Petechia
    Hypopigmentation, transitory
    Hyperpigmentation, transitory
  Complications
    Persistent erythema
    Infection
      Bacterial
      Viral
    Scarring
      Accutane therapy pre- or postoperative
      Infection; bacterial or viral (HSV)
      Patient manipulation
      Deep dermabrasion

HSV, herpes simplex virus.

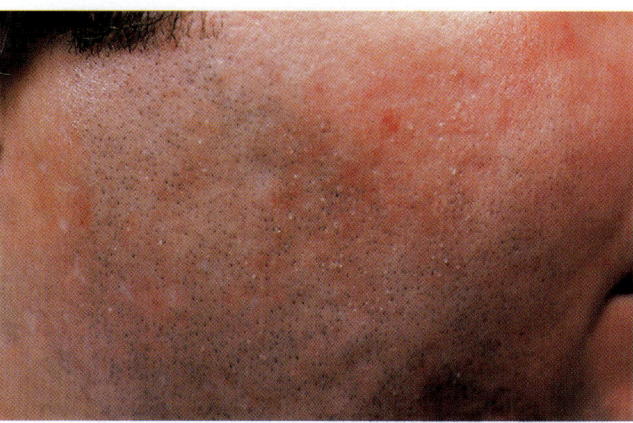

FIG. 230. Virtually all patients develop postoperative milia. This patient shows only a modest number. Some patients have larger numbers and larger size milia. This is an expected postoperative response and is usually self-limited and usually requires no treatment. Persistent milia may be treated with the use of a BufPuf or by incision and drainage using a surgical blade.

Lilly, Indianapolis, IN) may prevent the development of hypertrophic scars. Intralesional triamcinolone acetonide (Kenalog10, Bristol-Myers Squibb, Princeton, NJ) may be used in strengths of 2.5 mg to 10 mg per cc. If used, the injection should be limited to only several drops rather than cubic centimeters of volume. The liquid should not extend beyond the confines of the scar. Higher doses and infiltration into the adjacent normal tissues can cause atrophy. Repeat injections of this potent and long-lasting intralesional corticosteroid should be separated by 4-week intervals.

Other anticipated reactions are postoperative milia (Fig. 230). Virtually every patient develops milia, which are usually self-limiting. If they persist, the gentle use of a BufPuf or incision and drainage may be performed. Alternatively, unroofing of the milia may be achieved using an electrosurgical device on a low setting. Approximately 50% of patients who exhibit preexisting acne at the time of surgery will develop a flare but may not respond to systemic or topical antibiotics (Fig. 231). This response usually begins by the 6th postoperative week, is self-limiting, and usually subsides by the 4th to 6th postoperative months. I have never seen this flare extend beyond 1 year, and the severity of this flare is usually mild and does not lead to further scarring.

An uncommon but predictable response is a vascular flush that will occur in the previously frozen sites when the patient comes inside after exposure to cold air during the winter. This represents mild vascular instability. I have never seen a patient become more susceptible to frostbite following a dermabrasion, although patients are routinely warned to avoid excessive cold exposure during the first postoperative winter. A common postoperative side effect is pruritus, which may lead to excoriations, particularly while the patient is sleeping. The patient will note linear red lines after awakening, (Fig. 232). These are petechiae resulting from trauma and leakage from the incompletely healed vascular tree. The petechiae resolve within several days (see Fig. 232). Topical 2.5% hydrocortisone cream or similar mild corticosteroids, oral antihistamines, aspirin, and the use of cotton gloves worn at night are usually sufficient.

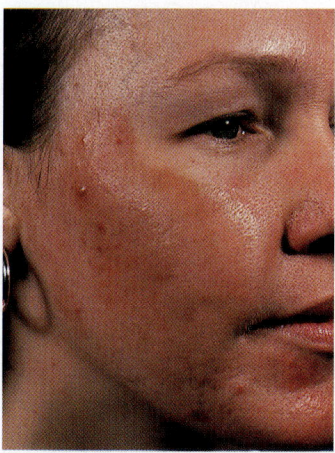

FIG. 231. This patient demonstrates two common postoperative effects. Postinflammatory hyperpigmentation is apparent over the entire cheek but is accentuated over the malar and zygomatic areas. This can occur from minimal sun exposure, sometimes as little as 15 minutes. The second common side effect is the recurrence of pustular acne, which is self-limited but usually unresponsive to systemic or topical antibiotic treatment.

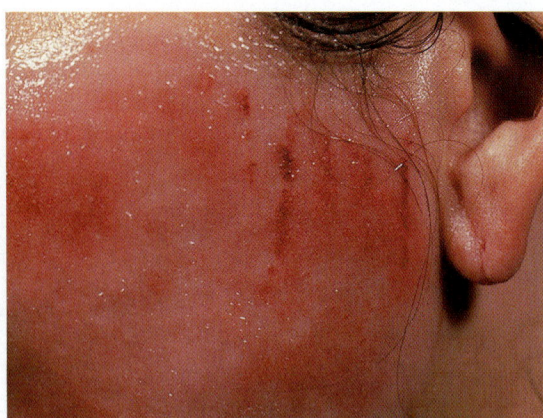

FIG. 232. Excoriation can result from pruritus which produces petechiae that are seen in linear patterns. This almost always occurs while the patient is sleeping and therefore the patient is unaware of the cause. Questioning reveals that the patient found these linear areas of petechiae upon awakening in the morning. These petechiae are self-limiting but can be prevented by the judicious use of mild topical steroid creams and/or systemic antipruritic medications.

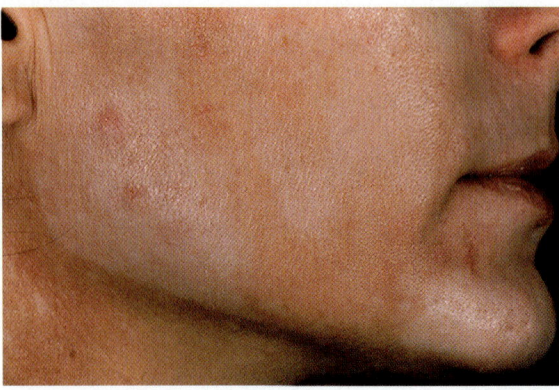

FIG. 234. Permanent hypopigmentation is uncommon. It is usually seen in dark-complected patients or individuals who have moderately severely sun-damaged skin. Permanent hypopigmentation is not a usual postoperative event and is not always related to the depth of the dermabrasion.

Petechiae can be observed. They are the result of a torsional effect on incompletely healed skin even though reepithelialization has occurred. In women, it is most commonly caused by whisker burn and is most frequently seen between the 3rd and 6th postoperative week (see Fig. 233). Almost universally, physicians misinterpret this vascular change as the onset of telangiectasia. Close observation with magnifying loupes will reveal that these areas are petechiae and do not blanch with pressure. This will resolve quickly once the patient is made aware of the cause. Men will experience the same effect when involved in contact sports such as basketball, football, or wrestling. This may also occur with the use of a safety razor, the sites most affected being inferior to the sideburns and on the chin. Petechiae may also result from increased intravascular pressure. Weightlifting or a Valsalva maneuver will increase vascular pressure in the head and can cause transitory petechiae (Fig. 233).

Temporary postoperative hypopigmentation is a usual and anticipated response. Permanent hypopigmentation is considered by me to be a side effect rather than a complication. It should be anticipated in dark-skinned white and Oriental patients (Figs. 234, 235). Yarborough has reported that the darker the preoperative color of African-Americans, the less likely there will be a significant color change, if any at all (59). Hypopigmentation is more commonly temporary than permanent and most patients regain normal pigmentation within 3 months. When present, usually only subtle changes

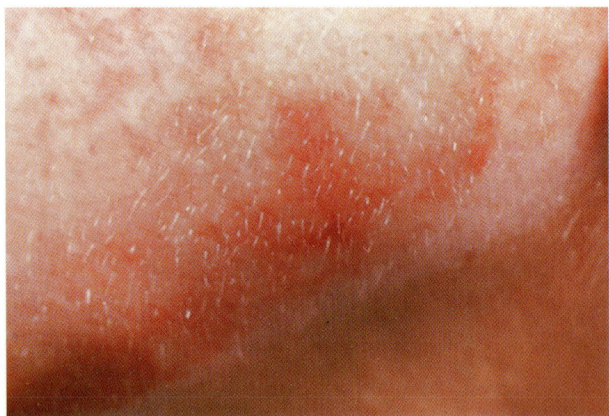

FIG. 233. Both petechiae and purpura are the result of injury to the newly formed capillaries. This frequently results from whisker burn, which causes a torsional injury to the newly reepithelialized epidermis. These frequently occur during the 4th and 6th weeks following dermabrasion. Running, lifting, or other strenuous activity will also cause a rupture of the capillaries, presenting as purpura or petechiae. This patient developed petechiae on the 18th postoperative day while lifting heavy boxes. Strenuous activity should be avoided for 4 to 6 weeks following dermabrasion.

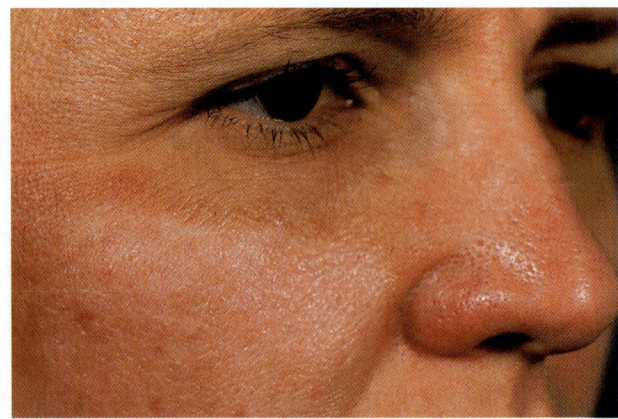

FIG. 235. Temporary hypopigmentation is a common postoperative event, particularly in people who live in sunny climates and possess a summer tan. This patient underwent a dermabrasion in the autumn while she still possessed her summer tan. Most patients will regain normal color blending by 6 months or earlier.

occur. The border of the dermabraded areas will be hidden under the mandibular body if the patient has been dermabraded to this point. This is the major reason why the surgeon should not dermabrade below the mandibular body, despite the fact that the patient may have significant scarring of the neck. I recall a case in which I abraded scars below the mandibular angle and body in a farmer who had considerable actinic damage on his neck, the rejuvenated skin at the surgical site was much lighter in color than the adjacent neck skin. I had improved one cosmetic defect and replaced it with another.

Postinflammatory hyperpigmentation is frequently seen in patients who are exposed to sunlight while the postoperative erythema persists (see Fig. 231). Sun exposure will promote melanogenesis in the erythematous skin. Minimal exposure of as little as 15 minutes can produce subtle hyperpigmentation. Some surgeons believe that it is more commonly found in patients with dark eyes. I have not noted a strong correlation. The response usually appears during the 3rd or 4th week after dermabrasion. Hyperpigmentation is temporary. Prevention consists of the regular use of sunscreens coupled with strict avoidance of sunlight exposure during the phase of postoperative erythema. It is best to apply sunscreens of at least 15 SPF value, two or three times a day when sunlight exposure is possible. Hyperpigmentation can be reduced by the application of a compounded bleaching cream consisting of equal parts of Eldoquin Forte, 4% cream (I.C.N. Pharmaceuticals, Costa Mesa, CA) and 0.1% Retin-A cream (Ortho Pharmaceutical, Raritan, NJ) to the darkened areas one to three times per day. I devised this compounded cream over 20 years ago and have used it with excellent results. I do not compound the cream with triamcinolone (Aristocort, Fujisawa USA, Deerfield, IL) because the corticosteroid can cause atrophy since this skin is temporarily thinned and lacking an effective keratin layer. This regime is most effective when the cream is applied shortly after the hyperpigmentation appears. The patient should expect to develop some erythema and slight desquamation when the cream is initially applied. In light-complected individuals, it is best to start with night-time applications, which may be increased to twice a day until bleaching is apparent. In some sensitive patients, the Retin-A cream cannot be tolerated but the Eldoquin Forte can be used. One should continue the bleaching cream for at least several weeks after the hyperpigmentation has faded. In geographic areas where sunlight exposure is great, the continuation for several months may be beneficial.

Complications consist of persistent erythema, scar formation, and infection from either bacterial or viral etiology. These are complications rather than side effects since they are not anticipated or predictable events. Some authors have referred to conditions such as milia, hypopigmentation, and hyperpigmentation as complications of dermabrasion. I disagree with this position, since these events occur frequently following the normal postoperative course of dermabrasion.

Persistent postoperative erythema, particularly if indurated or mottled, represents incipient scar formation (Fig. 236). Persistent erythema is most often seen in the danger zones (i.e., mandibular body and angle, bossing of the chin and forehead, the zygomatic arch, the malar eminence, and the infraorbital rim) and areas of marked contour definition such as the philtrum and the cleft of the chin. The changes of incipient scarring may also be seen when patients have rubbed or excoriated and in patients who have undergone Accutane therapy. When persistent erythema occurs, it is advised to require frequent postoperative visits to monitor patients carefully. When there is evidence of early scar formation, I start applications of mild topical steroid creams, followed by Cordran Tape applied overnight 5 days per week if the erythema does not improve with the corticosteroid cream alone. The use of short-acting injectable systemic steroids such as Celestone Soluspan 8 to 12 mg every 2 to 4 weeks used early after the recognition of these incipient scars is quite beneficial. More severe hypertrophic scars may require intralesional triamcinolone acetonide, which should initially be used in dilute concentrations (2.5 to 5 mg/cc) and in droplet volumes. Persistent scars may require increasing the concentration of the mixture (10 mg/cc). Because this agent is active in the skin for 4 weeks, a 1-month interval between injections is advisable. Overaggressive use of triamcinolone will result in telangiectasia and atrophy. Silastic gels have recently been introduced. My experience with their use is limited but satisfactory.

Keloids are very rare after dermabrasion. Individuals with a history of keloids should be warned that this is a possible complication, although rare. A spot dermabrasion to determine the mode of healing may be helpful but does not guar-

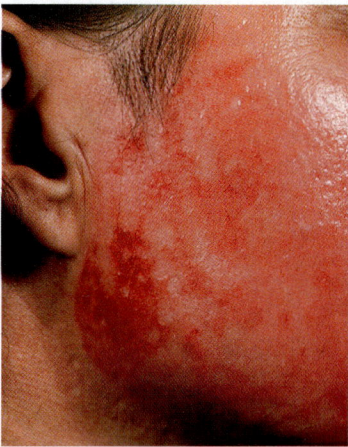

FIG. 236. Persistent erythema associated with induration is a sign of an incipient scar. When these changes are related to a dermabrasion that has been carried excessively deep, they are usually found in the danger zones of the mandibular body, bossing of the chin or forehead, the zygomatic arch, malar eminence, and infraorbital rim. This complication may also be seen as the result of patient manipulation, sometimes from aggressive rubbing during wetpacking or secondary to scratching to relieve postoperative pruritus. The most common cause is seen in post-Accutane patients who are developing postoperative scars.

antee that other areas of the face will heal similarly. In my experience, the only patients to develop keloids following dermabrasion were those who had been previously treated with Accutane. The treatment of keloids is the aggressive use of intralesional triamcinolone, Cordran Tape, silastic gel dressings, and external pressure dressings.

Bacterial and viral infections complicating the recovery phase of dermabrasion may lead to scarring. I have seen only one patient in 25 years who has developed a postoperative bacterial infection. When the patient was redermabraded several years later, another infection occurred and the same bacterial species was cultured, suggesting that the patient was a chronic carrier, with the bacteria probably residing in the nasal passages. The bacterial culture revealed coagulase-positive *Staphylococcus aureus*, which was sensitive to cephalexin (Keflex, Eli Lilly, Indianapolis, IN). I recently performed a taped Baker's phenol peel on this patient. He was placed on cephalexin and did not develop an infection. I routinely use 250 mg of erythromycin three times per day for 15 days as a precautionary antibacterial agent on all dermabrasion patients who tolerate this drug.

Viral infections with herpes simplex are not uncommon (Fig. 237). Although Orentriech states that he has never seen scarring occur after reactivation of herpes simplex when the involved areas are kept moist with wetpacks and ointment, I have seen several patients in whom very superficial scars have developed following viral reactivation (71). With the prophylactic use of acyclovir, the reactivation rate has decreased significantly. When reactivation occurs in a patient who has not provided a history of herpes simplex virus (HSV), the prompt institution of oral acyclovir has always prevented the occurrence of permanent scarring in my experience. If the patient is infected by another individual with an active HSV infection, the resulting primary herpes infection can be quite severe and may result in postherpetic scarring. The appearance of HSV infection is not typical in patients who have undergone facial dermabrasion, because the epidermal layer has been removed. Grouped erosions are the usual clinical finding since no vesicles will appear. When there is a positive history of preexisting herpes simplex of the facial areas, I use 200 mg of Zovirax five times per day for 2 days prior to the surgery and continue until the patient is completely reepithelialized. The dosage should be doubled or tripled if herpetic reactivation is suspected or occurs. If severe or extensive involvement occurs, hospitalization with intravenous administration of acyclovir and the use of wetpacks is advised.

Another complication that can cause injuries is the improper use or the presence of defective dermabrasion equipment. Lacerations, full-thickness penetration, and chipped teeth have followed dermabrasion. If a defective fraise or brush disintegrates during use, the resulting flying objects may cause injuries to the patient or operating room personnel.

POSTOPERATIVE RESULTS

Postoperative results may be divided into three categories: short-term, mid-term, and long-term. The short-term period is mentioned as a caution to the patient, the surgeon, and the reader of surgical literature because evaluations done during this period are misleading. The short-term period is that time span that begins at the completion of reepithelialization and continues through the 12th postoperative week. During this 3-month period from the day of surgery, there is edema and erythema present. The edema provides a fullness to any remaining depressed scars, and erythema masks the preexisting hypopigmented scars. Because of these facts, this period will provide the greatest cosmetic improvement. Only after the edema and erythema subside completely can the true results of surgery be appreciated. Photographs taken during this 3-month period can be grossly deceptive. Also during this short-term phase, some patients who have undergone a dermabrasion for the treatment of chronic or uncontrollable acne will experience a recurrence of their active acne with pustule formation. The surgeon should not confuse this with milia formation, which is an anticipated and predictable postoperative occurrence. An acne flare that occurs during the first 3 months will usually subside by the 6th postoperative month and only occasionally persist up to 1 year. This recurrence of acne will mask the therapeutic and cosmetic value of the surgery at least temporarily. Systemic antibiotics are often of little or no value during this period of acne flare, suggesting that its cause is more a sebaceous obstructive phenomena than a response to skin bacteria. This acne flare is usually minor and in my own experience of over 25 years has never caused residual scarring. I encourage all surgeons to caution their patients to avoid the use of Accutane during at least the first 6 months following dermabrasion or chemical peeling because of possible hypertrophic scarring.

Mid-term or intermediate results are those evaluated between the 4th and 12th months. During the initial short-term phase, all of the edema will subside but some erythema may persist. The flare of acne that has occurred will usually

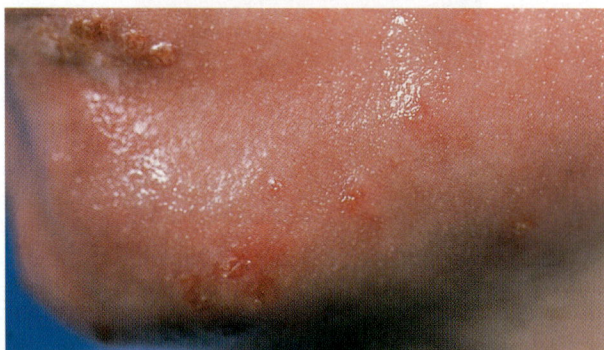

FIG. 237. Postoperative reactivation of herpes simplex can occur. Since the dermabrasion removes the epidermis, no vesicles will be seen. The diagnosis can be made when multiple grouped erosions on an erythematous base are observed. Sometimes, discomfort is associated.

diminish by the 6th month and the therapeutic value of the dermabrasion with a significant decrease compared to the preoperative chronic acne will be apparent before the 12th month. The compensatory seborrhea and milia that have occurred during the short-term phase have now subsided and the patient can expect to attain maximum cosmetic and therapeutic benefit. I usually evaluate permanent improvement between the 6th and 12th months but have assessed this as late as 1 year following the procedure.

Long-term results are those that remain more than 1 year following the surgery. I have found that it is often difficult for patients to return for an objective evaluation. Also, patients have difficulty in remembering their preoperative appearance. Without the aid of multiple preoperative photographs, this evaluation is of little or no value because the passage of time will dull the patient's memory. Evaluation of results more than 1 year after surgery, particularly when done in a written questionnaire without the use of photographs, are too inaccurate to be useful.

Standardization of evaluation methods remains elusive. Despite this, I have found that, surprisingly, both patients and I usually arrive at a similar percentage of improvement. In this evaluation, neither I nor the patient counts the individual scars that have been completely corrected or attempts to estimate the relative percentage of improvement of scars that remain. In essence, if the patient looks at his or her face and likes what he or she sees, then the outcome has been worthwhile and the patient has gained a better self-image. The old adage that "beauty is in the eye of the beholder" holds true. I have never seen a patient who could thoroughly recall the degree and extent of their preoperative cosmetic defect. This is not only true of dermabrasion but all other forms of cosmetic surgery. It is therefore obligatory that high-quality photographs that honestly portray the scarring be taken during the preoperative phase. Oblique light producing shadows is necessary to display scarring, but excessive shadowing distorts the natural appearance and exaggerates the defects. I believe that the best way to show these defects photographically is through the use of photo floodlamps (3200° Kelvin) in combination with Ektachrome tungsten slide film (ET 135-24 or 36, ISO 160, Kodak Industries, Rochester, NY) (see Fig. 78). Conversion of this film for outdoor use or use with artificial flash may be accomplished by the use of a Wratten filter 85B over the lens when shooting in daylight conditions or when using an artificial flash. This light-brown filter is available at most photographic supply houses.

The advantage of tungsten photoflood illumination is that the light source may be placed in front of and above the patient, producing oblique light that can be moved at will to produce the desired effect during the composition of the photograph. These photofloods provide oblique light that delineates the contour defect in a manner similar to that which occurs when the patient's face is exposed to overhead sunlight or indoors overhead artificial light. Professional photographers use multiple photoflood or photoflash units that provide flat light as opposed to oblique light. This flat light washes out the contour defects of the scarring, allowing the patient to appear to have excellent skin contour. The most common combination of camera and photo illumination are a photoflash unit attached to a camera body. This light will wash out scars, giving patients a normal-appearing skin. The surgeon should be alerted that this combination is inadequate for preoperative photographs.

When the postoperative evaluation is performed, I and the patient carefully review the standardized series of preoperative pictures to recall the patient's preexisting scars. With the aid of an overhead oblique light source and a mounted wall mirror, the remaining scars will be apparent. Both I and the patient independently arrive at a percentage of improvement. If several patients or office staff also participate in the final evaluation of improvement, all participants are instructed to write their results on a piece of paper so that evaluations are made independently and the opinion of one person will not influence another. When two evaluators are used, it is rare for the appraisal to vary more than 5%. If more individuals participate, the variation is usually 10% or less.

Although I have been performing dermabrasion since 1970, records of postoperative evaluation have been kept only since 1980. I can recall only two patients who felt their improvement was less than 50%. Most of my patients experience improvement of between 75% and 85% when cosmetic improvement is considered. All patients who have been treated for persistent or uncontrollable acne have experienced improvement of at least 50% or greater. Some patients, even those with extremely severe pustular and cystic acne, have shown complete resolution after a facial dermabrasion.

Patients occasionally rate their improvement as 100% although there are obvious scars remaining. When I have asked these patients why they rated their improvement at 100%, their answer has been "I achieved at least 100% of the improvement I had hoped for." This type of evaluation skews the statistics to the right but does demonstrate clearly that patients are satisfied with the results of this procedure (Figs. 238–262).

Facial dermabrasion, particularly for postacne scarring, provides a definitive cosmetic improvement when performed by an experienced and skilled surgeon using the principles that I have outlined above. These results are gratifying for both the surgeon and the patient. There is no adequate alternative treatment to dermabrasion. Other procedures may improve acne scarring such as the injection of filler substances, fat transfer, scar excision, scar elevation, or punch replacement grafting. However, none of these techniques replace dermabrasion. They act as adjunctive procedures. In addition to cosmetic improvement, facial dermabrasion provides therapeutic improvement for chronic or uncontrollable pustular or cystic acne. Because of these definitive and permanent improvements, dermabrasion has rightly earned a respected place in the armamentarium offered by the dermatologic surgeon.

Text continues on page 144

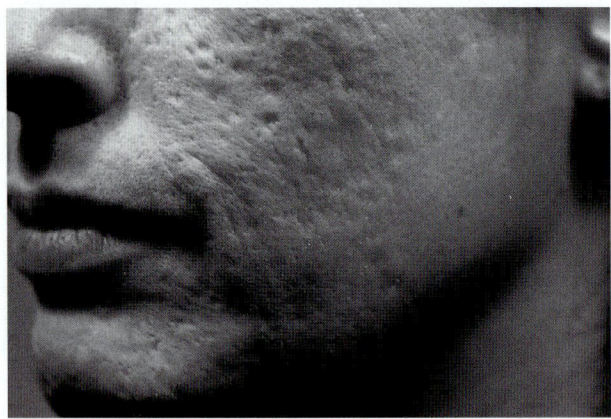

FIG. 238. This is a preoperative picture of a 38-year-old patient with extensive scarring of her cheeks, chin, and anterior mandibular areas resulting from cystic acne. These scars were depressed and hypopigmented. There are also icepick scars present.

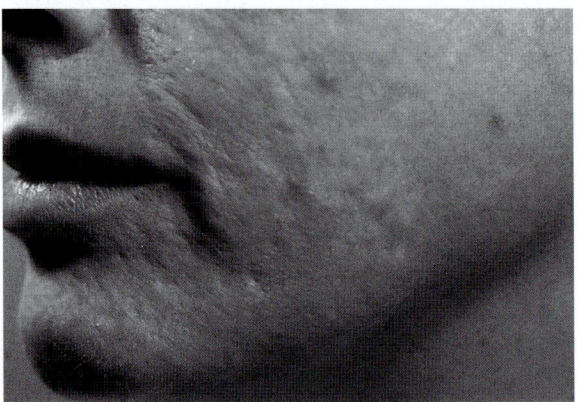

FIG. 239. The same patient as in Figure 238, 4 months following a facial dermabrasion using the Schumann Derma III Dermabrader. This patient experienced a slight flare of pustular acne but no cystic component occurred. There is marked improvement of her scarring, which she considered to be an 85% to 90% improvement.

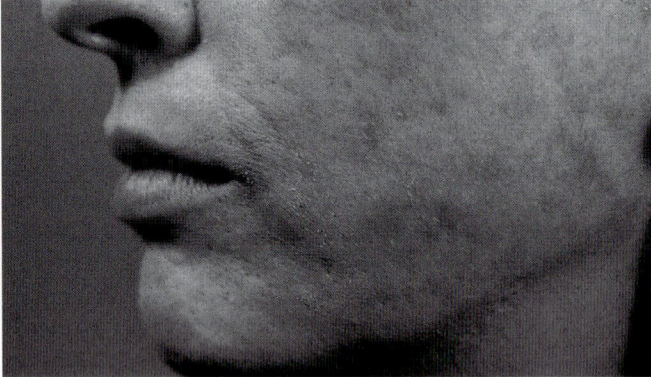

FIG. 240. This is the same patient as seen in Figure 239 after having undergone a second dermabrasion several years later using an extra-coarse diamond fraise. Note that there is additional improvement following this second procedure with almost complete correction of all preexisting scars. Several icepick scars persist and can be treated with punch grafting. The skin color is not blended well yet, as seen in the line of demarcation along the inferior border of the mandible. Ultimately, the pigment did attain a normal color.

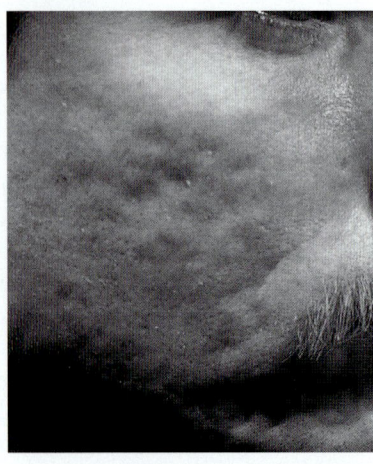

FIG. 241. This is a 27-year-old male patient with moderately severe depressed atrophic scars of his central cheeks and chin following long-term cystic acne. He will be instructed to shave his mustache prior to the dermabrasion so the Vigilon and Saran Wrap can be taped to his upper lip.

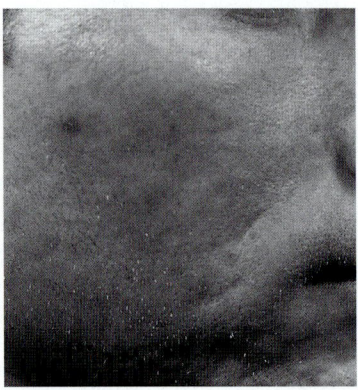

FIG. 242. This is a postoperative picture of the patient in Figure 241 after a dermabrasion using an extra-coarse diamond fraise. Significant improvement, particularly in the central cheeks, is evident. The depressed areas in the nasolabial fold and lateral to the angle of the mouth can be improved by using a filling substance. Fat would be successful in this case, because the depression is primarily the result of fat atrophy.

FIG. 243. This is a 25-year-old woman with extensive scarring of moderate severity that involves the entire cheeks, temporal areas, and chin. Because there are so many icepick scars, I chose not to perform transfer grafting.

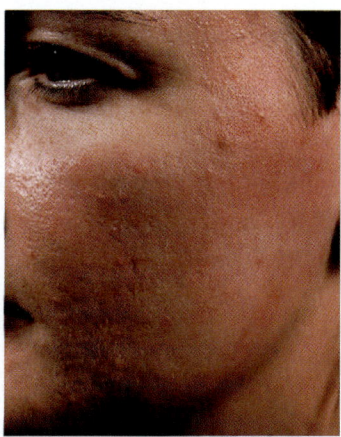

FIG. 244. This is the same patient as in Figure 243 following a facial dermabrasion using an extra-coarse diamond fraise. Note there is marked improvement of all scars, with almost no defect remaining. The patient is experiencing a slight flare of pustular acne. The dermabrasion was effective enough to remove almost all of the preexisting icepick scars.

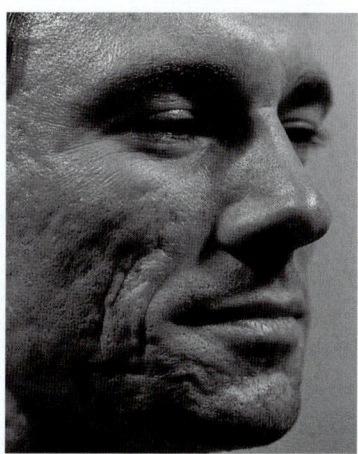

FIG. 245. This is a 22-year-old male patient with very severe depressed atrophic scars and marked fat atrophy of his central cheeks, chin, and temporal areas. This resulted from long-term severe cystic acne unresponsive to systemic and topical antibiotic therapy.

FIG. 246. This is the same patient as in Figure 245 following a facial dermabrasion using the Schumann Derma III Dermabrader. Despite the significant preexisting fat atrophy, there is marked improvement of his cutaneous scars. The color blending has been excellent. This patient evaluated his improvement at 80%. Lipotransfer would be helpful to the central cheeks and chin. A second dermabrasion would also be helpful.

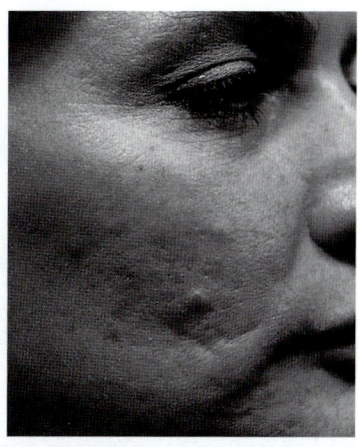

FIG. 247. This 43-year-old female patient had moderate acne scarring involving the cheeks and chin. Note there is also some fat atrophy in the midcheek secondary to acne, and the presence of a marionette line originating from the angle of her mouth secondary to aging.

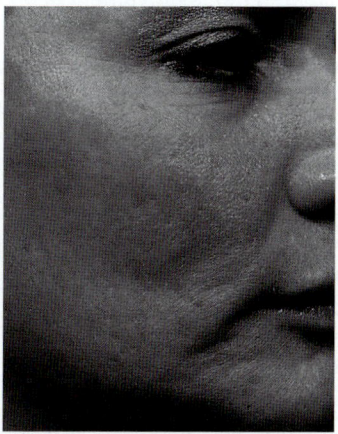

FIG. 248. This is the same patient as Figure 247, 3 months following a facial dermabrasion using an extra-coarse diamond fraise. Significant improvement of her postacne scarring is present in her central cheek. The dermabrasion has flattened the pigmented nevi that were present on her right cheek. Shave biopsies were performed on these lesions prior to the dermabrasion. Dermabrasion has not improved the elasticity of her skin. This patient would benefit from a rhytidectomy.

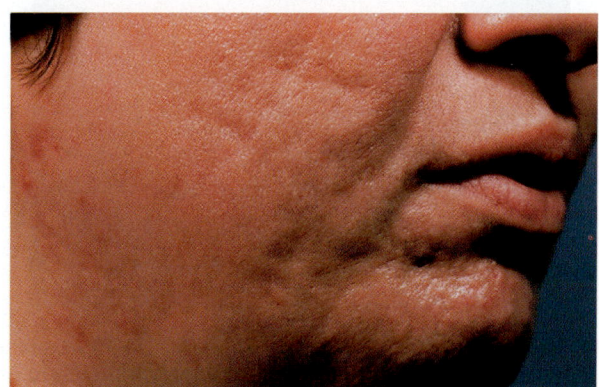

FIG. 249. This is a 32-year-old female patient with severe atrophic depressed scars of her central cheek, mandibular area, and chin, resulting from cystic acne. There is also a major component of fat atrophy.

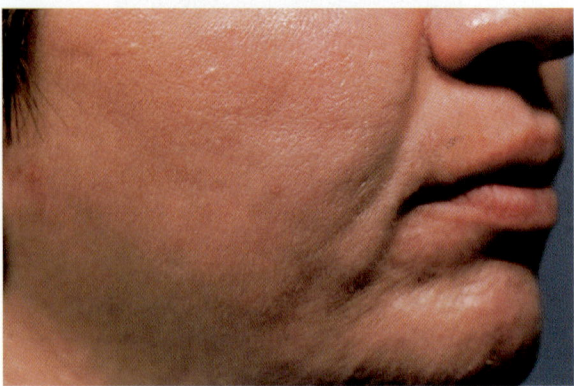

FIG. 250. This is the same patient as Figure 249, 4½ months postdermabrasion using the Schumann Derma III Dermabrader. There is marked improvement of the overall scarring. There is no edema at this stage. Only minimal contour defects persist in the area lateral to the angle of her mouth. This patient estimated her improvement at 95%.

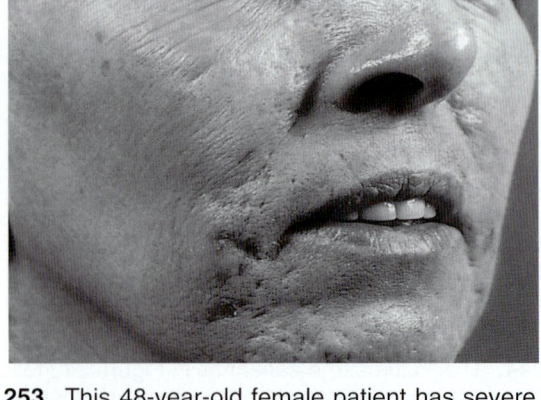

FIG. 253. This 48-year-old female patient has severe scarring of limited involvement on her cheeks lateral to the angle of her mouth and on the lateral portions of her chin. There is severe depression and atrophy in the involved areas that is secondary to cystic acne and compulsive excoriation.

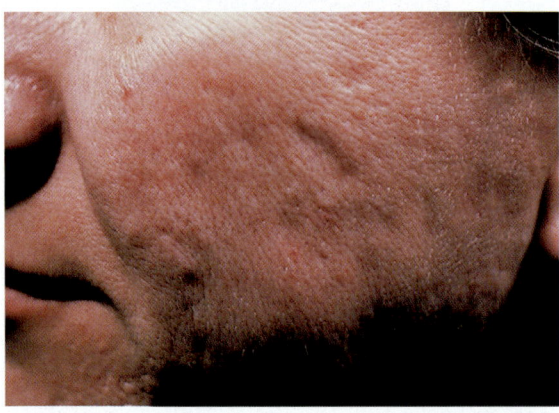

FIG. 251. This 40-year-old female patient has severe scarring of moderate extent involving her central cheeks and chin. The scars are atrophic and depressed and a number demonstrated hypopigmentation.

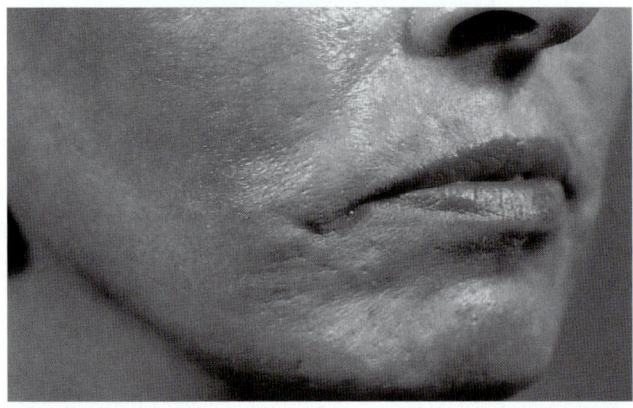

FIG. 254. This is the same patient as Figure 253. This photo was taken 3 months following a dermabrasion using the Schumann Derma III Dermabrader. There is marked improvement with only minimal contour defects remaining on her chin. Note the significant improvement of the area lateral to the angle of the mouth. This patient estimated her improvement at 95%.

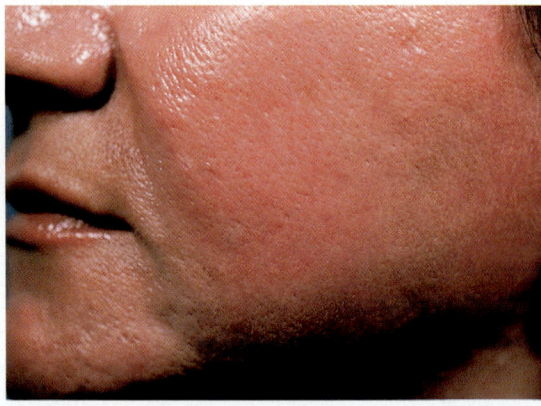

FIG. 252. Same patient as Figure 251. This photo was taken 3 months following a dermabrasion using the Schumann Derma III Dermabrader. Significant improvement, with essentially no evidence of preexisting scars, can be appreciated. The skin color is good and matches well with the nondermabraded sites. The patient estimated her improvement at close to 100%.

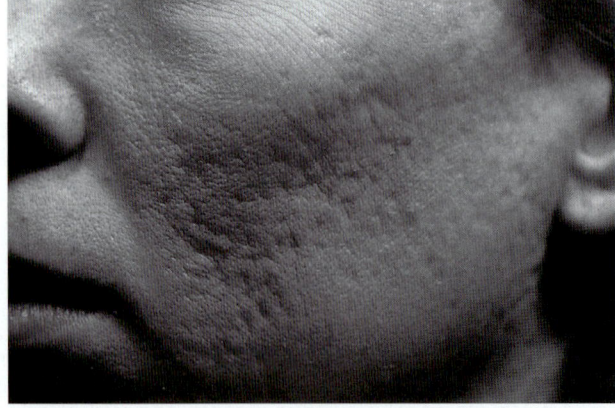

FIG. 255. This 28-year-old woman had many moderately severe broad-based depressed scars over an extensive portion of her cheeks. Many scars are atrophic and hypopigmented.

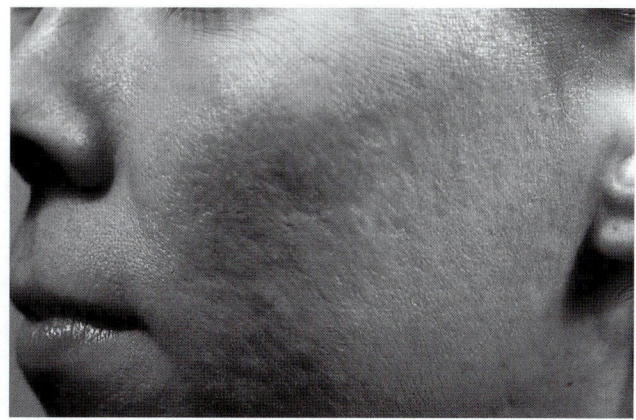

FIG. 256. This is the same patient as Figure 255 at 11 months postdermabrasion. She has excellent color blending and improvement of all of her preexisting scars. The scars over the lower cheek, anterior cheek, and zygomatic arch have been completely corrected. Only the deep atrophic hypopigmented scars of her malar area remain. There is excellent skin color with no evident line of demarcation at the inferior border of the mandible.

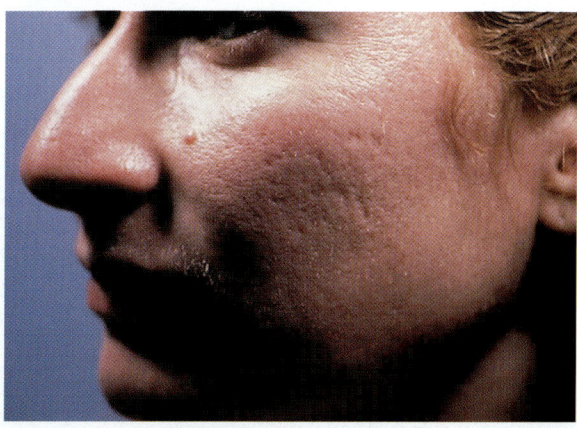

FIG. 259. This is a 29-year-old woman with extensive involvement of moderately severe scarring of her left central cheek. There is a pigmented nevus present on her medial cheek.

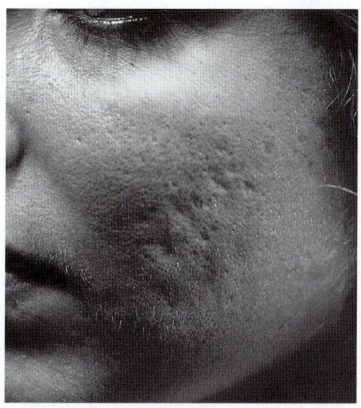

FIG. 257. This is a 29-year-old woman with severe scarring of her central cheek consisting of large depressed atrophic scars and many icepick scars. Fat atrophy can be seen at the lower central cheek and lateral to the angle of the mouth.

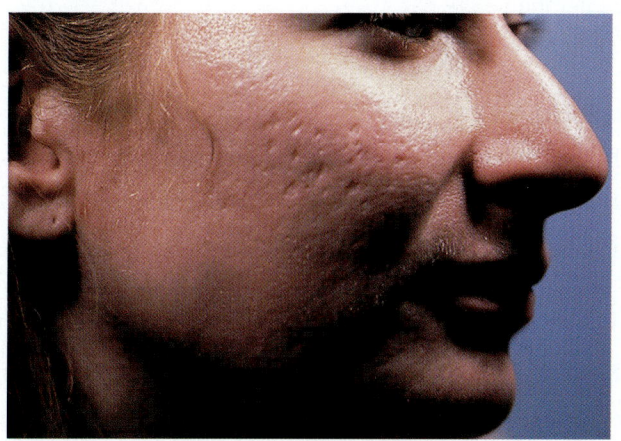

FIG. 260. Same patient as Figure 259 with deeper and more extensive scars present on her right cheek. These scars were so severe, I was doubtful that dermabrasion would be effective enough to provide a significant improvement.

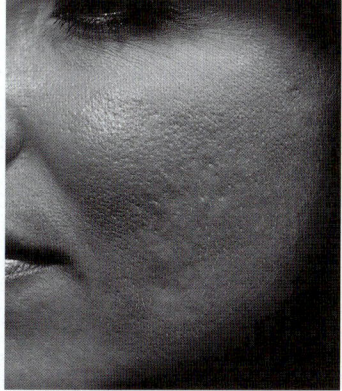

FIG. 258. This is the same patient as Figure 257 at 3 years postdermabrasion. There are both excellent results and color blending. Almost none of the preexisting scars can be identified. The remaining defects are subtle and primarily exist because of underlying fat atrophy. This long-term follow-up shows that using the principles outlined in this chapter can produce excellent long-term results.

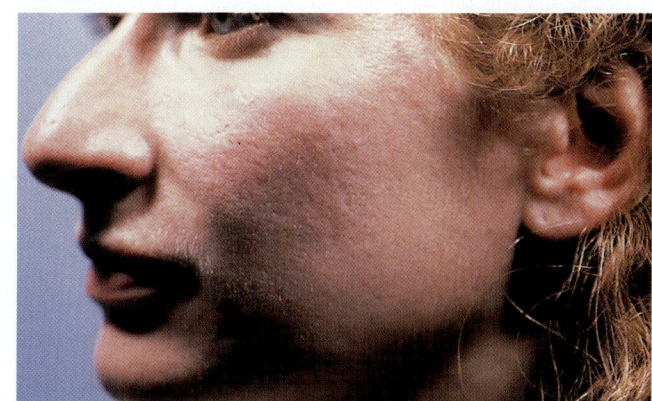

FIG. 261. Same patient as Figure 259 at 4½ months postdermabrasion. The color has now blended and is normal. The edema has completely resolved. The results on her left cheek are so dramatic that no preexisting scars can be identified

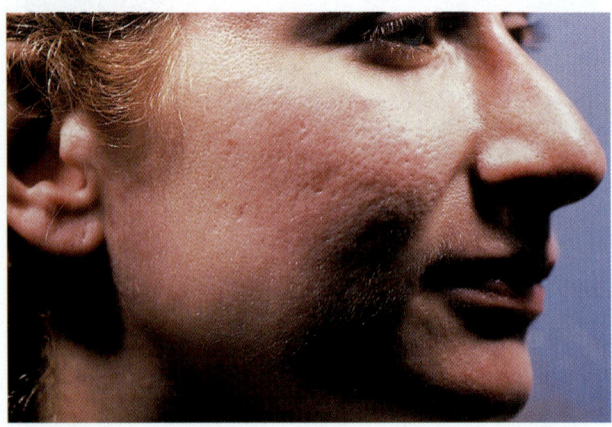

FIG. 262. Same patient as 260 at 4½ months postdermabrasion. There has also been remarkable improvement on her severely scarred right central cheek. Only subtle depressed areas remain at the locations of the most severe scarring. The patient rated her overall cosmetic improvement at greater than 95%.

REFERENCES

1. Ebbell B (translator). *Papyrus Ebers* Copenhagen: Levin and Munksgaard, Ejnar Munksgaard, 1937.
2. Kromayer E. Rotationsinstrumente: ein neues technisches Verfahren in der dermatologischen Kleinchirurgie. *Dermatol Z* 1905;12:26.
3. Kromayer E. Die Heilung der Akne durch ein neues narbenloses Operationsverfahren: Das Stanzen. *Illustr Monatsschr Aerztl Polytech* 1905;27:101.
4. Kromayer E. Die Heilung der Akne durch ein neues narbenloses Operationsverfahren: das Stanzen. *Munchen Med Wochenschr* 1905;52:942.
5. Kromayer E. Eine neues sichere Epitationsmethode: das Stanzen. *Deutsche Med Wochenschr* 1905;31:179.
6. Kromayer E. *Cosmetic treatment of skin complaints*. English translation of the second German edition (1929). New York: Oxford University Press, 1930;9.
7. Kromayer E. Das Frasen in der Kosmetik. *Kosmetalogische Rundschau* 1933:4–61.
8. Kromayer E. Kosmetische Resultate bei Anwedung des Stanzverfahrens. *Dermatol Wochenschr* 1935;101:1306.
9. Iverson PC. Surgical removal of traumatic tattoos of the face. *Plast Reconstr Surg* 1947;2:427.
10. Iverson PC. Further developments in the treatment of skin lesions by surgical abrasion. *Plast Reconstr Surg* 1953;12:27.
11. Kurtin A. Corrective surgical planing of the skin. *Arch Dermatol Syph* 1953;68:389.
12. Kurtin SB. A look back at Abner Kurtin, MD. *J Dermatol Surg Oncol* 1987;13:602.
13. Robbins N. Dr. Abner Kurtin, father of ambulatory dermabrasion. *J Dermatol Surg Oncol* 1988;14:425.
14. Coleman WP III, Alt T. Dermatologic cosmetic surgery. *J Dermatol Surg Oncol* 1990;16:170.
15. Lowenthal I. Punch biopsy with autograft. *Arch Dermatol Syph* 1953;67:629.
16. Blau S, Rein CR. Dermabrasion of the acne pit. *Arch Dermatol Syph* 1954;70:754.
17. Burks JW. *Wire brush surgery*. Springfield, IL: Charles C Thomas, 1956.
18. Wilson J, Ayres S, Luikart R. Mixtures of fluorinated hydrocarbons as refrigerated anesthetic. *Arch Dermatol* 1956;74:310.
19. Luikart R, Ayres S, Wilson J. Surgical skin planing. *NY State J Med* 1957;59:3413.
20. Yarborough J. Dermabrasive surgery. *Clin Dermatol* 1987;5:75.
21. Yarborough JM. Scar revision by dermabrasion. In: Roenigk RK, Roenigk HH, eds. *Dermatologic surgery*. New York: Marcel Dekker, 1989;909–933.
22. Johnson W. Treatment of pitted scars: punch transplant technique. *J Dermatol Surg Oncol* 1986;12:260.
23. Hanke CW, O'Brian JJ. A histologic evaluation of the effects of skin refrigerants in an animal model. *J Dermatol Surg Oncol* 1987;13:664.
24. Hanke CW, Conner AC, Reed J. Treatment of multiple facial neurofibromas with dermabrasion. *J Dermatol Surg Oncol* 1987;13:631.
25. Mandy SH. Tretinoin in the pre and post operative management of dermabrasion. *J Am Acad Dermatol* 1986;15:878.
26. Pinski JB. Dressings for dermabrasion: new aspects. *J Dermatol Surg Oncol* 1987;13:673.
27. Yarborough J, Alt TH, eds. Dermabrasion. *J Dermatol Surg Oncol* 1987;13:577–700.
28. Katz BE, Oca AG. A controlled study of the effectiveness of spot dermabrasion ("scarabrasion") on the appearance of surgical scars. *J Am Acad Dermatol* 1991;24:462.
29. Benedetto AV, Griffin TD, Benedetto EA, et al. Dermabrasion: therapy and prophylaxis of the photoaged face. *J Am Acad Dermatol* 1992;27:439.
30. Nelson BR, Majmudar G, Griffiths CE, et al. Clinical improvement following dermabrasion of photoaged skin correlates with synthesis of collagen I. *Arch Dermatol* 1994;130:1136.
31. Frank W. Therapeutic dermabrasion: back to the future. *Arch Dermatol* 1994;130:1187.
32. Coleman WP III, Klein JA. Use of the tumescent technique for scalp surgery, dermabrasion, and soft tissue reconstruction. *J Dermatol Surg Oncol* 1992;18:130.
33. Goodman G. Dermabrasion using tumescent anesthesia. *J Dermatol Surg Oncol* 1994;20:802.
34. Dzubow LM. Dermabrasion. *J Dermatol Surg Oncol* 1994;20:302.
35. American Academy of Dermatology Committee on Guidelines of Care: Guidelines of care for dermabrasion. *J Am Acad Dermatol* 1994;31:654.
36. Burks JW. *Dermabrasion and chemical peeling in the treatment of certain cosmetic defects and diseases of the skin*. Springfield, IL: Charles C Thomas, 1979.
37. Alt TH. Technical aids for dermabrasion. *J Dermatol Surg Oncol* 1987;13:638.
38. Solotoff S. Treatment for pitted acne scarring: postauricular punch grafts followed by dermabrasion. *J Dermatol Surg Oncol* 1986;12:1079.
39. Field L. Dermabrasion versus 5 fluorouracil in the management or actinic keratoses. In: Epstein I, ed. *Controversies in dermatology*. Philadelphia: WB Saunders, 1984;96–102.
40. Burks J, Marascalco J, Clark W. Half-face planing of precancerous skin after five years. *Arch Dermatol* 1963;88:140.
41. Stegman SJ. Sleep creases. *Am J Cosm Surg* 1987;4:277.
42. Stough DB III. The chemical face peel. *Cutis* 1976;18:100.
43. Roenigk HH Jr. Dermabrasion for miscellaneous cutaneous lesions: exclusive of scarring for acne. *J Dermatol Surg Oncol* 1977;3:322.
44. Wright MR. How to recognize and control the problem patient. *J Dermatol Surg Oncol* 1984;10:389.
45. Wright MR. Psychological evaluation of a cosmetic surgical patient. In: Coleman WP III, Hanke CW, Alt TH, Asken S, eds. *Cosmetic surgery of the skin*. Philadelphia: BC Decker, 1991;373–379.
46. Wentzell JM, Robinson JK, Wentzell JM, Jr. Physical properties of aerosols produced by dermabrasion. *Arch Dermatol* 1989;125:1637.
47. Update: human immunodeficiency virus infections in health care workers exposed to blood of infected patient. *MMWR* 1987;36:285.
48. Strauss JS. *Personal communication*. Iowa City, IA, 1982.
49. Roenigk HH Jr, Pinski JB, Robinson JK, Hanke CW. Acne, retinoids, and dermabrasion. *J Dermatol Surg Oncol* 1985;11:396.
50. Rubenstein R, Roenigk HH, Stegman SJ, Hanke CW. Atypical keloids after dermabrasion of patients taking isotretinoin. *J Am Acad Dermatol* 1986;15:280.
51. Zachariae H. Delayed wound healing and keloid formation following argon laser treatment or dermabrasion during isotretinoin treatment. *Br J Dermatol* 1988;118:703.
52. Fulton J. *Personal communication*. Newport Beach, CA, 1989.
53. Alt TH. Dermabrasion. In: Coleman WP III, Hanke CW, Alt TH, Asken S, eds. *Cosmetic surgery of the skin*. Philadelphia: BC Decker, 1991;147–195.
54. Katz BE. *Personal communication*. New York, NY, 1989.
55. Lucek RW, Colburn WA. Clinical pharmacokinetics of retinoids. *Clin Pharmacokinet* 1985;10:38.

56. Tromovitch TE, Stegman SJ, Glogau R. *Basic dermatologic surgery.* Chicago: Year Book Medical, 1984.
57. Kahn AM, Cohen MJ, Kaplan L, et al. Vitiligo: treatment by dermabrasion and epithelial sheet grafting: a preliminary report. *J Am Acad Dermatol* 1993;28:773.
58. Lontz W, Olsson MJ, Moellmann G, et al. Pigment cell transplantation for treatment of vitiligo: a progress report. *J Am Acad Dermatol* 1994;30:591.
59. Yarborough JM Jr, Beeson WH. Dermabrasion. In: Beeson WH, McCollough EG, eds. *Aesthetic surgery of the aging face.* St. Louis: CV Mosby, 1986;142–181.
60. Shelton RM, Grekin RC. Sterilization of the handengine. Is it a necessity? *J Dermatol Surg Oncol* 1994;20:385.
61. Hanke CW, O'Brian JJ, Salow EB. Laboratory evaluation of skin refrigerants in dermabrasion. *J Dermatol Surg Oncol* 1985;11:45.
62. Stegman SJ, Tromovitch TA. *Cosmetic dermatologic surgery.* Chicago: Year Book Medical, 1984;47–76.
63. McCollough KG, Langsdon PR. *Dermabrasion and chemical peel.* New York: Thieme Medical, 1988.
64. Abadir DM, Abadir AR. Dermabrasion under regional anesthesia without refrigeration of the skin. *J Dermatol Surg Oncol* 1980;6:119.
65. Panje W. Nerve block anesthesia of the head and neck. In: Epstein E, Epstein E Jr, eds. *Skin surgery,* 6th ed. Philadelphia: WB Saunders, 1987;36–43.
66. Strauss JS, Kligman AM. Dermabrasion and anatomy of acne pit. *Arch Dermatol* 1956;74:397.
67. Winter GD. Formation of the scab and the rate of epithelialization of superficial wounds of the skin of the young domestic pig. *Nature* 1962;193:293.
68. Winter GD, Scales JT. Effect of air drying and dressing on the surface of a wound. *Nature* 1963;197:91.
69. Hinman CD, Maibach HI. Effect of air exposure and occlusion on experimental human wounds. *Nature* 1963;200:377.
70. Pinski JB. Dressing for dermabrasion: occlusive dressings and wound healing. *Cutis* 1986;37:471.
71. Orentreich N. *Personal communication.* New York, NY, 1986.

8

Cosmetic Laser Surgery

Tina S. Alster

Although lasers have been in existence for decades, it has only been in the past few years that general interest in their use for cosmetic dermatologic applications has exploded. This rise in laser popularity has been due, in large part, to the development of a new class of "pulsed" lasers that can treat skin without unwanted thermal damage.

Physicians have been treating photodamaged skin and such dermatologic lesions as tattoos, birthmarks, and scars for many years with a wide array of therapies, including excision, dermabrasion, and chemical peels. These treatments, which essentially served to mechanically remove the top layers of lesional skin, were limited in terms of their risk-to-benefit ratio—scarring being the most undesirable, yet most encountered, side effect. Even with the advent of laser technology in the 1960s and continued advancement in the 1970s, the risk of scar formation remained high because of significant heat diffusion from the "continuous wave" lasers. It was not until the 1980s, when the concept of "selective photothermolysis" was introduced (meaning that a target in the skin could be selectively destroyed using a wavelength and pulse duration that matched its maximal absorption coefficient), that a variety of cutaneous lesions could be eliminated with minimal risk of side effects.

The first lasers to accomplish such selective cutaneous destruction were the pulsed-dye lasers. At wavelengths of 577 to 585 nm (yellow light spectrum), vascular lesions could be treated, whereas green light lasers (510 to 532 nm) could successfully treat superficial pigmented lesions. The Q-switched (QS, or quality-switched) lasers, including the QS ruby, QS alexandrite, and QS Nd:YAG (neodymium: yttrium-aluminum-garnet) lasers, were next. These Q-switched systems produce a single powerful pulse of stored energy and the red to near-infrared wavelengths of light that they emit can be used to treat deeply pigmented and tattooed lesions. The most recent additions to the laser armamentarium are the short-pulse, high-peak power or scanned CO_2 lasers, which, in comparison to the continuous wave systems, do not char tissue, but instead, remove or vaporize layers of photodamaged or scarred skin in a precisely controlled manner. The narrow zone of thermal damage that is produced by these newest lasers minimizes the risk of scarring and other untoward sequelae.

LASER TREATMENT OF VASCULAR LESIONS

Patient Selection

A variety of cutaneous vascular lesions are amenable to treatment with currently available vascular-specific lasers (Table 1). One of the most commonly encountered vascular lesions, facial telangiectasias, can be successfully treated with a 585-nm pulsed-dye laser, an argon-pumped tunable dye laser at 577 nm, a copper vapor or copper bromide laser at 578 nm, the krypton laser at 568 to 577 nm, and a KTP laser at 532 nm. These latter quasi-continuous-wave lasers, while not as vascular specific as the 585-nm pulsed-dye laser, are very useful in the treatment of larger-caliber linear vessels because of improved tissue penetration. In addition, they do not produce the purpuric tissue response that is characteristic of 585-nm pulsed-dye laser irradiation, making their use most desirable when cosmetic considerations are an immediate concern. On the other hand, for smaller-caliber vessels or for vascular birthmarks, such as port-wine stains, or when treating children, it is most advisable to use the 585-nm pulsed-dye laser because of its unsurpassable vascular specificity and low-risk profile in terms of scarring. Spider and linear telangiectasias of the legs that are larger than 1 mm in diameter are best treated with routine sclerotherapy. Those vessels that measure less than 1 mm in diameter, however, can now be treated with photothermal sclerosis using either a noncoherent pulsed beam at a wide spectrum of wavelengths (550 to 1000 nm) or long-pulsed-dye laser irradiation (595 to 600 nm). The use of longer wavelengths theoretically can provide deeper penetration of target vessels and improve light absorption by the deoxyhemoglobin that is prominent in the target venules.

TABLE 1. *Response of vascular lesions to laser treatment*

Laser type	Laser specifics	Facial telangiectasias	Leg telangiectasias	Port-wine stain	Hemangioma	Poikiloderma
Copper vapor	511 nm Quasi-CW	++	0	+	Unknown	Unknown
Krypton	520–530 nm Quasi-CW	++	0	+	Unknown	Unknown
Frequency-doubled Nd:YAG	532 Q-switched	++	0	0	Unknown	Unknown
KTP	532 nm Quasi-CW	++	0	0	Unknown	Unknown
Argon-pumped tunable dye	577 nm Quasi-CW	++	0	+	+	Unknown
Flashlamp-pumped pulsed dye	585 nm pulsed	+++	+	+++	+++	+++
Long-pulse dye	590 nm pulsed	+++	++	++	Unknown	Unknown
Photoderm VL	550–900 nm noncoherent pulsed	++	++	+	Unknown	Unknown

0, no effect; +, fair; ++, good; +++, excellent. CW, continuous wave; Nd:YAG, neodymium: yttrium-aluminum-garnet; KTP, potassium tritanyl-phosphate.

It is best to treat patients with lighter skin tones (Fitzpatrick skin phototypes I to III) for optimal penetration of the dermal blood vessels. The increased amount of melanin in darker skin tones decreases the amount of laser light available to the underlying oxyhemoglobin, as both melanin and oxyhemoglobin have similar absorption curves. This is not to say that darker skin tones cannot also be treated, but patients must be made aware that additional laser treatments may be necessary to achieve the desired clinical response. In addition, fluences (or laser energy) will need to be adjusted to maximize the efficacy of each laser treatment.

Patient Preparation

Patients undergoing pulsed-dye laser treatment should be forewarned not only of the rubber-band-like snapping sensation experienced with each laser pulse, but also of the immediate purpuric reaction that occurs in the laser-irradiated skin. The purpura may also be associated with local tissue swelling, and it typically lasts for 7 to 10 days postoperatively. Once the purpura fades, additional lesional lightening occurs over the next 4 to 6 weeks, commensurate with histologic clearing of the laser-induced vasculitis. Young patients who are apprehensive about the uncomfortable snapping sensation may require topical or even intravenous anesthesia.

Patients should be encouraged to avoid sun exposure of the lesional skin prior to and after laser irradiation. Tanned skin will actually reduce the amount of energy delivered to the intended vascular target because of competition for the yellow laser light by the overlying melanin. Although transient pigmentary alteration of the skin can occur after laser treatment, it is rare that permanent hypo- or hyperpigmentation will result. Nonetheless, patients should be informed of the possibility of postoperative cutaneous pigmentation changes.

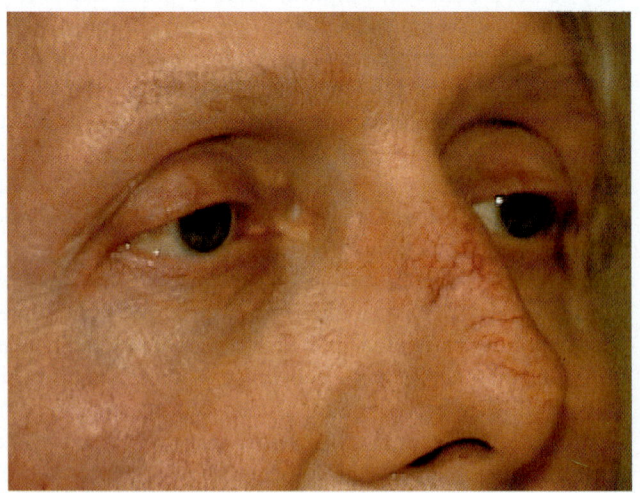
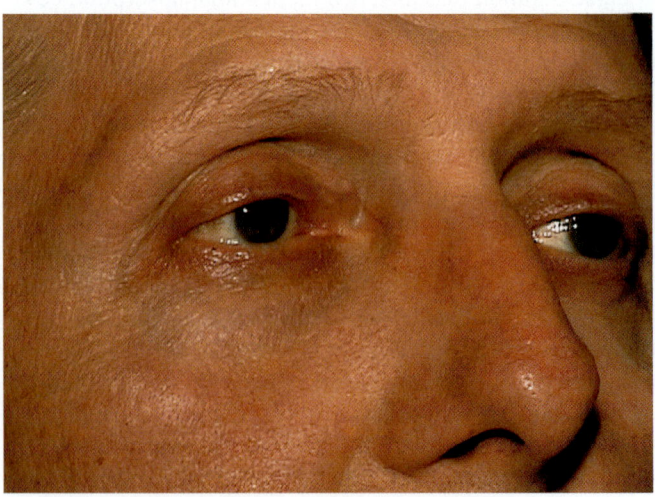

FIG. 1. Linear telangiectasias in the perinasal creases of a 41-year-old man before **(A)** and 6 weeks after **(B)** two treatments with a 585-nm flashlamp-pumped pulsed-dye laser at 7.0 J/cm² and 7-mm spot size.

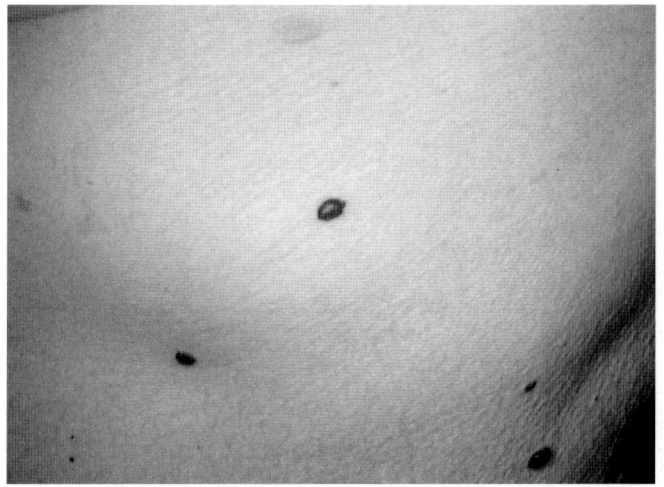 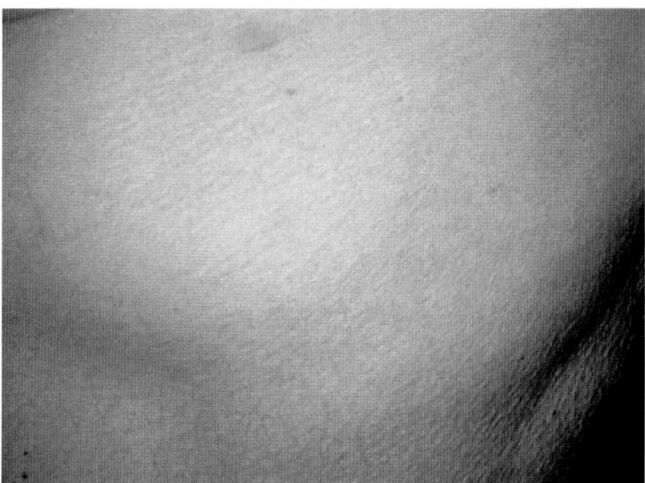

FIG. 2. Truncal angiomas in a 52-year-old woman before **(A)** and after **(B)** two treatments with a 585-nm pulsed-dye laser at 6.5 J/cm^2 using a 7-mm spot.

Last, patients should be counseled that more than one treatment is typically necessary to achieve total lesional eradication—even for telangiectasias. Vascular birthmarks, such as port-wine stains and hemangiomas, generally require several laser sessions (six or more), separated at bimonthly intervals to allow maximal clearing. Patients who have had prior treatment that produced tissue fibrosis (i.e., from electrodesiccation or continuous-wave laser irradiation) should be cautioned that the fibrosis may necessitate more than the normal number of treatments.

Laser Procedure and Treatment Parameters

Telangiectasias, when present as arborizing spiders or papular angiomas, are treated with spot sizes ranging from 3 to 10 mm at fluences of 4.0 to 7.5 J/cm^2 when using the 585-nm pulsed-dye system (lower fluences are used with larger spot sizes) (Figs. 1, 2). In general, lesions located in delicate tissue areas, such as on the eyelids, neck, and anterior chest, require the use of lower fluences, as do treatments in children or on pale, type I skin (Table 2). Additional treatments, if necessary, are usually delivered at the same or slightly increased fluence, depending on the initial clinical response. Fluences are decreased if an excessive tissue response is elicited, such as blistering, following treatment. Evaluation of response to treatment and retreatment should be scheduled 6 to 8 weeks after the initial treatment to allow time for optimal clearing.

Telangiectasias of the lower extremities measuring less than 1 mm in diameter can be treated with a long-pulse laser (ScleroLaser, Candela Laser Corporation, Wayland, MA) at 595 to 600 nm and fluences of 15 to 20 J/cm^2 with an elliptical handpiece. Photothermal sclerosis of small-diameter leg telangiectasias can also be achieved with the use of an intense pulsed light source (Photoderm VL, ESC Medical Systems, Haifa, Israel) using a 550-nm cut-off filter, 25 to 70 J/cm^2 irradiance, double pulses of 3.0 to 7.7 msec, and pulse delays ranging from 50 to 100 msec. Treatments using the Photoderm VL are separated by 2- to 4-week time intervals.

Port-wine stains and hemangiomas are optimally treated with a 585-nm pulsed-dye laser, applying adjacent, nonoverlapping laser spots at fluences ranging from 4.0 to 7.0 J/cm^2 (Fig. 3). Larger spot sizes of 7 to 10 mm are best used in order to reduce the number of pulses delivered (thereby decreasing treatment-associated pain) and also to improve tissue penetration (especially important for deeper, thicker, more nodular, or advanced lesions).

Postoperative Skin Care and Patient Follow-Up

Patients are instructed to apply an antibiotic ointment to the laser-treated sites daily. They are permitted to shower but must use a mild soap and gently pat (not rub) the areas dry. Regular sunscreen use is necessary once the purpura resolves, and patients are discouraged from tanning the areas for the reasons described previously.

A follow-up appointment is scheduled 6 to 8 weeks after laser treatment to allow complete healing and to assess the degree of improvement obtained. If mild hyperpigmentation

TABLE 2. *Factors affecting laser parameters*

Lesional factors
Lesion type
Lesion location
Prior treatment to lesion
Lesional response to laser
Patient factors
Patient age
Skin type
Activity (sun exposure) or social obligations
Expectations of treatment
Laser factors
Laser type (pulsed or continuous wave)
Spot size
Wavelength

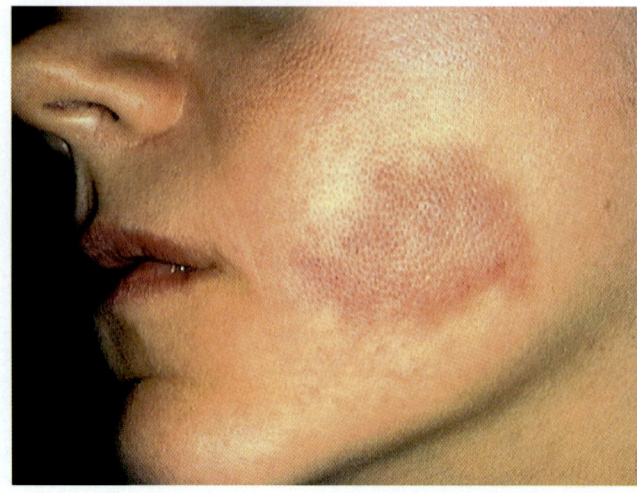 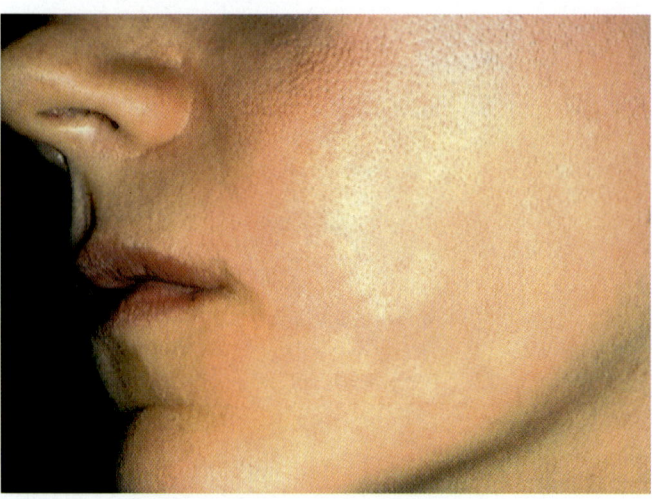

FIG. 3. A 34-year-old woman with a port-wine stain birthmark before **(A)** and 2 months after **(B)** the sixth laser treatment using a 585-nm pulsed-dye laser at average fluence 6.5 J/cm^2 and 7-mm spot.

is observed in the laser-treated skin (an orange-brown discoloration representative of residual hemosiderin deposition from the laser-induced vasculitis), the patient should wait an additional 2 to 4 weeks to be re-evaluated, to allow the skin to heal further. If the laser-irradiated area is improved, but residual vascular lesion remains, another laser treatment can then be delivered.

LASER TREATMENT OF PIGMENTED LESIONS

Patient Selection

Laser treatment of pigmented lesions has traditionally been limited to those lesions that are benign with little to no risk of malignant degeneration, such as solar lentigines and pigmented birthmarks (i.e., café-au-lait [CAL] macules and nevus of Ota). Most recently, investigators have also been evaluating the use of lasers in congenital and benign melanocytic nevi. Various lasers at different wavelengths have been used successfully to treat pigmented lesions because of the broad absorption spectrum of melanin—the primary lesional target, or chromophore.

Green light lasers, such as the pulsed-dye laser at 510 nm and the frequency-doubled Nd:YAG laser at 532 nm, can best eliminate superficial epidermal pigment, whereas the Q-switched red light lasers, such as the ruby at 694 nm, alexandrite at 755 nm, and Nd:YAG at 1064 nm, are better at treating deeper dermal pigment (Table 3). The pulsed-dye laser and QS laser systems follow the basic principles of selective photothermolysis—not only are the wavelengths optimized for the target chromophore (melanin), but their pulse durations are briefer than the thermal relaxation time of a melanosome (less than 1 μsec). Thus, excess thermal conduction with unnecessary cutaneous damage is avoided and the risk of scarring or other adverse sequelae is minimized. Pigment cells are selectively destroyed by these lasers, presumably either as a result of extreme temperature gradients created within melanosomes, or from shock-wave and cavitation damage resulting from the rapid thermal expansion of irradiated tissue. Other pigment-specific lasers such as the copper vapor or copper bromide, although emitting light at melanin-specific wavelengths, do not have pulse durations short enough to comply with these basic principles. These latter lasers are, therefore, best-suited for small lesions (i.e., lentigines) or whenever slight textural or pigmentary irregularities are of less cosmetic importance.

TABLE 3. *Lasers used to treat pigmented lesions*

Laser type	Wavelength	Solar lentigines	Café-au-lait	Nevus of Ota	Benign nevi	Melasma/PIH
Pulsed dye	510-nm pulsed	+++	+++	0	+	0
Copper vapor	511-nm Quasi-CW	++	+/−	0	+/0	0
Freq-doubled Nd:YAG	532-nm Quasi-CW	+++	+/++	0	+	0
Krypton	520–530-nm Quasi-CW	++	+/−	0	0	0
QS ruby	694-nm Q-switched	+++	+/++	+++	+/++	0
QS alexandrite	755-nm Q-switched	+++	+/++	+++	+/++	0
QS Nd:YAG	1064-nm Q-switched	+++	+/0	+++	+/++	0

0, no effect; +, fair; ++, good; +++, excellent. PIH, postinflammatory hyperpigmentation; CW, continuous wave; Nd:YAG, neodymium yttrium-aluminum-garnet.

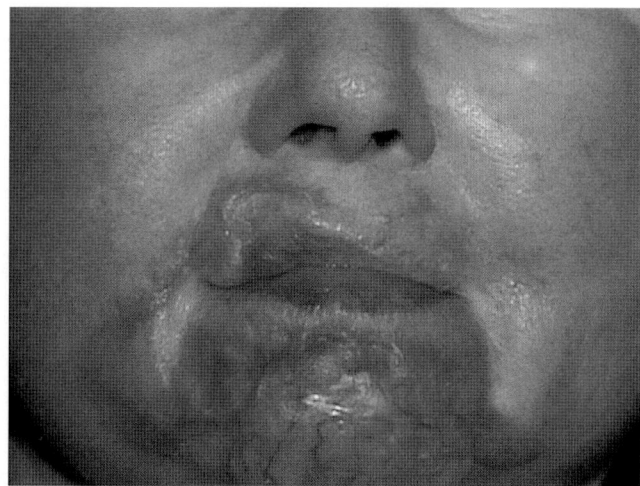 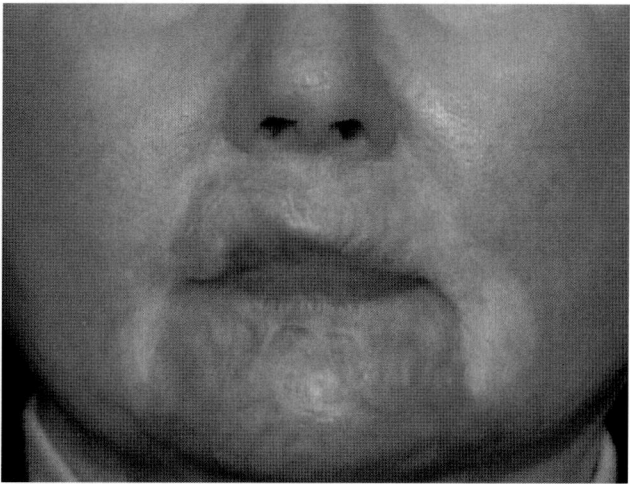

FIG. 13. Hypertrophic scars occurring within 4 weeks of perioral laser resurfacing, before **(A)** and 6 weeks after **(B)** three treatments with a 585-nm pulsed-dye laser at average fluence of 4.5 J/cm^2 using a 10-mm spot size.

bleaching creams mixed with glycolic or retinoic acid can be started to facilitate the fading process. Alternatively, a light (30%) glycolic acid treatment can be applied and repeated at biweekly intervals until the dyspigmentation resolves. Topical vitamin C application may also allow more rapid dissolution of this undesirable side effect if the patient's skin can tolerate it (many patients are still too sensitive at this point to begin regular acid application).

Another undesirable side effect is hypopigmentation. It may be several months before it is clinically apparent. It is most often seen in areas that have had extensive resurfacing (i.e., an increased number of laser passes). All skin types can be affected. Unfortunately, there does not appear to be a uniformly effective way to combat this problem and it may be permanent.

Other undesirable and more concerning side effects, such as scarring and ectropion formation, should they occur, become evident within the first month after the resurfacing procedure. Patients may complain about limited mouth opening if the perioral regions were treated. Simply feeling "tight" and looking red is typical of a normal healing response and does not imply any untoward effect. On the other hand, distinct areas of fibrosis or even hypertrophy are indicative of scar formation and patients should be started on a suitable scar treatment plan (Fig. 13). Although intralesional and topical steroids or silicone gel application can improve hypertrophic scars, more immediate and significant improvement is achieved with 585-nm pulsed-dye laser treatment (see Laser Treatment of Scars and Striae).

It is important to remember that whereas the actual laser resurfacing procedure may only last an hour or so, postoperative skin care and follow-up typically persist for several months. It is therefore imperative that a proper postoperative protocol be designed and implemented for all patients undergoing laser resurfacing, regardless of the size or area of skin being treated.

OTHER COSMETIC USES OF LASERS

CO_2 and Nd:YAG lasers are being used to facilitate blepharoplasties, face and neck lifts, and hair transplants. They can decrease intraoperative bleeding and, with practice, can actually decrease intraoperative times and eventual cosmetic outcomes. Laser vaporization of a wide variety of epidermal and dermal lesions, such as verrucae, keratoses, and intradermal nevi, allow rapid treatment and cosmetically improved results because of the elimination of sutures. Last, initial reports of permanent hair removal using long-pulsed ruby, alexandrites, or Nd:YAG lasers with or without topical carbon-based solutions have been promising. It is anticipated that laser targeting of hair follicles is a more expedient and effective method to remove undesirable hair with a lower rate of hair regrowth.

In conclusion, laser surgery is no longer reserved for disorders or lesions without effective alternative treatments, such as port-wine stains and nevus of Ota. In fact, laser surgery is being favored as the treatment of choice for a number of conditions, such as rhytides and scars, which have been responsive to other, older forms of therapy. There will, no doubt, be further advances in dermatologic laser applications as laser technology continues to evolve. Given the recent laser "hysteria" that has hit the medical and public mainstream, it will be especially important to maintain an objective eye to ascertain the distinct advantages of using this technology in the future.

SUGGESTED READINGS

Alster TS. *Manual of cutaneous laser techniques.* Philadelphia: Lippincott–Raven, 1997.
Alster TS. *Lasers in dermatology.* Dermatologic Clinics, Philadelphia: WB Saunders, 1997.
Alster TS, Apfelberg DB. *Cosmetic laser surgery.* New York: John Wiley & Sons, 1996.
Goldman MP, Fitzpatrick RE. *Cutaneous laser surgery: the art and science of selective photothermolysis.* St. Louis: Mosby Year-Book, 1994.

› 9 ›

Tumescent Liposuction

Jeffrey Alan Klein

In a broad sense, the tumescent technique is a novel method for drug delivery, with applications far beyond local anesthesia for liposuction. The tumescent technique was invented to allow liposuction using local anesthesia and to eliminate surgical blood loss and the dangers of general anesthesia. It has achieved that and much more. The aim of this chapter is to enlighten physicians about some of the fine points of modern tumescent technique for liposuction totally by local anesthesia. After a general discussion, liposuction of the lateral thigh will be used as a specific example of the newer concepts of liposuction.

Tumescent liposuction is not evolutionary, it is revolutionary. It is much more than a mere extrapolation of previous liposuction techniques that use general anesthesia or subcutaneous infiltration merely for hemostasis. It is the only technique that permits large-volume liposuction totally by local anesthesia. Although the tumescent technique is now the standard of care for liposuction, it is surprising that the technique has been so slow in finding acceptance among some groups of surgeons. The inertia of clinical dogma requires an energetic intellectual effort to change direction. There is similar resistance to more recent improvements for liposuction. These improvements include the use of microcannulas, as well as postoperative care involving incisions that are not sutured, to encourage maximal postoperative drainage of blood-tinged anesthetic solution, which in turn minimizes postoperative inflammation.

PRIOR LIPOSUCTION TECHNIQUES

The dry technique for liposuction relied on general anesthesia without any preoperative infiltration of vasoconstrictive solution. It is now widely regarded among dermatologic surgeons as substandard care because of the massive bleeding with which it is associated. The wet technique for lipoplasty, a slight modification of the dry technique, achieves a moderate decrease in surgical bleeding by injecting a minuscule volume of a relatively concentrated solution of epinephrine.

The tumescent technique is as different from the dry and the wet technique as local anesthesia is from general anesthesia. Virtually all deaths connected to liposuction have been associated with general anesthesia or excessive surgical blood loss. The tumescent technique for liposuction has eliminated these risks.

The use of any form of anesthesia should be based on strict indications. The convenience of general anesthetics is not an indication for their use. Local anesthesia should be used whenever possible because it is safer than general anesthesia or intravenous (IV) sedation.

Among those patients who have previously had liposuction by general anesthesia and subsequently had tumescent liposuction, the vast majority unquestionably prefer tumescent liposuction because of its superior comfort and rapid recovery.

Dermatologic surgeons have been doing tumescent liposuction since 1985 and have openly taught this technique to surgeons of other specialties. The tumescent technique was invented and developed because of the intuitive appeal of local anesthesia in terms of safety and hemostasis. Tumescent liposuction has proved to be safer, to provide superior aesthetic results, and to provide more rapid postoperative recovery and return to normal activities.

Dermatologic surgery and plastic surgery differ in one transcendent aspect. Dermatologists believe that surgery of the skin can *usually* be done more effectively and more safely using local anesthesia alone than with the concomitant use of general anesthesia or heavy IV sedation.

The reason that many surgeons do not use pure local anesthesia is lack of training and experience. The ability to do large surgical procedures totally by local anesthesia requires empathy, patience, and compassion when dealing with awake patients during surgery. Not all surgeons possess such interpersonal skills. The assumption that general anesthesia and heavy IV sedation are acceptable risks is based on the dogmatic and erroneous belief that IV sedation and general anesthesia are safer and more humane than local anesthesia.

The training of dermatologic surgeons is almost exclusively limited to the use of local anesthesia in an outpatient setting. The tumescent technique for local anesthesia is an invention of dermatologic surgery. For other surgical specialties, training predominantly concentrates on the use of general anesthesia for hospitalized patients.

With the tumescent technique, dermatologic surgeons can perform virtually any plastic surgical procedure of the skin totally by local anesthesia without parenteral sedation, narcotic analgesics, or general anesthesia. Thus, with appropriate training and skill, the tumescent technique allows dermatologic plastic surgical procedures such as liposuction, facelift, and abdominoplasty, to be accomplished with less pain, quicker recovery, better aesthetic results, and dramatically lower risk of complications.

Application of the tumescent technique has been extended to a number of procedures beyond the traditional boundaries of dermatologic surgery. Plastic surgeons have applied the tumescent technique to breast surgery (mastectomy, breast reduction, breast augmentation), and to large split-thickness skin grafts for burn patients.

LATERAL THIGH LIPOSUCTION

Modern aspects of tumescent liposuction are quite different from the procedure that was performed more than 10 years ago. The following discussion of tumescent liposuction of the outer thigh will give the reader some appreciation for the current state of the art of liposuction totally by local anesthesia, without IV or intramuscular (IM) sedation or narcotic analgesics.

Aesthetic Considerations

For many women, fat tends to preferentially accumulate on the thighs. Despite vigorous exercise and physical conditioning programs, the lack of visible improvement in the shape of their thighs is frequently frustrating. There is a common desire to change the look of disproportionate thighs and legs. It is not surprising that thighs are among the areas most frequently treated by liposuction.

From an aesthetic perspective, dolichocnemia, or the presence of long, slender lower extremities, is frequently desired. Long slender thighs suggest youth, athleticism, self-esteem, optimism, and vitality. In contrast, fat, thick, stumpy, lumpy thighs imply an image of older age, an inactive life style, humiliation, antipathy, and lethargy. Throughout the history of art and sculpture of the female figure, long legs are portrayed as elegant, graceful, artistic, and beautiful. Short, stumpy, thick legs, on the other hand, are not presented as being alluring or desirable. The aesthetic appeal of long legs seems to transcend culture and time. Artists, regardless of their sex, seem to find long legs attractive and refined.

The English language lacks a word to accurately designate the entire aesthetic unit of subcutaneous fat that includes the outer thigh. For the purposes of liposuction, the usual designations of "outer thigh, jodhpur, or trochanteric" area are not sufficiently inclusive. The outer thigh by itself, without the rest of its cosmetic unit, has an obovate (inverted egg) form. When liposuction is restricted to just the outer thigh, the result may be insufficient. Liposuction that leaves excessive fat in the inferolateral buttock and banana-form fold appears amateurish and artless.

The term *lateral thigh complex* defines an area of subcutaneous fat composed of the lateral trochanteric area, the inferolateral buttock, and the banana-form fold of the proximal posterior thigh. The periphery of this anatomic area is somewhat cordiform or cordate (heart-shaped). This grouping of smaller areas into a larger combined aesthetic unit has more artistic relevance.

Lipotrops and Liponots

One of the most common problems with liposuction of the lateral thigh is the risk of doing too much liposuction. The two areas of the lateral thigh most at risk for lipotrop are the pseudobulge and the proximal lateral posterior area. Lipotrop (*lipo* is short for liposuction, and *trop* [pronounced trō] comes from the French meaning too much) is defined as a localized area that has been treated excessively by liposuction (Fig. 1).

A liponot is an area of insufficient liposuction. Although not as disfiguring as a lipotrop, a liponot is nonetheless a source of considerable disappointment for the patient. A timid approach to liposuction is ultimately ineffectual and unsatisfactory. Superior liposuction results require a self-assured thoroughness in removing enough fat to achieve definite improvement while cautiously avoiding excessive extraction. Correct intraoperative positioning of the patient provides the confidence to remove enough fat for a significant cosmetic improvement while simultaneously avoiding a lipotrop.

Surface Anatomy and Preoperative Evaluation

Often, the patient is certain that her only area of concern is the obovate lateral thigh. However, it is usual for adjacent areas to be of equal or greater cosmetic importance. Polaroid photographs from both a posterior and anterior view help give the patient an objective perspective. Often, the hips are far more capacious and pose more of an aesthetic problem than the lateral thighs.

It is important to evaluate and discuss the need to treat the infragluteal-crease banana-form fold, as well as the inferolateral buttocks. Not treating these areas when doing liposuction of the lateral thigh can lead to a disappointed patient.

The shape of the buttocks changes with age. Inferolateral buttocks tend to sag with age. Perhaps the suspensory liga-

Abdomen Incision Sites

A preferred technique for incisional sites of the abdomen includes three openings in the suprapubic area (one in the midline, two laterally) (see Fig. 3), one incision in the superior umbilicus, and two or three incisions on each side of the abdomen along the anterior axillary line (one in the upper lateral abdomen, one in the mid-lateral abdomen, and an optional one in large patients in the lower lateral abdomen) (Fig. 7). This allows good crisscrossing and a complete treatment of the abdominal area.

The mid-lateral incision site is very important for good sculpting of the waist and lower abdomen. It allows good access to the deeper fat below Scarpa's fascia when suctioning laterally or inferiorly through that incision site. Fat is compartmentalized in the lower abdomen by layers of fascia, Camper's fascia, the superficial indistinct fatty layer, and Scarpa's fascia, which forms a distinct plane in the mid layer. In many patients, if the surgeon does not suction below Scarpa's fascia, adequate removal of the fat-pad in both the waist area and the lower abdomen will not be possible.

The lateral flank is crisscrossed from approximately four incision sites: two incisions inferiorly just superior to the natural depression, one incision anteriorly approximately at the waistline, and one incision posteriorly approximately at the waistline (Fig. 8).

The posterior flank is treated by crisscrossing from the two posterior lateral flank incisions and an extra incision in the midline back (Fig. 9). Two additional incisions are made

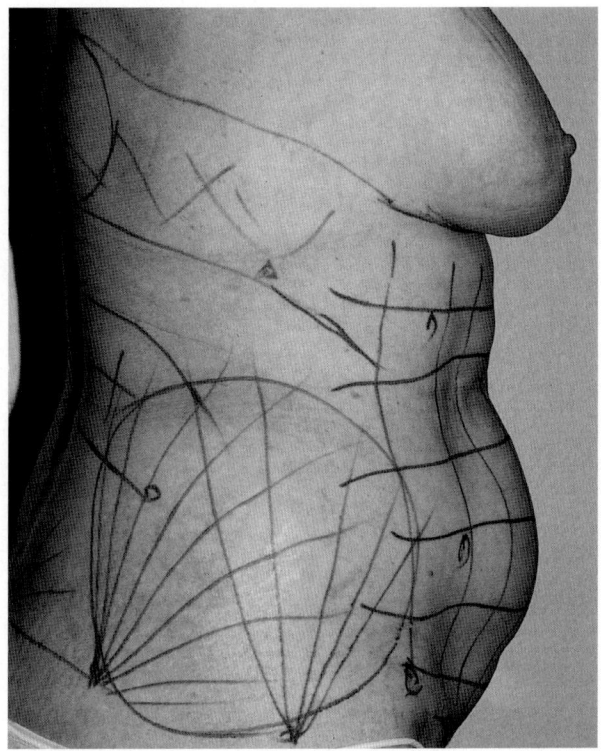

FIG. 8.

for the infrascapular pad at the midline back and posterior axillary line. Care must be exercised to place the incision just above the natural crease so that the crease will not be suctioned. The third incision used for the infrascapular pad is the superior lateral abdominal incision made previously.

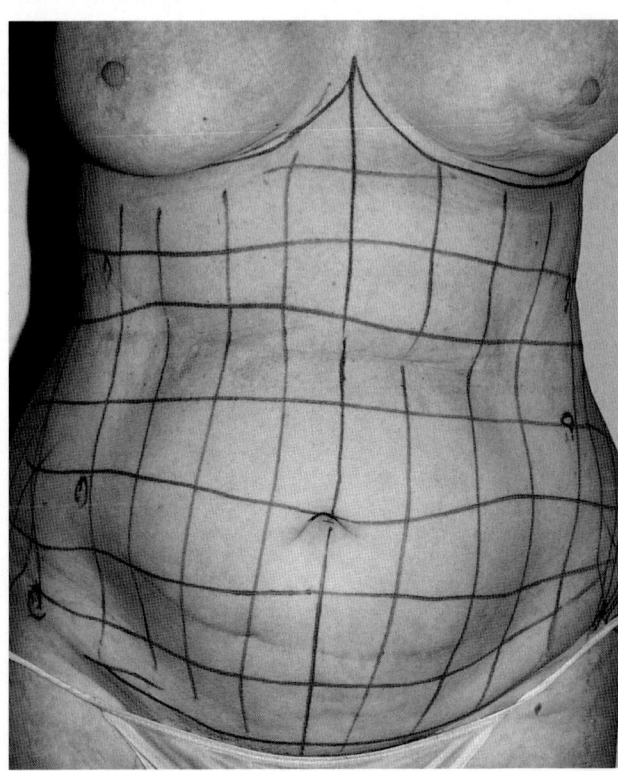

FIG. 7.

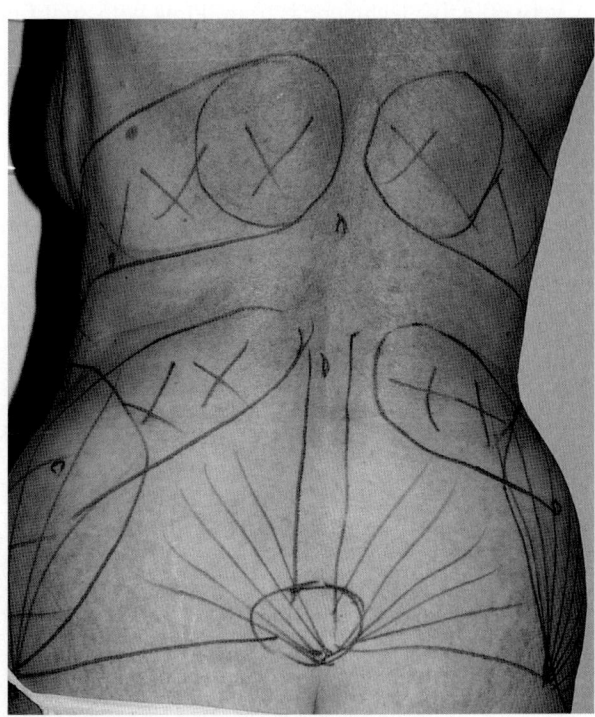

FIG. 9.

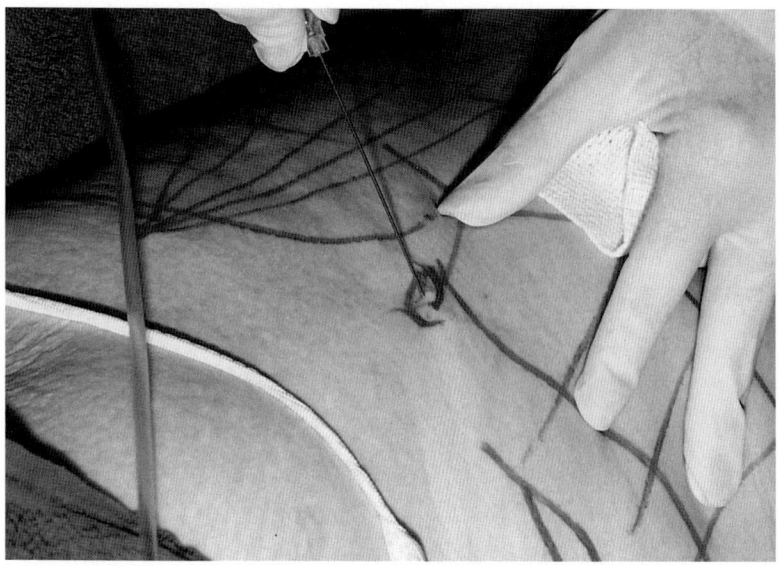

FIG. 10.

The Tumescent Infiltration

When the marking is finished, the patient is placed in the supine position and infiltration of the tumescent solution is begun. Monitoring is performed (pulse oximeter, blood pressure, and continuous electrocardiography [ECG]), and oxygen is given by nasal cannula. The premarked incision sites are first infiltrated with a small amount of 2% lidocaine with 1:1,000,000 epinephrine. This provides good anesthesia as well as good vasoconstriction to the sites, as they will be traumatized from the cannula insertions.

A very effective technique is to infiltrate with an infiltration pump, beginning with a 22-gauge spinal needle, until the patient is no longer sensitive (Fig. 10). This preanesthesia with the spinal needle is introduced through all marked sites. Careful monitoring and awareness of the total amount of lidocaine that is being infiltrated is essential.

The tumescent solution for the abdomen contains 0.1% lidocaine, and for the flanks and infrascapular area 0.05% lidocaine. The composition of the 0.1% and 0.05% tumescent solutions is prepared by adding, per total volume of 1000 ml of normal saline, either 50 or 25 ml, respectively, of 2% lidocaine with 1 ml of epinephrine (1:1000) and 12.5 mEq of sodium bicarbonate. Triamcinolone acetonide suspension (Kenalog) 10 mg per 1000 ml of normal saline may be added to reduce inflammation.

After this preanesthesia, the remainder of the tumescent solution is infused using a 14-gauge, multiport infusion cannula that allows the solution to diffuse to all regions (Fig.

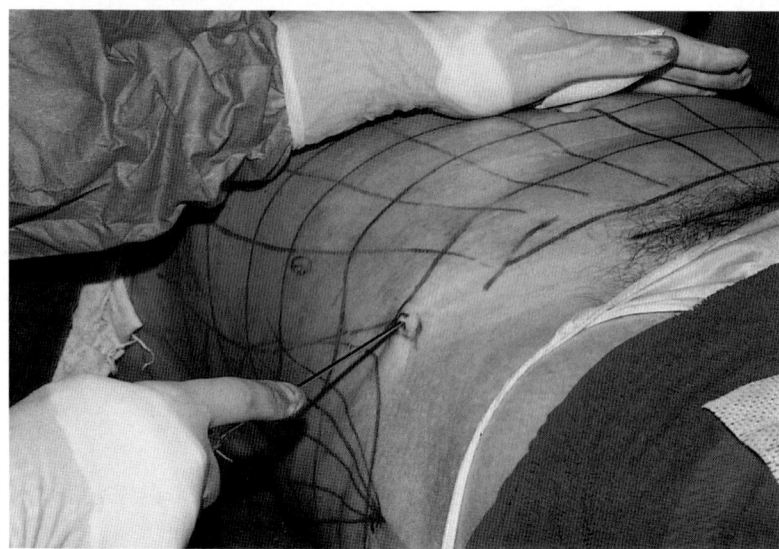

FIG. 11.

FIG. 12. A Cook cannula.

FIG. 14. A Klein cannula.

11). This ensures good preparation of the tissues with hydration, anesthesia, and vasoconstriction. In addition to the tumescent solution, one may sedate the patient with intramuscular (IM) Demerol, usually 50 to 100 mg, and IM Versed, 2.5 to 5 mg. Neither general anesthesia nor IV anesthesia is used. The Demerol and Versed relax the patient and relieve any slight discomfort during the infiltration.

SURGICAL TECHNIQUE—SUCTIONING

After the infiltration, the patient is prepared and draped for the suctioning procedure. Smaller cannulas, ranging from 14 gauge to 3 mm, are used. Cook, Pinto, and Klein cannulas (Figs. 12–14) are preferred for the trunk, starting with a 14-gauge, increasing to a 12-gauge, then to 3-mm, and completing with the smaller 12-gauge. A 3.5-mm cannula is used only in large-volume body-reduction cases.

With the patient in the supine position, the suctioning is begun on the right abdomen through the three suprapubic incision sites, usually with a 14-gauge cannula with two ports, always placed in a downward position (Fig. 15). Suctioning is begun at a fairly deep plane, thus allowing the surgeon to

FIG. 13. A Pinto cannula.

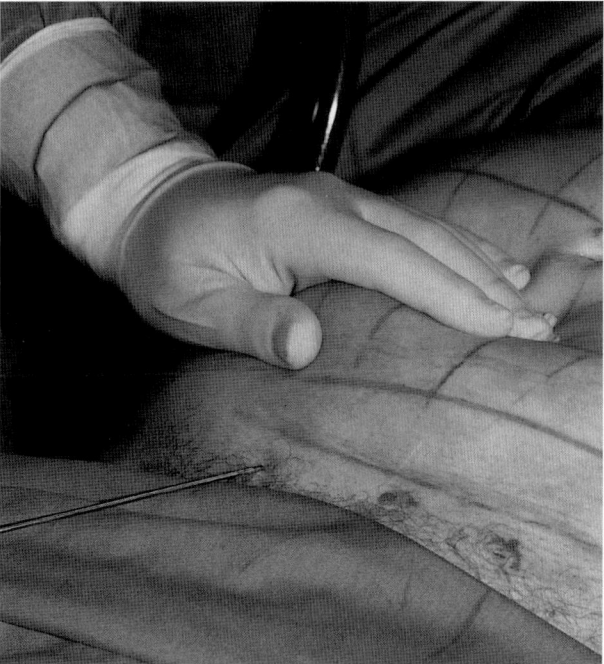

FIG. 15.

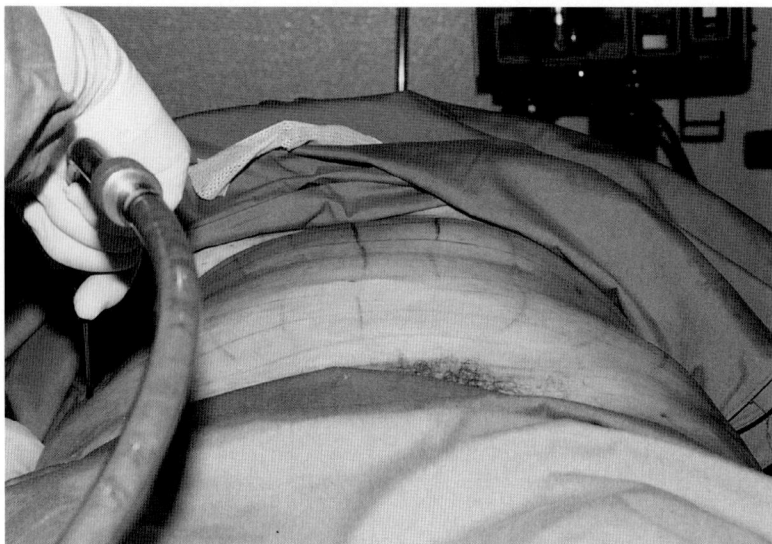

FIG. 16.

determine the firmness of the various areas of the adipose layer, to establish early tunneling, and to develop a pattern for removal of fat.

Next, the deep layers of the superior and inferior abdomen are treated by suctioning through the mid-lateral abdominal incision sites (Fig. 16). Remember to suction carefully deep to Scarpa's fascia, both at an inferior angle and at a lateral angle for the waistline. Suction the deep plane and gradually work up to the mid plane.

Suctioning is begun with a 4-inch, 14-gauge Klein cannula, and then a 6-inch, 14-gauge Klein cannula is used (Fig. 17). If the adipose layer is extremely firm or cicatricial, keep using the Klein 14-gauge until it is soft enough to change cannulas. Then switch to a more aggressive 3-mm Pinto, or a less aggressive 3-mm Cook cannula, which should be used in the upper and lower abdomen only from the lateral incision sites. Proceed in a uniform orderly and organized fashion throughout the fat-pad. Do not randomly sweep an area with the cannula (in the manner of a windshield wiper). Pull the cannula back and forth in a to-and-fro motion.

It is important to transect the fatty layer uniformly in an orderly progression throughout and not to repeat strokes in one place, thus digging a hole and then having to match the surrounding areas to the newly created depression.

With the abdomen treated on the right half, the procedure is repeated on the left half, beginning to crisscross the midline, to adequately connect all the interlacing tunnels. Carefully suction the lower abdomen below the Scarpa's fascia. Elevate any depressed scars by using a dissector instrument superficially just below the skin (Fig. 18). This ensures that the scar will elevate to the level of the surrounding areas that were just sculpted. If it appears that the scar may not easily be released from underlying structures, do not try to elevate it.

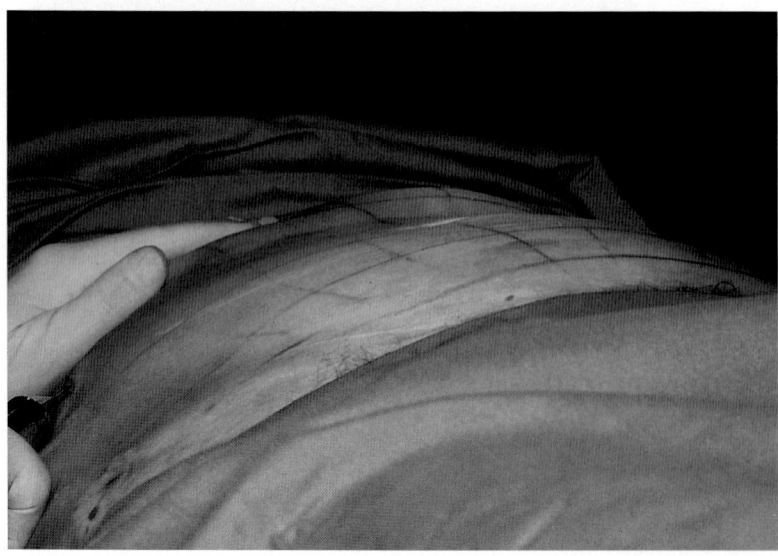

FIG. 17.

flection from moving red blood cells to be seen so that blood vessels and flow are shown (13). Color units have circuitry to indicate flow away from the tranducer in one color and flow toward the transducer in another color. Duplex scanners are found in fully equipped vascular laboratories, but laboratory personnel must be instructed in the examination of the superficial venous system. This must include an assessment of the saphenofemoral junction and the saphenopopliteal junction with the patient standing. A complete duplex ultrasound examination will also map superficial and deep veins with precise identification of sources of venous reflux (24,25).

Once the evaluation of the patient is complete, the presence and source of significant venous reflux should have been identified. If the patient has significant saphenofemoral reflux, treatment may include surgical control of that origin point of reflux prior to sclerotherapy or ambulatory phlebectomy of more distal branches. Although success rates for sclerotherapy of the saphenofemoral junction have been reported as high as 93%, this has not been our experience (26–28). A classic comparison of surgery and sclerotherapy caused Hobbs to conclude that saphenous vein insufficiency is best managed by surgery, whereas sclerotherapy is superior for treatment of isolated perforator incompetence (29).

Once the patient is judged to be a candidate for treatment, it is necessary to obtain informed consent. In our office, a video is shown detailing causes of varicose and spider veins, all treatments including laser and intense pulsed light, and possible complications such as hyperpigmentation, matting, and ulceration. The necessity for multiple treatment sessions is emphasized. Once the patient understands the risks and signs the consent form, photographs (35-mm slides) of the areas to be treated are taken. These serve to evaluate treatment progress and allow patients to recognize improvement.

Patients are told to wear shorts and not to use moisturizers or shave their legs on the day of treatment. Shaving the leg may cause erythematous streaks, making it difficult to visualize patterns of reticular and telangiectatic veins. Use of moisturizers causes poor adhesion of tape used to secure compression after injections, and it causes slower evaporation of alcohol used to prep the leg. More alcohol retention on the skin will cause increased stinging with skin puncture.

Patients are encouraged to eat at least a small meal beforehand to minimize vasovagal reactions. The room in which sclerotherapy is performed is kept cool to minimize vasovagal reactions; however, a warm room would cause vasodilatation and easier visualization of telangiectasias. The first treatment session, usually limited to one or two sites, is used to observe the patient for any allergic reactions to detergent-based sclerosants, to test his or her ability to tolerate the burning or cramping of a hypertonic solution, to judge the effectiveness of a particular concentration and class of sclerosing agent, and to observe any reactions to the tape or wrap used for compression.

The patient returns in 4 to 6 weeks to compare the test site with pretreatment photographs. At each session, all sites treated are noted in anatomic diagrams in the chart (Fig. 6). Concentration and volumes of all sclerosing solutions are recorded.

TREATMENT OF VARICOSE AND RETICULAR VEINS BY SCLEROTHERAPY

Because the technique of cannulating and injecting sclerosing solution is essentially the same whether a large varicose vein or a smaller blue reticular vein is being treated, the two sizes can be discussed together. Sclerotherapy may be utilized to treat any size of varicosity as long as certain conditions are met and certain principles followed (Table 2).

One never starts sclerotherapy of telangiectasias before treatment of larger-diameter reflux sources flowing into the telangiectatic area. Reflux may originate proximally or distally. The order of treatment is first varicose veins, then reticular veins, purple venulectases, telangiectatic webs or networks, and finally the smallest and most isolated telangiectasias. The finishing touches may be performed with laser or intense pulsed light sources, as many of these final remaining blemishes are too small to cannulate and inject with a 30-gauge needle.

The use of transillumination may help identify the sources of reticular veins connected to telangiectatic webs (Fig. 7). Another method is to use Doppler to trace reflux to its loudest point and initiate injections there. Once the common patterns of the LSVS are easily recognized, the use of Doppler or transillumination is reserved for cases in which the reticular veins are difficult to visualize.

When no clear feeder vessel is identified by Doppler or transillumination, then the point at which the telangiectasias begin to branch out is the site at which to begin injection. Alternatively, one may use the arrowhead sign as a guide for initiating injections (Fig. 8). This saves time by decreasing the number of injection sites per telangiectatic group. Injecting the telangiectasias directly is more successful than relying solely on the sclerosing solution reaching the telangiectasia through reticular vein injection. We often perform the injection of telangiectasias simultaneously with injection of

TABLE 2. *Principles of varicose vein sclerotherapy*

Reflux at the saphenofemoral junction is eliminated surgically
Larger veins treated prior to smaller veins
Proceed from most proximal veins distally
Reflux points determined initially and treated specifically
Vein must be emptied of blood by various maneuvers before injection
Direct finger pressure in a spreading and compressing motion following injection
Entire varicosity is treated at one session
Immediate and adequate compression

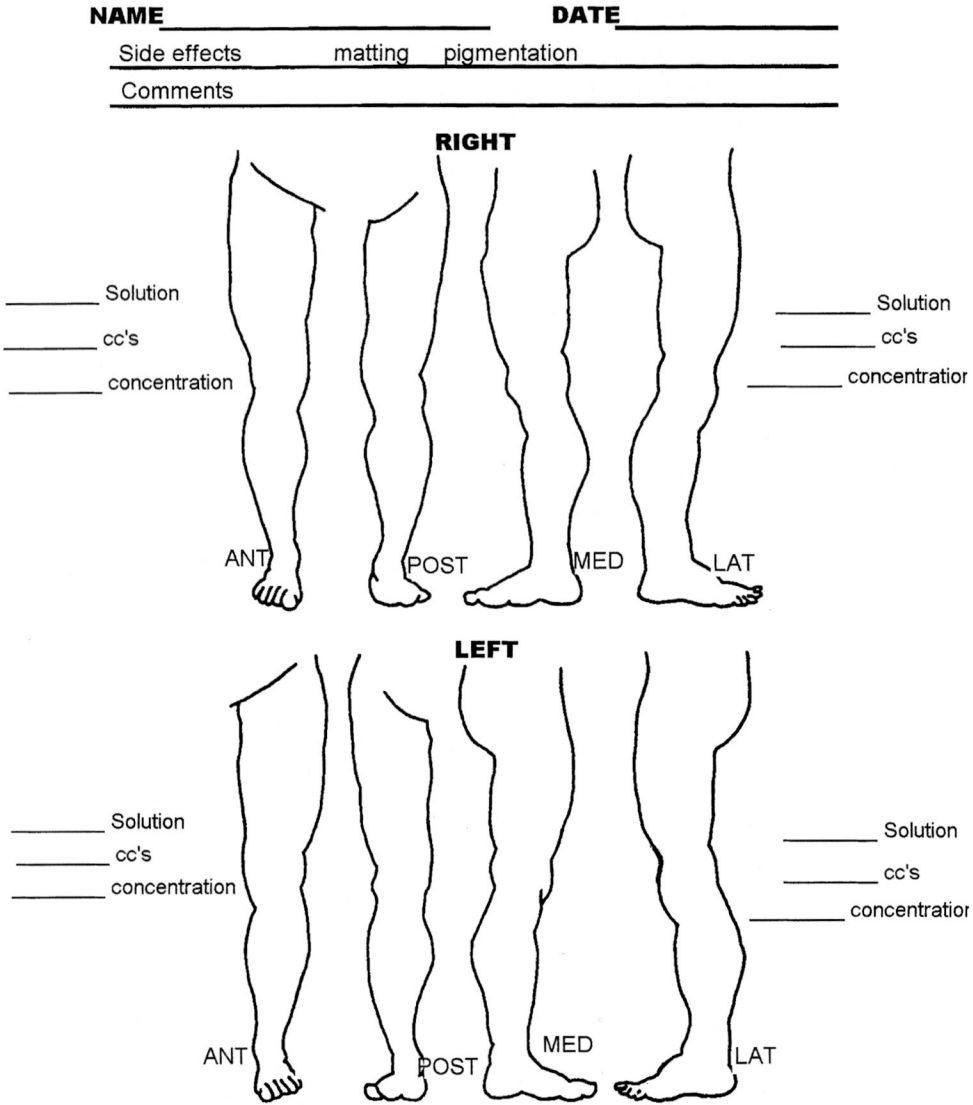

FIG. 6. Sclerotherapy record. Anatomic diagram for recording of injection sites during a single treatment session. Four views are necessary for each leg. Areas in which each sclerosing solution has been used are clearly marked using a separate color for each concentration or type of sclerosant. Total volume injected can easily be seen or calculated.

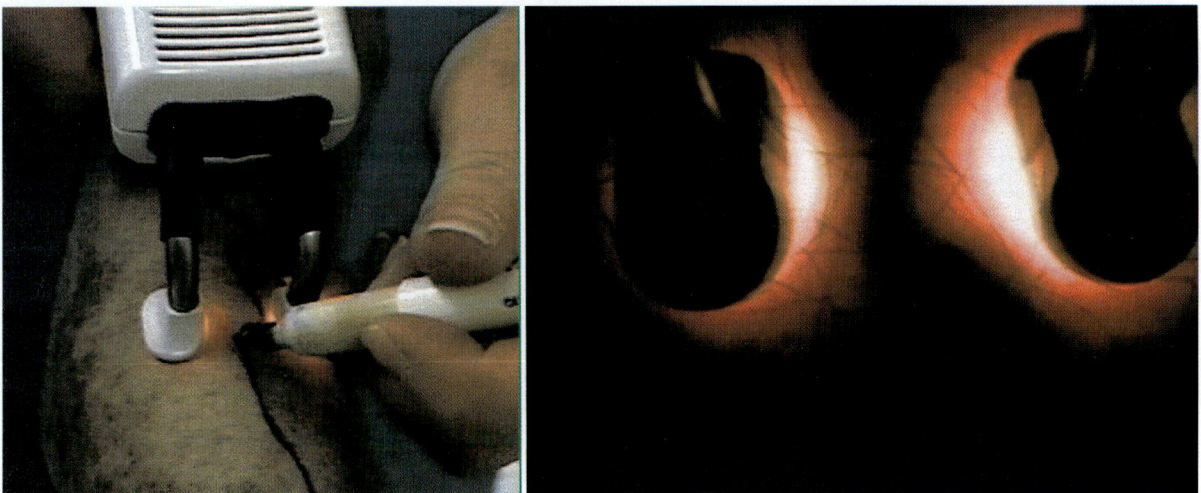

FIG. 7. A: Venoscope for transillumination allows marking of superficial veins targeted for ambulatory phlebectomy. **B:** Transillumination allows visualization of a feeding reticular vein as a dark shadow against a red background.

reticular veins in the hopes of decreasing the total number of treatments (3,30).

To begin the injection process of larger veins, the patient is recumbent and a 3-ml syringe with a 27- to 30-gauge needle bent to an angle of 10 to 30 degrees is inserted into the reticular vein, which is usually superficial and visibly blue and therefore usually does not require preliminary marking by pen (Fig. 9). When the sensation of piercing the vein is felt, the plunger is pulled back with the thumb of the dominant hand gently until blood is seen beginning to backup into the transparent plastic hub. This is possible even with a 30-gauge needle. If the wall of the reticular vein is very thin, the suction created by pulling back on the syringe may cause the wall to adhere to the needle bevel, preventing aspiration of blood. In this case, one can move the needle gently forward and backward and if no resistance is felt, the vein has probably been cannulated and the injection may proceed very cautiously.

Reticular veins have a tendency to spasmodically shrink and virtually disappear from view after a cannulation attempt. When this occurs, another injection site along the reticular vein must be sought. The cannulation of a reticular vein can be more difficult than protuberant venulectases or telangiectasias. Usually, the volume per injection site is no more than 0.5 ml but the capacity of long reticular veins may even exceed 1 ml. The progress of solution may be followed visually and the injection stopped when the entire reticular vein has cleared of blood. The reticular vein often appears to be undergoing a muscular contraction as well.

Sclerosants for the treatment of reticular veins are used in the following strengths: 0.2% to 0.5% sodium tetradecyl sulfate (STS; Sotradecol); 0.5% to 1% polidocanol (POL; Aethoxysklerol [not FDA approved]); and 23.4% hypertonic saline or hypertonic saline and dextrose (Sclerodex [not FDA approved]) (31–34) (Table 3). Until the physician gains experience cannulating reticular veins, cautious injection with the FDA-approved sclerosants cannot be overemphasized. A bruise will usually occur almost immediately and resistance to injection will be felt when the reticular vein has not been properly cannulated.

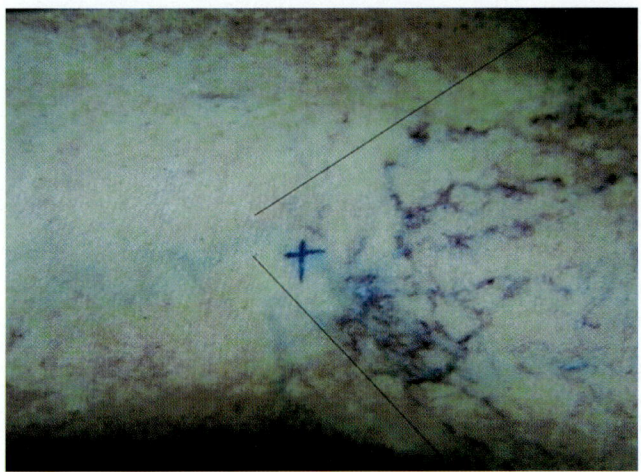

FIG. 8. *Arrowhead sign* denotes the drawing of intersecting vectors from each end of a telangiectatic web. The points of intersection typically land in the exact site of the associated reticular vein. This reticular vein is the source of pressure into these telangiectasias. One injection will fill this entire network, but it may take up to 1.5 ml of sclerosing solution.

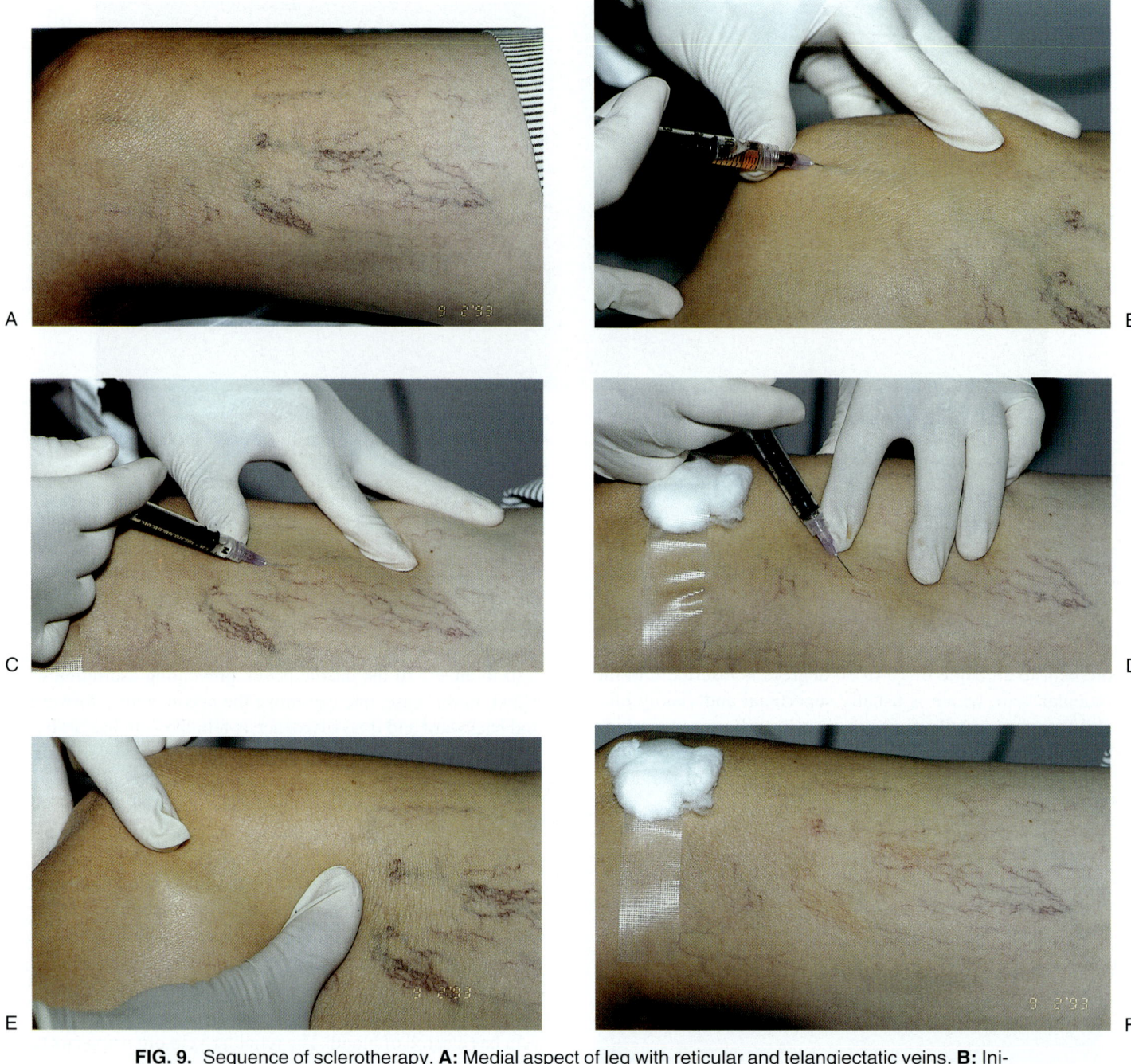

FIG. 9. Sequence of sclerotherapy. **A:** Medial aspect of leg with reticular and telangiectatic veins. **B:** Initial injection (0.5 ml) is placed into reticular vein, which is seen as blue just below the surface of the skin. **C:** Next site of injection is at the base of a telangiectatic web. Pressure into this region has been eliminated by previous injection site. Proper positioning of syringe is seen. The thumb of the nondominant hand lends additional support. **D:** The large telangiectatic web is approached from another site. **E:** Pressure is held over the previous injection site while the needle is moved to another access point to complete the injection of the entire telangiectatic web. **F:** Blanching is observed after injection of just a few drops of sclerosing solution. The injection must be stopped after this blanching occurs. Extreme blanching as shown here is usually indicative of solution backing up into the precapillary arterioles. Continued injection runs the risk of delayed necrosis.

TABLE 3. *Sclerosing solutions commonly used in the United States*

Chemical name	Brand name	Category	Advantages	Disadvantages
Sodium tetradecyl sulfate	Sotradecol Fibro-Vein Thrombovar	Detergent, rapid dissolution of endothelium	Painless intravascular Painful extravascular Strong for varicose veins Effective at low concentration	Skin necrosis with extravasation at concentrations >0.25% Expensive Pigmentation (postsclerosis)
Polidocanol[a]	Aethoxysklerol Sclero-Vein	Detergent	Always painless Cutaneous necrosis low Effective at low concentration	Urticaria (immediate) at injection site Skin necrosis from painless arterial injection Not FDA approved[a]
Hypertonic saline (23.4%)	None	Hyperosmolar, slow crenation of endothelium	Low risk of allergic reaction Readily available Rapid action	Painful stinging and cramping Skin necrosis
Saline and dextrose	Sclerodex	Hyperosmolar	High viscosity; remains in treated veins Low allergic risk Low risk of necrosis	Too weak for larger varicosities Slight stinging One concentration only Not FDA approved[a]

[a] under FDA review

INJECTION OF TELANGIECTASIAS

The patient is recumbent as for the larger veins. The dermatologic surgeon must have access to a typical sclerotherapy tray set-up, which includes the following:

Cotton balls soaked with 70% isopropyl alcohol
Protective gloves
Disposable 3-ml syringes
Disposable 30-gauge transparent-hub needles
Cotton balls or STD pads for compression
Transpore or paper tape
Nitroglycerine paste (for prolonged blanching)
Sclerosing solutions
Sodium tetradecyl sulfate (concentrations 0.1% to 0.5%)
Hypertonic saline (11.7% to 23.4%)
Hypertonic saline (10%) and dextrose (25%) (mixed by local pharmacy)
Polidocanol (concentrations 0.2% to 1%) (pending FDA approval)

The patient is placed in either the prone or the supine position on a hydraulic motorized table with height adjustment, allowing easy access to all regions of the leg. Treatment sites are repeatedly wiped with cotton balls heavily saturated with 70% isopropyl alcohol. Not only does this reduce infection risk, but also it permits better visualization of the vessels by increasing light transmission through otherwise reflective white scale on the epidermal surface. After complete evaporation of the alcohol, a 30-gauge needle, bent to an angle of 10 to 30 degrees with the bevel up, is placed on the skin so that the needle is parallel to the skin surface. A 3-ml syringe filled with 1.5 to 2.0 ml of solution is held between the index and middle fingers while the fourth and fifth fingers support the syringe against the leg in a fixed position, facilitating accurate penetration of the vessel (see Fig. 9). The nondominant hand is used to stretch the skin around the needle and may offer additional support for the syringe.

The firmly supported needle is then moved slowly 1 to 2 mm forward, piercing the vein just sufficiently to allow infusion of solution with the most minimal pressure on the plunger. Magnifying lenses on the order of 1.5× to 3× may help visualization of cannulation of the smallest telangiectasias, particularly for physicians over 40 years old.

Sclerotherapy technique requires a gentle, precise touch, as one learns to appreciate a subtle pop or "give" on entering the vessel. A very sharp needle is critical for this fine touch; the needle is changed as often as every three to four punctures to minimize tearing of the vessel. Similarly, one learns to recognize visually the appearance of the bevel of the needle within the lumen of the telangiectasia. If the solution does not flow easily, minimal withdrawal of the needle (fractions of a millimeter) may allow the easy flow of sclerosing solution since the likely scenario is that the needle has been advanced too far. The use of 32- to 33-gauge needles is not advised because they veer off course, tending not to move in the intended direction.

Injection of a tiny bolus of air (less than 0.05 ml) may be helpful to establish that the needle is within the vein, as slight clearing 1 to 3 mm ahead of the bevel can be seen. A larger air bolus theoretically allows the arborizing vessels to clear instantly, allowing greater spread of the sclerosing solution (35,36), but we and others have found this to occur infrequently and generally find a larger air bolus not necessary (1,37,38).

The sclerosing solution is refrigerated in 2-ml aliquots to enhance vasoconstriction by cold and to sequester the solutions so that the possibility of accidental injection of a sclerosing solution during routine procedures in the treatment room is minimized. Solutions of STS greater than 0.5% cannot be stored in syringes but are stored in glass vials until just prior to injection. STS will dissolve some of the rubber of the syringe plunger, causing difficulty moving the plunger and contaminating the sclerosing solution with rubber breakdown products (personal communication, Wyeth-Ayerst Laboratories, 1991).

Concentrations of sclerosants utilized for telangiectasias are less than those used for reticular veins: 0.1% to 0.2% STS, 0.1% to 0.5% POL (not FDA approved), or 11.7% to 23.4% hypertonic saline or hypertonic saline and dextrose (not FDA approved). The initial concentration is typically the lowest concentration listed above, termed the minimal effective sclerosant concentration (39). If one starts with too high a concentration, the risks of matting and pigmentation will be greater. On the other hand, when ineffective sclerosis occurs (as judged at a subsequent visit), the concentration can always be increased. An important concept is to increase the concentration but not the volume per injection to increase sclerosis success.

Injection of telangiectasias is performed extremely slowly using drops of sclerosant (0.1 to 0.2 ml or less) with minimal or no pressure on a 3-ml syringe to maintain filling of the veins and contact with the vessel wall for approximately 10 to 15 seconds. Rapid flushing of the vessels with large volumes of sclerosant causes unnecessarily large quantities to be injected. Larger quantities increase risks of extravasation injury or entry into the deep system. This theoretically increases risks for necrosis and deep venous thrombosis, respectively.

Particularly when using a hypertonic solution, the injection of sclerosant is stopped when blanching in a radius of 2 cm has occurred, or when 15 seconds has passed, thus minimizing the cramping and burning. When using painless detergent sclerosants, small volumes with small amounts of short-duration blanching will minimize side effects such as telangiectatic matting (40,41). Occasionally, no blanching occurs at the site of injection and the sclerosing solution flows easily through the telangiectasia or can even be seen flowing through adjacent telangiectasias or reticular veins several centimeters away from the injection site. In this case, the injection is stopped after no more than 0.5 ml of sclerosant has been injected. After the injection, immediate manual compression is applied. As a general rule, no more than 0.5 ml is injected into any single site.

By minimizing volume, pressure, and duration of injection, not only is pain minimized, but the risks of extravasation are minimized as well. Multiple areas (for example, at least ten 2- to 4-cm areas of telangiectasias on one thigh) can be treated with as little as 2 to 3 ml of sclerosant. This is more easily achieved with a nonpainful sclerosing solution. To minimize skin necrosis, extravasation must be avoided. If resistance to the easy injection of sclerosant or the beginning of any "bleb" at the injection site is noted, the injection is stopped immediately. The physician needs to keep an eye on the injection site at all times to notice the bleb at the moment of its occurrence. Some physicians keep a syringe of 5 to 10 ml of normal saline nearby to flush and dilute any areas of extravasation that may develop. Sclerosant thought to have extravasated may also be diluted with 0.5% to 1.0% lidocaine without epinephrine (further vasoconstriction must be minimized). A prolonged time of blanching after injection indicates possible arteriolar compromise, and then immediate use of topical nitroglycerine paste is recommended. Application is made in small dabs rubbed in until a faint blush replaces the blanch.

Immediately after injection, the treated area is gently massaged, usually in the desired direction of further spread of sclerosant. This may help to reduce pain and hasten the spread of the sclerosant through the targeted vessels (39). Any vessel larger than approximately 0.5 mm, or, more importantly, any size that protrudes above the surface of the skin, benefits from compression (42–44). After spreading the solution by massage for 5 to 10 seconds, cotton balls are secured over the injection sites by paper tape or Transpore tape. This is followed, particularly for protuberant telangiectasias or telangiectasias in association with reticular veins, with graduated 20- to 30-mm Hg or 30- to 40-mm Hg–support hose for 2 weeks (45–47). Patients are encouraged to walk and to not restrict their activities, with the exception of heavy weightlifting with the legs or any activity that results in sustained forceful muscular contraction leading to venous pressure elevation.

Treatment intervals vary, but allowing 4 to 8 weeks between treatments helps to minimize the number of necessary sessions. Often, telangiectasias will ultimately improve with at least partial clearing after exhibiting no initial response within the first 2 weeks. Typically, a patient will undergo three to five treatments separated by 1 month each. After the initial series of treatments, a rest period of 4 to 6 months will allow pigmentation and matting to clear, and the remaining reticular veins will establish new routes of drainage. Approximately 80% of patients will clear satisfactorily during the first course of treatment. The physician may then judge and reevaluate any remaining telangiectatic webs or new telangiectasias for the best approach for another round of sclerotherapy.

When patients have had a poor response to sclerotherapy after the initial series of treatments, the following may be considered. If one class of sclerosant achieves poor results, switch to another class, such as from hypertonic to detergent or vice versa (48). One must reassess whether the source of reflux from a reticular vein into a group of telangiectasias was adequately treated, both by physical examination and handheld Doppler, if necessary (9). The question of larger areas of reflux from axial varicosities that might have been overlooked must be considered. The patient must be carefully questioned about proper compliance with compression, as many patients abandon compression within several days of the sclerotherapy and fail to comply with our recommendation of 2 weeks. The age of the patient must be considered as well, as younger patients respond more quickly and thoroughly than older individuals. Some postmenopausal women taking high doses of estrogen and progesterone may improve the results of sclerotherapy by temporarily suspending hormonal supplementation (49–52). Alternatively, stubborn or resistant telangiectasias can be treated with other methods such as intense pulsed light or various lasers.

13

Hair Transplantation Using Micro- and Minigrafts

James Arnold

Hair transplantation is undergoing a burgeoning popularity that was inconceivable at the beginning of the 1990s. Not only are more cosmetic surgeons currently seeking training in this specialty than ever before, but there has been a new wave of acceptance by the general public of the more natural-appearing transplants available today. Even at the earliest signs of premature hair loss, today's patients are more apt to burst into a surgical office demanding, "When can we get started?"

The principal reason for this recent surge of interest from physicians and patients is the revolutionary development of micro- and minigrafting. Using large numbers of small grafts, today's transplant surgeons are able to offer patients significant amounts of hair distributed in very natural patterns. Consequently, patient satisfaction has grown dramatically and the number of prospective candidates has increased exponentially.

Despite this growth in professional and public interest, many cosmetic surgeons still seem reluctant to take the first step toward becoming a hair transplant surgeon. They may feel confused and overwhelmed by the wide range of surgical options available: most textbooks on this subject review dozens of procedures, each with several variations. Furthermore, the majority of workshops conducted include training not only in transplanting, but also in reductions, flaps, lifts, and even cadaver dissection. Entire sections of international meetings for hair replacement surgeons are devoted to major surgical procedures, some of which require the support of a fully equipped operating room and the assistance of an anesthesiologist. Is it any wonder that the typical office-based physician is hesitant to step into the hair replacement arena?

One simple solution to this predicament is for the surgeon to narrow his scope and concentrate solely on learning the art of micro- and minigrafting. After all, many internationally recognized transplant surgeons have quite successful practices limited exclusively to the transplantation of micro- and minigrafts. Most discriminating patients today have little interest in surgical procedures that go much beyond grafting: the majority of patients can easily reach their level of expectation and satisfaction with small grafts alone. Furthermore, the skills required for micro- and minigrafting can be easily mastered by any experienced dermatologic surgeon. And last, the wider margin of safety with these procedures allows the surgeon to comfortably operate in an out-patient office setting. In conclusion, the consensus today is that there is more intrinsic value in the art of micro- and minigrafting than in all the other hair replacement surgical options combined. There is no question that today's micro/minigrafting surgeon can effectively compete in the marketplace without performing flaps, reductions, expansions, lifts, or large-plug transplants.

Here are a few suggestions for getting started using this approach. First, concentrate solely on micro- and minigrafting. The opportunity to expand your skills to include other hair replacement procedures will come with time, if you so desire. Second, read and study everything you can on the subject, and familiarize yourself with state-of-the-art instruments and techniques (many of which are described in this chapter). Third, assemble a small team of assistants at the onset. Remember that acquiring the art of micro- and minigrafting demands coordinated team effort and interactive complementary learning. To get the work done, it is important to recognize that each member is a vitally important contributor to the team. Plan to help your assistants as much as you expect them to help you. Fourth, start small. Limit your initial micro/minigrafting sessions to 100 to 200 grafts. Be sure to always include some single-hair micrografts for the hairline. Although transplanting single-hair micrografts may at first seem more difficult than working with larger minigrafts, the reality is that micrografting can be learned quickly and is indispensable for re-creating natural-looking hairlines. Expect to spend approximately 1 year practicing and perfecting these newfound skills on those first 10 to 20 patients. Gradually strive to move more grafts in less time without sacrificing quality. Set an ultimate goal of transplanting 500 grafts or more to ensure that patients receive an appreciable amount of hair.

Despite the fact that hair transplantation still has limitations in creating density and providing extensive coverage, almost all transplant patients are pleased with the results. Of equal importance is the fact that the surgeon often feels satisfied as well. The ability to mimic nature's work calls on a surgeon's creativity. Finding creative expression can be a revelation for physicians accustomed to working in areas of medicine that did not previously provide such outlets. The artistic reward may ultimately be the transplant surgeon's greatest reward, stimulating interest and challenging creativity with each new patient.

MISSION

This chapter is designed to guide a dermatologic surgeon through a typical micro/minigrafting transplant procedure. The presentation makes two assumptions: (a) that the surgeon already possesses the surgical skills routinely used in dermatologic surgery, and (b) that the surgeon has at least observed or assisted with transplant surgery cases. For the novice surgeon who has not had any prior experience with hair transplantation, additional sources of information may be helpful. An abundance of textbooks, videos, seminars, and opportunities to observe transplant surgery are widely available.

The method described here separates the transplant procedure into four major tasks: (a) harvesting donor tissue, (b) sectioning donor tissue into individual grafts, (c) creating slits and holes in the recipient area to receive the grafts, and (d) inserting grafts into recipient sites.

The literature describes many ways to accomplish each of these four tasks. Novice surgeons presented with this multitude of choices often select a method for one task that may not mesh well with the subsequent task, thereby complicating the overall procedure. The procedure described in this chapter follows a logical sequence of steps designed to complete the four tasks in a simple, efficient, and coordinated manner. The quickest and easiest way to add micro- and minigrafting to a surgeon's repertoire of skills is by concentrating on a coordinated technique that carries the surgeon from beginning to end. Once a surgeon is capable of successfully completing a micro/minigrafting session, he or she can then experiment with alternative approaches to each of the four major tasks.

This author's particular approach to micro/minigrafting stems from a strong personal interest in mechanical engineering, time efficiency, and ergonomics. Many of the techniques described here have evolved from his personal quest to simplify and streamline the entire procedure for efficiency[1]. This simple, straightforward, and reliable method of micro/minigrafting is easy to learn. It is presently the same method used by the author in his own practice.

Besides the four major tasks involved with the actual surgery, the surgeon must also have knowledge of several other related tasks, including candidate selection, hairline design, and pre- and postoperative care. These tasks will be addressed briefly. Should the reader need additional information on these topics, the literature contains multiple references.

Please note that the technique described in this chapter refers to the patient in a sitting position. Donor strips are easily harvested by the surgeon as the patient bends his head forward from a seated position, and the recipient area is readily accessible to the transplant team as the patient leans his head backwards against the headrest. By trial and error, the author has discovered that patient comfort and surgical efficiency are maximized by using a dental chair. If, however, the surgeon is limited to a surgical table, several adaptations are possible. First, if the table is adjustable, one end can be elevated to re-create a chair-like configuration. Second, if the table is not adjustable, the patient can lie prone with his head supported by a Prone pillow, and the procedure can be adapted for this position.

As with all surgical procedures, hair transplantation can do "good" when applied properly and do "harm" when applied improperly. This chapter includes some philosophical guidelines to help steer the reader through the decision-making process that each surgeon and patient must confront. These guidelines are based on the tradition to "First, do no harm," and second, to provide maximum benefit to the patient for the work performed.

TRANSPLANT VOCABULARY

Transplant surgeons speak a language of their own. Fortunately, this language is easy to learn as it blends well with traditional "medicalese" and the new vocabulary is limited. The terminology is useful in written correspondence, verbal communication, and in recording information on patient charts. To avoid embarrassing situations, it is advisable to learn basic transplant talk before attending a national transplant meeting. During a lull in the meeting, the person sitting next to you may well lean over and say, "I transplanted the front of a Norwood class III last year with two sessions of 200 micros and 400 minis, mostly in slits. Now he's returned and appears more like a Norwood V, and some of the minis show compression. How do you treat such cases?"

---

[1] As a part of this quest, the author developed a number of the innovative instruments that are used in this procedure. These instruments have been designed to simplify specific tasks and to give greater precision and control to the surgeon overall. The same instruments are available commercially and the author receives benefit from their sale. This statement is intended as a financial disclosure to the reader.

The following list of terms describes the most important components of a transplant vocabulary. The same terms will be used throughout this chapter. While many other expressions can be found in the literature, their meaning can usually be deciphered from the context. The words presented below are listed roughly in order of frequency of usage rather than in alphabetical order.

Micrograft. The smallest of grafts, usually containing one hair, sometimes two. Micrografts are used mostly along the hairline.

Minigraft. A multihair graft, usually containing three to five hairs. A minigraft is the largest graft size that does not stand out visually as a tuft of hair. They are typically used to give a diffuse addition of hair to broad areas behind the hairline.

Large Minigraft. A multihair graft, usually containing 6 to 12 hairs. Visible as a tuft of hair in some situations. Large minigrafts are occasionally used to increase hair density in selected areas.

Macrograft. These are also known as full-size grafts. Macrografts typically measure 4 mm in diameter and contain 12 to 18 hairs. These large-size grafts predate micro- and minigrafts by 30 years. In their day, these large grafts were the standard graft and in essence the only size graft available for hair transplantation. Since the development of micro- and minigrafts, macrografts have been largely abandoned by transplant surgeons. The exceptions are a few veterans who are familiar with their use and who continue to place them judiciously well behind the hairline to add density.

Follicular Unit. An organized structure in the dermis of the scalp that contains one to four hairs, a single convoluted sebaceous gland, and the encircling ill-defined connective tissue. Individual units are separated from each other by intervening dermal tissue. The term *follicular unit* is rapidly replacing the older expression *hair bundles*, a phrase that continues to be popular in Asia.

Microslit. The smallest linear incision in the skin capable of accepting a micrograft. Usually measuring 1.5 mm or less in length, microslits tend to heal with no visible scaring.

Minislit. A linear incision in the skin capable of accepting a minigraft, ranging in length from 1.5 to 4 mm.

Hole. A round incision in the skin that results from removing a cylindrical core of tissue. Holes vary in diameter from 1 mm (accommodating one to three hair grafts) up to 3.75 mm (for macrografts.) The size of the hole is always measured by the diameter in millimeters.

Baldie. A colloquial term for the hairless central core of skin removed from a recipient hole.

Norwood Classification. The Norwood scale provides a method for describing and classifying the relative degree of hair loss in an individual. This simple method of classification allows the surgeon to quickly record the degree of hair loss for any individual (Fig. 1).

Density. Density is related to the concentration of hairs in a given area. A 4-mm circle is a common area used for a hair count to determine density. In the donor area, a concentration of 26 or more hairs in a 4-mm circle is considered high density; 20 to 26 hairs, average; and less than 20, low or poor density. When patients request "more hair," they usually are expressing a desire to increase density rather than to extend the transplant area.

Texture. Hair texture denotes both the degree of curl and the diameter of each hair. Many transplant surgeons specifically separate curl and hair diameter, whereas others combine the two. The gradation of texture is divided into three categories: poor, average, and good.

Diameter. By virtue of using the term hair *diameter*, one implies that the cross-section of hair is round. This, however, is not always the case. Whereas straight hair tends to be round, curly and especially crispy hair types tend to be oval or flattened. The diameter or the thickness of the individual hair is generally recorded as fine, average, or coarse.

Curl. The natural tendency of some hair to bend or coil can be observed and graded on a spectrum from straight (no curl) to wavy to curly to crispy.

Crispy. Originally, the first definition listed in an older dictionary for the word *crispy* was "excessively curly." Although the potato chip industry has changed the meaning of the word *crisp* for most people, the original definition can still be applied to tightly curled hair. Although crispy hair is strongly associated with people of African descent, the expression of this trait is not exclusively limited to this ethnic group. Furthermore, not all Africans or African-Americans have crispy hair. A certain percentage actually have wavy or simply curly hair. Therefore, rather than describe extremely curly hair as African, crispy is a more useful adjective. Regardless of the patient's ethnic heritage, the term *crispy* is generally perceived as an amicable term by all those affected.

Coverage. The degree of illusion that the scalp is hidden or covered by hair.

Color. Color indicates the amount and type of pigment naturally incorporated in the hair shaft, or the amount of stain artificially applied to the hair shaft. Color is important because, like texture, it can add or detract from the cosmetic results of transplanted hair. Hair tones that complement the color of the scalp appear to give better coverage than tones that contrast with the color of the scalp; for example, light-brown hair on a tan scalp covers better than jet-black hair on a white scalp.

Fringe. The superior border of the hair-bearing scalp, juxtaposed to the bald area. The fringe is notorious as an impermanent migrating line, and the migration is never in a favorable direction.

Compression. Scarring around a minigraft can compress the hair units together, giving the appearance of multiple hairs emerging from a single opening in the skin. This grouping of hairs appears as a small but distinct tuft. Compression seems to occur more commonly when minigrafts are placed in slits rather than in holes.

Popping. During the insertion process, the introduction of a graft into a recipient site may cause the extrusion of

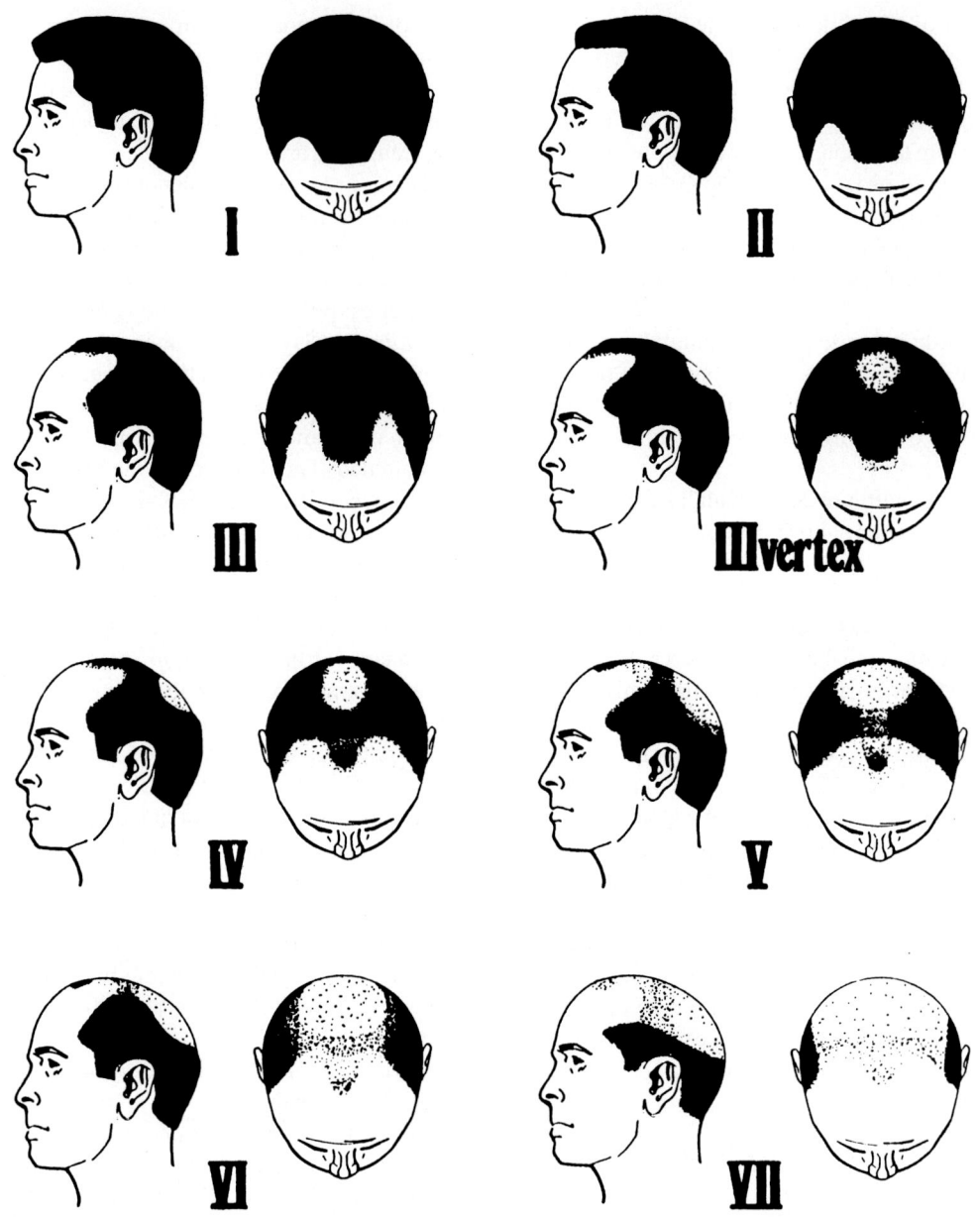

FIG. 1. These illustrations demonstrate the Norwood classification of the most common form of male-pattern baldness. (From Norwood OT. In: Norwood OT, Shiell R, eds. *Hair transplant surgery,* 2nd ed. Springfield, IL: Charles C. Thomas, 1984;5–10. With permission.)

nearby, previously inserted grafts. This extrusion, or tendency of nearby grafts to pop out of their sites, is termed *popping*. The phenomenon of popping is universally viewed as frustrating since each graft extruded must be reinserted. The Japanese term for this event, translated accurately into English, is *jump-up*.

Bald. An area of scalp completely devoid of terminal hair.

Thin or Thinning. Partial loss of terminal hair in a specific area of scalp. The amount of thinning tolerated by patients varies greatly. On the one hand, a patient with only 1% of his original hair may admit that he is thinning. As he struggles to comb his last dozen strands, he expresses the wish, "Do something before I'm bald!" Another patient with the absolute minimum of hair loss may exclaim, "Quick! Do something! I'm getting thin."

BASIC CONCEPTS UNDERLYING THE USE OF MICRO- AND MINIGRAFTS

In the past, relying on large grafts for hair transplantation created two major problems. First, the grafts were sufficiently large, measuring 4 mm in diameter and containing 12 to 18 hairs, that each one stood out as a conspicuous tuft of hair. Second, the grafts were placed in contrived, symmetrical patterns, such that curved rows at the hairline appeared unnatural. Unfortunately, these tufted grafts looked more like rows of corn or toothbrush bristles than something normally encountered in nature.

The revolutionary development of micro- and minigrafting has promptly eliminated these two difficulties. With this latest technique, the size of the grafts, and therefore the number of hairs in each graft, have been markedly reduced. Consequently, each hair unit now is barely detectable as a separate entity and certainly the unattractive tufts of hair from the past are no longer an issue. In addition, the smaller grafts are now placed in a random distribution to purposefully avoid the development of any obvious rows or gridlike patterns. These two important changes in modern hair transplantation allow the surgeon to produce a diffuse addition of hair with a much more natural appearance.

There are a variety of factors regarding graft size that must be considered to avoid a tufted appearance. In general, the grafts must be small and contain an average of three to five hairs. In particular, the color, texture, and diameter of the hair, as well as the color of the scalp, all affect the appearance of the graft. Dark hair or hair of large diameter tends to be more visible against a pale scalp. Under these circumstances, the graft size is best limited to two to three hairs. In contrast, light-colored, curly, crispy, and salt-and-pepper hair all allow for the use of larger grafts, averaging four to six hairs, before a tufted appearance becomes of concern.

Single-hair micrografts are used for special effect at the hairline. In nature, hairlines are not distinct but are created by a zone of transition from the hairless forehead to the hairy scalp. The transition begins with a few randomly scattered individual hairs; as one moves away from the forehead, the population of the individual hairs increases until full density is observed. This zone of transition ranges from 5 to 10 mm in width. To mimic nature, single-hair micrografts are used by the surgeon to create a similar zone of transition. Behind the narrow zone of transition, the three- to five-hair minigrafts are used to give some density to the remainder of the scalp.

Further enhancement of the transitional effect can be made by judicious selection and placement of the individual micro- and minigrafts used in and near the hairline. Micrografts usually contain a single hair, but 10% to 20% often contain two hairs. In the separation of single hairs from the donor tissue, pairs of closely adjoined hairs are often encountered. Rather than risk injuring either hair, the pairs may be left together as two-hair micrografts. When placed along the hairline, the single hairs are placed in front and the two-hair grafts are placed behind, giving a subtle transition from single to pairs of hairs. Similarly, minigrafts are created uniform in size when cut from the donor strips. Although of uniform size, the grafts usually contain three to five hairs. When placed in the recipient area, minigrafts with fewer hairs are selected for placement near the hairline. In this manner, the transition back from the forehead begins with single hairs, followed by two- and three-hair grafts. Finally, the average three- to five-hair grafts are used to cover the rest of the transplanted area.

The simplicity of this micro/minigrafting system will be appreciated by surgeons who have used grafts of multiple sizes to obtain a natural gradation back from the hairline. In this simplified approach, all the micrografts and their corresponding microslits are of one uniform size, while all the larger minigrafts and their corresponding holes are of a second, larger uniform size. Consequently, the surgeon and assistants deal with only two sizes of grafts and two sizes of recipient openings. The results imitate nature beautifully.

Since graft size is small, a greater number of grafts must be used to move sufficient hair. The number of grafts required in a single session to give the patient a sense of accomplishment over his hair loss is in the range of 500. Typically, the 500 grafts will consist of 100 to 150 micrografts for the hairline plus 350 to 400 minigrafts for some density behind the hairline. Experienced surgeons continually strive to increase the number of grafts per session. Accomplished surgeons are presently transplanting 700 to 800 grafts, usually 200 or more as micrografts and the remainder as minigrafts.

The factor limiting the number of grafts that can be transplanted in a single session is not the ability to generate and place grafts; the limit is set by the amount of donor tissue that can be reasonably harvested. Harvesting a band of donor scalp 1.2 cm wide and 18 to 20 cm in length (ear to ear) is a practical limit. The number of hairs removed from a donor area of this size typically ranges from 2000 to 2500. The resultant wound can be closed without undo tension and without undermining. The scar produced is generally minimal, leaving the donor area in a healthy state for future harvesting.

The patient and surgeon have some choice on how the 2000 to 2500 hairs will be transplanted. In the author's opinion, selecting approximately 200 single-hair micrografts for the hairline and dividing the remaining donor tissue into three to five hair minigrafts is cost effective, work effective, and makes aesthetic use of the available hair. The 200 micrografts are adequate for producing a natural look at the hairline. The remaining 500 to 600 minigrafts can be efficiently and effectively used to create a diffuse addition of hair behind the hairline.

Other surgeons limited to the same amount of donor hair may prefer to take a different approach and transplant greater numbers of even smaller grafts. Generating 600 single-hair grafts, 400 two-hair grafts, and the remainder as three-hair grafts can produce a total of 1500 to 2000 grafts for transplantation. Although the total number of grafts is greater, the amount of hair is the same. Whether the additional work, time, and cost are worth the subtle variation in the final result is debatable. There is also concern that the additional manipulation of donor tissue and recipient area needed to transplant larger numbers of grafts may be detrimental to the overall rate of hair survival.

The majority of transplant surgeons blend the use of micrografts for the hairline and minigrafts behind, much as the author describes. This approach is chosen in part for its efficiency. Of greater importance, the majority of patients find this approach meets their aesthetic demand for naturalness as well as their need for density and cost effectiveness.

THE PATTERNS OF MALE-PATTERN BALDNESS AND OTHER PHILOSOPHICAL CONSIDERATIONS

Most people perceive baldness as a single large area of bare scalp. The drawings of the Norwood scale tend to show a coalescence of hair loss from the anterior and posterior regions into a single area. In the most extreme case, the frontal view reveals a total absence of hair on the upper forehead. This area of follicularly deprived scalp continues back as far as the eye can see, and then over the horizon as a single continuous plane to the far reaches of the posterior fringe. The existing or anticipated expanse of such an area can overwhelm the patient and discourage the surgeon as they both wonder where to start the restorative process. Their bewilderment arises from the mistaken belief that the entire area of loss must be treated equally. In reality, selectively transplanting hair to specific areas and minimally treating or avoiding treatment to other areas can produce marked improvement for the patient.

An alternative approach to this singular view of hair loss looks at baldness as a process that affects two distinctly different areas; a posterior area and an anterior area. There are several valid reasons to differentiate between these two locations. On the one hand, posterior loss is highly unpredictable and advances relentlessly over the lifetime of the patient, posing unique treatment problems. The extent of the anterior loss, on the other hand, tends to be relatively stable and is limited by the more modest confines of the area. Furthermore, anterior hair loss carries a much greater psychosocial consequence for the patient than does posterior hair loss. Therefore, understanding the difference between anterior and posterior loss greatly simplifies the surgeon's formulation of the treatment plan and aids the patient in deciding what course to follow.

Posterior loss is easy to define. Beginning as a small round area of involvement on the back of the scalp, out of direct view from the patient, posterior loss progresses as an ever-enlarging circle. This circle of hair loss is known to expand in the latter decades of life. The unpredictable rate of loss plus the unknown ultimate extent of the loss complicate treatment. Because of the evolution of this process, what was considered a complete surgical correction of the area at one point in time may well be judged inadequate as the loss continues and the circle enlarges (Fig. 2).

Anterior loss is also progressive, but the ultimate size and location of the margins are more predictable. Anterior loss essentially involves all the hair loss forward of the posterior circle. Unlike posterior loss, this hair loss is visible to the patient daily. The front margin of the anterior loss is the hairline, while the rear margin is the anterior rim of the posterior circle (beyond the patient's view). With the area of loss defined by these two fixed margins, only the narrow lateral margins are subject to move over time. If and when the lateral margins do recede, a minimal amount of hair restoration is needed for repair (Fig. 3).

A key element for success with micro- and minigrafting is to understand that anterior loss has a significantly greater impact on the patient than does posterior loss. Anterior loss negatively affects the patient's (a) self-image, (b) public image, and (c) ability to maintain a youthful appearance.

The patient's self-image originates in the mirror. The image is brought into sharp focus and the memory updated daily as the patient routinely shaves, dresses, and grooms. Of all the factors initiating visits to the transplant surgeon, anterior hair loss viewed head-on by the patient is the strongest. If mirrors did not exist, most hair transplant surgeries would not take place. Of the thousands of hair transplants that have been performed, there is no record of a blind man requesting this procedure. By the same token, improving the frontal view, thereby improving the patient's self-image, generally fulfills the purpose and intent of hair restoration. After one or several transplant sessions, the patient eventually peers into the mirror and either likes or at least is somewhat relieved by what he sees. The moment the patient accepts his anteriorly viewed image generally marks the end of the doctor–patient relationship.

The image the public sees is typically the image the patient sees reflected in the mirror. After all, most interactions

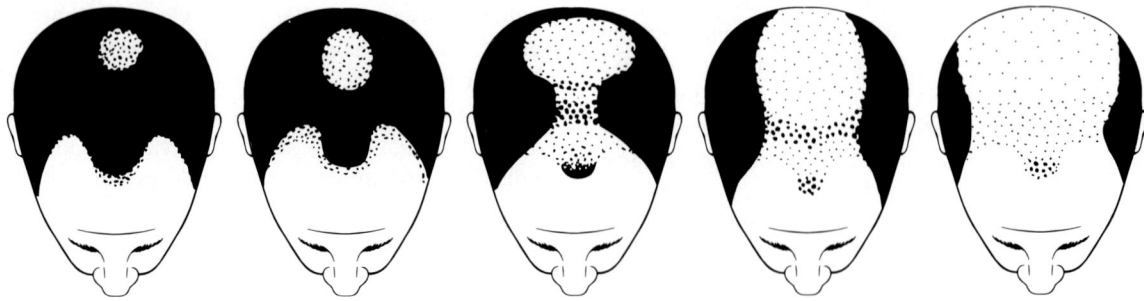

FIG. 2. Norwood classes III through VII illustrate how posterior hair loss begins as a small circle of involvement. The circle then continues to enlarge over the lifetime of the patient. Early treatment of this circle of hair loss is often judged to be incomplete later on as the circle enlarges.

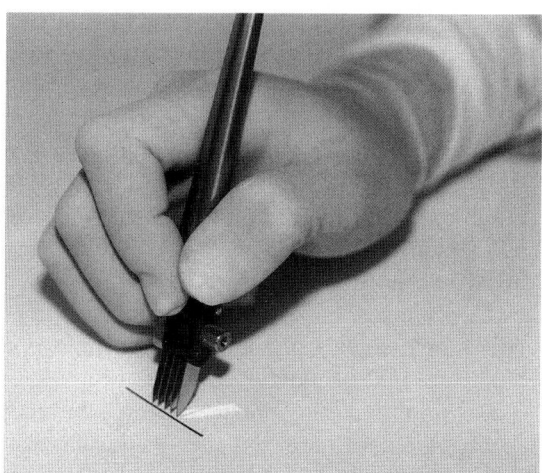 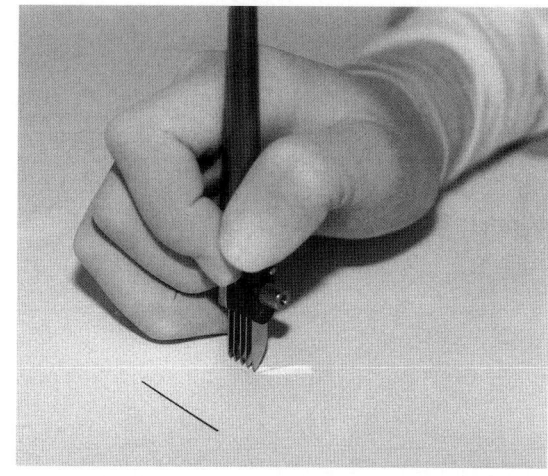

FIG. 20. A: The multiblade knife is held like a pen in an upright position. **B:** Fine finger movements advance the blade, while the hand, arm, and elbow remain stationary. This refined control allows for slow, deliberate, and precise cutting motions.

donor strips. This task of obtaining long, narrow strips of follicle laden scalp is of paramount importance for cutting high-quality grafts. The surgeon's technique must be flawless to avoid damage to the individual follicles. When donor strips are cut with care, intact follicles are visible along the entire length of each strip; when cut haphazardly, many follicles are transected and destroyed, leaving less than a full complement of viable hairs available for patient use. Fortunately, it is easy to acquire the skill of cutting high-quality strips. Experience has shown that when novice surgeons follow the instructions given here, good results are attainable even on initial attempts.

The ability to consistently cut long, narrow donor strips of high quality requires strict adherence to proper technique. To gain insight into this technique, the surgeon must fully appreciate the following concepts: (a) Hair emerges from the donor scalp at an angle that is unique to each patient and varies widely from one individual to the next. (b) In any individual patient, the angle of the hair growth changes as one moves laterally across the donor area. (c) While cutting donor strips, the blades of the scalpel must be held perfectly parallel to the angle of the emerging hair at all times. In this manner, the blades are directed between the hairs to avoid transection of the follicles. (d) The angle of the blades must be continually realigned as the surgeon moves laterally across the donor area, to mimic the changing angle of the emerging hair.

Once these basic concepts are understood, the surgeon must diligently apply three rules to his or her cutting technique:

1. The cuts must be made slowly.
2. The angle of the knife must be constantly readjusted.
3. The cutting process must be continuously monitored.

Slow, deliberate cuts are best made by adopting a new technique for holding the scalpel. Traditionally, the surgical scalpel is held in the hand and gripped by all five fingers. With this type of grip, the power to control the instrument comes from the arm and elbow. This gross motor movement, however, is too forceful and too rapid to execute the refined task of harvesting donor strips. A stroke of the arm can execute a 20-cm incision, the approximate length of a donor strip, in 2 to 3 seconds. Such rapidity leaves no time for the surgeon to stop, evaluate, and reposition the knife when the blade and emerging hairs are out of alignment.

By contrast, when the knife is securely held by a three-finger grip (much as one holds a pen), slow, deliberate, controlled cutting motions are possible. With this grip, the arm and hand remain stationary while the fingers alone advance the knife (Fig. 20). Consequently, instead of the surgeon executing a single sweeping slice across the donor bed, driven by the major muscle groups of the upper extremity, now fine finger movements can deliver a series of short, deliberate, highly precise incisions. Additional benefit from this style of controlled cutting is that the knife can be stopped instantaneously at any point along the way. Thus, a single slice is replaced by a series of multiple short cutting strokes. The several minutes needed to incise 20-cm lengths of donor strips with these short strokes adds insignificantly to the overall surgical time while adding exponentially to the surgeon's sense of control and precision. This slow cutting method is reminiscent of the way a fine woodworker carves a delicate line: when the surgeon implements this style of cutting, he or she may actually feel as though he or she is "carving" the donor strips from the scalp rather than just cutting them.

Application of the second rule concerning constant readjustment of the angle of the knife is also simplified by this new technique. Now that the knife is held upright like a pen, the cutting angle may be easily redirected by simply rotating the wrist. With this new hold, rotating the wrist at any point along a 60° arc effectively changes the angle of the knife. In this way, increments of change in the angle as small as 1° may be produced (Fig. 21).

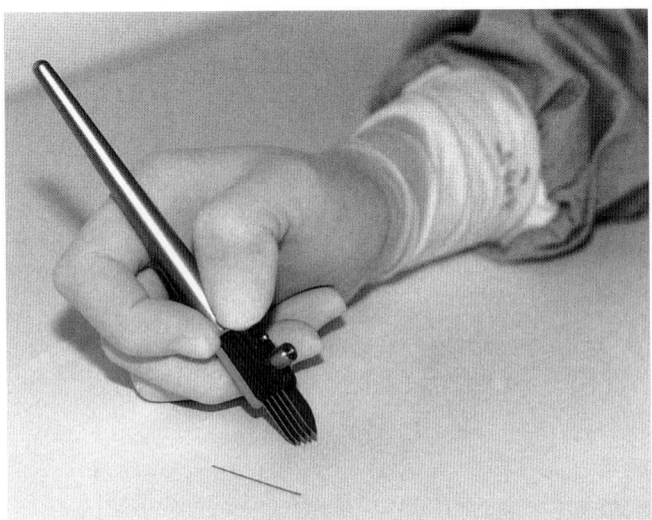

FIG. 21. The angle of the knife can be controlled and changed by rotating the wrist. Increments of change as small as 1° can be made over a 60° arc.

The third rule emphasizes the importance of continuously monitoring the parallel alignment between the scalpel blades and the emerging donor hairs during all phases of the cutting process. Immediately preceding each cutting stroke, the surgeon must take all precautions to ensure that the alignment is correct and have visual confirmation of that fact before proceeding. Similarly, after each cutting stroke, the freshly cut surface of the strips must be inspected. If the inspection reveals transected hairs, the knife must be properly realigned before continuing.

This fundamental switch in technique, from holding the multiblade knife with the entire hand to using a three-finger grip, provides the control needed to enhance the precision of cutting. With this new approach, each 1- to 2-cm long cutting stroke is controlled and deliberate. The surgeon keeps the scalpel blades within direct view as they are advanced, all the while ensuring that they are continually held in parallel alignment with the emerging hair. The multiple stops along the way at the end of each cutting stroke give the surgeon ample opportunity to look at the work, reposition his or her hand, and realign the angle of the knife with the angle of the emerging hair. With all details properly evaluated, each deliberate, controlled cutting stroke is executed under the vigilant eye of the surgeon. At all times, the entire cutting process and the continual repositioning of the knife blade relative to the angle of the emerging hair are under the direct observation and sensitive control of the surgeon.

Technique

Maximal tumescence of the donor area is essential. First, the surgeon quickly injects tumescent solution subcutaneously along the donor path a minimum of 5 mm below the surface to raise the scalp 10 to 15 mm above the skull and the large blood vessels lying near the periosteum. Next, additional tumescent solution is injected intradermally 1 mm beneath the surface to induce partial piloerection of the hairs. The zone of tumescence should extend several millimeters above and below the donor area to ensure that both the upper and lower blades of the multiblade knife will pass through fully tumid scalp (Figs. 22–24). Following the injection of tumescent fluid, the scalp appears blanched and taut. A donor path 20 cm long typically requires the introduction of 80 to 100 ml of saline to achieve maximum tumescence. Once maximum tumescence is established, the cutting process should begin without delay as the turgor will dissipate within several minutes.

Just prior to cutting the donor strips, the surgeon actively secures the position of the patient's head by firmly placing his or her nondominant hand on the patient's crown area. Stabilization is important to prevent the patient's head from moving during the crucial cutting process. At the same time, the surgeon's stance is stabilized by this pose, allowing better control over his or her cutting hand. The surgical assistant stands to the side of the patient and reaches around the patient's head, giving the surgeon full access to the donor area (Fig. 25).

Next, the surgeon takes up the multiblade knife in his or her dominant hand with a secure three-finger grip, much the way one holds a pen. Right-handed surgeons then begin harvesting the strips at the far right-hand side of the donor area; left-handed surgeons start at the far left-hand side. After the blades of the scalpel are aligned parallel with the emerging hair, they are introduced straight into the scalp. The surgeon will first notice appreciable resistance as the blades penetrate the full thickness of the dermis. In contrast, once the blades reach the 1.0- to 1.5-cm-thick, turgid, fatty layer below the dermis, the resistance becomes negligible. This marked less-

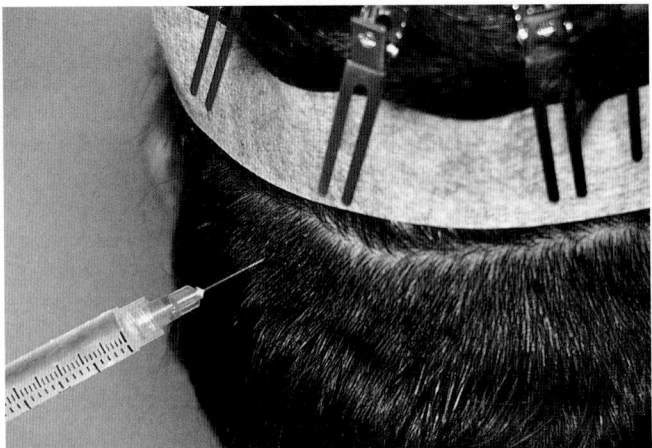

FIG. 22. Once the donor area is fully anesthetized, a solution of saline with epinephrine 1 : 200,000 is injected to produce tumescence. Maximal tumescence will be used in the donor area as an aid to harvesting the donor strips. In this figure, a 1-inch-long 25-gauge needle pressed through to the periosteum demonstrates the normal depth of the scalp prior to the induction of tumescence.

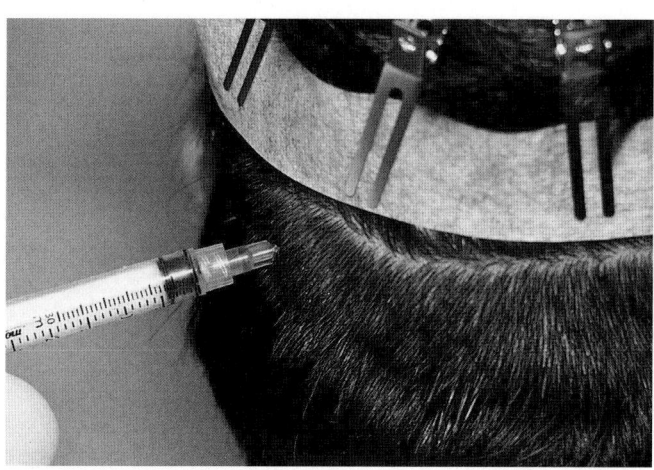

FIG. 23. The small diameter of the plunger of a 3-ml syringe produces great hydraulic pressure. The tumescent fluid can be injected easily with minimal strain placed on the surgeon's fingers. Most of the 80 to 100 ml of tumescent saline is injected into the subcutaneous fat, lifting the dermis 1.5 to 2.0 cm, well away from larger blood vessels near the skull. In this figure, a 1-inch needle completely buried in the scalp demonstrates the extent to which the scalp is fully lifted following induction of tumescence. The area of tumescence needs to extend several millimeters above and below the area to be excised.

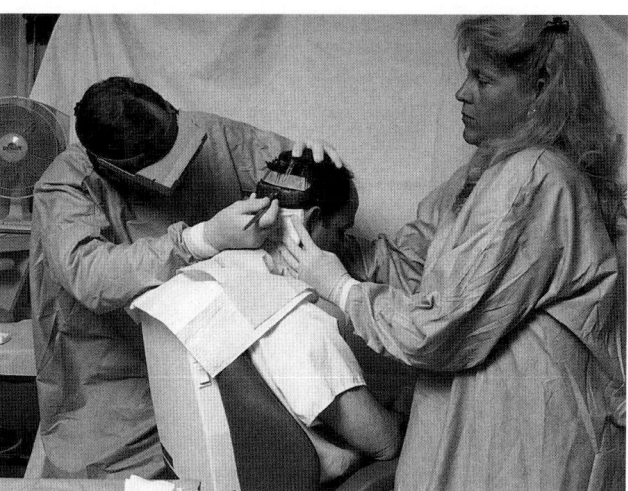

FIG. 25. The surgeon's free hand is placed on the patient's head to help stabilize both the surgeon and the patient. The surgical assistant positions him- or herself in front of the patient, giving the surgeon unobstructed access to the donor area. It is easier for the surgeon to monitor the two views needed for the cutting process from a standing position. The first view confirms parallel alignment of the knife blades with the donor hair, as seen in Figure 26.

ening in resistance notifies the surgeon when the blades have reached an adequate depth (Fig. 26).

After the blades penetrate the dermis, the surgeon initiates a series of short, precise cutting strokes that will eventually traverse the entire length of the donor area. Fine finger-controlled movements are used exclusively to deliver these abbreviated strokes while the hand, arm, and elbow are kept perfectly still. Each brief cut extends 1 to 2 cm in length, a distance equal to the range of motion of the fingers. At the end of each cut, the surgeon must pause to inspect the results and realign the scalpel blades as needed to maintain parallel alignment between the blades and the emerging donor hair. Also, at the end of each cut, the hand and arm need to be repositioned for the upcoming cut. By using refined finger motions alone, the surgeon advances slowly with great precision, while maintaining the proper knife angle during the cutting process.

At the end of each cutting stroke, the freshly cut surface can be inspected by using the knife to partially lift and separate the strips. The strips can be viewed from above to ex-

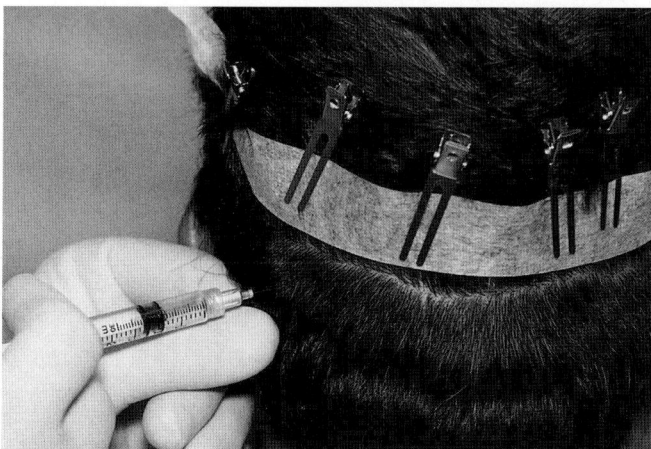

FIG. 24. With the subcutaneous space under tension, additional fluid is injected intradermally. The intradermal injections are quite shallow in the skin and cause the donor hairs to stand erect. The effect of this intradermal tumescence is similar to inducing "goose bumps": the hairs are made to stand on end.

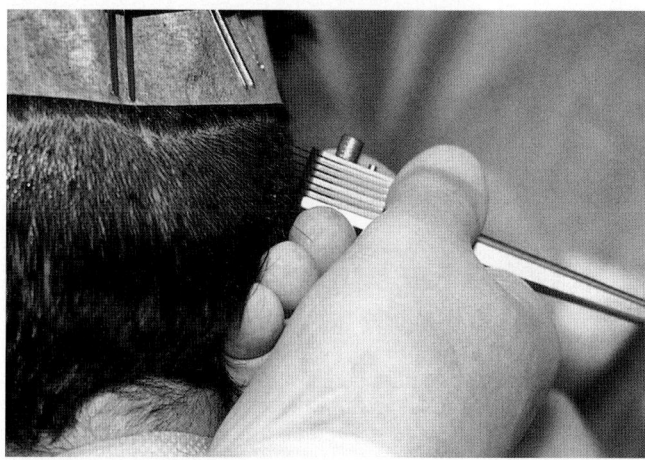

FIG. 26. With the multiblade knife held at the same angle as the emerging donor hair, the knife blades are introduced completely through the dermis. The fingers slowly advance the knife while the hand and arm remain stationary.

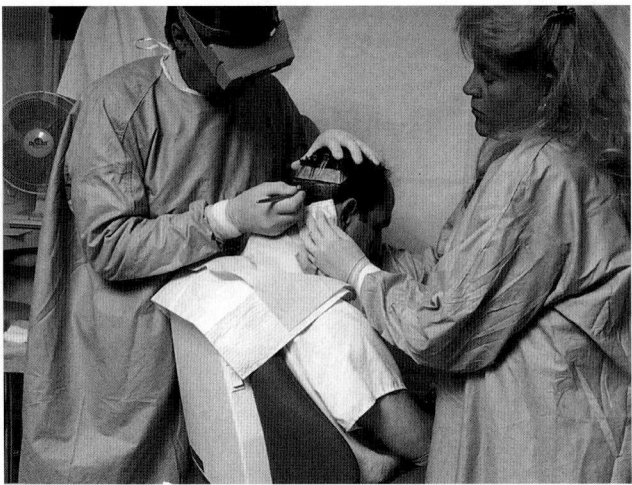

FIG. 27. The second view used by the surgeon to monitor the cutting process is almost 90° from the first and is easily achieved from a standing position. In this second view, the surgeon looks down on the cut surface of the strips.

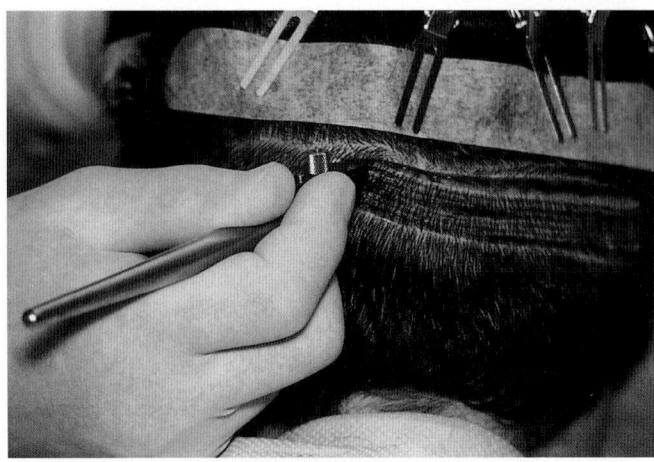

FIG. 29. The angle of the knife must constantly follow the changing angle of the donor hair. Near the center line, the angle of the donor hair is at a minimum: it stands nearly erect. The knife is positioned accordingly.

amine the cut surface for transected hairs. If transected hairs are found, the surgeon must decide whether to increase or decrease the cutting angle before the next stroke. It is important to properly align the knife with the angle of the emerging hair at the start of each cut. Thereafter, the surgeon must periodically check the alignment as the cutting proceeds, making sure to change the angle of the knife as the angle of the emerging hair changes (Figs. 27, 28).

Note that the two views used for monitoring the cutting process are from two different perspectives. The view to check alignment of the knife with the emerging hair is from the side. The view to check the freshly cut surface of the strips is an overview. It is helpful for the surgeon to have freedom of movement to gain multiple views from both angles. This freedom of movement is generally best accomplished by standing rather than sitting.

If hairs are still being transected despite the routine precautions described previously, one last maneuver can be considered. In 80% of cases where transection of hairs occurs, the angle of the emerging hair differs from the angle of the hair buried beneath the scalp. Consequently, in these instances, decreasing the angle of the knife by lifting the knife handle slightly cephalad, or up toward the top of the head, brings the angle of the blades back into alignment with the angle of the emerging hair (Figs. 29, 30).

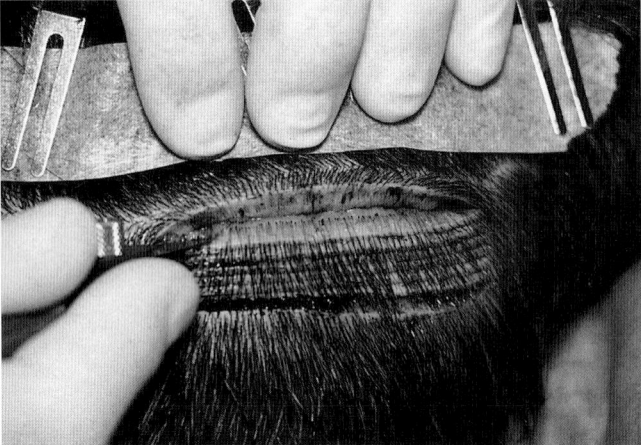

FIG. 28. This second view, used to monitor the cutting process, allows the surgeon to examine the cut surfaces of the strips for possible transection of the donor hairs. When the knife blades are passing properly between the hairs, transection of follicular units is avoided and the full length of individual hair units should be visible. If this second view confirms that the knife angle was correctly positioned, the surgeon returns to the first view to realign the knife with the angle of the hair in preparation for the next cutting stroke.

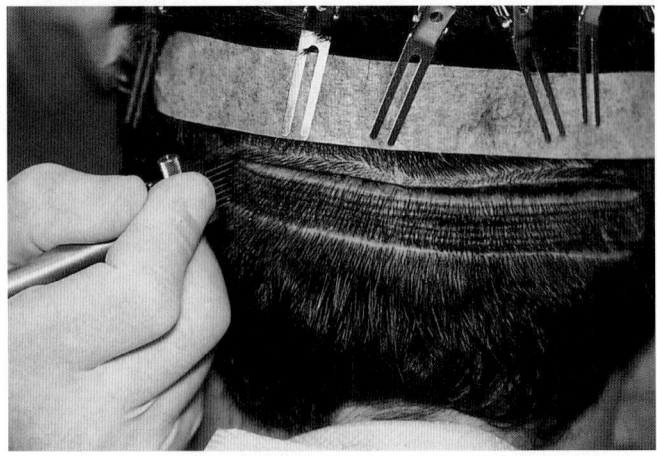

FIG. 30. At the lateral ends of the donor area, the knife angle must be increased to match the increasing angle of the emerging donor hair.

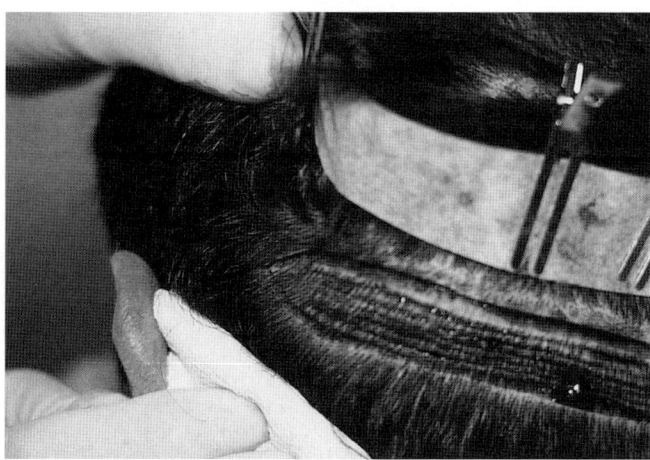 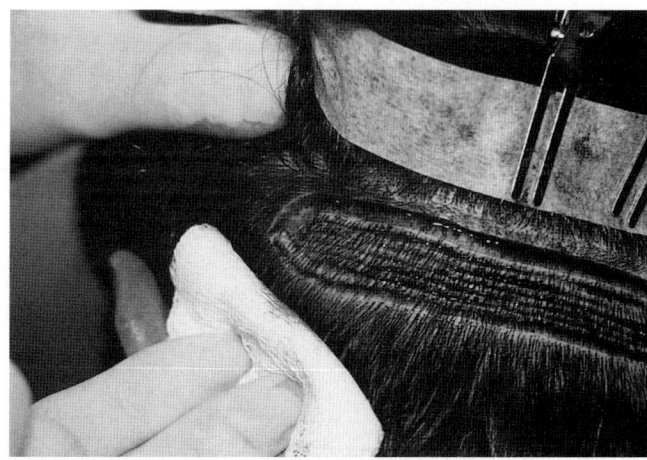

FIG. 31. A: The lateral margins of the donor strips are tapered *in situ* with a single No. 15 scalpel blade. **B:** Similarly, the individual donor strips are extended out to this lateral margin by use of the same blade. These incisions are best made while the donor strips are still stabilized by the underlying attachment to the subcutaneous tissue.

While the sensation of cutting through the skin between hairs is relatively smooth, cutting across actual hair follicles feels gritty or raspy. Although subtle, this change in texture is real. If the surgeon detects a gritty or raspy sensation while cutting, he or she should immediately stop and examine the cut surface for transected hairs.

After the full length of the donor strips has been carved out by the multiblade knife, a standard scalpel with a No. 15 blade is used to taper the lateral ends of the incision. The scalp can tolerate a relatively short or blunt taper without producing dog-ears. The same blade is then used to extend the cuts between the strips out to the lateral margins. In this manner, each strip is completely separated from the adjoining strip (Fig. 31). Last, the strip is best removed by first dividing it in half at the midline and then undercutting each segment through the subcutaneous fatty layer with a No. 15 scalpel blade or small scissors (Figs. 32, 33).

Once cut away from the donor bed, the strip should be placed between two layers of gauze for 2 to 3 seconds and gently patted and rolled clean by the assistant. After blood and debris have been removed, the strip is promptly placed in a cup of chilled saline (Figs. 34–36). After all the strips from one side have been removed, hemostasis should be achieved before proceeding to the alternate side (Fig. 37).

The surgeon can separate the individual strips *in situ* with greater precision than if all the strips are removed *en bloc* and then separated by the assistants. Also, since the surgeon is the sole team member isolating the strips, the assistants are at liberty to start the time-consuming task of sectioning grafts as soon as the first strips are made available.

After all the strips have been removed, there are two options available to the surgeon to close the donor site: sutures and staples. Most patients find that staples are more comfortable and create less irritation to the scalp. Also, many sur-

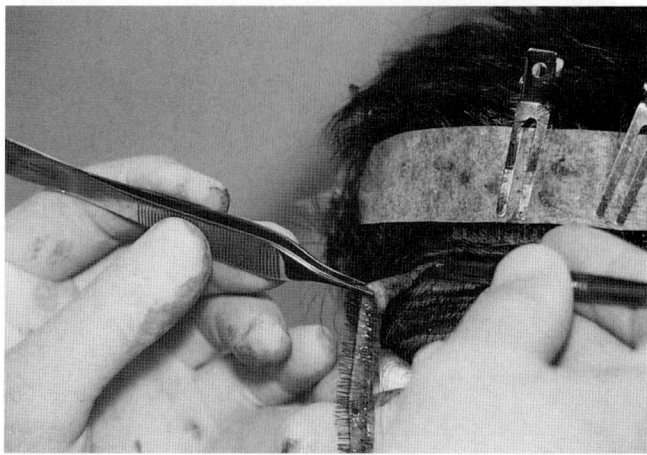

FIG. 32. It is often helpful to divide the donor strips in half at the midline. Shorter segments are easier to remove and handle.

FIG. 33. The strips are removed individually. After gently lifting a strip with forceps, a No. 15 scalpel blade can easily cut through the subcutaneous fat.

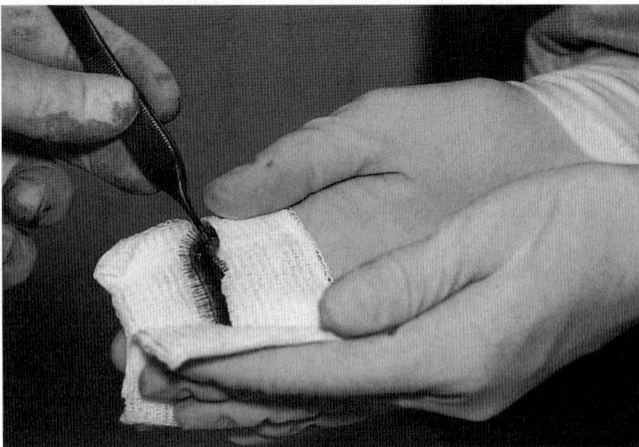

FIG. 34. After removing a long narrow strip from the donor area, the surgeon promptly lays the tissue out on a dry sponge held by the assistant.

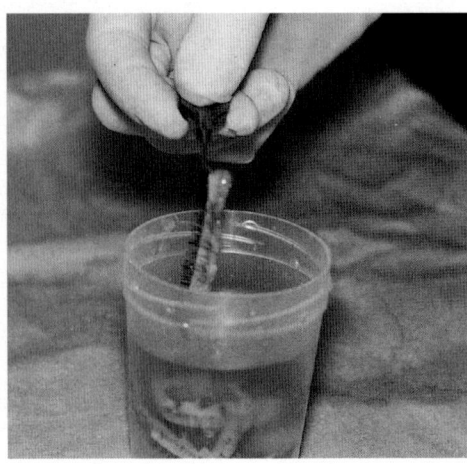

FIG. 36. The cleaned strip is promptly placed into a container of chilled saline.

geons believe that the cosmetic appearance of the wound closure is superior with staples. Some patients nevertheless prefer sutures. When sutures are used, they are best limited to the upper dermis to avoid injury to the deeper-lying follicles.

When staples are preferred, the 3M-DS25 stapler is ideally suited for the task. The surgeon begins by slowly advancing the first staple until the sharp prongs are partially exposed. The inferior prong is then pressed into the lower edge of the wound, functioning as a skin hook to lift the tissue. Next, the upper edge of the wound is partially everted with forceps as the upper and lower edges are approximated. Once the edges are well approximated, the staple is pressed closed. Using the "rule of halves," the surgeon places the first staple at the midline of the incision, and the subsequent staples in the middle of each remaining half. Thereafter, additional staples are inserted into the middle of each smaller segment until all the staples are 4 to 6 mm apart (Figs. 38–42).

A widely held opinion maintains that undermining wound edges is rarely necessary and preferably avoided. Common practice dictates that donor wounds as large as 12 to 14 mm wide can be easily closed without resorting to this traumatic intervention. The drawbacks of undermining include excessive bleeding from occult sites and the formation of adhesions. The adhesions in particular bind the scalp in these undermined areas and make future removal of donor strips and wound closure more difficult.

After the wound has been closed by sutures or staples, the medical assistant cleans the surgical field, removes the tape and hair clips from the surrounding area, and combs the overlying hair down over the donor area. Staples or sutures are removed in 7 days.

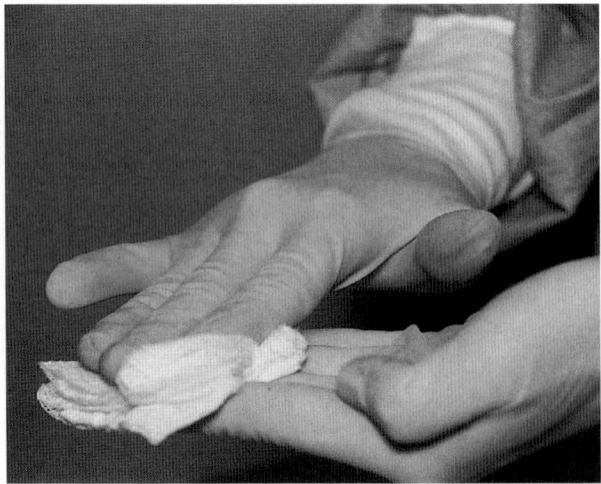

FIG. 35. The assistant next places a second dry sponge over the strip, sandwiching the tissue between gauze sponges. As the sponges are gently pressed and rolled together for 2 to 3 seconds, free blood and debris from the tissue is absorbed into the gauze.

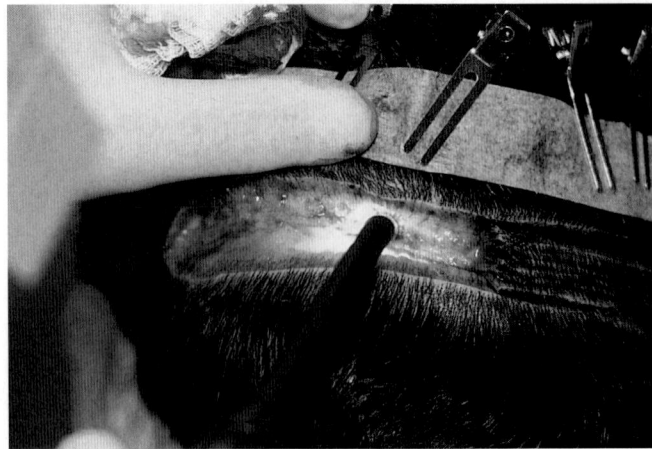

FIG. 37. After all the strips are removed from one side of the donor area, hemostasis of significant bleeders is achieved before proceeding to the alternate side.

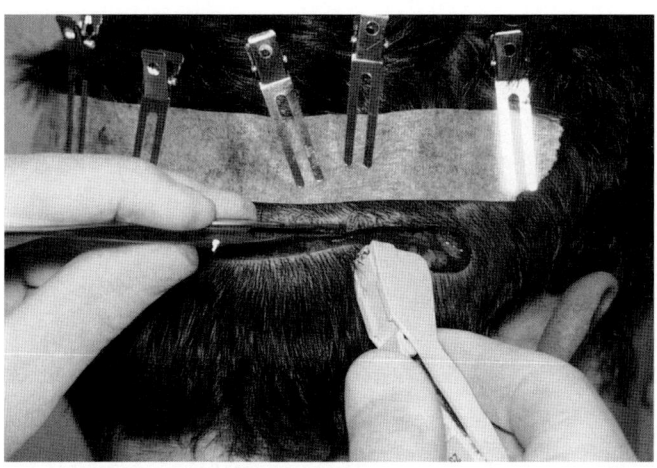

FIG. 38. A skin stapler, manufactured by 3M (Precise DS-25), is ideal for closing the donor site. A partially advanced staple can be used as a skin hook to lift the lower edge of the wound.

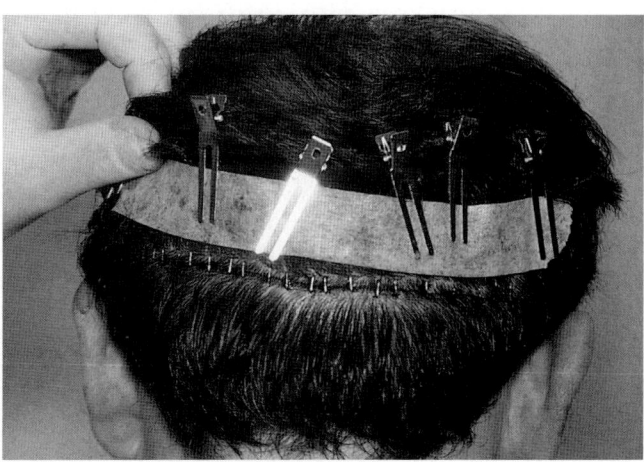

FIG. 41. Wound closure by staples is neat and fast. Most patients tend to prefer this particular staple system over sutures. The staples can be easily removed in 7 days by a disposable staple remover.

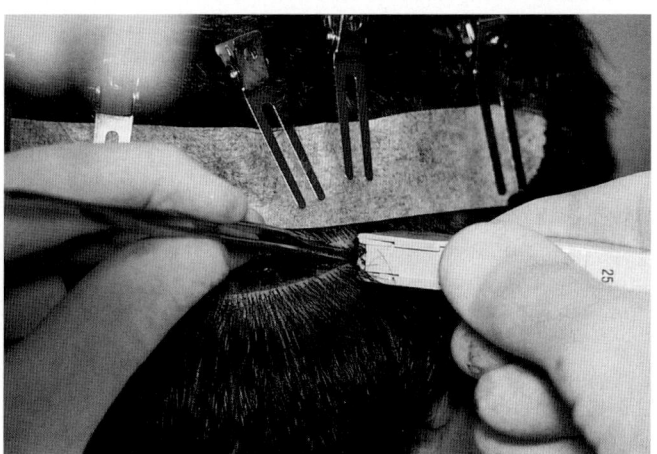

FIG. 39. The upper edge of the wound is everted by the Adson-Brown forceps to facilitate effective placement of each staple.

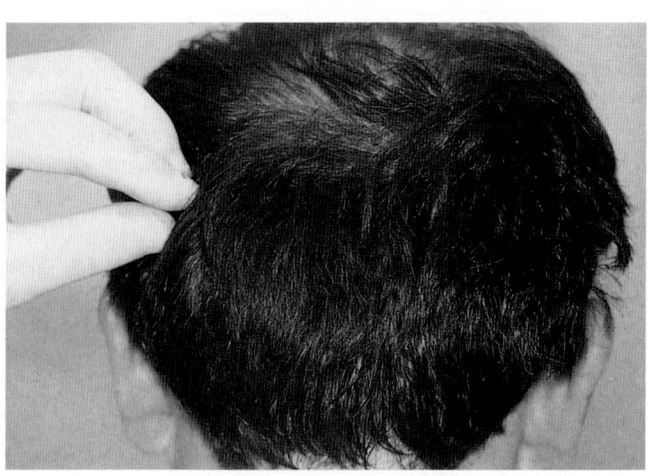

FIG. 42. After cleaning the donor area, the hair above the surgical wound is combed down over the donor site to conceal the incision.

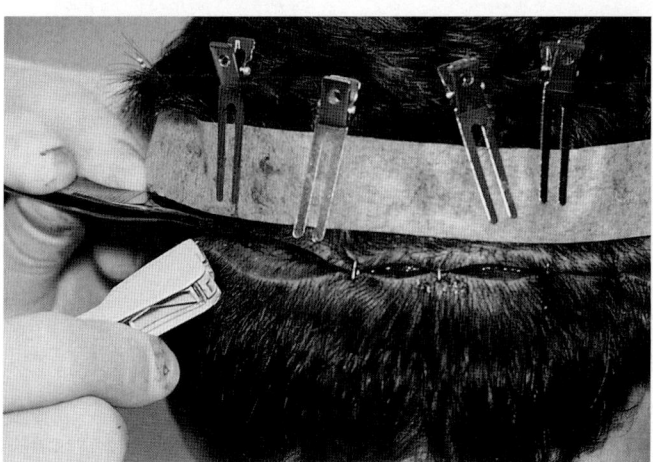

FIG. 40. The two edges of the wound are best approximated by closing with a series of widely spaced staples. In this manner, dog-ear formations at the ends can be avoided. If residual tumescent fluid interferes with the approximation of the edges, excess fluid can be pressed from the tissue. Pressure applied with a sponge mobilizes the fluid. This phenomenon is similar to that seen in the clinical condition of pitting edema.

SECTIONING GRAFTS FROM DONOR TISSUE

Although previously considered a cumbersome, time-consuming task, the following technique for sectioning grafts from donor tissue can generate large numbers of quality grafts in rapid succession. To minimize the time required for this task, a simple technique utilizing rapid, deft finger movements has been developed.

Fine finger movements are capable of executing highly precise and controlled maneuvers. Cursive handwriting is an excellent example of this activity. Finely controlled finger movements are responsible for producing a legible script while the hand is held at rest in a stationary position. The same principle can be applied to creating small grafts: the precision of finger-controlled movements allows for both rapid and accurate sectioning of donor strips into high-quality grafts.

Four pieces of equipment are used in this technique: (a) Personna surgical prep blades, (b) Foerster forceps, (c) a graft cutting board, and (d) magnifiers (Fig. 43).

Personna surgical prep blades are chosen for their sharpness and durability, and, most importantly, they can be manipulated solely by the fingers. When used for cutting grafts, these blades are held perpendicular to the cutting surface by the fingers of the dominant hand.

Foerster forceps also can be manipulated exclusively by the fingers. Octagonal rings in the handles allow them to be easily grasped by the thumb and forefinger. Consequently, rapid fine finger movements control this instrument in lieu of slower coarse hand motions. The rings also act as reference points for the fingers, maintaining a constant distance to the end of the serrated tips. Operators quickly learn to accommodate to this distance as if the instrument were an extension of the fingers. This design enables assistants to rapidly pick up and place the smallest grafts without hesitation (Fig. 44).

The graft cutting board is simply a wooden tongue de-

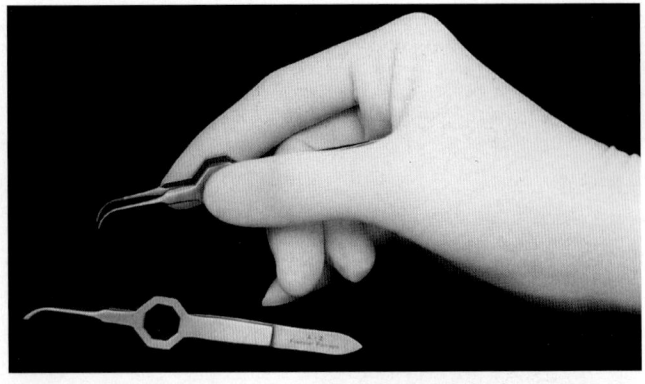

FIG. 44. Foerster forceps can be comfortably grasped by the thumb and forefinger, and they are easily manipulated by subtle finger movements. These special forceps enable the operator to maneuver hundreds of small grafts gently and rapidly while maintaining a high degree of precision.

pressor that has been soaked in saline for 10 minutes. The presoaking is important to moisten the wood, because a dry board quickly draws moisture away from the grafts (Fig. 45). Also, because the soaking process often warps or cups the wood, it is best to use the convex side of the curved board as the working surface (Fig. 46). There are a number of advantages to using a tongue depressor as a cutting board: not only is the board small, lightweight, and highly maneuverable, but it is the perfect length to accommodate a stretched-out strip of donor tissue. One challenge during the sectioning process is to be able to pick up and repeatedly move the donor strip about in a quick and easy manner. This is no simple feat because the tissue feels and acts much like a wet slippery piece of overcooked fettucine. However, by overlaying the strip on the cutting board, the two items together can be readily moved about as a single unit.

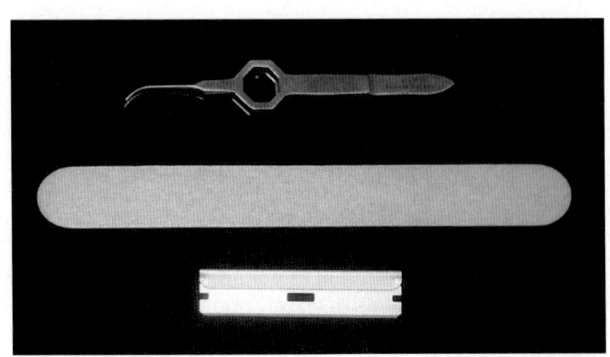
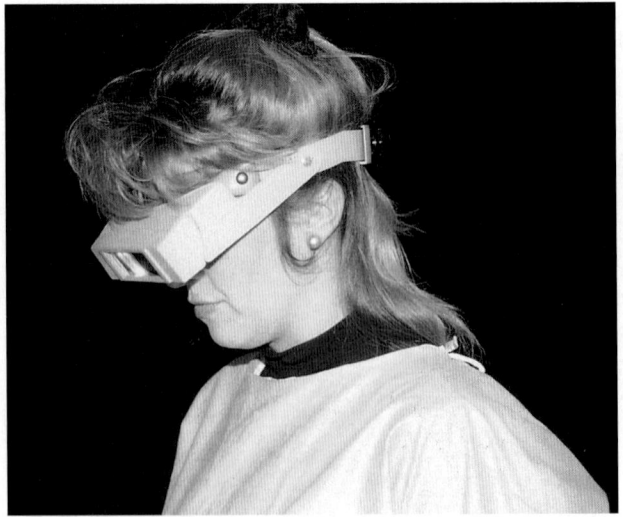

FIG. 43. A: These three items are most useful for sectioning donor strips into micro- and minigrafts: a pair of Foerster forceps, a graft cutting board, and Personna surgical prep blades. **B:** 1.75× magnifiers may be helpful for some assistants.

FIG. 45. Graft cutting boards (also known as sterile tongue depressors) are presoaked in saline to help prevent the donor strips from drying out.

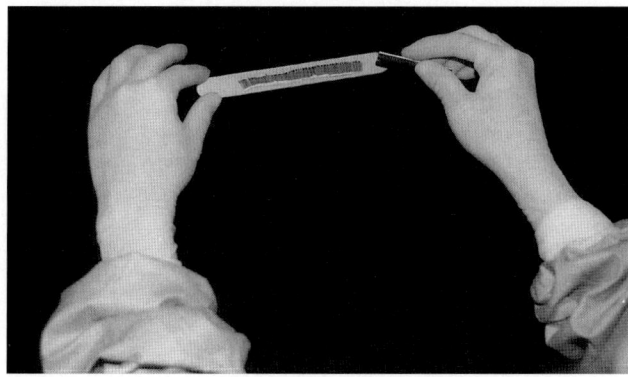

FIG. 47. A donor strip is placed lengthwise on a graft cutting board. The board is laid horizontally in front of the assistant.

The 1.75× magnifiers are a fourth piece of equipment useful for some assistants. This visual aid consists of two lenses of 1.75× magnification, which are mounted individually in front of each eye and attached to a headband. The unit can be worn comfortably on the head. This modest increase in magnification can significantly aid an assistant in avoiding the accidental transection of partially hidden hairs. Although many assistants have eyesight sufficiently good to cut grafts without magnification, an equal number may well benefit from the use of magnifiers. Ironically, the assistants who have the most to gain from magnification are often the ones who are unable to see the inferior quality of their grafts. In general, a good office policy is to require that all assistants first use the magnifiers on a routine basis during training. Then the decision of whether or not to continue the aid can be made depending on the quality of grafts they produce with and without magnification.

Technique

The donor strip is stretched out lengthwise on a graft cutting board while the board is placed horizontally on the work surface directly in front of the assistant (Fig. 47). The fatty tissue on the lower margin of the strip should be facing the assistant. The assistant applies gentle pressure to the upper half of the strip with the nondominant index finger. This pressure will cause the subcutaneous fat to be extruded. Once extruded, the fat can be trimmed away by the prep blade held in the assistant's dominant hand. As much fat as possible should be removed, as excess fat left on the grafts can interfere with graft insertion later on (Figs. 48, 49).

After removing the fatty tissue, the assistant turns the cutting board 90°. From this position, the strip can be viewed "on end" while the assistant sits with his or her hands resting comfortably along each side of the cutting board. Furthermore, the assistant's hands and forearms can rest naturally on the work surface while the surgical instruments are manipulated exclusively by the fingers (Figs. 50, 51).

Next, the surgical prep blade is held by the dominant hand as it is brought into parallel alignment with the hairs in the donor strip (Fig. 52). If the blade is not in alignment, it is better to reposition the cutting board than to strain the hand in an awkward position (Fig. 53).

Once the blade is comfortably held in alignment with the donor hairs, a period of labor-intensive graft production can begin. First, as the blade is positioned between adjacent hairs, a quick vertical downward stroke easily cleaves a graft from the near end of the strip. This motion is reminiscent of the infamous French guillotine in operation. Next, the forceps held by the nondominant hand swiftly moves the newly created graft a few millimeters away from the blade, "out of harm's way." Last, the fingers of the dominant hand lift up the blade in preparation for the next cut (Fig. 54). The distance the blade moves up and down is a mere 3 to 4 mm. This abbreviated distance allows a series of quick mincing strokes to be executed in rapid succession with a minimal amount of effort (Fig. 55).

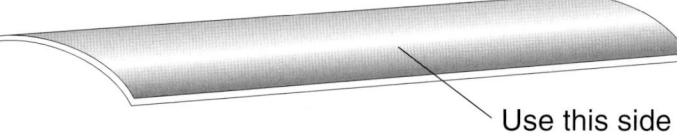

Use this side

FIG. 46. After soaking in saline, graft cutting boards tend to bow or cup. Use the convex side of the wet board as the cutting surface.

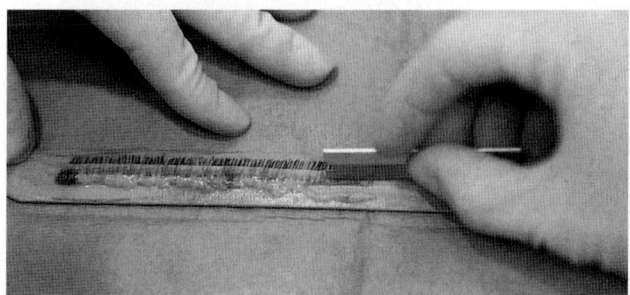

FIG. 48. A Personna surgical prep blade is used to trim as much fat as possible from the donor strip. Care is taken to not injure the lower portion of the follicles.

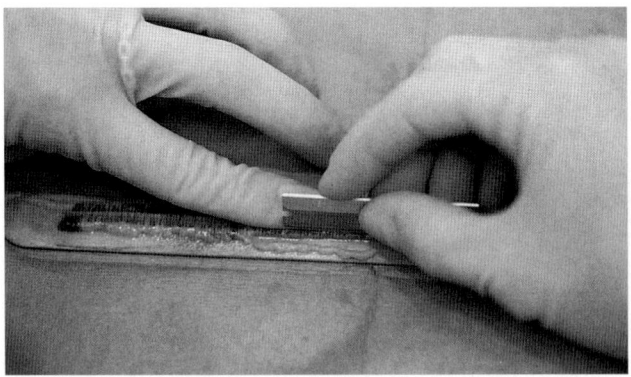

FIG. 49. The index finger applies firm pressure to the donor strip to help extrude the fatty layer. This excess fat is then easily trimmed away.

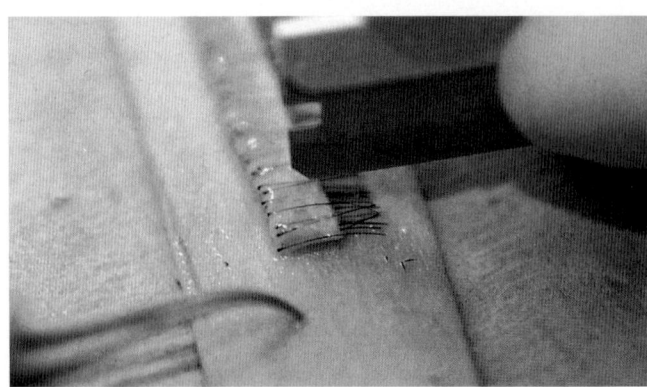

FIG. 52. The cutting board is turned to bring the hairs into parallel alignment with the blade.

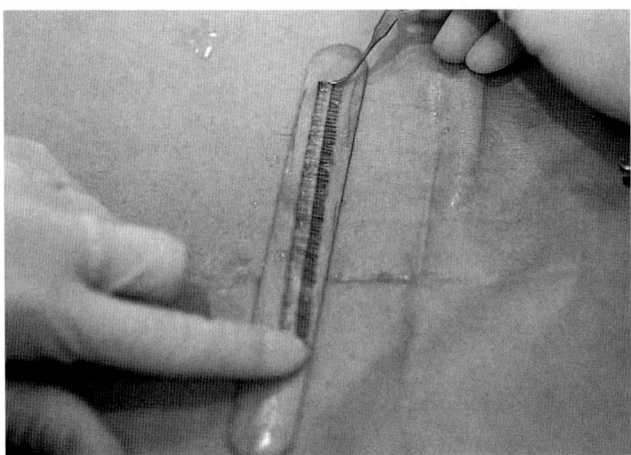

FIG. 50. Once the excess fat is removed from the donor strip, the cutting board is turned 90° away from the worker. The strip is then straightened by gentle stretching.

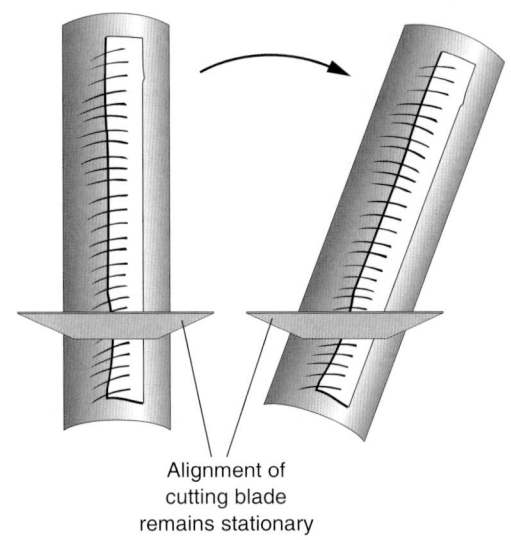

FIG. 53. When the cutting blade is aligned parallel to the hair follicles in the donor strip, the blade can pass directly between the hairs. If the blade and hair follicles are not in parallel alignment, it is better to turn the cutting board than to strain the hand in an uncomfortable position.

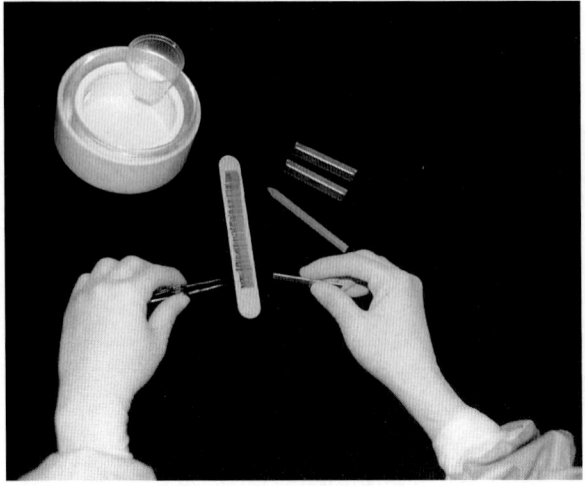

FIG. 51. Delicate finger movements do all the work while the assistant's hands and forearms rest comfortably on the work surface in a natural position.

The technique of rapidly tapping the knife in a random pattern can be practiced with a pen and piece of paper. First, a curved line is drawn on the paper to represent a hairline. Next, the pen is rapidly tapped, at least one tap per second, as the hand moves along the line. The pen dots should fall within a band 5 to 10 mm wide. With this approach, one can quickly learn to place the dots in a random pattern. Ultimately, this skill can be transferred to creating microslits along the hairline with a random distribution.

Holes for Minigrafts

In the majority of cases, this author favors using holes in lieu of slits to transplant minigrafts. The size of the holes is dictated by the size of the grafts. Minigrafts containing an average of three to five hairs are used in most instances. As soon as the donor strips are removed, an assistant cuts 15 to 20 test grafts, making sure that each graft contains three to five hairs. The size of these first few grafts is carefully assessed. An experienced assistant monitoring the grafts can inform the surgeon of the hole size needed. For three- to five-hair grafts, most often the hole size needed is 1.3 mm in diameter; occasionally, the limit extends to 1.5 mm. If there is any uncertainty concerning the proper size, a few test holes can be made for trial insertion of several grafts. Once the size of the graft and the size of the hole are selected, the transplant team enters a phase of intense productivity. The assistants stop counting the hairs in each graft and simply cut all the remaining grafts one uniform size. The surgeon can then proceed with a one-size punch to create all the holes needed in the area behind the hairline.

The instrument preferred by this author to cut holes for minigrafts is the Super Punch (A to Z Surgical). This particular punch supersedes all the other hand-held punches for a variety of reasons: it is lightweight, it is highly maneuverable, and it has an ultra-sharp cutting edge. The superior sharpness of the cutting edge enables this punch, more than any other, to readily pass through the skin without the need to rotate the handle. Consequently, lightly taping the instrument on the surface of the scalp, much as one does with the Lightning Knife to create microslits, is all that is needed to create miniholes. In this manner, multiple recipient holes can be made as fast or faster than a motorized punch, thereby simplifying the procedure and reducing the total surgical time.

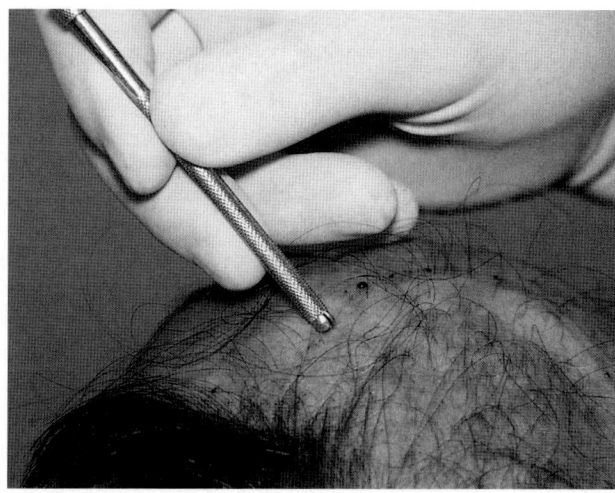

FIG. 65. The blade of the Lightning Knife is advanced fully into the scalp. The handle will reliably stop penetration of the blade at a preset depth, ensuring a uniform depth for all the incisions. If the tip of the blade tends to strike the bony surface of the skull, a small amount of tumescent fluid can be injected subcutaneously to lift the skin surface an additional 2 to 3 mm.

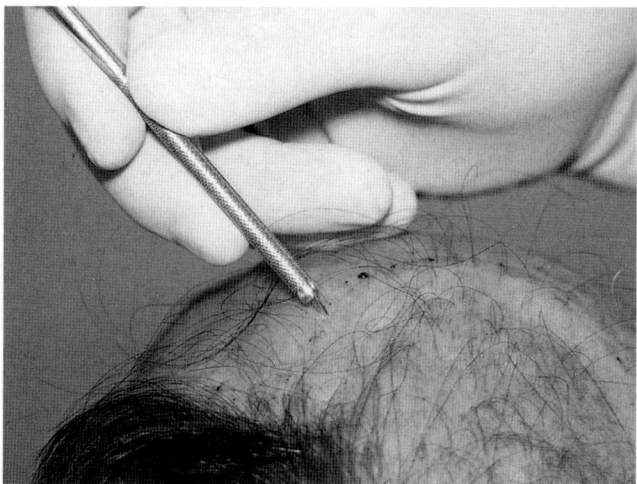

FIG. 64. Recipient slits are easily created by repeatedly tapping the Lightning Knife on the surface of the scalp. It is important to introduce the knife at an angle that parallels the angle of the natural growth of existing hairs.

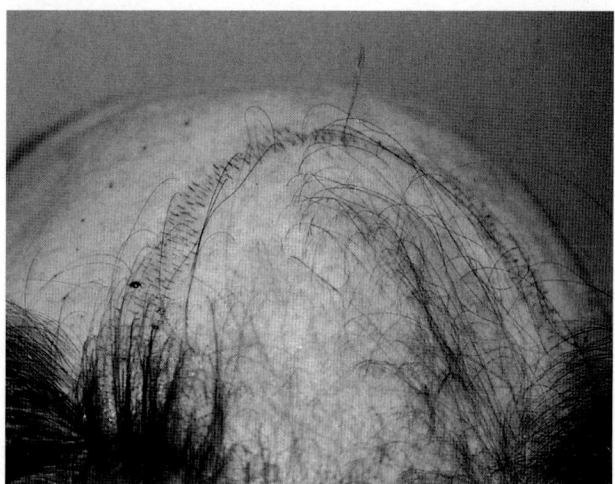

FIG. 66. The microslits are placed in a random pattern throughout the hairline zone. Making the zone slightly wider in the lateral regions produces a softer, less dense, more natural-appearing hairline zone. The length of each incision projects radially at a 90° angle from the hairline.

Technique

The punch is held upright like a writing instrument, between the second and third fingers and the opposing thumb. Movement to drive the punch comes from the wrist, much the way one would tap a pencil on a piece of paper. Near the hairline, holes are made slowly and diligently while being placed as close as possible to the microslits (Figs. 67–70). While moving away from the hairline, holes are made at varying rates depending on the density of the surrounding hair. Holes are created at a rate of two per second where scalp is void of hair and one per second where there is minimal density of preexisting hair or grafts. The pace slows even further where there is moderate density of hair, as great care is needed to avoid injury to the surrounding follicles. Last, when existing hair is densely packed and sufficient scalp space no longer exists to accommodate the size of the punch, the punch must be abandoned. In this instance, slit incisions are preferable to holes to avoid injury to the existing hair.

When choosing recipient sites, it is of course desirable to place the holes side by side as close as possible. By general consensus, leaving a bridge of skin between the holes equal to the diameter of the holes is considered sufficient to foster good healing and good hair survival.

During the actual cutting of each hole, a central core of skin is created. It is most important that this core be properly removed to avoid accidental burial under a minigraft. In the event that the core is not properly removed, a small cyst is likely to develop within 1 to 2 months postoperatively. Cysts from this source present a nuisance to both the surgeon and the patient. Proper treatment of these cysts consists of incision and drainage. To avoid this complication, great care should be taken to remove all cores at the onset.

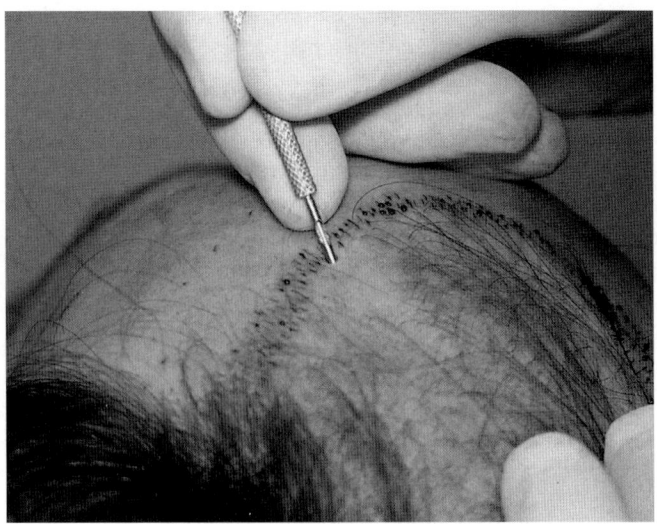

FIG. 68. A distinctive advantage of the Super Punch is that it has an ultra-sharp cutting edge that allows the holes to be created by simply pressing the punch through the skin without rotation.

Cores from holes can also be lost beneath the skin during the cutting of the holes. This is especially true if tumescence is used in the recipient area. Most of the tumescent fluid expands the subcutaneous fat layer. Loose skin cores are easily lost in this subcutaneous expanded space. In the absence of tumescence, the central cores have no place to go and thus remain in the hole where they are visible to the surgeon. It is therefore important to not use tumescence in the recipient area where holes will be placed.

A few central cores of skin may get trapped in the lumen

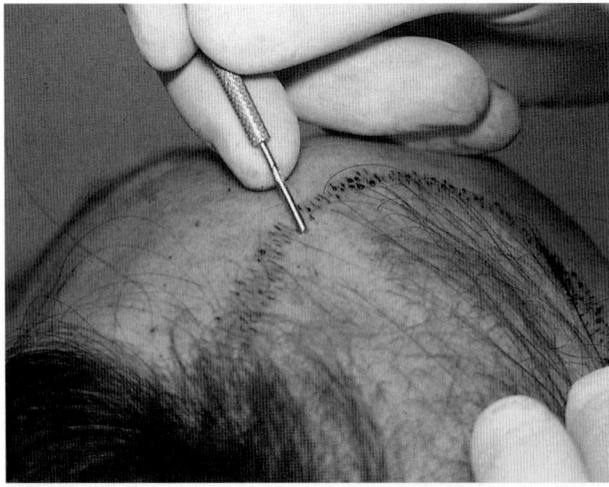

FIG. 67. Recipient holes for minigrafts are created by the Super Punch. In 80% of patients, the punch size used for three- to five-hair minigrafts is 1.3 mm. The remaining 20% of patients generally have less density in the donor areas and therefore require a slightly larger graft size to encompass these three to five hairs. A 1.5-mm punch is used for this latter group of patients.

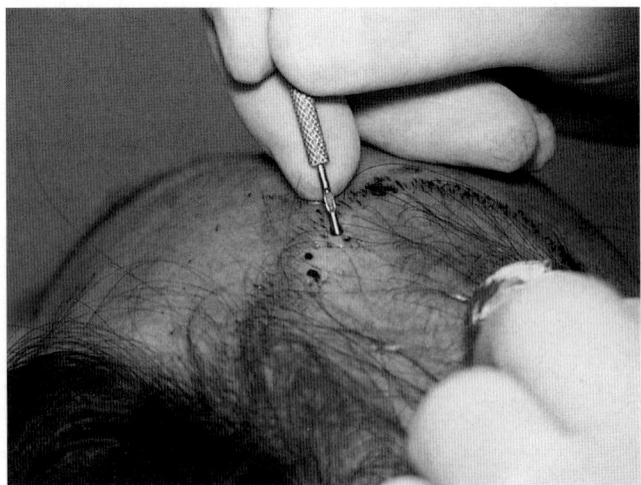

FIG. 69. The punch is usually tilted forward as the recipient holes are cut at an angle that parallels the natural growth of preexisting hairs. Holes are carefully placed in a random pattern just behind the microslits. The microslits and holes are juxtaposed as close as possible. Where they interface, the microslits and holes slightly interdigitate for a seamless transition.

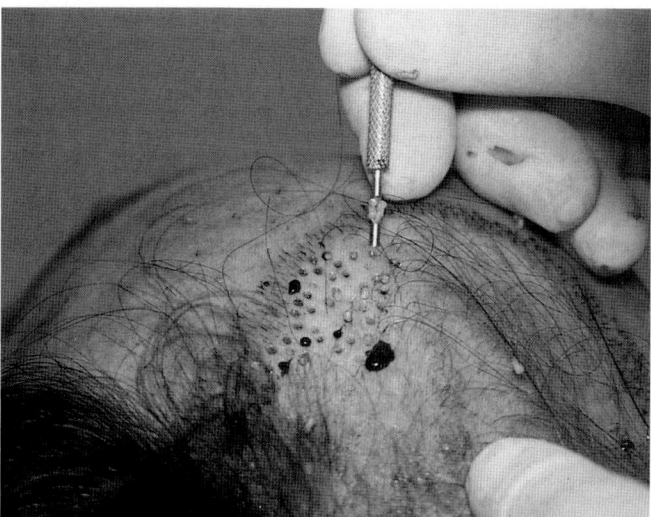

FIG. 70. After the first holes are meticulously placed near the hairline, subsequent holes may be generated more quickly to fill in the area behind the hairline. Surgeons can learn to punch holes faster than one per second and still maintain a random pattern. Since tumescence is not used, central cores of skin tend to remain high in the holes. The few cores trapped in the lumen of the punch escape via the side tissue-escape port. Cores extruded from the tissue-escape port tend to accumulate on the punch.

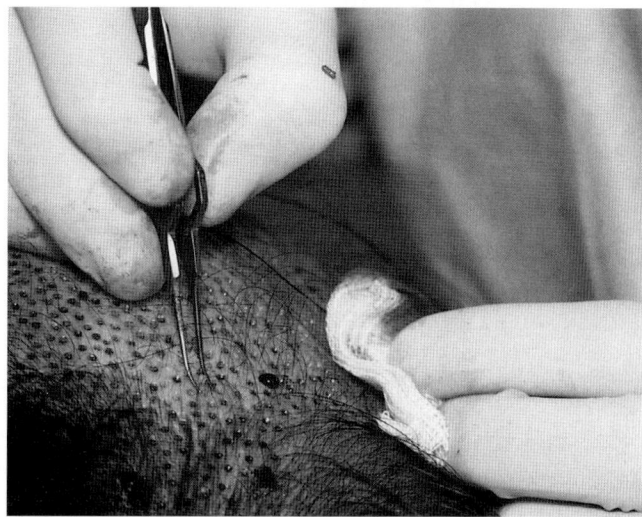

FIG. 71. Foerster forceps are used to remove the central cores. When the forceps are held upside down with the curved tips slightly open, minimal downward pressure on the scalp partially expresses each core. The cores can then be quickly whisked away.

of the punch after several holes are cut. Fortunately, the Super Punch is designed with a self-cleaning tissue-escape port that allows excess cores to escape freely from the side of the punch. The surgeon is thus spared the inconvenience of repeated interruptions to clean out an occluded punch. Also, the risk of a partially occluded punch driving a core beneath the skin is eliminated.

The majority of cores are manually removed after all the holes have been cut. Foerster forceps are ideally suited to help with this task. With the forceps held upside down and the curved tips slightly open, downward pressure on the scalp partially expresses each core. The forceps can then grasp one or two partially extruded cores at a time and extract them from the remainder of the holes. In this manner, the process of expressing and extracting the cores can be repeated over and over again with very little effort in rapid succession. Any free cores that tend to adhere to the forceps or adjacent hair can be ignored as the extraction process continues. Assistants can readily learn to complete a cycle of expressing and extracting the cores in less than 1 second. Experienced assistants often work at a rate of 100 cycles per minute (Figs. 71, 72).

Once or twice during the process of removing the cores, the recipient area and forceps are sprayed with saline and gently wiped clean of dried blood and debris with a dry compress. Keeping a disposable spray bottle filled with saline close at hand is most convenient for this purpose. If hair is present on the scalp, a disposable plastic comb is used to remove any cores adhering to the hair (Fig. 73). In conclusion, with this approach the transplant team can both remove cores from several hundred holes, and cleanse the scalp within 5 minutes.

Slits for Minigrafts

The Lightning Knife is an ideal instrument for creating minislits. The technique described previously for creating microslits is easily adapted for creating minislits. For mini-

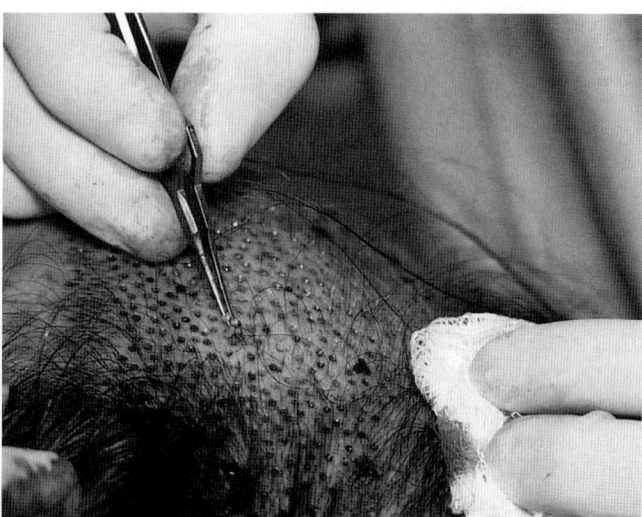

FIG. 72. Ignoring the cores that tend to adhere to the forceps, the assistant quickly repeats the cycle of expressing and whisking away the cores from the newly created holes. Experienced assistants can complete one or two cycles per second, rapidly clearing the recipient area of all remaining cores.

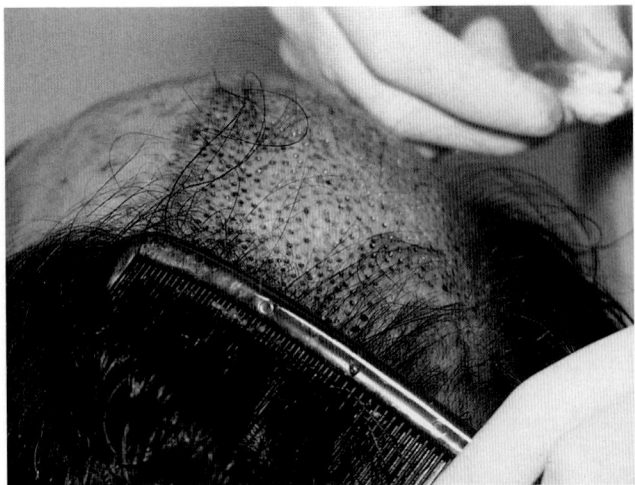

FIG. 73. A sponge is used to wipe away most of the blood and debris. A disposable comb removes residual cores from the hair.

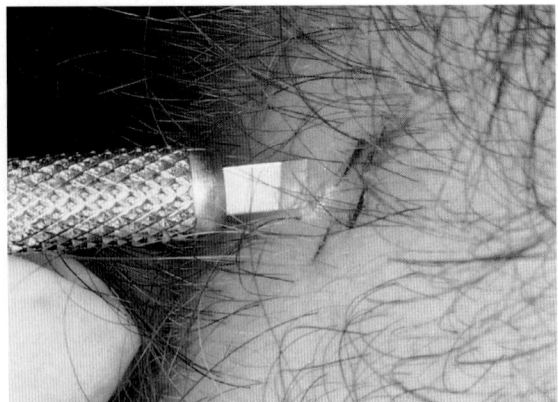
A

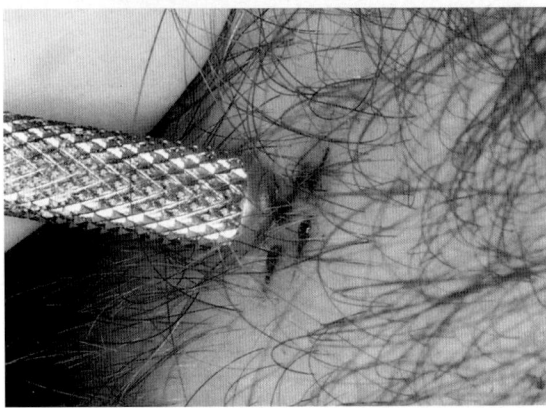
B

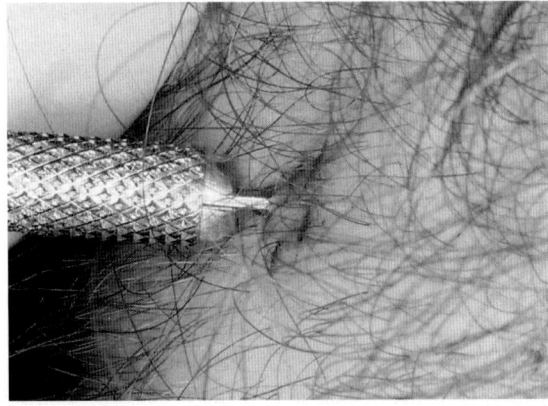
C

FIG. 74. A: For minigrafts of three to five hairs, a No. 62 miniblade will create a 3-mm incision. **B:** The blade is thrust fully into the scalp, allowing the handle to control the depth. Usually, the blade is immediately withdrawn. **C:** Alternatively, to stretch the incision open for greater dilation, the blade is rotated within the incision prior to removal.

grafts, a larger slit is required. Minigrafts in the three- to five-hair range generally fit well into slits 3 mm in length. This length of incision can be produced by using a No. 62 miniblade in conjunction with the Lightning Knife. The No. 62 miniblade is adjusted to protrude from the handle approximately 5 mm. Tapping the knife on the surface of the scalp will rapidly produce a series of incisions uniform in size and depth. The surgeon should not hesitate to drive the blade fully into the scalp, relying on the handle to stop penetration at the preset depth. If there is concern that the blade may reach the bony surface of the skull, enough tumescent fluid can be injected to raise the scalp several millimeters. Again, with the extra width of the mini blade, the incisions are partially dilated (Fig. 74).

When additional dilatation of minislits is desired, a technique called the California twist can be applied. This new technique simply calls for the surgeon to twist or rotate the blade of the Lightning Knife one half-turn (180°) within the incision before withdrawing the blade. This extra rotary movement stretches out the walls of the incision and thereby leaves an enlarged residual space in its path. The technique is most efficient if the surgeon alternates the direction of rotation for each incision from clockwise to counterclockwise. This alternating action is similar to rolling a pencil between the thumb and second and third fingers, and allows the surgeon to maintain a constant grip on the instrument when moving from one incision to the next. The augmented dilatation of the incisional opening is particularly useful in highly resilient or "tight" scalps, and allows for easier insertion of grafts and less popping after placement.

Surgeons first discovering the ease and rapidity of creating slit incisions often wonder why they should bother cutting holes for minigrafts at all. Clearly, creating holes requires the extra step of removing cores, and a lost core may reappear postoperatively as a cyst. The author originally used holes for minigrafts, switched to slits for approximately a year, and then returned to holes for the past several years. The preference for holes incorporates several observations, all of which lend themselves to a common conclusion: the final results produced with holes tend to be less detectable and to appear more natural.

GRAFT INSERTION

The task of inserting grafts into recipient sites is the most time-consuming step of the entire transplant procedure. Typically, 60% or more of the total procedural time is spent on this process. The surgical time needed for two assistants to place 500 grafts into recipient openings in a routine transplant is approximately 1 to 2 hours.

It is essential that the transplant team not only adopt a technique for inserting grafts that is quick and easy, but that the assistant's physical comfort is ensured during this extended period of intense labor and concentration. For when the insertion process goes well, the work is free flowing and the staff is relaxed and in good spirits. When the process does not proceed so well, the staff dreads this portion of the surgery and views the work as tedious, difficult, and frustrating. The key factors that aid assistants during the graft insertion process include (a) maintaining adequate hemostasis in the recipient area, (b) correctly matching the graft size with the size of the recipient sites, (c) employing fine finger motions with appropriately sized surgical instruments, (d) limiting the work area to a small space to minimize hand, finger, and eye motions, and (e) providing comfortable work stations.

Maintaining adequate hemostasis is crucial for graft insertion to proceed. Bleeding not only obscures visibility in the surgical field but demands immediate intervention to ensure patient comfort and safety. Control of bleeding must always take first precedence. The key to establishing adequate hemostasis in the recipient area is judicious use of epinephrine. Injecting small amounts of a concentrated epinephrine solution throughout the recipient area generally provides sufficient vasoconstriction to prevent bleeding. An epinephrine concentration of 1:50,000 is usually effective. However, a higher concentration of 1:25,000 may be required in refractory patients. The increased concentration is obtained by adding stock epinephrine 1:1000 to either saline or lidocaine. The volume of concentrated epinephrine utilized during the insertion process ranges from 5 to 15 ml. Many surgeons new to hair transplantation express concern about the high concentrations of epinephrine used to achieve hemostasis. The gravest concern comes from the possible systemic effects of the drug, with cardiac arrhythmias leading the list. In reality, systemic effects are either minimal (a rise in pulse rate less than 10 beats/min) or not observed at all. The primary explanation for this observation relates to the fact that the recipient area was initially anesthetized with a solution containing epinephrine 1:100,000. The effect of this initial bolus of epinephrine is a moderate amount of persistent vasoconstriction in the recipient area. It is the persistent vasoconstrictive effect that in turn greatly slows or prevents the release of subsequent boluses of epinephrine from leaving the recipient area and reaching the general circulation. Despite the importance of maintaining hemostasis, it is not uncommon to find inexperienced transplant surgeons hesitant to use adequate amounts of epinephrine. Even with 100% of the staff's time spent wiping, sponging, compressing, or otherwise trying to control oozing, and with graft insertion at an absolute standstill, the novice transplant surgeon may still withhold the necessary epinephrine. The single greatest saving of time is when the surgeon finally realizes that *more liberal use of epinephrine is not only safe, but prevents bleeding and enables assistants to resume their primary task of inserting grafts.*

Correctly matching the size of the graft with the size of the recipient site is also important for fast, efficient insertion. When grafts are properly matched, they insert easily and stay in place. When grafts are mismatched, however, several problems arise. Undersized grafts tend to move, either extruding after several minutes or migrating below the skin surface. Oversized grafts may be difficult or even impossible to insert and subject to crush injury. Furthermore, forcing oversized grafts into recipient sites often produces popping of nearby grafts. Popping is a setback that requires additional time for reinsertion. When the surgeon unexpectedly encounters oversized grafts, two solutions are possible. First, the recipient holes or slits can be enlarged with a No. 11 or No. 15 scalpel blade. This is a practical solution, especially if a large number of mismatched grafts are present. Second, assistants can trim away excess tissue or even a single hair if need be from each graft, especially if only a small number of oversized grafts are involved. The best solution, however, is always prevention. All members of the transplant team must communicate clearly and tailor the graft to match the recipient opening perfectly.

Learning to minimize wasteful motions by substituting nimble finger movements for slower hand and arm movements comes with practice. The application of these principles will be discussed further in the upcoming section on insertion techniques. Of importance is the awareness that significant time can be saved by minimizing and simplifying movement. The insertion of each graft requires several steps and motions. With a transplant procedure of 500 grafts, each small saving of time or motion is multiplied by 500. A saving of 4 seconds per graft, for example, multiplied by 500 reduces the overall insertion time by half an hour.

Concentrating the work area, by bringing the worker's hands and eyes relatively close to the recipient area as well as by having the grafts close at hand, improves efficiency. With the instruments and grafts in close proximity to the recipient sites, simple and direct finger motions can be employed. Minimizing distance and movement maximizes speed and precision in graft insertion.

Although often overlooked, an issue of utmost importance is the assistant's comfort during the lengthy insertion process. Unfortunately, most transplant assistants have no choice but to stand during the insertion process due to physical constraints of the surgical room. Even when there is adequate space for seating, simple stools are usually provided, which offer no upper body support. Consequently, whether the worker is standing or sitting, the tendency is for the assistant to lean forward to reach the surgical field. This unsupported leaning forward creates low back strain, a condition that commonly manifests itself as a need to "take a break," to stretch and walk around. As the strain increases in severity, the individual may complain of blatant back spasm, pain, or both. Not only does each interruption add to the overall procedural time but fatigue in general accounts for workers slowing down and making careless mistakes. There are several ways to increase comfort and thereby optimize assistant productivity. The key lies in applying ergonomics to the workspace, by designing the workspace with the worker's comfort in mind. Two concepts can be used to accomplish this.

The first concept has to do with all the assistants working at eye level with the task both close at hand and within a comfortable viewing distance. One way is to have everyone gathered around the recipient area, standing tall with good posture and elevating the surgical chair or table as need be to bring the subject up to the assistants' eye level. Individual adjustments can be made by offering the shorter workers footstools to stand on. At this new height, all the assistants have the work area at eye level and close at hand. More importantly, the need to lean forward has been eliminated, sparing the assistant low back strain.

The second concept has to do with providing the assistant upper body support by means of a specially designed ergonomic chair. This comfortable chair includes a padded arm rest, against which the assistant can lean to support his or her body weight. As the assistant leans forward into the surgical field, the weight of the upper body can be fully supported by the elbows, thereby eliminating any strain placed on the lower back muscles (Fig. 75). Assistant chairs work particularly well when used in conjunction with a dental chair for the patient. The narrow back of a dental chair affords several assistants close access to the patient (Fig. 76). Traditional surgical tables tend to be excessively wide or bulky in the region of the patient's head and shoulders and do not permit access from these chairs. In the latter situation, the assistants may find ways to support their arms on the edge of the surgical table or the headrest. Any front support the assistant can make use of will go a long way to decrease back strain and increase the ability to work nonstop for extended periods.

Technique: Insertion of Micrografts

This procedure is best streamlined for efficiency when the assistants first gather all the instruments and supplies they will need for this step and then locate them in one area near the patient. A portable Mayo stand pulled up beside the head of the dental chair can serve as an additional work surface. This stand easily holds a number of items, including cotton tip applicators, forceps, gauze sponges, a disposable spray bottle with saline, one or two graft coolers containing the grafts, and perhaps one or two syringes with the 1:50,000 epinephrine solution.

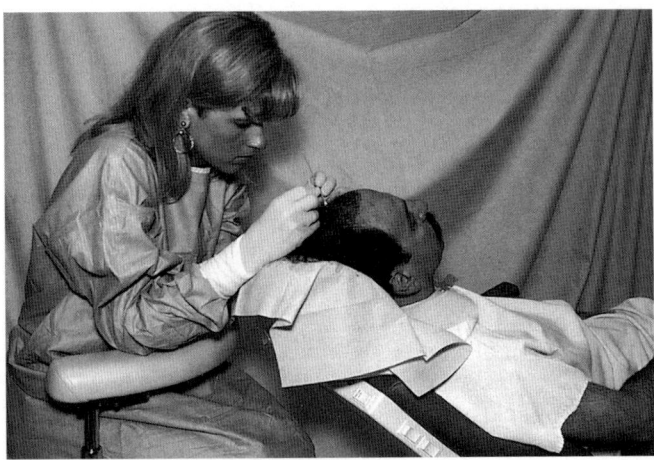

FIG. 75. An ergonomic chair allows the assistant to lean forward into the work site, while supporting the elbows and upper body against the padded arm rest. This kind of frontal support is crucial for preventing back strain and enables the assistant to work comfortably for long uninterrupted periods.

Immediately before starting the insertion process, the assistants clean and recheck the recipient scalp for bleeding one last time. A fine mist of saline is sprayed over the scalp and gently wiped away by dry gauze sponges to produce a blood-free surface. Punch holes are rechecked to ensure that all central skin cores have been removed. Small volumes of epinephrine 1:50,000 can be infiltrated into any areas where oozing or active bleeding persist. Once the scalp is clean and dry, the assistants can turn their full attention to the placement of grafts (Fig. 77).

Placement of micrografts is similar to placement of minigrafts except for the instruments used. Whereas Foerster forceps are quite suitable for placing minigrafts, more refined micro-sized forceps called Micro Foerster forceps are needed for placing micrografts. Basically, the tips of the Fo-

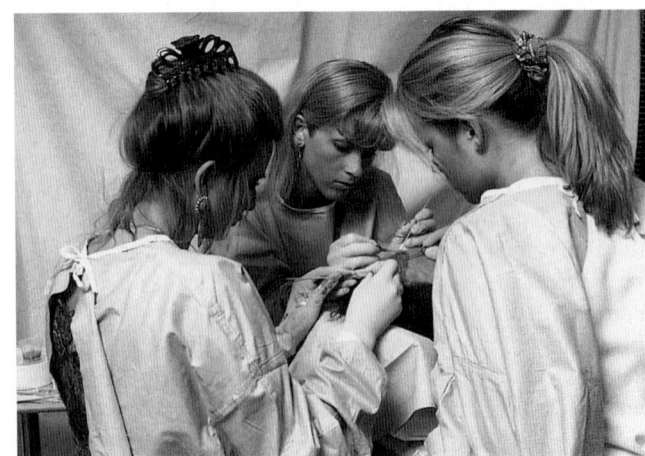

FIG. 76. Unlike traditional surgical tables, the narrow design of a dental chair and headrest affords several assistants close access to the patient. The unobstructed area beneath the back and headrest provides space for the workers' knees and legs.

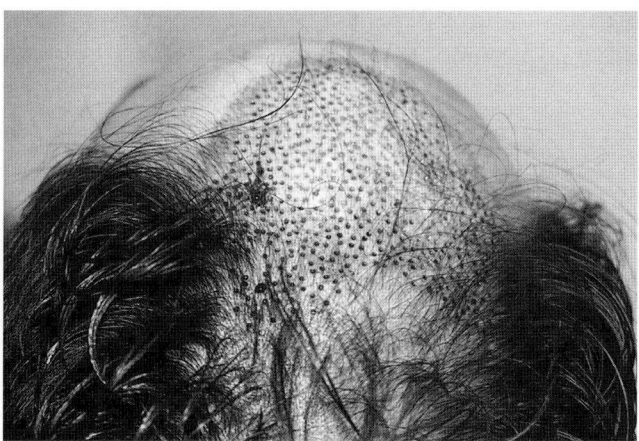

FIG. 77. Final cleansing of the recipient area is accomplished by lightly spraying saline over the area with an inexpensive, disposable spray bottle. Dry sponges are used to wipe away the saline and any remaining blood. The excellent hemostasis produced by the concentration of epinephrine 1:50,000 can be appreciated. This photo records 200 microslits and 626 holes of 1.3 mm in diameter.

erster forceps are too large to fit into the microslit incisions. Micro Foerster forceps, on the other hand, have been specifically designed to work with micro-incisions. Also, this finer instrument has been modified with smooth, narrow, nonserrated tips to facilitate gentle handling of single-hair grafts, and easy insertion and withdrawal of forceps from the opening.

To begin the insertion process, the forceps are used to transfer 20 to 30 micrografts from the graft cooler to the dorsum of each assistant's nondominant hand. Excess saline is absorbed with a cotton tip applicator, leaving just enough moisture for the grafts to adhere to the glove surface (Figs. 78, 79). After the assistant organizes the grafts into a pile at the base of the thumb, the nondominant hand comes to rest

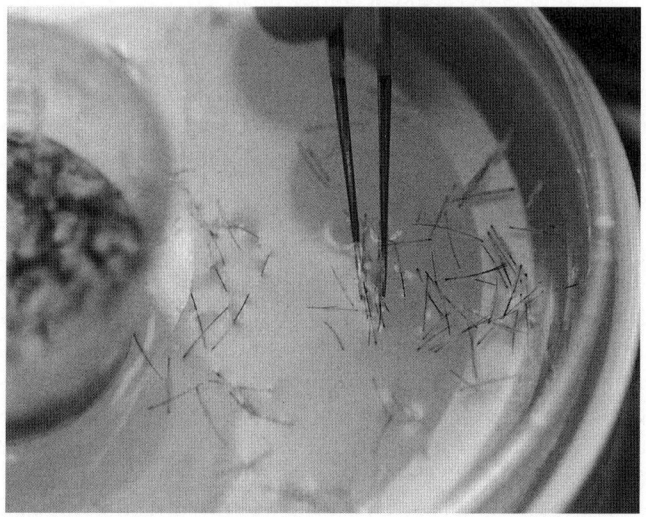

FIG. 78. Using the fine tips of the Micro-Foerster forceps, a group of 15 to 20 micrografts is gathered and gently transferred.

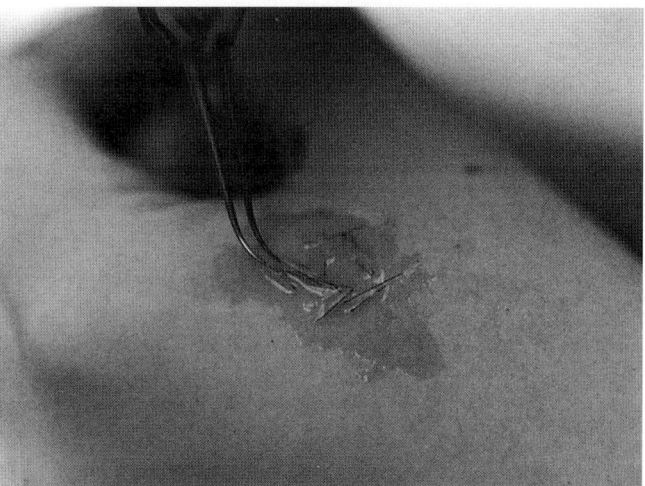

FIG. 79. The micrografts are placed near the base of the left thumb. A cotton tip applicator absorbs excess saline, encouraging the grafts to adhere to the glove.

on the patient's scalp near the recipient sites, holding a cotton tip applicator between the thumb and index finger.

Next, the assistant gently lifts and moves an individual graft toward a recipient site. The forceps are used by the dominant hand to delicately grasp the graft by the dermal tissue near the follicle. Care is taken to avoid squeezing the follicle directly, as direct insult may damage or destroy critical elements in the unit. Poor growth or low yield of the micrografts can result from crush injury sustained by the follicles at the time of insertion.

After a graft is inserted into the micro-incision, it is released by the forceps. Most often, the forceps slide out easily without dislodging the graft. After the forceps are withdrawn, a cotton tip applicator held in the nondominant hand gently taps the top of the graft both to blot away any oozing of serous fluid or blood and to help secure the position of the graft. Grafts that are not fully seated in the micro-incisions are maneuvered into place by the cotton tip applicator or forceps. The cotton tip applicator advances the graft by gentle tapping while the forceps grasp the exposed portion of the graft or the hair itself and maneuver the graft into place (Figs. 80–82).

The stub of exposed hair left on the graft as a marker, or "flag," is especially useful during micrograft insertion. The stub indicates the direction of hair growth, which enables the assistant to orient the graft properly. Also, if a graft drops below the skin surface, the stub marks the presence of the graft and thereby prevents accidental insertion of a second graft into the same incision. Third, the stub can be used as a convenient handle for leveling the graft in the incision. By grasping the hair with the forceps, the assistants can jiggle the graft up and down to bring it to the proper level.

Two assistants work simultaneously in order to minimize the time needed for micrograft insertion. One assistant starts at the lateral aspect of the hairline and moves toward the midline, while the second assistant begins at the midline and

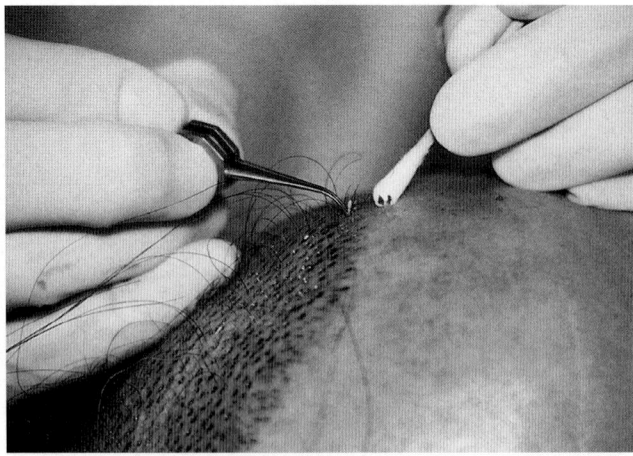

FIG. 80. A micrograft is delicately held by the dermal tissue near the base of the follicle and gently introduced into the micro-incision.

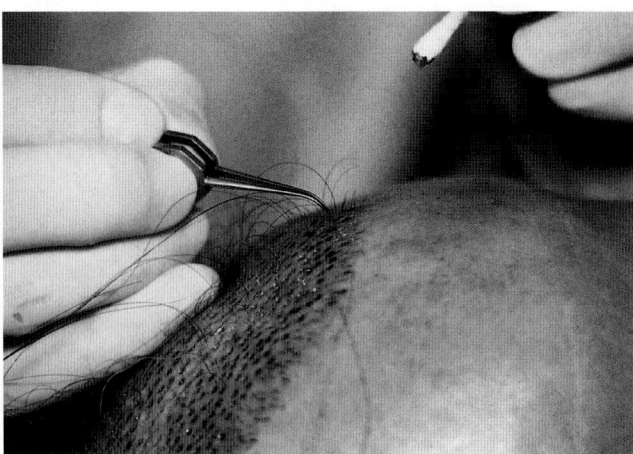

FIG. 82. Usually, the forceps can be withdrawn without dislodging the graft. A cotton tip applicator can be used to hold the graft in place as the forceps are withdrawn. Both the forceps and the cotton tip applicator are useful for adjusting the final level of the graft.

moves toward the contralateral margin of the hairline. Both work along the hairline in the same direction (e.g., from right to left), keeping the two work areas completely separate.

Assistants often prefer to insert micrografts along the hairline first while hemostasis and local anesthesia are most pronounced. Insertion of minigrafts generally follows completion of the micrografts. However, whenever three assistants are available, two can place micrografts along the hairline while a third worker simultaneously inserts minigrafts in the posterior portion of the recipient area.

New assistants generally find that micrografts are more challenging to place than minigrafts. With practice, the ability to place single-hair micrografts improves. Most experienced assistants can place single-hair grafts as fast or faster than minigrafts.

Technique: Insertion of Minigrafts

Placing multihair grafts into a hole or slit incision differs only slightly from the method used for micrografts. The larger minigrafts are handled more effectively with the larger Foerster forceps.

Foerster forceps and 6-inch cotton tip applicators are the two items used for inserting minigrafts. Assistants working from a seated position generally prefer Foerster forceps with curved tips, whereas assistants working from a standing position have a different angle of approach and usually prefer forceps with straight tips.

The cotton tip applicators are useful in several ways. Grafts protruding from recipient sites can be gently pressed or tapped down to the correct level with an applicator. If the insertion initiates bleeding at the site, an applicator can be used to apply gentle direct pressure. Also, applicators are used to keep the work area clean, allowing good visualization.

The minigrafts are kept chilled in the graft coolers as long as possible. One or more graft coolers are placed near the assistants, allowing quick access to the supply of chilled grafts.

Foerster forceps are used to transfer 20 to 30 grafts to the dorsum of the assistant's nondominant hand. Locating this small group near the base of the thumb will position the grafts near the recipient sites.

The Foerster forceps gently grasp the lower edge of the graft. Care is taken to hold the grafts by the dermal tissue, avoiding the individual hairs. The forceps introduce the graft into the recipient site as far as possible. Often, the forceps will draw the graft completely into the hole or slit. Occasionally, the graft will not remain fully seated after the forceps are withdrawn. To avoid this dislocation, the forceps and the cotton tip applicator are used to press the graft home (Figs. 83, 84).

The graft must also be oriented for direction of hair growth. This direction is designated by the 3-mm stub of exposed hair. When round holes are the recipient sites, it is most expeditious to first place the graft and then orient it sec-

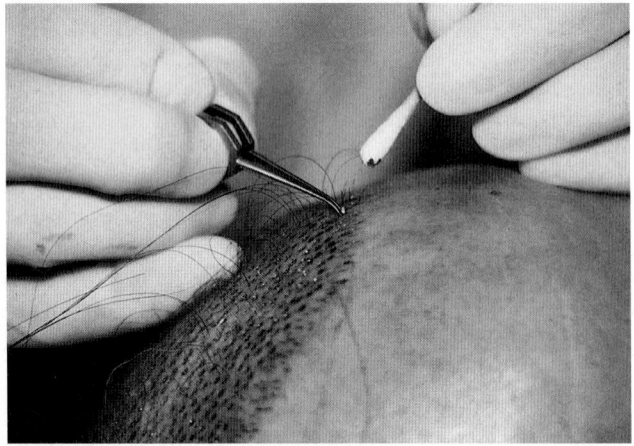

FIG. 81. The forceps slide the graft deep into the incision before releasing the hair.

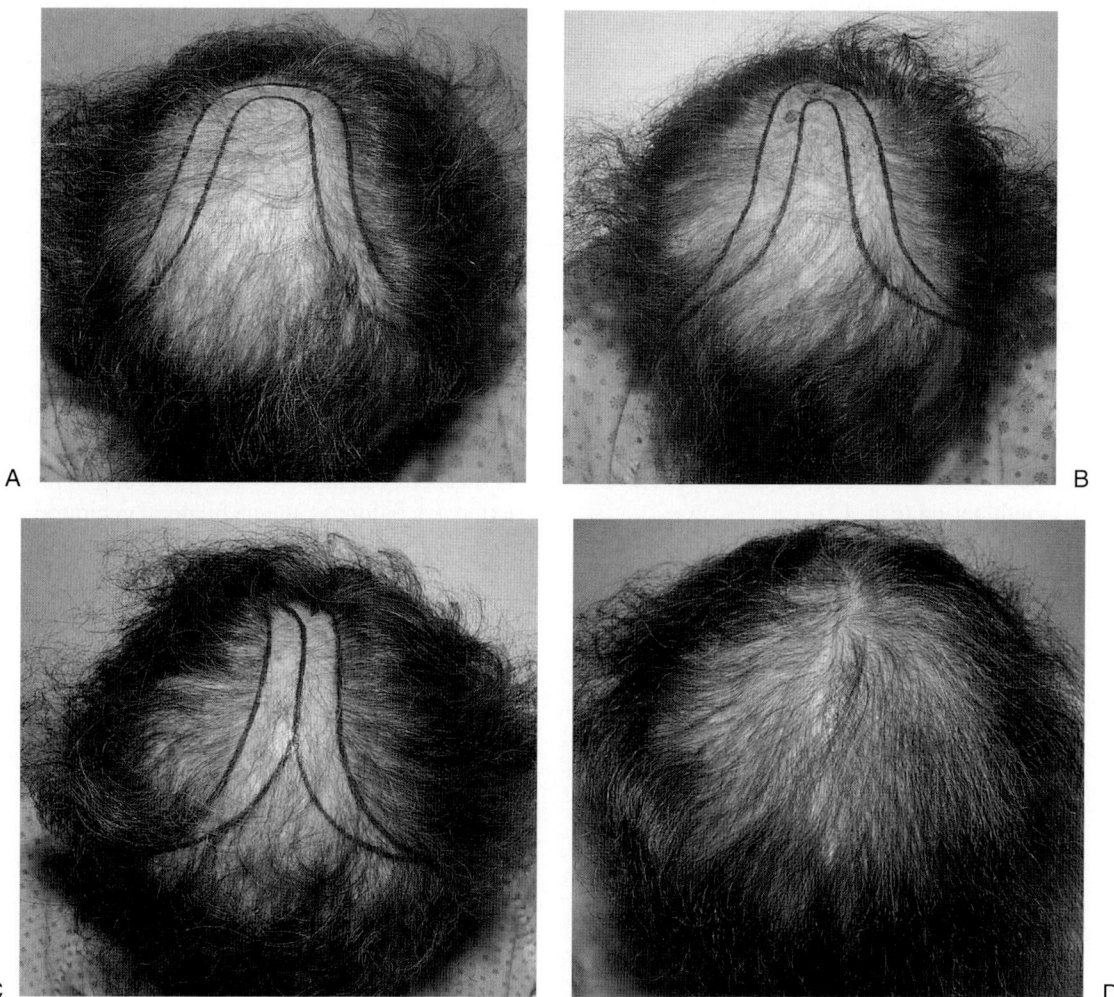

FIG. 10. A: Patient with average laxity before a circumferential scalp reduction. The patient had two unsuccessful lazy-S scalp reductions previously. **B:** Same patient after the first circumferential and immediately before the second scalp reduction. **C:** Same patient after the second circumferential and immediately before the third. **D:** Same patient after the third procedure.

negated. The primary advantage of circumferential scalp reduction over curvilinear scalp reduction is that a much greater area of alopecia is excised because of the ability to undermine much more aggressively. In fact, if the temporal incisions are extended down to the mid sideburn (something I do frequently), the occipitalis and periauricular muscles can be cut, which adds a tremendous amount of upward mobility to the procedure. Additionally, more aggressive undermining lateral and medial to the occipital neurovascular bundles can be accomplished quite easily. These extra capabilities allow complete elimination of alopecia in three procedures for a patient with average laxity, resulting in excellent cosmesis in the vast majority of patients (Fig. 10A–D).

The Marzola Scalp-Lift

As previously mentioned, this procedure was the original scalp reduction performed from the outside working in. This technique is essentially a paramedian scalp with more aggressive undermining down to the hairline of the nape and no undermining of the contralateral alopecic bald scalp (see Fig. 4).

The other keys to this procedure are that (a) it advances the hair-bearing skin significantly into the temporal recessions, (b) it advances hair-bearing skin into the vertex, (c) it advances much more hair-bearing skin when compared to a paramedian or conventional scalp reduction, and (d) it does all of this with minimal to no alopecic stretch-back.

I use this technique when a patient has had previous grafting performed by me or another practitioner. In a study that I published several years ago, I found that if a bilateral scalp-lift was carried through on patients with prior hair-grafting, the probability of obtaining a postoperative necrosis was approximately 12% (7). When two Marzola lateral scalp-lifts were performed, instead of one bilateral lift, the incidence went down to 1%. And although it takes the patient a little while longer to achieve his or her results, the final cosmesis is as good as when the bilateral procedures are performed (Fig. 11).

The Bilateral Occipitoparietal Scalp-Lift

This technique is basically a bilateral Marzola lateral scalp-lift with the incision permeating from one mid sideburn, along the donor dominant fringe, to the other mid sideburn (see Fig. 5). The undermining is performed all the way down to the hairline of nape bilaterally and around the posterior rim of the ears. This extra undermining allows a prodigious removal of baldness, and it does it in an aesthetically pleasing way. The primary advantage of this approach over the Marzola lift is that it much more expeditious, allowing most class VI patients to be completely closed in two procedures over a 3-month period (Fig. 12).

The Brandy Bitemporal Scalp-Lift

The bitemporal scalp-lift evolved as a method to completely eliminate the alopecia after the bilateral occipitoparietal scalp-lift. This flap is essentially a C-shaped flap that fits into a complementary S-shaped flap (Fig. 13). There are four sequential incision lines that have been described at length in the original article (5) (Fig. 14). Following these four lines sequentially makes this procedure progress in a very quick and methodical manner.

Another important aspect of the bitemporal scalp-lift is that it can also be used to treat patients with mild vertex baldness and temporal recessions (Fig. 15). This treatment entails only one operation, but it must be certain that the patient's baldness is not going to progress to a class V or VI baldness. If it is believed that the patient is going to progress to a more extensive baldness, then a bilateral occipitoparietal scalp-lift

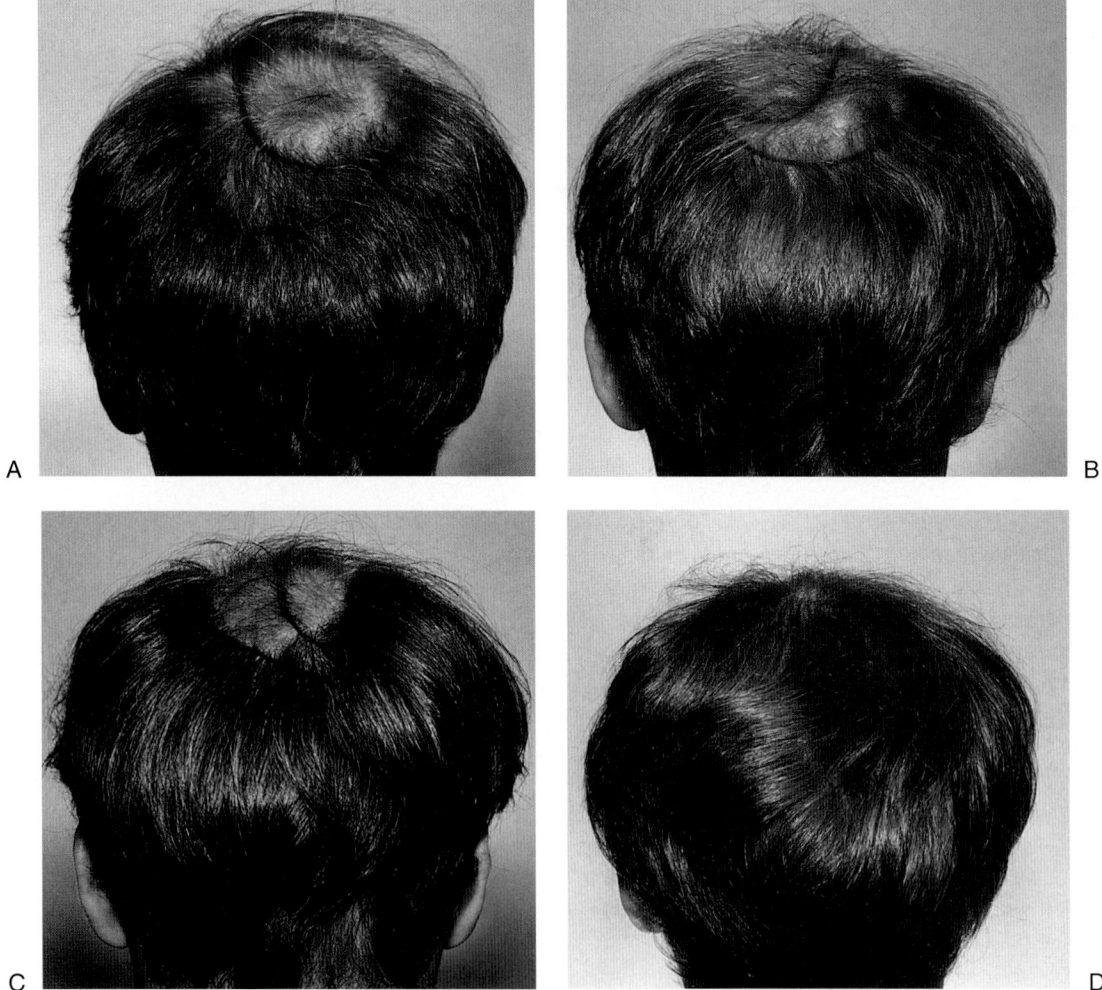

FIG. 11. A: This patient had prior punch-grafting by another surgeon. A Marzola lateral lift was therefore to be performed instead of a bilateral occipitoparietal scalp-lift. **B:** After the first lateral and immediately before the second. **C:** After the second lateral and immediately before the bitemporal scalp reduction. **D:** After two lateral lifts, one bitemporal scalp reduction, and one transposition flap.

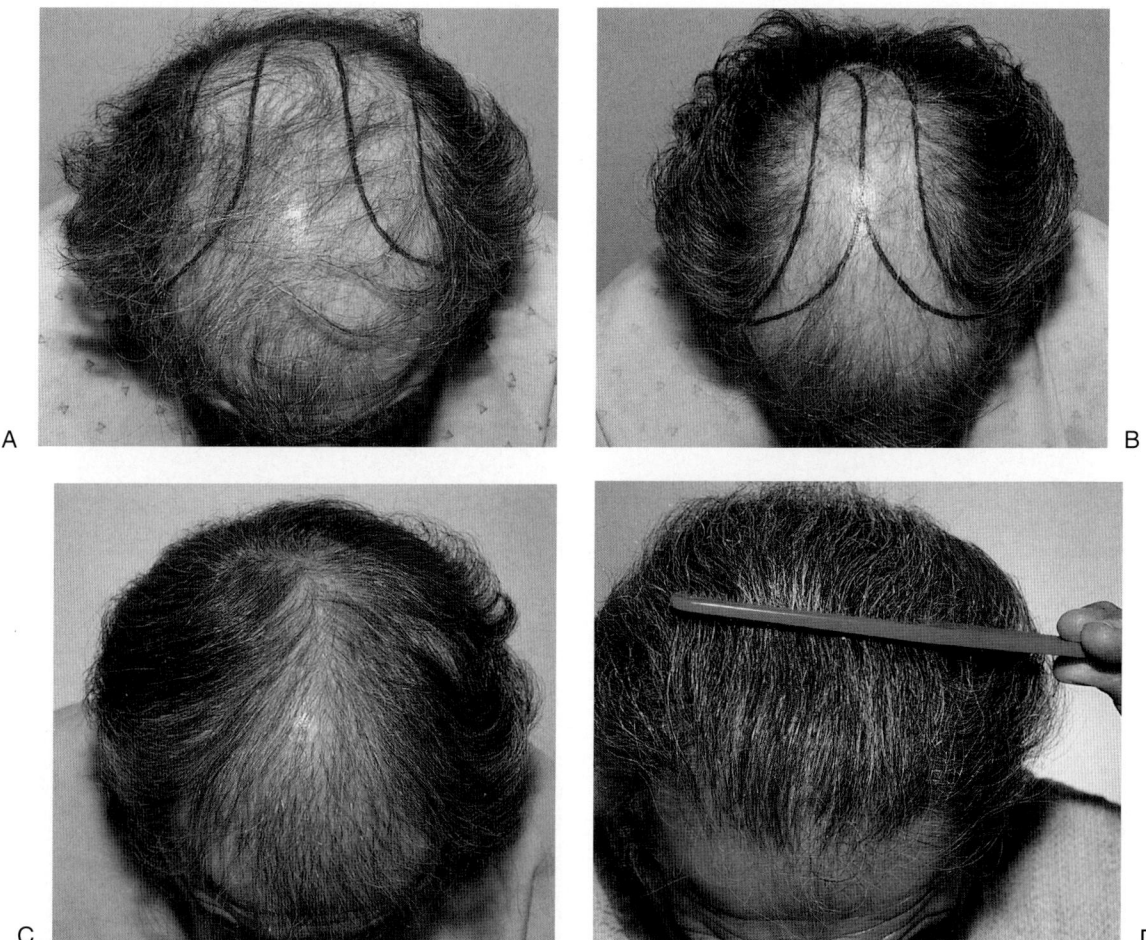

FIG. 12. A: Patient before a bilateral occipitoparietal scalp-lift. **B:** Same patient after the bilateral occipitoparietal scalp-lift and immediately before a bitemporal scalp reduction. **C:** Same patient after the bitemporal scalp reduction and one grafting session. **D:** Same patient after three sessions of mini- and micrografting to the frontal area.

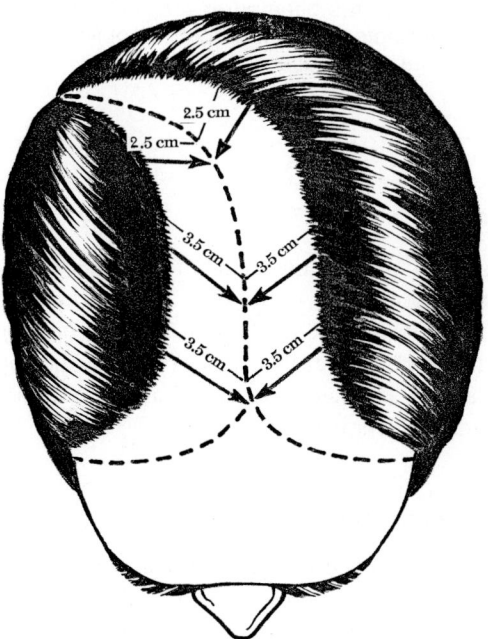

FIG. 13. The bitemporal scalp-lift. Notice the average amount of alopecia excision and the anterior and medial vector forces for this procedure.

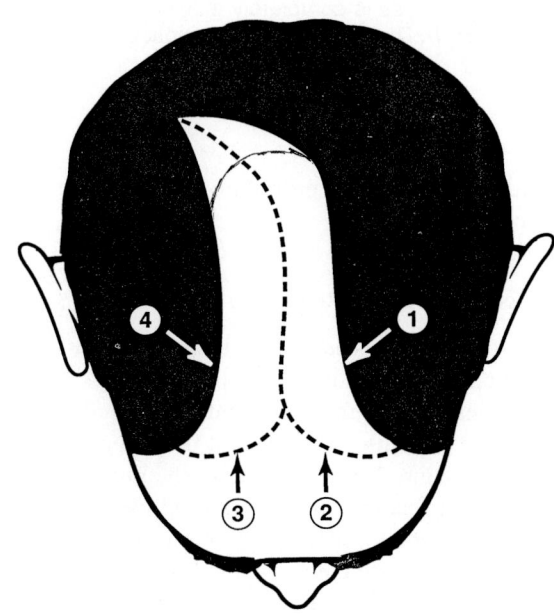

FIG. 14. The four basic incision lines of the bitemporal scalp-lift and scalp reduction.

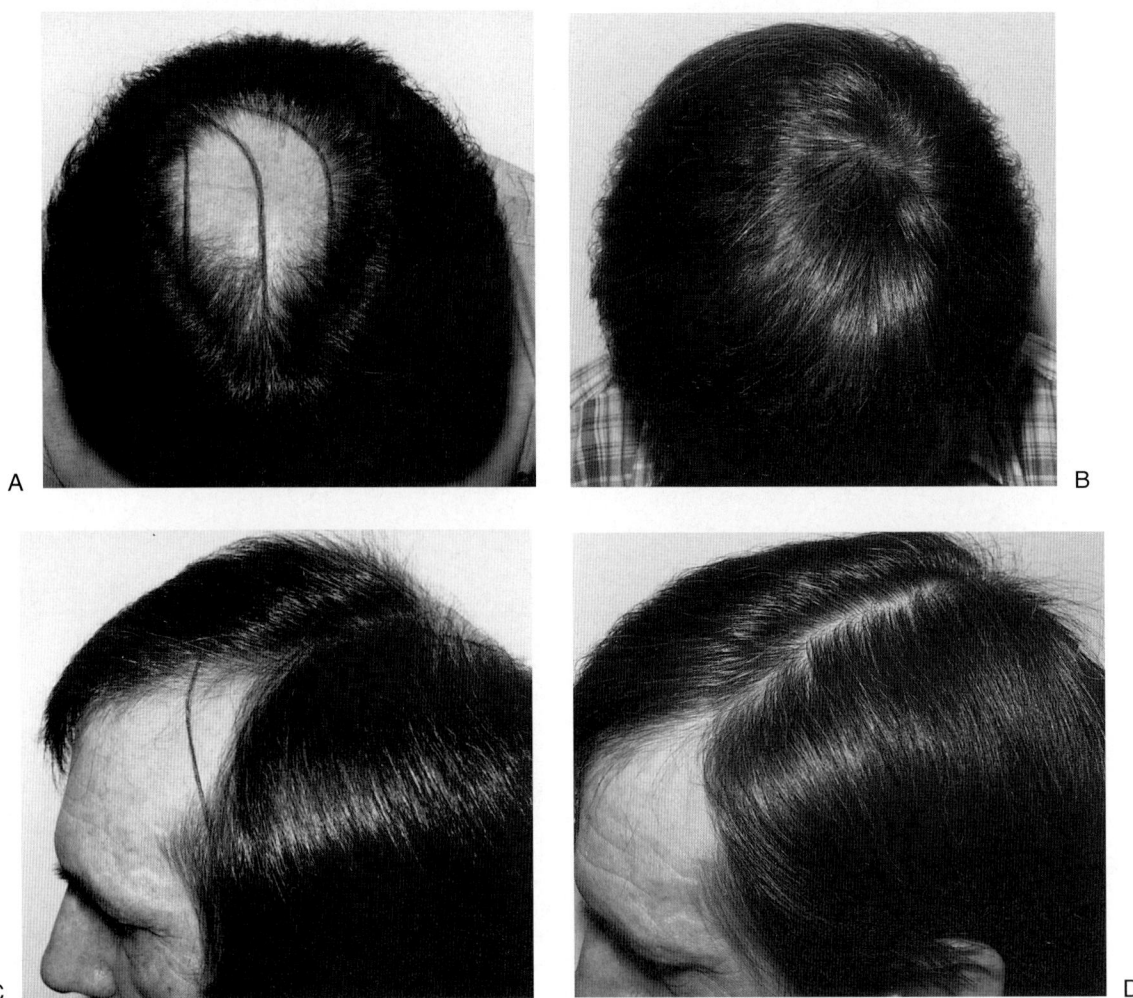

FIG. 15. Patient with a class III vertex alopecia that I believed was not going to significantly progress. **A:** Immediately before a bitemporal scalp-lift from the top view. **B:** After the bitemporal scalp-lift. The baldness is completely eliminated with one surgery. **C:** Same patient before surgery, from the oblique view. **D:** After the surgery, notice the forward advancement into the temporal recession.

followed by a bitemporal procedure should be the protocol of choice.

The Bitemporal Scalp Reduction

This procedure is essentially a bitemporal scalp-lift except that the undermining stops at the nuchal ridge. This is the procedure that is used most frequently to completely eliminate the bald area after the bilateral occipitoparietal scalp-lift. This procedure is used instead of the bitemporal scalp-lift because the nape hair is usually already thinned out somewhat after the first scalp-lift, and further lifting in that area would exacerbate the problem. Also, the alopecia area is usually small enough after the first bilateral occipitoparietal scalp-lift that a full lift is not needed to accomplish closure (see Fig. 12A–C).

METHODS

This section involves the actual mechanics of some of the procedures mentioned—primarily those procedures performed from the outside working in. It is my opinion that if one can markedly reduce the chance of getting postoperative stretch-back of alopecic skin, then that approach should be the procedure of choice in most cases.

The Circumferential Scalp Reduction

The patient first signs the appropriate consent forms, and presedation is orally administered with 20 mg of diazepam and two oxycodone tablets. While these are taking effect, the incision line for the circumferential scalp reduction is scribed with Bonnie Blue ink. When drawing in these lines,

I usually decide between two different methods—starting at the mid sideburn or starting at the temporal region. If the patient has a tight scalp, I usually draw the initial incision line beginning at the left mid sideburn, up to the temporal recession, around the donor dominant fringe, and back down to the contralateral mid-sideburn. *Note: At this time, one should use Doppler ultrasonography to identify and scribe the base of the superficial temporal artery.* The incision at the mid sideburn is approximately 1 cm anterior to this structure. I extend the incision on these "tight" patients because their scalps typically do not move away from the skull very well when undermining. This stiffness, of course, affects my visualization tremendously. When the incision is extended down to the mid sideburn, all of a sudden a new world appears, and my ability to perform better and more intricate surgery increases dramatically.

Once the lines are completed, we take the patient to the operating room and begin adminstering anesthesia. To ensure that an excellent ring block is going to be achieved, I make dots 1 cm apart in the areas that are going to be injected. I make these in a ring, starting at the mid-frontal area, extending down to the mid sideburn, around the ear, and along the nuchal ridge. I also make extra dots below the nuchal ridge lateral and medial to the nuchal line. These extra dots are used to obtain the extra anesthesia needed in case the additional maneuvers of occipitalis muscle division and deeper undermining are desired.

I then use 2% lidocaine hydrochloride with 1 : 100,000 epinephrine, and, with a 30-gauge needle, I inject into the dots, full thickness, on a 90-degree angle. Once all the dots are injected into, I inject between the dots with 1% lidocaine hydrochloride with 1 : 200,000 epinephrine. These injections are also administered full thickness. However, a 25-gauge needle is utilized instead of a 30-gauge needle. The larger needle is used on the second round because the patient usually does not feel the second set of injections, so I do not have to worry as much about the burn of the lidocaine. This larger needle therefore allows me to be a little more aggressive with the amount of anesthesia that I administer, which in turn improves the block.

Once the ring block anesthesia is completed, it is time to begin the operation. The first incision is at the left mid sideburn, anterior to the temporal artery, and is swung around the donor dominant fringe to the mid-posterior region at the vertex. Light cauterization is then performed. After completing the incision and cautery, I have my assistants take skin hooks, hook onto the temporofrontal galea, and retract in an upward direction. I then take a No. 10 Bard Parker blade and undermine over the temporal fascia, only halfway down to the base of the ear (Fig. 16A). Once I get to that point, I take a facelift scissors (with a cutting edge on both sides of each blade) and make tunnels with an outward motion down to the base of the ear. While I am making these tunnels, one of my assistants is holding the patient's head downward while the other assistant pulls the scalp upward with two hands at the point that I am working. *The coordination between the two assistants is probably the most important aspect of all the lifting procedures that I am going to discuss in this chapter.* Remember, one assistant holds the head down with one hand and holds up the flap edge with the other—the other assistant pulls with two hands in the area that I am undermining.

Additionally, I am using a suction retractor that elevates and tightens the scalp above my scissors. Without this retractor and the assistants pulling and pushing in opposing directions, the scalp moves about aimlessly, which makes the surgery much more difficult than it needs to be.

After a series of tunnels are made down to the base of the ear, I connect them by cutting the bridges with an inward motion of the scissors (see Fig. 16B). With this technique, the undermining process can proceed very quickly. Once it is completed over the parietal scalp, I push a few gauze pads under the elevated flap.

The patient's head is now shifted straight ahead and then completely to the right. The incision is continued during these head movements so that it extends from the mid-posterior vertex region, around the donor dominant scalp, and to the right mid sideburn anterior to the temporal artery (see Fig. 16C). The same undermining is then performed on the right side of the head.

Once the undermining is completed laterally on both sides, the patient's head is moved straight onto the Prõn Pillõ. At this point, each assistant takes hold of his or her respective side of the flap and each pulls the flap inferiorly and posteriorly. I then take a No. 10 blade and begin undermining down to the occipitalis muscles with broad left-to-right motions. Very quickly, I am able to reach the point where the occipitalis muscles attach to the skull (see Fig. 16D).

Upon reaching the occipitalis muscles, I now have five options:

1. I can stop and advance the flap.
2. I can divide the occipitalis muscles, releasing the inhibitory contractile forces of those muscles (see Fig. 16E).
3. I can divide the occipitalis muscles and the periauricular muscles, releasing the inhibitory contractile forces of both of these muscles.
4. I can divide the occipitalis and periauricular muscles and undermine an extra 1 to 2 cm medial and lateral to the occipital neurovascular bundle (see Fig. 16F).
5. I can do all the above plus undermine all the way down to the hairline of the nape, making certain to dissect around the occipital neurovascular bundle. This in essence becomes a modified scalp-lift, a technique that will be discussed in more detail later.

In most cases, I will proceed to option 4. Option 5 is performed only if option 4 does not produce the movement desired. Once the undermining is completed, regardless of the degree, the flap is now advanced. The first area to be excised is the mid-posterior vertex. The flap is advanced straight for-

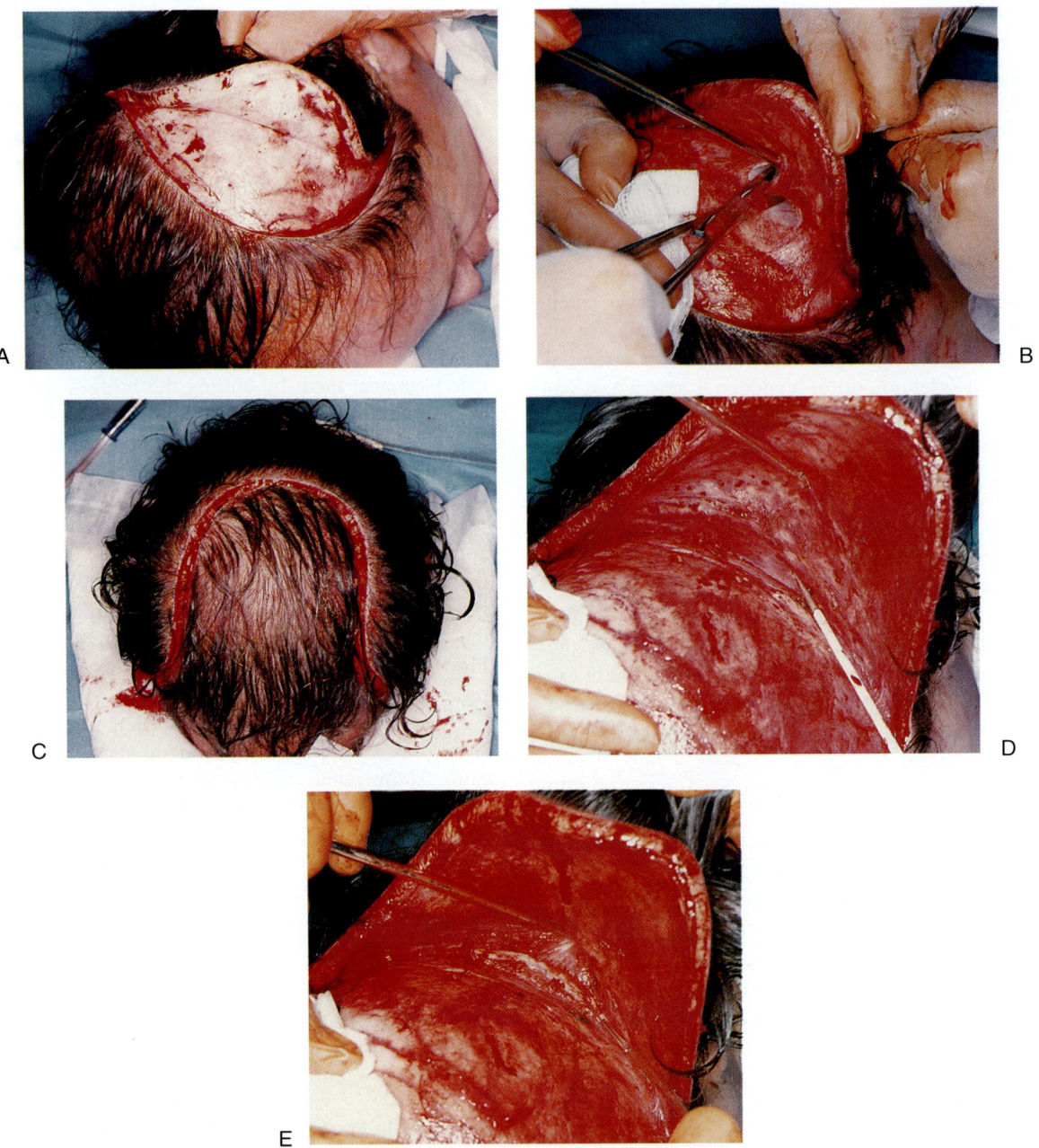

FIG. 16. A: The initial incision line of the circumferential scalp reduction is made from the mid sideburn and the area is initially undermined with a No. 10 Bard Parker. **B:** Tunnels are made with blunt outward dissection and these are then connected with inward sharp dissection. **C:** The circumferential is then completed around the entire donor dominant fringe. **D:** After undermining down to the nuchal ridge with the tunneling technique, the occipitalis muscles are nicely exposed. **E:** The occipitalis muscles are then lightly divided with either cut-cautery or a No. 10 Bard Parker. *(Continued)*

ward and a blood stain marking is made where the flap can be reached. An incision is then made at the blood stain line (see Fig. 16G). At this point, I take a staple gun and staple this part of the hair-bearing flap to the alopecic skin. The other option is to place a deep temporary 0-PDS II at this same location (see Fig. 16H).

Once the posterior part of the flap is stabilized, I take both sides of the scalp and advance them *simultaneously*. It is critical to advance these flaps superiorly at the same time or else there will be a marked advancement on one side and a much smaller advancement on the other. After this is accomplished, the flaps also are pressed down onto the alopecic skin so that blood stains are created bilaterally. These blood stains dictate where the incisions will be made, in a manner similar to that done at the mid-posterior incision.

Upon completion of the alopecic excision (see Fig. 16I), the staple or deep galeal suture at the mid posterior is removed and the undersurface of the flap is thoroughly cauter-

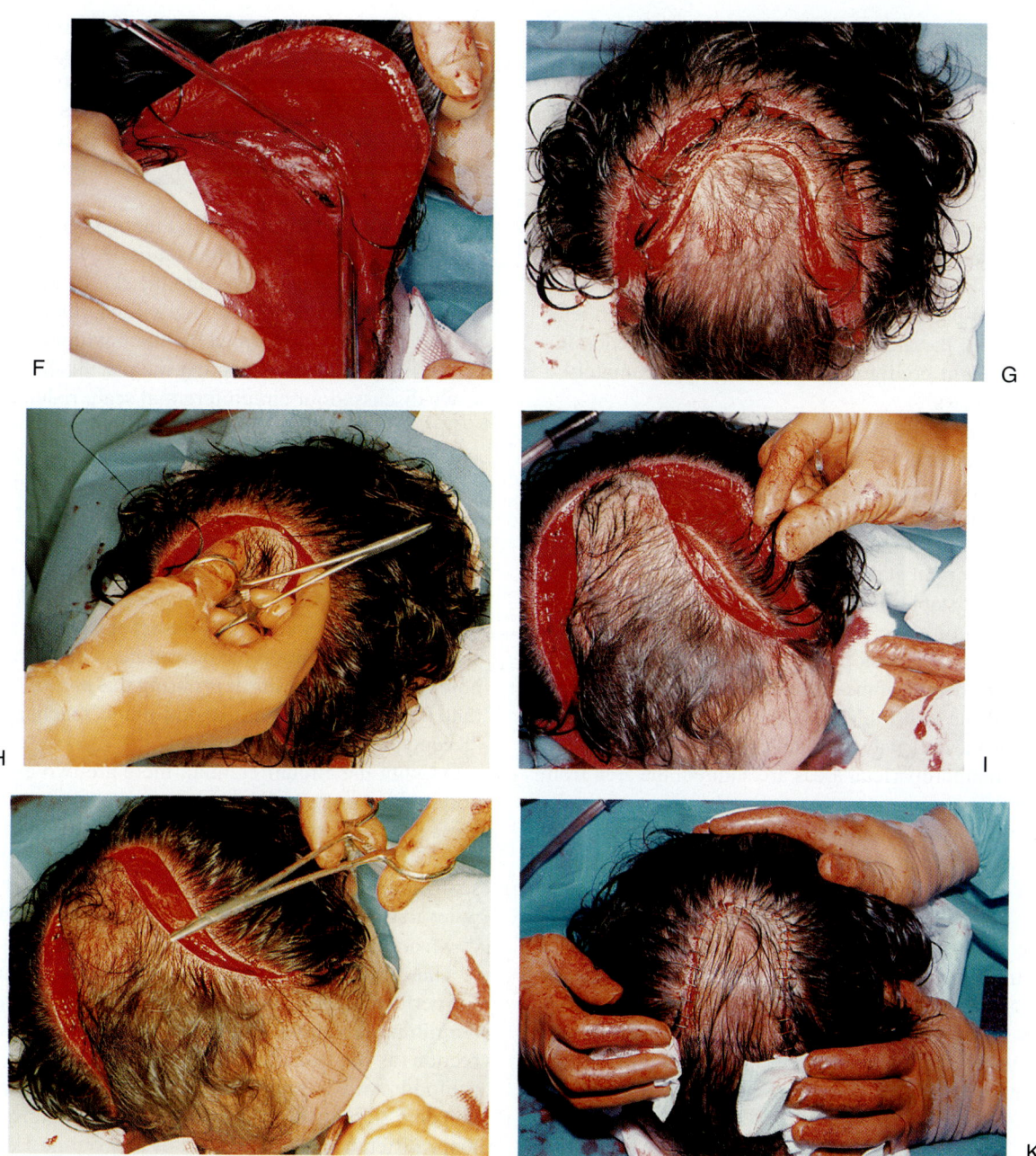

FIG. 16. *(Continued)* **F:** Once the occipitalis muscles are divided, more aggressive undermining can be accomplished lateral and medial to the occipital neurovascular bundles. **G:** Once this more aggressive undermining is accomplished, the flap is advanced anteriorly. This photo demonstrates an average amount of alopecia excision at the vertex region. **H:** A galeal suture (used here) or cutaneous staple can be placed at the mid-posterior area at this time. **I:** The parietal and temporal excisions are done at this point. It is crucial to predict the excisions by advancing *both* sides of the scalp medially at the same time and making blood stains bilaterally. If one side is marked at a time, marked asymmetry will occur. **J:** The figure-of-eight suture is the key to developing good eversion and approximation of the wound edges. This technique also eliminates the fascioliasis of the galea. In this photo, there are figure-of-eight sutures at each of the temporal recessions. **K:** After the galeal sutures are completed, the skin edges are closed with either staples or 4-0 PDS II clear. Sutures are actually preferred, but staples were used in this case because of the photographer's time constraints.

ized. To facilitate this, I take a hooked retractor and place it under the right side of the flap. I irrigate thoroughly with normal saline and cauterize aggressively on that side. The same process is repeated on the opposite side. Usually, drains are not inserted for this procedure, but if there was excessive bleeding or if the undermining proceeded down to the hairline of the nape, drains are placed at the lowest point in the postauricular sulcus.

The flap edges are now sutured. I first suture the galea at the mid-posterior region with a 0-PDSII. When performing this attachment, I take a bite through the periosteum before taking 1-cm bites through the galeal surfaces of the alopecic and hair-bearing flap edges. After this stabilization takes place, I use a figure-of-eight suture at each of the temporal recessions (see Fig. 16J). This figure-of-eight configuration is critical to obtain the eversion that I desire and to prevent galeolysis that can so commonly occur when only one suture bite is utilized. After these key three galeal sutures are completed (i.e., mid-posterior, right temporal recession, left temporal recession), the areas between them are sutured using the figure-of-eight configuration, leaving approximately 2 cm between throws.

Upon completion of the galeal sutures, I suture the skin surface with a running 4-0 PDSII clear suture (see Fig. 16K). I begin at the mid-posterior region and run the suture to the patient's left temporal recession. I then run the same type of suture from the right temporal recession to the mid-posterior region. It is important at this point in the operation to (a) use suture instead of staples because of their improved accuracy, (b) use clear sutures so that the patient does not have a grotesque appearance postoperatively, and (c) use wide differentials in the depths of the suture bites because of the wide fluctuation of the scalp thickness on both sides of the flap edges. This is the only way to achieve the best scars possible.

Once the temporoparietal areas are sutured, the area from the temporal recessions down to the mid-sideburns are sutured. These areas are sutured exactly as the aforementioned areas were, except that (a) a drain is placed at the most inferior aspect of the incision, (b) a 5-0 PDSII is used on the skin instead of 4-0 PDSII, and (c) care must be used not to take a galeal bite through the superficial temporal artery.

After suturing the entire incision line and cleaning the head thoroughly with hydrogen peroxide, we spread K-Y Jelly over all of the incisions. We place a circumferential dressing over the head and discharge the patient into the care of a responsible adult.

The Bilateral Occipitoparietal Scalp-Lift

This procedure is simply an extension of the circumferential scalp reduction. It is performed pretty much the same as a circumferential reduction except for the following points: (a) An occipital artery ligation (through vertical 2-cm incisions) is performed 2 to 6 weeks before the actual operation. (b) Undermining proceeds down to the hairline of the nape. (c) Undermining proceeds around the posterior rim of the ear down to the inferior earlobe.

As previously alluded to, the bilateral occipitoparietal scalp-lift is similar to the circumferential scalp reduction until the occipitalis muscles are reached. It is at this point that the procedure becomes more aggressive.

The first tunnel below the nuchal ridge is a subcutaneous one in the postauricular skin. This tunnel is usually made looking at the skin from the surface (not looking under the flap), and it is extended all the way down to a horizontal line that I draw preoperatively and that extends from one ear lobe to the other ear lobe (Fig. 17A). Once this initial tunnel is formed on the patient's left side, I gradually move medially with my undermining, getting into a deeper plane as I progress toward the midline.

The first step in this medial undermining is to lightly incise the patient's left occipitalis muscle. This muscle should be incised where it attaches into the skull and it is along this incision where the undermining will be guided. This undermining is usually performed by making tunnels with a blunt dissection and then connecting them with sharp dissection, as we discussed for circumferential scalp reduction.

Initially, I am in the fat layer in the postauricular skin. But as I dissect toward the midline, I will attempt to divide the fascia of the trapezius muscle. This deeper undermining at the middle 8 cm of the subnuchal region is probably one of the most critical parts of the operation, aside from the occipital artery ligation. If I see fat in the area below the mid-nuchal line, I immediately get my scissors in a downward direction. To always keep the scissors at a proper angle, either stand when performing the procedure or sit with the scissor-holding elbow in the air. It is during this part of the operation that I remember my childhood piano teacher reiterating, "Keep your elbows up!"

As with the circumferential, there are two extremely important forms of retraction taking place: (a) A suction retractor is used to push the undersurface of the flap in an upward direction. (b) The assistants coordinate to give optimum visualization—one pulls the hair upward with two hands at the point that I am undermining, and the other holds the head down and gently elevates the flap edge.

These two activities are, without doubt, the most crucial for performing this procedure well and easily. Once the undermining is completed, I advance the flap in an anterior direction (as was done for the circumferential scalp reduction), a blood stain is made where the flap advances, and the alopecic skin at the mid-posterior area is excised. The primary difference is that instead of an average 1- to 2-cm advancement, we typically achieve 4 to 5 cm of advancement at the vertex (see Fig. 17B,C).

After completion of the posterior advancement, very thorough cauterization is performed under the flap. Is it not unusual for me to spend a good 10 to 15 minutes taking care of bleeders. Once we achieve good hemostasis, I make 1-cm incisions immediately behind the earlobes. These are made with a long-handled No. 10 Bard Parker and are carried through from the undersurface of the postauricular skin.

A Penrose drain is now taken in hand and a small divot is made in the drain, approximately 4 cm from the end. The other end of the drain is then grabbed with a hemostat, placed under the flap, and pushed through the postauricular stab incision. The small divot is made to rest immediately behind the skin so that blood and serum can exit from the postauricular skin. Once this position is achieved, the drain is sutured

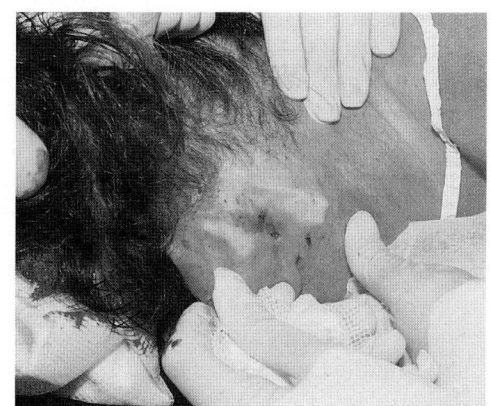
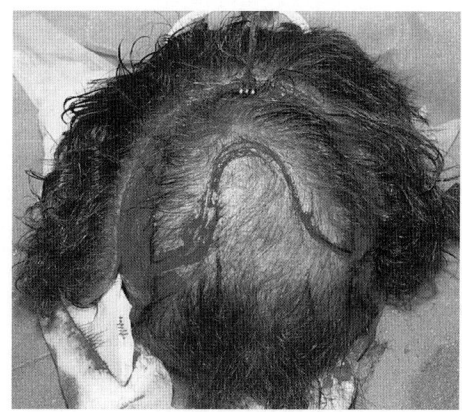
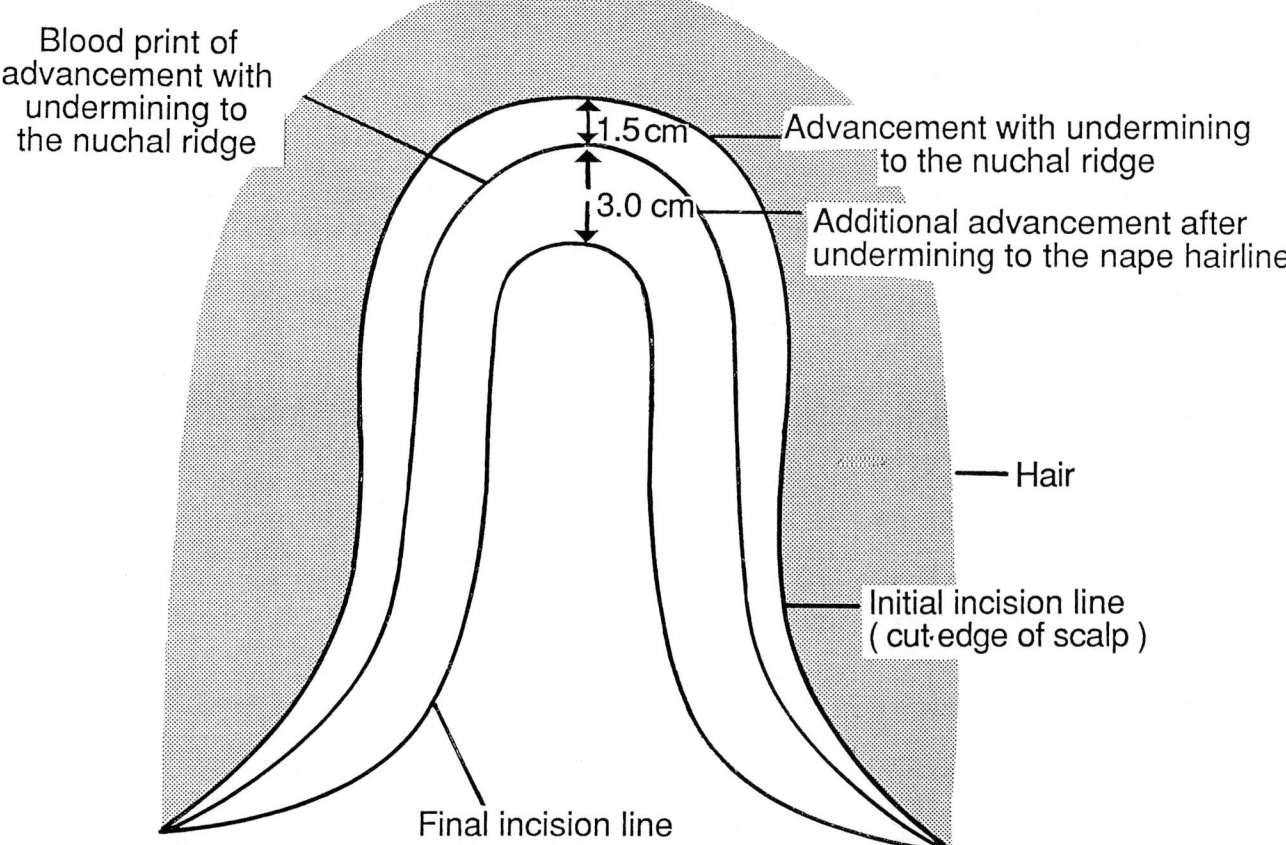

FIG. 17. A: Subcutaneous tunnels made in the postauricular area are the first areas to be undermined below the nuchal line when performing scalp-lifting. **B:** A typical advancement into the vertex with the bilateral occipitoparietal scalp-lift. **C:** The difference between the advancements of scalp-lifting and circumferential scalp reduction. Notice the much greater elevation into the vertex with scalp-lifting.

into place with a 4-0 chromic suture. The same protocol is performed on the opposite side.

Once the drains are in place, another careful cauterization is performed. After it is decided that the flap is indeed blood free, a topical thrombin–marcaine solution is administered under the flap. The topical thrombin helps with clotting and the marcaine with prolonging the anesthesia effect.

From here on, everything is done exactly as in the previous section for the circumferential scalp reduction. The primary difference is that there will be a much greater advancement into the temporal recession and parietal area (see Fig. 4). Another difference is the circumferential dressing that is applied. There are two gynecologic pads placed horizontally over the nape area and forehead, there are two stacks of gauze pads over each posterior drain site, and there is a 6-inch Ace bandage wrapped firmly around these. After this initial part of the dressing is completed, the routine circumferential dressing of gynecologic pads and cling is applied over the Ace bandage. This combination of applications affords more pressure over the nape area and also helps blood to be siphoned from the drain sites on the stacks of gauze pads.

The Bitemporal Scalp-Lift

Because the bitemporal scalp-lift is a technique that sprang from the bilateral occipitoparietal scalp-lift, and because it is so different in its configuration, I will take the reader through each important step. It must be reiterated that this operation can be used either as a closure procedure after the bilateral occipitoparietal scalp-lift or as a one-step procedure for an individual who has class V baldness. In regard to the latter, however, it is important that the patient is not going to progress much further at the vertex. Because of this, I usually perform the one-step approach only on patients over 40 years of age who have an extremely stable delineation after hair wetting.

The presedation is performed the same as the bilateral occipitoparietal scalp-lift. When scribing this procedure, I first use Doppler ultrasonography to identify the base of the superficial temporal arteries. These vessels will almost always be at the same vertical level as the posterior rim of the beard. A line is then drawn 1 cm anterior to the base of the temporal artery and is extended upward to permeate along the donor dominant fringe up to the vertex. At this point I stop. I then do the same thing on the other side of the patient's head. Once these two lines are accomplished, I draw a line sagittally right down the middle of the two lines that were previously drawn. When this middle line reaches approximately 1 cm from the mid-posterior donor dominant scalp, I begin to veer at a 45-degree angle into the donor dominant hair. Once I hit the donor fringe, I usually continue this line an additional 4 cm at the same 45-degree angle. After this middle line is completed, it is just a matter of continuing the outer lines into the donor scalp to meet the posterior endpoint of the middle line. On average, one outer line will be at a 60-degree angle and the other at a 30-degree angle (see Fig. 13).

After the lines are completed, the patient's presedation has taken effect and we now take the patient in for the appropriate intravenous anesthesia. Incision line 1 is usually the first incision of this procedure, which I usually begin at the left mid sideburn, anterior to the temporal vessel. I swing this incision around the parietal area (see Fig. 14) and then follow the prescribed line on that side into the donor dominant scalp, usually at a 30-degree angle. Once this incision is completed, I undermine down to the occipitalis muscle on the patient's left side. Then I advance the flap and see where I can reach medially and anteriorly. *It is at this point in the operation that an extremely important precept becomes evident: The more one advances medially, the less one advances laterally, and vice versa.* This concept is true for all scalp-reduction procedures, but it plays out most importantly with the bitemporal scalp-lift, the bitemporal scalp reduction and the modified bitemporal scalp-lift.

Once the flap is advanced, I push the flap down and make a blood print. If I can make it to 40% of the distance to the predrawn incision line 2, I can go ahead and make that new incision. If I am not sure, I usually undermine all the way down to the hairline of the nape on the same side. Once I do this additional undermining, and if there is no doubt as to where the flap will be advanced, incision line 2 is made!

Incision line 3 is the exact opposite of incision line 2. I make this incision from the midline all the way down to the patient's right mid sideburn (anterior to the temporal vessel). I then take a Lahey clamp and grab some of the alopecic skin at the midline and begin sharp dissection with a No. 10 Bard Parker blade. I continue this dissection down the mid-parietal area and I do it with the help of my two assistants holding skin hooks for additional retraction. Once I get to this point, my assistants and I undermine the rest of the scalp all the way down to the hairline of the nape and around the posterior rim of the ears. This dissection is done exactly the way that I described it in the previous sections.

After completing the dissection, I staple incision line 1 to incision line 2, and I usually do this with the flap stretched as medial as possible. I then take a small D'Assumpcao clamp at this point and hook it onto the area of incision line 3. It is at this point that I try to reach the anterior portion of the scribed incision line 4 with my D'Assumpcao clamp. As far as I can reach with the small clamp is where I will push down and have one of my assistants hold the clamp in position. I subsequently take a larger D'Assumpcao clamp and place the instrument on incision line 1 at the parietal area. This larger clamp is then extended across the entire length of the midline alopecia toward the parietal aspect of the proposed incision line 4 (Fig. 18). It is pushed down until three small marks are imprinted onto the scalp. The same procedure is repeated at one or two other points along the parietal area.

The anterior small clamp is now released by the assistant, and the small marks imprinted onto the scalp are exposed by washing with saline solution. These marks are now connected by a scribe and will constitute incision line 4. If the D'Assumpcao clamps were able to hit the proposed incision 4, that is where the incision will be made. However, if the clamps end up short, the incision line must be made at that point, which will leave an elliptical area of alopecia remaining on the top of the patient's head (see Fig. 18). This area, of course, will be removed at a future surgery with a small midline scalp reduction.

Once incision line 4 is completed, the temporary staples are removed and thorough cauterization of the undersurface is performed, the posterior drains are placed, and the topical thrombin–marcaine solution is administered under the flap. The flap edges must now be brought together. The first area of approximation is at the frontotemporal area on the side where the flap veers into the donor dominant scalp. This is brought together with a galeal 0-PDS II figure-of-eight suture. The opposite side is then done in the same fashion. After these two initial sutures are placed, a deep figure-of-eight suture at the vertex is performed. This suture is placed at the

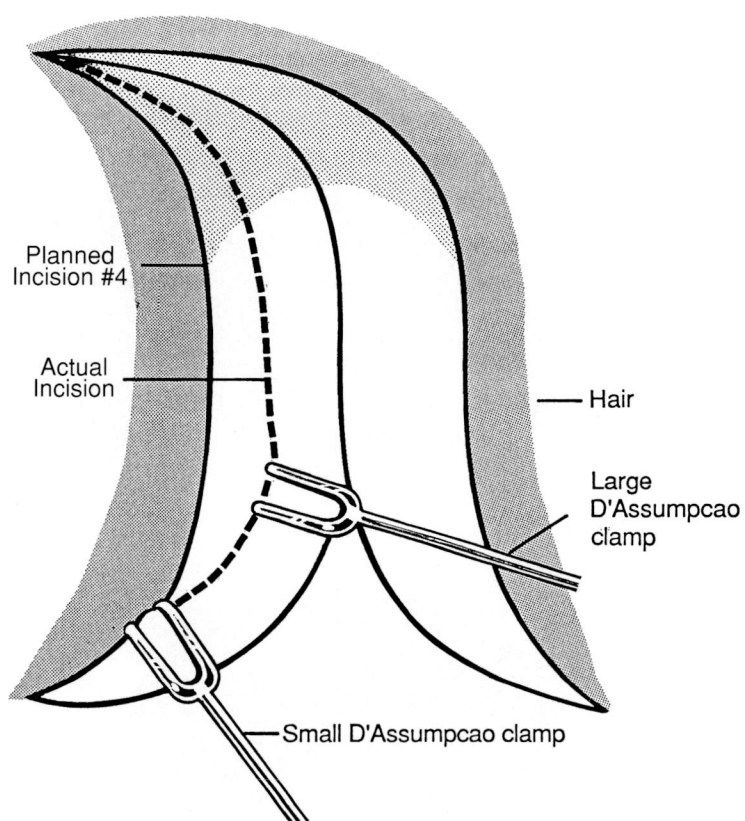

FIG. 18. D'Assumpcao clamps are used to determine where incision line 4 will be. A small one is used to hook incision line 3 to incision line 4. A large one is used to hook incision line 1 to incision line 4. If the predetermined line 4 cannot be reached, a new one must be made based on the tiny point-incisions created by the D'Assumpcao clamps.

point where the flap edges meet at the top of the head; I refer to this point as the Three Rivers (in commemoration of the Allegheny, Ohio, and Monongahela Rivers flowing into the Pittsburgh area). When this suture is completed, the three keystone sutures are in place. All other deep sutures are inserted approximately 2 cm apart and are done along the entire length of the incisions. The skin is then brought together with a combination of clear 4-0 PDS II and 5-0 PDS II. Upon completion of suturing, the K-Y Jelly and circumferential dressing is done exactly as described in the previous section.

Bitemporal Scalp Reduction

As previously stated, the bitemporal scalp reduction is basically a miniature version of the bitemporal scalp-lift with undermining stopping at the nuchal ridge medially and proceeding a little deep to the nuchal ridge laterally. This procedure is almost always used as a closure after the bilateral scalp-lift instead of a full bitemporal scalp-lift for three reasons: (a) The remaining horizontal distance of alopecic skin is usually narrow enough that it does not require that deep undermining be performed. (b) The nape hair thins out a fair amount during the first bilateral occipitoparietal scalp-lift—a second will only further exacerbate the problem if the patient's hair is already thin. (c) The temporal recessions have already been advanced into with the bilateral occipitoparietal scalp-lift. Another anterior advancement, in most cases, makes the hairline "ape-like." The primarily medial vectors of the bitemporal scalp reduction prevents this from occurring (Fig. 19).

On the other hand, if the patient has a very wide area remaining after the first bilateral occipitoparietal scalp-lift and the nape hair is still maintaining good density, I will go ahead and perform a full bitemporal scalp-lift for the complete elimination of the patient's alopecia.

Modified Bitemporal Scalp-Lift

The modified bitemporal scalp-lift is performed in the same manner as the bitemporal scalp-lift, except that the vectors are in a more anterior direction (Fig. 20). This procedure is rarely performed, primarily because it was developed for the patient with temporal recessions in combination with excellent prospects for not losing his or her hair at the vertex of the head. Because of these well-defined criteria, the only patients who really qualify, in most instances, are those patients over the age of 40 with no sign of vertex thinning after hair wetting. Although the criteria are very well defined and few patients qualify, when I do come across the proper patient, the results can be extremely dramatic (Fig. 21).

The primary difference between the modified bitemporal scalp-lift and the conventional bitemporal scalp-lift is that only approximately 1 to 2 cm is removed at the midline with the modified, as compared to 6 to 8 cm with the conventional bitemporal lift. The other difference is that the temporal hair is advanced approximately 5 cm into the temporal recessions

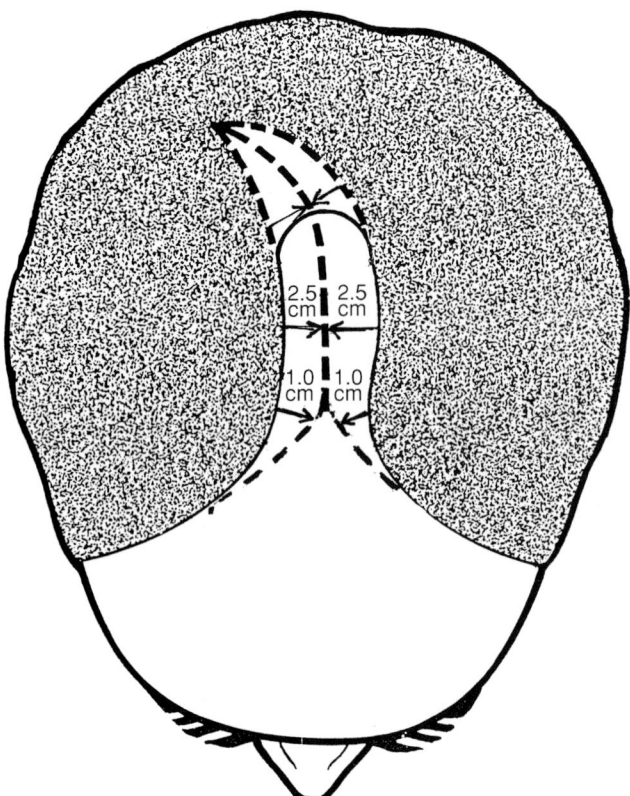

FIG. 19. The more medial and less anterior vectors of the bitemporal scalp reduction when compared to the bitemporal scalp-lift. Notice that less is removed at the center of the excision, and barely any is removed anteriorly. This finding occurs because there is little undermining below the nuchal ridge.

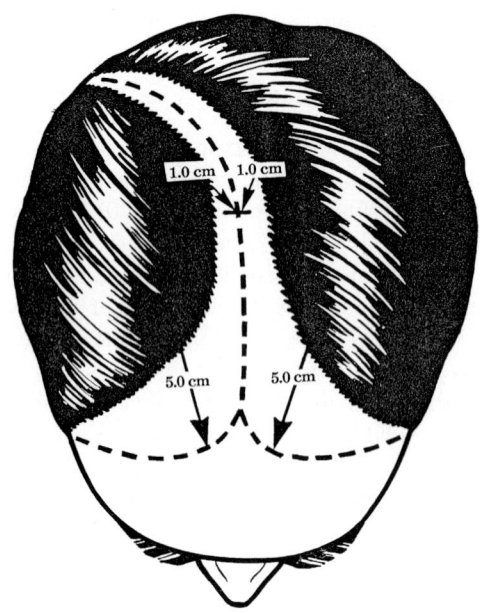

FIG. 20. The more anterior and less medial vectors of the modified bitemporal scalp-lift when compared to the bitemporal scalp-lift.

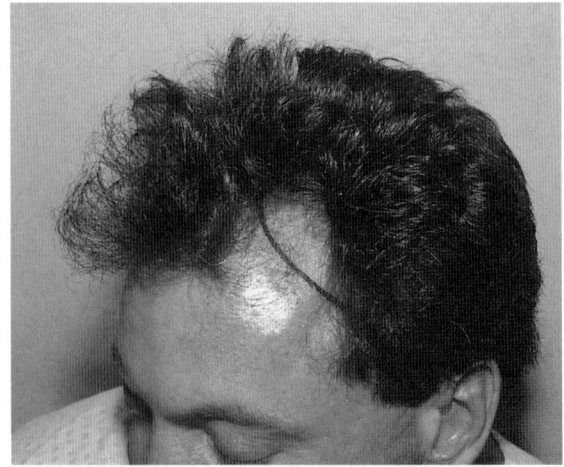

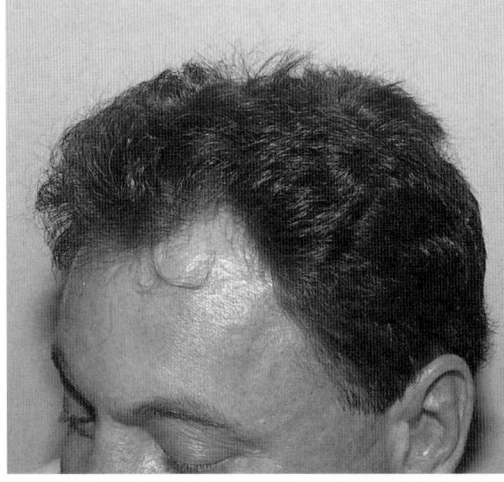

FIG. 21. Patient (about 40 years old) with bitemporal recessions and no evidence of thinning at the vertex. **A:** Immediately before a modified bitemporal scalp-lift. **B:** After the modified bitemporal scalp-lift. One procedure is all this patient needed.

with the modified, as opposed to the 2.5 cm commonly found with the conventional bitemporal scalp-lift.

These statements indicate that there is an exchange of vectors that can be manipulated in an infinite number of ways. When performing the modified bitemporal lift, the bitemporal lift, and the bitemporal scalp reduction, I always have the flexibility of advancing more medially in exchange for losing some on the anterior advancement. On the other hand, if I want to achieve more anterior advancement, I can do that, but at a price—I lose the amount of alopecia that I can remove at the midline. These relationships are crucial to learn if one wants to perform these procedures with finesse and precision.

The Frontoparietal Advancement Flap

The frontoparietal advancement flap evolved as a method to develop the frontal hairline without getting into the technique of hair transplantation. Before the days of fine mini- and micrografting, it was not uncommon for patients to totally reject the idea of the "hair plug" being utilized on their head. It was on these patients that I would sometimes perform the frontoparietal advancement flap.

This procedure is always performed after a bitemporal scalp-lift or scalp reduction. Approximately 2½ months after the bitemporal procedure, a delay must be performed (Fig. 22A). This movement must be carried through, because to get the anterior movement toward the new hairline, the superficial artery must be divided. The incision for the delay must therefore follow the midline scar of the bitemporal procedure, and then veer toward the top of the ear, once the incision hits the frontoparietal temporal recession. It is with this downward diagonal incision toward the ear that the posterior branch of the superficial temporal artery will be severed.

Once the diagonal incision is completed, the flap is undermined approximately 8 cm from the distal tip. The flap is then laid back down and sutured into place. Two weeks later, the frontoparietal flap is performed, with the undermining being the same as the lateral Marzola lift. Once the first one is performed (see Fig. 22B), the second is typically done 3

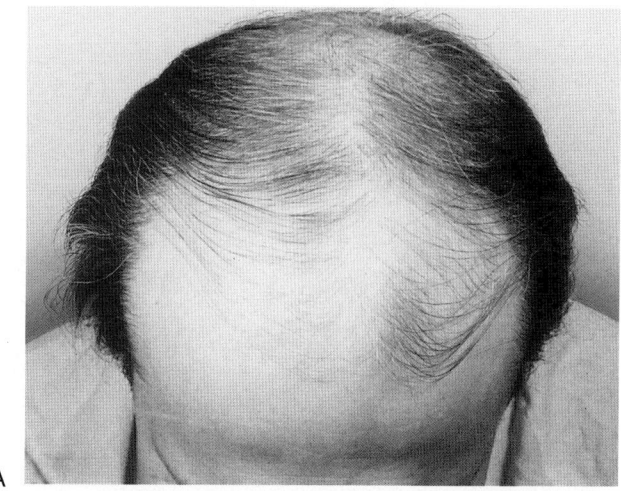

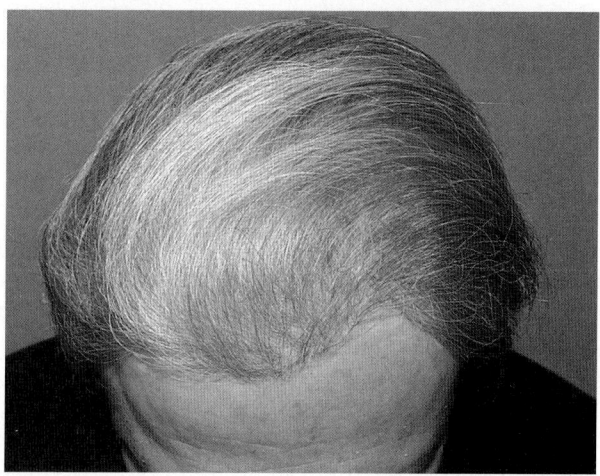

FIG. 23. A: Patient with extensive baldness prior to surgery. **B:** Same patient after a bilateral occipitoparietal scalp-lift, a bitemporal scalp-lift, and two frontoparietal advancement flaps.

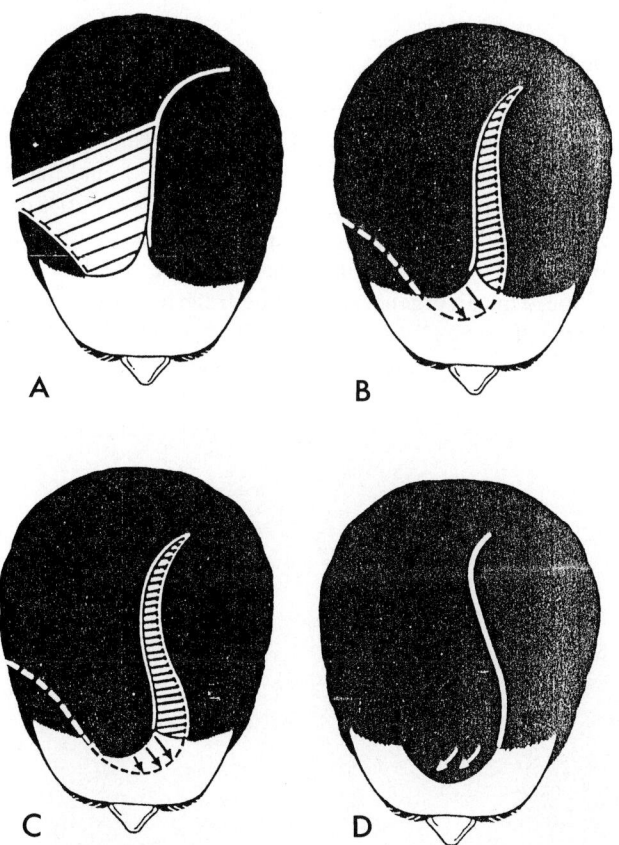

FIG. 22. A: The delay procedure for the frontoparietal flap. Note how the posterior branch of the superficial temporal artery will be cut during the incision and elevation of the delay. **B:** The first frontoparietal flap advances in a primarily anterior direction. **C:** The second frontoparietal flap. **D:** After two, the hairline flows downward and to the side.

months afterward (see Fig. 22C,D). It is after this second one that the desired hairline is usually achieved (Fig. 23).

One area of concern with this procedure is the elevation of the periauricular hairline that can occur when consecutive procedures are performed. This sequela can occur because each procedure involves the undermining of postauricular skin, which in turn causes a stretching of that region. It is not hard to imagine that after a bilateral occipitoparietal scalp-lift, followed by a bitemporal scalp reduction, followed by two frontoparietal advancement flaps, the periauricular hairline on the side of the frontoparietal advancement flaps could get rather high. This is one reason that I usually do not perform this technique on patients with high periauricular hairlines at the initial consultation.

Preauricular Flap

If the hairline is becoming a significant problem after the first frontoparietal advancement flap, I will sometimes perform a preauricular flap from the opposite side. Typically,

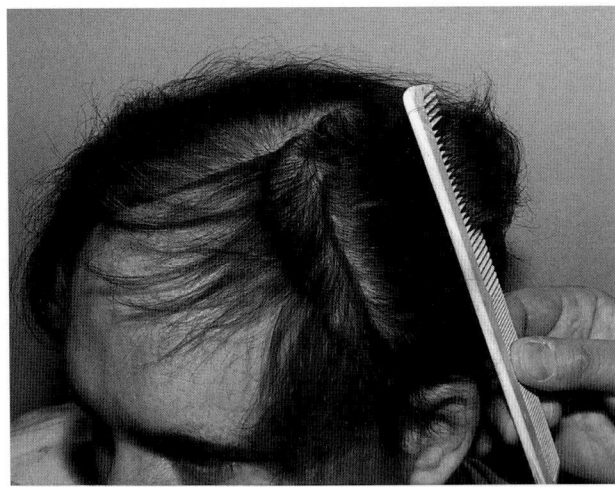

FIG. 24. The preauricular flap is usually 2.5 cm at its base and extends down to the base of the ear. Every attempt is made to spare the superficial temporal artery. There is also a small expander under the scalp just posterior to the designed flap. This is usually placed 2 to 3 months before the transposition so that minimal to no tension will be present at the preauricular incision line.

however, I will insert a very small tissue expander under the parietal scalp on the side that the flap is going to be performed. This insertion is usually done 2 to 3 months before the actual flap operation, and it is done to ensure a loose closure at the temporal area.

The base of this flap is typically 2.5 cm and extends all the way down the mid sideburn. As can be seen from Figure 24, the vertical anterior scar from the scalp-lift is used as the anterior edge of the flap. The expander allows enough laxity that the original scar can be excised and the new incision closed under minimal to no tension. When designing this flap, I like to round the distal tip and, if I can, avoid the superficial temporal artery.

The actual procedure is a simple transposition flap (Fig. 25). I do excise away the recipient area, but I make certain to make this opening a little smaller than the size of the flap. I use deep 0-PDS II sutures for the galeal layer at the vertical incision preauricularly, and I use only fine 5-0 prolene sutures cutaneously for the flap itself. I also use the fine 5-0 prolene sutures for the cutaneous layer of the vertical scar.

Typically, frontoparietal advancement flaps and preauricular flaps need additional micrografting anterior to the frontal scar. This can entail two to three sessions, and it is one of the reasons that I use flaps infrequently for creation of the hairline. It is my present belief that if you are going to need two to three grafting sessions anyway, why not just graft the entire frontal zone and save the patient the time and expense of the flap surgery?

COMPLICATIONS OF SCALP REDUCTION AND SCALP-LIFTING

When one speaks of the typical complications from any surgery (e.g., infection, necrosis, fistula), the techniques in this chapter are extremely safe. It is in the area of the natural sequelae of these procedures where one can get into problems. Each one will now be carefully addressed.

Slot Formation

All midline procedures will develop a severe slot down the back of the head (see Fig. 6). This phenomenon was studied by Nordstrom in the early 1980s, and he found that the length of the bald area elongates by approximately 10% of its original length with each procedure (9). Furthermore, a more problematic divergence of the hair becomes evident at the midline. This divergence, sometimes referred to as "the parting of the Red Sea," occurs because hair normally grows perpendicular to the midline along the sides of the head. When

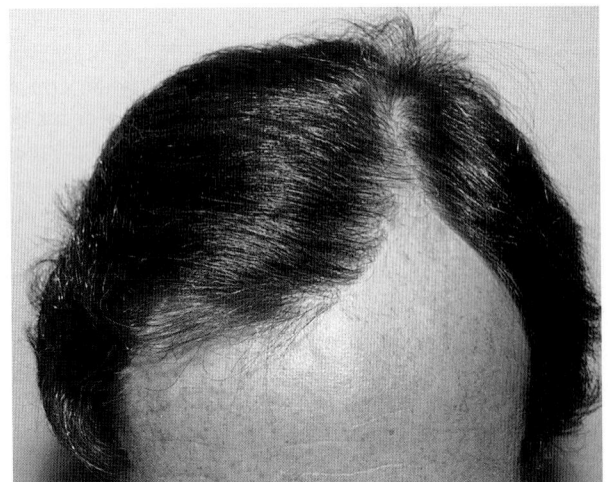
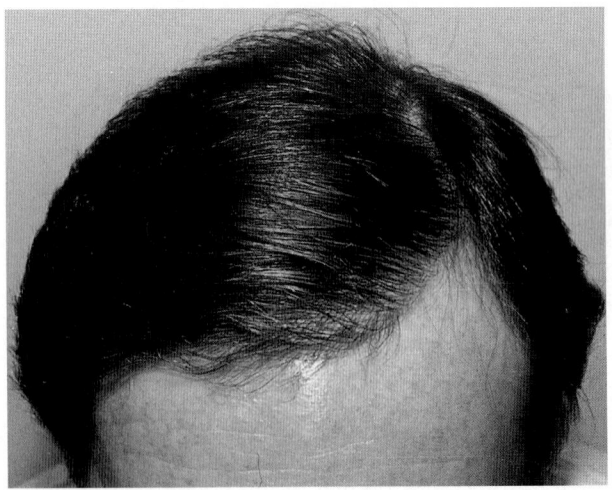

FIG. 25. A: Patient after a frontoparietal advancement. It was noticed that this patient's periauricular hairline was elevating too much after three consecutive surgeries. It was therefore decided to proceed with a preauricular flap from the opposite side. **B:** Same patient after the preauricular was transposed into place.

this perpendicular hair is pulled toward the midline (a place where hair normally grows in a straight-forward direction) an unsightly, unnatural appearance results.

Of all of the procedures, midline scalp reduction creates the worst amount of slot formation and divergence. Scalp-lifting produces the least amount because the scalp is elevated an average of 4.5 cm into the vertex and because the inferior aspect of the bitemporal procedures tails off into the donor dominant scalp. Both, however, are plagued by this problem. Today, transposition flap techniques make this difficulty manageable and will be discussed later in this chapter.

Numbness

Temporary anesthesia at the vertex is a problem that is innate with all hair restoration procedures. This occurs secondary to division of either the main trunks or branches of the occipital and lesser occipital nerves. Over time, this numbness improves by a physiologic process called the adoption phenomenon of nerve regeneration, in which new nerve endings develop from the peripheral nerves that have not been violated. These nerve endings usually develop from the nodes of Ranvier and the various synapses of these peripheral intact nerves.

Of all of the scalp reduction procedures, scalp-lifting produces the most severe anesthesia at the vertex. In a recent survey that I sent out to 177 patients, I discovered that almost all patients had a return of sensation, although this return was usually 50% to 100% of normal. The size of the area was 0 to 2 inches in diameter at the vertex. The average time of return was approximately 12 months.

Wide Scarring

One of the most difficult problems of scalp reduction, and probably a common reason that some do not perform the procedure, is that a small percentage of patients get wide scars. I have found that the younger patient, the greater the chance of developing a wide scar. I don't know why this is so, but it can be hypothesized that younger patients have a greater amount of collagen deposition secondary to their increased metabolism.

Another reason for wide scarring can be Ehlers-Danlos syndrome or mild variants thereof. I had one patient with full-blown Ehlers-Danlos who ended up with a donor scar after hair transplantation that was literally 3 to 4 cm wide. Mild variants of that syndrome can sometimes be picked up by noticing a velvety skin, increased laxity of the skin, ability to touch the tongue to the nose, and hypermobility of the joints. These criteria, however, do not consistently correlate with poor healing.

In most patients, it is just impossible to predict the healing capability. To convey this reality, I tell patients at the consultation that there is a 1% chance that they may get a wide scar. If they happen to be in that 1% group, then the appropriate transposition flap or hair transplantation techniques will be required to help ameliorate the problem.

High Periauricular Hairline

It is essential to evaluate the periauricular hairline on all patients contemplating scalp reduction surgery, because this hairline will elevate somewhat with each procedure that is performed. If the hairline is high before the surgeries, it certainly will be in an abnormally high position after the surgeries. It is therefore important to have the patient grow his or her hair 1 to 2 inches before the surgery to hide this abnormality and to explain to them that micrografting with one- to two-haired grafts may be required in that region. This micrografting is usually done at the time of the hair-grafting to the frontal area and, in most cases, results in a beautiful reconstruction. The key to this reconstruction is to simply direct the hair *steeply* in the direction of the hair immediately superior to it.

Deepening of the Temporal Recession

The problem of deepening temporal recessions occurs with all scalp reduction procedures, except for the bilateral occipitoparietal and bitemporal scalp-lifts. All other procedures mentioned in this text will deepen the temporal recession somewhat. Because of this phenomenon, it is important to explain this sequela to the patient and to also predict this movement if hair-grafting is being performed before scalp reduction.

Infection

Although infection is considered a risk with any surgery, I have not found any scalp surgery to be highly susceptible to bacterial invasion. In more than 4000 scalp reductions over a 15-year period, I have not been able to document one single infection.

Necrosis

The most feared complication of scalp-lifting is necrosis at the nuchal ridge. As mentioned, this complication has virtually been eliminated with the addition of the vertical incision occipital artery ligation. There is, however, still a very small chance of developing this problem over the nuchal line. To date, the incidence is 0.3% with the vertical ligation procedure. In light of that fact, it is crucial to mention the possibility of necrosis in all consent forms and communications with the patient.

If the patient happens to develop a necrosis, it will almost always be over the nuchal ridge. In these cases, I have simply informed the patient to keep the area clean and not pick at the scab. Typically, the scab falls away in approximately 1 month, at which time a pinkish smooth scar remains. This scar can then be repaired by carrying through a donor harvest right over the problem area during one of the hair-grafting procedures performed subsequent to the lifts.

MAINTAINING THE NEUROVASCULAR BUNDLE

Because of the area of numbness that can occur after scalp-lifting, some patients wish to forego the procedure. In these cases, I will sometimes perform the procedure with the occipital neurovascular bundle intact. The disadvantage, however, is that the amount of advancement is significantly less.

Recently, I compared advancements with the neurovascular intact to those with the neurovascular bundle divided. I did these measurements on ten patients who were undergoing lateral scalp-lifts, chosen primarily because I normally do not ligate such patients prior to their first lateral lift. I could, therefore, perform the lateral lifts with the neurovascular bundle intact (since there was no prior division), do my measurements, and then divide the bundle and do subsequent measurements.

The way that this technique is performed is to first undermine to the occipitalis muscle and then cut the muscle horizontally where it attaches to the skull. I subsequently gently dissect adjacent to the bundle vertically with a dull Metzenbaum scissors and then get completely around it with a curved Thorek scissors.

Once the occipital neurovascular bundle is completely dissected, I take a vessel loop and place it around the bundle and bring the two ends of the loop together with a hemostat (Fig. 26). Now, when I dissect deeply to the right of the neurovascular bundle, I move the hemostat to the left. Likewise, when I dissect to the left of the neurovascular bundle, I move the hemostat and let it hang to the right. This back and forth movement of the hemostat allows me to get the visualization I need and prevents me from nicking the occipital neurovascular bundles.

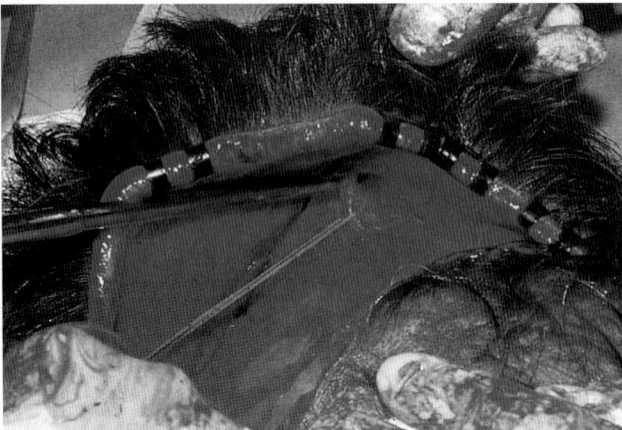

FIG. 26. The occipital neurovascular bundle has been dissected away, and there is a vessel loop around it. This technique decreases the amount of postoperative vertex hypesthesia, but it does not achieve the same amount of advancement medially and anteriorly.

In the study that I performed with these 10 patients, I measured three advancements: (a) a mid-posterior sagittal measurement, (b) a medial measurement directly above the ear, and (c) a 45-degree measurement at the widest point of the temporal recession. What I found was interesting. At all three points, there was approximately 1 cm less advancement, which would indicate approximately 2 cm less advancement at all three areas if a bilateral procedure was performed. These findings must therefore be seriously considered and discussed with the patient when contemplating this modification of the conventional scalp-lifting procedure.

ADJUNCTS TO SCALP REDUCTION SURGERY

To make scalp reduction an easier procedure, I have developed a few instruments that I believe greatly facilitate the operations. The instrument that is the most important to me is the suction retractor briefly mentioned previously. I developed this instrument with Robbins Instruments Company several years ago, primarily because I needed something that was going to keep the field clean while giving me the flap elevation and stabilization that I needed to perform the procedure quickly and accurately. Initially, I used a Poole suction cannula, but this approach caused undo pain to the extensor muscles of the forearm. To relieve this discomfort, I simply added a handle to the Poole cannula and changed a few details on the cannula, winding up with an instrument that, although very simple, changes the whole perplexity of the procedure.

The other instrument that we developed that has had a great facilitating effect on the cauterization phase of the operations is the hook retractor, also previously mentioned. This instrument was also developed with Robbins Instruments Company many years ago and has, like the suction retractor, been found to be extremely invaluable during these scalp reduction procedures. This instrument consists of a handle connected to a serrated wire frame, with a hook connected at its base. This instrument is simply hooked into the superior edge of the galea, and, once the hook has stabilized the retractor, the wire frame allows me to see the undersurface of the flap and cauterize any significant bleeders.

Finally, a scalp-stretching device that we use preoperatively has come to be an integral part of our scalp reduction procedure. It consists of a headband and two elastic bands that are crisscrossed on top of the head. When the elastic bands are stretched and attached with Velcro to the sides of the headband, a linear stretching or biologic creep occurs on the scalp. This headband is adjusted by the patient in such a way that it should pop off every 5 minutes or so. Typically, it is used for 30 minutes per day starting 30 days before the first procedure and then 30 minutes per day starting 1 month after each surgery. This latter usage prevents scar tissue under the flap from hardening, which can hinder scalp mobility during subsequent operations. By starting the stretching 1 month after the scalp reduction procedures, the scar is kept soft, allowing maximum alopecia removal.

SCALP EXTENSION IN RELATIONSHIP TO SCALP REDUCTION

Scalp extension is another adjunct to scalp reduction surgery and entails the linear, two-dimensional, stretching of the scalp. This can be done in several ways: (a) the scalp stretching device just described, (b) manual stretching, (c) the Sure-Closure system developed by Dr. Hirshowitz, and (d) silicone sheeting stretched beyond its resting state.

Silicone sheeting stretched beyond its resting state is what most hair restoration surgeons think about when hearing the word *scalp extension*. There are two basic types of extenders being utilized: (a) the Frechet extender and (b) the Brandy custom-made extender. I use the latter system. This extender is made by taking a 0.05-inch-thick sheet of plain silicone sheeting and cutting away an extender the size that is desired, plus 2 cm. For example, if a 3-cm length is desired for the stretchable section of the extender, the silicone sheet should be cut to 5 cm by 5 cm.

After the plain silicone sheet is cut, two 1-cm by 5-cm sheets of Dacron-reinforced silicone sheeting are cut away. These are then glued to the distal ends of the plain silicone sheet (Fig. 27A). This special glue, which can be obtained from the manufacturers of the sheeting (Pillar Surgical, Allied Biomedical Corporation, Applied Biomaterials Technology Corporation), can be cured overnight by letting it sit in room air, or it can be placed into an autoclave, which will cure the silicone glue in 20 minutes. Once the glue is cured, the special hook plates that I developed with Applied Biomaterials Technology Corporation are crimped onto the Dacron-reinforced endpieces (see Fig. 27A). The extender is now ready to go.

The only time that I use an extender is with a circumferential scalp reduction. I do not use it with scalp-lifting because the circulation is more tenuous and necrosis might ensue. The point in the procedure that I insert the extender is after total alopecia excision and the temporal deep galeal sutures are placed. Then, I simply release the temporary suture or staple at the mid-posterior end of the U-shape and undermine the central alopecic area up to the position of the anterior sutures. This undermining gives incredible exposure and allows for the simple insertion of both a circumferential extender posteriorly and a rectangular one anteriorly (see Fig. 27B). These are simply inserted by pushing the hookplates under the scalp flap edges with the superior ends of two Bard Parker blade handles. Once these are in place, the alopecic flap is laid atop the extenders and the skin is closed with the appropriate suture.

Equation for Predicting Amount of Extension

Understanding scalp extension is not difficult, if one simply remembers that the scalp can stretch only as far as the material is stretched beyond its resting length. To help explain this concept, I developed an equation, $L - E = I$, where L is the length that the extender is stretched beyond its resting length, E is the expected removal from the second scalp reduction based on the first reduction with concomitant preoperative massaging, and I is the improved amount of alopecia removal from extension use.

Let us put this equation into action so that the principles are better understood: A patient comes into the office with 12 cm of alopecic width on the top of his or her head, and we perform a circumferential scalp reduction, removing 2 cm from each parietal area. In essence, we have removed 4 cm of alopecic width. After the alopecia is removed, we undermine the central remaining baldness and insert our rectangular extenders and stretch it 6 cm from the resting state. How much more alopecic excision will we achieve than if we did not use the extender? Using the equation, 6 cm (L) − 4 cm (E) = 2 cm (I), and the improved amount of alopecia re-

 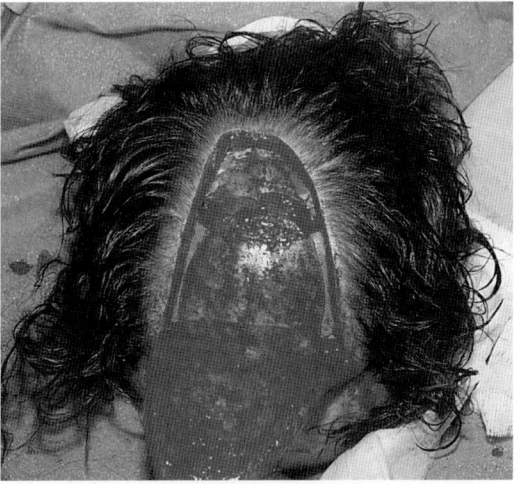

FIG. 27. A: Two small Dacron-reinforced sheets are glued to a larger sheet of plain silastic with a special silicone glue. Hook plates are pushed onto the distal Dacron ends. These plates can then be hooked under the scalp with the use of the blunt ends of blade handles. **B:** A rectangular and circumferential extender in place during a circumferential scalp reduction. Notice the incredible visibility that the circumferential scalp reduction affords.

moval is 2 cm with the extender. The other important point is that this extension is accomplished in 4 weeks, which makes the improvement even more dramatic.

Determining Extender Length

To be able to use the previous equation, one must know how to determine the resting length of the extender. First, one must understand that the resting length is the distance between the two Dacron-reinforced portions of the extender, that is, the entire length minus 2 cm, as each Dacron-reinforced portion is 1 cm in width.

The equation to determine the necessary width for a given procedure is: $W - D = R$, where W is the width of the alopecia remaining after the first scalp reduction, D is the desired amount of alopecia removal during the next surgery, and R is the resting length of the extender.

Again, let us put this equation into practice so that we can better understand it. Let us take a patient with 12 cm of alopecic width on whom we just performed a circumferential scalp reduction and removed 3 cm of total width. The remaining width will thus be 9 cm (12 cm − 3 cm = 9 cm). Therefore, W = 9 cm. If we would like to remove 5 cm during the next procedure, we must stretch the silastic sheeting 5 cm beyond its resting state. Since the desired amount of alopecia removal is 5 cm, D = 5 cm. Now all we need to do is plug in the numbers to the equation and the resting length is found to be 9 cm − 5 cm = 4 cm. Thus, the distance between the Dacron-reinforced portions of the extender should be 4 cm in length.

If one is performing "inside-out" procedures, the scalp extension technique described must be done, because scalp extension most definitely eliminates the stretch-back problem. Under these conditions, most class VI, extensively bald patients should be able to be closed in three procedures if average laxity exists. If one performs "outside-in" scalp reductions, scalp extension *primarily* helps in expediting the procedures (1-month spacing instead of 3 months). It will also improve alopecia removal in those patients with extremely tight scalps.

TRANSPOSITION FLAPS FOR THE CORRECTION OF SLOTS

As we have discussed, alopecia-reducing surgery will almost always cause slot formation and divergence of the hair at the midline. It can also be generalized that the more intense the hair loss, the more intense the problem postoperatively.

To deal with this difficulty, Dr. Patrick Frechet developed a triple hair-bearing flap that takes the hair from its diverging position and converts it to a more normal conformation (Fig. 28). I performed this technique on many patients and found it to be exceptional for some patients, but for others I found some problems: (a) The narrow flaps with pointed tips were prone to necrosis. (b) Hair transplantation could not be performed simultaneously because too much scalp laxity was being taken up from too many different directions. (c) It was difficult to judge the appropriate widths of the flaps based on the scalp laxity that was being estimated. (d) The technique was rather difficult. (e) Scarring was at times apparent.

In an attempt to simplify and improve the procedure, I converted the three narrow flaps into one large wide flap. I also made the distal tip round, instead of pointed, and kept the width the same along the entire length of the flap. This transposition flap is usually 3 cm wide by 7 cm long when performed the first time. It is 3 cm wide by 8 cm long if per-

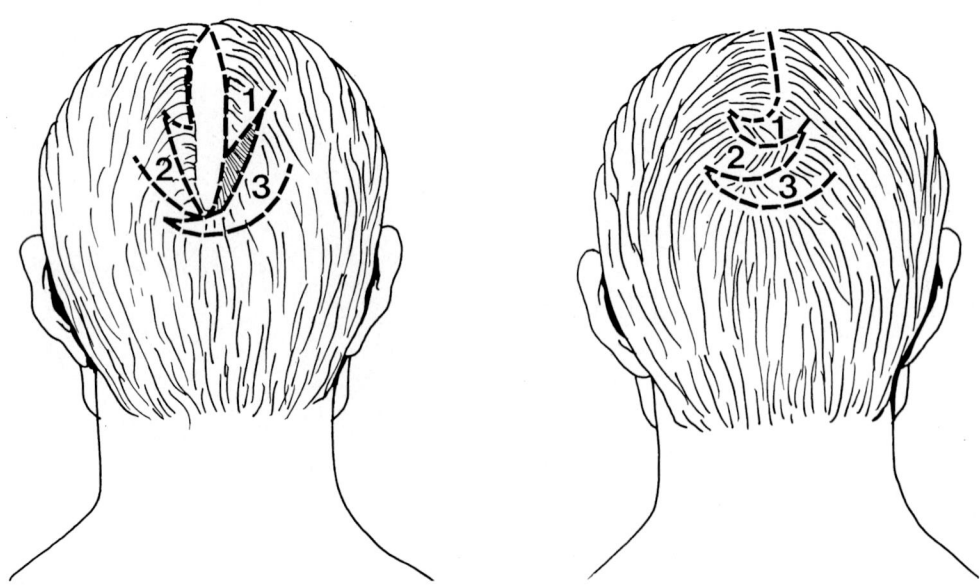

FIG. 28. The triple flap technique of Frechet. Notice the pointed tips, which make these flaps prone to necrosis.

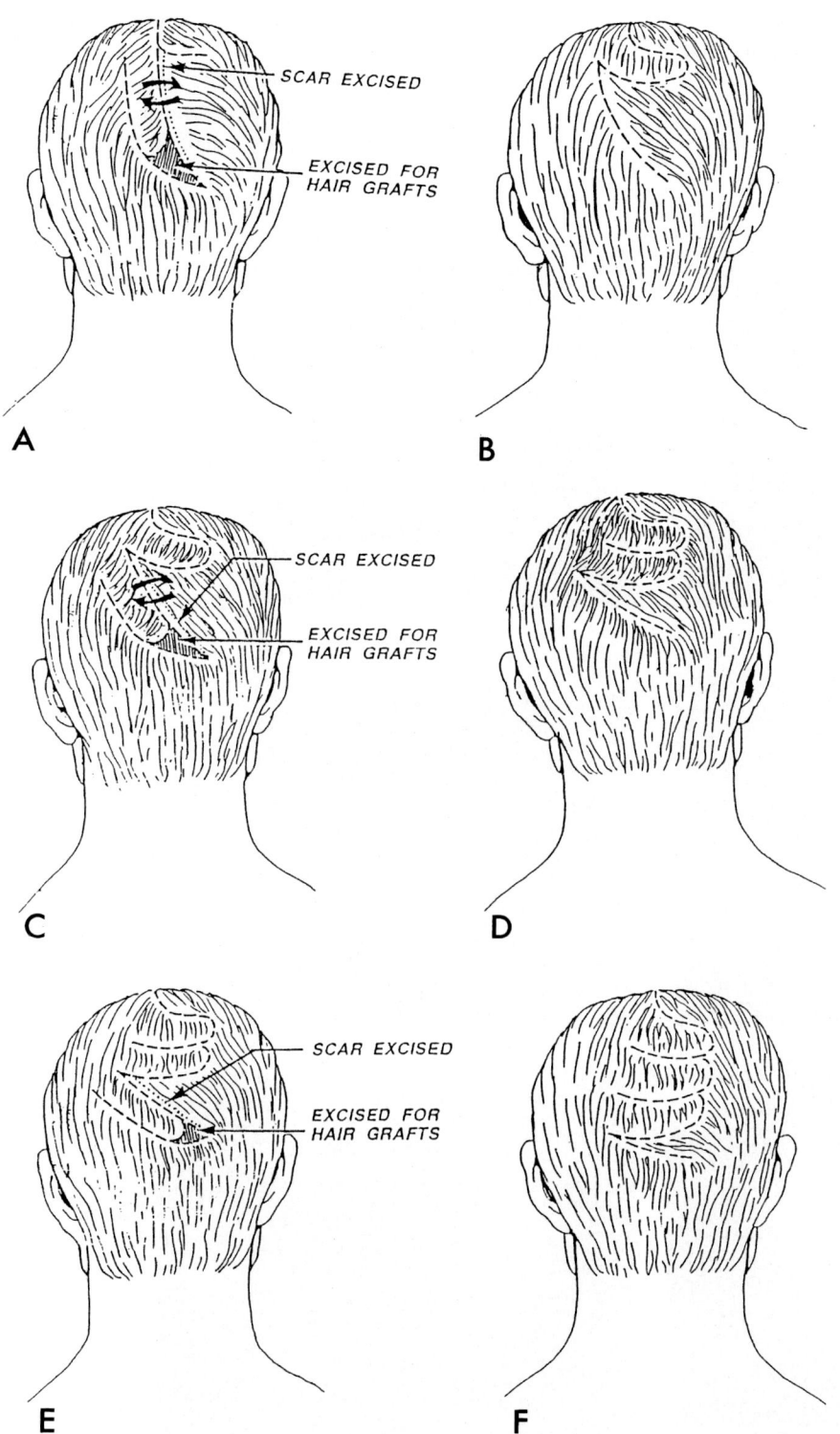

FIG. 29. A: The first flap is usually 3.0 cm by 7.0 cm and is transposed into position. Hair grafts are taken from the area distal to the flap and from the area that the flap is transposed into. **B:** The hair is oriented in a much more normal direction after this first flap. **C:** If it is believed that another flap is needed, a second is done under the first. This flap is usually 3.0 cm by 8.0 cm. **D:** The first and second flaps in place. **E:** If a third is needed, it is performed exactly as the first two, except that the length is usually 9.0 cm. **F:** All three flaps in place.

formed under the first flap, and 3 cm wide by 9 cm long if performed under the second flap.

The first flap is usually turned 1 cm posterior from the highest point on the head. It is rotated at this point to take advantage of the shingling effect that can be accomplished on the descending part of the head. The hair grafts are taken from the hair at the distal part of the flap and the area that the flap is being turned into (Fig. 29A,B). This negates the need to perform a donor harvest below the transposition flap.

If, after the first flap, I believe that the vertical scar, which has been shifted laterally and inferiorly, is still a little noticeable, a second flap is performed under the first (see Fig. 29C,D). As stated previously, this flap is somewhat longer than the former and is performed under the first one. The prior vertical scar is excised and the vertical component is moved further inferiorly and laterally. If a third is needed, the same sequence is repeated (see Fig. 29E,F).

The key to this procedure is that the scars that are in a cosmetically noticeable position usually heal imperceptibly (Fig. 30), because there is absolutely no tension in the area that the flap is rotated into. In fact, there is usually compression (negative tension) in the area of the flap's new home. This highly desirable surgical environment makes beveling techniques highly effective at getting hair to grow through

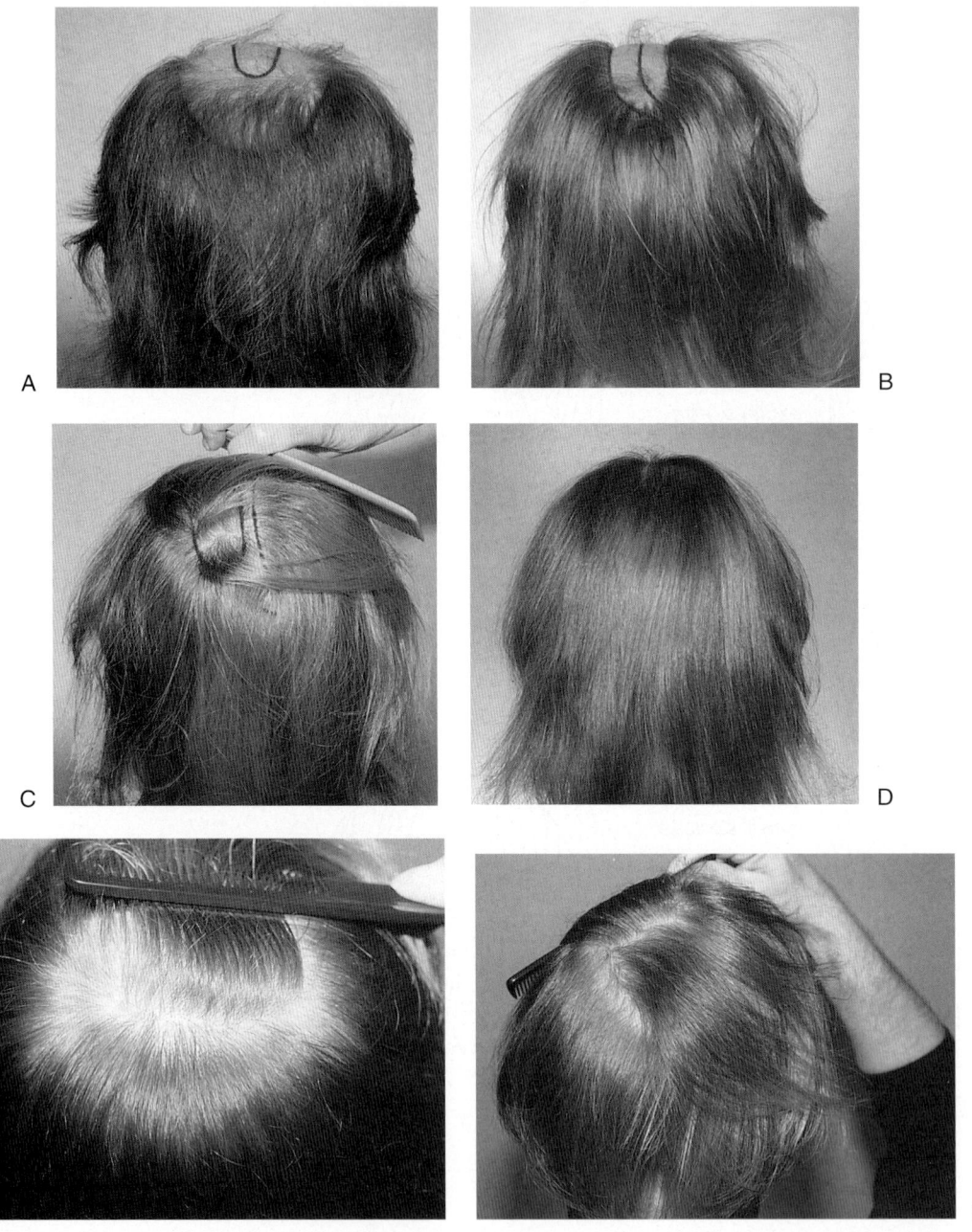

FIG. 30. A: Patient with an extensive baldness immediately before a bilateral occipitoparietal scalp-lift. **B:** After the bilateral occipitoparietal scalp-lift and immediately before a bitemporal scalp reduction. **C:** After the bitemporal scalp reduction, there is an element of divergence and slot formation. The first transposition flap is scribed immediately before the surgery. **D:** With the first flap in place, the patient's result is dramatically improved. **E:** When observing the most superior scar of the transposition flap, one notes that hair is growing through the scar. This occurs almost routinely because of the compression (negative tension) that occurs in this region and the beveling technique utilized. **F:** The inferior incision, which takes up almost all of the tension, can widen at times during the scarring process, but it is in an inferolateral position. This allows easy camouflage, especially after two of these flaps are performed.

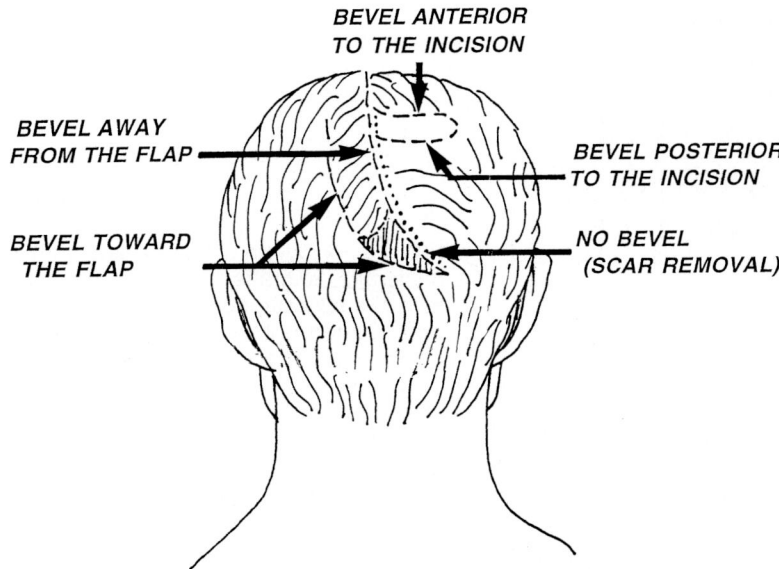

FIG. 31. The critical bevels that are needed to accomplish consistently good results.

the scar tissue (Fig. 31). The vertical component is where all of the tension exists with this technique and thus wider scars can occur in this area. But this scar should be extremely well hidden after one or two of these wide transposition flaps (see Fig. 30D).

INTEGRATION OF MINI- AND MICROGRAFTING

Hair grafting to the frontal area is usually performed simultaneously with the transposition flap and is carried through immediately anterior to the transposition flap. The technique that I use is a systematic three-step approach that has been documented in the *Journal of Dermatologic Surgery* (8). Usually, the first session consists of approximately 100 six- to eight-hair grafts (Fig. 32), 120 three- to four-hair grafts and 75 one- to two-hair grafts. Each session thereafter is performed with the same approximate number of grafts based on the three-step systems (Fig. 33).

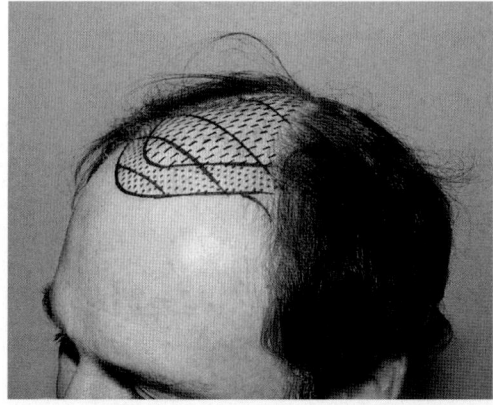

FIG. 32. Stencil marks in place. Note the graduation from six- to eight-hair grafts, to three- to four-hair grafts, to one- to two-hair grafts.

The two stencils that I use to develop the fully staggered pattern consist primarily of (a) 20 slit openings per square inch, 6 mm apart, for six- to eight-hair grafts (Fig. 34A) and (b) 40 hole openings per square inch, 6 mm apart, for three- to four-hair grafts (see Fig. 34B). Typically, there is an 8-square-inch area in the frontal area that needs hair grafting. Usually, the most anterior area, which is 6 inches long and ½ inch wide, is grafted with the three- to four-hair grafts. Therefore, the 40-grafts-per-square-inch stencil is utilized. The length is 6 inches, the width is ½ inch; therefore, the area is 3 square inches. Three square inches times 40 grafts per square inch equals 120 three- to four-hair grafts at the frontal area.

The remaining area is therefore 5 square inches. Since six- to eight-hair grafts are used in this remaining area for increased volume, the other stencil is utilized. Five square inches times 20 slits per square inch equals 100 six- to eight-hair grafts. The remaining area at the most anterior edge is done randomly with one- to two-hair grafts.

The blades that I now use for each graft are No. 15 Bard Parkers for the six- to eight-hair grafts; Swann Morton No. 91s for the three- to four-hair grafts; and Swann Morton No. 90s for the one- to two-hair grafts. These blades stay sharp through the entire array of incisions and typically do not need to be changed during a single procedure.

During the following procedure, the second transposition flap is performed if needed and the donor material is taken from the end of the flap. If a transposition is not being performed, a conventional donor harvest is done at the most inferior point where good hair is available. These grafts are performed 2 mm to the right of the first growing set of hair grafts. To carry this through efficaciously and expeditiously, I make a small mark with a Pilot marker over each growing graft. I then make the appropriate incision 2 mm to the right of each marking.

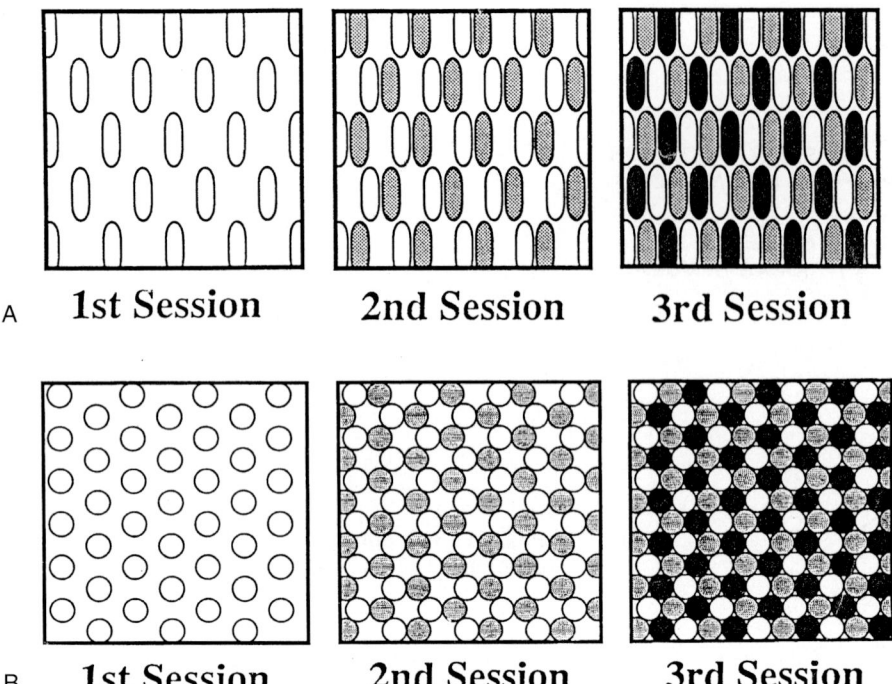

FIG. 33. A: When using six- to eight-hair minigrafts, 20 grafts are placed per square inch in a fully staggered pattern. The second session is then performed 2 mm to the right of the first set of growing grafts. The third is performed between, and slightly posterior to, the first and second sessions. A fourth session, if needed, would be performed with a random session of three- to four-hair minigrafts into Swann Morton 91 incisions. **B:** When using three- to four-hair minigrafts, 40 grafts are placed per square inch in a fully staggered pattern. The second session is then performed 2 mm to the right of the first set of growing grafts. The third is performed in between the first and second sessions.

Four months later, when the hair from the second session is growing, I place a large dot over the first and second session together and place my incisions between and slightly posterior to these dots. If a fourth session is needed, it is usually performed 6 months after the third session and is done randomly to fill in the "nooks and crannies" that may remain after the three sessions are completed.

The primary advantages of performing the surgery in this systematic fashion, as opposed to the more random approaches utilized by most physicians, are the following: (a) We accomplish even coverage with each procedure because of the fully staggered patterns (Fig. 35). (b) We optimize our chances of achieving even growth because of the even nutritive circulation that each graft receives. (c) We minimize the chances of crushing grafts during the placement phase, because each graft is an equal distance from the adjacent one. (d) We minimize the damage to the recipient area during the epinephrine injections. Because we have stenciled out our pattern previously, we can inject into the lines and avoid damage to the skin that is going to supply nutrition to the hair grafts just planted. (e) We improve the assistants' speed at placing the grafts, because, as a result of the equal spacing, there is less popping. (f) We improve the surgeon's speed, especially in the later sessions, at which time finding a randomly growing mini- or micrograft in thinning hair can be a grueling experience.

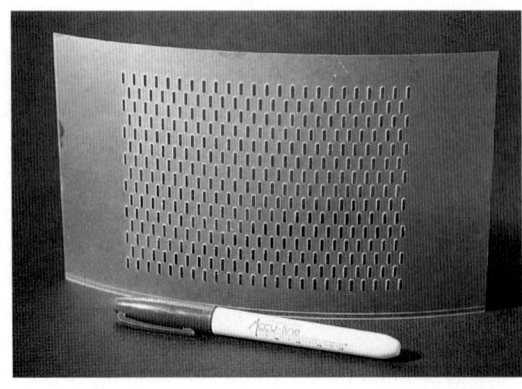 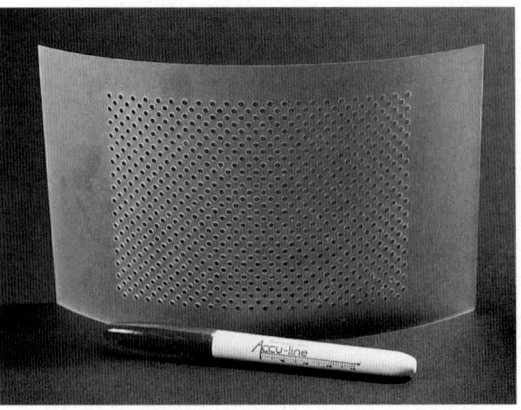

FIG. 34. A: The stencil that is used for the six- to eight-hair minigraft approach. **B:** The stencil that is used for the three- to four-hair minigraft approach.

technique of, 107–122
temperature control for, 107, 119
test, 88, 95–96
transfer grafting with, 84, 87, 132–134
for trichoepitheliomas, 86
tumescent, 85, 97, 105
of vegetarians, 92
Derma III Dermabrader, 100–101
Diamond fraises, 101, 102–103
Diazepam (Valium)
for hair transplantation, 236
for Jessner's-TCA chemical peel, 68
for TCA chemical peel, 56
Diplopia, due to BTX-A, 10
Discoid lupus erythematosus (DLE), dermabrasion with, 87
Donor strips, for hair transplantation
harvesting of, 238–245
sectioning grafts from, 246–251
Doppler ultrasound, of varicose veins, 208–209
Dressing
for dermabrasion, 122–132
for hair transplantation, 262
for liposculpture of circumferential thighs and buttocks, 197–199
Drool grooves, collagen implants for, 25–29
Dry ice, with TCA chemical peel, 53, 56–58, 65
Duplex ultrasound, of varicose veins, 210–211
Dysport, toxicity of, 2

E

Edema, after dermabrasion, 138
Ehlers-Danlos syndrome, hair transplantation with, 285
Electromyography (EMG), BTX-A with, 16–17
Epinephrine, for hair transplantation, 236, 257
Erythema, after dermabrasion, 134–135, 137
Excoriation, compulsive, dermabrasion for, 81–83
Extrinsic aging, 84
Eyelid ptosis, due to BTX-A, 10

F

Facial asymmetry, BTX-A for, 15–16
Facial muscles, 5–6, 11
Facial telangiectasias, laser treatment of, 147, 148
Fascia, superficial, 203
Feathering, in liposculpture, 203
Fibrel, 35–42
allergic reaction to, 42
commercial kit for, 37
contraindications to, 37
indications for, 37
inflammation due to, 39, 40, 41
mechanism of action of, 35–37
postoperative care for, 39, 40
results of, 39–41, 42
side effects and complications of, 41–42
skin test for, 37
technique for, 37–39, 40
Fibro-Vein (sodium tetradecyl sulfate), for sclerotherapy, 213, 215, 216
Fitzpatrick skin classification, for TCA chemical peel, 53–54, 65
Flanks, liposculpture of, 171–184
complications of, 179–181
incision sites for, 174–175
marking prior to, 172–174
patient selection for, 171
postoperative treatment of, 179
preoperative evaluation for, 171–172
preparation of patient for, 172
results of, 181–184
surgical technique for, 177–179, 180
tumescent infiltration for, 176–177
Fluoro Ethyl, 103, 109
5-Fluorouracil (5-FU), chemexfoliation vs., 69
Foerster forceps, in hair transplantation, 246, 255, 260–261
Follicular unit, 225
Forehead lines, horizontal
BTX-A for, 12–15
collagen implants for, 22–23
Forelock, 235
Freezing
for dermabrasion, 105–106, 109, 119, 120–122
for TCA chemical peel, 53, 56–58, 65
Frigiderm, 103
Fringe, 225
Frontalis muscle, BTX-A for, 12–15
Frontoparietal advancement flap, 282–283
Frown lines
BTX-A for, 4–10
collagen implants for, 23–24
5-FU (5-fluorouracil), chemexfoliation vs., 69
Furrows, Fibrel for, 39, 40

G

Gas sterilizing system, 100, 101
Gentian violet marking, for dermabrasion, 108, 119
Glabellar frown lines
BTX-A for, 4–10
collagen implants for, 23–24
Glogau skin classification, for TCA chemical peel, 53–54
Glogau type II wrinkles, BTX-A for, 4–10
Glogau type IV crow's-feet, BTX-A for, 10–12
Glycolic acid peel, 43–51
buffered, 43
choice of formulation for, 43
classification of, 43
consent form for, 46, 47
consultation prior to, 44
esterified, 43
free acid formulations for, 43
indications for, 43, 44
materials for, 46
medical history and examination prior to, 44–46
medications affecting, 44
partially neutralized, 43
patient instructions and preparation prior to, 46, 47, 48
pitfalls and adverse reactions to, 47, 51
procedure for, 48–50
relative exclusions to, 44–46
role of nurse/aesthetician in, 50
sensitivity to, 44
with TCA chemical peel, 65
treatment and instructions after, 50, 51
Graft cutting boards, in hair transplantation, 246, 247
Grafts
dermabrasion with, 84, 87, 132–134
micro- and minigrafts, for hair transplantation. See Micrografts; Minigrafts
Greater saphenous vein (GSV), 205, 206
Gynecoid shape, liposculpting and, 185, 186

H

Hair
crispy, 225
curly, 225
Hair bundles, 225
Hair color, 225
Hair coverage, 225
Hair density, 225
Hair diameter, 225
Hairline
adolescent vs. adult, 231
central point of, 233–234
design of, 233–235
height of, 233–234
high preauricular, 285
Hair loss
alopecia reduction for. See Alopecia reduction
hair transplantation for. See Hair transplantation
Norwood classification of, 225, 226
patterns of, 228–230
Hair texture, 225
Hair thinning, 226
Hair transplantation, 223–264
with alopecia reduction, 291–293

Hair transplantation (contd.)
  anesthesia for, 236–238, 252
  concepts underlying, 226–228
  consultation for, 230–232
  creation of recipient sites in, 251–256
  design of hairline in, 233–235
  ergonomic chair for, 258
  graft insertion in, 257–262
  harvesting donor strips in, 238–245
  hemostasis in, 257
  male-pattern baldness and other philosophical considerations in, 228–230
  number of grafts for, 227
  patient preparation for, 237–238
  placement of micro- and minigrafts in, 226–228
  postoperative care for, 262–264
  sectioning grafts from donor tissue in, 246–251
  teamwork and team efficiency in, 232–233
  vocabulary for, 224–226
Hemangioma, laser treatment of, 148, 149
Hemostasis, in hair transplantation, 257
Herpes simplex virus (HSV)
  after dermabrasion, 138
  and dermabrasion, 88
HIV (human immunodeficiency virus), and dermabrasion, 88
Holes, for hair transplantation, 225, 251–252, 253–255
Hook retractor, for scalp reduction, 286
Hooks, for phlebectomy, 217, 218
Horizontal forehead lines
  BTX-A for, 12–15
  collagen implants for, 22–23
HSV (herpes simplex virus)
  after dermabrasion, 138
  and dermabrasion, 88
Human immunodeficiency virus (HIV), and dermabrasion, 88
Hydroquinone, with TCA chemical peel, 54–55
Hydroxyzine hydrochloride (Vistaril)
  for dermabrasion, 118
  for Jessner's-TCA chemical peel, 68
Hyperpigmentation
  after dermabrasion, 97, 137
  dermabrasion for, 85
  postinflammatory
    laser treatment of, 150
    TCA chemical peel for, 65
Hypertonic saline and dextrose (Sclerodex), for sclerotherapy, 213, 214, 215
Hypertrophic scars, and dermabrasion, 97
Hypopigmentation, after dermabrasion, 97, 136–137

I

Icepick scars, transfer grafting and dermabrasion for, 132–134
Immune response, to BTX-A, 1–2
Infection, after dermabrasion, 138
Infragluteal banana-form fold, in liposuction, 165, 195
Infragluteal crease, in liposuction, 165
Infrascapular pad, marking for liposculpture of, 173–174
Insurance coverage, for dermabrasion, 76–77
Intrinsic aging, 84
Isotretinoin (Accutane)
  and dermabrasion, 88–97
  and glycolic acid peels, 44, 51

J

Jessner's-trichloroacetic acid peel, 65, 67–74
  complications of, 73
  consultation for, 67–68
  formulation for, 68
  indications for, 67
  mechanism of action of, 73–74
  method for, 67–69
  preoperative preparation for, 68
  recovery from, 69
  results of, 69–73
  sedation for, 68
J-pattern scalp reduction, 265, 266, 269
"Jump-up," 226

K

Keloidal scars, and dermabrasion, 97
Keloids, after dermabrasion, 137–138
Keratoses, actinic
  dermabrasion for, 84
  Jessner's-TCA chemical peel for, 69, 70
  TCA chemical peel for, 65
Klein cannula, 177, 178
Kling dressing, for dermabrasion, 122, 124
Kojic acid, with TCA chemical peel, 55

L

Laser treatment, 147–161
  other uses of, 161
  of photodamaged skin, 157–161
  of pigmented lesions, 150–152
  of scars and striae, 154–157
  of tattoos, 152–154
  of vascular lesions, 147–150
Lateral subdermic venous system (LSVS), 205, 206
Laughing gas, for hair transplantation, 236
Lazy-S scalp reduction, 265, 266, 269
Leg telangiectasias, 205–221
  ambulatory phlebectomy for, 217–221
  injection of, 215–217
  laser treatment of, 147, 148, 149
  sclerotherapy for, 211–215
  steps prior to treatment of, 208–212
  superficial anatomy of, 205–208
Lentigines, solar, laser treatment of, 150, 151
Lesser saphenous vein (LSV), 205, 206
Lidocaine, for hair transplantation, 236, 237
Lightning Knife
  for microslits, 252–253
  for minislits, 255–256
Light reflection rheography (LRR), of varicose veins, 209
Liponots, 164
Liposculpture
  of abdomen, flanks, and back, 171–184
    complications of, 179–181
    incision sites for, 174–175
    marking prior to, 172–174
    patient selection for, 171
    postoperative treatment of, 179
    preoperative evaluation for, 171–172
    preparation of patient for, 172
    results of, 181–184
    surgical technique for, 177–179, 180
    tumescent infiltration for, 176–177
  of circumferential thigh and buttocks, 185–203
    and gynecoid shape, 185, 186
    instrumentation for, 188
    in lateral position, 193–195
    patient marking for, 188–190
    postoperative course of, 197, 199
    postoperative dressings for, 197–199
    preoperative evaluation for, 187–188
    prerequisites to, 186–187
    in prone position, 195–197
    results of, 200–202
    in supine position, 192–193
    thoughts and observations on, 202–203
    touch-up of, 186, 200
    tumescent anesthesia for, 191–192
    unanticipated sequelae to, 199–200
    vs. liposuction, 185–186
Liposuction
  of lateral thigh, 164–169
    aesthetic considerations in, 164
    cannulas for, 169
    gross anatomy in, 165
    lipotrops and liponots in, 164, 165
    lipowarp and, 166
    midline and, 166–168
    positioning for, 165–168
    postoperative care after, 169
    preoperative topographic markings for, 165
    staging of, 169

surface anatomy and preoperative evaluation for, 164–165
surgical technique in, 169
trochanteric bulge and, 166, 167
vs. liposculpture, 185–186
machine vs. syringe, 203
tumescent
of abdomen, flanks, and back, 176–177
anesthesia in, 163–164, 168
infiltration in, 168
of lateral thigh, 163–169
pitfalls and unique considerations with, 169
vs. prior techniques, 163–164
Lipotrops, 164, 165
Lipowarp, of lateral thigh, 166
Lips, collagen implants for, 29–31, 32
LRR (light reflection rheography), of varicose veins, 209
LSV (lesser saphenous vein), 205, 206
LSVS (lateral subdermic venous system), 205, 206
Lupus erythematosus, discoid, dermabrasion with, 87

M

Macrografts, for hair transplantation, 225
Magnifiers, in hair transplantation, 247
Male-pattern baldness
alopecia reduction for. See Alopecia reduction
hair transplantation for. See Hair transplantation
Norwood classification of, 225, 226
patterns of, 228–230
Marzola scalp-lift, 265–267, 271–272
Median scalp reduction, 265, 266, 268
Melasma
dermabrasion for, 85
Jessner's-TCA chemical peel for, 70–71, 72
laser treatment of, 150
TCA chemical peel for, 54–64, 65
Mentalis muscle, BTX-A for, 15
Meperidine, for Jessner's-TCA chemical peel, 68
Mercedes scalp reduction, 265, 266, 268–269
Mesolabial folds
BTX-A for, 15, 16
collagen implants for, 25–29
Microcannulas, for liposuction of lateral thigh, 169
Microfoam tape, in dermabrasion, 108, 119
Micro Foerster forceps, for hair transplantation, 258–259
Micrografts, for hair transplantation, 223–264
with alopecia reduction, 291–293
anesthesia for, 236–238, 252
concepts underlying, 226–228
consultation for, 230–232
creation of recipient sites in, 251–256
defined, 225
design of hairline in, 233–235
ergonomic chair for, 258
harvesting donor strips in, 238–245
hemostasis with, 257
insertion of, 257–260
male-pattern baldness and other philosophical considerations in, 228–230
microslits for, 225, 251–253
number of, 227
patient preparation for, 237–238
placement of, 226–228
postoperative care for, 262–264
sectioning grafts from donor tissue in, 246–251
single-hair, 227, 249, 250
teamwork and team efficiency in, 232–233
vocabulary for, 224–226
Microslits, for hair transplantation, 225, 251–253
Midazolam (Versed), for hair transplantation, 236
Midline scalp reduction, 265, 266, 268
Mid-pupillary line, BTX-A injection into, 7, 9
Milia, after dermabrasion, 135
Minigrafts, for hair transplantation, 223–264
with alopecia reduction, 291–293
anesthesia for, 236–238, 252
concepts underlying, 226–228
consultation for, 230–232
creation of recipient sites in, 251–256
defined, 225
design of hairline in, 233–235
ergonomic chair for, 258
harvesting donor strips in, 238–245
hemostasis with, 257
holes for, 225, 251–252, 253–255
insertion of, 257–258, 260–262
large, 225
male-pattern baldness and other philosophical considerations in, 228–230
minislits for, 225, 251–252, 255–256
number of, 227
patient preparation for, 237–238
placement of, 226–228
postoperative care for, 262–264
sectioning grafts from donor tissue in, 246–251
teamwork and team efficiency in, 232–233
vocabulary for, 224–226
Minislits, for hair transplantation, 225, 251–252, 255–256
Molluscum contagiosum, TCA chemical peel for, 64–65
Muller hook, 217, 218

N

Naloxone hydrochloride (Narcan), after dermabrasion, 125
Nasal flare, BTX-A for, 15
Nasolabial folds, collagen implants for, 25–29
Neurofibromatosis, dermabrasion for, 86
Neurovascular bundle, in alopecia reduction, 267, 286
Nevi, benign, laser treatment of, 150
Nevus of Ota, laser treatment of, 150
Nitrous oxide, for hair transplantation, 236, 238
Norwood classification, of male-pattern baldness, 225, 226

O

Occipital neurovascular bundle, in alopecia reduction, 267, 286
Occipitoparietal scalp-lift, bilateral, 267, 272, 273, 278–280
Occlusive dressings, for dermabrasion, 131–132
Oesch's hook, 216, 217
Omniderm, for dermabrasion, 132
Orbicularis oculi muscle, BTX-A injection into, 7, 8

P

Paramedian scalp reduction, 265, 266, 269
Pear fraise, 102
Periorbital wrinkles
BTX-A for, 10–12
collagen implants for, 24–25
Personna surgical prep blades, in hair transplantation, 246, 247
Petechiae, after dermabrasion, 136
Phenol solution, chemical peel with, 118
Phlebectomy, ambulatory, 217–221
Photoaging, Jessner's-TCA chemical peel for, 67–74
Photodamaged skin, laser resurfacing of, 157–161
Photoplethysmography (PPG), of varicose veins, 209–210
Pigmentary changes, after dermabrasion, 97
Pigmentary disorders, dermabrasion for, 85
Pigmented lesions, laser treatment of, 150–152
Pinski bullet fraise, 102, 112

Pinto cannula, 177, 178
Platysmal bands, BTX-A for, 14, 15
Poikiloderma, laser treatment of, 148
Polidocanol (POL, Aethoxysklerol, Sclero-Vein), for sclerotherapy, 213, 215, 216
"Popping," in hair transplantation, 225–226, 257
Port-wine stain, laser treatment of, 147, 148, 149, 150
Postacne scarring
    dermabrasion for, 79–82
    Fibrel for, 37–41, 42
    TCA chemical peel for, 54–64, 65
Postsurgical scars, dermabrasion for, 84
PPG (photoplethysmography), of varicose veins, 209–210
Preauricular flap, 283–284
Presacral pad, marking for liposculpture of, 174
Procerus muscle, BTX-A injection into, 7, 8
Pruritus, after dermabrasion, 135, 136
Psychological status, and dermabrasion, 86, 87, 99
Ptosis, due to BTX-A, 10

R
Radiation therapy, dermabrasion after, 87
Ramelet's hook, 217, 218
Refrigerant
    for dermabrasion, 103–104, 109, 119, 120–122
    for TCA chemical peel, 53, 56–58, 65
Rest-On foam, after liposuction, 169
Resurfacing, BTX-A with, 12
Reticular veins, 205–221
    ambulatory phlebectomy for, 217–221
    sclerotherapy for, 211–215
    steps prior to treatment of, 208–211
    superficial anatomy of, 205–208
Retinoic acid
    and dermabrasion, 88–97
    and glycolic acid peels, 44, 51
Rhinophyma, dermabrasion for, 85
Rhytides
    dermabrasion for, 84–85
    Fibrel for, 39, 40
    laser treatment of, 158, 159
    postinflammatory, 65
Ring blocks, for hair transplantation, 236, 237, 238

S
Scalp extension, 287–288
Scalp-lift
    bilateral occipitoparietal, 267, 272, 273, 278–280
    Brandy bitemporal, 272–274, 280–281
    complications of, 284–286
    Marzola, 265–267, 271–272
    modified bitemporal, 281–282
    neurovascular bundle in, 267, 286
Scalp reduction, 265–293
    adjuncts to, 286
    bitemporal, 274, 281, 282
    Burow's triangle, 269–270
    circumferential, 270–271, 274–278
    complications of, 284–286
    curvilinear, 270
    frontoparietal advancement flap for, 282–283
    history of, 265–267
    from inside out, 267–269
    J-pattern, 265, 266, 269
    lazy-S, 265, 266, 269
    Mercedes, 265, 266, 268–269
    methods of, 274–284
    midline (median), 265, 266, 268
    mini- and micrografting with, 291–293
    from outside working in, 270–274
    paramedian, 265, 266, 269
    partially from outside working in, 269–270
    preauricular flap for, 283–284
    scalp extension and, 287–288
    transposition flaps for corrections of slots from, 288–291
    Y-pattern, 265, 266, 268–269
Scalp-stretching device, 286
Scars and scarring
    after dermabrasion, 137
    with Accutane, 88–97
    dermabrasion for, 79–84, 140–144
    Fibrel for, 37–41, 42
    laser treatment of, 154–157
    TCA chemical peel for, 54–64, 65
Schumann Derma III Dermabrader, 100–101
Sclerodex (hypertonic saline and dextrose), for sclerotherapy, 213, 215, 216
Sclerotherapy
    for telangiectasias, 215–217
    for varicose and reticular veins, 211–215
Sclero-Vein (polidocanol), for sclerotherapy, 213, 215, 216
Sedation
    for Jessner's-TCA chemical peel, 68
    for TCA chemical peel, 56
Serrated wheels, for dermabrasion, 102
Silicone sheeting, for scalp extension, 287
Skin classification, for TCA chemical peel, 53–54, 65
Skin contour, in dermabrasion, 104–105
Skin grafts, dermabrasion with, 84, 87, 132–134
Skin retraction, 202
Slits, for hair transplantation, 225, 251–253, 255–256
Slot formation
    with median scalp reduction, 268
    with scalp reduction, 284–285
    transposition flaps for correction of, 288–291
Smallpox scars, dermabrasion for, 80
Sodium pentobarbital, for dermabrasion, 107
Sodium tetradecyl sulfate (STS, Sotradecol, Fibro-Vein, Thrombovar), for sclerotherapy, 213, 215, 216
Solar lentigines, laser treatment of, 150, 151
Spandex garment, for liposculpture of circumferential thighs and buttocks, 197, 198, 199
Stretch-back
    with paramedian scalp reduction, 269
    with Y-pattern scalp reduction, 269
Striae, laser treatment of, 154–157
STS (sodium tetradecyl sulfate), for sclerotherapy, 213, 215, 216
Suction retractor, for scalp reduction, 286
Sunscreen
    after dermabrasion, 131
    for melasma, 54
Superficial fascia, 203
Super Punch, for holes for minigrafts, 253–255
Supraorbital nerve block, for hair transplantation, 236

T
Tattoos
    dermabrasion for, 85–86
    laser treatment of, 152–154
TCA peel. See Trichloroacetic acid (TCA) peel
Telangiectasias
    facial, laser treatment of, 147, 148, 149
    leg, 205–221
        ambulatory phlebectomy for, 216–221
        injection of, 215–217
        laser treatment of, 147, 148, 149
        sclerotherapy for, 211–215
        steps prior to treatment of, 208–211
        superficial anatomy of, 205–208
Temperature control, for dermabrasion, 107, 119
Temporal recession, deepening of, 285
Thigh
    circumferential, liposculpture of, 185–203
        and gynecoid shape, 185, 186
        instrumentation for, 188
        in lateral position, 193–195
        vs. liposuction, 185–186
        patient marking for, 188–190

postoperative course of, 197, 199
postoperative dressings for, 197–199
preoperative evaluation for, 187–188
prerequisites to, 186–187
in prone position, 195–197
results of, 200–202
in supine position, 192–193
thoughts and observations on, 202–203
touch-up of, 186, 200
tumescent anesthesia for, 191–192
unanticipated sequelae to, 199–200
lateral, liposuction of, 164–169
aesthetic considerations in, 164
cannulas for, 169
gross anatomy in, 165
lipotrops and liponots in, 164, 165
lipowarp and, 166
midline and, 166–168
positioning for, 165–168
postoperative care after, 169
preoperative topographic markings for, 165
staging of, 169
surface anatomy and preoperative evaluation for, 164–165
surgical technique in, 169
trochanteric bulge and, 166, 167
tumescent infiltration for, 168
Thigh midline, 166–168
Thrombovar (sodium tetradecyl sulfate), for sclerotherapy, 213, 215, 216
Toxicity, of BTX-A, 2
Transfer grafting, dermabrasion with, 132–134
Transposition flaps, for correction of slots from scalp reduction, 288–291
Traumatic scars, dermabrasion for, 83–84
Trichloroacetic acid (TCA) peel, 53–66
for acne scarring, 54–64, 65
additives to, 55–56
combination agents for, 53, 65
complications of, 65
concentration of, 55–56
consent form for, 53
contraindications to, 53
with deeper resurfacing, 65–66
follow-up of, 63–64
freezing agent with, 53, 65
frosting from, 61, 68
with glycolic acid, 65
histologic depth studies of, 66
indications for, 65
with Jessner's solution, 65, 67–74
medium-depth, 53, 67
for melasma, 54–64, 65
for molluscum contagiosum, 64–65
patient instructions after, 61–63
preoperative evaluation and preparation for, 53–56
repeating of, 64
sedation for, 56
with solid carbon dioxide, 53, 56–58, 65
technique of, 56–61
Trichoepitheliomas, dermabrasion for, 86
Trochanteric pseudobulge, 166, 167
Trunk, liposculpture of, 171–184
complications of, 179–181
incision sites for, 174–175
marking prior to, 172–174
patient selection for, 171
postoperative treatment of, 179
preoperative evaluation for, 171–172
preparation of patient for, 172
results of, 181–184
surgical technique for, 177–179, 180
tumescent infiltration for, 176–177
Tumescent liposuction, 163–169
of abdomen, flanks, and back, 176–177
anesthesia in, 163–164
of circumferential thighs and buttocks, 191–192
infiltration for, 168
of lateral thigh, 164–169
pitfalls and unique considerations with, 169
postoperative care after, 169
vs. prior techniques, 163–164

U
Ultrasound, of varicose veins, 208–211

V
Valium. See Diazepam (Valium)
Varicose veins, 205–220
ambulatory phlebectomy for, 217–221
sclerotherapy for, 211–215
steps prior to treatment of, 208–211
superficial anatomy of, 205–208
Vascular lesions, laser treatment of, 147–150
Vegetarians, dermabrasion of, 92
Versed (midazolam), for hair transplantation, 236
Vigilon, for dermabrasion, 122, 123, 131–132
Vistaril (hydroxyzine hydrochloride)
for dermabrasion, 118
for Jessner's-TCA chemical peel, 68
Vitiligo, dermabrasion for, 97
Von Recklinghausen's disease, dermabrasion for, 86

W
Wetpacks, after dermabrasion, 126
Wire brushes, for dermabrasion, 101–102
Wrinkles
dermabrasion for, 84–85
Fibrel for, 39, 40
Glogau type II, BTX-A for, 4–10
periorbital
BTX-A for, 10–12
collagen implants for, 24–25

Y
Y-pattern scalp reduction, 265, 266, 268–269

Z
Zyderm I Collagen Implant (ZC-I), 21
Zyderm II Collagen Implant (ZC-II), 21
Zyplast Implant (ZP), 21